Social and Organizational Developments through Emerging E-Government Applications:
New Principles and Concepts

Vishanth Weerakkody
Brunel University, UK

Information Science REFERENCE

INFORMATION SCIENCE REFERENCE
Hershey · New York

Director of Editorial Content: Kristin Klinger
Senior Managing Editor: Jamie Snavely
Assistant Managing Editor: Michael Brehm
Publishing Assistant: Sean Woznicki
Typesetter: Michael Brehm, Carole Coulson
Cover Design: Lisa Tosheff
Printed at: Yurchak Printing Inc.

Published in the United States of America by
Information Science Reference (an imprint of IGI Global)
701 E. Chocolate Avenue
Hershey PA 17033
Tel: 717-533-8845
Fax: 717-533-8661
E-mail: cust@igi-global.com
Web site: http://www.igi-global.com/reference

Library of Congress Cataloging-in-Publication Data

Social and organizational developments through emerging e-government applications : new principles and concepts / Vishanth Weerakkody, editor.
p. cm.
Includes bibliographical references and index.
Summary: "This book offers reflective accounts of the key research themes that have emerged in the last few years as electronic government services have become commonplace in the world"--Provided by publisher.
ISBN 978-1-60566-918-2 (hardcover) -- ISBN 978-1-60566-919-9 (ebook) 1. Internet in public administration. I. Weerakkody, Vishanth.
JF1525.A8S625 2010
352.3'802854678--dc22

2009044466

British Cataloguing in Publication Data
A Cataloguing in Publication record for this book is available from the British Library.

Table of Contents

Detailed Table of Contents

IT enabled e-governance in India seeks to achieve a more equitous, efficient, transparent, speedy, and corruption free service delivery system. But in the Indian context the challenge for e-governance is how to reduce the gap between the rich and poor towards a more inclusive governance system, benefiting particularly the poor in backward regions as in Chhattisgarh State, India.

Proactive economic policies combined with the ICT revolution of the past decade have brought about many changes in managing businesses and organizations in developing countries like India. The prowess achieved through this revolution has also led to exploitation of ICT for better governance and rural development. As a result, several ICT projects have been initiated to foster improved governance and facilitate rural development by appropriately linking public and private institutions. RASI (Rural Access to Services through Internet) is one such government-private initiative to promote e-governance and ICT enabled rural development. This longitudinal research is to analyze the factors related to access to and usage of the services offered through this project in Erode district of the state of Tamilnadu in India. Data for this empirical research was collected through survey and interviews during two time periods (2004 and 2006). Findings show that the project has largely deviated from its objectives due to lack of government support, non-scalable technology and ownership issues. Based on these findings, the authors provide a set of recommendations to policy makers and implementing agencies.

The objective of this chapter is to design an e-government organizational performance framework and to suggest ICTs solutions through a case study of Haryana state government in India so as to enhance efficiency and effectiveness of services provided to citizens. The framework is suggested using responses collected from 150 government departments. The ICTs solutions were validated by data collected from 90 e-government experts. A log linear regression analysis is used to develop the framework. The framework with minor modifications can be developed for similar other e-government settings.

The purpose of this study is to explore the connection between the stages of e-government development and collaboration demands in local government. Specifically, this study analyzes the demand for intergovernmental, interagency, and intersectoral collaborations during the three stages of local e-government development, including e-government initiation, application development, and integration. Based on an in-depth case study, this chapter identifies specific collaboration types demanded during local e-government development in the Gangnam district government in Seoul, Korea. In each stage of e-government development, the local government encountered varying degrees and types of resource dependence upon internal and external organizational units. A particular type of collaboration became dominant in each stage as the relative importance of each collaboration type changed.

Although efforts for developing e-democracy have been underway for over a decade, recent literature indicates that its uptake by citizens and Elected Members (EMs) is still very low. This chapter explores the underlying reasons for why this is so from the perspective of local EMs in the context of UK local authorities. It draws on findings reported in earlier works supplemented with primary case study data. Findings are interpreted through the lens of Giddens structuration theory, which assists in drawing out issues related to three dimensions of human agency: communication of meaning, exercising power and sanctioning behaviour. The chapter abstracts categories of agency from the findings and uses these to formulate eight propositions for creating an e-friendly democratic culture and enhancing EMs uptake of e-democracy. These propositions provide an indication for future e-democracy research direction.

Much has been written about the benefits of e-government, but far less has been written about how the e-government revolution will be staffed. Many questions remain about whether we have the capacity to develop and provide new e-government services. This chapter seeks to add to our knowledge in this area by examining three perspectives on the readiness of administrative leaders for effective development of e-government systems and strategies. The authors examine the lingering division of policy and administration, present an assessment of the technology knowledge of city managers, and finish with an examination of the leadership strategies available to administrative leaders in city government for achieving the kind of comprehensive changes that many e-government initiatives require. The authors find challenges in each of these important areas and also opportunities. The chapter concludes with recommendations for administrative leaders to break free from these different barriers to success.

Preface: A Reflection of the Past, Present and Future of E-Government Research

EXECUTIVE SUMMARY

Government and industry e-commerce agendas have become more closely linked in recent times and more people are now less tolerant of poor, impersonal service in the public sector as they become aware of the power of the web and experience good service in the private sector. With the advancement of Information and Communication Technologies, electronic government (e-government) has emerged as an effective means of delivering government services to citizens. It is in every government's interest to make their public services more efficient and available in order to gain citizens' trust, which has often eluded many governments and political leaders in modern society. While e-government has already established itself as the primary enabler for transforming the way government services are offered to citizens in developed countries, it is now beginning to show promising results in many developing countries. This article offers a reflective account of the key research themes that have emerged in the last few years in the International Journal of Electronic Government Research and in the wider published domain. The article suggests that e-government research has evolved from initially focusing on strategy and implementation issues to later examining adoption and diffusion of services from a citizen perspective, followed by exploring technical complexities of implementation and finally to the current studies of transformational government.

INTRODUCTION

Electronic government (e-government) can be broadly viewed as the adoption of information and communication technology (ICT) in government organisations to improve public services. For many countries, e-government implementation efforts began in the late 1990s. The e-government led implementation of ICT in public administration during the last ten years has offered better, faster and more transparent means for citizens and businesses to interact with government organisations. Equally, it has also created a platform for better collaboration and information sharing between various government agencies. Implementation efforts in most countries have now evolved from basic information provisioning to more integrated service offerings that involve cross-agency process and information systems (IS) transformation to enable more joined-up and citizen-centric e-government services. However, public sector service transformation is a complex undertaking involving distributed decision-making that requires a good understanding of the political context, business processes and technology as well as design and engineering methods capable of breaking through the traditional boundaries that exist between public organisation units. Conversely, from a demand perspective extensive efforts are required to increase citizens' awareness about the transformation of the delivery of government services and their online availability.

In order to prevent digital divide in terms of using e-government services, it is also necessary that citizens from all facets of society are equipped with basic ICT skills as well as private and or public access to high-speed Internet connections. Yet, despite the availability of innovative technologies, government agencies are faced with many technical, organisational and socio-economic challenges and barriers that need to be addressed when developing, adopting and diffusing e-government systems and services. Furthermore, from an organisational perspective e-government has introduced an environment where most public institutions such as healthcare, social services, education and employment have struggled with the need to balance issues such as transparency and opaqueness, or social inclusion and professionalism. Consequently, there has been increasing pressure on the academic and practitioner communities for research that focuses on bridging the gap between e-government theory and practice.

In the aforementioned backdrop, various researchers and practitioners have attempted to offer insights into the implementation, acceptance and diffusion of e-government services. The last few years has seen e-government being regarded with the same level of importance that e-business was treated with in the mid 1990s. Consequently, in the last two years in particular, transformational government (or t-government for short) has emerged as the parallel of business process reengineering (BPR) that the private sector witnessed in the early 1990s. While early e-government efforts focused on e-enabling customer facing, front-office processes, t-government entails the same principles as BPR and focuses on ICT enabled transformation of both front- and back-office processes in public sector organisations. In this context, when examining e-government literature, it can be concluded that principally four key themes have emerged in published research on e-government. These include: a) articles that examine the implementation of e-government from a policy-oriented perspective that includes strategic, organisational and wider socio-political dimensions; b) papers that take a citizen-centric perspective on e-government through adoption and diffusion research; c) papers that explore the technical complexities of delivering e-government that cover aspects such as interoperability, integration and information sharing; and finally, d) articles that explore the transformational aspects of e-government development.

In this article, the aforementioned themes will be examined briefly in the context of previously published research and conjectures will be drawn on how these themes will evolve in the future. This article is structured as followed. The next section will offer a review of research that examines e-government implementation from a wider organisational and policy viewpoint. This will be followed by an analysis of e-government adoption and diffusion literature from a citizen-centric perspective in section 3. Research that examines the technical aspects of e-government will then be discussed in section 4 followed by the concept of transformational stage e-government in section 5. Finally, conclusions will be drawn in section 6 and presumption of future research directions will be offered in section 7.

E-GOVERNMENT IMPLEMENTATION: STRATEGIC, ORGANISATIONAL AND SOCIO-POLITICAL INFLUENCES

The implementation of e-government projects in various countries has taken different strategic approaches concerning key issues such as financial, technological, project management and control of programmes. For instance, while some European countries such as the UK has maintained central control of the national e-government project using a top-down management style, other countries such as Norway, Denmark and the Netherlands take a more decentralised bottom-up approach (Weerakkody *et al*, 2006).

E-government is currently embryonic and can be viewed as a concept operating in a dynamic and changing environment. Therefore, it is as yet unknown whether a more rigid, comprehensive approach to e-government strategic planning (Sambamurthy *et al.*, 1994; Earl, 1993; Galliers, 1991; McFarlan 1971) or a more flexible, incremental approach (Sambamurthy *et al.*, 1994; Earl, 1993) is suitable. While advocates of comprehensive planning (Mintzberg, 1994) suggest that this approach will succeed in a turbulent environment such as e-government, critics such as Johnson and Scholes (1999) argue that a more flexible, incremental approach is suited for such environments.

According to Hunter and Jupp (2001), a true Internet strategy must examine all aspects of the business model, interactions with customers and stakeholders, and should identify those areas where more value can be created for all stakeholders by moving processes and interactions online. The plan of action for e-government should therefore include: a clear definition of e-government that covers key areas to be addressed and identification of all customers; a vision that is easily understood and succinctly expresses the concept of and plans for e-government; specific goals and objectives that can be monitored and measured; and identification of policies necessary to support e-government (Weerakkody, *et al.*, 2006). Holmes (2001) argues that from the various e-government strategies and actions there are five underlying principles emerging: put information and services online and do everything online; ensure easy and universal access to online information and services; skill government employees to be knowledge workers; work in partnership to make it happen; and remove barriers and lead by example.

Many studies have also captured organisational level influences that have impacted upon e-government efforts including reluctance to embrace change (Irani *et al.*, 2008; Mansar, 2006; Beynon-Davies and Martin, 2004), bureaucratic organisational structures (Hu *et al.*, 2006; Altameem *et al.*, 2006; Fang, 2006; Kraemer and King, 2005), and the lack of leadership in change efforts (Irani *et al.*, 2008; Beynon-Davies and Martin, 2004; O'Donnell *et al.*, 2003).

In addition to the strategic level and organisational level influences, the next most prominent research theme has to be social and political aspects of e-government. Much has been written about the various social level benefits of e-government (Irani *et al.*, 2008; Al-Shafi and Weerakkody, 2008; Raffat, 2003; Hazlett and Hill., 2003; Silcock, 2001), whilst on the contrary political level issues have been discussed in a more negative light as they have often been seen as barriers to e-government (Irani *et al.*, 2008; 2007; Ramaswamy and Selian, 2007; Beynon-Davies and Martin, 2004; O'Donnell *et al.*, 2003).

E-GOVERNMENT ADOPTION AND DIFFUSION: THE CITIZENS AS USERS

E-government diffusion is an international phenomenon that has received much attention and publicity in the last five years or so. This coincides with the implementation and widespread availability of e-services in the public sector. In particular, the lack of demand and adoption of e-government services has resulted in the need for research into understanding the factors influencing the adoption and diffusion of e-government from the citizens' perspective. This line of inquiry has been pursued vigorously by scholars who have an interest in Internet related IT service adoption and diffusion research. This is no surprise given the impact of the Internet on modern society. For instance, according to a global study conducted by comScore there are over 694 million Internet users worldwide. However, in light of the increased ubiquity of e-government, most countries, including the United States (US) which accounted for the largest number of Internet users (152 million users) and the United Kingdom (UK) which rounded out the top five with 30,190 million users, are eager to increase citizen acceptance of this innovation (ComScore, 2006).

The European Union (EU) and United Nations reports ranked both the US and the UK in the top tier of its e-government readiness index (UNPAN 2008; European Union, 2004). However, despite the UK e-enabling many of its services, its government is encountering several barriers to e-government adoption (Weerakkody and Choudrie, 2005; Al-Sebie and Irani, 2005). A study by Gilbert *et al*., (2004) indicates that citizens' potential usage of e-government services in the UK is extremely low (Al-Sebie and Irani, 2005). Despite marketing efforts to increase awareness (Adeshara *et al*., 2004), many local government councils in the UK (www.direct.gov.uk) have stated that the usage of their services is sparse. Cross (2007) reports that a £5m campaign to persuade citizens to contact their local council via the central e-government web portal (www.direct.gov.uk), has had little effect in the UK. In a wider European context, other research by the European Commission's Eurostat service has found that the UK is behind Germany, Sweden, Norway, Iceland and Finland in the number of individuals interacting online with public authorities (Kablenet.com, 2005). According to this research the UK is also behind most EU countries in the number of businesses obtaining information and transacting with the government over the Internet. According to the European Commission, 31 percent of businesses in the UK get information from the government online, placing the country behind Sweden (90 percent), Lithuania (63 percent), Poland (57 percent) and Italy (51 percent) in this category (Kablenet.com, 2005).

Although the aforementioned context is encouraging, according to the latest survey by the United Nations, universal access to the Internet is still in the distant future for many countries (UNPAN, 2008). In the US, 50 percent of citizens use the Internet compared to a global average of 6.7 percent whereas in the Indian sub-continent, it is a mere 0.4 percent (UNPAN, 2008). Studies have shown that even in developed countries online transactional systems have achieved only modest levels of usage (Carter and Weerakkody, 2008).

Given the aforementioned context, researchers have argued that the rate of e-government adoption and diffusion will depend on some key factors (Carter and Weerakkody, 2008; Al-Shafi and Weerakkody, 2008). Among these, trust (Carter and Belanger, 2005; Warkentin *et al*., 2002; Welch *et al*., 2005) and ICT divide (Huang, 2007; Wright, 2002) are seen as an integral part of e-government adoption.

The Influence of Trust on E-Government Adoption

Research has shown that citizens' confidence in the ability of an agency to provide online services is imperative for the widespread adoption of e-government initiatives. In this context trust is seen as an imperative for e-government adoption. Trust of the government refers to one's perceptions regarding the integrity and ability of the agency providing the service (McKnight *et al*., 2002; Beccera and Gupta, 1999; Ganesan and Hess, 1997; Jarvenpaa *et al*., 1998; Lee and Turban, 2001; Mayer *et al*., 1995; McKnight *et al*., 1998). Gefen *et al*. (2005) posit that trust in the agency has a strong impact on the adoption of a technology. Before endorsing e-government initiatives, citizens must believe government agencies demonstrate the competence and technical savvy necessary to implement and secure e-government systems. Transparent, accurate, reliable interaction with e-government service providers will enhance citizen trust and acceptance of e-government services. On the contrary, broken promises and fraudulent behaviour from government officials and employees will decrease trust and increase opposition to these initiatives (Carter and Weerakkody, 2008). Oxendine *et al*. (2003) compare citizen adoption of electronic networks in different regions of the US (Oxendine *et al*., 2003). They found that system adoption was more prominent in localities where citizens are more trusting. Due to the impersonal nature of the Internet, citizens must believe that the agency providing the service is reliable. Wang and Emurian (2005) posit a lack of trust as one of the most formidable barriers to e-service adoption, especially when financial or personal information is involved.

The Impact of ICT Divide on E-Government Adoption

As governments worldwide increasingly implement e-government services, concerns about the potential impacts of a digital divide continue to grow. While definitions of the concept of the digital divide vary, it generally refers to the distinction between the ICT haves and have-nots: the difference between those who have Internet access and computer skills and those who do not. Regarding access, Internet connections are still not distributed evenly across racial, regional and socio-economic lines. According to Wright (2002) in 2001, 60 percent of white households in the US had Internet access, while only 34 percent of African American and 38 percent of Latino households did. Similarly, roughly 78 percent of households with an income between $50,000 and $75,000 had Internet access compared to only 40 percent of those with household incomes between $20,000 and $25,000 (Wright, 2002). Thomas and Streib (2003) suggest that among Internet users, ethnicity and education are important predictors of which Internet users will also utilize government Web sites, with those users more likely to be white and better educated. They construe that government web sites seem to draw an even more exclusive audience than the already somewhat elite audience for the Internet in general (Thomas and Streib, 2003). Further, Huang (2007) finds that in US counties' adoption of e-government is highly correlated with various socio-economic factors.

The ICT divide is even stronger for the skills needed to use technological innovations (Wellman and Haythornthwaite, 2002). Mossenberger *et al.* (2003) suggest many people lack the basic skills needed to interact with computer hardware and software. Researchers have found that the elderly, less-educated, poor and minority individuals were more likely to need computer assistance, such as help with using the keyboard or e-mail (Jackson *et al.*, 2004; Weerakkody *et al.*, 2004). Even those who obtain basic computer skills are frequently unable to use a computer or the Internet to retrieve and interpret information (Mossenberger *et al.*, 2003).

Trust and ICT divide surface as two of the most significant factors that influence e-government adoption and diffusion. The other factors mentioned in the literature revolve mainly around commonly cited ICT adoption and diffusion themes such as usefulness, usability and accessibility (Venkatesh *et al.*, 2003; Rogers, 2003; Davis, 1989) of e-government services. These are not exceptional to the e-government context and therefore not discussed here. Certainly, adoption and diffusion studies are still emerging in the e-government context and comparatively small when examined against the wider ICT and e-commerce adoption research. Nevertheless, these emerging studies are helping to advance the understanding of the concept from a user (or citizen) perspective and continue to shed light on the challenges facing governments in respect of citizens' adoption of their services. However, this is only the tip of the iceberg as there are many technical complexities and challenges that need to be tackled when implementing e-government services as outlined in the next section.

E-GOVERNMENT IMPLEMENTATION: TECHNICAL COMPLEXITIES AND CHALLENGES

As more and more citizens become Internet savvy they demand faster delivery of public services and better insight into the status of their requests. While integrated service delivery requires the sharing of information among the information systems of public agencies and harmonization of cross-organisational business processes, a debate that is facing many European governments' on-line agenda, at least in the short term, is how to proceed best with this integration. Existing systems are typically build-using architectures that do not readily support enterprise-wide integration, thus requiring the development of new architectures to link on-line government (Allen *et al.*, 2001; Weerakkody *et al.*, 2007). The challenge is that many e-government initiatives require information exchange in networks across different governmental organisations. Most public institutions today manage technology in what is popularly described as 'stove pipes' or 'isolated islands of technology' (Weerakkody *et al.*, 2007), with individual institutions implementing their own channels, web applications and supporting infrastructure. Traditionally, government agencies are organised vertically around departments. Cross-organisational processes can only be created by integrated IS delivering timely and accurate information, and supporting cross-departmental processes (Champy, 2002; Weerakkody *et al.*, 2006). Current systems are often developed within the boundaries of departments without having in mind the 'big picture' capturing the enterprise architecture of the whole organisation. The existence of isolated, overlapping in function and content, highly fragmented and unrelated computerized applications within the same public organisation has resulted in a major interoperability problem and has led to 'isolated islands of technology' (Peristera and Tarabanis, 2000; Kamal *et al.*, 2009).

Having largely evolved from e-business ideas, e-government requires the collaboration of various stakeholders and integration of business processes and IS in disparate organisations in order to deliver on-line-real-time services. As such, an e-government environment needs business processes that can be continuously optimized and expanded outside the enterprise and outside internal enterprise systems (Fustes, 2003; Champy, 2002). While the linking of these processes and IS require enterprise application integration (EAI) technologies, EAI has been an expensive and often problematic solution for many organisations engaged in e-business (Linthicum, 1999; Sutherland and Willem, 2002; Kamal *et al.*, 2009); these problems are multiplied in the public sector, where inefficient and bureaucratic business processes and disparate legacy IS/IT systems need to be integrated in an e-government environment (Weerakkody *et al.*, 2006; Kamal *et al.*, 2009). In a resource limited environment such as government agencies, enterprise architectures should therefore not be merely about service delivery, but also about integrating and sharing resources and using common systems (Hanafin, 2004; Weerakkody *et al.*, 2007). Opportunities for joint-development, pooling of resources and coordination of efforts are often neglected due to the lack of an overview. Although there are a number of enterprise architectures available (e.g. Zachman, 1987; Bernard, 2004; Nora, 2006; Schekkerman, 2004; Office of the e-envoy, 2002; Danish Ministry of Science, 2003) public managers find it difficult to translate the architecture to their specific situation, use these architectures to guide their decision-making and use these architectures as guidance for development from the existing situation. One of the reasons is that concepts are only vaguely defined, and too abstract or too technically defined (Kunda and Brooks, 2000; Peristera and Tarabanis, 2000)

A key research question that is often asked in e-government literature is, 'what are the process integration and enterprise architecture challenges faced by government when implementing integrated e-government services' (see for instance, Janssen and Cresswell, 2005; Weerakkody *et al.*, 2007; Kamal *et al.*, 2009). In this respect, the technical infrastructure and IS used in public agencies have to come under heavy scrutiny. In the last few years substantial investments have been made by governments around the world to improve their infrastructure and technology. Despite these investments, improving interoperability and integration in the context of e-government still presents a significant challenge, as the public sector can be characterized as largely non-process-oriented, legacy system driven. In the last few years various technologies have offered a new context for addressing some of these integration issues. From an organisational perspective, the implementation of e-government demands the reengineering of business processes and supporting IS in a way that is more radical than any other form of change seen in the public sector (Irani *et al.*, 2008; Weerakkody *et al.*, 2007). Consequently, there are many technical, semantic and organisational challenges needing to be solved.

Figure 1. Dimensions and stages of e-government development (Adapted from Layne and Lee, 2001)

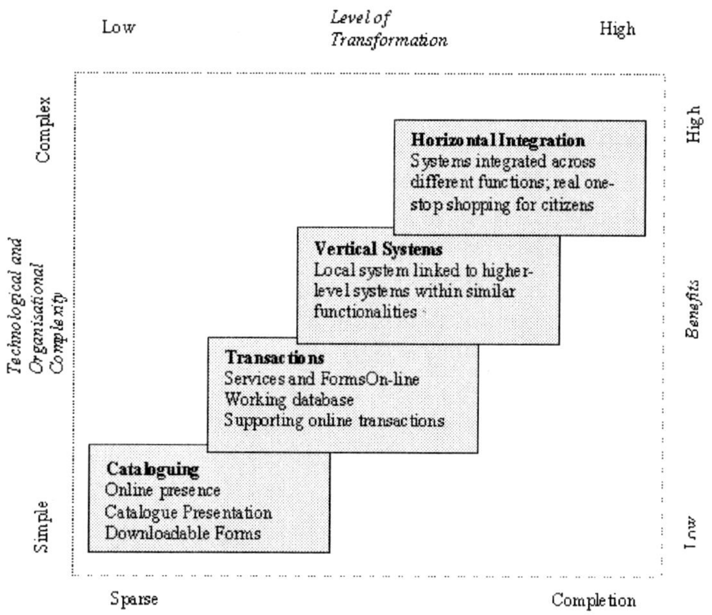

In respect of integration, the two main challenges facing government agencies are related to *Process Integration* and *Enterprise Architecture. Process integration* refers to the ability to connect systems in one way or another. In general this is complicated as there are many systems that need to be connected to many other systems (Weerakkody *et al.*, 2007). In addition, there are often many connections necessary between systems, as each message or data exchange requires a connection. There are various methods and change management approaches to deal with this aspect. *Enterprise architecture* (EA) lacks a universally accepted description. An EA identifies the main components of the enterprise, its information systems, the ways in which these components work together in order to achieve defined objectives and the way in which the systems support integration (ibid). As such, it can be used as an umbrella for guiding and supporting integration activities.

Integration challenges are further compounded by the different implementation focus, objectives and levels of transformation in public services in different countries. For instance, in the USA, the main objective is to automate and integrate different islands of information to simplify and maximize the benefits of technology (Navarra and Cornford, 2003), whereas in Europe the emphasis is to modernize public services and offer better services to citizens (Weerakkody *et al.*, 2004; 2006; 2007). Given this context, examining one of the most cited representations of the different stages and dimensions of e-government development (see Layne and Lee, 2001) is appropriate (figure 1). Figure 1 captures the process transformation and integration aspects and the scope needed for a one-stop e-government web portal according to Layne and Lee (2001).

In the cataloguing stage in figure 1, governments focus on establishing an online presence by publishing index pages or a localised site where electronic documents offer the public information relating to government services (Layne and Lee, 2001). This is the simplest and least expensive form of web presence and from the government's perspective it helps to save staff time spent on answering basic questions (Bonham *et al.*, 2003). In the transaction stage the focus is on connecting the internal government systems to online interfaces thus allowing citizens to electronically transact with government institutions. While the speed of which this sector has progressed is disappointing, the process of developing and maintaining services in this stage are more complex than at the first stage (Vasilakis *et al.*, 2003). In the third stage, vertical integration, federal, state and local governments are expected to connect to each other to offer a higher level of integrated service. The main challenge is to ensure compatibility and interoperability between various government databases (Layne and Lee, 2001). The most complex stage is horizontal integration where different services and functions within the same level of government are integrated to provide a one-stop-shop for all major services (Raffat, 2003). This, according to Bonham *et al.*, (2003) requires a transformation of how government functions are conceived, organised and executed and is more difficult to realize than the first three stages.

Developed countries (in North America and Western Europe) have managed to realise a few horizontal level integration of key services (such as taxation, social security and licensing) and many transaction level services such as e-billing, e-payments, e-voting and e-forms.

Although the abovementioned cases are encouraging, it can be argued that the transfer of public administrative processes that are organised around functional silos to an e-enabled, real-time, automated and process-based state would involve the rethinking and redesign of processes and IS at both local and national government levels (Irani *et al.*, 2008; Weerakkody *et al.*, 2008. There are also many instances where information is clearly not available locally (within the organisation) to execute processes and service specific customer demands. This adds a further complexity to the process, as information now may need to be obtained from sources outside the organisational boundaries of local government/councils. Organisations that are part of different hierarchies need to collaborate to ensure integrated service provisioning. Therefore, it is fair to state that progressing from the cataloguing stage to the horizontal integration stage (in figure 1) will require a radical redesign of established business processes and legacy systems utilizing techniques such as business process redesign as suggested by Hammer and Champy (1993); this is a complex undertaking (Hazlett and Hill, 2003; Halachmi, 1997). The next section reviews recent developments that have influenced the evolution of e-government from the current state of largely transaction level services to a more integrated one-strop environment. As explained in the next section, this evolution has largely been enabled by various governments' strategies to transform public administration processes across their organisations using ICT.

REALISING TRANSFORMATIONAL STAGE E-GOVERNMENT: FROM VISION TO REALITY

Recent e-government efforts have shifted their focus from e-enabling front-end to reengineering back-office processes. These efforts closely resemble the principles of business process redesign (BPR) seen in the private sector in the early 1990s and governments have commonly labelled them as transformational government (or t-government). In most western countries, t-government has naturally evolved from e-government. Yet, there still remains considerable confusion about t-government. The definitions offered for e-government differ according to the varying e-government focus and are usually centred on technology (Zhiyuan, 2002), business (Wassenaar, 2000), process (Bonham *et al.*, 2001), citizen (Burn and Robins, 2003), or a functional perspective (Seifert and Peterson, 2002). These different schools of thought show that there is no universally accepted definition of the e-government concept (Yildiz, 2007). However, we can distinguish between transformational government and e-government; t-government covers broader organisational and socio-technical dimensions which involve radically changing the structures, operations and most importantly, the culture of government (O'Donnell *et al.*, 2003; Ramaswamy and Selian, 2007; Irani *et al.*, 2007). Thus, a suitable definition for t-government that encapsulates a wider perspective of the transformational aspects of e-government would be: "*t-government is the ICT-enabled and organisation-led transformation of government operations, internal and external processes, structures and culture to enable the realisation of citizen-centric services that are transparent, cost effective and efficient*" (Weerakkody *at al*., 2008). In this definition it is proposed that the creation of citizen-centric services require considerable changes at all levels, which might be radical changes rather than incremental improvement.

Lee *et al.,* (2005) and Norris and Moon (2005) have found that local e-government efforts remain primarily informational (i.e. offering basic online services) and seldom achieve joined up service delivery or the potential positive impacts claimed by its most dedicated advocates. In this context, authors such as Kraemer and King (2005) have also argued that e-government is not transformational [as implied by Hammer and Champy (1993) in the case of BPR], but is incremental [for instance as suggested by Davenport (1993), Harrington (1991) or Carr and Johansson (1995)]. Kraemer and King (2005) further predict that the path of local e-government efforts that has been observed to date (i.e. incremental change) is likely to continue into the foreseeable future. Even though many governmental entities have built one-stop-shops to streamline the efficiency of services, the basic paper-based forms are continuing to rule the day (Conklin, 2007). Therefore, it is arguable that many government agencies are focusing on incremental improvements that are wrongly being branded as transformational. Moreover, some argue that more than 70 percent of e-government initiatives have failed to meet initial transformation objectives in the early stages of implementation (Gandhi and Cross, 2001; Beynon-Davies and Martin, 2004; Di Maio, 2006). Most of these failures can be attributed to the inability of governments to change business processes in response to the e-government model (Joia, 2004; Davison *et al.,* 2005; Ferlie *et al.,* 2003). Therefore, these early failures have resulted in an even more pressing need to integrate the front-end and back-end systems and processes (West, 2004; Kim *et al.,* 2007; Jas and Skelcher, 2005).

Many researchers have suggested that governments should be willing to change their business processes in order to reap the full potential of an e-government initiative (Kim *et al.,* 2007; Andersen and Henriksen, 2006; O'Donnell *et al.,* 2003; Swedberg and Douglas, 2003). In particular, to achieve t-government and the associated benefits, government departments and agencies need to actively co-ordinate and align with one another through the integration of processes and IS/IT systems (Murphy, 2005; Andersen and Henriksen, 2006; Weerakkody and Dhillon, 2008). T-government will enable government services to be fully integrated (vertically and horizontally) and citizens can expect to have access to a variety of services through a single portal (one-stop-shop) (Gil-Garcia and Martinez-Moyano, 2007). However, governments find it difficult to reach mature stages of e-government and a superior customer-focus as joined-up service delivery will require a considerable level of integration of back-end information systems such as electoral registers, land and property systems, council tax systems and benefits systems (Beynon-Davies and Martin, 2004; Holmes, 2001; Sarikas and Weerakkody, 2007).

Ultimately transformational government will require the ability to rethink processes in a cross-functional way as championed by BPR approaches (Hammer and Champy, 1993; Champy, 2002; Fagan, 2006). Whilst this has proven difficult in the private sector, research suggests that local authorities will face even more severe challenges in the bureaucratic, functionally oriented, legacy systems driven environment of government (Weerakkody *et al.,* 2007; Fagan, 2006). Moreover, as discussed in the previous section this will require concepts such as EA and service oriented architecture (SOA) that are capable of seamless integration of cross-agency processes and IS.

It is arguable that t-government is seen by many as the final phase of e-government, which focuses upon cost savings and service improvement through back-office process and IS/IT change. The t-government vision will require three key transformations, which firstly includes services enabled by ICT that are designed around the citizen and not the provider. Secondly, governments must move towards a

Table 1 Challenges Affecting Transformational Change: An E-Government Literature Perspective

Challenges Affecting T-Government	Literature Source
Organisational Challenges	
Reluctance to embrace change	Irani et al. (2008); Mansar (2006); Beynon-Davies & Martin (2004)
Bureaucratic organisational structure	Hu et al. (2006); Altameem et al. (2006); Fang (2006); Kraemer & King (2005)
The lack of leadership in change efforts	Irani et al. (2008); Beynon-Davies & Martin (2004); O'Donnell et al. (2003)
Process Change Challenges	
Confusing existing processes	Wimmer (2001); Gouscos et al. (2006); Altameem et al. (2006)
Information fragmentation	Irani et al. (2008); Gouscos et al. (2006)
Incremental and modest change	Beynon-Davies & Martin (2004)
Cultural and Social Challenges	
Organisational culture	Irani et al. (2008); Montagna (2005); Ebrahim & Irani (2005)
Unwillingness to share IS/IT systems and processes	Ebrahim & Irani (2005); Murphy (2005); Conklin (2007)
Employee resistance to change and fear of change	Robinson & Griffiths (2005); Murphy (2005)
Data sharing and data protection laws	Murphy (2005); Janssen et al. (2007)
IS/IT Integration Challenges	
Inflexible and incompatible legacy systems	BCS (2006); Gichoya (2005); McIvor et al. (2002); Sarikas & Weerakkody (2007)
Existing legacy systems increase costs	Sarikas & Weerakkody (2007); Ezz & Papazafeiropoulou (2006); Ebrahim & Irani (2005); Holden et al. (2003)
Lack of technology and BPR skills by IT staff	Ramaswamy & Selian (2007); Weerakkody et al. (2007)

shared services culture, thus eliminating data duplication, and integrating and re-engineering back-office processes (Janssen *et al.*, 2007). Thirdly, there must be broadening and deepening of government's professionalism in terms of planning delivery, management and governance of IT-enabled change (www.cio.gov.uk; Palanisamy, 2004).

Many scholars and practitioners have identified challenges that are facing e-government efforts and in particular in reaching the transformational stage of e-government (Irani *et al.*, 2008; Mansar, 2006; Gupta and Jana, 2003; Fang, 2006; West, 2004; Margetts and Dunleavy, 2002; Raffat, 2003; Palanisamy, 2004; Weerakkody *et al.*, 2007; Sarikas and Weerakkody, 2007). When drawing upon the normative literature on e-government in order to distinguish the key challenges affecting governments' progression onto the transformational stage of e-government (or t-government), the key challenges identified in e-government literature can be broadly classified under four key themes which capture the organisational, process change, socio-cultural and IS/IT integration aspects (Lee *et al.*, 2005) (Table 1).

The complexity of transformational change in the public sector (as outlined in table 1) is reflected in the fact that in practice only 4 percent of e-government initiatives are in fact aiming to reach t-government (Balutis, 2001; Conklin, 2007). This is reminiscent of the BPR era during the early 1990's, where many private sector organisations failed in their transformation efforts with BPR type changes (Willcocks, 1995; Hazlett and Hill, 2003; Coram and Burnes, 2001; Motwani *et al.*, 2004; Hammer and Champy, 1993; Peters *et al.*, 2004). Given BPR's chequered history, it coveys more negative signals than positive indicators. Consequently, many researchers (such as Gupta and Jana, 2003; Palanisamy, 2004; Andersen and Henriksen, 2006; Mansar, 2006; Fang, 2006; Irani *et al.*, 2008; Weerakkody and Dhillon, 2008) have begun to focus their immediate research efforts in the t-government area.

CONCLUSION

This article has attempted to offer a snapshot of how e-government research has progressed over the last few years, from inception to implementation, and through to adoption and diffusion. In doing so, the article has touched on the past, present and future of e-government in the context of governments' role (as the service provider) and citizens' role (as the user). Four themes have emerged in e-government research: a) strategy formulation and policy making in the context of implementation; b) adoption and diffusion of services; c) technical challenges in implementation; and d) the transformational stage of e-government or fully functional e-government.

E-government research indicates that the diffusion of digital services has been slower than anticipated and that many governments are not making use of available technology for transforming government processes and offering value added services. In cases of successes ICT enabled change; the impact of e-government has been only incremental rather than transformative. According to the literature, a number of challenges have impacted upon the successful implementation and diffusion of e-government. Many researchers have shown that several social, economic and political barriers constrain the scope of transformation and restrict successful e-government implementation from an organisational and strategic perspective. Conversely, digital divide and the socio-political nature of public sector reforms are cited by many as key factors affecting e-government diffusion from a citizen centric perspective.

When examining the papers published in the International Journal of Electronic Government Research (IJEGR) and the wider e-government domain, it is evident that early research on e-government was very much focused on examining the strategy, policies and the electronic service delivery plans of various governments. In this phase many researchers also looked into the complexities of implementation from an organisational perspective. Subsequently, after basic e-government services were successfully implemented by governments and became available on a more widespread scale, researchers were beginning to focus on adoption and diffusion aspects, particularly due to poor take-up of these services. Well established theories such as the technology acceptance model (Davis, 1989), diffusion of innovation (Rogers, 2003) and unified theory of acceptance and use of technology (UTAUT) (Venkatesh *et al.* 2003) have been used to study adoption and diffusion. Thereafter, in parallel, when e-government services that were offered became more advanced (i.e. as per figure 1) and implementation efforts were beginning to undergo process and IS integration problems, a number of researchers began to focus on the technical complexities. Finally, in the last two years, the concept of transformational government or t-government has emerged, which encompasses a broader perspective of public administration, as t-government is seen as the final stage of fully functional electronic service delivery for the public sector.

In the transformational e-government stage, greater cost-savings, transparency and efficiency and effectiveness are offered in all government services. To date, few countries have excelled in reaching the transformational stage of e-government. This is due in part to the complexity of reaching this high level of maturity for e-government. The literature suggests that e-government efforts in most countries are incremental and seldom is a joined-up service delivery created. In addition, Kraemer and King (2005) and Weerakkody and Dhillon (2008) further predict that the path of local e-government efforts observed to date (i.e. incremental change) is likely to continue into the foreseeable future, whereas there is a need for more radical changes. From this perspective many academics and practitioners have identified a variety of change barriers and challenges affecting t-government such as the lack of compatible IS/IT infrastructures, lack of standardised data definitions, management commitment, bureaucratic organisational structures and employee resistance towards change to name a few. Therefore, transformational change in the public sector poses many challenges to governments that are reminiscent of the BPR era in the private sector in the early 1990s. It is reasonable to assume that most developed countries will spend the next five to ten years tackling these challenges, while in the developing world many countries are only beginning to implement basic transactional level services. In this context, it is predicted here that e-government will remain a major research theme for the foreseeable future.

FUTURE RESEARCH DIRECTIONS

Current research into e-government indicates that the concept of electronic service delivery in the public sector will continue to grow at an accelerated pace, but its diversity and impact will be determined by the extent to which citizens adopt it as well as various governments' efforts to diffuse the concept. While most research into adoption and diffusion point a less than encouraging picture, lessons are beginning to emerge which indicate that citizens are demanding more value added services before they could be fully enticed to use e-government. The early e-government efforts have focused very much on e-enabling existing front-office services without much consideration on reengineering the back-end business processes and IS/IT systems that support these customer facing processes. Therefore, it is fait to state that most e-government initiatives were offering an e-business front end to existing, often inefficient and ineffective business processes that were experienced by citizens for many years. In this context, many governments have realised that the present and future e-government efforts should be focused very much on transforming the way services are delivered, not only in terms e-enabling them, but also in terms of efficiency, effectiveness, transparency and most importantly the value-added features offered to citizens through e-government.

Future research on e-government will no doubt explore the key facets of process transformation and reengineering including strategic, organisational, socio-cultural and human influences. Most significantly, the technical complexities that arise in a transformational context, including integration of legacy systems with new and reengineered IS/IT systems will be a major challenge that will need much research effort. Finally, the economic and efficiency aspects will be as important for governments where new and relatively unproven concepts such as *shared services* will need major research efforts on the part of the academic community in order to generate a better understanding and help effective exploitation. In a broader context, the potential impact of e-government on reforming socio-economic, political and democratic policies to establishing the notion of 'e-governance' will be an interesting area to observe in the future.

REFERENCES

Adeshara, P., Juric, R., Kuljis, J., & Paul, R.J. (2004). A Survey of Acceptance of e-Government Services in the UK. In *Proceedings of the International Conference on Information Technology Interfaces*. Cavtat, Croatia.

Allen, B.A., Juillet, L. Paquet, P., & Roy, J. (2001). E-Governance and Government On-Line In Canada: Partnerships, People and Prospects. *Government Information Quarterly*, 18, 93-104.

Al-Sebie, M., & Irani, Z. (2005). Technical And Organisational Challenges Facing Transactional E-Government Systems: An Empirical Study. *Electronic Government, an International Journal*, *2*(3), 247-276.

Al-Shafi, S., & Weerakkody, V. (2008). Adoption of Wireless Internet Parks: An Empirical Study in Qatar. In *Proceedings of the 5th European and Mediterranean Conference on Information Systems (EMCIS).*

Altameem, T., Zairi, M., & Alshawi, S. (2006). Critical Success Factors of E-Government: A Proposed Model for E-Government Implementation. *IEEE*, 1-5

Andersen, K., & Henriksen, H. (2006). E-Government Maturity Models: Extension of the Layne and Lee Model. *Government Information Quarterly*, 23, 236-248.

Balutis, A.P. (2001). E-Government 2001. Part I: Understanding the Challenge and Evolving Strategies. *The Public Manager*, Spring, 33-37.

BCS British Computer Society. (2006). Sweating the Assets, *ITNOW article*, p.18 available at: http://www.bcs.org/, [Accessed on: 25 May 2007]

Becerra, M. and Gupta, A. K. (1999). Trust Within the Organization: Integrating the Trust Literature with Agency Theory and Transaction Costs Economics. *Public Administration Quarterly, 23*(2), 177-203.

Bernard, S. A. (2004). *An Introduction to Enterprise Architecture*. Indiana: Author House.

Beynon-Davies, P., & Martin, S. (2004). Electronic Local Government and the Modernisation Agenda: Progress and Prospects for Public Service Improvement, *Local Government Studies*, *30*(2), 214-229

Bonham, M.G., Seifert, J. W., & Thorson, S.J (2001). The Transformational Potential of e-Government: The Role of Political Leadership. In *Proceedings of the 4th Pan European International Relations Conference*, UK.

Burn, F., & Robins, G. (2003). Moving Towards E-Government: A Case Study of Organisational Change Processes. *Logistics Information Management*, *16*(1), 25–35.

Carr, D., & Johansson, H. (1995). *Best Practices in Re-engineering: What Works and What Doesn't in the Re-engineering Process*. New York: McGraw-Hill.

Carter, L,, & Belanger, F. (2005). The Utilization of E-government Services: Citizen Trust, Innovation and Acceptance Factors. *Information Systems Journal, 15*(1), 5-25.

Carter, L., & Weerakkody, V. (2008), E-Government Adoption: A Cultural Comparison, *Information Systems Frontiers*, *10*(4), 473-482.

Champy, J. (2002). *X-Engineering the Corporation: Reinventing Your Business in the Digital Age*. Warner Books.

Cio.gov.uk. (n.d.). Retrieved July 18, 2007 from http://www.cio.gov.uk

ComScore. (2006). 694 Million People Currently Use the Internet Worldwide According to Comscore Networks. Retrieved January 18, 2008 from http://www.comscore.com/press/release.asp?press=849

Conklin, A. (2007). Barriers to Adoption of E-Government. In *Proceedings of the 40th Hawaii International Conference on Systems Sciences* (pp. 1-8). IEEE.

Coram, R., & Burnes, B. (2001), Managing Organisational Change in the Public Sector: Lessons from the Privatisation of the Property Service Agency, *The International Journal of Public Sector Management*, *14*(2), 94-110.

Cross, M. (2007). £5M E-Government Awareness Campaign Flops. *The Guardian.* Retrieved April 15, 2008 from http://www.guardian.co.uk/technology/2006/oct/12/marketingandpr.newmedia

Danish White Paper on Enterprise Architecture, (2003). *Danish Ministry of Science, Technology and Innovation*. Retrieved November 20, 2007 from http://www.oio.dk/arkitektur/eng

Davenport, T.H. (1993). *Process Innovation: Reengineering Work through Information Technology*. Boston, MA: Harvard Business School Press.

Davis, F.D. (1989). Perceived Usefulness, Perceived Ease of Use, and User Acceptance of Information Technology. *MIS Quarterly,* 13, 319-340.

Davison, R.M, Wagner, C., & Ma, L.C.K. (2005), From Government to E-Government: A Transition Model, *Information Technology and People*, *18*(3), 280-299.

Di Maio, A. (2006) Moving from E-Government to Government Transformation, *Business Issues* (pp.1–3). Retrieved June 2, 2007 from http://www.gartner.com

Direct.gov.uk. (n.d.). Retrieved July 18, 2007 from http://www.direct.gov.uk/en/index.htm

Earl, M.J. (1993). *Experiences in Strategic Information Systems Planning. MIS Quarterly, 17*(1), 1-24.

Ebrahim, Z., & Irani, Z. (2005). E-government Adoption: Architecture and Barriers, *Business Process Management Journal, 11*(5), 589-611.

European Union (2004). United Nations Global e-Government Readiness Report 2004 – Towards Access for Opportunity. Retrieved September 11, 2006 from http://www.epractice.eu/document/2948

Ezz, I., & Papazafeiropoulou, A. (2006). Inter-organisational Collaboration Towards Process Integration in the Public Sector. E-government Collaboration in Egypt, In *Proceedings of the 39th Hawaii International Conference on System Sciences* (pp. 1-10). IEEE.

Fagan, M. (2006). Exploring City, County and State E-government Initiatives: an East Texas Perspective, *Business Process Management Journal*, *12*(1), 101-112.

Fang, Z. (2002). E-Government in Digital Era: Concept, Practice and Development, *International Journal of the Computer, The Internet and Information*, 20,193-213.

Ferlie, E., Hartley, J., & Martin, S. (2003). Changing Public Service Organisations: Current Perspectives and Future Prospects, *British Journal of Management*, 14, S1–S14.

Fustes, M. (2003, July). The Unconstrained Business. *Insight*, 3, 15-17.

Galliers, R.D. (1991). Strategic Information Systems Planning: Myths, Reality and Guidelines for Successful Implementation. *European Journal of Information Systems*, *1*(1), 55-63.

Ganesan, S. and Hess, R. (1997). Dimensions and Levels of Trust: Implications for Commitment to a Relationship. *Marketing Letters*, *8*(4), 439-448.

Gefen, D., Rose, G.M., Warkentin, M. & Pavlou, P.A. (2005). Cultural Diversity and Trust in IT Adoption: A Comparison of USA and South African e-Voters. *Journal of Global Information Management, 13*(1), 54-78.

Gandhi, S., & Cross, C. (2001). E-Government Initiative at City of Orlando: Current Trends and Future Directions. In *Proceedings of the URISA Conference*, October 2001 (pp.1–12).

Gichoya, D. (2005). Factors Affecting the Successful Implementation of ICT Projects in Government, *The Electronic Journal of e-Government, 3*(4), 175-184. Retrieved May 29, 2007 from http://www.ejeg.com

Gil-Garcia, J., & Martinez-Moyano, I. (2007). Understanding the Evolution of E-Government: The Influence of Systems of Rules on Public Sector Dynamics, *Government Information Quarterly,* 24, 266-290.

Gilbert, D., Balestrini, P., & Littleboy, D. (2004). Barriers and Benefits in the Adoption of E-government. *International Journal of Public Sector Management, 17*(4/5), 286-301.

Gouscos, D., Kalikakis, M., Legal, M., & Papadopoulou, S. (2006). A General Model of Performance and Quality for One-stop E-Government Service Offerings. *Government Information Quarterly*, 1-26.

Gupta, M.P., & Jana, D. (2003). E-Government Evaluation: A Framework and Case Study, *Government Information Quarterly*, 20, 365–387.

Halachmi, A. (1997). Government Reforms and Public Productivity: Do We Have All The Answer? *Work Study, 46*(7), 233-245.

Hammer, M., and Champy, J. (1993). *Re-engineering the Corporation: A Manifesto for Business Revolution*. New York: Harper Collins Publishers Inc.

Hanafin, M. (2004). *Welcomes Speech Minister of State*. European E-Government Conference ECEG2004, Dublin, Ireland.

Harrington, H. (1991). *Business Process Improvement: The Breakthrough Strategy for Total Quality, Productivity and Competitiveness*. New York: McGraw Hill.

Hazlett, S.A. and Hill, F. (2003). E-Government: the Realities of Using IT to Transform the Public Sector. *Managing Service Quality, 13*(6), 445-452.

Holden, S., Norris, D., & Fletcher, P. (2002). Electronic Government at the Grass Roots: Contemporary Evidence and Future Trends. In *Proceedings of the 36th Hawaii International Conference on System Sciences* (pp.1-8).

Holden, S.H., Norris, D.F. and Fletcher, P.D. (2003). Electronic Government at the Local Level: Progress To Date And Future Issues. *Public Performance and Management Review, 26*(4), 325–344.

Holmes, D. (2001). *E.gov E-Business Strategies for Government*. London: Nicholas Brealey Publishing.

Hu, P., Cui, D. & Sherwood, A. (2006). Examining Cross-Agency Collaborations in E-Government Initiatives, *Proceedings of the 39th Hawaii International Conference on System Sciences*, pp.1-11.

Huang, Z. (2007). A Comprehensive Analysis of U.S. Counties' E-Government Portals: Development Status and Functionalities. *European Journal of Information Systems,* 16, 149-164

Hunter, D. R., & Jupp, V. (2001), *E-government Leadership: Rhetoric vs. Reality - Closing the Gap.* Retrieved March 12, 2004 from http://www.accenture.com/Global/Services/By_Industry/Government_and_Public_Service/PS_Global/R_and_I/GovernmentsRhetoric.htm

Irani, Z., T. Elliman, & Jackson, P. (2007). Electronic Transformation of Government in the U.K.: A Research Agenda. *European Journal of Information Systems, 16*(4), 327-335.

Irani, Z, Love, P.E.D., & Jones, S. (2008). Learning Lessons From Evaluating Egovernment: Reflective Case Experiences That Support Transformational Government, *The Journal of Strategic Information Systems*, *17*(2), 155-164.

Jackson, L. A., von Eye, A., Barbatsis, G., Biocca, F., Fitzgerald, H.E., & Zhao, Y. (2004). The Impact of Internet Use on the Other Side of the Digital Divide. *Communications of the ACM, 47*(7), 43-47.

Janssen, M., & Cresswell, A. (2005). The Development of a Reference Architecture for Local Government. In *Proceedings of the Hawaii International Conference on System Sciences (HICSS-38).*

Janssen, M., Joha, A., & Weerakkody, V. (2007). Shared Service Arrangements in the Public Sector: An Exploratory Study, *Transforming Government: People, Process and Policy, 1*(3), 271-284.

Jarvenpaa, S. L., Knoll, K., & Leidner, D.E. (1998). Is Anybody Out There? Antecedents of Trust in Global Virtual Teams. *Journal of Management Information Systems, 14*(4), 29-64.

Jas, P., and Skelcher, C. (2005). Performance Decline and Turnaround in Public Organizations: A Theoretical and Empirical Analysis. *British Journal of Management,* 16, 195-210.

Johnson, G., & Scholes, K. (1999). *Exploring Corporate Strategy*. Upper Saddle River, NJ: Prentice Hall.

Joia, L. (2004). Developing Government-to-Government Enterprises in Brazil: A Heuristic Model Drawn from Multiple Case Studies. *International Journal of Information Management*, 24, 147-166.

Kablenet.com (2005). UK Lagging on E-government. Retrieved April 12, 2006 from http://news.zdnet.co.uk/internet/0,1000000097,39198581,00.htm

Kamal, M., Weerakkody, V., & Jones, S. (2009), The Case of EAI in Facilitating E-Government Services in a Welsh Authority. *International Journal of Information Management, 29(*2).

Kim, H., Pan, G., & Pan, S. (2007). Managing IT-Enabled Transformation in the Public Sector: A Case Study on E-Government in South Korea. *Government Information Quarterly*, 24, 338-352.

Kraemer, K., & King, J. (2005). Information Technology and Administrative Reform: Will E-Government Be Different? *International Journal of Electronic Government Research*, 1, 1-18.

Kunda, D., & Brooks, L. (2000). Identifying and Classifying Processes (Traditional and Soft Factors) That Support COTS Component Selection: A Case Study. *European Journal of Information Systems, 9*(4), 226-234.

Layne, K.J.L., & Lee, J. (2001). Developing Fully Functional E-Government: A Four Stage Model, *Government Information Quarterly, 18*(2), 122-136.

Lee, M. K. O., & Turban, E. (2001). A Trust Model for Consumer Internet Shopping. *International Journal of Electronic Commerce, 6*(1), 75-91.

Lee, S.M., Tan, X., & Trimi, S. (2005). Current Practices of Leading E-Government Countries. *Communications of the ACM, 48*(10): 99–104.

Linthicum, D. (1999). *Enterprise Application Integration*. Addison Wesley.

Mansar, S. (2006). *E-Government Implementation: Impact on Business Processes* (pp. 1-5). *IEEE.*

Margetts, H., & Dunleavy, P. (2002). *Cultural Barriers to E-Government* (Working Paper). University College London and London School of Economics for National Audit Office.

Mayer, R. C., Davis, J. H., & Schoorman, D.F. (1995). An Integrative Model of Organizational Trust. *Academy of Management Review, 20*(3), 709-734.

McFarlan, F.W. (1971). Problems in Planning the Information System. *Harvard Business Review, 42*(2): 75-89.

McIvor, R., McHugh, M., & Cadden, C. (2002). Internet Technologies: Supporting Transparency in the Public Sector. *The International Journal of Public Sector Management, 15*(3), 170-187.

McKnight, D. H., Cummings, L. L., & Chervany, N.L. (1998). Initial Trust Formation in New Organizational Relationships. *Academy of Management Review, 23*(3), 473-490.

McKnight, H., Choudhury, V., & Kacmar, C. (2002). Developing and Validating Trust Measures for E-commerce: An Integrative Typology. *Information Systems Research, 13*(3), 334-359.

Minzberg, H. (1994). *The Rise and Fall of Strategic Planning.* Prentice Hall International.

Montagna, J. (2005). A Framework for the Assessment and Analysis of Electronic Government Proposals. *Electronic Commerce Research and Applications*, 4, 204-219.

Mossberger, K., Tolbert, C.J., & Stansbury, M. (2003). *Virtual Inequality: Beyond the Digital Divide.* Washington, D.C.: George Washington University Press.

Motwani, J., Kumar, A., & Antony, J. (2004). A Business Process Change Framework for Examining the Implementation of Six Sigma: A Case Study of Dow Chemicals. *The TQM Magazine, 16*(4), 273-283.

Murphy, J. (MP Parliamentary Secretary Cabinet Office Report) (2005). Beyond e-government the world's most successful technology-enabled transformations, executive summary, INSEAD the business school for the world (pp.1-124). Retrieved May 29, 2007 from http://www.localtgov.org.uk

Navarra, D. D., & Cornford, T. (2003). A Policy Making View of E-Government Innovations in Public Governance. In *Proceedings of the Ninth Americas Conference on Information Systems*, Tampa, Florida.

Nora (2006). Nederlands OverheidsReferentieArchitectuur. Samenhang en samenwerken binnen de elektronische overhead. ICT Programma Architectuur Elektronische overheid. Retrieved April 2006 from http://elo.asp4all.nl/atlas/referentiearchitectuur

Norris, D.F., & Moon, M.J. (2005). Advancing E-Government at the Grass Roots: Tortoise or Hare? *Public Administration Review, 65*(1), 64–75.

O'Donnell, O., Boyle, R., & Timonen, V. (2003). Transformational Aspects of E-Government in Ireland: Issues to be addressed, *Electronic Journal of e-Government, 1*(1), 23-32. Retrieved May 24, 2007 from http://www.ejeg.com

Office of e-Envoy UK (2002). *E-Services Development Framework Primer v1.0b.*

Oxendine, A., Borgida, E., Sullivan, J.L., & Jackson, M.S. (2003). The Importance of Trust and Community in Developing and Maintaining a Community Electronic Network. *International Journal of Human-Computer Studies,* 58, 671-196.

Palanisamy, R. (2004). Issues and Challenges in E-governance Planning, *Electronic Government, an International Journal*, *1*(3), 253–273.

Peristera, V., & Tarabanis, K. (2000). Towards An Enterprise Architecture For Public Administration Using A Top-Down Approach. *European Journal of Information Systems*, 9, 252-260.

Peters, R., Janssen, M., & Van Eagers, T. (2004). Measuring e-Government Impact: Existing Practices and Shortcomings. In *Proceedings of the Sixth International Conference on Electronic Commerce* (pp.480-489). ACM.

Raffat, R. (2003). *Developing a Successful E-Government* (Working Paper). School of Architecture, Design Science and Planning, University of Sydney, Australia.

Ramaswamy, M., & Selian, A. (2007). E-Government in Transition Countries: Prospects and Challenges. In *Proceedings of the 40th Hawaii International Conference on System Sciences* (pp.1-10). IEEE.

Robinson, O. and Griffiths, A. (2005). Coping with the Stress of Transformational Change in a Government Department,.*The Journal of Applied Behavioral Science*, *41*(2), 204-221. Retrieved June 25, 2007 from http://jab.sagepub.com

Rogers, E. M. (2003). *Diffusion of Innovation*, The Free Press, New York.

Sambamurthy, V., Zmud, R.W., & Byrd, T.A. (1994). The Comprehensiveness of IT Planning Processes: A Contingency Approach. *Journal of Information Technology Management*, *5*(10), 1-10.

Sarikas, O.D., & Weerakkody, V. (2007). Realising Integrated E-Government Services: A UK Local Government Perspectives. *Transforming Government: People, Process and Policy*, *1*(2), 153-173.

Schekkerman, J. (2004). *How to Survive in the Jungle of Enterprise Architecture Frameworks*. Victoria: Trafford Publishing.

Seifert, J., & Petersen, E. (2002). The Promise of All Things E? Expectations and Challenges of Emergent Electronic Government. *Perspectives on Global Development and Technology*, *1*(2), 193–213.

Silcock, R. (2001). What is e-Government? *Parliamentary Affairs*, 55, 88-101.

Sutherland, J., & Willem, J. (2002). Enterprise Application Integration and Complex Adaptive Systems, *Communications of the ACM, 45*(10), 59-64.

Swedberg, D., & Douglas, J. (2003). Transformation by Design: An Innovative Approach to Implementation of e-Government. *Electronic Journal of e-Government*, *1*(1), 51-56. Retrieved May 24, 20007 from http://www.ejeg.com

Thomas, J. C., & Streib, G. (2003). The New Face of Government: Citizen-Initiated Contacts in the Era of E-Government. *Journal of Public Administration Research and Theory, 13*(1), 83.

UNPAN (2008). *United Nations E-Government Survey: From E-government to Connected Government*. New York: United Nations.

Vasilakis, C., Laskaridis, G., Lepouras, S., Rouvas, S., & Georgiadis, P. (2003). A Framework for Managing the Life Cycle of Transactional E-Government Services. *Telematics and Informatics*, 20, 315-329.

Venkatesch, V., Morris, M., Davis, G., & Davis, F. (2003). User Acceptance of Information Technology: Toward a Unified View. *MIS Quarterly*, 27, 425-478.

Wang, Y. D., & Emurian, H. H. (2005). An Overview of Online Trust: Concepts, Elements, and Implications. *Computers in Human Behaviour*, 21, 105-125.

Warkentin, M., Gefen, D., Pavlou, P.A., & Rose, G.M. (2002). Encouraging Citizen Adoption of E-Government by Building Trust. *Electronic Markets*, *12*(3), 157-162.

Wassenaar, A. (2000). E-governmental Value Chain Models. In *11th International Workshop on Database and Expert Systems Applications* (pp.289-293).

Weerakkody, V., & Choudrie, J. (2005), Exploring E-Government in the UK: Challenges, Issues and Complexities. *Journal of Information Science and Technology*, *2*(2), 25-45.

Weerakkody, V., & Dhillon, G. (2008), Moving from E-Government to T-Government: A Study of Process Reengineering Challenges in a UK Local Authority Context. *International Journal of Electronic Government Research*, *4*(4), 1-16.

Weerakkody, V., Baire, B., & Choudrie, J. (2006). E-Government: The Need for Effective Process Management in the Public Sector. In *Proceedings of the Hawaii International Conference on System Sciences (HICSS-39).*

Weerakkody, V., Choudrie, J., & Currie, W. (2004). Realising E-Government in the UK: Local and National Challenges. In *Proceedings of the 10th Americas Conference on Information Systems.*

Weerakkody, V. Dhillon, G. and Dwivedi, Y.K. (2008), Realising Transformational Stage E-Government: Challenges, Issues and Complexities, *Proceedings of the Americas Conference on Information Systems (AMCIS)*.

Weerakkody, V., Janssen, M., & Hjort-Madsen, K. (2007). Realising Integrated E-government Services: A European Perspective. *Journal of Cases in Electronic Commerce*, *3*(2), 14–38.

Welch, E. W., Hinnant, C. C., & Moon, M.J. (2005). Linking Citizen Satisfaction with E-Government and Trust in Government. *Journal of Public Administration Research and Theory*, *15*(3), 371-391.

Wellman, B., & Haythornthwaite C. (2002). *The Internet in Everyday Life.* Oxford: Blackwell.

West, D. (2004). E-Government and the Transformation of Service Delivery and Citizen Attitudes, *Public Administration Review*, *64*(1), 15–27.

Willcocks, L. (1995). False Promise or Delivering the Goods? Recent Findings on the Economics and Impact of Business Process Reengineering. In *Proceedings of the 2nd European Conference on IT Investment Evaluation.*

Wimmer, M. (2001). European Development Towards Online One-stop Government: The "eGOV" Project. In *Proceedings of the ICEC2001 Conference* (pp.1-8).

Wright, N. (2002). *The Economics of Privacy in the Information Age*. Annual Meeting for the Academy of Marketing Studies.

Yildiz, M. (2007). E-Government Research: Reviewing The Literature, Limitations, and Ways Forward. *Government Information Quarterly*, 1-20.

Zachman, J.A. (1987). A Framework for Information Systems Architecture. *IBM Systems Journal*, *26*(3), 276-292.

Zhiyuan, F. (2002). E-Government in Digital Era: Concepts, Practice and Development. *International Journal of the Computer, the Internet and Management, 10*(2), 1-22.

Chapter 1
E-Government Capabilities for 21st Century Security and Defense

Roy Ladner
Stennis Space Center, USA

Fred Petry
Stennis Space Center, USA

Frank McCreedy
Stennis Space Center, USA

ABSTRACT

In this article we provide an overview of e-government as it pertains to national security and defense within the Department of Defense (DoD) and Department of Homeland Security (DHS). We discuss the adoption of Web services and service-oriented architectures to aid in information sharing and reduction of IT costs. We also discuss the networks on which services and resources are being deployed and explain the efforts being made to manage the infrastructure of available services. This article provides an overview of e-government for national security and defense and provides insight to current initiatives and future directions.

INTRODUCTION

With the growth of the Internet, e-commerce has become prevalent for the exchange of information, goods, and services. Electronic government or e-government refers to the government's utilization of the tools of e-commerce in order to accomplish its mission. Typical e-government services include online driver's license renewal, federal income disbursement, and even filing federal or state income tax returns. In this article we provide an overview of e-government as it pertains to national security and defense within the Department of Defense (DoD) and Department of Homeland Security (DHS). The DoD is the lead federal agency for homeland defense and includes military departments such as the Navy, Air Force, and Army as well as defense agencies such as the Defense

Information Systems Agency (DISA) and the Defense Threat Reduction Agency (Department of Defense, 2000). The DHS is the lead federal agency for homeland security and includes the U.S. Coast Guard; Customs & Border Protection; U.S. Secret Service; Federal Emergency Management Agency; Transportation Security Administration; and so forth (Department of Homeland Security History, 2006; O'Rourke, 2005). We describe how the capabilities available through e-government are changing the way these agencies provide homeland defense and homeland security.

This article is organized as follows. We begin with a general description of e-government. We then describe the functional components of Web services. Following this we show how service-oriented computing is being adopted for homeland security and defense. We describe the Global Information Grid (GIG) and other networks on which services and resources are being deployed and explain the efforts being made to manage the infrastructure of available services. We conclude with a description of the Integrated Web Services Broker (IWB) being developed by the Naval Research Laboratory as an example of how Web services can be efficiently identified, selected, and used in service-oriented environments such as the GIG.

E-GOVERNMENT OVERVIEW

E- is also known as e-gov, digital government, and online government. E-government deals mostly with Internet applications to assist in government functionality. Although not a focus of this article, the term has also been applied to some non-Internet applications such as citizen tracking systems that deal with omnipresent surveillance and biometric identification (What is e-government, 2007).

The overall objective of e-government may be characterized as streamlining government operations in some form. This can take a number of forms, including those listed in a 2002 e-government implementation strategy (United States Office of Management and Business [OMB], 2002, p. 4) as:

- Eliminating layers of government management;
- Making it possible for citizens, businesses, other levels of government and federal employees to easily find information and get service from the federal government;
- Simplifying agencies' business processes and reducing costs through integrating and eliminating redundant systems;
- Enabling achievement of the other elements of the President's Management Agenda; and
- Streamlining government operations to guarantee rapid response to citizen needs.

In the course of achieving e-government, delivery of services may follow a number of models similar to those found in e-commerce, namely, government-to-citizen, government-to-business, government-to-government and intra-governmental: Internal efficiency and effectiveness (IEE) (OMB, 2002).

The U.S. government has established an e-government office having online presence at http://www.whitehouse.gov/omb/egov/. The following statement on this Web site indicates the significance of the transformation taking place, "E-Gov does not mean putting scores of government forms on the Internet. It is about using technology to its fullest to provide services and information that is centered around citizen groups." In order to facilitate access to federal, state, and local e-government, the federal government has also established a Web portal, http://www.usa.gov/. Additionally, recent developments in e-government news are routinely published in *Federal Computing Week* and available online at the following Web site: http://www.fcw.com/e_government.asp?topic=egov

The Geospatial One-Stop is an example of a presidential initiative that provides federal and state agencies with Web portal access to mapping related data. This single point of access allows the sharing of data in a way that makes better use of resources. The portal is found at geodata.gov and includes the tools for finding and analyzing the multiple sources of information that are available. These tools support functions such as search, interactive mapping, and metadata publishing. Mapping data available through the Geospatial One-Stop is accessible via the Open Geospatial Consortium's Web Mapping Service (WMS) specification. The Geospatial One-Stop can also make use of other portals to maximize available data. One example of how it makes non-WMS data available is seen in its access to the Geospatial Information Database (GIDB) portal system developed at the Naval Research Laboratory. The GIDB provides a portal to over 1,500 data servers. Many of these servers are not WMS compliant. In order to enable non-WMS compliant data to be accessible together with WMS compliant data on the Geospatial One-Stop, the GIDB portal provides a WMS entry point to its portal. This is illustrated in Figure 1.

An example of e-government within the DoD is the Air Force Innovation and Technology Knowledge Management Web site. This site was launched in April 2006 in order to coordinate knowledge sharing among many innovation communities that are working on new technology and solutions. The Air Force Knowledge Now (AFKN) service is accessed through the Air Force portal and is pictured in Figure 2. Other agencies, such as the U.S. Navy, and Army also have Web portals that are similar in nature.

One example of DHS e-government is the Homeland Security Digital Library (HSDL). This Web-based service is an online library that provides access to several hundred thousand documents pertaining to U.S. policy, presidential directives, and national strategy. It also includes specialized resources such as theses, reports from various universities, organizations, and local and state agencies. The library is intended to help federal, state, and local government agencies develop future policies as well as assist students/faculty to research the decision-making processes since the September 11 terrorists attack. It would have been difficult for each government official, student, or faculty member to individually obtain a copy of these documents. It also would have been a duplication of efforts (Department of Homeland Security at Naval Post Graduate School, n.d.). The goals of e-government are achieved here by providing the information in a speedy manner and eliminating redundant efforts (Lamont, 2006).

WEB SERVICES IN E-GOVERNMENT

E-government is aimed at "simplified and timely delivery of services to the citizens" (OMB, 2002) of a community. In its simplest form, this may involve e-government solutions that make government services conveniently available via Web pages as shown through the e-government solutions mentioned previously. In contrast, many DoD and DHS application areas call for

Figure 1. Geospatial one-stop access to data via GIDB portal

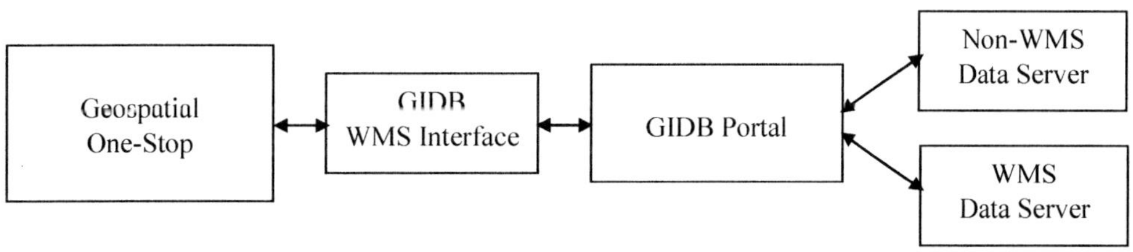

Figure 2. Air Force portal (Source: Adkins, R., n.d.)

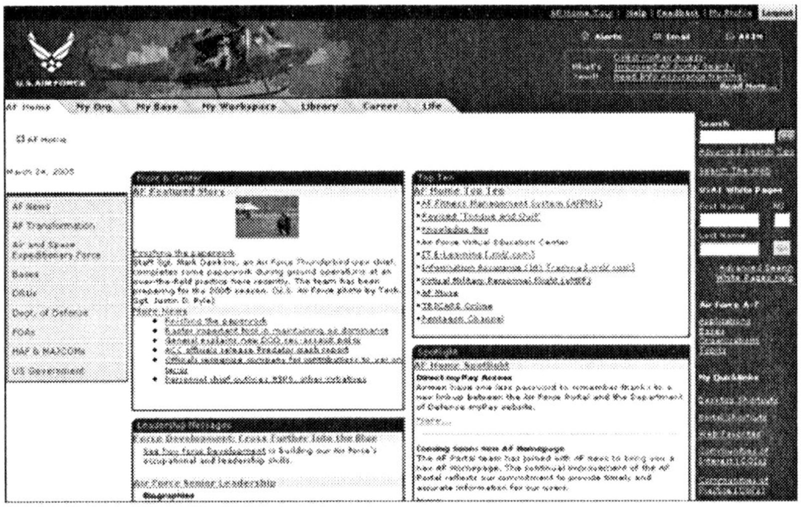

more complex machine-to-machine interaction with e-government services and even data interoperability across multiple communities. E-government solutions in these cases utilize Web services technology.

Web services provide data and services to applications and users over a network via a set of standards and protocols. Commonly used standards and protocols include, but are not limited to, the extensible markup language (XML), simple object access protocol (SOAP), the web services description language (WSDL), and universal discovery description and integration (UDDI) (Cerami, 2002).

XML is a language that provides a means to describe data in a platform and programming language independent manner; thus providing a means of decoupling client and server applications. A WSDL file is a document that uses XML to define a Web service interface or "contract" for a Web service. The contract details the syntax and structure of requests that a Web service will accept and responses that the Web service will generate. In addition, the contract defines the XML messaging mechanism of the service. SOAP will most likely be the messaging mechanism identified in the WSDL file as SOAP allows for the exchange of information between computers regardless of platform or language. The WSDL or Web service contract may be registered in a UDDI Web service registry much like a phone number is published in a phone book. Figure 3 illustrates the use cycle of Web services.

A Web service registry provides a way for consumers to find data providers and desired services. A registry provides a means for data providers to advertise their Web services. Registering or publishing a Web service with a registry is optional; however, not registering a Web service with a registry is comparable to not publishing a phone number in the phone book. It will be difficult for a potential consumer to locate the Web service. Not publishing a Web service may be a desired security measure for the providers of some Web services such as those involved in the nation's security and defense.

There are applications on the Internet that provide services to consumers without using the commonly used Web service standards and protocols. These applications are "Web-based services" and they employ diverse methods for discovery, description, messaging, and transport (Ladner et al., 2006a). In this article, the use of the term *Web services* refers to the services that

Figure 3. Illustrated use of Web services

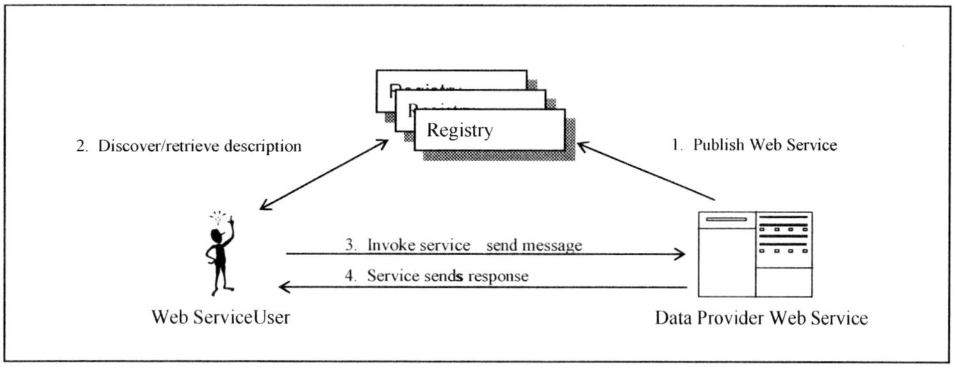

employ at least XML, WSDL, and SOAP standards and protocols.

SERVICE-ORIENTED COMPUTING

The significance of Web services and Web-based services for e-government is found in the service-oriented computing paradigm. Service-oriented computing is a means of organizing Web services and Web-based services around a conceptual service-oriented Architecture (SOA). The SOA has been technically described as "a conceptual business architecture where business functionality or application logic is made available to users or consumers as shared reusable services on an IT network. Services in an SOA are modules of business application functionality with exposed interfaces and are invoked by messages" (Marks & Bell, 2006, p. 1). The SOA is the means by which business functionality is published, discovered, and consumed on a network. Services offer resources in a loosely coupled manner and users are able to build composite applications that draw on multiple sources.

DoD Service-Oriented Computing

Service-oriented computing is being embraced by major DoD initiatives such as the GIG, Net-Centric Enterprise Services, the Navy's ForceNet, the Army's Future Combat System, and the Air Force's Joint Battlespace Infosphere and Joint Battle Management/Command & Control (Paul, 2005). The following sections explain some of these initiatives in more detail and reveal some of the challenges associated with the DoD's service-oriented e-government for its internal customers.

Global Information Grid

In short, the GIG proposes to provide the framework in which to connect all technology within the DoD and outside the DoD as needed. The GIG can be thought of as a global network that will support data and service needs to all DoD functions at all times (in war, in crisis, and in peace). By providing a global network with connectivity and resources available to all DoD users, a free flow of information will be established that will provide a significant edge over adversaries (National Security Agency, n.d.).

However, the GIG must allow this free flow of information to authorized users only. Security of this system is of utmost concern. This same free flow of information in the hands of an adversary could prove to be detrimental.

Figure 4. Portal to the global information grid

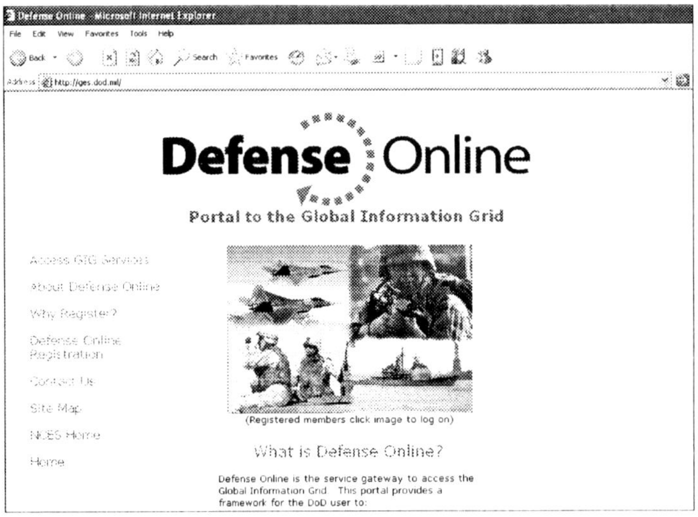

Net-Centric Enterprise Services (NCES)

The GIG is the global network on which DOD services and resources can be deployed. These deployed services and resources should have an over-arching organization on the global network in order to prevent information overload and chaos for users. NCES, which was created by DISA, is an attempt to organize and manage the proliferation of resources available on the GIG.

Any user within the DoD community who needs to share and retrieve information is considered to be an NCES customer. This includes war fighters. Resources on the GIG should be available 24/7/365 and the information available should be of the highest quality. In addition, the user should have the capability to pull data with minimum latency to support time critical decisions. (Defense Information Systems Agency, Department of Defense, 2006)

The NCES Program has four product lines of services: Enterprise Service-Oriented Architecture Foundation, DoD Enterprise Collaboration, Content Discovery and Delivery, and Portal. Enterprise Service-Oriented Architecture Foundation enables the reusability of services and helps to reduce the complexity of the DoD's information technology environment. The foundation services include, for example, the NCES Mediation Service, which provides for XML translations using eXtensible Stylesheet Language Translation (XSLT) style sheets. Enterprise Collaboration provides collaboration tools such as conferencing and white board sessions. Content Discovery & Delivery supports efficient information advertisement, discovery, and delivery.

The Portal provides secure Web access to NCES services and the capability to leverage an application throughout the GIG thereby reducing the creation of redundant functionality. The portal to the GIG, named Defense Online, is pictured in Figure 4. (Defense Information Systems Agency, Net-Centric Enterprise Services [DISA-NCES], 2006)

NCES describes users of the program as either end users, service providers, service consumers, or data providers. End users directly access services via a portal environment. Accessible services include the portal, messaging, search, and service discovery. Service providers make services available through NCES. Service consumers support programs of record through applications that make use of NCES services. For example, a developer may integrate an application with NCES mediation services (described previously). Sample applications are made available to assist developers with writing their own applications to make use of the mediation services for specific needs. Data providers support programs of record by making data available via NCES. Users learn about and retrieve this data using Content Discovery and Delivery services.

Net-Centric Enterprise Solutions for Interoperability (NESI)

Currently, NESI is a joint effort between DISA, Air Force, and Navy. NESI provides concrete guidance for the life cycle management of a service to be deployed on the GIG. NESI brings to life the concepts and ideas expressed in higher level abstract directives, policies, and mandates regarding net-centric warfare (Netcentric Enterprise Solutions for Interoperabilty, 2006). While NESI provides life cycle guidance, NCES provides a registry in which to publish a service along with other tools which enhance the reusability of the service. A service that has been created using NESI guidance and registered with NCES is deployed on the GIG. This net-centric enterprise is depicted in Figure 5 (Navy PEO C4I, 2004). End users at various nodes on the GIG access needed services that may be co-located or located at other nodes. Among the core enterprise services offered through NCES are data discovery, service discovery, mediation, security, and enterprise service management. Through this core services, for example, a war fighter at Node C may be able to discover a source of needed data that is available from a service at Node B and then use the NCES mediation service to retrieve the data. The same war fighter may then transmit the same data to a service offered by Node A that provides defensive strike power.

DHS Service-Oriented Computing

The DHS, like the DoD, is moving toward service-oriented computing (Stevens, 2007). Through an

Figure 5. Net-centric DoD enterprise

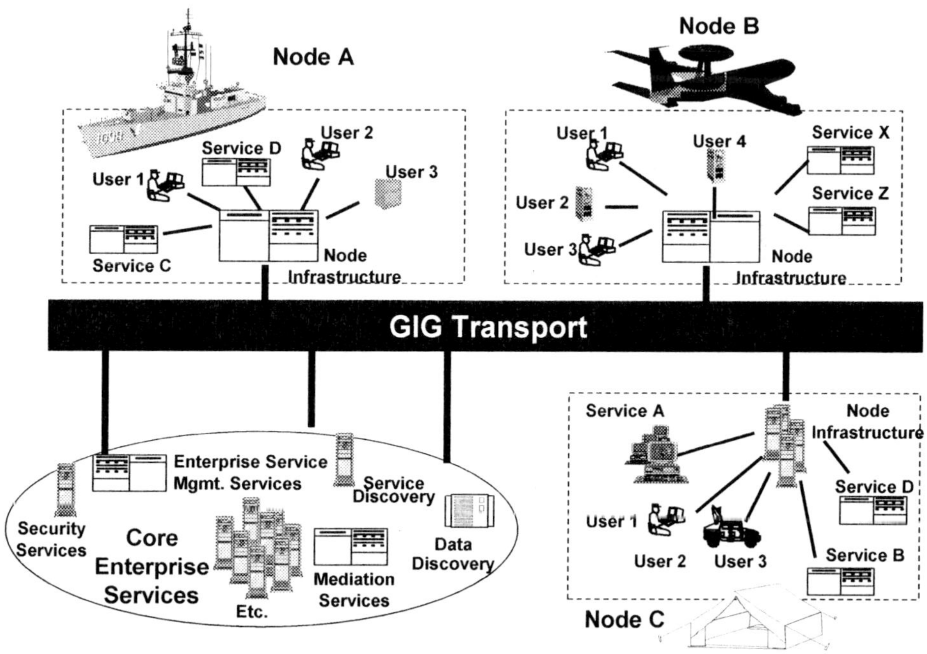

Figure 6. Autonomous Web service discovery

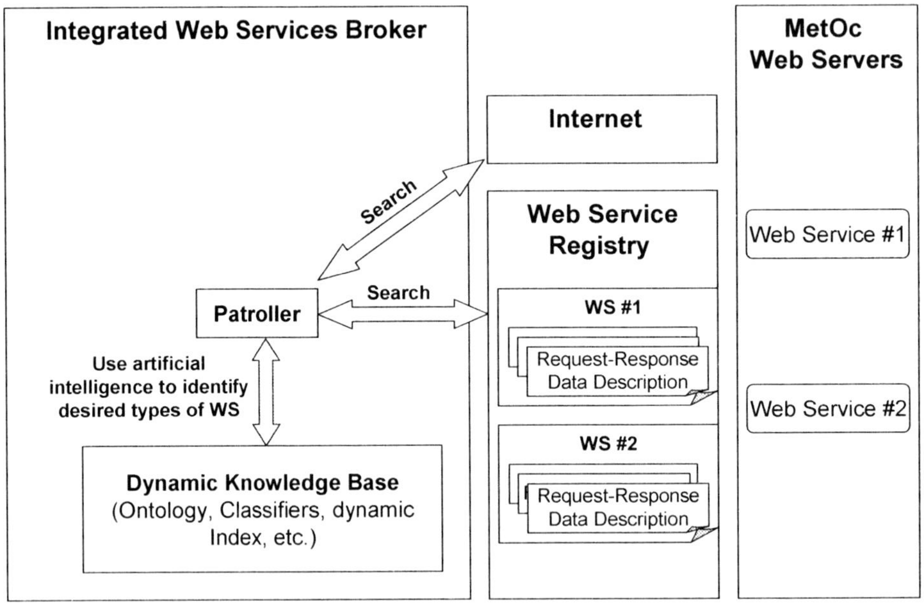

effort called OnetNet DHS is seeking to achieve maximum data sharing and service reuse by connecting the various networks that were put under the DHS umbrella when the department was formed (DHS Special Report | Component Approach, 2006). OneNet is distinct from DoD's GIG and is focused on sharing unclassified but sensitive data (DHS Special Report | Forward Motion, 2006; Magnuson, 2006). However, the need for DHS to collaborate with DoD agencies is obvious and communication bridges are being established so that multiple components from the two departments can share information over a network (DISA DMZ, 2006). One example of this is the Maritime Domain Awareness project in which the U.S. Navy, the U.S. Coast Guard, and the Office of Naval Intelligence share information over a network.

The Integrated Common Analytical Viewer (iCAV) is a noteworthy service-oriented effort within DHS. Using an integrated geographic information system and SOA, this software provides Web-based dissemination, analysis, and visualization of shared data. The effort connects systems that previously could not share information so that a consistent, mission-specific common operating picture is provided to DHS and its mission partners. The intent of this geospatial-intelligence analytic tool is to enable better preparation, prevention, response, and recovery from natural and man-made disasters ("ManTech awarded," 2006).

E-GOVERNMENT AND THE SEMANTIC WEB

With the growth of e-government much more relevant data is available for decision making. Within DoD, for example, the proliferation of service-oriented computing on the GIG means that services must be effectively and efficiently identified, selected, and used. Yet the identification and retrieval of data from heterogeneous sources in such a distributed system poses many difficulties. Assimilation of data from heterogeneous sources means that differences in notation, terminology, usage, and so forth prevents simple querying and retrieval of data. Approaches utilizing manual translations or interface mappings as with XSLT

Figure 7. Autonomous mediation

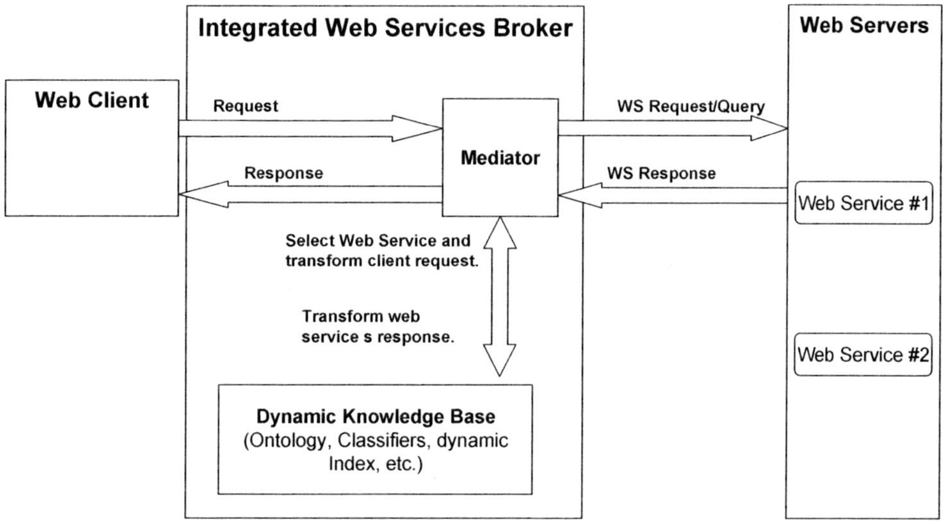

style sheets (an approach taken by NCES Mediation Services) require an application developer to write new software or prepare new style sheets.

The recognition of such integration difficulties has influenced many of the concepts that are embodied in the Semantic Web. Semantic technologies such as ontologies have been developed to support the goal of sharing knowledge for various domains of interest. An ontology captures terms, concepts, and relationships within a domain to provide a model and the semantics of a domain. Part of the power of an ontology is that it can capture the semantics of a single domain as shared by different communities (Korotkiy & Top, 2006).

The Knowledge Management Working Group and the Semantic Interoperability Community of Practice are two federal working groups that are focused on semantic technologies and the promise they hold for information sharing challenges within e-government. Additionally, various methodologies for applying ontologies to exploit the semantics of Web services have been explored (Korotkiy & Top, 2006; Ladner et al., 2006b; Medjahed & Bouguettaya, 2005). One approach being developed by the Naval Research Laboratory is the IWB.

Integrated Web Services Broker

The IWB is an example of middleware for use in a services-oriented environment such as the GIG to achieve semantic interoperability between clients and Web services. The goal of the IWB is to give client applications net-centric plug-and-play capabilities with regard to retrieving needed data.

To accomplish this goal, the IWB is being engineered to independently decompose and analyze ad hoc Web services interface descriptions in order to identify Web services of interest and then cache information about each service in order to support an autonomous mediation process. The mediation process does not require a priori knowledge of any particular service for specialized code development, pre-prepared taxonomies of available services or end-user resolution of structural and syntactic differences inherent in varying Web services interfaces. The approach is intended to avoid the necessity of client application software enhancements to address changes in services' interfaces as the service evolves.

The IWB utilizes semantic Web technologies (ontologies) and artificial intelligence techniques (classifiers) in order to carry out its functions.

Although the IWB is being prototyped for the meteorological and oceanographic (METOC) domain, the techniques employed are generic enough to apply to many other domains.

The approach followed in the IWB is in contrast to other approaches to Web service data brokers that assume that Web service providers will deploy an ontological description of their Web service (Paolucci, Soudry, Srinivasan, & Sycara, 2004). The IWB assumes that ontological descriptions of Web services have not been provided by the service provider; the IWB instead assumes that only the Web service WSDL and associated schemas have been provided. Through the use of ontologies and classifiers, the IWB seeks to avoid the need for Web service providers to supply an ontological description of their service (Ladner et al., 2006b).

The primary functions of the IWB can be described as Web service discovery and client request mediation. These functions are depicted in Figures 6 and 7. The IWB first discovers Web services that supply data for the domain of interest by searching Web service registries and the Internet for WSDLs. It then classifies the WSDLs and methods contained therein using classifiers that have been trained on the domain of interest.

Upon finding WSDL operations that provide the desired domain data, the IWB then caches information about the Web service interface needed to support mediation of client requests. In this process, the IWB uses its own domain ontology to create critical on-the-fly XML schema to ontology concept mapping that the software records during this phase. This is similar to an ontology alignment or schema mapping task. Additionally, the software determines and records instructions for composing a valid request to this Web service. All of this information is used to populate an index of Web services within the dynamic knowledge base. In doing so, an additional classifier is used to identify data specializations within the domain for which the Web service supplies data. The cached information allows the IWB to select the Web service as an appropriate target for filling a client application request, to invoke the Web service when selected and also to transform the client application's XML terminology and structure to that of the Web service.

In the mediation process, the IWB receives and decomposes client application requests to determine the data that is being requested. The software consults the domain ontology to determine key concepts in the current decomposed request. A list of appropriate Web services are selected based on the intersect of Web services providing the key concepts. The selected Web services are ordered by confidence ranking. The Web service with the highest confidence ranking will be contacted first in attempt to fill the client request.

Mediating a data request to a Web service requires the IWB to compose a valid request for the selected Web service operation. To do this the IWB must resolve terminology and structure differences between the client request and the selected Web service operation. If the highest ranked Web service does not supply an answer, then the IWB moves on to contact the next highest ranked Web service in the list. This continues until the desired data is received or until there are no more Web services to contact to fill that particular client request. Upon receiving a response from a Web service, the IWB must perform a reverse transform of XML terminology and structure from that of the Web service to the client.

The IWB should not be confused with middleware that provides composite Web services, that is Web services composed of at least two other Web services to form a business process. IWB can be thought of as a "façade" as defined in NESI implementation guidance in that provides a unified interface to a dynamically changing set of interfaces in a subsystem (Netcentric Enterprise Solutions for Interoperabilty, 2006). However, "façade" is simplistic and does not disclose the real power of the IWB. The IWB is a run-time discovery and mediation engine. The set of interfaces that it represents are undetermined at the startup of the IWB software. The IWB educates itself on the topic of which Web service interfaces to represent by finding Web services and then using artificial intelligence to determine if these services are within the desired domain. The IWB then uses knowledge management techniques to record instructions for itself regarding how to construct valid XML messages to those Web services, which includes resolving terminology and XML structure differences between the client XML and the Web service XML. During mediation, the IWB provides a smart dynamic reconfiguration mechanism (Paul, 2005). The IWB is charged with representing the Web service interface that has the highest confidence score to fulfill an individual user request. However, when the service with the highest confidence score does not return an answer (for whatever reason) another service will contacted by the IWB to fill the client request. This will be the service with the next highest confidence score. The IWB will again resolve terminology and structure differences; this time between the client request and the newly substituted Web service. It will also construct an appropriate XML message using instructions that it determined and recorded for itself previously. This dynamic reconfiguration allows for mission-critical client applications to proceed without interruption (Paul, 2005). The ontology is key in the mediation process as it acts a pivot device for terminology mapping between client Web service requests.

SUMMARY

We have described how the DoD and DHS are expanding e-government capabilities through several major initiatives to support security and defense. These initiatives are centered on service oriented computing to support the internal customers and partners of DoD and DHS. The adoption of service-oriented computing provides the DoD and the DHS with the opportunity to better leverage information and data to provide enhanced protection for U.S. assets while reducing the long term IT budget. However, moving toward service-oriented computing also provides challenges such as managing a massive SOA, like the GIG, so that information overload does not negate the possible gain from such an architecture. The strategies and full benefits of utilizing a SOA are a field of much research interest. The application of the Semantic Web through work such as the IWB should bring new methodologies that will most likely play a significant role in realizing the full benefits of this SOA.

ACKNOWLEDGMENT

The authors would like to thank the Naval Research Laboratory's Base Program, Program Element No. 0602435N for sponsoring this research.

REFERENCES

Adkins, R. (n.d.). *Air Force knowledge now.* Retrieved February 22, 2007, from http://www.e-gov.com/events/2005/km/downloads/KM05_2-3_Adkins.pdf

Cerami, E. (2002). *Web services essentials.* CA: O Reilly & Associates.

Defense Information Systems Agency, Department of Defense (DISA). (2006, November 3). *Core services—Net-centric enterprise services.* Retrieved February 22, 2007, from http://www.disa.mil/main/prodsol/cs_nces.html

Defense Information Systems Agency (DISA)—Net-Centric Enterprise Services. (2006, September 8). *Net-centric enterprise services user guide, Version 1.0/ECB 1.2.* Retrieved February 20, 2007, from http://www.disa.mil/nces/NCES_UG_Final_v1_0.pdf

Department of Defense (DoD). (2000, March). *Organizational chart*. Retrieved April 20, 2007, from http://www.defenselink.mil/odam/omp/pubs/GuideBook/Pdf/DoD.PDF

Department of Homeland Security (DHS). (2006, September). *History: Who became part of the department?* Retrieved April 20, 2007, from http://www.dhs.gov/xabout/history/editorial_0133.shtm

Department of Homeland Security (DHS). (2006, June 26). *Special report | Component approach aiding IT infrastructure consolidation*. Retrieved January 31, 2007, from http://www.gcn.com/print/25_17/41104-1.html

Department of Homeland Security (DHS). (2006, June 26). *Special report | Forward motion, amid widely documented IT failures, security advances and infrastructure upgrades are gaining traction at DHS*. Retrieved January 31, 2007, from http://www.gcn.com/print/25_16/41076-1.html

Department of Homeland Security at Naval Post Graduate School. (n.d.). *Homeland security digital library*. Retrieved January 19, 2007, from https://www.hsdl.org/

Korotkiy, M., & Top, J. (2006). Onto SOA: From ontology-enabled SOA to service-enabled ontologies. In *IEEE International Conference on Internet and Web Applications and Services*.

Ladner, R., Warner, E., Petry, F., Gupta, K., Moore, P., & Aha, D. (2006a). Design of an integrated Web services brokering system. *International Journal of Web Services Research*.

Ladner, R., Warner, E., Petry, F., Gupta, K., Moore, P., & Aha, D. (2006b). Soft computing techniques for Web services brokering. *Web Intelligence Journal*.

Lamont, J. (2006, May 26). *E-government: Enhancing national security*. Retrieved February 22, 2007, from http://www.kmworld.com/Articles/ReadArticle.aspx?ArticleID=15806

Magnuson, S. (2006, August). Homeland security mission creates more complications. *National Defense Magazine*. Retrieved April 20, 2007, from http://www.nationaldefensemagazine.org/issues/2006/August/HomelandSecurity.htm

ManTech awarded disaster-mapping contract from DHS. (2006, November 12). *SOA World Magazine*. Retrieved February 22, 2007, from http://webservices.sys-con.com/read/299259.htm

Marks, E., & Bell, M. (2006). *Executives' guide to service-oriented architecture (SOA): A planning and implementation guide for business and technology*. Wiley.

Medjahed, B., & Bouguettaya, A. (2005). Customized delivery of e-government Web services. *IEEE Intelligent Systems, 20*(6), 77-84.

National Security Agency. (n.d.). *Global information grid, Scope and objectives*. Retrieved February 22, 2007, from http://www.nsa.gov/ia/industry/gigscope.cfm?MenuID=10.3.2.2

Navy PEO C4I & Space RAPIDS Team, Air Force ESC C2ERA Team. (2004, December). *Net-centric enterprise solutions for interoperability*. Retrieved April 17, 2007, from http://nesipublic.spawar.navy.mil/files/NESI-Overview-v1e.ppt

Netcentric Enterprise Solutions for Interoperabilty. (2006, June). *Netcentric enterprise solutions for interoperability part 5: Developer guidance* version 1.3. Retrieved April 20, 2007, from http://nesipublic.spawar.navy.mil/part5/releases/1.3.0/WebHelp/nesi_part5_v1_3.htm

O'Rourke, R. (2005, June 2). *Homeland security: Navy operations—Background and issues for Congress.* Retrieved February 22, 2007, from http://www.history.navy.mil/library/online/homeland_security.htm

Paolucci, M., Soudry, J., Srinivasan, N., & Sycara, K. (2004). A broker for OWL-S Web services. In *Proceedings of the AAAI Spring Symposium on Semantic Web Services* (pp. 562-567).

Paul, R. A. (2005). *DoD towards software services.* In *Proceedings of the 10th IEEE International Workshop on Object-Oriented Real-Time Dependable Systems (WORDS'05)* (pp. 3-6).

Stevens, L. (2007, February). *The in and out of SOA.* Retrieved April 20, 2007, from http://www.fedtechmagazine.com/article.asp?item_id=257

United States Office of Management and Business (OMB). (2002, February 27). *Implementing the President's management agenda for e-government.* Retrieved January 19, 2007, from http://www.usa.gov/Topics/Includes/Reference/egov_strategy.pdf

What is e-government? (n.d.). Retrieved January 19, 2007, from http://www.wisegeek.com/what-is-e-government.htm

This work was previously published in International Journal of Electronic Government Research, Vol. 4, Issue 1, edited by M. Khosrow-Pour, pp. 1-13, copyright 2008 by IGI Publishing (an imprint of IGI Global).

Chapter 2
Unclassified Information Sharing and Coordination in Security, Stabilization, Transition and Reconstruction Efforts

Ranjeev Mittu
U.S. Naval Research Laboratory, USA

Suleyman Guleyupoglu
ITT Corporation, USA

Al Johnson
Office of Secretary of Defense Networks and Information Integration, USA

William Barlow
Office of Secretary of Defense Networks and Information Integration, USA

Michael Dowdy
Femme Comp, Inc. (FCI), USA

Sean McCarthy
Femme Comp, Inc. (FCI), USA

ABSTRACT

The emergence of new doctrine is enabling security, stabilization, transition and reconstruction (SSTR) operations to become a core U.S. military mission. These operations are now given equal priority to combat operations. The immediate goal in SSTR is to provide the local populace with security, restore essential services, and meet humanitarian needs. The long-term goal is to help develop indigenous capacity for securing and providing essential services, therefore, many SSTR operations are best performed by indigenous groups with support from foreign agencies and professionals. Large scale disasters, however, are an example where military support can enhance the value of SSTR operations. Without the means to effectively coordinate groups across the civil-military boundary, basic assistance and relief operations may be severely impeded. This paper will describe a conceptual portal, ShareInfoForPeople, which incorporates advanced Information and Communication Technology to enable collaboration, coordination and information sharing across the civil-military boundary in support of SSTR.

INTRODUCTION

With the signing of the Department of Defense Directive (DoDD) 3000.05, *Military Support for Security, Stabilization, Transition and Reconstruction (SSTR) Operations* into policy (U.S. DoD, 2007), SSTR operations have become a core U.S. military mission that the DoD must be prepared to conduct and support. These operations are now given equal priority to that of combat operations. The immediate goal is to provide the local populace with security, restore essential services, and meet humanitarian needs. The long-term goal is to help develop and maintain: indigenous capacity for securing essential services, a viable market economy, rule-of-law, democratic institutions, a robust civil society. These operations are conducted to help establish order, while promoting and advancing U.S. interests and values.

This article will begin by briefly describing SSTR operations and provide notional examples. Next, we will describe the capabilities of the ShareInfoForPeople portal (https://www.ShareInfoForPeople.org) to enable coordination and information sharing across the civil-military boundary during SSTR operations. We will then discuss the utilization of this portal in the Navy's Trident Warrior experiment. Lastly, we describe future development activities and technical challenges that remain to be investigated within our portal environment. We will conclude with a brief summary.

SECURITY, STABILIZATION, TRANSITION, AND RECONSTRUCTION

SSTR operations are conducted outside the boundaries of U.S. lands and territories, and information and communication technology (ICT) capabilities are critical enablers for the conduct of these missions. While there are similarities within the ICT systems for the employment of automated information systems between domestic and international partners, policy and structural frameworks create a different workflow for each side with regard to information dissemination and coordination. We will limit our scope to examples of military operations outside of U.S. borders.

Many SSTR operational tasks are best performed by indigenous groups, with support from foreign or U.S. civilian professionals. Complex disasters are an example where military involvement and support for SSTR operations can provide significant value to foreign governments and non-governmental organizations (NGOs), which may already be under great stress to respond in a timely and effective manner. The command and control structure, resources, and assets that the military can offer in such situations can shorten the response time line. However, without the means to properly coordinate the efforts of such a large and diverse group which spans the civil-military boundaries, basic assistance and relief operations may be severely impacted leading to delays or waste in the overall response cycle.

In SSTR operations, the U.S. military supports the Department of State and works with non-DoD partners, which may include select military units of other nations NGOs, international organizations (IO), and private volunteer organizations. Large-scale disasters are one example where proper coordination between participating organizations can increase the effectiveness of the overall response. A key element in the success of SSTR operations is the ability of the U.S. (or other lead activity) to obtain and process information about the situation and status of participating partners, while disseminating (or making accessible) the widest amount of relevant information to the partners in the ad-hoc coalition. Through the sharing of unclassified information via an appropriate ICT framework, the goal is to increase the level of coordinated activity among all of the participants. As illustrated in the following notional scenarios,

SSTR operations are subjected to non-traditional and unanticipated partners:

- **Disaster relief:** Following a tsunami in the western Pacific, the U.S. Navy has been designated Combined/Joint Task Force Commander for U.S. military disaster relief operations involving an island nation that experienced severe destruction from several 50-foot waves. Coalition partners include naval elements from various Pacific Rim nations, for example, Australia, Thailand, Japan, China, South Korea, and India. Ground/air elements from these same countries are involved in delivering relief supplies and distribution of those supplies is being managed by a combination of efforts by the host nation, the United Nations, USAID, and international relief organizations such as the Red Cross.
- **Humanitarian assistance:** Following a period of severe drought and dislocation of local peoples, the U.S. Army is designated Combined/Joint Task Force Commander for humanitarian assistance operations in a region of sub-Saharan Africa. Coalition partners include the United Nations, Doctors without Borders, and the International Red Cross.

While these are notional examples, recent history reveals that the initial years of the 21st century have witnessed numerous large-scale crises such as the Indian Ocean tsunami and Kashmir earthquake. There have also been longer-term, multi-faceted emergencies such as those in Sudan. The United States has been involved as a part of multi-national coalition missions, including the Balkan states, Afghanistan, and Iraq. The U.S. has also provided humanitarian assistance in response to devastating natural disasters around the world. Increasingly, the scale and scope of such events involve both civilian and military components.

The next section will describe the ShareInfoForPeople portal that is being developed to enable collaboration and information sharing across the civil-military boundaries in support of SSTR operations. The purpose is to enable non-traditional and unanticipated partners to share information and better coordinate activities with the civilian and military components.

INFORMATION AND COMMUNICATIONS TECHNOLOGIES FOR SSTR

The Internet is driving emergent behavior in personal and group communications and is leading to new forms of interaction, as witnessed through many social network Web sites that are growing in popularity such as MySpace.com, Flickr.com, Craigslist.org, Wikimapia.com, and so forth. These, and similar Web sites, are leveraging new trends in collaboration such as Web 2.0 (e.g., mashups) to enable social networking. A few characteristics of the Web 2.0 may include the use of Real Simple Syndication (RSS), Weblogs (aka blogs), wiki's and social book marking which enable Web sites to be highly interactive (at a personal level). Some of the capabilities associated with mashups may include the ability to aggregate or transform content from remote sites through Web-browser-based applications. These applications generally provide simple and convenient programming interfaces to easily ingest or interact with new content. The benefits of aggregating, transforming, or even creating new content enables new ideas and concepts to emerge, which then become discoverable and accessible from within the site, or to other sites through mechanisms such as RSS.

The DoD is also embracing Web 2.0 and is actively leveraging these technologies in order to understand their value in improving collaboration and helping to achieve coordinated activity in SSTR operations. This article will describe a specific implementation of such a system called ShareInfoForPeople that is being funded by Office of Secretary of Defense—Networks and Information Integration to explore methodologies for unclassified information-sharing capabilities across the civil-military networks in support of SSTR operations.

As can be seen in Figure 1, ShareInfoForPeople provides a set of tools through a Web browser interface to enable real-time coordination and information sharing based on open standards and frameworks. The infrastructure is implemented using the Drupal (2007) content management system (CMS) and many of the baseline information sharing and collaboration tools have been contributed through the Drupal open source community. Drupal is a very modular open source software written in PHP hypertext processor language. It was chosen due to the very broad development community and user base, as well for its many "off-the-shelf" modules that can be extended as needed to suit the particular problem domain. While other frameworks have the potential to provide similar advantages ("Ruby," 2007), Drupal was chosen as the framework since it is already a complete CMS, without requiring additional programming effort to build CMS functionality. In addition, the fact that it is a community driven open source project means that it is easier to transition the system to the partner organizations without imposing an investment burden on them for expensive software licenses. Furthermore, the use of open source software has been approved in IT systems within the Department of the Navy, which also demonstrates a paradigm shift within DoD towards the acceptance and use of open source software (Rendleman, 2007). This should lead to an opportunity to improve collaboration and coordination between the civil groups and military components as both are migrating towards open source software, and our portal may be able to serve as a baseline. The primary capabilities of ShareInfoForPeople include the following:

- **Fully indexed site:** Content is indexed based on user-specified meta-data tags to enable searching of local content. When a user creates and uploads content to the site such as images, audio, blogs, and so forth there is an opportunity for the user to specify meta-

Figure 1. The ShareInfoForPeople.org opening screen

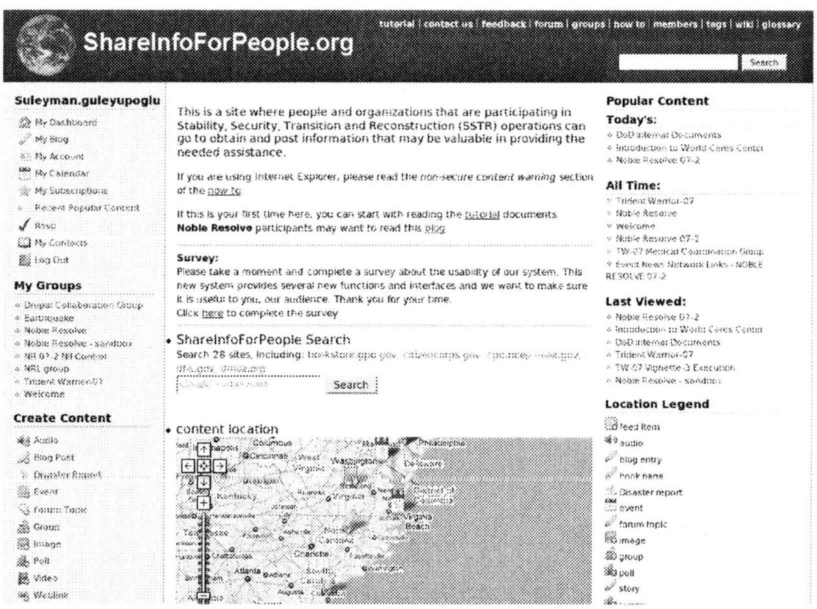

data tags that serve as an index mechanism, in order to facilitate searching from within the site.

- **GeoRSS and RSS feeds:** RSS and GeoRSS technology is utilized to incorporate the latest content from TRITON and Information Management and Mine Action Programs (iMAPP) as well as from other sites that support such feeds. The use of GeoRSS enables the coding of geospatial information within traditional RSS feeds and allows ShareInfoForPeople to display these geospatially referenced feeds using its local mapping interface.
    - TRITON (https://maps.nswc.navy.mil) is a scalable Web application architecture engineered to integrate and visualize geospatial data. It can be linked to databases or information and near real-time data feeds. It integrates imagery on-the-fly and dynamic map services from other organizations. TRITON is currently serving static images via GeoRSS to ShareInfoForPeople to demonstrate the initial proof-of-concept. User feedback on desired future capabilities within ShareInfoForPeople will enable us to expand our interactions with TRITON.
    - The iMMAP focuses on the larger concerns of war including the realities of an overstretched military; how America goes to war; and the civilian casualties of war. The iMMAP is involved in public education/news gathering and supports distribution of such information. Similar to TRITON, iMMAP is providing GeoRSS feeds to ShareInfoForPeople to demonstrate proof-of-concept.
- **Collaborative authoring:** ShareInfoForPeople currently supports a wiki capability (Figure 2) to promote collaboration and dissemination of shared knowledge. A community-driven approach should enable convergence towards accurate and reliable information being shared.
- **Upload or create content:** ShareInfoForPeople provides tools to upload content such as video, audio (Figure 3), and images within a group-based structure. Users can provide a title to what is being uploaded; upload the files by browsing their local directory; provide a description of the content; and define meta-data tags describing the content so that

Figure 2. The ShareInfoForPeople Wiki pages

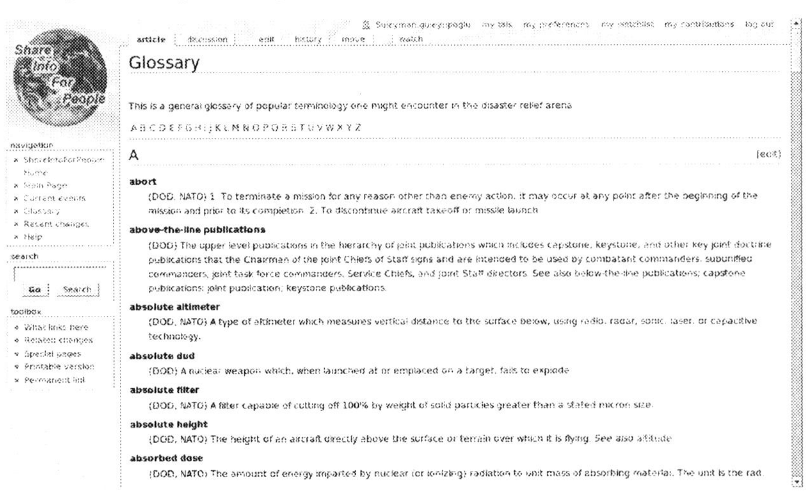

Figure 3. Screenshots showing how to upload audio content

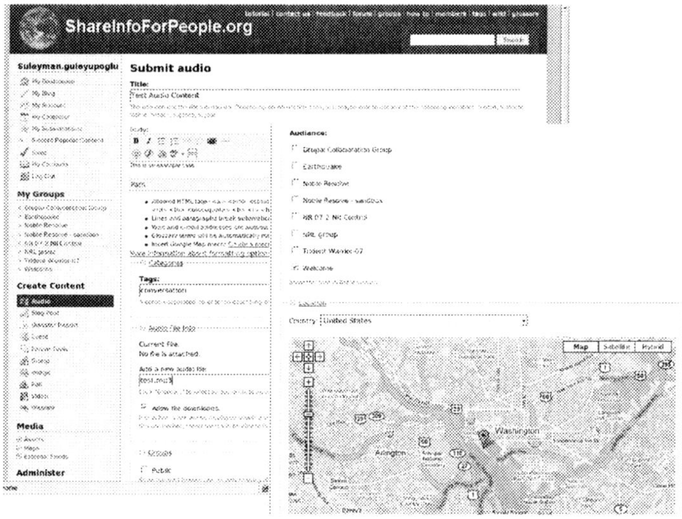

the tags can be indexed and used to facilitate search. The user can specify the group in which to make that content visible and can also place the content on a map by specifying a latitude and longitude coordinate (or by clicking directly on the map). Only a few of these items are mandatory during the upload process. Additional content such as blogs, events, and disaster assessment reports can be created within the site.

- **Image annotation capability:** ShareInfo-ForPeople permits users to annotate images as well as describe the annotation through free-form comments. A user can click on a particular image that is stored within the site, which will subsequently reveal an interface as shown in Figure 4. This interface permits the user to add, edit, delete, or hide notes. After the user clicks on "add note," a note is created by drawing a bounding box over the area of interest on the image, which can be

Figure 4. Image-annotation capability

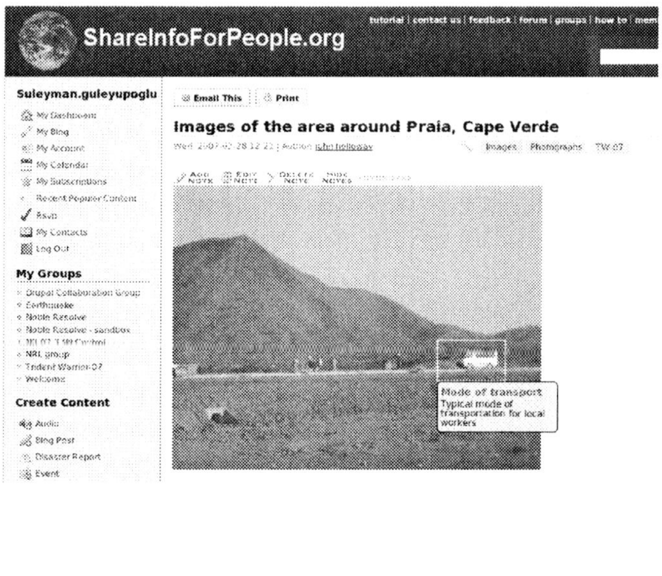

Figure 5. ShareInfoForPeople map display

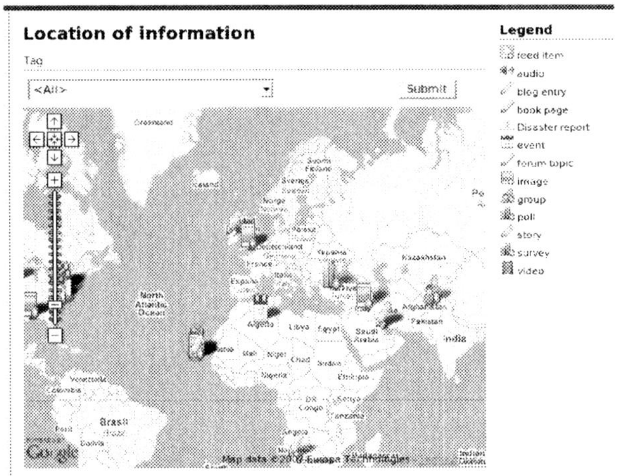

moved or resized by the user. These notes can contain a subject and free-form comments describing the overlaid note. Furthermore if coordinates are associated with the image, it can be geo-referenced on a corresponding map (seen at the lower right corner of the Web page in Figure 4).

- **Content can be geo-tagged and displayed on a map:** The mapping capability leverages COTS solutions to maximize interoperability (e.g., Google Maps). Figure 5 shows the Google Map interface within ShareInfoForPeople. The content on the map can be clicked, and a pop-up area will appear that provides additional description.
- **Subscription-based e-mail notifications:** All *subscribed-to* content generates e-mail alerts. For example, one can enable e-mail notifications through the user account settings. This will allow users to receive e-mail notification when new content has been posted to a group. Furthermore, e-mail notifications can also be provided when a user has replied to a discussion thread within a group.
- **Searchable subject matter expert (SME) registry:** When users complete their personal information such as expertise or skill sets through the account preferences area in ShareInfoForPeople, this information gets indexed. This will facilitate searching, so that users can easily find individuals who are able to offer specific services, support, or other assistance during a crisis situation. People publish as much information about themselves as they are comfortable in sharing with other users of the site.
- **Multi-lingual chat:** In addition to the typical asynchronous mode of communication associated with Web portals, the site offers a multi-lingual chat capability. Each user is assigned a Jabber ("What is Jabber," 2007) chat account that can be used with a locally installed application or through Web-based interface. This allows on-the-fly translation and communication between users who do not share a common language.
- **JPEG metadata discovery tool (JMDT):** As a means of discovering additional information, ShareInfoForPeople interfaces with JMDT (2007). This allows users to run keyword queries from ShareInfoForPeople to search for images indexed within JMDT. In addition, GeoRSS feeds can update site users on any new image indexed by JMDT. These feeds can be filtered by keywords to provide only relevant images.

The current implementation of ShareInfoForPeople provides the foundation on which to build more sophisticated capabilities, as specific requirements emerge from experimentation and other forms of user feedback. Furthermore, the philosophy of ShareInfoForPeople has been to use free and open software and standards to enable interoperability with other systems. We envision this approach will offer an increased opportunity to instantiate an enterprise-wide capability composed of loosely coupled, agile systems that provide synergistic capabilities. The next section discusses our involvement in experimentation, followed by a discussion of near term development activities.

EXPERIMENTATION IN TRIDENT WARRIOR 2007

The ShareInfoForPeople portal underwent user experimentation during the Trident Warrior experimentation in March 2007. Trident Warrior is a yearly exercise designed to provide a venue for technology experimentation that supports the Navy's FORCEnet vision. The focus of the experimentation in March addressed Maritime Domain Awareness (MDA). However, there were additional, related scenarios as a complement to MDA.

The ShareInfoForPeople portal was used by various civil and military groups to coordinate and share information in response to a hypothetical scenario consisting of a bird-flu outbreak on the Cape Verde Islands off the coast of West Africa. The portal was used by various groups from the NGO medical communities as well as those from Commander, Second Fleet in response to the events in the scenario to discuss medical logistics issues, post information on status of activities, share images on local geography, and so forth. Through participation in this experiment we were afforded an opportunity to collect valuable feedback from the civil and military communities in order to improve the future capabilities of our portal. Future experiments are also being planned in the Joint Forces Command's Noble Resolve experiment series which also focuses on civil-military information sharing.

NEAR TERM DEVELOPMENT ACTIVITIES

While the current implementation of ShareInfoForPeople provides a basic set of capabilities and functionality needed for collaboration and information sharing, there are still a number of areas to investigate and further prototype. Since our system is architected using the Drupal framework, we expect to leverage modules already being developed by the Drupal community and modify those as needed to meet the requirements of our user community. In addition, three primary areas for future exploration include social network analysis (SNA), OpenID, and task management capabilities.

Social Network Analysis

The current capabilities of ShareInfoForPeople provide a mechanism to search for users based on their skill set or expertise. The emerging concepts and ideas associated with SNA have the potential to add significant value within the information sharing environment. Research and tools from the SNA community may allow users to understand who the experts are in the SSTR community and to whom and how they are linked. As a simple example, social maps that depict connectivity between users in the context of their discussion threads, and the ability to filter the social map based on specific keywords are likely to provide the foundation to enable the community to identify service providers or those that may offer similar services or capabilities. The ability to rate individuals within the social network may also be an important aspect in building trust within the community of users. This is particularly important during pre-deployment prior to any crisis situation so that some level of trust and common understanding can be achieved. Furthermore, pre-deployment interactions can help in the development of concept of operations or doctrine to provide guidance during real-life situations by helping people or organizations form the bonds of working together. One of the challenges, however, will be to effectively visualize such a network or efficiently filter through the various dimensions of information contained in the social network.

Identity and Site Access Management

The need to protect sites from malicious behavior and limit participation to those actually involved in responding to a crisis, in addition to the sheer number of sites that one needs to interface with to gather information with which to respond to complex emergencies drives users to have multiple accounts/passwords to accomplish their work. The ability to get timely access to new sites, as well as remember and manage passwords can be a significant obstacle in gaining access to critical information in real-life emergency situations. Having single-sign-on access to a federation of sites that have agreed to common security criteria would improve tremendously the user's ability to discover and access the appropriate information. An ability to logon to the site using the OpenID (2007) standard will likely provide those advantages and benefits. This will enable users to log on once and seamlessly navigate to and from sites that must be password protected by relying on the OpenID service provider to verify the identity of the user.

Effectively Delegating and Managing Tasks

Another key area that is currently being explored is the application of techniques to coordinate tasks across a large and diverse group of users such as first responders and those in command centers. While information-sharing capabilities are a necessary first step, in a real disaster or crisis situation it is very likely that there will be thousands of groups containing hundreds of discussion threads. The discussion threads are likely to evolve to contain descriptions of who can offer services such as shelter (service providers) or who may need shelter and where they are currently situated (service requestors). The biggest challenge will be to automatically extract such information from the discussion threads. Manual processes are likely to be slow and inefficient. Therefore, techniques to automatically extract these descriptions from the online discussions and translate those into representations that can be manipulated by tools will be required. This is an area where we expect to leverage other work from natural language processing. Capturing such information could also be achieved by users completing structured templates or forms, and it is likely that some combination of free text extraction and forms would be used or available to the users.

Once information can be extracted and translated into a more structured representation (or is already available in a structured form) then it becomes easier to manipulate and use that information to match service providers to service requestors. We expect to develop algorithms that provide the underlying capabilities to enable such a matching. As an example, in related research we have developed several approaches for the global optimal assignment of resources, such as people or organizations, to activities based on the *Hungarian algorithm* (2007). These algorithms will be further enhanced to enable users or organizations to negotiate between the allocated assignments (e.g., accept, decline, etc.).

TECHNICAL CHALLENGES

On one end of the spectrum, activities may be (re) allocated or negotiated at emergency command centers, which have a reliable communications backbone, and promulgated to those in the field. However, at the other end of the spectrum, where actual users are likely to negotiate activities with each other, the communications environment may be unreliable. These "disadvantaged users," however, may be able to access a mobile version of the ShareInfoForPeople portal and maintain minimal functionality for uploading or creating content, annotating images, participating in discussion threads as well as negotiating activities between each other. However, given the chaotic and communications-challenged environments in which these types of systems will likely operate, it is conceivable that there may be users who get disconnected from each other in the field or with those at some remote command centers. There is a real challenge, from a network perspective, to ensure connectivity. This presents an opportunity to leverage research from the field of mobile wireless networking and intelligent agent-based applications to help alleviate these problems.

Mobile Ad-Hoc Network Environments

Critically damaged areas with degraded or no infrastructure (e.g., transportation, communication, etc.) provide a challenge in SSTR operations. We focus our discussion on the communications infrastructure. The ability to coordinate a large and diverse group of first responders begins with the ability to communicate guidance or orders, while receiving situation reports from those in the field. The lack of a stable communications infrastructure will negatively impact the efforts of those that need to coordinate and share information. Recent technological advances in mobile ad-hoc networks (MANET) are key enablers in the deployment of net-centric cooperative multi-agent systems in disaster areas. MANET technology holds the promise of enabling communications between first responders when the local communications infrastructure is unusable. These networks support mobile entities, connected through a wireless network that supports discovery and self-organization through peer-to-peer message exchanges, leading to an increase in the robustness of the overall network. Figure 6 shows a comparison of MANET with high performance networks and the mainstream Internet.

Although MANET technology is advancing to enable connectivity between mobile users, there still may be circumstances in which users get disconnected (examples such as distance between users or the affects of the environment on signal propagation). In order to improve the overall success of the deployment of MANET, new approaches and techniques that enable users to communicate to the maximum extent possible utilizing whatever network bandwidth is available will be needed.

The concept of "network-aware" coordination is emerging and is depicted in Figure 7. In such an approach, the users or application are aware of the state of the network, thereby allowing the applications to adapt in order to "work around" network constraints, while the network is aware of the state of the applications or mission needs in order to better handle traffic flows. Such cross-layer information exchange is important to enable a more robust communication strategy for the first responders in order to support their coordination activities. To the extent possible, coordination strategies also have to be robust against message loss and equipment failures.

A few of the research issues in network-aware coordination include defining measures for determining network congestion or other types

Figure 6. Communications and networking issues

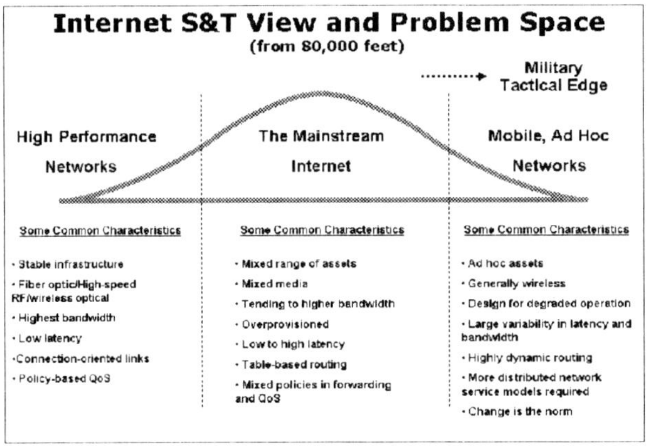

Figure 7. Network-aware coordination

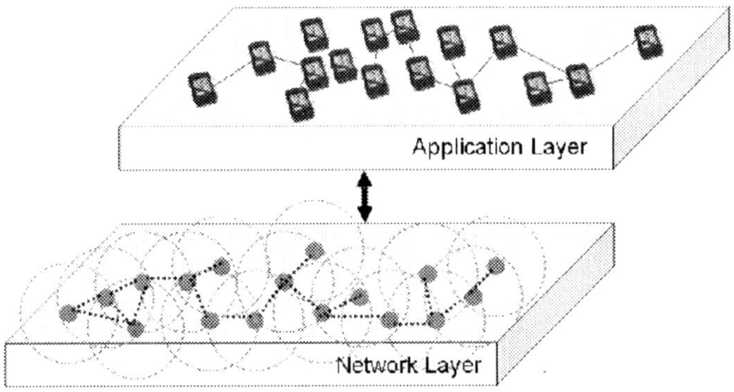

of failures such as loss of connectivity within the network, in order to provide such measures and parameters to the application layer. The key challenges for the application layer include how to best utilize that information in order to adapt communication strategies (e.g., sharing images that are smaller in size, prioritizing certain information, or identifying certain nodes to act as communications relays). Such a feedback loop may be continuous, so that the network could support larger bandwidth exchanges as congestion is proactively alleviated in the network.

Distributed Planning and Multi-Agent Systems

Research may also be leveraged from the field of multi-agent planning, re-planning, and scheduling between heterogeneous coordination entities. Distributed techniques such as automated plan merging and negotiation tools between responders may resolve local conflicts and issues without an entire re-planning effort. While coordination tools have been directed towards assisting human-to-human collaboration, software agents can be introduced to reduce interdependence by providing fast and robust solutions, bypassing delays in human response such as information gathering tasks. Specifically, coordination software agents may help incident commanders in directing large-scale teams and to gather information for situational awareness.

SUMMARY AND CONCLUSION

This article has described the ShareInfoForPeople portal to enable coordination and information sharing between the civil and military communities in support of SSTR operations. The architecture is based on the Drupal framework, an open source CMS being managed under General Public License (GPL). Furthermore, the philosophy of ShareInfoForPeople is to embrace free and open source software and standards as much as possible to enable future interoperability with other portals that provide similar or complementary capabilities. We have also briefly described how ShareInfoForPeople was used at the Trident Warrior 2007 experiment in order to gather user requirements.

The article has also described future development activities such as the planned leverage of modules already being developed by the Drupal community, which will be tailored to meet the needs of the ShareInfoForPeople users. In addition, technologies such as social maps will be investigated, as well as single-sign-on to enable users to seamlessly interact with other sites and portals. Because the latter technology is in its infancy, the challenge will be to find supporting hubs or portals that will be prepared to integrate with our portal using this capability. The ability to manage and negotiate tasks across the civil-military boundary are also worthy of exploration in order to improve coordination. Lastly, we have described some of the open challenges that remain such as network aware coordination, to enable ShareInfoForPeople to be robust in response to an increase in the number of mobile users during a real crisis situation.

REFERENCES

Drupal. (2007). Retrieved July 23, 2007, from http://www.drupal.org

Hungarian algorithm. (2007). Retrieved July 23, 2007, from http://en.wikipedia.org/wiki/Hungarian_algorithm

JPEG Metadata Discovery Tool (JMDT). (2007). Retrieved July 23, 2007, from http://metadata.solers.com

OpenID. (2007). *Open ID—Free secure identity.* Retrieved July 23, 2007, from http://www.openid.org

Rendleman, J. (2007). Navy CIO approves open-source software use. *Government Computer News.* Retrieved July 23, 2007, from http://www.gcn.com/print/26_14/44462-1.html

Ruby, Ruby on rails and Drupal, what is the difference? (2007). Retrieved July 23, 2007, from http://groups.drupal.org/node/2176

U.S. Department of Homeland Security. (2007). *National response plan.* Retrieved July 23, 2007, from http://www.dhs.gov/xprepresp/publications

U.S. Department of Defense (DoD). (2007). *DoD directive 3000.05, Military support for stability, security, transition, and reconstruction (SSTR) operations.* Retrieved July 23, 2007, from http://www.dtic.mil/whs/directives/corres/html/300005.htm

What is Jabber? (2007). Retrieved July 23, 2007, from http://www.jabber.org/about/overview.shtml

This work was previously published in International Journal of Electronic Government Research, Vol. 4, Issue 1, edited by M. Khosrow-Pour, pp. 36-48, copyright 2008 by IGI Publishing (an imprint of IGI Global).

Chapter 3
In-Stream Data Processing for Tactical Environments

Marco Carvalho
Institute for Human and Machine Cognition, USA

ABSTRACT

Data dissemination and information management technologies for tactical environments are quickly becoming major areas of research for both military and civilian applications. Critical to the problem is the need for fully distributed information management technologies that are efficient, adaptive and resilient. In this paper, we introduce and discuss a new strategy for tactical data dissemination and processing based on distributed online learning. Starting from a formal description of the problem we introduce our proposed solution and its theoretical properties. We also present and discuss a number of simulation experiments for different data dissemination scenarios, and conclude the work with a discussion on how such techniques may be applied to critical e-government environments under different assumptions of service availability and information release policies.

INTRODUCTION

Tactical networks are generally characterized as mobile ad hoc networks under policy and resource constraints. These types of network environments are commonly found in military and disaster recovery operations and represent a percentage of the types of environments where government agencies are required to effectively operate and collaborate.

Generally, the primary objective of tactical networks is to support fast formation of ad hoc groups and systems to share data, processing capabilities, and communication resources. One of the most critical and challenging problem in these types of environments is the distributed coordination of resource allocation for data distribution and processing. The decentralized and dynamic natures of tactical environments require resource coordination strategies that are distributed, efficient, and adaptive. Furthermore, coordination mechanisms are expected to be resilient to environmental changes and failures, with minimum requirements for maintenance and configuration.

Conceptually, the problem of dynamic resource allocation in tactical networks consists of finding and maintaining the best data distribution trees that together minimize the global utilization of resources for data processing and data transmission, while complying with policy constraints both at the levels of the nodes an network.

In this work we revisit a reinforcement learning-based strategy proposed by Carvalho (2006) for the resource allocation problem in tactical networks. The goal is to formulate the problem in a way that supports the application of a resource coordination protocol that will leverage from previously established localized learning techniques.

BACKGROUND AND PREVIOUS WORK

The resource allocation problem for data processing in mobile ad hoc networks can be generally classified into three main groups: (1) local data processing, (2) remote data processing, and (3) distributed (or in-stream) data processing. In each case, the goal is to allocate resources for data processing and distribution from a source node to multiple sink nodes requiring (possibly) different variations of the data.

In the first type of problems (i.e., local data processing), the source of the data is responsible for providing the necessary transformations required by each client. Similar to conventional client-server models, local data processing essentially allocates all processing to the data source (i.e., the server). The research focus on these types of problems is basically in the allocation of resources for data distribution (i.e., data routing).

Curran (2003) proposed a reinforcement learning-based algorithm for routing in ad hoc networks. The SWARM protocol is data agnostic, focused only on packet routing. When receiving a data packet, each node chooses the appropriate action (next hop) based on current policies. The work was later extended by Dowling, Curran, Cunningham, and Cahill (2004) who proposed the collaborative reinforcement learning-based routing protocol called SAMPLE, for mobile ad hoc networks. Chang, Ho, and Kaelbling (2004) have also proposed the use of reinforcement learning techniques for data routing in mobile ad hoc networks. Although the approach did not address tactical issues such as service decomposition and distribution, it did allow for interaction between data routing and node mobility. Peng and Deyun (2006) also leverage from reinforcement learning algorithms to improve quality of service (QoS) routing strategies. In his work, Peng proposes a heuristic-based algorithm that utilizes reinforcement learning to estimate best QoS routing paths from previous experience, reducing the number of QoS flood and probing packets for path maintenance in mobile networks.

Remote data processing problems try to identify a node in the network that is the best candidate for the data processing task. Like in the previous types of problems, the task of allocating resources for data processing is separate from the allocation of resources for data transmission in the network. For example, if a number of clients require data to be retrieved and processed from a server in the field, a remote data processing strategy will essentially identify a proxy node in the network (based on CPU, memory, and storage capabilities) to act as the point for data processing and re-distribution. Costs related with data transmission from the source to the proxy and from the proxy to each client are independently calculated.

In 2004, Baehni, Eugster, and Guerraoui proposed a data aware variation of conventional multicast protocols that took into account the nature of the data being transmitted when building the multicast trees. Other topic-based publish/subscribe systems such as such as TPS (Eugster, Guerraoui, & Damm, 2001) and JORAM (Maistre, 2003) also leverage from multicast protocols and the assumption of a clear hierarchy on data and events to build efficient multicast groups for topic-based data distribution. Similar approaches were also proposed by Katz and Brewer (1994), Chen and Schwan (2005), Carvalho and Breedy (2002), and others.

Most of the agent-based negotiation strategies or economical-model perspectives have also targeted remote data processing. Carvalho, Pechoucek, and Suri (2005), Pechoucek, Marık, and Stepankova, (2001), Kothari, Sabhash, and Zhou (2003), and Buyya, Stockinger, Giddy, and Abramson (2001), are all examples of such approaches.

Reinforcement learning techniques are also not new for remote data processing. They have been previously proposed for several data routing algorithms (Boyan & Littman, 1994; Choi & Yeung, 1996; Littman & Boyan, 1993; Miikkulainen & Kumar, 1999; Stone, 2000; Tao, Baxter, & Weaver, 2001).

A third and perhaps more interesting type of data processing in mobile ad hoc networks is distributed data processing. In these types of problems, a task is actually fragmented into sub-tasks that can be allocated to multiple nodes in the network in order to jointly minimize data processing and distribution costs.

The way in which tasks are fragmented and distributed (in-stream data processing) is a function of the capabilities of network nodes, topology, and policies. While a number of data-centric routing protocols such as SPIN-IT (Woodrow & Heinzelman, 2001) and Directed Diffusion (Intanagonwiwat, Govindan, & Estrin, 2001) have been proposed for data streaming in MANETs, the research on in-stream data processing is relatively new.

PROBLEM DESCRIPTION

For the purpose of this work, the formal description of the resource allocation problem is based on three concepts that, together, characterize the network environment and a task to be performed. These concepts are the network, the data-state transition (i.e., data transformation), and the data task.

The Environment and Task Description

The physical environment consists of a mobile ad hoc network represented by a network diagram. The network describes the current physical constraints of the system, both in terms of nodes (hosts) and communication (links) capabilities. The tasks, referred to as "data tasks" define both processing (data transformation) and transmission jobs to be accomplished by the network.

The Network Diagram

Definition 1: *A **Network Diagram** (NET) is defined as a graph structure NET (N,L) where $N = \{ n_1, n_2, ..., n_n\}$ is a set of vertices representing nodes (hosts) in the network and $L = \{ l_1, l_2, ..., l_n\}$ is a set of edges representing the communication links between nodes. Data transmission between nodes can only occur through a link (l_i) in the graph, and all links are assumed to be bi-directional and symmetric.*

There is a link-specific transmission cost factor (*tfactor*) associated with each edge, and a processing cost factor (*pfactor*) associated with each node (Figure 1). Communication edges are assumed to be symmetric so the same *tfactor* is valid for communications in both directions. At any given time, a node is aware of its current *pfactor* and the *tfactor* for the connected links. Both the *pfactor* and the *tfactor* are used to estimate the costs for processing and transmitting a data packet respectively.

Figure 1. A NET (network) and a DST (data-state transition) diagrams

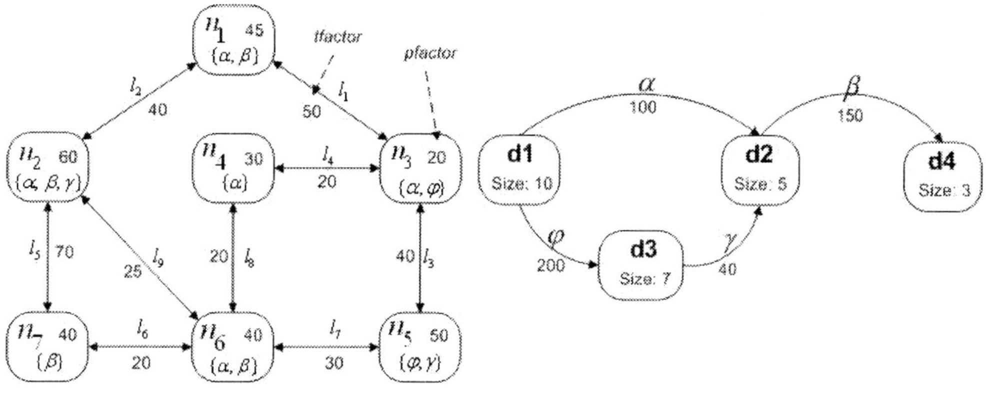

A data transition diagram (Figure 1) essentially specifies (through a graph structure) all possible state transitions supported by a data type. An instance of a data type (i.e., a datum) can be duplicated, processed, or transferred between nodes. Examples of data types are video images (snapshots), documents, and sensor data-captures in general. Each data type in the framework has a finite, well-defined number of possible states and state-transition paths. A data type is fully described by a data state transition graph (*DST*), defined as follows:

Definition 2: *A* ***Data State-Transition Diagram*** *(DST) is a directed graph DST(D, F), where D* = { $d_1, d_2, ..., d_n$ } *is a set of vertices representing all possible states that a datum can assume and* $F = \{f_1, f_2, ..., f_n\}$ *is a set of edges representing all functions* f_i *that can be applied on the data.*

The data information provided by the DST is static. It depends only on the data-type and it does not change in time or location in the network. Given an instance of a datum, every host in the network knows (or can obtain) the DST for the datum's data type. The proposed framework simultaneously supports multiple data types and data transactions competing for shared network resources.

Data Task Description

A data task is defined as a combined data processing and data transmission job assigned to a node in the network. It is constrained (in the context of this work) to a single source and potentially multiple destinations. A network node is capable of handling one data task at a time, but multiple data tasks can be simultaneously processed at multiple nodes in the network.

A data stream is a sequence of data packets that are individually processed. In this discussion a data task is defined as a task for handling a single data packet. A data stream implies a sequence of data tasks. To simplify the formal definition of a data task, the concepts of a source pair and a target pair will be first introduced.

Definition 3: *For a given NET(N,L) and DST(D,F), define a* ***Source Pair*** *sp(NET, DST) and a* ***Target Pair*** *tp(NET, DST) as tuples* $\langle n_i, d_j \rangle$ *where* $n_i \in$ N *and* $d_j \in$ D. *A* ***Target Pair Set,*** *denoted by TP* = { $tp_1, tp_2, ..., tp_h$ }, *is an unordered set of target pairs.*

To simplify notation, for discussions where a single data type is considered over a fixed (or temporarily fixed) network, the source pair (*sp(NET, DST)* $\langle n_i, d_j \rangle$) and the target pair (*tp(NET, DST)* = $\langle n_k, d_k \rangle$) will be simply denoted as *sp* and *tp* respectively, under the implied assumption that n_i, $n_k \in$ N and d_i, $d_k \in$ D. Leveraging from the pervious definitions, a data task can be defined as follows:

Definition 4: *For a given NET(N,L) and DST(D,F), a* ***Data Task*** *is defined as a tuple dT(NET, DST) = ⟨sp, TP, phist⟩ where sp is a source pair sp(NET, DST) = ⟨n_i, d_j⟩, TP a target pair-set in (NET,DST), and phist an unordered set of nodes {n_i},$n_i \in$ N.*

In a data task, the source pair identifies which node has which datum, and the set of target pairs defines the target nodes and the datum they should receive. A data task essentially specifies a source pair (node/datum) and a set of destination pairs (node/datum) as part of a task to be accomplished. To simplify notation, a data task *dT(NET, DST)* = ⟨*sp, TP, phist*⟩ is simply denoted as *dT* in contexts where a single data type *DST* and *NET* are considered. Furthermore, in order to facilitate the notions introduced in subsequent discussion, we should also define two auxiliary functions f_n and f_d as follows:

Definition 5: *Define a* ***Node Function****, denoted by $f_n(\gamma)$ for ($\gamma = sp$) or ($\gamma = tp$), as a function $f_n(\langle n_i, d_j\rangle) = n_i$ that returns the node n_i of the argument γ.*

Definition 6: *Define a* ***Datum Function****, denoted by $f_d(\gamma)$ for ($\gamma = sp$) or ($\gamma = tp$), as a function $f_d(\langle n_i, d_j\rangle) = d_i$ that returns the datum d_j of the argument γ.*

Both the node and the datum functions can be applied to a data task (*dT* = ⟨*sp, TP, phist*⟩), which is equivalent to applying the functions in the *source pair* (*sp*) of the data task. That is f_n(*dT* = ⟨*sp, TP, phist*⟩) = f_n(*sp*) and similarly f_d(*dT* = ⟨*sp, TP, phist*⟩) = f_d(*sp*).

A data task fully specifies the source node *sp* = ⟨n_i, d_j⟩ and the task to be performed. It is, by definition, assigned to the node $n_i = f_n(sp)$ specified in the source tuple (*sp* = ⟨n_i, d_j⟩) and can have an arbitrary finite size for the target pair set and the path history.

The path history (*phist*) rather than specifying part of the task, defines constraints on how the task can be handled or delegated. The *phist* essentially defines a blacklist for the tasks, that is, a list of nodes in the network that must not be relied upon for assistance with this specific task. A valid data task must satisfy two conditions:

a. All data d_j specified in the source pair (*sp* = ⟨n_i, d_j⟩) or target pairs *tp* = ⟨n_i, d_j⟩ ⊂ *TP* must be of the same data type. That is, all datum instances must be part of the same DST diagram. Furthermore, there must be at least one data transition path (in the DST graph) from the source datum $d_j = f_d(sp)$ and each of the data $dj = f_d(tp) \mid tp \in TP$.
b. None of the nodes specified in the target pairs must be part of the *phist* set, unless the task is defined as a *terminal task*. A terminal task is defined as follows:

Definition 7: *A* ***terminal task*** *is a data task dT = ⟨sp, TP, phist⟩ where the target pair set TP is a singleton {tp}$\mid$ $\mid${tp}$\mid$=1 $\mid$, and the following conditions hold: $f_n(sp) = f_n(tp)$ and $f_d(sp) = f_d(tp)$.*

An example of a terminal task is $dT^{final} = n_1$: d_1 # n_1: d_1 # *phist*. Terminal tasks are *void* tasks that require no further processing or transmission of data. By definition, a non-terminal data task *dT* = ⟨*sp, TP, phist*⟩ assigned to node *sp* = ⟨n_i, d_j⟩ must be handled by that specific node, however, the concept of handling a task (as it will be described later) includes the notion of converting the task to another "equivalent" task (or a set of "equivalent" tasks) to be delegated to other nodes in the network.

For notational purposes, a data task can be represented as a single string, separated by '#' symbols to indicate each of the three elements of the tuple. For instance, the data task *dT* = ⟨*sp, TP, phist*⟩ = ⟨(n_1, d_1), {(n_2, d_3), (n_4, d_4)}, {n_0}⟩, can be represented by the string $dT = n_1: d_1 \# n_2: d_3, n_4: d_4 \# n_0$. In this example, node n_1 is given datum d_1 and the task of ultimately delivering datum d_3 to node n_2 and datum d_4 to node d_4 (without relying on node n_0 (in *phist*).

In the general case, the string notation for the data task is defined as follows:

$$dT = \langle sp, TP, phist\rangle$$
$$dT = f_n(sp): f_d(sp) \# \{f_n(tp_i): f_d(tp_i)\} \# \{n_j\} \mid tp_i \in TP \wedge n_j \in phist$$

This notation will be extensively used for the description of the problems, simulations and results. The column symbols between nodes and datum types are optional in the notion and might be dropped when there is no risk of ambiguity, allowing for the task $n_2: d_1 \# n_3: d_2, n_4: d_2 \# n_1$, to be also represented as $n_2d_1 \# n_3d_2, n_4d_2 \# n_1$.

The State of a Node

A node $n_i \in N$ can be in one of two types of states: idle or active. The default state of a node is in idle. When a node receives a data task from one of its neighbors, it transitions from an idle to an active state (s_i^{active}). If the received task is a terminal-task (i.e., if it is addressed to the node itself), the node simply consumes the datum and immediately transitions to back to an idle state (s_i^{idle}). In this case, the node is not required to choose an action for handling the task.

If, on the other hand, the task received is non-terminal the node must choose an action that will locally handle the task. The local handling of task might involve data transformations or task delegation to one or more of its neighbors. After applying the selected action, the node state will transition to idle, and the node becomes ready to receive new data requests from its neighbors.

An **active state** of node n_i, denoted as s_i^{active}, is always equal to a *single data task* being handled by node n_i at the time, and is defined as:

$$s_i^{active} = dT = \langle sp, TP, phist\rangle \left| \begin{cases} f_n(sp) = n_i, \text{ and} \\ dT_i \text{ is not a terminal state} \end{cases} \right. \qquad (1)$$

An **idle state** of node n_i, denoted as s_i^{idle}, is always equal to a *set of data tasks* and defined as follows:

$$s_i^{idle} = DT \mid \forall dT_i \in DT \left| \begin{cases} dT_i \text{ is a terminal state, or} \\ f_n(dT_i) \neq n_i \end{cases} \right. \qquad (2)$$

where $DT = \{dT_0, dT_1, ..., dT_k\}$ is a finite (possibly empty) set of data tasks. Recall that $f_n(dT_i)$ is equal to $f_n(sp_i)$, where sp_i is the source pair of data task dT_i.

Actions

An *action* is defined as a transition from any active state (s_i^{active}) to an idle state (s_i^{idle}), as follows:

Definition 8: *For a given NET(N,L) and DST(D,F), an action $a(s_i^{active})$, or $a(dT)$, represents a state transition $s_i^{active} \to s_i^{idle}$, where $s_i^{idle} = DT' = \{dT'_0, dT'_1, ..., dT'_k\}$ and $s_i^{active} = dT_i$ is defined in Box 1.*

In Definition 8, $DST_{path}(d_i, d_j)$ denotes a path in $DST(D, F)$ connecting states d_i to d_j and indicates that a data conversion between the two states is theoretically possible.

Note that not all $s_i^{active} \to s_i^{idle}$ transitions constitute valid actions. For instance, the action $a_i(n_1 : d_1\#n_3 : d_2\#) = \{dT' = n_2 : d_1\#n_3 : d_2\# n_1\}$, corresponds to a state transition $dT \Rightarrow \{dT'\}$, that is, $(dT = n_1 : d_1\#n_3 : d_2\#) \Rightarrow \{(dT' = n_2 : d_1\#n_3 : d_2\# n_1)\}$. The results of this action is the state transition $s_i^{active} \to s_i^{idle}$ (and $s_i^{idle} \to s_i^{active}$) and the semantics is that node n_1 with datum d_1 and the task to deliver d_2 to n_3 (i.e. $dT = n_1 : d_1\#n_3 : d_2\#$) delegates the job to node n_2, providing it with datum d_1, that is, $\{(dT' = n_2 : d_1\#n_3 : d_2\# n_1)\}$. This is a valid action and it will result in having node n_2 responsible for the next move.

Box 1.

$$a(dT = sp, TP, phist) = DT' \left| \begin{cases} (dT_i')^{final} \vee f_n(sp) \neq f_n(dT_i'), & \forall dT_i' \in DT' \\ (dT_i')^{final} \vee f_n(dT_i') \notin phist, & \forall dT_i' \in DT' \\ \bigcup_{dT_i'} (TP_{dT_i'}) = TP_{dT}, & \forall dT_i' \in DT' \\ \exists DST_{path}(f_d(dT), f_d(dT_i')), & \forall dT_i' \in DT' \\ f_n(sp) \text{ is a neighbor of } f_n(dT_i') \text{ in NET}, & \forall dT_i' \in DT' \end{cases} \right.$$

However, the action $a_j(n_1 : d_1\#n_3 : d_2\#) \Rightarrow \{dT' = n_2 : d_1\#n_5 : d_2\# \, n_1\}$ would be invalid because the "job" delegated to node n_2 (i.e. to deliver d_2 to node n_5) is different than the original job for which n_1 was responsible (i.e., n_3: d_2). Note that in the first case, the target pair-set is maintained through the conversion, which constituted a valid delegation of the task to a neighbor node thus a valid action. In the second example, the target pair-set was modified, which will result in a different outcome as node n_2 continues to handle the task.

Intuitively, in the first transition, the same data task (or an equivalent of it) is "delegated" to node n_2, which is now responsible for delivering datum d_2 to node n_3. In the second example, the target pair-set no longer includes the original task of delivering datum d_2 to node n_3. This constraint on the formation of the target pair set for a valid action is formally stated in the action definition (third condition in the list).

The example shown in Figure 2 satisfies all the conditions specified in the Definition 8. The example specifically highlights the fourth condition in the definition, that is, the required existence of a $DST_{path}(f_d(dT), f_d(dT'_i))$ in DST for all data transitions.

Note that the validation of the action relies solely on information available to node n_2. Aside from the list of neighbors (usually available to any node through the lower layer data link protocols) there are no assumptions or dependencies made on the capabilities of neighbor nodes.

Action Cost Estimation

In general, an action combines a data processing step with a data transmission. In its simplest form, an action simply consists on delegating the task to a neighbor node (data transmission) but it could also include local processing of the datum into one or more states.

The weights provided in both the DST and NET diagram allow for the cost estimation of both data transfer and data processing costs.

Figure 2. An example of a valid action

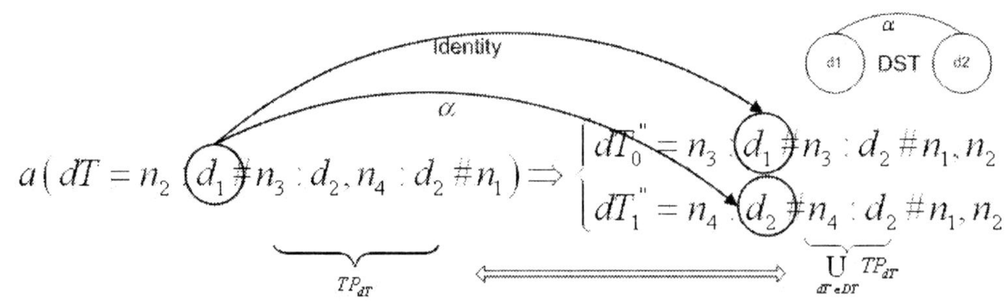

Equation 3, for instance, shows an example for cost estimation for a simple task ($dT = n_i d_k \# n_j d_p \# phist$) between two neighbor nodes n_i and n_j in a given environment.

$$Cost(a(dT)) = f_{st}(d_k, d_p) \cdot n_i^{pfactor} + d_p^{size} \cdot l_{i,j}^{tfactor} \tag{3}$$

Equation 3 shows the cost estimate for having node n_i (with datum d_k) deliver datum d_p to its neighbor node n_j (assuming that datum d_k can be converted to d_p through a function $f_{st}(d_k, d_p)$ available at n_i).

The equation considers that the data conversion from states ($d_k \rightarrow d_p$) happens at node n_i, before the transmission to node n_j. In this case, the data cost for the data conversion is given by $f_{st}(d_k, d_p) \cdot n_i^{pfactor}$, while the cost for the transmission is given by $d_p^{size} \cdot l_{i,j}^{tfactor}$.

Conversely, if the datum d_k was first transferred to node n_j to be then converted to d_p, the associated costs would be given by Equation 4, where the transmission portion is now weighted by d_k^{size}, and the processing cost by $n_j^{pfactor}$ (under the assumption that the transformation function $f_{st}(d_k, d_p)$ was also available at n_j).

$$Cost(a(dT)) = d_k^{size} \cdot l_{i,j}^{tfactor} + f_{st}(d_k, d_p) \cdot n_j^{pfactor} \tag{4}$$

Equations 3 and 4 produce exactly the same outcome at node n_j (i.e., datum d_p), however at different costs. An interesting decision to be made by node n_i is to determine which of the solutions (3) or (4) is the best (lowest cost) for the given task, namely, provide node n_j with datum d_p, without necessarily knowing the capabilities or data transformation costs of node d_j.

For a generalized action converting dT to a set $DT = \{dT'_0, dT'_1, ..., dT'_k\}$ (Equation 5), where $|DT| = k$, the overall costs consists in the sum of all transmission and data transformation tasks.

$$a(dT = \langle sp, TP, phist \rangle) \Rightarrow \{\langle sp'_0, TP'_0, phist' \rangle, \langle sp'_1, TP'_1, phist' \rangle, ..., \langle sp'_k, TP'_k, phist' \rangle\} \tag{5}$$

The data transmission sub-tasks are assumed to be independent from each other and their costs can be summed directly. The costs for the data conversion tasks, however, are estimated through a combined function $f_{st}(d_s, \{d_{sp_0}, d_{sp_1}, ..., d_{sp_k}\})$, where $d_{sp_j} = f_d(sp_j)$, that leverages from the commonality in the data. The data cost, in this case, can be estimated by Equation 6.

$$Cost(a(dT)) = f_{st}\left(d_s, \{d_{sp_0}, d_{sp_1}, ..., d_{sp_k}\}\right) n_j^{pfactor} + \sum_{j=1}^{k} \left(d_{sp_j}^{size} \cdot l_{i,f_n(sp_j)}^{tfactor}\right) \tag{6}$$

In Equation 2, the first term describes the combined costs for data processing while the second term aggregates all data transmission costs. The data processing costs are defined by the cost transformation of the minimum spanning tree from d_s (source) to $\{d_{t1}, d_{d2}, ..., d_{tp}\}$ (destinations), over the DST graph.

For example, consider the task shown in Figure 3. The graph shows only the local information available to the node, including its local neighbors and the DST for the data type described in the task.

If, given the state described in Figure 3, node n_2 chooses the action:

$$a(dT = n_2 : d_1 \# n_8 : d_2, n_5 : d_4, n_9 : d_5 \# n_2) \Rightarrow$$

$$\begin{cases} dT'_0 = n_1 : d_2 \# n_8 : d_2 \# n_2 \\ dT'_1 = n_6 : d_4 \# n_5 : d_4 \# n_2 \\ dT'_1 = n_7 : d_5 \# n_9 : d_5 \# n_2 \end{cases} \tag{7}$$

The outcome of the action is shown in Figure 4. At the left side of the figure, the network graph shows the actual data transmissions from node n_2 to nodes n_1, n_6 and n_7, as defined in Equation 7.

Figure 3. A sample data task for cost estimation

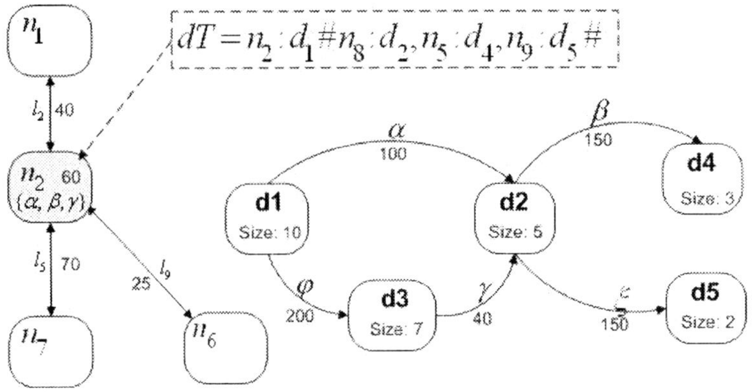

Figure 4. The minimum spanning tree for data processing cost estimation

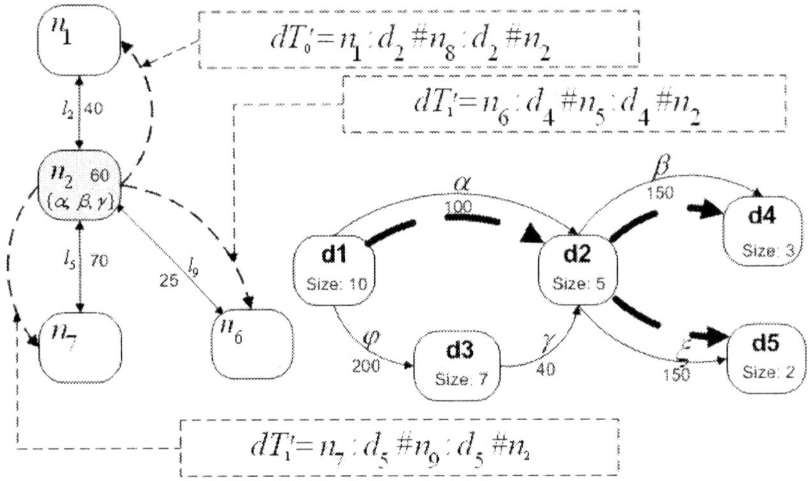

At the right side of the Figure 4, the minimum spanning tree for the data conversion is shown over the DST diagram. The cost of the action is show in Equation 8 (see Box 2), where the $f_{st}(d_1, \{d_8, d_9, d_5\})$ is defined as the cost of the minimum spanning tree from d_1 to $\{d_2, d_4, d_5\}$.

In the general case the cost of an action $a(dT)$ is given by Equation 9,

$$Cost\left(a(dT) = DT'\right) = f_{st}\left(f_d(dT), \left\{f_d\left(dT'_j\right)\right\}\right) f_n(dT)^{pfactor} + \sum_{j=1}^{|DT|}\left(\left(f_d\left(dT'_j\right)\right)^{size} \cdot l^{tfactor}_{f_n(dT), f_n(dT'_j)}\right)$$

$$, for \quad \forall dT'_j \in DT'sCost \qquad (9)$$

The resource allocation problem consists of finding the best allocation of resources in the network that would realize the task successfully with the lowest possible cost ($\arg_A \min(TotalCost)$).

Each node has to make a local decision (that is not necessarily the best local choice) in order to allow for a global solution that will evolve to a minimum aggregate cost (in the optimum case).

Finding a solution for the resource allocation problem essentially consists of minimizing, at run-time, the global cost for all concurrent data requests in the network, that is, to solve the cost estimation problem in a dynamic environment. In practice, the problem consists of incrementally improving the cost estimate at each node,

Box 2.

$$\begin{aligned} Cost(a(dT)) &= f_{st}\left(d_1,\{d_2,d_4,d_5\}\right)\cdot n_2^{pfactor} + \sum_{j=1}^{|DT|}\left(\left(f_d(dT'_j)\right)^{size}\cdot l_{2,f_n(dT'_j)}^{tfactor}\right) \\ &= f_{st}\left(d_1,\{d_2,d_4,d_5\}\right)\cdot n_2^{pfactor} + \left(d_2^{size}\cdot l_{2,1}^{tfactor} + d_4^{size}\cdot l_{4,6}^{tfactor} + d_5^{size}\cdot l_{2,7}^{tfactor}\right)n_7 \end{aligned} \tag{8}$$

recognizing that the cost functions themselves are dynamic.

LEARNING STRATEGIES FOR THE RESOURCE ALLOCATION PROBLEM

For all practical purposes, the combinatorial nature of the resource allocation problem makes it very difficult to use strategies based on global information. Sub-optimal solutions are usually well accepted as long as they can be quickly identified and initialized to minimize latency.

One way to find the best action is to try each possibility and, through an exhaustive search identify which task would yield the lowest cost. There are, however, more efficient ways to choose the next action based on the incomplete experience acquired in early trials. Under certain constraints and assumptions, the problem can be reduced to a well known online learning problem in game theory known as the k-arm bandit problem.

The k-Arm Bandit Problem

The k-arm bandit problem proposed by Robbins (1952) defines a scenario where a gambler must choose one of "k" slot machines to place a bet. At each bet (which are assumed to have fixed value) the player pulls the arm of the slot machine and collects the reward in cash, if any. The objective of the game is to maximize the gains of the gambler over a fixed number of plays.

In order to achieve his/her goals in maximizing the gains, the gambler must be able to identify, as early as possible which of the machines gives the best odds for wining. Assuming, for now, that each arm returns its rewards based on a fixed pre-defined distribution that is unknown to the gambler, the challenge in the problem is to decide at each play, when to exploit a "known" distribution versus exploring a new one.

The dichotomy "exploration" and "exploitation" is a characteristic of most online learning problems and have been addressed in detail in the context of *Reinforcement Learning* by Sutton and Barto (1998), who enumerates a number of strategies for balancing exploitation and exploration for maximizing gains in the long run.

Among the strategies presented by Sutton and Barto (1998), two groups are of particular interest for this work, the ε-*greedy* and the softmax exploration strategies. The ε-*greedy* strategies essentially define a ε value that determines the ratio between exploratory and exploitative plays. It establishes that ε percent of the time, the gambler will not use its best known "arm" and will choose, instead, one of the other arms with equal probability.

Conversely, Softmax action selection strategies choose the next action (or "arm" to be played) through a probability distribution of the expected reward of all available arms. A very common distribution used for these types of strategies is the Gibbs or Boltzmann distribution. After a few plays, the probability of choosing arm "a" for the next play is proportional to the exponential of the accumulated observed for that action (Equation 10):

$$P_a(t) = \frac{e^{Q_t(a)/\tau}}{\sum_{b=1}^{n} e^{Q_t(b)/\tau}} \qquad (10)$$

where $P_a(t)$ is the probability of choosing action (a) at play (t), $Q_t(a)$ is the accumulated rewards for action (a) up to time (t), and τ is a parameters known as the "temperature" for the distribution. The higher the temperature the more uniform-like the distribution will seem and the lower the temperature the greater will be the differences in the probabilities arising from differences in accumulated values.

Action Selection using SoftMax and ε-greedy Strategies

The selection of an action starts with a node first checking if the message is addressed to itself. If the node receiving the data task is listed in the target pair list it will first create a sub-task that is terminal.

For example, if node n_3 receives task $dT = n_3d_2 \# n_3d_4, n_2d_3 \# phist$, it must verify that the task is to be (at least partially) consumed by node n_3 itself, as it is listed in the target pair set. If there were no remaining nodes in the target pair set, the task would be completed and would no longer be forwarded. Node n_3 in that case would simply send a broadcast message announcing the success of the task, with the attached cost for handling the final conversion.

In the general case however, based on the received data task dT and the current set of neighbors, the selection of an action first requires the complete set of possible actions to be built for cost evaluation. The list of neighbor nodes is first pruned to remove any neighbors that are also listed in the *phist* of the data task. The remaining neighbors will be considered as candidates for receiving the task.

Consider for instance, the example shown in Figure 5, where node n_4 receives message $n_4d_1 \# n_6d_2, n_7d_2 \# n_1$ from n_1 and that the transition between datum d_1 and d_2 is done through function α.

Figure 5 shows the list of all actions available to node n_4. The set of actions are created based on the received task $n_4d_1 \# n_6d_2, n_7d_2 \# n_1$ and the list of neighbors $\{n_1, n_2, n_6\}$ from which node n_1

Figure 5. A list of possible actions

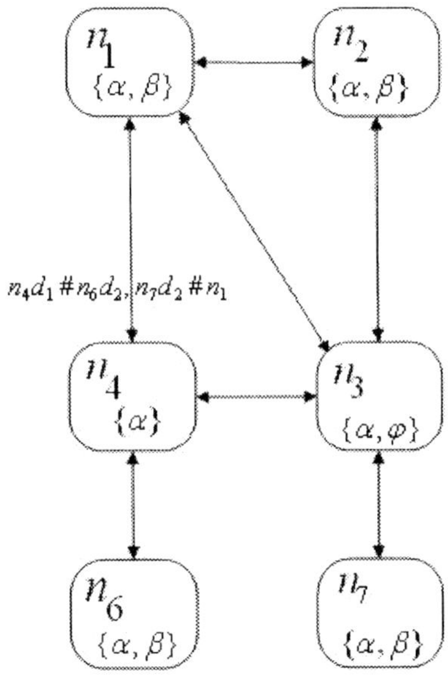

$$a_0(dT) = n_6d_1 \# n_6d_2, n_7d_2 \# n_1, n_4$$
$$a_1(dT) = (n_6d_1 \# n_6d_2 \# n_1, n_4)(n_3d_1 \# n_7d_2 \# n_1, n_4)$$
$$a_2(dT) = (n_6d_1 \# n_7d_2 \# n_1, n_4)(n_3d_1 \# n_6d_2 \# n_1, n_4)$$
$$a_3(dT) = (n_6d_1 \# n_6d_2 \# n_1, n_4)(n_3d_2 \# n_7d_2 \# n_1, n_4)$$
$$a_4(dT) = (n_6d_1 \# n_7d_2 \# n_1, n_4)(n_3d_2 \# n_6d_2 \# n_1, n_4)$$
$$a_5(dT) = n_3d_1 \# n_6d_2, n_7d_2 \# n_1, n_4$$
$$a_6(dT) = n_6d_2 \# n_6d_2, n_7d_2 \# n_1, n_4$$
$$a_7(dT) = (n_6d_2 \# n_6d_2 \# n_1, n_4)(n_3d_1 \# n_7d_2 \# n_1, n_4)$$
$$a_8(dT) = (n_6d_2 \# n_7d_2 \# n_1, n_4)(n_3d_1 \# n_6d_2 \# n_1, n_4)$$
$$a_9(dT) = (n_6d_2 \# n_6d_2 \# n_1, n_4)(n_3d_2 \# n_7d_2 \# n_1, n_4)$$
$$a_{10}(dT) = (n_6d_2 \# n_7d_2 \# n_1, n_4)(n_3d_2 \# n_6d_2 \# n_1, n_4)$$
$$a_{11}(dT) = n_3d_2 \# n_6d_2, n_7d_2 \# n_1, n_4$$

Figure 6. Four nodes network for test and DST

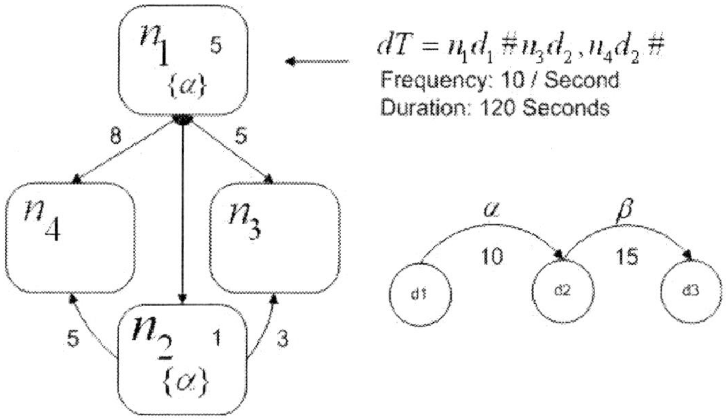

was eliminated because it is listed in *dT*'s *phist*. The selection of an action will follow either an ε-greedy or a SoftMax strategy, using the Boltzmann distribution. Even before receiving any feedback from neighbors, a prior can be estimated for the actions based on their local cost estimations. If there is absolutely no information about any prior probability for the actions, all tasks are considered equiprobable and the selection is based on a uniform random draw. The most likely scenario, however, is that node n_4 might have collected information reported by both nodes n_3 and n_6 either due to direct interactions with them in previous requests, or through promiscuously listening to messages from these nodes.

EXPERIMENTAL EVALUATION

The proposed algorithm was implemented and tested on a simulated network for several network topologies and data flows. The purpose of these tests was to verify the behavior of the algorithm, rather than benchmark its performance given that the current implementation is a not optimized and intended as a proof of concept version of the algorithm. In order to demonstrate and discuss the algorithm, a few scenarios were defined and simulated. In this section, we present some of our simulation results for different topologies and topology-change conditions.

The 4-Node Fixed Topology

The first simulation test is a fixed network with four nodes and a three-state data transition graph. Both the network topology (NET) and the DST diagram are shown in Figure 6. The figure also shows all costs associated with data processing (*pfactors, function costs*) and transmission (*tfactors, datum size*).

One single data stream was created for this test. The stream will consist of 10 tasks ($dT = n_1d_1 \# n_3d_2, n_4d_2 \#$) per second to the system (i.e., to node n_1) for a period of 120 seconds. The target nodes (target pair-set) for the task are nodes n_3(datum d_2) and n_4(datum d_2), with no processing capabilities (no functions available) as illustrated in Figure 6.

Nodes n_3 and n_4 will report (log) all successful tasks and their costs. A successful task, from a node's perspective, consists of having the specified datum delivered at the target node (i.e., receiving a terminal task). If both nodes report that the same task was completed (which can be matched by a task ID), then the overall task ($dT = n_1d_1 \# n_3d_2, n_4d_2 \#$) is said to have succeeded and the cost of completion is the sum of the costs from both n_3 and n_4.

Figure 7 shows the average aggregate cost results from four independent runs for each of

Figure 7. Four node fixed topology Boltzman vs. ε-greedy

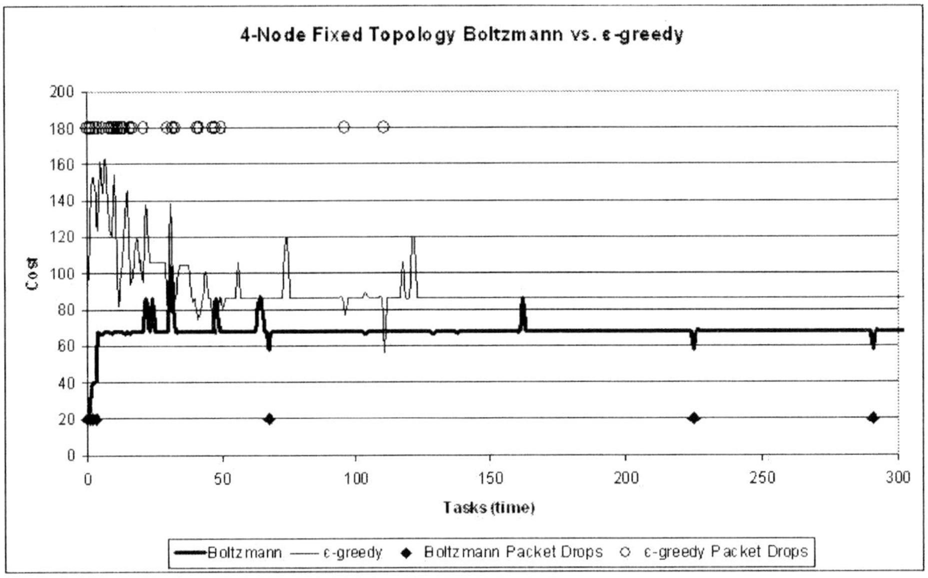

the policy selection strategies. Packet drops for each strategy are also shown in Figure 7.

In this example, the epsilon coefficient for the ε-greedy strategy is calculated at each iteration as the ratio of actions flagged as "unknown" and the total number of strategies available. Initially, with several unknown actions available the algorithm using an ε-greedy strategy will be more proactive on searching for new possibilities.

Out of 300 data tasks, the ε-greedy strategy lost an average of 28 tasks while Boltzmann lost nine tasks on average. Note that most of the loss in the ε-greedy occurs at the beginning of the process, while unknown actions are being explored.

The 4-Node Changing Topology

A more interesting scenario is when a change in topology occurs during the flow of a data stream. This example is shown in Figure 8, where the four node topology is used for the same scenario as the previous example.

In this case, however, node n_2 is initially removed from the topology and added at a later time. Figure 8 presents the average of four tests showing how the algorithms reacted to the insertion of the node in the topology. The time of the insertion was approximately the same in each run (dotted zone in the figure). In this example, both algorithms quickly detect the new neighbor and extend their set of available actions and find a better solution for the DDT.

The ε-greedy implementation, as expected fluctuates a little longer until it explores the new set of known solutions. Because the probability of exploration drops as new solutions become "known" (that is, recently tested), the curve stabilizes with the Boltzmann implementation after a while.

The costs, in both cases is the minimum cost available to in the network, the fact that the Boltzmann line at some point goes below that value (right after the addition of the node) indicates packets being dropped in some of the runs, resulting in a lower average cost.

The 7-Node Changing Topology

Another test involving the addition and removal of nodes is shown in Figure 9 for a 7-node topol-

Figure 8. Four-node network with changing topology

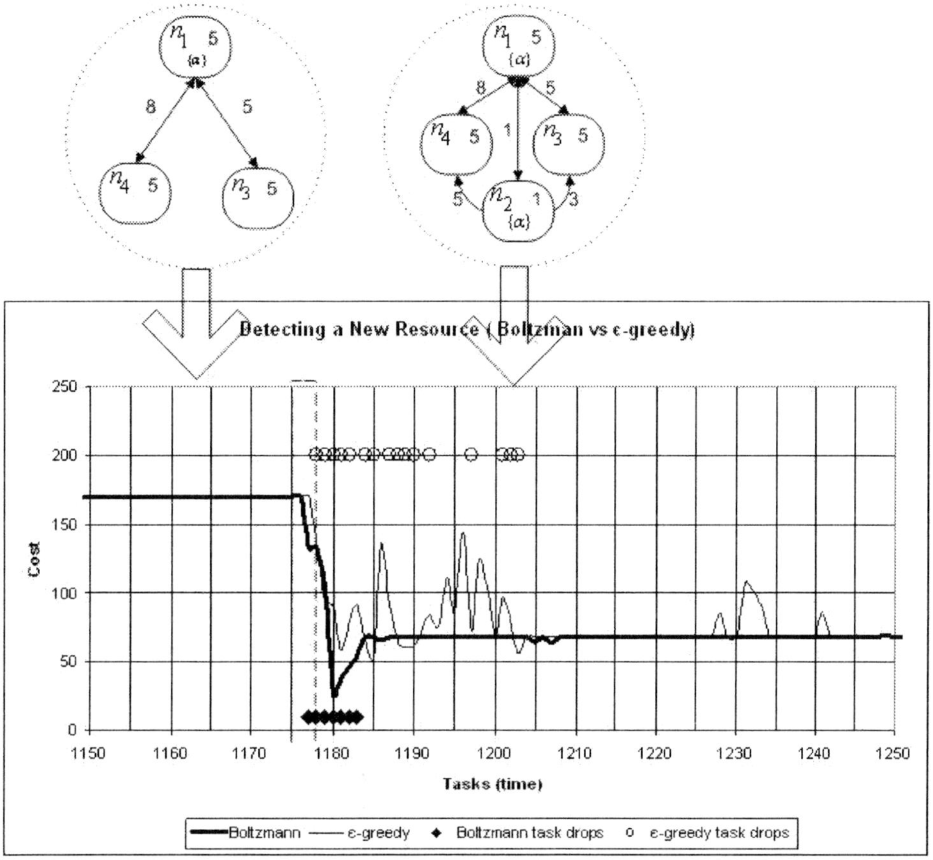

Figure 9. A 7-node network with changing topology

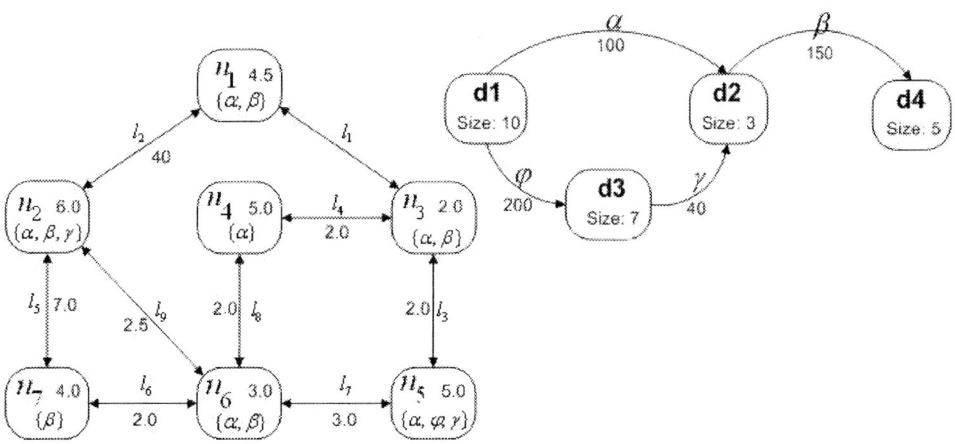

Figure 10. A 7-node network changing topology

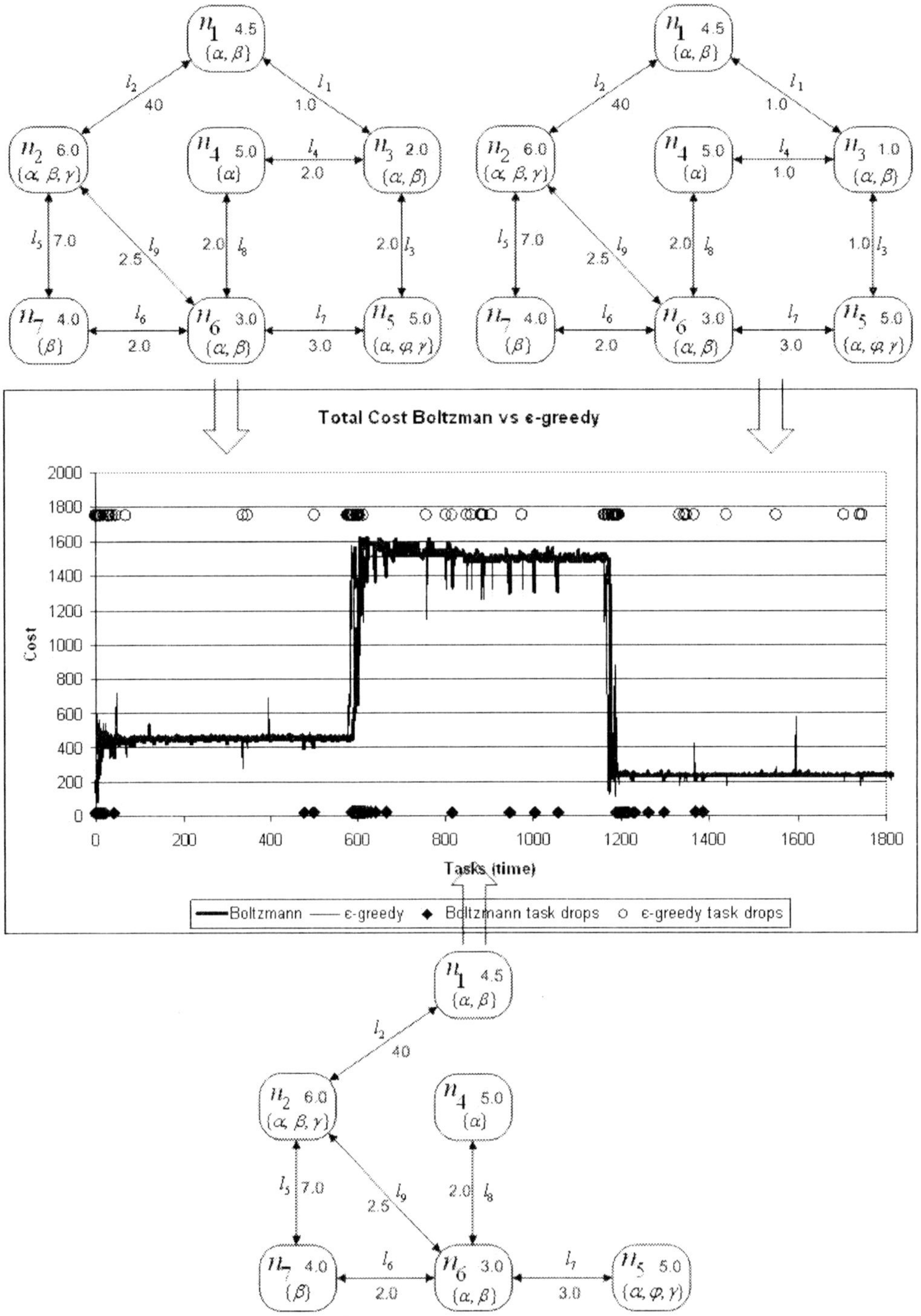

ogy and associated data task. The data stream in this example is given by $dT = n_1d_1 \# n_4d_2, n_3d_2\#$, injected in n_1 at a rate of 20 requests per second for 120 seconds.

In this simulation, the minimum cost path is through node n_3, which performs a transformation and then splits the stream to n_4 and n_3.

The resulting aggregate costs for the algorithm using both the Boltzmann and the ε-greedy strategies are shown in Figure 10.

At 20 requests per second, the horizontal axis in the figure provides an indirect measurement of "time." In this example, 30 seconds into the simulation, node n_3 is removed from the network (shown at the bottom of Figure 10) and the processing of the task is switched to flow through nodes n_2 and n_6.

Coincidentally in this case, this is also the shortest communication path for the flow, but

Figure 11. Removing node n3 from the 7-node topology

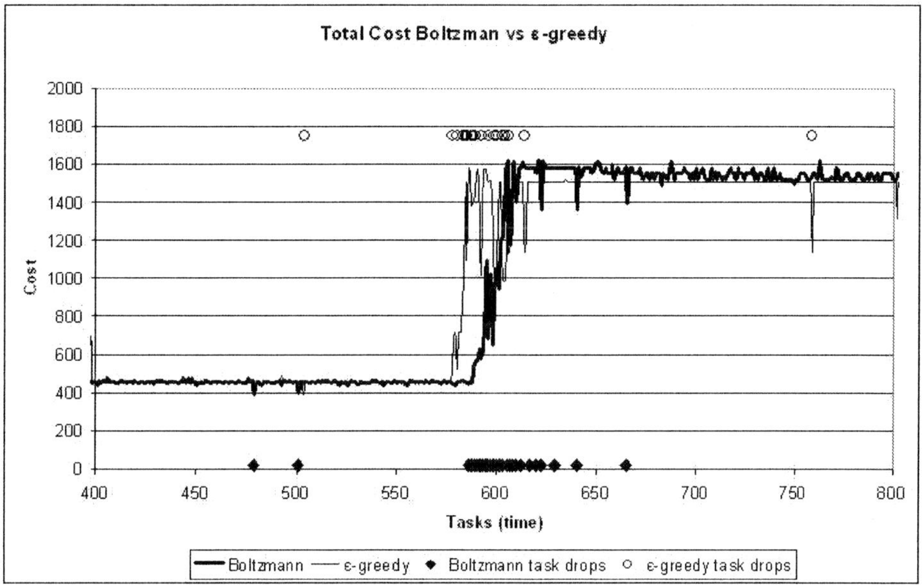

Figure 12. Re-inserting node n3 from the 7-node topology

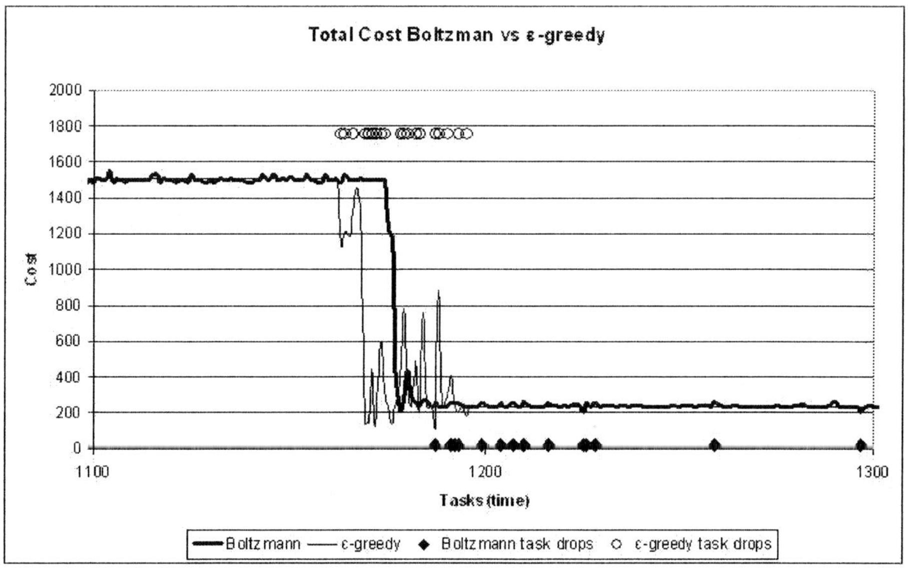

in other simulations (not shown in this specific figure) if the processing cost of node n_6 increases, the transformation tasks starts happening at node n_2, as opposed to n_6. The effects of the removal of node n_3 are shown in detail in Figure 11.

Node 3 is added back to the network at time 60 (around 1200 in the x-scale) with a different set of edge costs. Note that both strategies move the processing flow back again to node n_3. Figure 12 shows in detail the recover to a lower cost configuration after node n_3 is re-added to the network.

CONCLUSION

In this article we have revisited and summarized the data distribution strategy for tactical environments proposed by Carvalho in 2006. The main contribution of this work was the design and proof-of-concept implementation of a novel approach for the resource allocation problem in tactical networks. In our approach, we leverage from pervious research on reinforcement learning and game theory to design a distributed algorithm for resource allocation that simultaneously addresses the requirements for resource constrained in-stream data processing in mobile ad hoc networks, an important capability for tactical environments.

The algorithm introduced in this work proposes the simultaneous allocation of resources for both data processing and data transmission in the network. This combined approach to the resource allocation problem differs from techniques commonly found in the literature that are: (1) centered at the application (or middleware levels) and rely on models and estimates of the underlying communications framework for resource allocation or, (2) data-agnostic techniques centered at the network level that attempt to infer data processing requirements to better allocate routes.

In this work, the resource allocation problem was first defined and formally described in the context of an online learning in order to be mapped, under certain assumptions, to the well known k-arm bandit problem at the node level. From that formulation, two standard strategies for policy selection (ε-greedy and SoftMax) were slightly modified and integrated with the algorithm.

The resource allocation algorithm proposed in this work is reactive, efficient, flexible, and adaptive. The experimental results, although preliminary at this stage, have provided some evidence that the algorithm is capable of adapting to changes in both environment and task requirements. Further tests are necessary to validate the algorithm in large scale settings and benchmarking.

ACKNOLWEDGMENT

This work has been partially supported by the U.S. Army Research Laboratory under contract W911NF-04-2-0013, by the U.S. Army Research Laboratory under the Collaborative Technology Alliance Program, Cooperative Agreement DAAD19-01-2-0009, by the Office of Naval Research under grant N00014-03-1-0780, and by the Air Force Research Laboratory under Cooperative Agreement FA750-06-2-0064.

REFERENCES

Baehni, S., Eugster, P. Th., & Guerraoui, E. (2004, June). Data-aware multicast. In *Proceedings of the 5th IEEE International Conference on Dependable Systems and Networks (DSN '04).*

Boyan, J. A., & Littman, M. L. (1994). Packet routing in dynamically changing networks: A reinforcement learning approach. *Advances in Neural Information Processing Systems, 6.*

Buyya, R., Stockinger, H., Giddy, J., & Abramson, D. (2001, August 20-24). Economic models for management of resources in peer-to-peer and grid computing. In *Proceedings of International Conference on Commercial Applications for High-Performance Computing,* Denver, CO. SPIE Press.

Carvalho, M. (2006). *Distributed resource coordination strategies for mobile ad hoc networks.* Unpublished PhD dissertation, Tulane University, New Orleans, LA.

Carvalho, M., & Breedy, M. (2002, October). Supporting flexible data feeds in dynamic sensor grids through mobile agents. In *Proceedings of the 6th International Conference in Mobile Agents (MA 2002),* Barcelona, Spain.

Carvalho, M., Pechoucek, M., & Suri, N. (2005, July). A mobile agent-based middleware for opportunistic resource allocation and communications. In *Proceedings of the Fourth International Joint Conference on Autonomous Agents and Multiagent Systems; Defense Applications of Multi-Agent Systems (DAMAS).*

Chang, Y., Ho, T., & Kaelbling, L. (2004). Mobilized ad-hoc networks: A reinforcement learning approach. In *Proceedings of the First International Conference on Autonomic Computing (ICAC '04)* (pp. 240-247).

Chen, Y., & Schwan, K. (2005, November). Opportunistic overlays: Efficient content delivery in mobile ad hoc networks. In *Proceedings of the 6th ACM/IFIP/USENIX International Middleware Conference (Middleware 2005).*

Choi, S. P. M., & Yeung, D. Y. (1996). Predictive q-routing: A memory-based reinforcement learning approach to adaptive traffic control. In *Proceedings of NIPS-8* (pp. 910-945).

Curran, E. (2003). *Swarm: Cooperative reinforcement learning for routing in ad hoc networks.* Unpublished MSc thesis, Trinity College, Dublin, Ireland.

Dowling, J., Curran, E., Cunningham, R., & Cahill, V. (2005, May). Using feedback in collaborative reinforcement learning to adaptively optimize MANET routing. *IEEE Transactions on Systems, Man, and Cybernetics—Part A: Systems and Humans, 35*(3).

Duran-Limon, et al. (2000). *Context-aware middleware for pervasive ad hoc environments.* (Tech. Rep.). Project CORTEX.

Eugster, P., Th., Guerraoui, R., & Damm, C. H. (2001, October). On objects and events. In *Proceedings of the 16th ACM Conference on Object-Oriented Programming Systems, Languages and Applica-tions (OOPSLA 2001)* (pp. 131-146).

Intanagonwiwat, C., Govindan, R., & Estrin, D. (2000, August). Directed diffusion: A scalable and robust communication paradigm for sensor networks. In *Proceedings of the Sixth Annual International Conference on Mobile Computing and Networking (MobiCOM '00),* Boston, MA.

Katz, R., & Brewer, E. (1996). Wireless overlay networks and adaptiveApplications. In *Proceedings of MobiCom.*

Kothari, A., Sabhash, S., & Zhou, Y. (2003). Bandwidth-constrained allocation in grid computing. In *Proceedings of WADS.*

Littman, M., & Boyan, J. (1993). *A distributed reinforcement learning scheme for network routing* (Tech. Rep. No. CMU-CS-93-165).

Maistre, F. (2003). *JORAM.* Retrieved May 2005, from http://joram.ob-jectweb.org

Miikkulainen, R., & Kumar, S. (1999). Confidence based dual reinforcement q-routing: An adaptative on-line routing algorithm. In *Proceedings of the Sixteenth International Joint Conference on Artificial Intelligence* (pp. 758-763).

Pechoucek, M., Marık, V., & Stepankova, O. (2001). Towards reducing communication traffic in multi-agent systems. *Journal of Applied Systems, 2*(1), 152-174.

Peng, F., & Deyun, Z. (2006). *Hybrid optimize strategy based QoS route algorithm for mobile ad hoc networks.* Department of Computer Science and Technology, Xi'an Jiaotong University, Xi'an, China.

Robbins, H. (1952). Some aspects of the sequential design of experiments. *Bulletin American Mathematical Society, 55,* 527-535.

Stone, P. (2000). Tpot-rl applied to network routing. In *Proceedings of the 17th International Conference on Machine Learning.*

Sutton, R. S., & Barto, A.G. (1998). *Reinforcement learning: An Introduction.* Cambridge, MA: MIT Press/Bradford Books.

Tao, N., Baxter, J., & Weaver, L. (2001). A multi-agent, policy-gradient approach to network routing. In *Proceedings of the 18th International Conference on Machine Learning.*

Woodrow, E., & Heinzelman, W. (2001). *SPIN-IT: A data centric routing protocol for image retrieval in wireless networks.* Retrieved November 20, 2003, from http://www.ece.rochester.edu/~wheinzel/GroupWeb/papers/spin-it_icip02.pdf

This work was previously published in International Journal of Electronic Government Research, Vol. 4, Issue 1, edited by M. Khosrow-Pour, pp. 49-67, copyright 2008 by IGI Publishing (an imprint of IGI Global).

Chapter 4
Implementing Interoperability Standards for Electronic Government:
A Case Study of the E-Ping Brazilian Framework

Ernani Marques dos Santos
University of São Paulo, Brazil

ABSTRACT

Interoperability standards play an important role in the integration of systems and information sharing for electronic government. However, these processes do not just mean exchange of data but, mainly, integration of processes and transactions. Therefore, the implementation of these standards depends not only on technological aspects, but also on other variables of the institutional, organizational and economical contexts. Based on this scenery, this chapter discusses the implementation of the standardization process in an electronic government environment. It presents the findings from a case study of the Brazilian interoperability framework (e-PING), based on documents content analysis and face-to-face semi-structured interviews. As a result, it points out some aspects that may be conditioning in the setting of these standards.

INTRODUCTION

Standardization can bring several benefits for the public administration, such as improvement of data management, contribution for the information infrastructure, expansion of the contexts of action of the programs of the public policies, improvement of the accountability and promotion of the coordination of programs and services, among others.

DOI: 10.4018/978-1-60566-918-2.ch001

In the electronic government's case, the ideal environment should be a single access point to the information and services. In this context, it is easy to identify the relevance of the adoption of standards due to the need of systems integration and information sharing. Akbulut (2003), Dawes (1996) and Landsbergen and Wolken (2001) already investigated these processes among government agencies and they identified the standards adoption as an enabler factor.

Standardization is necessary to facilitate the data exchange, their re-use along the time, and also to prevent the lock-in to proprietary tools and formats (EPAN, 2004). However, in order to a standard be succeeded is necessary its use and its acceptance by all of the agents involved in the transactions affected by its implementation.

Several factors can be conditioning in the adoption of standards by the government agencies, such as incompatible technologies, internal interests of each agency, dominant professional standards, external influences on the decision makers, and the level of decision power of the agency.

Based on these premises it can be clearly seen that the adoption of standards of interoperability by the government agencies is a complex process, due to the number of agents involved in the process, the environment where it takes place, the level of interrelation between the agents and the environment, besides the likely conflicts of interests originated by this interrelation. Therefore, it needs to be analyzed and understood, since the understanding of this process allows the creation of better conditions for dissemination and evolution of the specified standards.

The objective of this paper is, therefore, to identify what factors can be conditioning in the adoption of interoperability standards in electronic government's environment. It presents a case study of the e-PING - Standards of Interoperability for Electronic Government, a framework that has been implemented by the Brazilian Federal Government since 2004 (Brasil, 2008).

STANDARDS AND STANDARDIZATION

A standard is a group of specifications to which all of the product elements, processes, formats, or procedures under its jurisdiction have to adhere (Tassey, 2000). For David and Greenstein (1990), a standard is a group of technical specifications adhered by a group of suppliers, tacitly or as a result of a formal agreement.

David and Steinmueller (1994) classify the standards in four categories: reference, minimum quality, interface and compatibility. The compatibility standards play a relevant role in the Information Technology field, because they enable data exchange among components of a specific system or between different inter-organizational systems.

According to Williams at all (2004), the development and implementation of compatibility standards not only technically define an inter-operational method among the different components in a network, but it also represents a proposal for the future of the complex socio-technical systems that are the form of an inter-organizational network.

Standards can also be classified according to the processes by means of which they are established. A distinction is frequently made among formal, *de facto* and *de jure*. Formal standards are created through standardization entities; *de facto* are technologies established by market mechanisms, and the *de jure* are the ones imposed by law (Hanseth & Monteiro, 1998).

According to Graham *at all* (1995), the standardization process represents an attempt to align interests, practices of businesses and expectations of a group of people with one interest to develop and to use the system that will be standardized. Therefore, the standardization is not just to provide a usable solution but, mainly, to articulate and to align expectations and interests (Williams, 1997).

In the context of Information Technologies (IT), the standardization can be defined as the process in which two or more agents agree and adhere to a group of technical specifications of a system, their parts or their functionality, tacitly or as a result of a formal agreement (David & Greenstein, 1990). Consequently, these standards enable and constrain at the same time the behavior of several agents in the future (Garud, Jain & Kumaraswamy, 2000).

Standardization is an important action to enable information sharing in information systems. Therefore, it is necessary to define compatibility standards to be adopted among those systems (Dos Santos & Reinhard, 2007).

INTEROPERABILITY

Interoperability can be defined as the ability of two or more systems of interacting and exchanging data in agreement with a defined method, in order to obtain the results expected. However, this definition can not be taken as a consensus. IEEE (2000), for instance, presents four definitions:

- The ability of two or more systems or elements of exchanging information amongst themselves and to use the information that were exchanged;
- The capacity for units of equipments in working together to accomplish useful functions;
- The capacity, promoted but no guaranteed by the adhesion to a certain group of standards, that it makes possible heterogeneous equipments, usually manufactured for several suppliers, to work together in network.
- The ability of two or more systems or components to exchange information in a heterogeneous network and to use these information.

Interoperability can be also defined as the ability of government organizations to share information and integrate information and business processes by use of common standards (State Services Commission, 2007). According to Archmann and Kudlacek (2008), it is the ability of ICT systems to communicate, interpret and interchange data in a meaningful way.

E-government interoperability is the process by which independent or heterogeneous information systems or their components managed by different jurisdictions/administrations or by external partners work together in predefined and agreed terms and specifications (Gottschalk & Solli-Saether, 2009).

The interoperability can bring several benefits, such as more effectiveness (interconnection instead of isolated solutions), efficiency (reduction of the transaction costs and increase of the involved agents' participation), and responsiveness (better access to more information, making possible the fastest resolution of the problems) (Landsbergen & Wolken, 2001).

Goldkuhl (2008) states that interoperability is perhaps the most important issue of e-government. According to the author, the establishment of advanced solutions with integrated e-services and one stop government imply high demands on e-government interoperability. Several other authors have pointed out the importance of e-government interoperability, e.g. Cava and Guijarro (2003), Benamou et al (2004), Klischewski (2004), Bekkers (2005), Klischewski and Scholl (2006).

However, there are significant barriers to achieve interoperability in an effective and wide way. These barriers can be classified as politics, organizational, economical and technical (Anderseen & Dawes, 1991):

- **Political:** Definition of the guidelines of the adopted policies; conflicts in the definitions of the levels of privacy in the accesses to the information; predominant organizational culture; ambiguity of the authority in the collection and use of the information; administrative discontinuity.
- **Organizational:** Lack of experience and absence of the predisposition of sharing; level of the personnel's qualification involved in the processes; organizational culture;

- **Economical:** Lack of resources for disposing the information for other agencies; form of acquisition of the resources (usually acquired based on the smallest price and not on the best value);
- **Technical:** Incompatibility of adopted hardware and software; property rights; ignorance of the data generated and stored by the systems; multiple definitions of data.

Scholl and Klischewski (2007) also argue that there are several constraints that influence the interoperability. According to these authors, these constraints can be classified as constitutional and legal, jurisdictional, collaborative, organizational, informational, managerial, cost, technological and performance.

Although the information sharing is a common objective for government agencies, the scope of this share is still limited (Dawes & Bloniarz, 2001). The benefits that this share can bring to the policy makers, public agents and citizens are considered highly important, but the government agencies fail to implement it due to these technological, organizational, politics and economics barriers (Dawes, 1996; Landsbergen and Wolken, 2001; Rocheleau, 1997).

Information sharing and interoperability are mainly interactions processes. Several internal and external variables act at the same time and can become critical factors to their successes. Landsbergen and Wolken (2001) point out that to implement interoperability is easier when:

- Exists a previous history of the involved agencies in working together
- The share focus is on transactional and not on operational or strategic information
- The agents perceive benefits in the short time

Therefore, interoperability standards setting can be considered as a hard task to achieve, since the defined specifications have to overcome several barriers to be adopted.

METHODOLOGY

The research consisted of a case study based on documents analysis, data collection through questionnaire, and semi-structured interviews. The research object was the e-PING framework, a set of standards specified by the Brazilian Federal Government to be used by the government agencies.

The research consisted of two stages. The first one was the analysis of the documents that specify the standards to be adopted and the reports about the actions carried out by the e-PING coordination group to implement them. In the second stage the level of adoption of the e-PING by the government agencies was investigated through the analysis of the data collected in a survey conducted by the coordination group of the project.

The objective of this survey was to examine the use of the interoperability standards by the Federal Government's agencies, as well as to identify the barriers in its adoption. The survey was conducted through one web questionnaire consisted of 46 questions made available in the internet on a page managed by the Ministry of Planning, Budget and Administration, the executive agency of the project. The request for completion of the questionnaire was sent by email to IT managers from 66 agencies of the direct and indirect administration of the Federal Executive Branch and it was obtained a total of 45 answers (approximately 68%). The questions included issues as general vision of the e-PING, policies of the researched institution in relation to the use of ICT and specific topics for each segment covered by the architecture.

Three semi structured interviews were conducted with the coordinator and with a technical advisor of the project in order to clarify how decisions about the specifications of the standards and the adopted strategies to conduct the survey with the agencies were taken.

THE E-PING FRAMEWORK

The architecture e-PING - Standards of Interoperability of Electronic Government - defines a minimum set of premises, policies and technical specifications that regulate the use of Information and Communication Technologies (ICT) in the interoperability of services of the Brazilian electronic government, establishing the interaction conditions with other government institutions (besides states and municipal districts) and with the society. These standards include five broad segments: (1) interconnectivity, (2) security, (3) means of access, (4) organization and exchange of information and (5) areas and issues for electronic government integration (Brasil, 2008). The Table 1 presents the covered issues for each defined segments.

For each one of these segments, there is a process to analyze the corresponding proposed standards that will compose the architecture. This process includes the selection, approval and classification of the selected specifications in five levels (Brasil, 2008):

- **Adopted (A):** Evaluated and formally approved;
- **Recommended (R):** It should be used by the government agencies, but it was not formally approved yet;
- **Transition (T):** Not recommended because it does not conform to some technical requirement. It may be used only temporarily;
- **Under evaluation (E):** Still under evaluation;

Table 1. Definition of the segments of the and-PING

Segments	Covered issues
Interconnectivity	Conditions for government agencies to connect to each other and to external institutions.
Security	Security aspects to assure operations validity and privacy
Means of access	Devices for accessing to the services of electronic government.
Organization and exchange of information	Issues related to the management and transfer of information.
Areas and issues for electronic government integration.	New ways of integration and exchange of information based on the definitions of e-PING.

Table 2. Classification of the standards of the e-PING

Segments	Total of specified standards	Classification				
		(A)	(R)	(T)	(E)	(F)
Interconnectivity	23	9	8	2	2	2
Security	34	9	18	-	7	-
Means of access	129	22	47	33	2	25
Organization and exchange of information	7	4	-	-	2	1
Areas and issues for electronic government	17	4	5	-	6	2
Total	210	48	78	35	19	30

- **Future evaluation (F):** Not yet evaluated. Left for future consideration.

In the version 4.0, published in December 2008, the e-PING established specifications for 210 standards. Table 2 presents the standards statistics, classified according to levels and segments.

The e-PING framework defined guidelines for standardization in the Brazilian electronic government based on experiences from United Kingdom, USA, Canada, Australia and New Zealand. These countries have invested intensively in policies and processes for the establishment of IT standards and structures dedicated to achieve interoperability and, consequently, to provide better quality and to decrease costs in the public services.

The e-PING architecture is defined as a basic structure for electronic government's strategy in Brazil and its initial specifications was based on the e-GIF (Government Interoperability Framework) project, implemented by the British government starting from 2000 and now in the version 6.1 (e-GIF, 2004). Due to its established time and constant evolution, the e-GIF has been considered as a reference for interoperability standards in electronic government.

Initially applied only to the Brazilian Federal Government's Executive Branch, the envisaged architecture covers the exchange of information among the Federal Executive Branch and citizens, state and municipal governments, the Legislative and Judiciary Branches of the Federal Government, the Federal Public Prosecutor's Office, international organizations, governments of other countries, Brazilian and international business and the Third Sector (NGOs, Civil Society Organizations, etc.)(Figure 1). The e-PING is mandatory for the Federal Executive Branch (including federal public agencies and other federal entities) for all the new information systems, for legacy systems involving the provision of electronic government services or integration between systems, and also for all other systems involved in electronic government services (Brasil, 2008).

In order to obtain a reference for the conception of the e-PING, a Brazilian Government committee visited the UK in June 2003 with the purpose of knowing the e-GIF, the interoperability framework implemented by the British Government starting from 2000. After that, the e-PING coordination group was created in November of 2003 and the work groups one month later. These groups were

Figure 1. e-PING relationships. (Source: Adapted from Brasil, 2008)

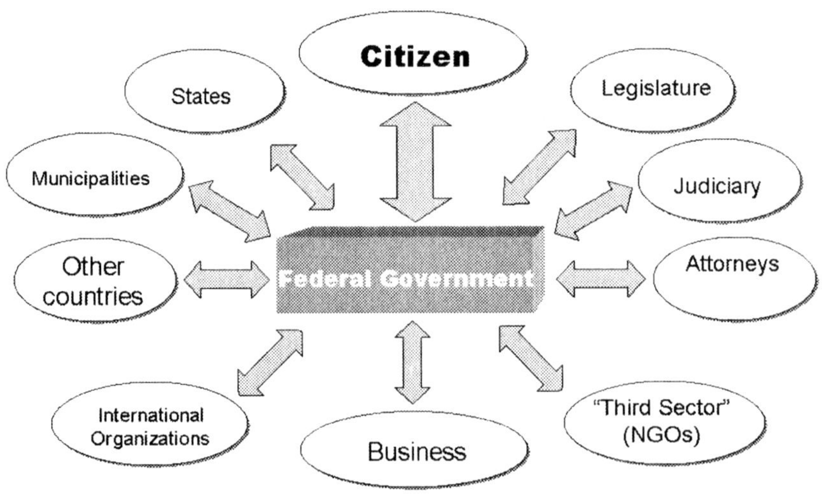

formed by members from several government agencies, in a partial time work basis.

Five work groups were created, one for each area covered by the architecture. Each group is responsible for promoting discussions about their related area and for presenting the results to the other groups during the meetings with the coordination. The coordination group is responsible for managing the activities of the work groups as well as presenting and discussing the project with other institutions from the public and private sectors (Figure 2). This group also reports to Electronic Government's Executive Committee (CEGE) on the project's progress, through its Executive Secretary.

The work groups began their activities in January 2004 to specify the preliminary version (version 0) of the architecture which was released in May. From June to August this document was submitted to public consultation on the project's website. During that same period six public hearings took place in different cities, with a total attendance of more than 600 people. These public consultations and hearings brought the contributions from public agencies, researchers and ICT suppliers to the project, with more than 90 suggestions submitted. After the analysis of the suggestions the document was updated and the version 1.0 was published in March 2005. A Federal Government's Law was published with the regulations for the use of the architecture in July.

The e-PING's reference document established the guidelines for implementing the interoperability among the several technological solutions used by the Brazilian Government. These guidelines covered topics as network security, computational infrastructure, technological requirements, standards for software development and data and information accesses.

As a result of the discussions driven by the work groups, two other versions of the reference document were published: the version 1.5 in December 2005 and the version 1.9 in August 2006. This last one was also submitted to public hearing and consultation. After the evaluation of the given suggestions, the version 2.0 was released in November 2006. Other versions were released: 2.9, in October 2007, 3.0 in December 2007, 3.9 in October 2008 and 4.0 in December 2008. The Figure 3 displays the e-PING versions publishing timeline.

Figure 2. Management model of the e-PING project (Source: Adapted from Brasil, 2008)

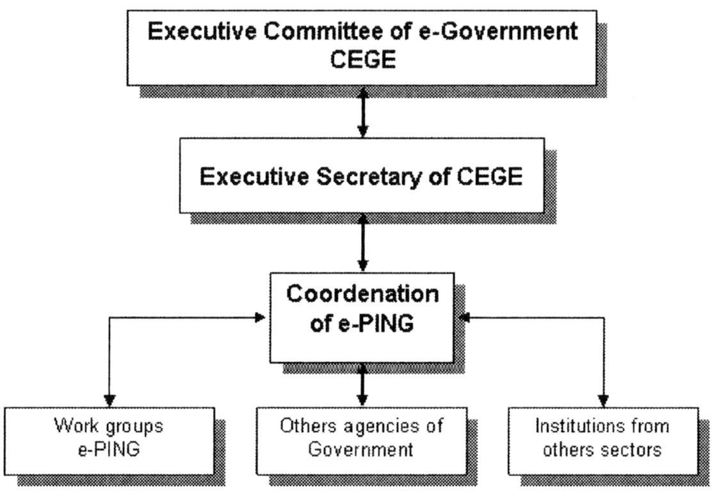

Figure 3. Timeline of the e-PING versions

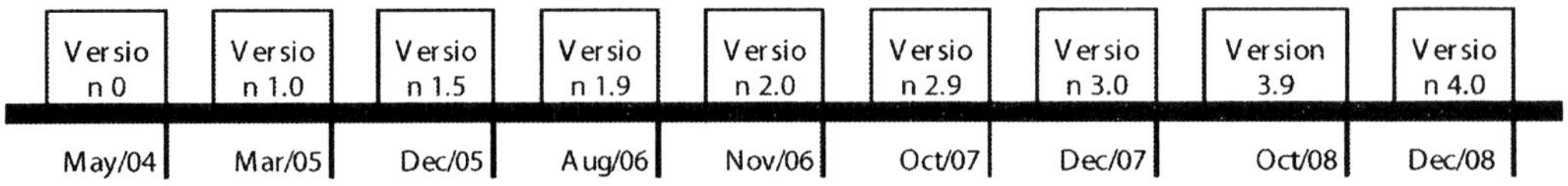

DISCUSSION

A strong point of the project has been its publishing and discussion strategies. From its beginning until the release of the version 4.0, 36 national and international presentations about the framework were made in seminars, workshops and conferences. This brought visibility to the project, making possible a high knowledge level about their guidelines not only for the public managers but also for the society in general. The public hearings and consultations helped to bring to a common forum the interested agents' expectations, which is likely to anticipate the identification and to reduce conflicts of interests.

Several standards specified by the coordination of the project are *de facto* standards (such as XML and web services), that can increase some agencies' willingness to adopt the framework. On the other hand, this can lead other potential adopters to become less interested, in case they consider this fact as a reducing factor of the relevance of their specifications.

In the version 4.0, the e-PING had 210 specified standards, out of which 78 were classified as recommended (R), corresponding to about 37% of the total. Only 48 were defined as adopted (A), i.e., less than 23%. This means that although the project has been active for more than four years, the level of standards already formally approved may be considered relatively low. This situation can be seen as an inhibiting factor, since that only a small part of the specified standards is already formally ratified.

In the survey conducted by the coordination of the project, more than 82% of the managers claimed that they knew the specifications of the architecture and about 53% affirmed to have already adopted it, at least partially. But just little more than 2% did not have difficulties in adopting the standards, while the rest had some kind of restrictions. More than 33% had technical resources or professional skills limitations to implement the specifications, and about 28% affirmed that they did not know what was being accomplished by other agencies. Approximately 17% stated to have time restrictions for implementation of projects and more than 12% declared they did not know the architecture specifications. Those results point out barriers for the effective adoption of the standards since the agencies do not have resources to implement them and to manage the changes imposed by the process. It is also necessary to notice that, although the coordination of the project has been promoting an intense publishing strategy about the architecture, still there is a significant number of managers in the researched agencies that ignores the subject.

The research also revealed that more than 58% of the information systems in use are aligned with the main internet and Web standards specifications. About 44% of the researched agencies already adopt XML as data exchange standard and more than 82% adopt browsers as the main information access mean and, in this group, approximately 78% use a minimum standard of the browse, to allow the systems to operate in multiple platforms. These standard adoption levels suggest a possibility of a high adherence to the e-PING since there is a low level of incompatibility between the technologies already implemented by the agencies and the framework specifications.

Finally, another point to be mentioned is that the level of adoption of the and-PING is not totally known. As the adoption is compulsory only for the Federal Executive Branch, the adopting agencies from other branches and from other government levels are not easily identified. On the other hand, the coordinators of the project have received requests from several institutions to help them in their implementations, which can mean an increase of the adoption of the standards.

CONCLUSION

The present study is expected to contribute to the understanding about the implementation of interoperability standards for electronic government and the likely conditioning factors of this process.

Standards are difficult of being developed and implemented. Some of them do not go further than its development phase, due to problems in the process of articulation of the discussions and their definitions. Others, although specified, are not adopted, some due to their implementation or institutionalization processes. Technological innovations or changes in the market can also sometimes make a standard becomes irrelevant or to demand significant adaptations in their specifications and, as a consequence, it is not adopted. After specified, a standard can be adopted more or less thoroughly, but it may become obsolete, creating the need of its substitution or even not being more applicable due to the changes in the technological context in which it was created.

This dynamic of the standardization, characterized as a continuous process of evolution and adaptation, also presents a constant tension between the definitions and the needed flexibility and generalization for the long-term persistence of the standard.

Based on these points, it is believed that the analysis and understanding of the adoption process of interoperability standards for electronic government allow the creation of a better spread condition and evolution of the specified standards. This includes identifying the conditioning factors of the process, their natures and possible interrelations. This paper points out some of these factors and some of their characteristics. A limitation of the findings of this research is that the survey questionnaire was designed by the e-PING coordination group and not by the author. There was not a clearly defined theoretical foundation to base the data collection and to rationally establish the questions to be included in the questionnaire and the main topics to be discussed in the semi-structured interviews. As a further research agenda can be suggested to draw a new questionnaire and to conduct another survey in order to get a deeper analysis of these factors to establish their interrelations and their likely correlations.

ACKNOWLEDGMENT

This research has been financially supported by the Conselho Nacional de Desenvolvimento Científico e Tecnológico – CNPq (Brazil).

REFERENCES

Akbulut, A. (2203). *An investigation of the factors that influence electronic information sharing between state and local agencies*. PhD Dissertation Thesis. Louisiana State University.

Andersen, D., & Dawes, S. (1991). *Government information management. A primer and casebook*. Englewood Cliffs, NJ: Prentice Hall.

Archmann, S., & Kudlacek, I. (2008). Interoperability and the exchange of good practice cases. European Journal of ePractice, 2(1), 3-12.

Bekkers, V. (2005). The governance of back office integration in e-government: some Dutch experiences. In M. Wimmer et al (Eds.), *EGOV 2005* (LNCS 3591, pp. 12-25).

Benamou, N., Busson, A., & Keravel, A. (2004). Impact of e-government interoperability in local governments. In R. Traunmüller (Ed.), *EGOV 2004* (LNCS 3183, pp. 82-87).

Brasil (2008). *e-PING: Padrões de interoperabilidade de governo eletrônico – versão 4.0*. Brasília: Comitê Executivo de Governo Eletrônico.

Cava, I., & Guijarro, L. (2003). Interoperability issues of shared infrastructures for e-government. In R. Traunmüller (Ed.), *EGOV 2003* (LNCS 2739, pp. 369-372).

David, P., & Greenstein, S. (1990). The economics of compatibility standards: An introduction to recent research. *Economics of Innovation and New Technology*, *1*(1-2), 3–41. doi:10.1080/10438599000000002

David, P., & Steinmueller, W. (1994). Economics of compatibility standards and competition in telecommunication networks. *Information Economics and Policy*, *6*(3-4), 217–241. doi:10.1016/0167-6245(94)90003-5

Dawes, S. (1996). Interagency information sharing: expected benefits, manageable risks. *Journal of Policy Analysis and Management*, *15*(3), 377–394. doi:10.1002/(SICI)1520-6688(199622)15:3<377::AID-PAM3>3.0.CO;2-F

Dawes, S., & Bloniarz, P. (2001). *Knowledge networking in the public sector*. New York: Center for Technology in Government, University at Albany/SUNY.

Dos Santos, E., & Reinhard, N. (2007). Setting interoperability standards for e-government: An exploratory case study. Electronic Government, an International Journal, 4(4), 379-394.

e-GIF (2004). *e-Government Interoperability Framework*. Office of the e-Envoy – Cabinet Office, UK.

EPAN – European Public Administration Network. (2004). *Key principles of an interoperability architecture*. Ireland.

Garud, R., Jain, S., & Kumaraswamy, A. (2000). Institutional entrepreneurship in the sponsoring of common technological standards: the case of Sun Microsystems and Java. *Academy of Management Journal*.

Goldkuhl, G. (2008). *The challenges of interoperability in e-government: towards a conceptual refinement*. Pre-ICIS 2008 SIG e-Government Workshop, Paris.

Gottschalk, P., & Solli-Saether, H. (2009). *E-government interoperability and information resource integration: Frameworks for aligned development*. Hershey, PA: Information Science Reference.

Graham, I., Spinardi, G., Williams, R., & Webster, J. (1995). The Dynamics of EDI standard development. *Technology Analysis and Strategic Management*, *7*(1), 3–20. doi:10.1080/09537329508524192

Hanseth, O., & Monteiro, E. (1998). Standards and standardization processes. In *Understanding information infrastructure* (manuscript).

IEEE Standards Information Network. (2000). *IEEE 100: The authoritative dictionary of IEEE standards terms*, Seventh Edition. New York: IEEE.

Klischewski, R. (2004). Information integration or process integration? How to achieve interoperability in administration. In R. Traunmüller (Ed.), *EGOV 2004* (LNCS 3183, pp. 57-65).

Klischewski, R., & Scholl, H. (2006). Information quality as a common ground for key players in e-government integration and interoperability. In *Proceedings of the 39th Hawaii International Conference on System Sciences.*

Landsbergen, D., & Wolken, G. (2001). Realizing the promise: government information systems and the fourth generation of information technology. *Public Administration Review*, *61*(2), 205–218.

Rocheleau, B. (1997). Governmental information systems problems and failures: a preliminary review. Public Administration and Management: An Interactive Journal, 2(3).

Scholl, H., & Klischewski, R. (2007). E-government integration and interoperability: framing the research agenda. *International Journal of Public Administration*, *30*(8), 889–920. doi:10.1080/01900690701402668

State Services Commission. (2007). *New Zealand e-government interoperability framework.* Retrieved from http://www.e.govt.nz.

Tassey, G. (2000). Standardization in technology-based markets. *Research Policy*, *29*(4-5), 587–602. doi:10.1016/S0048-7333(99)00091-8

Williams, R. (1997). Universal solutions or local contingencies: tensions and contradictions in the mutual shaping of technology and work organization. In I. Mcloughlin & D. Mason (Eds.), *Innovation organizational change and technology* (pp. 170-185). London: International Thompson Business Press.

Williams, R., Bunduchi, R., Gerst, M., Graham, I., Pollock, N., Procter, R., & Voß, A. (2004). Understanding the evolution of standards: alignment and reconfiguration in standards development and implementation arenas. In *Proceedings of the 4S & EASST Conference. Paris.*

Chapter 5
Ontological Mediation for Multi-Agent Systems

Shahram Rahimi
Southern Illinois University, USA

Pravab J. Rana
Southern Illinois University, USA

Raheel Ahmad
Southern Illinois University, USA

Bidyut Gupta
Southern Illinois University, USA

ABSTRACT

A major performance factor when gathering information across a platform like the World Wide Web is the efficiency of the search and retrieval system. The effectiveness of current search and retrieval systems is restricted as they do not use the semantics of the data but only utilize keywords. Using a multi-agent system where agents gather information and organize it, creating ontologies, is a very viable approach to the problem. Major difficulties that arise during collaboration among such information-providing agents are ambiguity and data misinterpretation. This is due to the diversity of ontology creators, differences in linguistics, and ontological overlapping. Users may also knowingly or unknowingly add incorrect information to ontologies. Ontological mediation tries to address such collaboration issues relating to ambiguous and unfamiliar information arising due to various reasons. We propose a communication-based approach for ontological mediation. In the process, we also present a classification model for ontological mediation.

INTRODUCTION

The way information is searched and retrieved across vast collections such as the Internet is still very raw. Generally, keywords are entered in search engines and documents are searched looking for the keywords. Any such enormous collection can be processed more efficiently if its data are organized. Organization here means data arrangement and representation in such a way that information retrieval is faster, relevant, and better, with machines themselves being able to understand the semantics. Creating ontology of terms and forming hierarchy of concepts is one such organization. Such organization of vast sets of data into a well-structured ontological representation presents difficulties. The data may be in different formats, using a variety of different languages and with conflicting ideas. Further it is not an easy task to verify the reliability of data, or for that matter, to update or alter any data and make it transparent across the system.

Even after organization of data into ontologies, effectiveness and efficiency are not guaranteed. To be effective the organized information should also form a cohesive interpretation. Without coherence, information will not be useful irrespective of how well it is organized. Uniformity in a multi-agent architecture like ours is not guaranteed without intervention. With different agents gathering and organizing information on different domains, inter-agent collaboration is needed. This collaboration with other information-providing agents (called information agents for the remainder of this article) can unfortunately lead to misunderstandings and ambiguities. Such problems are due to the inherent complexity that arises during automated information exchange, linguistic differences, overlapping information, and also due to the diversity of users who create ontological documents. Different information agents may reply with conflicting information for a single query. There can be a variety of reasons for conflicting information. Conflicting information may be the result of a conflicting domain. For example in response to an information request about "OWL," one agent may reply "OWL" as a Web Ontology Language while another agent might respond to the query as a nocturnal bird. Though both agents provide correct information, the information becomes futile as the receiving agent cannot process such an ambiguous response.

Conflicts arising from difference in domain are easier to mediate. Few questions relating to where the information is being used can help determine the domain and hence resolve the conflict. Nevertheless, conflicts do not always involve different domains. As different users may be involved in creating the ontology for the information agents, the information itself may be flawed and incorrect. This can result in conflicting information for a same term within the same domain. Linguistic difference can also be one of the causes of such conflicting information. For example, British English uses "first floor" to refer to the first floor above the ground, however in American English, it is another name for the ground floor itself. Among other reasons (discussed later) being able to identify and resolve linguistic difference as in the previous example is the goal of ontological mediation. The need for ontological mediation goes beyond the interactions between existing ontologies. It is also desirable that new ontologies bringing in new information are easily incorporated within the system. For this ontological reorganization, reconciliation, merging, and update are necessary.

Our model uses techniques suggested in "A Multi-Agent Architecture for Distributed Domain-Specific Information Integration" (Rahimi, Carver, & Petry, 2005) as the method for collecting data through knowledge discovery, information gathering, and integration from multiple sources. Similar to the Domain Model and the Information Source Model introduced in Rahimi et al. (2005), our agents have an ontology of terms (its knowledge base) and also partial information about other agents that provide further specialized information on a topic. The following sections present a simple and straight forward communication-based ontological mediation approach for efficient collaboration among such information agents. In the process, we also present a classification model of ontological mediation and the viability of our approach.

Previous Works

The field of ontological mediation is active with various past and current researches focusing on different aspects of mediation and negotiation. However, most of these works either cover aspects of mediation or are too specific. Two of the more comprehensive methodologies are introduced in Campbell and Shapiro (1998) and Hexmoor and Sabaa (2006). Campbell's (1999) research focuses on ontological mediation for dialect problem. Whenever a problem in dialect arises the agents try to find out the ambiguous word by making further queries. The queries may be simple yes or no answer queries. Campbell along with Shapiro, also developed algorithms for ontological mediation (Campbell & Shapiro, 1998). Their approach was used in the WordNet ontology (Miller, 1995) focusing on dialect problem. They however make an assumption that there are no conflicting terms. Their scope of mediation is, therefore, rather restricted.

A more recent approach is presented in "Towards Semantically Coherent Collaboration" (Hexmoor & Sabaa, 2006). In this approach each agent has two roles, that of an ordinary agent and a mediator. The mediator role is employed when the receiver does not understand some of the terms of the sender. They use functional specification to represent and match concepts. Functional specifications refer to key values or properties of a concept that can uniquely identify it. This approach focuses more on mediation between agents whose lower ontologies differ minimally.

DEVELOPMENT PLATFORM

In our model, a hierarchy of information agents is created following methods introduced in Kenoblock et al. (2007). Similar to the way current information sources are independently constructed, information agents are developed and maintained separately. They draw on other information agents and data repositories to provide a new information source that others can build upon in turn. Each information agent is another information source, but provides an abstraction of the many information sources available. In this network, each agent in addition to having an individual domain ontology, which is a representation of the information it can interpret, includes brief information about other specialized agents in the domain. The hierarchy of agents is built such that in lower levels the agents become more specific in the information (Kenoblock et al., 2007).

Figure 1 illustrates how the ontology of an agent's domain of expertise (domain model) and the model providing information from other agents that can provide relevant information (information source model) are utilized. The model providing information on other agents describes the content of interest available and the relationship between these concepts and the concepts in the domain

Figure 1. Mapping of models

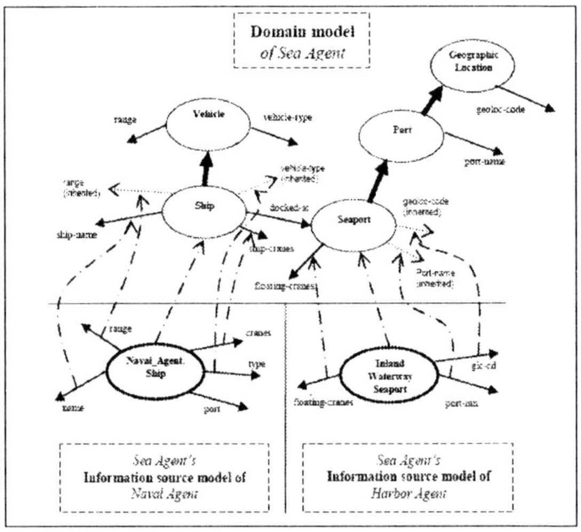

model. These mappings are useful for inter-agent querying. Such a model may not contain a complete description of the other agents, but rather only those portions that are relevant (Kenoblock et al., 2007).

Whenever an information request is issued, every agent initially queries its knowledge base, which is an ontological document, to retrieve information. Agents use query languages such as RDQL (Seaborne, 2004) and SPARQL (Prud'hommeaux & Seaborne, 2007) to retrieve information from their ontological bases. A RDQL query is similar to a SQL query with fields for documents from where information is to be retrieved, conditions that need to be matched for the query and restriction that should be considered. Figure 2 illustrates the syntax of an RDQL query. The RDQL query is based upon the idea that an RDF document can also be represented as collection of nodes and relationship between nodes. Such collections also known as "triples" have a subject, a predicate, and an object. The subject denotes a resource, the predicate denotes traits or characteristics of the resource, and the object expresses a value for the trait. The "where" condition specified in an RDQL query is used to match against such triples in the ontological document. If the required information is not available in the agent's ontology, information requests are sent to other agents using an agent communication language (discussed later on). Whenever an ambiguous or an unknown response arrives, mediation is required.

Figure 2. Syntax of a RDQL query

```
SELECT variable
FROM document (optional)
WHERE condition
AND Restriction
USING Namespace
```

Creating ontologies is a fundamental step as these ontologies serve as repositories for our agents. Thus any data we come across is represented and organized using an ontological language. Web Ontological Language (OWL) (McGuinness & Harmelen, 2004) is one such language that is utilized. Editors, similar to SWOOP (Kalyanpur, Parsia, Sirin, Grau, & Hendler, 2006) may be used for OWL to create ontologies as well as to write queries for retrieving information from such ontologies. Figure 3 is a screenshot of an OWL class tree created using SWOOP. In our system, OWL is chosen over some of the other existing languages such as Resource Description Framework (RDF) (Bray, 1998), Ontology Interchange Language (OIL) and Darpa Agent MarkUp Language (DAML) (Connolly et al., 2001). We selected OWL since much of the work done in OIL and DAML has been included in OWL. Furthermore, every OWL document is also an RDF document. As such OWL provides all the features provided by these languages while adding new tags to better describe classes, properties, and relations.

OWL has three sub-languages: OWL-Lite, OWL-DL, and OWL-Full. While OWL-Full provides high expressiveness of concepts with a large language vocabulary, OWL-DL supports automated reasoning as it is based on description logic. Thus when one requires greater expressiveness, OWL-Full can be selected and if automated reasoning is required OWL-DL may be preferred. Automated reasoning makes automatic inferencing possible. For instance, for basic statements such as (1) Maya is a student, and (2) All students have student ids, an inference that "Maya has a student id" can be made. Reasoners similar to Pellet (Sirin, Parsai, Grau, Kalyanpur, & Katz, n.d.) and Racer (Haarslev & Moller, 2003) that work with OWL-DL should be able to make inference like this and even more complex ones easily. This is what draws us to choose OWL-DL over other ontological languages.

The agents can be created using Java, and therefore we require interconnection between

Figure 3. SWOOP screenshot

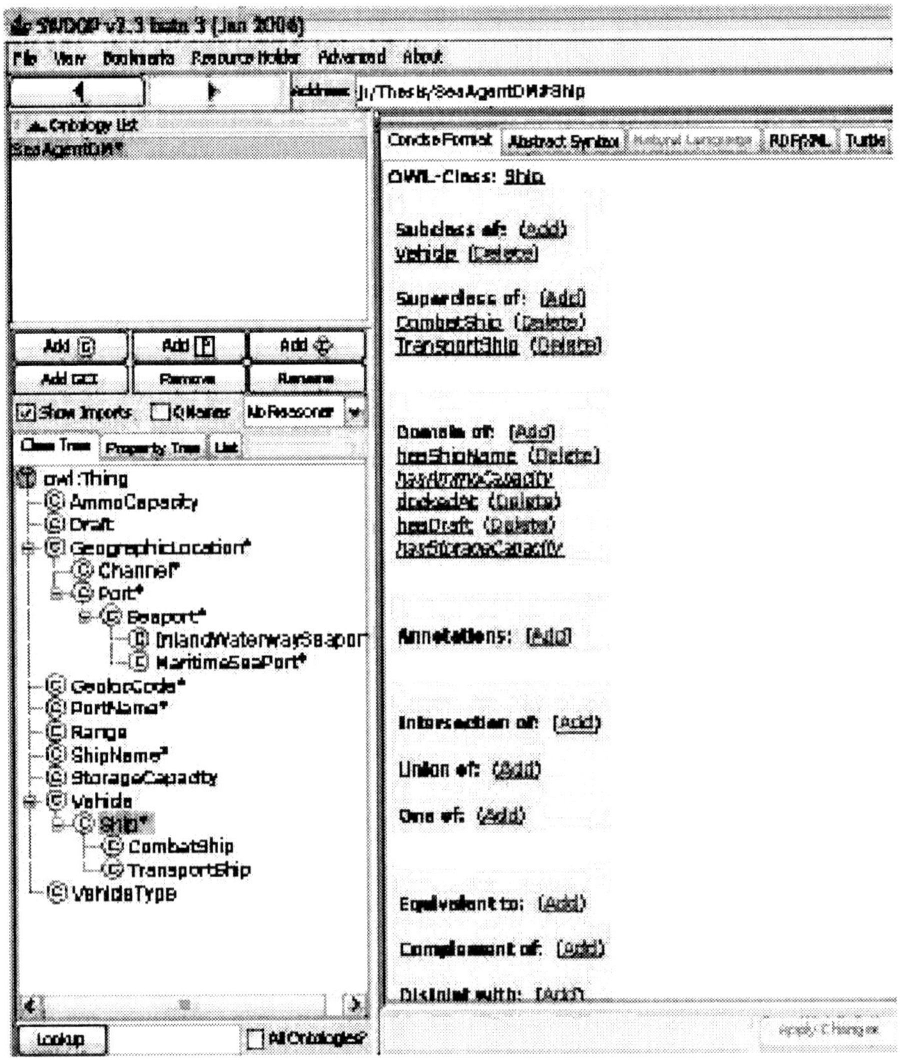

Java and the OWL-DL ontologies. The Jena tookit (Jena—A Semantic Web Framework for Java, n.d.) allows Java access to RDF and OWL-type languages. Using Jena, it is possible for the agents to create domain and information source models based on OWL-DL documents without losing their semantics. Jena also includes tools that allow the models to be modified and queried through the use of Java code. Reasoners can be accessed and applied to the models by using the DIG interface (Bechhofer, Moller, & Crowther, 2003) along with Jena or by using simple, built-in Jena reasoners.

During information retrieval, there is also the need of finding interpretation of unknown terms and making such meanings transparent to other information agents. These issues highlight the need for mechanisms to share information. To be effective the agents need to be able to share information with one another and to use others' services to understand ambiguous and unknown terms. An agent communication language is used for this purpose. Knowledge Query and Ma-

Figure 4. A sample KQML query

```
Ask about
        : Content "(Temperature, Carbondale)"
        : Language OWL-DL
        : Ontology Weather Ontology
        : Reply-with "Current Temperature"
        : Sender Weather Agent
        : Receiver Temperature Agent
```

nipulation Language (KQML) (Finin, Fritzson, McKay, & McEntire, 1994) is preferred as the agent communication language in our system. KQML is used by agents to communicate with one another as well as with the mediation agent to report and resolve ambiguity. Figure 4 illustrates a sample KQML query from a weather agent to a temperature agent asking for the current temperature reading at Carbondale. Such queries should be appropriately mapped for information retrieval from ontologies.

MEDIATION METHODOLOGY

As mentioned, even with the same sub-version of OWL, misinterpretations are possible owing to linguistic differences, interpretation differences across domains, faulty and overlapping information, and inherent complexity with machine interpretation. In the presented methodology, ontological mediation is carried out by mediation agents. These agents are also information agents. Any information agent possessing sufficient knowledge may act as a mediation agent. In our model, the higher level agents in the information agent hierarchy have brief information about what the agents below them contain (Rahimi et al., 2005). Thus higher level agents can act as mediation agents for the agents below them.

When an information agent comes across an ambiguous or unknown term, it reports to its mediation agent. To answer to an arbitration request, a mediation agent first uses a voting algorithm. It initially sends a message to the manager agent. Manager agent is a specialized agent that performs ontological verification and consistency checking and maintains a list of information agents and brief information about their ontologies so that when required it can provide a directory of agents capable of replying to a particular query. When the system becomes very large, the manager agent can delineate its task to different domain-specific manager agents.

Once the agent's list arrives, a multi-cast message is sent by the mediation agent to all the agents having information about the subject of the mediation. Using a simple counter, votes are collected for the different interpretations and the interpretation receiving higher than a threshold number of votes (currently 66%) is selected as the correct interpretation. If no clear interpretation emerges from voting, questioning method is used (described later). Any ambiguity or unfamiliarity that cannot be resolved over a long period of time is reported to human experts through the human aid agent. Mediation through voting and questioning mechanism (Figure 5) is described with more details in the following sub-sections.

Voting-Based Mediation

When a sender receives multiple interpretations or a response which it cannot understand, it reports to its mediation agent. The mediation agent first sends a message to the manager agent asking for all agents whose ontology has information related to the terms creating ambiguity or unfamiliarity. The mediation agent then sends a message to all the agents that are listed by the manager agent. Each agent receiving the message replies with its interpretation. A counter is maintained and incremented by the mediation agent for each interpretation. The interpretation receiving highest vote (66% or more) is assumed correct. The participating agents are informed by mediation agent about the interpretation.

Figure 5. Overview of proposed ontological mediation approach

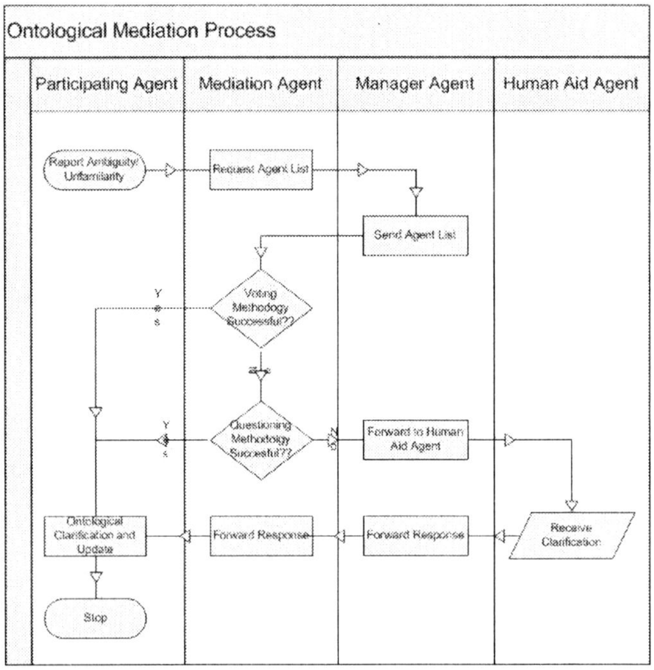

Communication Primitives for Voting Method

The voting-based approach uses the following communication primitives for mediation. The sequence of exchange of these communication primitives has been depicted in Figure 6.

- *Request_Agent_List:* The mediation agent asks the manager agent for the list of agents having knowledge on the ambiguous or unknown term. The domain of use is also provided to restrict the search.
- *Request_Term_Information:* The mediation agent sends a "Request_Term_Information" to all agents that are listed in the manager agent's response. "Term" here refers to the word that needs to be interpreted correctly.
- *Term_Information_Response:* Each Agent receiving the request sends its interpretation of the term to the mediation agent.
- *Counter_Update:* "Counter_Update" is an internal communication message used by the mediation agent. It is used for tallying different interpretations.
- *Voting_Success_Term_Interpretation:* This message is used to indicate that voting was successful. Success here means that we have an interpretation receiving greater than or equal to the threshold number of votes (currently 66%). The correct interpretation is then sent to the agents involved in the ambiguity or trying to interpret an unknown term.
- *Voting_Failure_Term:* This is also an internal communication primitive and is used to indicate that voting could not find a clear interpretation and that questioning method should now be employed.

Questioning-Based Mediation

If ambiguous and unknown terms cannot be resolved by voting, mediation agent starts the

Figure 6. Sequence diagram for voting-based mediation

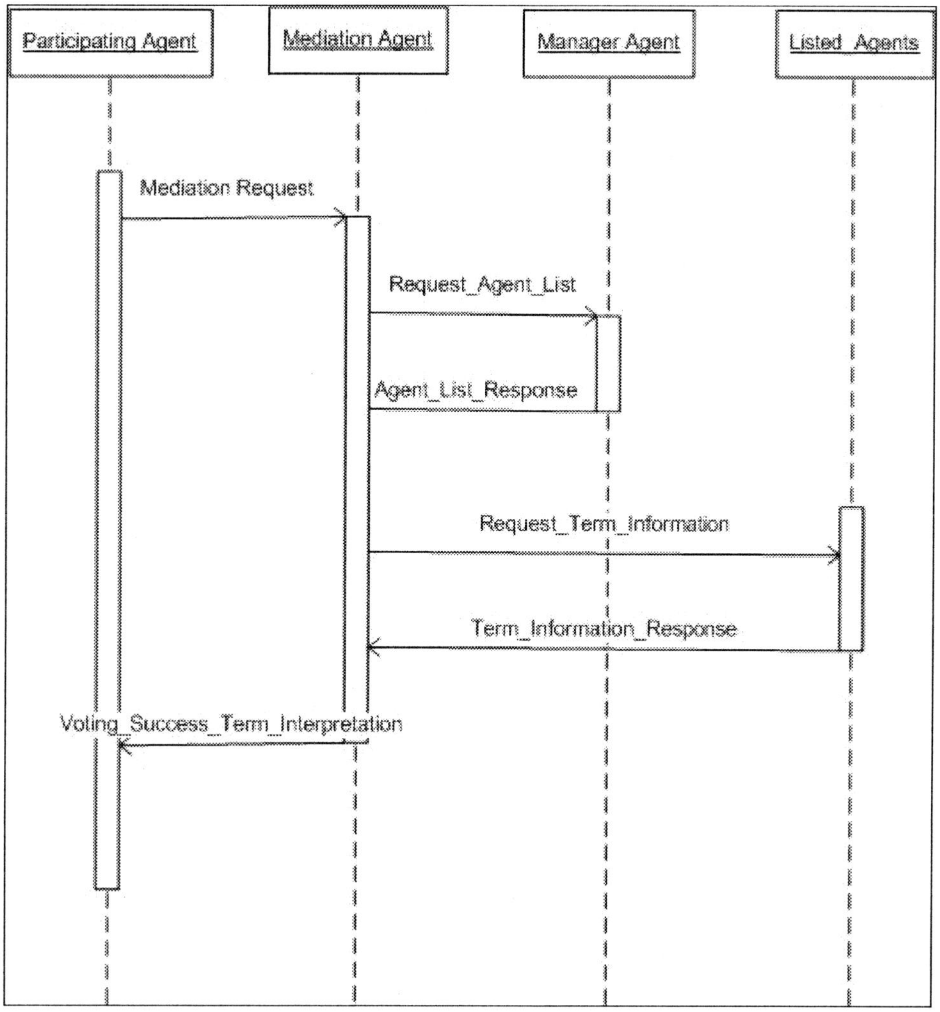

questioning method. Mediation agent initially inquires about the domain, the higher ontology and the hierarchy of the term among others. If mediation can be achieved through responses to these questions, the participating agents are informed about the correct interpretation. When such information is insufficient to resolve ambiguity, mediation agent asks further questions regarding properties, restrictions, and cardinality. If mediation agent cannot resolve the ambiguity through responses to these questions as well, the data is tagged as ambiguous and passed on to human aid agent for expert human assistance. Once the experts have clarified the ambiguity, all participating agents are informed through the manager agent.

Communication Primitives for Questioning Method

The questioning-based approach uses the following communication primitives for mediation. The sequence of exchange of these communication primitives has been depicted in Figure 7.

- *Request_Term_Hierarchy:* This is the initial communication primitive for the questioning method. It is used for requesting clarification

Figure 7. Sequence diagram for questioning-based mediation

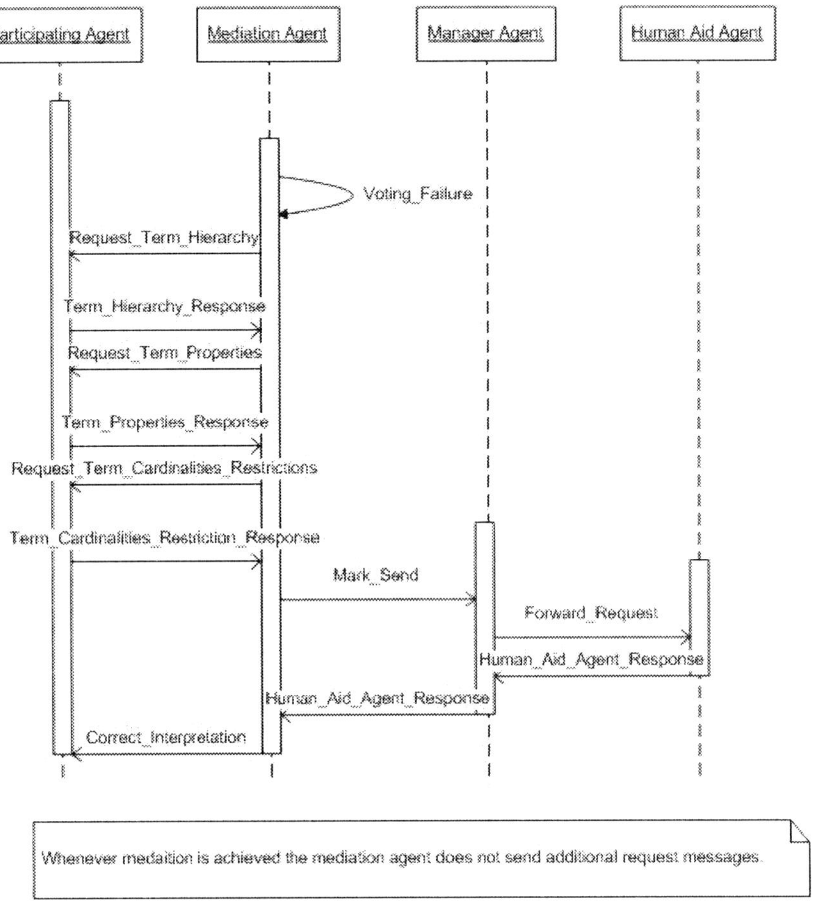

on the hierarchy of the term. This message is sent by the mediation agent to the agents involved in the ambiguity inquiring about the super class, the subclass, the domain, and any other synonym terms that may be present. For interpretation of an unknown term, this message is sent to the agent from where the request originated as well as agents involved in the earlier voting process.

- *Term_Hierarchy_Response:* Each agent receiving "Request_Term_Hierarchy" responds with a "Term_Hierarchy_Response." The response contains information about the super class, subclass, domain, and any other synonyms for the term.
- *Request_Term_Properties:* When mediation agent is unable to clarify the ambiguity or unfamiliarity through "Term_Hierarchy_Response," further information is requested through "Request_Term_Properties." The properties are requested in a manner of increasing significance. The properties that can uniquely identify the term are requested before any other properties. A similar approach has been used in Hexmoor and Sabaa (2006) for associating concepts and functional specifications.
- *Term_Properties_Response:* This is the message sent in response to the "Request_Term_Properties." It contains the list of properties ordered by increasing significance. One way to find the higher significance of a property is to monitor the associated use of the property in context to the term. It may also be accomplished

by adding certain identifying information for the properties that are significant.

- *Request_Term_Cardinalities_Restrictions:* Mediation agent uses this primitive when it is unable to mediate even after receiving the properties list. This is a request to list any cardinalities or restrictions associated with the sent properties.
- *Term_Cardinalities_Restrictions_Response:* This is the response for "Request_Term_Cardinalities_Restrictions" and it lists the associated cardinalities and restrictions.
- *Mark_and_Send_to_Manager_Agent:* When the mediation agent is unable to clarify the ambiguity or unfamiliarity through the aforementioned set of communication primitives, it marks it as "currently ambiguous" and passes it on to the manger agent using this message.
- *Forward_Request_Human_Aid_Agent:* Once a term marked as "currently ambiguous" is received by the manager agent, it prepares a data structure to store information relating to the agents involved, the date of reported ambiguity, the mediation agent used, and the ambiguous interpretations. It then forwards the term to the human aid agent.
- *Request_Human_Clarification:* This communication primitive is used by the human aid agent to inquire human experts. Human aid agent maintains lists of resource persons on various domains. Initially the use of this agent may be more frequent. With time as the system becomes more comprehensive, the role of human aid agent will become insignificant, while agents themselves are able to mediate the majority of ambiguity and unfamiliarity.
- *Human_Clarification_Response:* When the interpretation of the term has been established by human experts, it is reported to the manager agent through this message.
- *Human_Aid_Agent_Response:* Once human experts have clarified the meaning and sent it to the human aid agent, the human aid agent forwards it. It sends the corrected interpretation to the manager agent, mediation agent, and the agents involved in the mediation process.

Addressing Security and Other Issues of Concern

The following sub-sections present security and other issues of concern for the presented methodology. We have to be concerned about security issues such as trust among agents, dealing with malicious users, and agents and techniques for maintaining a quantitative measure of such concerns. We keep track of the degree of certainty value that is used as a reflection of percentage match among different concepts. For efficiency purpose, we also make a slight modification to our methodology when dealing with unknown terms.

Trust in Ontological Mediation

Here, we assume that whenever an ontology is created, it is formed as correctly as possible. This assumption helps to reduce the credibility issue regarding information received by an agent. Human experts to some degree also can help to verify the credibility of the ontology, but if such verifications have to be done frequently, the purpose of creating information agents will be futile. If we do not make this assumption, we will have to maintain a trust value for each participating agent that reflects the credibility of the agent and its ontology. When an agent is frequently the cause of ambiguity, its credibility will be reduced. The credibility of an agent not causing ambiguity will be increased as time passes. The trust value of an agent ranges between "0" to "1" with "0" signifying no trust in the agent and "1" signifying that the agent is fully trusted. Initially all agents have trust value of 0.5. Any information sent by an agent having a low trust value is subjected to further questioning by the receiving agent. Over time the trust value increases and the information from an agent with a higher trust value is accepted more readily. The trust value of an agent is decreased if it is found to be sending incorrect information.

History of Mediation

Each mediating agent maintains a log of participants, ambiguity, and correct interpretation for all mediations undertaken. With time such information will be helpful in identifying malicious agents in the system. An agent may be termed as malicious if it causes a high number of ambiguities and its interpretations are found to be incorrect most of the time. The history of mediation is also mapped to a value ranging between "0" and "1". A "0" value signifies that the history of the agent is dire while a value "1" represents an ideal history. As with trust value, information originating from agents with low mediation history value is subjected to further questioning and skepticism while information from agents having higher value is accepted readily.

Degree of Certainty

Degree of certainty is a quantitative scale associated with terms whose meanings are identified through inquiring and property matching. Such terms may be unknown or ambiguous. Degree of certainty is expressed as a numerical value ranging between "0" to "1." This value is also the measure of identical property and property values between two terms. If, for a term "staircase" being interpreted as "ladder," the degree of certainty value associated by an agent is 0.4, it reflects relatively low certainty. It also signifies that property and property values of terms "staircase" and "ladder" match by approximately 40%. On the other hand, a value of "1" expresses highest possible certainty and match. This value is determined by pattern matching properties. As mentioned, any OWL (RDF) type document can also be represented in form of triples and such triples may be matched in the model. Any interpretation having a degree of certainty value less than 0.5 should not be used as a possible synonym. Degree of certainty value is not used while determining unknown or ambiguous interpretations through existing synonyms.

Dealing with Unknown Terms

When a response is partially or completely unknown, an interpretation is required (an example is provided later). A slightly varied initial approach is undertaken when dealing with such terms. As the first step, the unknown term or terms are marked. The receiving agent then requests the domain in which the term is used. Once the domain is known, a request message is constructed using the unknown term and its domain-of-use information. The requesting agent sends this message to the agent from which it received the initial request asking for any known synonyms. If known synonyms are found, mediation will be simple and computationally very efficient. Figure 8 depicts an abstraction of such an exchange of messages between two agents. If the agent does not receive any known synonym term that can be interpreted, it then uses voting and questioning algorithms.

The domain-of-use information is also used to narrow down the search during execution of voting algorithm. When the agent is the foremost agent receiving the information request (for instance directly from human users) and the sender agent is absent, voting and questioning techniques are directly used.

EVALUATION OF A CLASSIFICATION MODEL FOR ONTOLOGICAL MEDIATION

When discussing ontology and ontological mediation, classification becomes important. Through classification of ontological mediation, not only

Figure 8. A sample of initial message exchanges for finding unknown term

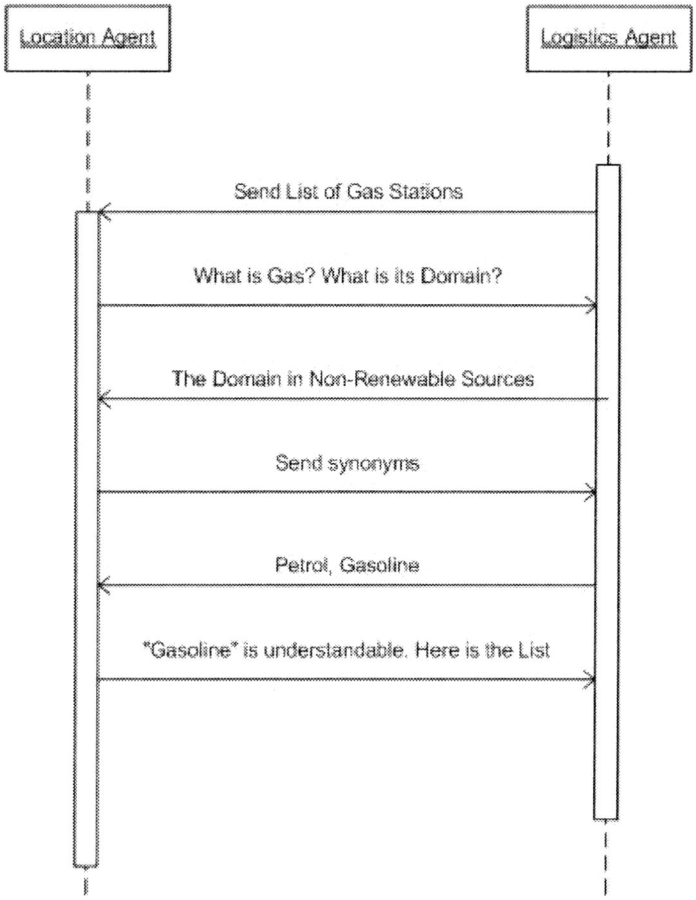

can we understand its importance and practical enormity, but we also can measure the effectiveness of our approach against different realistic scenarios. In this section, we have classified ontological mediation into five categories and discussed how our methodology addresses them.

Mediation of Dialect Problems

This is a classic ontological mediation problem arising from dialect problem. The dialect problem refers to the language differences owing to the region it is spoken. For example what British English refers to as "Lift" and American English as "Elevator," is the same thing. Let us consider another example with two synonyms, "motorbike" and "motorcycle" and see how the presented methodology will handle it. Inquiring about the higher ontology or super domain, the mediation agent will find that both terms refer to a kind of "two wheeler automobile." The mediation agent can now ask questions on properties, restrictions, and cardinalities of the terms for further clarification. Questions on properties such as engine, chassis, displacement, and fuel will reveal that in fact both terms refer to the same concept. In this case, the properties and property values are the same and hence it can be concluded that both terms refer to the same concept. The agents can now add a reference for the synonym terms in their individual ontology (Figure 9).

Figure 9. Resolving dialect problem

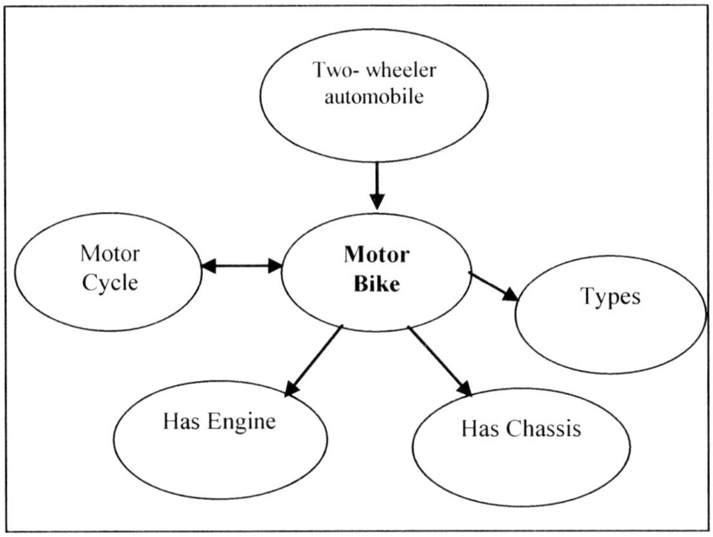

Ontological Reconciliation across Dissimilar Domains

Ontological mediation is also essential when a term has multiple interpretations across different domains. If a single term has multiple meanings, further questioning about the domain can clarify the context in which it is being used. Considering the previous example about "OWL," the mediation agent can ask the participating agents about the domain in which "OWL" is being used. One agent's domain of use is "nocturnal bird," where the other one is "Ontological Language." Since our model is built on a hierarchy of information agents and utilizes KQML (Finin et al., 1994), providing keywords to restrict domains, it can be assumed that we will rarely need to arbitrate such class of ontological mediation. However if we do, a simple question regarding the domain of interest would reveal the right meaning.

Ontological Reconciliation for Faulty Information

This is the most difficult class of mediation to arbitrate. Such ambiguities result from incorrect information or a malicious user. Let us consider an example where knowingly or unknowingly an agent has the term "ladder" listed in its ontological document as "staircase." Whenever any agent is trying to interpret the meaning of "ladder" or "staircase," this agent will propagate incorrect information. The use of standard registration procedures during creation of a new ontology can be utilized to check incorrect and malicious information. Yet, it can not be guaranteed that all the information can be verified. In the previous case, two meanings for ladder will exist within the system. First is the actual meaning of ladder and the second is "staircase." It will be very hard to clarify such ambiguities, if a third agent that can interpret "ladder" correctly does not exist. If even after voting and questioning algorithms a clear interpretation does not emerge, the term is marked as ambiguous by the mediation agent. Whenever an agent requests information on an ambiguous data, all meanings and interpretations are returned. Over time as the system grows, by monitoring the history of mediation, such faulty information and agents can be identified. The mediation agent also periodically asks the agents, who are involved in an ambiguity, if through knowledge discovery or from other sources, their interpretations have been modified. The aid of human experts shall be used to resolve long lasting conflicts and ambiguities.

Ontological Merges and Updates

There can be cases when a certain part or a whole response is unfamiliar. When a reply contains unknown terms, they have to be identified and interpreted. Considering the previous example, if the reply to a request asking for "information on motorbike parts" states "a motorbike engine has pistons and cylinders" and the agent cannot interpret what "piston" is, further queries have to be made by the receiving agent. As mentioned earlier, the receiving agent inquiries the sender agent for any synonyms of "pistons" in the domain of "motorbike." Voting and questioning methodologies are used when the unknown term cannot be interpreted through existing synonyms in the sender's or receiver's ontology. Once the meaning of the unknown term has been determined, the receiving agent can enhance its ontology to contain brief information about what a "piston" is and how it is related in the context of an engine.

One problem with such updates is determining what new information the agent should incorporate and what information it should leave for other agents to add to their ontologies. We should avoid situations where a single agent is burdened with a large volume of information just because it keeps on discovering new terms. The role of mediation agent comes into the picture here, deciding on what information should be passed on to the lower level agents for update and what should not. Any new term that is found unsuitable to be passed onto the lower agents should also be appropriately placed. This can also be accomplished by the mediation agent which itself is a higher level agent in the hierarchy with partial information about the contents of lower level agents. At times it is also suitable to merge two ontologies into a single one. Through the use of automated reasoning, Jena interface (Jena–A Semantic Web Framework for Java, n. d.), and KQML performatives (Finin et al., 1994), our approach permits such necessary merging and updates.

Ontological Reorganizations

Ontological reorganization is necessary as the agents find new terms and concepts. This reorganization is done not only to improve the arrangement of the agents but also for faster and more efficient information exchange.

Suppose initially a logistics agent drew information from agents such as temperature, wind, terrain, altitude, and location agents among others. With time as the number of agents and their ontologies grow, reorganization is needed. It may be efficient to reorganize some components of the logistics agent such as terrain, altitude, and location agents and place them under another agent say the geographical agent. The geographical agent now draws information from agents such as the terrain, altitude, and location agents. The logistics agent, being placed hierarchically above the geographical agent, knows when and for what the geographical agent should be approached. Our model permits such reorganizations.

Performance Analysis

In this section, the performance of the presented methodology is analyzed under some altering parameters. A simulation software was developed to aid the analysis. The software simulates mediation through some specific parameters. It takes into account constraints such as communication delay, agents' response delay, ontological knowledge, system comprehensiveness, and ambiguity level as values between 0 and 1. Ontological mediation algorithms of voting and questioning are simulated on a limited scale. We are mainly trying to analyze the success rate of voting approach, the effect of increasing number of agents on the overall delay (assuming voting fails), and also the effect of increasing levels of ambiguity on mediation time.

Initially, insufficient knowledge in the ontologies or incorrect ontologies can adversely effect voting. Mediation may also be complicated in scenarios where there are only two agents having knowledge on a term and they do not agree on its interpretation. As such, questioning and human intervention can be frequently needed at the beginning. When the individual ontological knowledge grows and the system becomes more inclusive, voting algorithm is able to arbitrate to a greater extent. With time, the comprehensiveness of the system increases, while incorrect ontologies can be marked and corrected. This is due to the dynamic nature of our approach that helps the ontologies to cultivate. Human assistance also aids in this process.

Voting however may never be 100% successful. New, partially incorrect, and ontologies having insufficient knowledge can always play a part in voting. Figure 10 illustrates the mediation success for voting approach against improving ontological knowledge, which is also supported by the simulation program. We based our analysis on the fact that mediation success is mainly a function of ontological knowledge, system comprehensiveness, and a randomness factor associated with the information request.

When there is an increase in the number of agents involved in mediation, we expect a symmetrical increase in the overall delay. As Figure 11 depicts, our simulation did support this hypothesis. Our expectation was based on the fact that overall delay for the mediation process is a function of communication delay, agent response delay, number of agents involved, ambiguity level, and processing time. Assuming that the number of agents is a factor that varies most often (new agents are added and ontologies are expanded over time), it can act as the prime factor in determining the overall delay. Exceptions can occur if voting methodology is successful and questioning delays are avoided.

In the proposed approach, the mediation agent requires longer processing time when faced with increasing scales of ambiguity. This is because our methodology uses incremental sub-levels for mediation. For example, if questions on hierarchy cannot resolve ambiguity, further questions on properties are asked, and if questions of properties cannot resolve the ambiguity, questions on cardinalities and restrictions are asked. Therefore, with increasing level of ambiguity, more time will be required for clarifications by the questioning method. When utilized, human aid agent also adds to the mediation time. Figure 12 depicts the expected performance of our approach in this re-

Figure 10. Mediation success vs. the quality of ontological knowledge

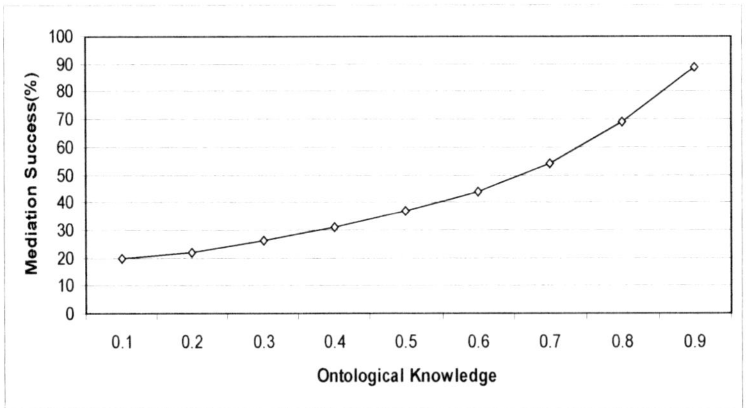

Figure 11. Number of agents vs. delay

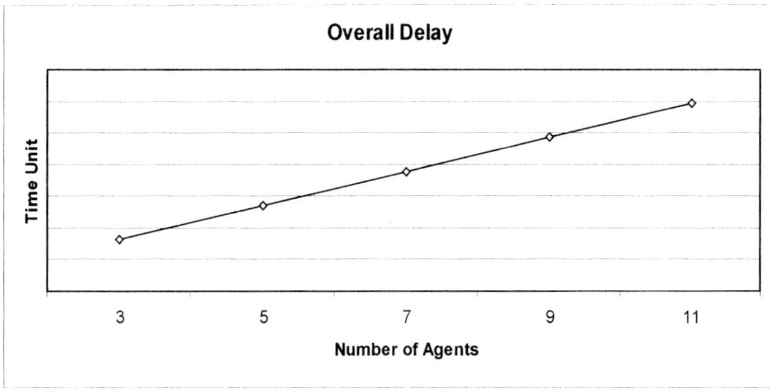

Figure 12. Mediation time vs. ambiguity level

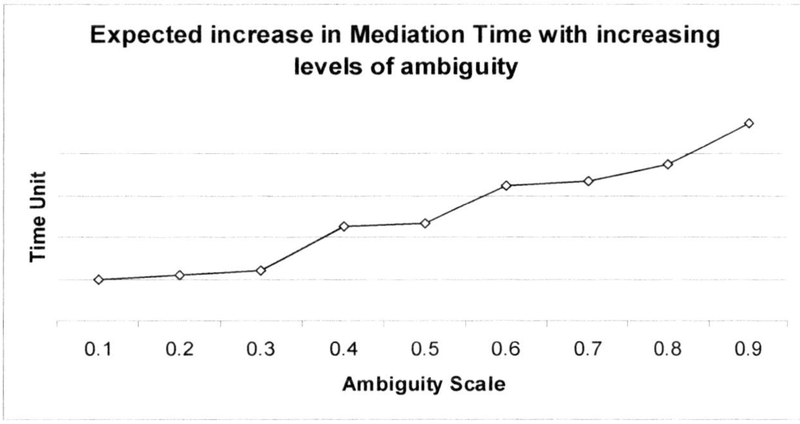

gard. Each sharp increase accounts for utilization of another sub-algorithm within the questioning methodology and for using the human aid agent. Note that in the analysis we have assumed 0.3, 0.5, and 0.8 as ambiguity levels that will call for further questioning.

APPLICATION AVENUES IN E-GOVERMENT

Ontology development is finding its way in diverse areas such as the Semantic Web (Ding et al., 2005), peer-to-peer systems (Parkhomenko, Lee, & Park, 2003), automobile projects (Golebiowska, Dieng-Kuntz, Corby, & Mousseau, 2001), simulation modeling (Miller, Baramidze, Sheth, & Fishwick, 2004), e-commerce (Obrst, Wray, & Liu, 2001), application servers (Oberle, Eberhart, Staab, & Volz, 2004), and e-government (Karyda et al., 2006). Whatever the avenue for applying ontology may be, ontological mediation is indispensable. In this section, we look into one such avenue, that is, e-government. E-government is the term used to define a system in which a government uses electronic means for communication. The communication may be with the citizens, other government agencies, internal communication, or with foreign governments. Due to its vast and growing nature, e-government itself has been sub-classified into different categories. Some of the categories are government-to-citizen or government-to-customer (G2C), government-to-business (G2B), and government-to-government (G2G) (Lee, Tan, & Trimi, 2005). Multi-agent systems (MAS) are starting to be applied to different aspects of e-government. Such automated systems are being introduced for applications ranging from online processing and citizen support to matters of security and defense among others.

Data Surveillance

Let us consider a scenario where an e-government is trying to monitor electronic activities of certain individuals. For such a task, an autonomous MAS such as the one introduced in Rahimi et al. (2005) could be of a great use. Agents are created drawing their knowledge, which in this case is the terms to be monitored, from domain-specific initial lists of terms. Such lists of terms should be organized into ontologies, using tools such as OWL-DL (as mentioned earlier). Via these reference ontologies, the agents can organize electronic data related to a target individual into an ontology. These data may be collected from various communication mediums such as e-mails, chats, and online search preferences. For such a case, a system based on Rahimi et al. (2005), which utilizes the previously mentioned ontological mediation approach to resolve ambiguity and unfamiliarity would be ideal. The suitability of our approach lies in the fact that with information agents we are not only focusing on keywords to perform search, but also are trying to understand the semantics of the contents. The importance of mediation in such an application is because of the agents' need to communicate with one another to organize the global view of the data being sent or received. During this process, new, ambiguous, or suspicious terms may come up that need clarification. Moreover, as new terms to be monitored are revealed, they are added to the suitable domain-specific lists and the administrative agent of the MAS is informed of them. Other agents can then interact with the administrative agent when needed.

Ontological mediation plays a vital role during the process of data organization as it requires inter-agent communication and knowledge from different ontologies. Our model uses a dynamic mediation methodology which over time produces comprehensive ontologies to be used by MAS for the purpose of automated monitoring and surveillance.

Viruses and Network Attacks/ Defense Mechanisms

Malwares are a constant threat to computers and electronic resources. An ontological-based application could be developed to create a comprehensive ontology of malwares with possible solutions and defense mechanisms. Such ontology can be built and maintained as part of an e-government resource. The ontology thus created will not only list the malwares but also provide information regarding its features, possible defend solutions, and precautionary steps. Figure 13 illustrates an abstract overview of ontology for malwares with solutions and precautionary steps for each type. Such ontology when completed will be significant for an MAS. Agents can use this knowledge as a reference to check for malwares, and if detected, carry out specified solutions. As with malwares, an ontology of network-related attacks and defense mechanisms can also be created. Such ontology will provide comprehensive information on detecting possible network-related attacks and appropriate means of defense. With time as these ontologies grow, they can be broken down into different sub-ontologies, each for a type of malware or network-related attack or even further into various sub-types. Once we have a network of collaborating ontologies, ontological mediation is indispensable.

Even with a single ontology of malwares or network-related attacks, ontological mediation is crucial. The proposed ontological mediation methodology facilitates materializing global knowledge bases and provides for locating and accessing the right resources.

Figure 13. An abstract overview of an ontology for malwares

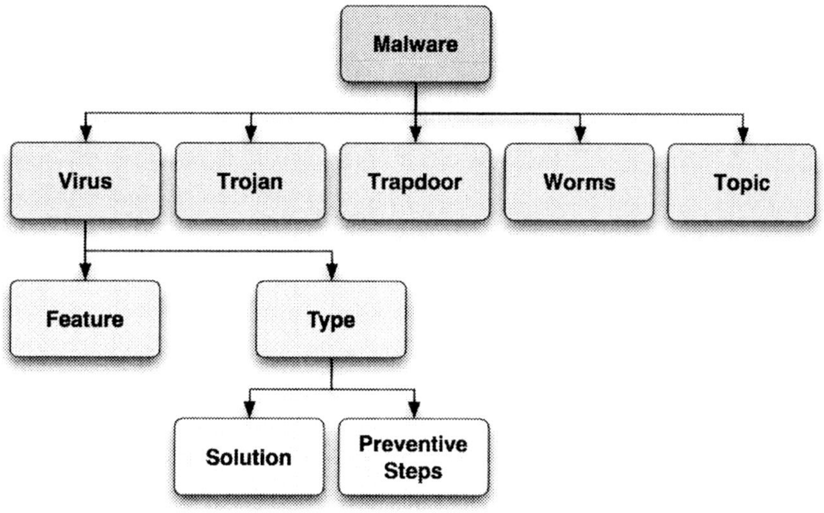

System Logs

To better serve and protect sensitive information in e-government servers, log files can be organized into ontologies. Whatever log files are generated in servers can be transformed into ontology of events, causes and effects (Figure 14). Different ontologies can be created for different events. Ontologies may also be based on servers, server locations, or domain of log messages. Agents could be built over such ontologies to automate part of the responsibilities of the system administrators. These ontologies are also valuable for system administrators as references with agents assisting in retrieving required information and monitoring the system efficiently. Here also mediation will be critical when retrieving information as these ontologies are large and may have duplicate or similar terms, events or causes.

Online Profile of Individuals

A central ontology of an online profile of individuals could be created by an e-government to better serve citizens and protect their personal data. For

Figure 14. An abstract overview of an ontology for system logs

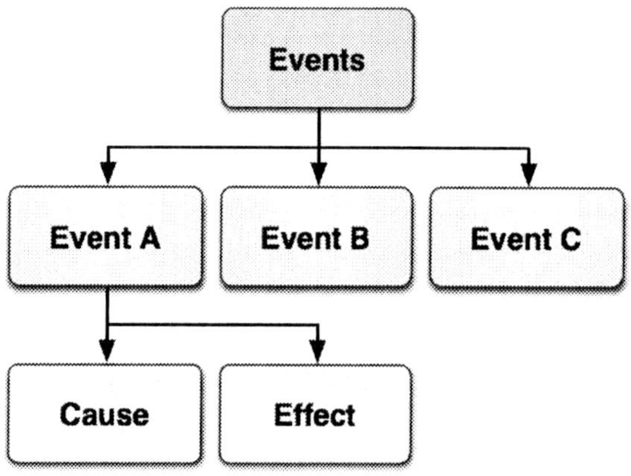

such an ontology, the government should have access rights, while the individuals are able to query, retrieve, and update their personal information. Such an ontology will serve a dual purpose. First it makes it easier for the users themselves to perform tasks such as updating mailing addresses and profile modification at a single portal with effects reflecting across all areas. Secondly, it would be easier to track and trace frauds and online mischief. With information being placed at a single location, personal data could be better protected.

Figure 15. Block representation of ontological mediation and inter-agent communication

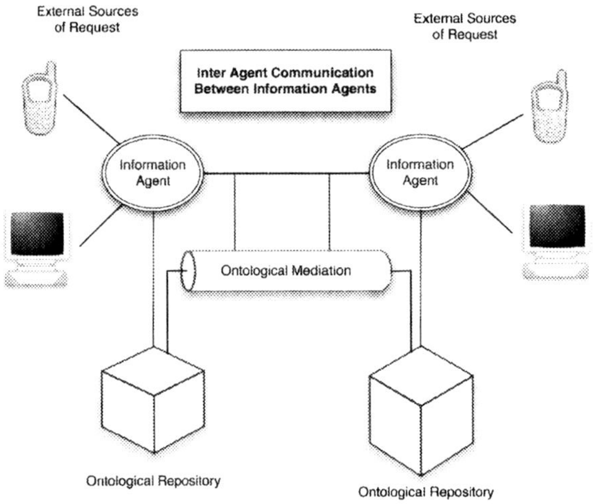

Instead of having multiple online accounts in banks, phone companies, and e-commerce sites, a single account can be created for all online activities. The online profiles can be extended to incorporate hotel and travel preferences, airline preferences, shopping preferences, and so forth. External information requests from third party companies could be granted based on predefined policies and access rights.

The proposed mediation methodology is effective in clarifying requests and responses between the central ontology and the agents trying to retrieve information from it. Development of such a system would not be possible without mediation capabilities (Ke & Wei, 2004).

In each of the previous examples, ontology serves as an excellent tool for information organization. Nevertheless as mentioned earlier, information organization by itself is insufficient. Ontological mediation methodologies become equally important whenever multiple ontologies are involved and inter-agent activities are required (Figure 15). Our methodologies of voting and questioning are simple but versatile enough to be suitable for different ontological applications in areas such as e-government. Having said that, appropriate reasoning tools and well–defined, inter-agent communication protocols are essential for effective mediation.

CONCLUSION

In the World Wide Web and the major intranets, information is constantly created and modified by thousands of users and hence may not be cohesive. MASs provide an efficient and effective approach for large-scale information gathering and dispersion by generating and maintaining ontologies. In this article, an ontological mediation methodology was presented for such MASs.

A collaborative mediation approach is preferred due to its effectiveness and simplicity. In our model, mediation agents are used to resolve ambiguity and unfamiliarity among agents. A mediation agent initially employs a voting algorithm. If voting does not produce a clear interpretation, specific questions are asked to resolve ambiguous or unknown terms. Our methodology also benefits from taking advantage of human experts when an ambiguity or unfamiliarity cannot be resolved by agents over a period of time. We have considered a benevolent environment; nevertheless, trust values and history of mediation are utilized to defend against ill intents and malicious agents. Our approach for mediation is thus simple yet practical and comprehensive, which provides for a high degree of mediation success. High mediation success in turn reflects efficiency in information search and retrieval.

This is important to note that automated reasoning is the heart of effective information retrieval as well as the mediation process. How well the semantics of the data can be understood and processed depends on how well the reasoners, working on top of the ontological documents, can make inferences. Although OWL-DL supports automated reasoning, its capability is restricted. With the introduction of more powerful ontology languages and reasoners, the system could perform with greater effectiveness and efficiency. This article does not comprehensively cover the implementation issues and is more concerned about the mediation framework and methodology.

REFERENCES

Austin, J. L. (1962). *How to do things with words.* Cambridge, MA: Harvard University Press.

Bechhofer, S., Moller, R., & Crowther, P. (2003). The DIG description logic interface. In *Proceedings of 2003 International Workshop on Description Logic (DL2003), Rome, Italy* (pp. 85-94).

Bray, T. (1998). *RDF and metadata.* Retrieved January 20, 2007, from http://www.xml.com/pub/a/98/06/rdf.html

Campbell, A. E. (1999). *Ontological mediation: Finding translation across dialects by asking questions.* Unpublished doctoral dissertation, University at Buffalo, The State University of New York, Department of Computer Science and Engineering.

Campbell, A. E., & Shapiro, S. C. (1998). *Algorithms for ontological mediation* (Tech. Rep. No. 98-2). University at Buffalo, The State University of New York, Department of Computer Science and Engineering, SNePS Research Group.

Connolly, D., Harmelen, F. V., Horrocks, I., McGuinness, D. L., Patel-Schneider, P. F. & Stein L. A. (2001). *DAML+OIL (March 2001) reference description.* Retrieved January 20, 2007, from http://www.w3.org/TR/daml+oil-reference

Ding, L., Kolari, P., Ding, Z., Avancha, S., Finin, T., & Joshi, A. (2005). *Using ontologies in the Semantic Web: A survey* (TR-CS-05-07). University of Maryland, Baltimore County, Ebiquity Research Group.

Finin, T., Fritzson, R., McKay, D., & McEntire, R. (1994). KQML as an agent communication language. In *Proceedings of the 3rd International Conference on Information and Knowledge Management* (pp. 456-463).

Golebiowska, J., Dieng-Kuntz, R., Corby, O., & Mousseau, D. (2001). Building and exploiting ontologies for an automobile project memory. In *Proceedings of the 1st International Conference on Knowledge Capture K-CAP* (pp. 52-59).

Haarslev, V., & Moller, R. (2003). Racer: An OWL reasoning agent for the Semantic Web. In *Proceedings of the International Workshop on Applications, Products and Services of Web-based Support Systems, in conjunction with the 2003 IEEE/WIC International Conference on Web Intelligence* (pp. 91-95).

Hexmoor, H., & Sabaa, H. (2006). Towards semantically coherent collaboration. In *Proceedings of the International Symposium on Collaborative Technologies and Systems* (pp. 264-269). Washington, DC: IEEE Computer Society.

Jena–A Semantic Web Framework for Java. (n.d.). Retrieved December 4, 2006, from http://jena.sourceforge.net/index.html

Kalyanpur, A., Parsia, B., Sirin, E., Grau, B. C., & Hendler, J. A. (2006). Swoop: A Web ontology editing browser. *Journal of Web Semantics, 4*(2), 144-153.

Karyda, M., Balopoulos, T., Gymnopoulos, L., Kokolakis, S., Lambrinoudakis, C., Gritzalis, S., et al. (2006). An ontology for secure e-government applications. In *Proceedings of the First International Conference on Availability, Reliability and Security (ARES'06), 00* (pp. 1033-1037).

Ke, W., & Wei, K. K. (2004). Successful e-government in Singapore. *Commnications of ACM, 47,* 95-99.

Knoblock, C.A. & Ambite, J.L. (1997). *Agents for Information Gathering, Software Agents*. J. Bradshaw, (Ed.), MIT Press, Menlo Park, CA.

Lee, S. M., Tan, X., & Trimi, S. (2005). Current practices of leading e-government countries. *Communications of ACM, 48,* 99-104.

McGuinness, D. L., & Harmelen, F. V. (Eds.). (2004). *OWL Web ontology language overview.* Retrieved December 4, 2006, from http://www.w3.org/TR/owl-features/

Miller, A. G. (1995). WordNet: A lexical database for English. *Communications of ACM, 38,* 39-41.

Miller, J. A., Baramidze, G. T., Sheth, A. P., & Fishwick, P. A. (2004). Investigating ontologies for simulation modeling. In *Proceedings of the 37th Annual Symposium on Simulation ANSS* (p. 55).

Oberle, D., Eberhart, A., Staab, S., & Volz, R. (2004). Application servers, enterprise computing and software engineering: Developing and managing software components in an ontology-based application server. In *Proceedings of the 5th ACM/IFIP/USENIX International Conference on Middleware* (pp. 459-477).

Obrst, L., Wray, R. E., & Liu, H. (2001). Ontological engineering for B2B e-commerce. In *Proceedings of the International Conference on Formal Ontology in Information Systems, 2001* (pp. 117-126).

Parkhomenko, O., Lee, Y., & Park, E. K. (2003). Ontology-driven peer profiling in peer-to-peer enabled semantic Web. In *Proceedings of the Twelfth International Conference on Information and Knowledge Management* (pp. 564-567).

Prud'hommeaux, E., & Seaborne, A. (Eds.). (2007). *SPARQL query language for RDF.* Retrieved June 16, 2007, from http://www.w3.org/TR/rdf-sparql-query/

Rahimi, S., Carver, N., & Petry, F. E. (2005). A multi-agent architecture for distributed domain-specific information integration. In R. Ladner & F. E. Petry (Eds.), *Net-centric approaches to intelligence and national security* (pp. 129-148). New York: Springer.

Seaborne, A. (2004). *RDQL—A query language for RDF.* Retrieved December 4, 2006, from http://www.w3.org/Submission/RDQL/

Searle, J. (1969). *Speech acts: An essay in the philosophy of language*. London: Cambridge University Press.

Sirin, E., Parsai, B., Grau, B. C., Kalyanpur, A., & Katz, Y. (n.d.). *Pellet: A practical OWL-DL reasoner.* Retrieved December 4, 2006, from http://mindswap.org/papers/PelletJWS.pdf

This work was previously published in International Journal of Electronic Government Research, Vol. 4, Issue 1, edited by M. Khosrow-Pour, pp. 68-88, copyright 2008 by IGI Publishing (an imprint of IGI Global).

Chapter 6
I-FGM as a Real Time Information Retrieval Tool for E-Governance

Eugene Santos Jr.
Dartmouth College, USA

Eunice E. Santos
Virginia Polytechnic Institute & State University, USA

Hien Nguyen
University of Wisconsin, USA

Long Pan
Virginia Polytechnic Institute & State University, USA

John Korah
Virginia Polytechnic Institute & State University, USA

Huadong Xia
Virginia Polytechnic Institute & State University, USA

ABSTRACT

Homeland security and disaster relief are some of the critical areas of E-governance that have to deal with vast amounts of dynamic heterogeneous data. Providing rapid real-time search capabilities for such applications is a challenge. Intelligent Foraging, Gathering, and Matching (I-FGM) is an established framework developed to assist users to find information quickly and effectively by incrementally collecting, processing and matching information nuggets. This framework has been successfully used to develop a distributed, unstructured text retrieval application. In this paper, we apply the I-FGM framework to image collections by using a concept-based image retrieval method. We approach this by incrementally processing images, extracting low-level features and mapping them to higher level concepts. Our empirical evaluation shows that our approach performs competitively compared to some existing approaches in terms of retrieving relevant images while offering the speed advantages of distributed and incremental process and unified framework between text and images.

INTRODUCTION

One of the main challenges in e-governance is to effectively and efficiently find relevant information from vast amounts of dynamic heterogeneous sources quickly under the pressures and limitations of time, supporting tools, and resources. For instance, when natural disasters such as Hurricane Katrina (2005) or the Asian Tsunami of 2004 happen, we need to quickly locate the areas that are most affected and collect information in order to estimate the needed aid for items such as medicines, foods, and drinking water. Unfortunately, in such a situation, frontline communications are typically chaotic (or non-existent) and/or there are too many channels of information from different sources that make the retrieval of relevant pieces of information a lot harder. For "hot spots" such as disaster relief areas, combat zones, and so forth information is changing rapidly and as such there is only a small window of time for information to remain valid. Additionally, various types of data representation are used such as images, blogs, maps, news reports, audios, and videos. Each type of data format contains important and indispensable information for the various governmental agencies. Therefore, in order to better assist these agencies in addressing these challenges, there is a clear and urgent need to develop a system that rapidly provides real-time retrieval capabilities of heterogeneous sources of information. There are three main issues that we need to address: (1) how to gather and retrieve information quickly in a real-time setting given the limitations of resources and time; (2) how to address the problem of heterogeneous data; and, (3) how to improve retrieval success.

We address the aforementioned issues by developing a framework for intelligent foraging, gathering, and matching (I-FGM) that incrementally and distributively gathers, processes, and matches information nuggets to assist users at finding information quickly and effectively. In our previous work (Santos, Santos, Nguyen, Pan, & Korah, 2005, Santos et al., 2006), I-FGM has been empirically demonstrated to be an effective tool for text retrieval on large and dynamic search spaces. Even though unstructured text is a typical format for most databases/sources, images are also popular with significant support from commercialized search engines such as Google, Yahoo!, and MSN. In order to demonstrate that I-FGM is a general framework for information retrieval, it is necessary to study the system's ability at effectively handling such heterogeneous data which contains at least text and images. In this article, we apply the I-FGM framework on image collections by using a concept-based image retrieval method. We approach this by incrementally processing the images, extracting low-level features, and then mapping them to higher level concepts. The novelties of our approach lie with the distributed storage and incremental processing and matching of information nuggets extracted from a region-based wavelet image retrieval scheme. We deploy a concept-based image retrieval algorithm that maps low-level features of the images to high-level concepts. In this way, we are also able to translate the visual information of images into document graphs (Santos et al., 2005), which are used in I-FGM as a common representation of information for heterogeneous data types. Thus, I-FGM provides a seamless integration of text and image through a single unifying semantic representation of content. By implementing and testing our image retrieval algorithm in I-FGM, we can validate the I-FGM framework as a method for future unified rankings of heterogeneous documents.

This article is organized as follows: In the methodology section, we first provide a brief background on current image retrieval systems. Next, we give an overview of the image retrieval algorithm that was implemented in I-FGM. We then describe the architecture of I-FGM and the implementation details of the current prototype. This section is followed by a description of our system evaluation procedure along with simulation results. We validate the performance of the image algorithm and show that it can be used in I-FGM for faster retrieval of images. Finally, we will present our conclusions and future work.

METHODOLOGY

Background and Related Work

The goal of the I-FGM framework is to facilitate real time searches in large and dynamic search spaces. In particular, I-FGM aims to integrate the retrieval of multiple data types; to enable a unified framework to compare heterogeneous documents; and to employ resource allocation policies facilitated by partial processing to conduct efficient anytime searches. In this article, we integrate image retrieval in I-FGM by employing an algorithm based on techniques from Content Based Image Retrieval (CBIR). We now present the current state of research in CBIR and the approaches that have been leveraged in I-FGM.

CBIR is an important sub-area of image retrieval that aims to classify, identify, and retrieve images based on its visual content rather than using human generated information such as meta-tags and annotations. Through the previous decade, there has been significant progress in this field, documented in various surveys (Rui, Huang, & Chang, 1999; Smeulders, Worring, Santini, Gupta, & Jain, 2000; Veltkamp & Tanase, 2000). Although, a general solution for image retrieval still eludes researchers due to the difficulties posed by the well-documented phenomena of sensory gap and semantic gap (Enser & Sandom, 2003), CBIR techniques have shown great promise in automating the process of interpreting images. We decided to employ CBIR in I-FGM because other methods require extra-image information such as meta-tags or HTML text from Web pages containing the image. In the CBIR methods, the visual content or low-level features of the images have to be converted into an intermediate form or signature before it can be interpreted. Our choice of low-level features and feature signature are important as it has a direct influence on the performance of the system. Examples of low-level features in images are color, texture, and contrast.

Region-based methods are a widely used type of CBIR. In these methods (Carson, Belongie, Greenspan, & Malik, 2002; Li, Wang, & Wiederhold, 2000; Ma & Manjunath, 1997; Natsev, 2001) images are divided into regions, each of which has similar pixel characteristics. This collection of regions forms a signature for the image. The premise behind these methods is that similar images will have similar regions. Methods such as WALRUS (Natsev, Rastogi, & Shim, 2004) and SIMPLIcity (Wang, Li, & Wiederhold, 2001) use wavelets (Daubechies, 1992) to represent the feature signature of regions. Methods such as (Natsev et al., 2004; Wang et al., 2001) generate regions by calculating a feature signature for a part of the image (window) at a time. The window is slid across the image such that every pixel of the image is contained in at least one window. These windows are then clustered based on a distance measure. Each cluster is then considered to be a region. These methods work well even with complex images containing multiple concepts or objects. One of the drawbacks in these methods is that they take query images instead of a text query. This is also one of the reasons preventing its direct usage within the I-FGM framework.

We will use the image segmentation and region clustering techniques from WALRUS in our image retrieval algorithm. The feature vector that we use to represent the low-level features of the image is similar to the one used in SIMPLIcity. Although SIMPLIcity is a well known regions method, it does only coarse-grained classification of images into semantic classes such as *"outdoor," "indoor," "texture," "non-textured,"* and *"photographs."* I-FGM on the other hand deals with more fine-grained classifications. Our algorithm seeks to map low-level features to high-level concepts by forming regions of similar pixel characteristics and then mapping them to the concepts. Although this is similar to the CAMEL (Natsev, Chadha, Soetarman, & Vitter, 2001) algorithm (a variant of the WALRUS method), there are significant differences. The concepts used in CAMEL are single object concepts such as "apple." It compares the feature vectors for this concept with incoming images and tries to determine if the concept is contained in the image using a distance-based similarity measure. We found that CAMEL does not deliver the required performance when implemented with the images that we typically deal with. The main reason is that it is difficult to accurately identify single-object concepts in images. Another important reason why we cannot use this method is that it uses a distance-based similarity measure that is adversely affected by the presence of non-relevant features in the images. A better option is to use machine learning techniques to match the low-level features of concepts and images. ALIPR (Li & Wang, 2006) is another automatic annotation method that tries to map low-level features to keywords. ALIPR is an established method that has given good performance. It has also been used commercially. Unfortunately, it cannot be used with the partial processing paradigm of I-FGM. In I-FGM, we incrementally process an image, using each partial step to gain an insight into the relevancy of image and proportionately grant resources. The information gathered from one step has to be reused in successive partial steps so as to minimize the overhead. In ALIPR, the probability distributions associated with its feature vectors cannot be calculated with the incomplete image information available at each partial step in I-FGM.

Another technology that we will leverage in I-FGM is the prevalent WWW image search engine. I-FGM uses the Internet as a search space in this article since it is a rich source of images and dynamic in nature. We will use image search engines such as Google and MSN to do a first order filtering on the search space similar to the Internet and narrow down the search space. These search engines cannot be used for real-time retrieval as they use static indexes that are built off-line (Kherfi, Ziou, & Bernardi, 2004). Also, they require human-generated information in the form of the html text surrounding the images (Tsymbalenko & Munson, 2001) or meta-tags. On the other hand, analysts using I-FGM must deal with images from various sources: satellite imagery, aerial reconnaissance images, and so forth, which may not be accompanied by annotations.

In this article, we seek to incorporate image search by implementing a concept-based image retrieval algorithm. Our algorithm will extract low-level features of images and map to predefined concepts. We will show how we can convert images into document graphs, which are the common knowledge representation in I-FGM. By doing so, we will validate our framework for unifying heterogeneous data types.

Image Retrieval for I-FGM

As mentioned earlier, we have validated I-FGM as a credible framework to provide real-time search in large and dynamic free-text databases. Here, we incorporate image retrieval into the framework. As such, our goal is not about presenting a new method for image retrieval but rather a method that is built on principles that have been tested and validated by the image retrieval research community that can be used in the I-FGM framework. We will use our image retrieval algorithm to validate the I-FGM framework on image collections. We also intend to show how smart resource allocation strategies can reduce computational costs and save time when dealing with large and dynamic databases. Furthermore, by representing the information in images as a document graph, we will have demonstrated how a unified representation can be applied to multimedia (text and/or image) documents.

As we mentioned earlier, the third point on heterogeneity is a particularly important issue in the databases that I-FGM expects to deal with in

Figure 1. Document graph for the text "Workers at coal mine on strike"

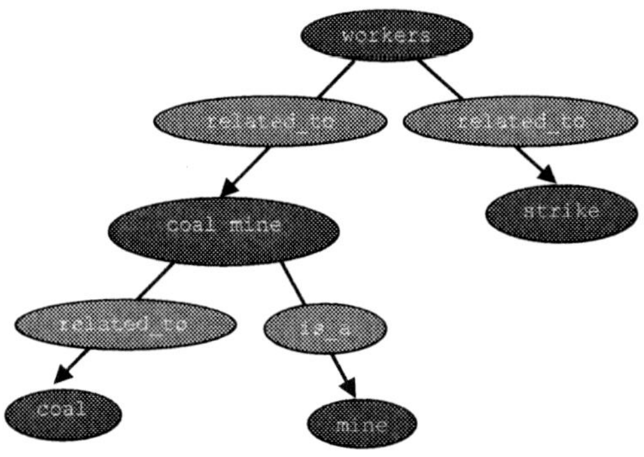

support of governmental agencies. Our databases may contain documents of different data type (images, text, multi-media files). Within each data type, another level of heterogeneity can occur. For example, images can occur in different forms such as photographs, satellite imagery, maps, and so forth. A straightforward method of dealing with this is to use separate retrieval methods for each data type and somehow combine their ranking results. This is a very ineffective method since the ranking measures used by the separate methods may share little or no semantic relationships. For example, it is unclear whether an image of similarity x based on texture and color values is equally relevant to users, or a text of the same similarity value based on keyword matches. We resolve this problem by extracting the information from a document using a given retrieval method and then representing the semantic contents of the document in a common graphical structure called the document graph. A document graph (example in Figure 1) consists of nodes representing concepts, and edges representing relations between nodes. This representation extracts the main information contained in any given document.

The image retrieval method that we use with I-FGM requires certain characteristics as we alluded to in the previous section. First, it should be amenable to partial processing where information gleaned from each partial step is re-useable by the next partial step. Next, the similarity measure calculated from each partial step should be a good indicator of the final similarity value, which helps in designing resource allocation strategies. Also, the time taken to process an image with partial processing should not be significantly larger than one-step processing. Finally, the method should also be able to convert the visual content of images into document graphs. All of this will allow us to accept natural language queries so as to be consistent with the text retrieval methodology already deployed within I-FGM.

Figure 2. Image retrieval in I-FGM

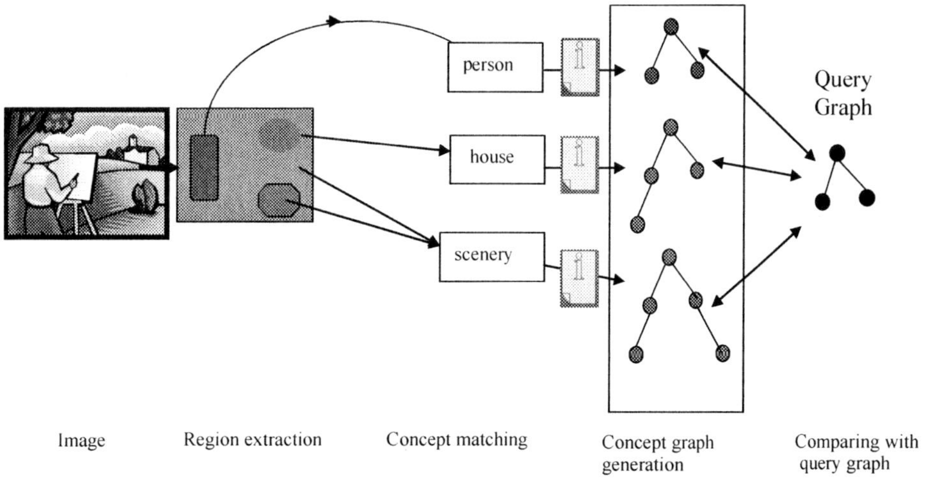

A step-by-step representation of the retrieval process is depicted in Figure 2. When a new image arrives in the system, it is incrementally processed to extract its low-level features in the images. These features are compared with those images found in the concept library and matching concepts are then noted. Here, the concept library is a collection of well-known concepts along with its annotation and an image feature vector representing its characteristics. The concept feature vector is modeled by a machine learning algorithm using a training set. The text annotations of these concepts are then combined to form the textual description of the image. The description is then converted into a document graph and compared with the document graph representation of the natural language query (query graph) to compute a similarity value. We now describe the steps in the image retrieval in detail:

1. **Low-level feature extraction:** Each image is represented by a 16-dimensional feature vector with each dimension representing a region of image. An image is said to have a maximum of 16 regions. This is borrowed from SIMPLIcity where it was found that 16 regions give good performance. Since we also use the same feature vector, we decided to use this value. Each region is represented by a six-dimensional vector representing the color and texture information of the images. In order to extract the regions from an image, the image is incrementally processed with a sliding window. We use the LUV color space. For each window, a signature is calculated from the average values of the color and the 2x2 wavelet transform on the L component. Haar wavelets are used as they are computationally efficient and have good performance (Natsev et al., 2004). The first three components of the signature are the average values of L, U, and V values of the pixels in the window, respectively. The high-frequency components of the wavelet transform form the remaining three components of the window signature. The signature of a window *w* is of the form:

$$h_w = \{l_w, u_w, v_w, m^1_w, m^2_w, m^3_w\}$$

where l_w, u_w, v_w are the average values of the pixel color in windows *w* and m^1_w, m^2_w, m^3_w are the high-frequency components of the Haar wavelet transform of the L values in *w*.

Based on their signatures, the windows are clustered together using a clustering algorithm. We use the BIRCH (Zhang, Ramakrishnan, & Livny, 1996) clustering algorithm as it is one of the most efficient clustering algorithms available. Each of the clusters form a region represented by its centroid. The area of each region is also calculated simultaneously. The regions are sorted according to its area and the largest region's signature form the first dimension of the image feature vector, the second largest region form the second dimension, and so on. Hence the image feature vector of an image *x* is represented by the vector:

$$f_x = \{l_{x,1}, u_{x,1}, v_{x,1}, m^1_{x,1}, m^2_{x,1}, m^3_{x,1}, \ldots\ldots \\ \ldots\ldots, l_{x,16}, u_{x,16}, v_{x,16}, m^1_{x,16}, m^2_{x,16}, m^3_{x,16}\}$$

where $l_{x,i}$, $u_{x,i}$ $v_{x,i}$ are the average color values in the centroid for region i and $m^1_{x,i}$, $m^2_{x,i}$ $m^3_{x,i}$ are the wavelet transforms for the L color space in the centroid for region i.

2. **Creation of the concept library:** The library is created off-line and this process is depicted in Figure 3. It consists of a set of concepts that are commonly found in the image databases that I-FGM is searching. Each concept is accompanied by a short textual description, which is generated manually. In our method the low-level features of images are mapped to concepts in the library. The descriptions

Figure 3. Off-line creation of concept library

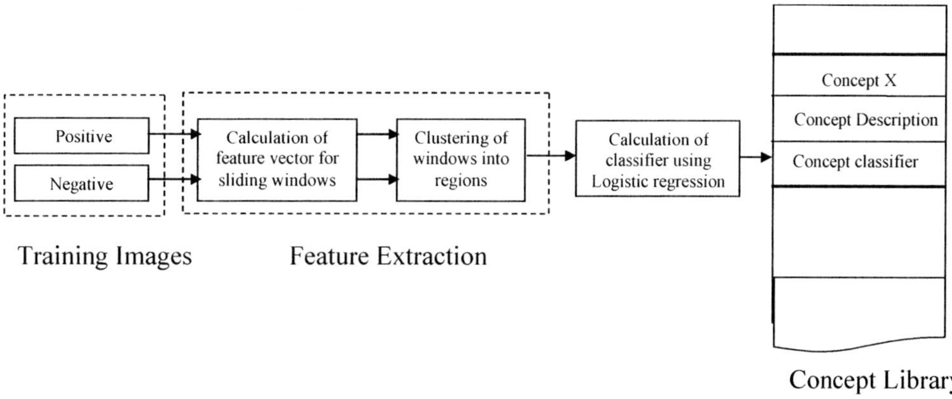

of the relevant concepts are then used to automatically generate the annotation for the images. This method of automatic annotation of images has less manual intervention than most other methods that generally require human generated metadata for each image. A classifier for each concept is generated by a machine learning algorithm based on logistic regression. A detailed description of the machine learning algorithm is presented later on. A set of training images are used to create the classifier. The training images are of two types: images that represent the concept (positive training) and images that do not represent the images (negative training). The image feature vector is extracted for each of these images and fed into the machine learning technique to create the classifier.

3. **Image matching:** This process matches low-level features of the images to high-level concepts (Figure 4). For each image, we incrementally compute its feature vector. During each incremental step, the image feature vector for the portion of the image that has been processed is calculated and compared against the concept classifiers in the library. A machine learning algorithm

Figure 4. Extraction of relevant concept from the image

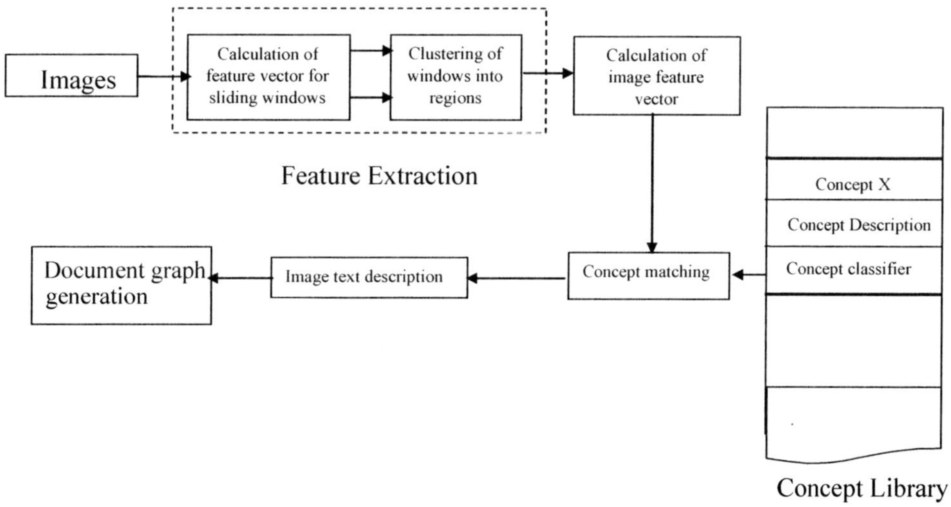

determines if a particular concept is relevant to the image or not. If a concept is relevant, its concept annotation is stored. At the end of the matching phase, the annotation of all matched concepts are combined together to form the image description. The description is converted in to a document graph and compared with the document graph of the query where the similarity is calculated.

4. **Machine learning algorithm:** Logistic regression (LR) is appropriate for matching concepts in the concept library with images because it can be modeled as a binomial classification problem. LR has been found to be appropriate for binary classification and can be improved to achieve fast speed and reliability (Komarek, 2004). Some studies have compared LR with some other popular classifiers used in machine learning such as tree induction (Perlich, Provost, & Simonoff, 2003), Naïve Bayesian classifier (Mitchell, 2005), and support vector machine (Vapnick, 1999). It has been found (Perlich et al., 2003) that LR performs better with small training data set while tree induction is better with a large data set. Naïve Bayesian classifiers require conditional independence among variables. Therefore, its application is limited, and in situations where such an assumption does not hold, LR is found to perform more accurately than Naïve Bayes (Mitchell, 2005). The loss function used in LR has been shown to be approximated by a support vector machine (Vapnick, 1999; Zhang, Jin, Yang, & Hauptmann, 2003). Algorithms based on LR have been used in CBIR (Ksantini, Ziou, Colin, & Dubeau, 2007) and in relevance feedback (Caenen & Pauwels, 2002) for image retrieval. Each concept is either relevant to the given image or not. The dependant variable (relevancy of the concept) can have two values: 0-not relevant and 1-relevant. The explanatory variables are the centroids of the regions in the image. The classifier for a particular concept is calculated by using positive and negative images. As mentioned before, the image vectors of each of these images are used to train the classifier. The training inputs are of the form:

$$t_j = \{l_{i,1}, u_{i,1}, v_{i,1}, m^1_{i,1}, m^2_{i,1}, m^3_{i,1}, \ldots$$
$$\ldots l_{i,16}, u_{i,16}, v_{i,16}, m^1_{i,16}, m^2_{i,16}, m^3_{i,16}, r_j\}$$

where $l_{x,i}$, $u_{x,i}$ $v_{x,i}$ are the average color values in the centroid for region i in the training image j. $m^1_{x,i}$, $m^2_{x,i}$ $m^3_{x,i}$ are the wavelet transforms for the L color space in the centroid for region i in the training image j

$$r_j = \begin{cases} 0 & \text{for negative images} \\ 1 & \text{for positive images} \end{cases}$$

The logit function for an image vector x is given as

$$g(x) = \alpha + \beta_1.l_{x,1} + \beta_2.u_{x,1} + \beta_3.v_{x,1} + \beta_4.m^1_{x,1}$$
$$+ \beta_5.m^2_{x,1} + \beta_6.m^3_{x,1} \ldots\ldots + \beta_{91}.l_{x,16}$$
$$+ \beta_{92}.u_{x,16} + \beta_{93}.v_{x,16} + \beta_{94}.m^1_{x,16}$$
$$+ \beta_{95}.m^2_{x,16} + \beta_{96}.m^3_{x,16}$$

where α, β_i $(1 \le i \le 96)$ are weights calculated by the maximum-likelihood method from the training images. The LR algorithm is implemented using the WEKA software (Witten & Frank, 2005).

System Architecture

I-FGM has a flexible architecture based on a multi-agent system that enables it to quickly deploy and redeploy computational resources. It also provides plug-and-play facilities for rapid deployment of any new retrieval method. Based on functionality, I-FGM can be decomposed into the following components:

1. I-Forager
2. gIG-Soup
3. gIG-Builder

4. I-Matcher
5. Blackboard

A detailed description of the various components of I-FGM can be found in Santos et al. (2005, 2006):

- **I-Forager:** This component uses third-party search tools to perform a first-order filtering of the documents in the search space. In our prototype, three I-foragers are used to download potentially relevant images into the gIG Soup. Google, MSN, and Yahoo are used in the I-Foragers. The query is sent to each of the I-Forager and the top 50 results are downloaded into the gIG Soup. I-Forager calculates the first order similarity that is based on the rank returned by the search engines.
- **gIG-Soup:** This component is the central data repository of I-FGM that holds the images as they are processed by I-FGM. The gIG-Soup is implemented using a NFS share directory to hold the image documents and a MySQL database that stores the document details such as image file name, similarity values, and first order similarity. MySQL tables are also used to synchronize the working of the different components of I-FGM.
- **gIG-Builder:** This component processes the document in the gIG-Soup into a document graph that is compared with the query graph to calculate its similarity. The gIG-Builders incrementally process the images and calculate the image feature vector. The feature vector is compared with classifiers in the concept library and matching concepts selected. The descriptions of the matched concepts are combined to form the text description of the concepts. Now that we have a text description of images, we can convert it into a document graph using the same method that we use for a text document (Santos et al., 2005, 2006). The image retrieval algorithm was described in detail in the previous sub-section. gIG-Builders select an image based on the priority values and calculate the signature of a certain number of windows, which is again dependant on the image priority. Pixel windows (8x8) and sliding distance of four pixels are used. The feature vectors of the windows processed until that moment are clustered using the BIRCH clustering algorithm with a threshold value of 70. The centroids and areas of the clusters or regions are stored. The feature vector of the image is updated and compared with the classifiers in the library using the LR algorithm. The text description of the matched concepts are combined together to provide the text representation of the image.
- **I-Matcher:** After the images have been converted into a document graph, it is compared with the query graph. The query graph is produced when the query is converted into a document graph. After comparison of the two graphs, a similarity measure is calculated. It is a numerical measure of how close the image is to the query. The similarity is given by the formula:

$$sim(q,d_i) = \left(\frac{n}{2*N} + \frac{m}{2*M}\right) * \rho$$

$$\rho = \begin{cases} 1 - \dfrac{C_1 - C_2}{L} & \text{where } C_1 \geq C_2 \\ 1 - \dfrac{C_1}{L} & \text{where } C_1 < C_2 \end{cases}$$

Where q is the query graph, d_i is the document graph, n and m are the number of concepts and relation nodes respectively, of the query graph found in the document graph, and N and M are the total numbers of concept and relation nodes of the query graph. Two relation nodes are matched if and only if at least their parent and their child are matched; ρ is a probability measure of our confidence in the similarity; C_1 is the number of concepts matched to the image and C_2 is the number of possible relevant concepts. We calculate C_2 from the number of concepts in the query graph. Since the concepts that are matched to the image are not always correct, we use ρ as a weight to the similarity value. For some images, the matched concepts are varied; for example "*dinosaur,*" "*snowstorm,*" and "*fruits.*" These images happen to have pixel characteristics found in all these concepts. By using a confidence measure, we are quantifying how sure the machine learning algorithms is about its matches. If the matches are small in number, that images have certain unique pixel characteristics that are found in only certain concepts. The confidence measure will be high for these images. For images that match a large number of concepts, we say that the machine learning algorithm is not so confident about its matches.

The priority value for the image is also calculated after each partial step. The priority function is used to determine the order in which the documents in the gIG Soup will be processed. This guides the allocation of computing resources. The amount of processing done during a particular step is also determined by the priority. The priority formula used is identical to the one in Santos et al. (2006) except for the weights that were calculated for images, are used in the formula.

- **Blackboard**: Since the documents are partially processed, its similarity values changes. In addition to this, the search space is dynamic. The documents having the top similarity values will change over time. Blackboard will display the most recent results in a rolling fashion. Such a display is essential when real time search results are required.

DISCUSSION

Results and Analysis

We validate the performance of our image retrieval algorithm in three steps. In the first set of experiments, we validate the ability of the LR-based machine learning technique to match image features to relevant concepts. We do this by comparing with another machine learning technique called C5.0 (Quinlan, 1993). C5.0 is an established data mining tool for discovering patterns that delineate categories, assembling them into classifiers, and using them to make predictions. It does automatic classification using decision trees. In the field of image classification, it has been used in classification of satellite imagery (Hurd, Civco, Gilmore, Prisloe, & Wilson, 2006) and protein crystallization (Zhu, Sun, Cheng, & Bern, 2004) images.

After we show the LR method to be an effective one in matching low-level features in images, we proceed to the second step in our validation, that is, validating the whole image retrieval algorithm. In our algorithm, we map regions in the image to known concepts. We now test if this matching is done effectively. We compare its performance with a previous prototype of I-FGM that implements WALRUS only. WALRUS is an established method and we have used WALRUS in I-FGM (Santos et al., 2007) to get good retrieval results. It may be noted that the concept-based I-FGM is built on top of the WALRUS sub-system. If we can show that the precision of the concept-based I-FGM is similar or better than the WALRUS based I-FGM, we can then conclude that matching of concepts and low-level features is effective and thus validate our algorithm.

Finally, we have to validate whether the image retrieval algorithm coupled with the distributed processing approach of I-FGM helps in fast retrieval of images. We do this by comparing its performance with two control systems that represent traditional distributed methods.

Creation of Testbed

For conducting the experiments, an image testbed containing a sizeable number of images and a set of queries is created. We chose a scenario titled "Natural disasters" as disaster relief is one of the areas of e-government where quick retrievals are required in large and dynamic databases. We select a set of five queries from this scenario. They are:

1. Building damaged by hurricane Katrina,
2. Firefighters fight wildfires,
3. Heavy snow storms in the winter,
4. Houses damaged by tornado, and
5. Houses damaged by tsunami.

For each query, a testbed is created by running the three I-Foragers and downloading the top 50 results from each search engine.

Creation of Concept Library

Before the concept-based I-FGM can be run, a concept library has to be constructed. Building a comprehensive library is difficult and time consuming. Instead, we tailor our library to contain concepts that are related to the "Natural disasters" scenario.

The library must also contain unrelated concepts to provide a fair assessment of our image retrieval algorithm. We use a set of 22 concepts listed in Figure 5. Each concept in the library consists of a brief concept description and the concept classifier. Examples of concept descriptions are shown in Figure 6. For each concept, two sets of images (20 each) representing the positive and negative images are used to train the classifier. These images are processed to extract its feature vector consisting of the centroids of its constituent regions. The feature vectors are used to train a classifier in LR. Details about the LR technique are given in the previous sub-section. The concept

Figure 5. List of concepts in the concept library

Beach	Damaged buildings	Cold weather	Dinosaur	Firefighter
Fires	Fruits	Tribal People	Snow Storm	Mud Slide
Mountains	Trees	Floods	Forest fires	Rainstorm
Tornado	Elephants	Flowers	Food	Tsunami
Hurricane	Katrina			

Figure 6. Examples of concepts and concept description in the concept library

	Concept	Concept description
1.	Beach	Beach has sand. Beach has lines with coconut trees. Beach has a blue ocean. People sunbathe on the beach. Waves can be seen on the beach. People lie on the beach. People watch boats on the beach. There are boats on the beach. It is windy on the beach. People relax on the beach. People play on the beach.
2.	Damaged buildings	Damaged buildings are caused by natural disasters. Damaged buildings are caused by flood, storm, and hurricane. Damaged buildings have damaged walls, leaking roots, broken doors, broken windows, and so forth. Damaged buildings can also be caused by terrorism attack. For example, the World Trade Center was damaged by terrorist attack.

library is stored in the memory of the gIG-Builders at the beginning of the experiment.

Validation of the Machine Learning Technique

In this section we validate the performance of LR-based machine learning technique implemented in the concept based I-FGM system by comparing it with C5.0. The existing studies in the machine learning community (Lim, Loh, & Shih, 2000; Perlich et al., 2003) have shown that LR performs competitively with other classifiers and performs better with small data sets than C4.5 (earlier version of C5.0). We would like to verify this finding on our own data set. The C5.0 algorithm was trained using positive and negative images for each concept in the concept library and classifiers were created. Our LR technique and the C5.0 algorithm was used on the image testbed created for query 4: "Houses damaged by tornado." For each image the algorithm delivered matching concepts from the concept library. The relevant concepts for this query are "Damaged Buildings" and "Tornado." When the matched concepts of the two algorithms were compared, we observe that the LR technique matched the relevant concepts "Damaged Houses" and "Tornado" for more relevant images than the C5.0 algorithm. This can be observed in the results tabulated in Figure 7. Due to space limitation, results for only four randomly picked images are displayed. Three of the images (1, 2, & 3) are relevant and the last one (4) is not relevant. For all the images, we see that the LR method retrieves more matched concepts (marked in red in Figure 7) than C5.0. It may be observed that most of the matched concepts of LR are also semantically similar. For example, for image 1 in Figure 7, two of the matched concepts are flood and rainstorm. Though non-relevant, they are semantically related to Tornado as they all belong to the class of natural disasters. For the relevant images 1, 2, and 3, the LR algorithm consistently matches the relevant concepts while C5.0 fails to match the concept "Tornado" to these images. Thus, we see that LR algorithm has a better performance than C5.0. In future work, user-based relevance feedback will be used to refine the matches made by the machine learning algorithm. Thus we have validated the performance of the LR-based machine learning technique implemented in our image retrieval algorithm.

Validation of Image Retrieval Algorithm

In this section, we will validate the image retrieval algorithm implemented in I-FGM. In the algorithm we map the image features to high-level concepts and obtain a textual description of the images. The document graphs are then generated from the text descriptions. The document graphs are then compared against the text query to determine the similarity measures. (The image algorithm was described in detail earlier.) We will compare the performance of the concept-based I-FGM prototype with a purely WALRUS-based I-FGM prototype that we developed in Santos et al. (2007). By getting comparable or better results in concept-based I-FGM prototypes, we will show that using the concept mapping on top of WALRUS does not have an adverse effect on performance and we get just as effective results.

The WALRUS-based I-FGM prototype was the first step towards deploying image retrieval in I-FGM (Santos et al., 2007). It was developed to show that a regions-based image retrieval algorithm like WALRUS can be easily incorporated into the I-FGM. The prototype has the same system architecture as the concept-based I-FGM prototype. The image retrieval algorithm used in the WALRUS-based I-FGM is identical to the concept-based I-FGM except for two differences: (1) the WALRUS system uses query images instead of text queries, and (2) the WALRUS system compares the regions of the query image with that of the search space images, instead of extracting concepts from images. I-matcher extracts the

Figure 7. Concepts matched by the logistic regression and C5.0 algorithms

	Image	Matching concepts	
		Logistic regression	**C5.0**
1		Damaged buildings, Dinosaur, Fruits, Snow- storm, Mountains, Flood, Tornado, Elephants Flowers	Damaged- building, Dinosaur, Elephant, Firefighter, Flood, Fruit, Rainstorm
2		Damaged buildings, cold weather, dinosaur, fruits tribal people, food, mountains, trees, forest fires, rainstorm tornado, flowers	Damaged- building, Dinosaur, Elephants, Firefighter, Flood, Fruit, Rainstorm
3		Beach, Flood, Damaged buildings, Cold weather, Snowstorm, Mountains, Rainstorm, Tornado, Elephants	Beach Damaged- building Elephants Flood Mountains Rainstorm
4	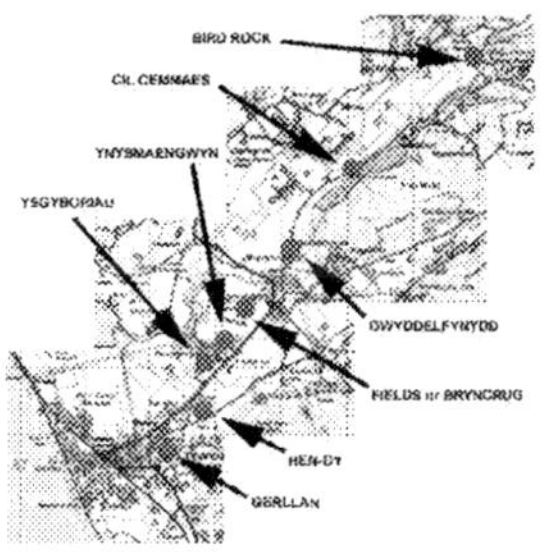	Fruits, Trees, Tribal people, Snowstorm, Mountains, Forest fires, Elephants	Beach, Tree Damaged-building, Elephants, Flood, Rainstorm, Snowstorm

image feature vector from the query image and compares it with image feature vector of the search space image. The similarity measure used is

$$Similarity(P,Q) = \frac{area(\cup_{i=1}^{n}(P_i)) + area(\cup_{i=1}^{n}(Q_i))}{area(P) + area(Q)}.$$

Here P and Q represent the retrieved image and the query image respectively. The set of ordered pairs $\{(P_1, Q_1), \ldots, (P_n, Q_n)\}$ form a similarity region pair set for P and Q, where P_i is similar to Q_i and for $i \neq j$, $P_i \neq P_j$, $Q_i \neq Q_j$.

Both WALRUS-based and concept-based I-FGM prototypes are run with the testbed of five queries. Precision (Salton & McGill, 1983) is the performance metric that we use to compare the performance of the concept-based and WALRUS-based I-FGM system. It is a commonly used metric in information retrieval and is defined as the ratio of the relevant documents (images) retrieved to the total documents (images) retrieved. In this article we use a slightly different definition: ratio of the relevant documents (images) among the top n retrieved documents (images). The two systems are run on each of the query testbed and the top 15 images for each query are analyzed to determine their relevance and finally calculate the precision.

Analysis of the Validation Results

The top 15 images retrieved by the WALRUS-based I-FGM prototype for each query are analyzed to determine if they are relevant or not. We do this using certain criteria. For example, in query 1: "Building damage by hurricane Katrina," we only consider images that depict damaged buildings, especially on the coast as relevant images. The precision results obtained by the two systems for all the queries are tabulated in Figure 8. For lack of space we present the top 15 image results for only query 1 (Figures 9a and 9b). Each image is tagged as x.y where x is the name of the search engine that downloaded the image and y is the rank provided by it. The images deemed relevant are indicated by a check mark in Figure 9. A quick glance shows that the performances of the systems are comparable as they retrieve around the same number of relevant documents in each query. The concept-based and WALRUS-based systems win in two queries each (queries 1 & 3 for the concept-based system and queries 2 & 4 for the WALRUS-based system) and have a tie for query 5. From these results, we can come to the conclusion that our concept-based image retrieval algorithm performs as well as WALRUS. It may be noted here that the concept mapping part of our current prototype is built on top of the WALRUS feature extraction sub-system. Relevant concepts are matched after the WALRUS sub-system extracts the regions in the images. The document graphs are then generated and compared with the query. We use this to provide a unified framework for heterogeneous data. Similar performance results for both WALRUS and concept-based IFGM show that the performance is not degraded when concepts matching are used with the feature extraction. This also leads us to conclude that the regions-based feature extraction methodology can indeed be used to effectively map low-level image features to higher level concepts.

Evaluation of Image Retrieval in I-FGM

In this section we will validate the effectiveness of I-FGM for image retrieval. We achieve this by comparing its performance with two other control systems that represent the traditional information and distributed processing paradigms.

The control systems differ from I-FGM only in the way the documents are chosen for processing. The control systems are baseline and partially intelligent systems. In the baseline system, the

Figure 8. Precision values attained by WALRUS-based and concept-based I-FGM

	Precision	
	WALRUS-based I-FGM	*Concept-based I-FGM*
Query 1	9/15	*10/15*
Query 2	10/15	*9/15*
Query 3	9/15	*11/15*
Query 4	13/15	*12/15*
Query 5	*10/15*	*10/15*

Figure 9a. Precision results for query1 using WALRUS-based I-FGM

documents are chosen at random for processing. Each document is given the exact same chunk of time for processing in each step. In the partially intelligent system, the priority of a document is static and is equivalent to the first-order similarity. We use the image testbed created previously to conduct the simulation experiments. The images are processed by the gIG builders and the final similarity measure recorded. The top *n* documents are selected as the target document set for each query.

The control systems and I-FGM systems are run on the testbed for each query. Two performance metrics calculated during each run are: (1) recall vs. time, and (2) document waiting times. Recall (Salton & McGill, 1983) is defined as the ratio of the relevant documents retrieved to the total number of relevant documents. We designate the top *x* documents selected by our image retrieval method as the set of relevant documents. We store the recall values for each control system at regular intervals throughout the period of simulation. The waiting time for a document is defined as the time spent in the gIG Soup before it is displayed on the blackboard. Since one of the goals of I-FGM is to

Figure 9b. Precision results for query1 using concept-based I-FGM

get to the relevant documents as quickly as possible, the waiting time is an important metric.

RESULTS AND ANALYSIS

As mentioned before, the control systems and I-FGM are run on the test beds of the five queries. The waiting times of relevant documents and recall values are monitored during the simulations.

It has the shortest waiting time for the most documents in queries 4 and 5. For query 3, it ties with baseline system to get the most number of documents in the shortest time. Overall, I-FGM is best in three queries, baseline in two queries, and partial in one query.

We now carefully analyze the results of each query. In query 1 (Figure 10a), baseline system is the best performing system getting 6 out of the 11 documents the fastest. Partial comes second getting four documents and I-FGM is third with two documents. When we analyze the documents closely, we see that I-FGM performs poorly for this query for one primary reason. The similarity measure fluctuates, decreasing in one step and increasing in another.

In I-FGM, a priority function (used for selecting from the gIG-Soup) decreases the priority of an image when its similarity at a particular step

Figure 10a. Document waiting time-query 1

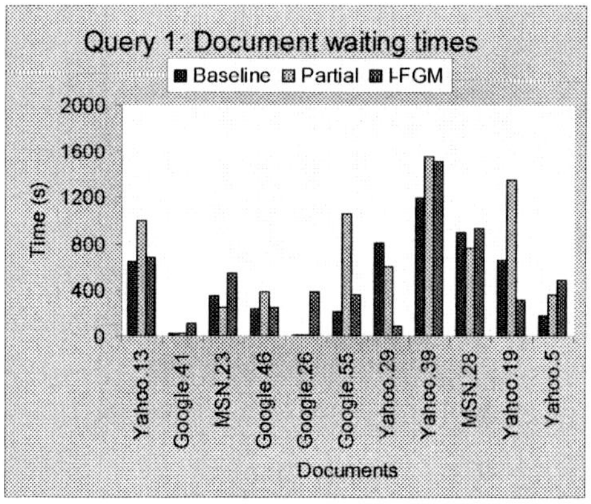

Figure 10b. Recall vs. time—Query 1

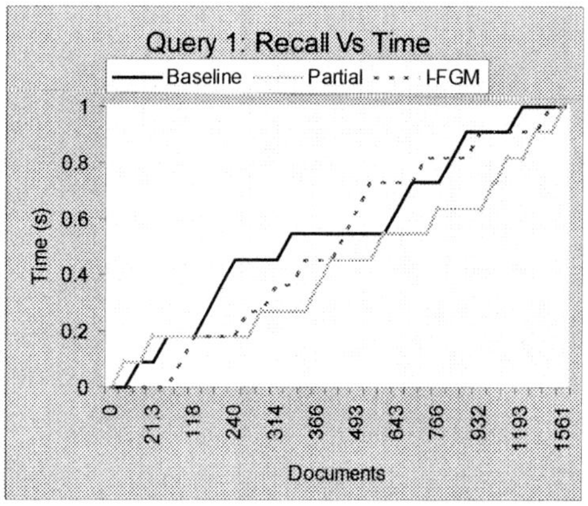

Figure 11a. Document waiting time—Query 2

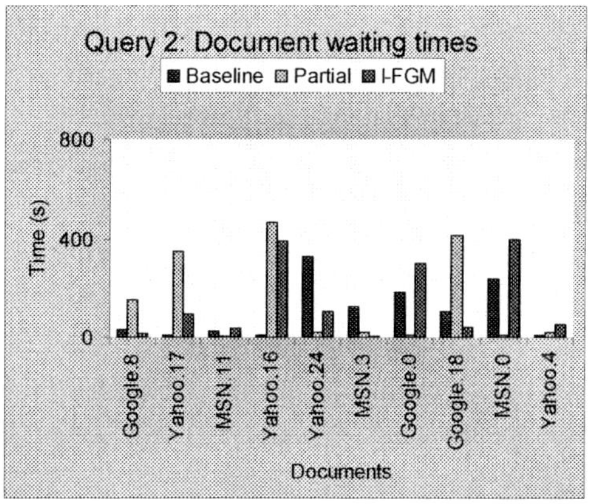

Figure 11b. Recall vs. time—Query 2

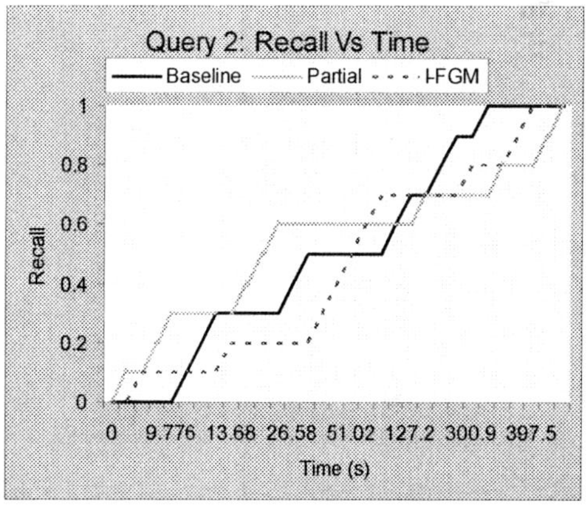

does not increase proportional to the processing time in that particular step or when the similarity decreases. Documents with rapid fluctuations in similarity do not work well with this priority function. Although we used an initial set of experimental results to determine the weights in the priority function, more work needs to be done in formulating a better priority function. As we obtain more experimental results, the priority function will be refined and this will be part of future work. From the precision graph (Figure 10b), we see that I-FGM has a better recall for part of the simulation time. For query 2 (Figures 11a and 11b), partial system has lowest waiting times for four documents while I-FGM and baseline system comes second with three documents each. We can easily see why this is the reason. The relevant documents are highly ranked by the I-Foragers, that is, they have a high expected first order similarity. Since the partial system processes the documents based only on the expected first order similarity, such documents are most likely to be picked by it sooner than the other systems. This is further helped by the fact that documents such as MSN.0 and Google.0 are small (around 2,000 windows). But it may be noted that the performance of I-FGM is not much worse than partial as it gets only one document less than the partial systems.

Figure 12a. Document waiting time—Query 3

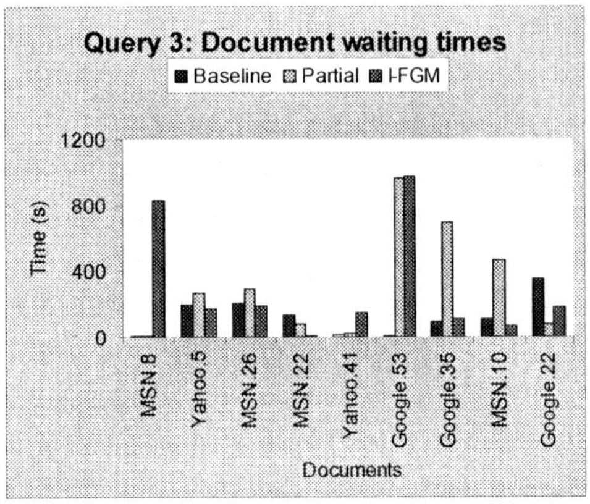

Figure 12b. Recall vs. time—Query 3

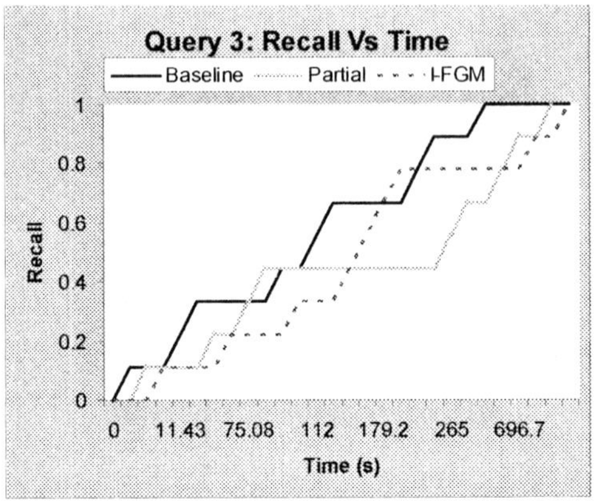

Figure 13a. Document waiting time—Query 4

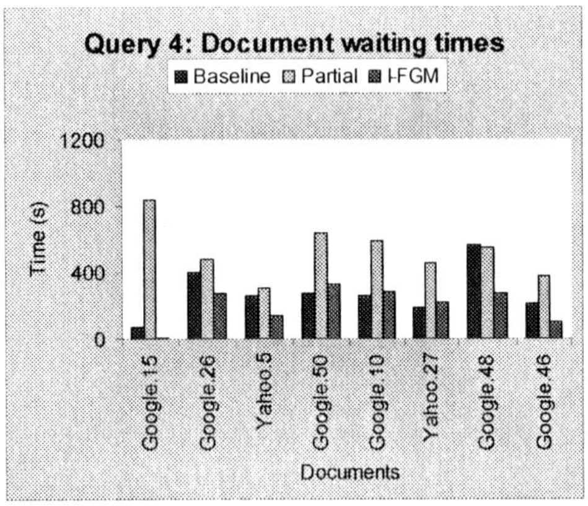

Figure 13b. Recall vs. time—Query 4

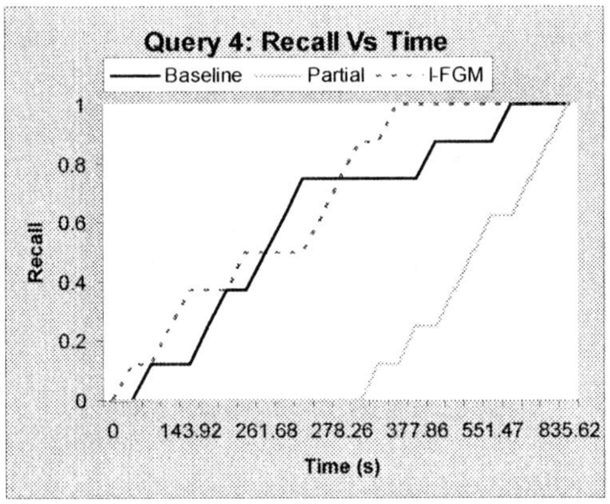

For query 3 (Figures 12a and 12b), both I-FGM and baseline systems perform the best, getting four documents each. Partial system comes in last with one document. When we analyze three documents (Yahoo.41, Google.53, Google.35), which is picked by baseline system the earliest, we see that these documents have a high similarity value after the first partial step itself. Since they are lowly ranked by the I-foragers, they have a low initial priority in the I-FGM system. Therefore I-FGM gets these documents only after a certain amount of simulation time has passed. Baseline system gets lucky by selecting these documents early. But since these documents give a high similarity value in the first processing step, they appear in the blackboard after the first processing step. I-FGM has better performance than baseline and I-FGM for queries 4 (Figures 13a and 13b) and 5 (Figures 14a and 14b). For query 4, I-FGM gets 5 out of the 8 relevant documents. Baseline system comes in second with three documents. In the recall graph also, I-FGM has a higher recall value than the other systems for most of the simulation time. For query 5, I-FGM gets 5 documents out of 11 target documents. Partial and baseline tie for the second place with 4 each. In the recall graph (Figure 15b), I-FGM has a better recall than other systems over the range (0.2-0.7). The similarity values for images can decrease over time (which does not happen in text retrieval) and fluctuate rapidly. These factors make the modeling of priority function for images a difficult task. Despite this, we have shown I-FGM to be better in the majority of queries, thus proving its feasibility as a quick and reliable retrieval method for images.

Figure 14a. Document waiting time—Query 5

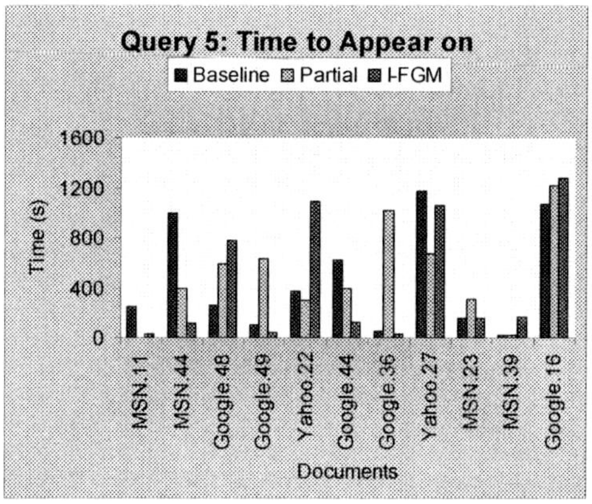

Figure 14b. Recall vs. time—Query 5

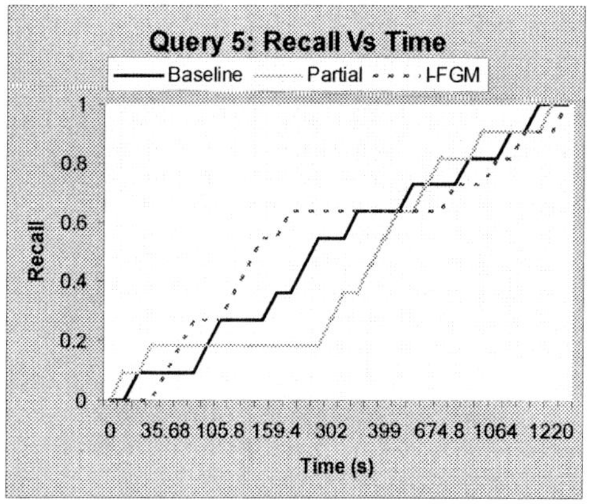

CONCLUSION

In this article we designed and implemented an image retrieval algorithm based on mapping low-level features of images to higher level concepts. We validated this algorithm on I-FGM and showed that it can be used to represent the visual information of images as concepts and relations. Consequently, we also validated the methodology in I-FGM of providing a unified ranking for heterogeneous data types. I-FGM was also compared against two control systems to show that the image retrieval algorithm works well with partial processing and helps in faster retrieval of images.

The simulations in this article were conducted on a static testbed. In the future, this will be extended to include simulation studies for different dynamic conditions in the search space. Furthermore, with our single unifying representation of semantic content in text and image via our document graphs, I-FGM will be readily modified for a mixed document search space containing both text and image documents. Documents that contain both text and image data will also be considered. Currently, I-FGM does not request any user input except the user's queries. We plan to incorporate relevance feedback to allow users to give their inputs on the retrieval quality. Users can be asked explicitly to indicate which images are most similar to what they are looking for. We may also observe the user's interactions with our system to infer implicitly which images might be of their interests. These retrieved relevant images then will be used to modify the user's original queries by adding both textual and image information to them. This process will help guide the retrieval task so that it returns more relevant images to the user.

ACKNOWLEDGMENT

The work was supported in part by the National Geospatial Intelligence Agency Grant Nos. HM1582-04-1-2027 and HM1582-05-1-2042. We would also like to thank Dr. Qunhua Zhao for his various comments and advice in this project.

REFERENCES

Caenen, G., & Pauwels, E. J. (2002). *Logistic regression models for relevance feedback in content-based image retrieval.* San Jose, CA: Storage and Retrieval for Media Databases.

Carson, C., Belongie, S., Greenspan, H., & Malik, J. (2002). Blobworld: Image segmentation using expectation-maximization and its application to image querying. *IEEE Transactions on Pattern Analysis and Machine Intelligence, 24*(8), 1026-1038.

Daubechies, I. (1992). *Ten lectures on wavelets.* Philadelphia: SIAM.

Enser, P., & Sandom, C. (2003). Towards a comprehensive survey of the semantic gap in visual image retrieval. (LNCS 2728, pp. 279-287).

Hurd, J. D., Civco, D. L., Gilmore, M. S., Prisloe, S., & Wilson, E. H. (2006, May 1-5). *Tidal wetland classification from landsat imagery using an integrated pixel-based and object-based classification approach.* Paper presented at the ASPRS 2006 Annual Conference, Reno, NV.

Kherfi, M. L., Ziou, D., & Bernardi, A. (2004). Image retrieval from the World Wide Web: Issues, techniques, and systems. *ACM Computing Surveys, 36*(1), 35-67.

Komarek, P. (2004, May). *Logistic regression for data mining and high-dimensional classification* (Tech. Rep. No. CMU-RI-TR-04-34). Pittsburgh, PA: Carnegie Mellon University, Robotics Institute.

Ksantini, R., Ziou, D., Colin, B., & Dubeau, F. (2007). *Logistic regression models for a fast CBIR method based on feature selection.* Paper presented at the International Joint Conference on Artificial Intelligence.

Li, J., & Wang, J. Z. (2006). *Real-time computerized annotation of pictures.* Paper presented at the ACM Multimedia Conference, Santa Barbara, CA.

Li, J., Wang, J. Z., & Wiederhold, G. (2000). *IRM: Integrated region matching for image retrieval.* Paper presented at the ACM Multimedia Conference, Los Angeles, CA.

Lim, T. S., Loh, W. Y. & Shih, Y. S. (2000). A comparison of prediction accuracy, complexity, and training time for thirty-three old and new classification algorithms. *Machine Learning, 40,* 203-228.

Ma, W. Y., & Manjunath, B. (1997). *NaTra: A toolbox for navigating large image databases.* Paper presented at the IEEE International Conference on Image Processing.

Mitchell, T. (2005). *Generative and discriminative classifiers: Naïve Bayes and logistic regression.* Retrieved from http://www.cs.cmu.edu/~tom/mlbook/NBayesLogReg.pdf

Natsev, A. (2001). *Multimedia retrieval by regions, concepts, and constraints.* Unpublished PhD thesis, Duke University, Durham, NC.

Natsev, A., Chadha, A., Soetarman, B., & Vitter, J. S. (2001). *CAMEL: Concept annotated iMagE libraries.* Paper presented at the Storage and Retrieval for Image and Video Databases, SPIE, San Jose, CA.

Natsev, A., Rastogi, R., & Shim, K. (2004). WALRUS: A similarity retrieval algorithm for image databases. *IEEE Transactions on Knowledge and Data Engineering, 16*(3), 301-316.

Perlich, C., Provost, F., & Simonoff, J. (2003). Tree induction vs. logistic regression: A learning-curve analysis. *Journal of Machine Learning Research, 4,* 211-255.

Quinlan, J. R. (1993). *C4.5: Programs for machine learning.* San Francisco: Morgan Kaufmann.

Rui, Y., Huang, T., & Chang, S. (1999). Image retrieval: Current techniques, promising directions and open issues. *Journal of Visual Communication and Image Representation, 10*(4), 39-62.

Salton, G., & McGill, M. (1983). *Introduction to modern information retrieval.* McGraw-Hill.

Santos, E., Jr., Santos, E., Nguyen, H., Pan, L., & Korah, J. (2005). Large-scale distributed foraging, gathering, and matching for information retrieval: Assisting the geospatial intelligent analyst. In *Proceedings of the SPIE* (Vol. 5803, pp. 66-77).

Santos, E., Jr., Santos, E., Nguyen, H., Pan, L., Korah, J., Zhao, Q., et al. I-FGM information retrieval in highly dynamic search spaces. In *Proceedings of SPIE* (Vol. 6229, pp. 1-12).

Santos, E., Jr., Santos, E., Nguyen, H., Pan, L., Korah, J., Zhao, Q., et al. (2007). Applying I-FGM to image retrieval and an I-FGM system performance analyses. In *Proceedings of the SPIE: Defense \& Security Symposium* (Vol. 6560), Orlando, FL.

Smeulders, A. W. M., Worring, M., Santini, S., Gupta, A., & Jain, R. (2000). Content-based image retrieval at the end of the early years. *IEEE Transactions on Pattern Analysis and Machine Intelligence, 22*(12), 1349-1380.

Tsymbalenko, Y., & Munson, E. V. (2001). *Using HTML metadata to find relevant images on the Web.* Paper presented at the Internet Computing, Las Vegas, NV.

Vapnik, V. (1999). *The nature of statistical learning theory* (2nd ed.). Springer Verlag.

Veltkamp, R. C., & Tanase, M. (2000). *Content-based image retrieval systems: A survey* (Tech. Rep. No. UU-CS-2000-34). The Netherlands: Utrecht University, Department of Computer Science.

Wang, J. Z., Li, J., & Wiederhold, G. (2001). SIMPLIcity: Semantics-sensitive integrated matching for picture libraries. *IEEE Transactions on Pattern Analysis and Machine Intelligence, 23*(9), 947-963.

Witten, I. H., & Frank, E. (2005, June). *Data mining: Practical machine learning tools and techniques* (2nd ed.). Morgan Kaufmann.

Zhang, J., Jin, R., Yang, Y., & Hauptmann, A. G. (2003). Modified logistic regression: An approximation to SVM and its application in large-scale text categorization. In *Proceedings of the Twentieth International Conference on Machine Learning 2003,* Washington DC.

Zhang, T., Ramakrishnan, R., & Livny, M. (1996). *BIRCH: An efficient data clustering method for very large databases.* Paper presented at the ACM SIGMOD International Conference on Management of Data, Montreal, Canada.

Zhu, X., Sun, S., Cheng, S. E., & Bern, M. (2004). *Classification of protein crystallization imagery.* Paper presented at the 26th Annual International Conference of IEEE Engineering in Medicine and Biology Society, San Francisco.

This work was previously published in International Journal of Electronic Government Research, Vol. 4, Issue 1, edited by M. Khosrow-Pour, pp. 14-35, copyright 2008 by IGI Publishing (an imprint of IGI Global).

Chapter 7
E-Governance and Development:
Service Delivery to Empower the Poor

Raul Zambrano
United Nations Development Program, USA

ABSTRACT

This article provides a quick assessment of current e-governance policies and programmes to then suggest an alternative approach to the issue of the use information and communications technology in governance process. By focusing on citizens and stakeholders needs and fostering their participation in decision-making processes, governments can be best prepared to provide them with basic services and information, especially to poor and marginalized areas excluded from the potential benefits of e-governance. Pro-poor basic delivery in turn has the potential of fostering stakeholder engagement in public policy discussions at the local level.

INTRODUCTION

Since the mid-1990s, information and communications technology (ICT) have raised to the forefront of discussions related to globalization and development (economic, sustainable, or human). Supported by the relatively fast expansion of both the Internet and (the even faster) mobile phone use (ITU, 2006), many developing countries now see the strategic use of ICTs as a new productive area to engage with the global economy while addressing, at the same time, some of their critical development challenges (RITA, 2000). The potential of ICTs as an enabler for development, and not as a goal in themselves (Accenture, Markle, & UNDP, 2001), is fostering the latter processes.

ICTS AND GOVERNANCE

The use of ICT in governance processes and by governments has been mostly centered in the deployment of ICT applications and solutions to streamline government's operations, reduce transactional costs, and (hopefully) increase transparency and accountability of public institutions. E-government (or online government) has indeed taken off since the end of the millennium. "Modernization" of public state institutions complemented by the delivery of specific government services has thus been the cornerstone of this approach. As a matter of fact, many developing countries have complemented existing national ICT strategies with e-government policies and/or ad hoc deployment of solutions for specific national sectors (Heeks, 2003).

The latest trend on e-government, in response in part to the many failures of many of related initiatives (Heeks, 2003), suggests a more citizen-centric approach in which e-government priorities are much more responsive to citizens' needs and development agendas (UNDESA, 2005). This has been complemented by a new and independent body on work that focuses on e-democracy or e-participation (Coleman, 2005) via access to information via ICT, content production, and dissemination across networks of state and non-state stakeholders, and interactive communications with government institutions and across other organizations.

CONCEPTUAL FRAMEWORK

A citizen centric approach has fundamental consequences of the use of ICT in governance processes. As shown in Figure 1, citizens are both "clients" and "stakeholders" in the overall process.

As "clients," citizens are the users and consumers of government services, including broadcasting (one-way delivery) of information and knowledge resources. This is the basic role that mainstream e-government programmes assign to citizens. It is essentially a *transactional* role where the final aim is to deliver a service, basic or not. Key indicators here are related to the transaction process itself (cost, time, quality, easy of use, etc.). Thus, ICTs can have a direct impact in the process in terms of production, distribution, and consumption of the services and information provided.

As stakeholders, citizens play a substantially different role. The essential aspect here is the role they can play in the design and implementation of public policies and development agendas if effective participation in these processes is feasible within a given political context. The focus here is on *empowering* citizens. The aim is to provide stakeholders with the capacity and tools to engage with local and national governments and other players in policy or development discussions.

Figure 1. E-governance framework (Source: UNDP)

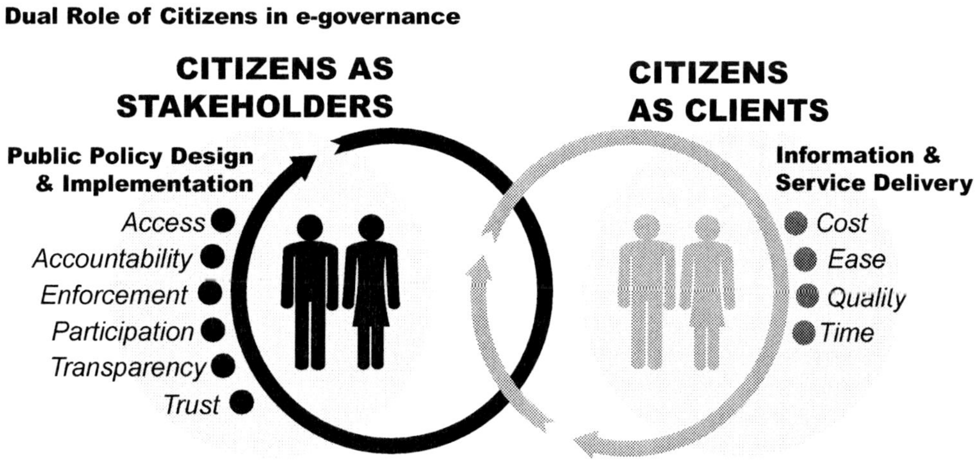

This is a two-way street where communications and interaction are basic components. Key indicators here are directly related to critical governance factors such as access, trust, participation, and so forth. The potential of ICTs for producing and reproducing information at very low cost and creating new and/or enhancing existing citizen's (and interactive) networks offers the possibility of supporting the role of citizens as active stakeholders (e-participation).[1]

There is also a clear connection between the two components. For example, citizen- centric e-government initiatives should involve stakeholders in the design and implementation of e-government strategies. Moreover, priority areas for e-government interventions should be identified in conjunction with stakeholders, on the basis of a multi-sectoral approach.[2]

This article will focus on the first dimension of this dual role of citizens to then explore potential links with e-participation. Information and service delivery to all are essential if governments are truly committed to addressing poverty and social exclusion.

E-GOVERNANCE AND THE POOR

Many if not most of the large e-government programmes and projects are centered in supporting and strengthening the internal and external capacities of national government institutions to fulfill their functions in a more effective and efficient fashion (UNDESA, 2003). In many cases, local governments and municipalities are not part of the equation, never mind the poorest areas and communities. Not surprisingly, most of these initiatives fail to reach the poorest and socially excluded sectors of the population (World Bank, 2003).

Does this mean that there are no clear links between e-governance, defined in the broad sense, and the poor?

To address this question, and based on the conceptual framework, a review of some of the existing literature on the subject is presented. This is complemented by the presentation of a case study followed by final conclusions and recommendations for further research.

E-SERVICES FOR THE POOR

Most e-government initiatives are focused on what has been called *e-administration* or the use of ICTs to strengthen public institutions and make them more efficient and transparent. This is an inward looking process where government institutions look at specific ICT solutions to streamline their operations. Most of these initiatives are not directly focused on service delivery and, at best, end up just providing public information to citizens usually through non-interactive Web portals. Such programmes are usually implemented in national government institutions located in large urban centers. Finally, most e-government national strategies are completed on a non-participatory basis excluding both local governments and non-state stakeholder in design and implementation (Bhatnagar, 2006).

There are, however, a handful of examples which in the last 5 years or so have attempted to focus on delivering basic services to the poor using ICTs (both old and new). Most of these are usually implemented by state and local governments that run them directly or through innovative public private partnerships with small enterprises and NGOs. These cases can be summarized by specific targets established from the onset, as follows:

1. Delivery of basic services to citizens. As illustrated by project Gyandoot in Madhya Pradesh, India is a solid example of how the use of ICTs could help a distant government reach a poor and drought-prone district and deliver some key services to them effectively and efficiently. It provides villagers access

to vital government information and to documents such as income and residence certificates through kiosks operated by local entrepreneurs (Blattman, Jensen, & Roman, 2003).

2. Foster economic well-being for the rural poor, as in Projects FRIENDS (fast, reliable, instant, effective network for disbursement of services) and AKSHAYA. The first is notable for enabling people to process bill payments in one local center, the second for the diverse information and government services local people can access in the same center. Both have been found instrumental in developing social networks and generating entrepreneurial activities that in turn enable local people to be productive (Madon, 2004).
3. Enhance local government administration and accountability. The ability to process various transactions directly with government and the elimination of middle-persons has been noted as key in the reduction of opportunities for corruption, which in turn contributes greatly to better perception of government by the citizens. Villagers attribute to projects such as Gyandoot and FRIENDS the tremendous reduction in the common practice of paying bribes in order to get public services transactions. Some projects even include a complaint mechanism through which villagers can report unfair prices, broken irrigation pumps, absentee teachers, and other local problems, the local people also become empowered to push for and monitor action from their government (Cecchini & Scott, 2003).
4. Increase trust in local government. As illustrated by the e-justice project, a portal designed to promote legal awareness and understanding (by simplifying laws, judgments, and procedures); provide access to legal information and services (legal aid and alternative remedies, range of information on human rights and issues relevant to people's lives in the rural area). One key service of e-justice is enabling the rural poor to submit grievances and requests for assistance from legal experts online for free; it evaluates grievances submitted and refers them to a court that will guide citizens (via assigned advocates) on appropriate ways to resolve problems (NISG & i4D, 2006).
5. Promote Public-Private partnerships. Most of the initiatives seek alliances with either small entrepreneurs and/or developmental NGOs to effectively reach the poor and deliver basic services. Thus local governments are aware of their limitations in reaching remote population on a sustainable basis and outsource functions and operations to third parties.

All in all, these initiatives still face many constraints including:

1. Model. Research and cases cited here confirm that there is not one *model* that could be pointed to as the definitive success model for the use of ICTs in enhancing democratic governance and empowering the poor for development. Perhaps of all challenges noted in various studies, it is this lack of a solid, unassailable model that many planning their own initiatives find pressing. As needs are different for each locale or group of people, pinning down what "design" may prove most suitable or replicable becomes problematic (Chen, Chen, Huang, & Ching, 2006).
2. Sustainability and cost. Although not all initiatives entail enormous costs, the general perception is that ICT initiatives require big investments that developing countries cannot find negligible and thus find these initiatives difficult to deem as priority. Some research confirms, however, that certain successful initiatives do not require prohibitive costs and are in fact self-sustaining. The

Kothmale program in Sri Lanka is the best example; another is the Boohmi project in India (De' & Sen, 2004).

3. Social and physical infrastructure. Some research points to citizens' lack of skills, existence of rural/urban and gender divides, lack of access to computers or other ICT tools, and so on, as barriers to the success of any initiative (Pigato, 2001). These are constraints, however, that did not impede those projects adopted in rural India where local people are noted to lack skills and education, and communities do not have the physical infrastructure deemed ideal (Bhatnagar, 2006).
4. Scalability and replicability. Many of the initiatives do not cover large segments of the poor population and indeed seem to work best in smaller environments. Also, the successful cases that happen to take place mostly in India are not being replicated in other countries with similar socio-economic conditions. However, this seems to be a factor that goes beyond the simple deployment of ICT and is more related to national policies on decentralization and public sector reform.
5. Lack of clear impact. There is still little evidence on the impact of these efforts on the poorest populations. Plenty of anecdotal evidence has been put forward but there is still very little factual data to provide harder facts about the impact these projects on local human development.

CASE STUDY: INDIA: PROJECT E-SETU (E-BRIDGE)—CITIZENS ACCESS TO INFORMATION AND GOVERNMENT SERVICES[3]

The E-setu project[4] was launched in 2003 by UNDP and the government of India in the island of Majuli, the largest inhabited river island in South Asia.[5] The island has no (real/analog) bridges connecting it to the mainland. The only access to Majuli is thus by ferry boat, a trip that takes at least 2 hours (one-way). From the island's population viewpoint, this means that getting a permit for a local fair, obtaining a land registration certificate, or registering a newly born child requires time-consuming and hazardous trips (especially during the rainy season) to the Deputy Commissioner (DC) Office in the mainland.[6]

With the support of the DC in the district headquarters in Jorhat, UNDP India launched the E-setu project with a budget of U.S. $ 70,000 and the specific objective of facilitating access to information and government services—and not just to provide connectivity or access to the Internet to islanders. Initially, two separate kiosks were setup in Majuli, one at the local government office (Sub-Divisional Office, SDO) and one run by a small local entrepreneur. Using store-and–forward technology over existing telephone lines and satellite links, both were linked to the kiosk setup at the DC office in Jorhat. The latter in turn was directly connected to the Internet and ran sophisticated hardware and software.

From the beginning, end-users were not expected to directly use the computer equipment installed by the project. Instead local operators were trained and asked to both serve the general public and handle the PCs and printers. This also provided an ideal human interface for those end users that were illiterate.[7] Indeed, the project spent important resources in training kiosk operators as well as government officials. Operators were also frequently rotated so that they quickly learned the in and outs of the new system.

Operators printed out the respective government forms requested by the public and assisted them in filling them out. Citizens arriving at the kiosks were registered in the system and provided a unique ID number. Once the request was completed and submitted, citizens were provided a receipt with a unique ID too, as well as a date when they could return to pick up their completed requests. Users who already had good knowledge of using PCs were welcome to handle the process on their own. This was particularly the case at the private operated kiosks—which also included several in the mainland that were associated to the project.

The project started by offering a total of 12 basic services which provided citizens in the island with rapid access to government certificates of diverse kind ranging from birth[8] to senior citizen certificates. Scaling fees were used for charging for services. For the first couple of months, services were provided for free to entice the population to use the kiosks. Then a flat fee of 2 Rs was charged for the next couple of months. This was increased to 5 Rs by the sixth month of operations. An additional 15 services were also added to the kiosks portfolio—for a total of 27. These now included copies of certificates to permits for land sales and possession of fire crackers. By November 2003, the main services the kiosks provided were:

Table 1 shows the main services demanded by the local population. Note the relation between the demand for Jamabandi (land registration) certificates and the issuing of land sale permissions. Land sales require that owners have in their possession a copy of their land titles and E-setu greatly facilitated this.

Table 2 shows the benefits of E-setu in terms of service delivery. There are clear benefits in terms of time, cost, access, and quality of service.

Data for Table 2 includes over 11,200 applications received through the E-setu kiosks. Citizens thus saved over Rs 400,000 and close to 14 thousand person days in getting these services. On the other hand, both kiosks collected in the first 6 months after starting applying fees, close to Rs 34,000 with over 90% coming from the government operated kiosk.

We thus have an effective local e-governance project that not only provides more access to services and information to poor people but also improves the quality of the services while substantially reducing the time invested by citizens in getting access to them.

Another key direct benefit should also be highlighted. By accessing the kiosks poor citizens learned about their own individual rights as well as the right to access information on government and the public services it is supposed to provide.

In locations where E-setu was not established, the so-called "black coats" act as intermediaries between the government and citizens and charge hefty fees for providing and expediting the various certificates and other government services. In such situations, citizens have no option but to make use of the "black coats" to obtain the service they require. E-setu on the other hand, has helped promote greater the transparency and accountability of government institutions involved in the project by eliminating intermediaries and provid-

Table 1. Key services provided by E-setu, 2003 (Source: UNDP India)

Service	Applications Received		Applications Attended	
	#	%	#	%
Jamabandi (land registration) Copy	4,830	43	4,765	43
Birth Certificate	1,725	15	1,702	15
Permanent Residence Certificate	1,607	14	1,600	15
Land Sale Permission	1,046	9	986	9
Other	2,090	19	2,025	18
Total	11,298	100	11,078	100

Figure 2. Demand for E-setu main services, 2003 (Source: UNDP India)

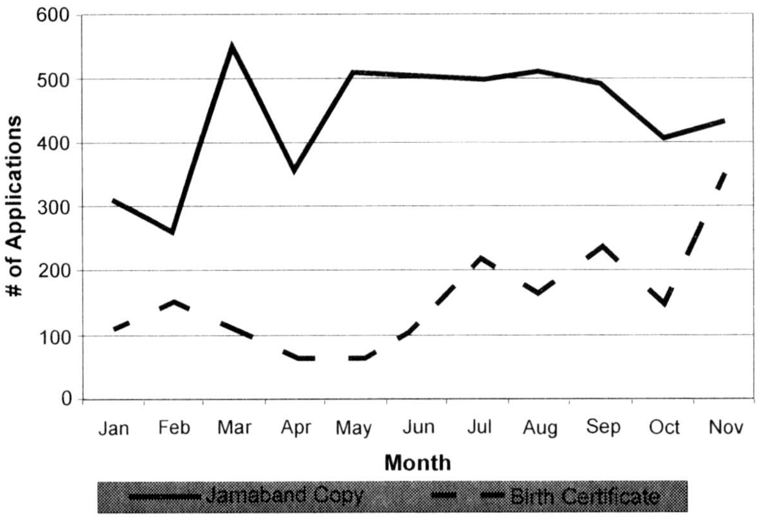

ing a friendly (and human) interface to citizens. Obtaining a birth certificate allowed citizens to also learn about both the benefits and rights this brings to them (access to education and health services in many states in India) and the 1989 UN Convention on the Rights of the Child.

By the end of 2003, when UNDP support and financing for the project ended, the project was rather successful. Majuli was now connected not only to the mainland but also to the Internet. The number of services and the number of users was constantly increasing and the quality of services was praised by the local people not only for being fast and efficient but also user-friendly. Kiosk operators were adequately trained and end-users did not have to use the computer equipment if they did not know how.

On the other hand, the project was also facing critical challenges. On the technology side, lack of constant power supply affected the performance of the kiosks as well as communications with Jorhat. Furthermore, the backend process of the delivery of certificates was yet to be enabled using ICT. But the main threat was the financial sustainability of the project as actual operating costs exceeded the revenue generated by the kiosks.[9]

Proposed solutions included increasing the price for services (charging at real costs for example) and enhancing the services offered to include items such as payment of the various

Table 2. E-setu benefits for the community (Source: UNDP India)

Item	**Before E-setu**	**With E-setu**
Transportation Costs	Rs 28.00/2 days	None
Incidental Expenses	Rs 20.00 /2 days	None
Processing Fees		Rs. 10.00
Intermediaries	One or more	None
Time required	Min. 2 persons-day	Half a person-day
Delivery	1–3 months	5 days max.
Total	Rs 48.00/2 person-days	Rs 10.00/Half person-day

consumer bills and taxes. Also considered were: health provision, agricultural and veterinary services, information on commodity prices (e-market), incorporation of electoral rolls and land records databases, video-conferencing services, and even academic counseling.

In 2004, the "E-setu society," a foundation of sorts under the chairmanship of the DC, was created with the purpose of supporting the overall project. The project increased the number of services to 50, and has reportedly become financially sustainable. As the project can be easily replicated in other districts, there are now plans to deploy it throughout the state of Assam. One example is the joint work with the Community Information Centers of the Ministry of Information Technology which setup a couple of centers in the island and was planning to adopt the E-setu model to enhance the services they offered (CIC, 2006).

It should be pointed out that "models" similar to E-setu seem to be proliferating in India. In 1999, the state of Maharashtra[10] launched the Integrated Citizen Facilitation Centers (SETU Project) which started in a mid-sized city and operates as a one-stop shop for citizens. The centers offer services for obtaining certificates, permits, affidavits, and so forth, and are now operating in 28 districts and 298 Taluka[11] places in the state. A 2002 case study on SETU described the initiative as a partial success given cumber paper procedures still in place and the limited range of services (Singh, 2002). Apparently, the latter still holds today, as reported by the programme's Web site.

But perhaps the best known and most successful example is e-seva (which means e-services) which started on a 1999 via a pilot launched in Hyderabad and which today also provides rural areas in the West Godavari district with access to government services ranging from certificates to payment of taxes while also supporting community based transactions.[12]

All in all, these examples show the great potential that ICTs can play in helping governments deliver basic services and information to the poorest communities.

CONCLUSION

To make a case for e-governance as a means for empowering the poor, a case in India which highlights successful efforts in applying ICT to improve basic service delivery in disadvantaged and marginalized areas was chosen. While the final impacts of these efforts are yet to be fully assessed and further research needs to be completed, the current evidence demonstrates the true potential ICTs have for empowering the poor.

The evidence also suggests that focusing on local governments (instead of national ones) where large segments of poor and marginalized populations inhabit (urban or rural), is a key entry point to make real impact on delivering primary services in an effective fashion. Correlation between these efforts and national policies for government decentralization seems to be a positive one, at least in the case of India.

One interesting link that emerges from this article is that between service delivery and people's awareness of their rights and duties as citizens via access to information. In principle, bringing basic services to poor/marginalized populations can indeed bring increased awareness of both the civic rights of people as well as the potential that ICTs can provide to them to have their voices heard in (local) public policy and decision making processes. And all this together can entice people in general and stakeholders in particular, to engage more directly with governance processes that will end up directly affecting their own lives.

REFERENCES

Accenture, Markle, & UNDP (2001). *Creating a development dynamic: Final report of the digital opportunity initiative*. New York: UNDP. Retrieved January 21, 2006, from http://www.opt-init.org/framework/onepage/onepage.html

Bhatnagar, A. (2006). *Paving the road towards pro-poor e-governance: Findings and observations from Asia-Pacific case studies*. Bangkok: UNDP, Asia Pacific Development Information Programme (APDIP). Available at http://www.apdip.net/projects/e-government/capblg/casestudies/Overview.pdf

Blattman, C., Jensen, R., & Roman, R. (2003). Assessing the need and potential of community networking for development in rural India. *The Information Society, 19*, 349-364.

Cecchini, S., & Scott, C. (2003). Can information and communications technology applications contribute to poverty reduction? Lessons from rural India. *Information Technology for Development, 10*, 73-84.

Chen, Y. N., Chen, H. M., Huang, W., & Ching, R. K. H. (2006). E-government strategies in developed and developing countries: An implementation framework and case study. *Journal of Global Information Management, 14*(1).

Coleman, S. (2005). New mediation and direct representation: Representation in the digital age. *New Media & Society, 7*.

Community Information Center, CIC. (2003). *E-setu: e-governance project in Jorhat*. East Jorhat, Assam, India: Nakachari. Retrieved August 15, 2007, from http://www.cic.nic.in/cicwebpages/Assam/jorhateast/About%20e-setu.htm

De', R., & Sen, C. (2004). The complex nature of e-government projects: A case study of Bhoomi, an initiative in Karnataka, India. *Lecture Notes in Computer Science, 3183*.

Governance Knowledge Center. (2004). *E-setu in Assam*. New Delhi: Department of Administrative Reform and Public Grievances, Ministry of Personnel, Public Grievances and Pensions, Government of India. Retrieved May 22, 2007, from http://203.200.1.75/GKC/GKC_WebUI/Portal/TaxonomyShowcase/ShowCaseStudy.aspx?CSID=404&tid=389

Harris, R., & Rajora, R. (2006). *Empowering the poor: Information and communications technology for governance and poverty reduction, a study of rural development projects in India*. Bangkok: UNDP, Asia Pacific Development Information Programme (APDIP). Retrieved May 23, 2007, from http://www.apdip.net/publications/ict4d/EmpoweringThePoor.pdf

Heeks, R. (2003a). *Understanding e-governance for development. IDPM i-government* (working paper 11). University of Manchester. Retrieved January 20, 2006, from http://www.sed.manchester.ac.uk/idpm/publications/wp/igov/igov_wp11.pdf

Heeks, R. (2003b). *Most e-government-for-development projects fail: How can risks be reduced?* (IDPM i-government working paper 14). University of Manchester. Retrieved January 20, 2006, from http://www.sed.manchester.ac.uk/idpm/publications/wp/igov/igov_wp14.pdf

ITU, International Telecommunication Union. (2006). *World telecommunication Iindicators database* (9th ed.). Geneva: ITU. Retrieved April 20, 2006, from http://www.itu.int/ITU-D/ict/publications/world/world.html

Macintosh, A. (2006). E-participation in policy-making: the research and the challenges. In P. Cunningham & M. Cunningham, (Eds.), *Exploiting the knowledge economy: Issues, applications and case studies*. IOS press.

Madon, S. (2004). Evaluating the development impact of e-governance initiatives: An explanatory framework. *Electronic Journal of Information System in Developing Countries, 20*(5).

NISG & i4D. (2006). ICTD project review workshop (Electronic version). *ICTD project newsletter, June*. Retrieved April 12, 2007, from http://www.i4donline.net/articles/current-article.asp?articleid=705&typ=Features

Pigato, M. (2001). *Information and communication technology, poverty, and development in sub-Saharan Africa and South Asia* (Africa region working paper series #20). Washington, DC: World Bank.

Rwanda Information Technology Authority, RITA. (2000). *Strategies towards the achievement of the missions for the realization of the vision for Rwanda by RITA*. Retrieved January 26, 2006, from http://www.rita.gov.rw/about/about_strategie.html

Serrao, S. A., & Sujatha, B. R. (2004). *Birth registration: A background note*. Bangalore, India: Community Development Foundation. Retrieved January 28, 2007, from http://www.ilpnet.org/news/BRWorkshop/BirthRegistration_Background.pdf

Singh, V. S. (2002). *SETU: A citizen facilitation center in India. E-government for development information exchange*. University of Manchester: IDPM. Retrieved February 2, 2007, from http://www.egov4dev.org/setu.htm

Souza, C. (2001). Participatory budgeting in Brazilian cities: Limits and possibilities in building democratic institutions. *Environment & Urbanization, 13*(1).

Tiku, K. M. (2004). *E-setu brings digital opportunities to Majuli helps island emerge out of time warp*. New Delhi: UNDP India News. Retrieved March 3, 2007, from http://209.85.165.104/search?q=cache:sDjuGxtf8rAJ:www.undp.org.in/UNDPNEWS/Jan-04/j-pg02.htm+undp+india+news+e-setu&hl=en&gl=us&ct=clnk&cd=1&client=firefox-a

United Nations. (2000). *Millennium development declaration*. Retrieved January 22, 2007, from http://www.un.org/millennium/declaration/ares552e.pdf

UNDESA. (2003). *World public sector report 2003: E-government at the crossroads*. New York: United Nations.

UNDESA. (2005). *Global e-governance readiness report*. New York: United Nations. Retrieved March 3, 2007, from http://www.lidec.futuro.usp.br/downloads/egovUN.pdf

UNDP. (2004). *Assam human development report 2003*. New Delhi: UNDP India. Retrieved January 25, 2006, from http://hdr.undp.org/docs/reports/national/IND_India/INDIA_2003_en.pdf

UNDP (2004). *Final evaluation report on sustainable development networking programme*. Retrieved January 28, 2006, from http://sdnhq.undp.org/docs/evals/SDNP-assessment-report-Final.pdf

UNDP. (2003). *Project e-setu: reaching the unreached*. New Delhi: UNDP India. Retrieved January 25, 2006, from http://www.undp.org.in/events/ict-goa/e-setu15-16dec03goa.PPT

UNHCHR. (1989). *Convention on the rights of the child*. Geneva: United Nations. Retrieved January 28, 2006, from http://www.unhchr.ch/html/menu3/b/k2crc.htm

World Bank. (2003). *World development report 2004: Making services work for poor people*. Washington, DC: World Bank. Retrieved Fabruary 3, 2007, from http://econ.worldbank.org/external/default/main?menuPK=477704&pagePK=64167702&piPK=64167676&theSitePK=477688

ENDNOTES

1 Participation is both a means and an in the process. Citizen-centric e-governance policies should end up enhancing stakeholder participation. But, on the other hand, this can be better achieved if stakeholders are involved in the process from the very start (Souza, 2001). Furthermore, e-participation can also be a tool on other non-ICT processes such as elections, parliaments, and many

public policy making issues not related to ICTs (Macintosh, 2006).

2 A citizens' survey in Brazil, conducted by Cisco, suggests that national priorities for e-government are exactly the opposite of those demanded by people. This seems to be the case in several other countries where applications such as e-visas or e-passports are being implemented while others more close to the poorest sectors of the population are not even in the launching pad. A similar point but from a different point of view is highlighted in World Bank (2003).

3 Sources for this case study include UNDP (2003), Tiku (2004), Community Information Center (2003), and Governance Knowledge Center (2004).

4 It is reported that the name E-setu was furnished by one of the dwellers of Majuli. This supposedly made the project even more attractive to local citizens and end users.

5 Majuli is located in the district of Jorhat, State of Assam. Full socio-economic and development details are depicted in the Assam Human Development Report (UNDP, 2003). In a nutshell, Assam is below the India average in terms of development with poverty rates around 35%. Furthermore, the ICT revolution that has taken place in India since the late 1980s has largely by-passed this state. At any rate, Jorhat, with a population of over 1 million is, by most indicators, the best-off district in the whole state. For details on the Majuli island, see http://en.wikipedia.org/wiki/Majuli. For a map of the Jorhat district, see http://www.mapsofindia.com/maps/assam/districts/jorhat.htm

6 The choice of Majuli to implement this project is intentional, given its physical isolation from the district itself. These conditions can also be easily found in most rural/underserved areas in developing countries. The difference is that in the former case building actual infrastructure would be very expensive vis-à-vis setting ICT solutions to deliver basic services and information.

7 In 2001, the literacy rate in the Jorhat district was 78%. See UNDP India HDR (2003).

8 The 1989 Registration of Birth and Death Act of the Government of India make such registration compulsory. However, 35 years later, only about 55% of the daily births were registered and even fewer had obtained birth certificates. See Serrao & Sujatha (2004).

9 This is a well known issue in the literature related to telecenters. For a presentation of this issue from a development point of view, see UNDP's Final Evaluation Report on Sustainable Development Networking Programme (2004).

10 For general information on Maharashtra, see http://en.wikipedia.org/wiki/Maharashtra. For SETU itself, see http://setu.maharashtra.gov.in/index.htm

11 Taluka is a unit of government in parts of India. See http://en.wikipedia.org/wiki/Tehsil for details.

12 Visit e-seva at http://esevaonline.com/ and the district project in http://www.westgodavari.org/. For a quick overview of district information see http://en.wikipedia.org/wiki/West_Godavari. A systematic case study of e-seva is included in Harris & Rajora (2006).

This work was previously published in International Journal of Electronic Government Research, Vol. 4, Issue 2, edited by M. Khosrow-Pour, pp. 1-11, copyright 2008 by IGI Publishing (an imprint of IGI Global).

Chapter 8
E-Governance in India:
From Policy to Reality—A Case Study of Chhattisgarh Online Information System for Citizen Empowerment (CHOICE) Project of Chhattisgarh State of India

Malathi Subramanian
University of Delhi, India

Anupama Saxena
Guru Ghasidas University Bilaspur, India

ABSTRACT

IT enabled e-governance in India seeks to achieve a more equitous, efficient, transparent, speedy, and corruption free service delivery system. But in the Indian context the challenge for e-governance is how to reduce the gap between the rich and poor towards a more inclusive governance system, benefiting particularly the poor in backward regions as in Chhattisgarh State, India.

INTRODUCTION

The concept of electronic governance (e-governance) covers the use of electronic technologies in crucial areas of public action in a democracy, particularly those affecting relations and interaction between public authorities and citizens in the provision and access of public services. It entails the incorporation of digital technology in the exercise of power which could be described as 'electronic democracy' and electronic public service delivery system. Thus, e-governance strengthens democratic institutions and processes in that it seeks to involve the public on a more regular basis in political choices so that their needs and priorities are respected and better addressed. This has led to electronic government (e-government), which has also led to the modernization of public administration while bringing it closer to civil society through the use of information and communication technologies. In order that e-governance becomes a reality, e-government must ensure that it involves the largest possible number of citizens through a participatory interaction and to this end employs information communication technologies. E-governance through information technology (IT) enabled services thus involves the re engineering and digitizing government processes, minimizing direct contacts between the government and citizens and institutionalizing transparency and accountability in public administration.

Theme and Purpose of the Study

This study aims at assessing some e governance schemes and mechanisms adopted for improving public service delivery in India from the perspective of the citizen. It explores the gap between the stated objectives of the ICT policies and their outcome. The study seeks to examine whether e-governance schemes and mechanisms adopted in public administration in India have improved service delivery systems for the citizens in a backward region. Have e-governance mechanisms and processes improved citizen access and brought the administration and citizen closer? Have the shortcomings of the earlier manual service delivery system been overcome? Are all citizens able to benefit from e-governance processes and mechanisms? These are some of the questions which this study attempts to address with the help of a sample survey of the working of some e-governance mechanisms grouped under Chhattisgarh online information system for citizen empowerment (CHOICE) in the Chhattisgarh state, which is one of the most backward regions in India.

The purpose of this study is to not merely take stock of the progress of the working of the e-governance processes and mechanisms which are expected to improve public delivery systems in Chhattisgarh State of India. The aim is also to share the lessons learnt with policy makers as well as with the development scholars in the field and to indicate further policy initiatives and correctives needed. The findings in this study are based on a sample survey of the working of the schemes grouped under CHOICE in Chhattisgarh State.

Methodology

The study is focused on one of the flagship projects of e-governance in the Indian state of Chhattisgarh called the Chhattisgarh online information system for citizen empowerment (CHOICE). So far it has been implemented only in the state capital, Raipur. Hence, the study is focused on Raipur and the sample survey pertains to that area. The study and the findings of the survey are based on both primary and secondary sources.

The primary sources included information collected directly from the citizens accessing services through both the operative modes, e-services, as well as the traditional/manual systems The secondary sources included information collected from the official government records, official Web sites, and records available at the CHOICE centres, CHOICE center agents, and other written and documented sources.

Design of the Survey, Sampling Method, and Size

The sample survey was carried out over 3 months during October to December 2006. The survey comprised unstructured interviews with three groups of citizens who visited the specific CHOICE centres for accessing the e-services. This was complemented by focused group discussions with some of the citizens accessing e-services. A total of nine group discussions were held in 3 of the 14 CHOICE centres involving 57 persons in all. Three group discussions were held separately in the government offices involving 22 participants in all.

Out of 14 CHOICE centers, 3 CHOICE centers were selected to collect information directly from the citizens visiting these centres. The three centres were chosen on the basis of the number of citizens availing the services during the 3 months duration. Thus, the three CHOICE centres chosen were: one with the maximum number of citizens, one with the minimum number of citizens, and one with the average number of citizens.

It was found that generally the centres located in crowded places, particularly those being run by persons already running cyber cafes or computer centres with a ready customer base, had more customers. Attempts were also made to ascertain whether the location, nature of public dealing, or anything else related to a CHOICE centre had any impact on the numbers availing the services, or on the quality of service delivered, but no such concrete evidence was found. Therefore the sample was based simply on the number of citizens availing the services.

Three focused group discussion comprising a minimum of 5 and maximum of 10 citizens selected randomly were conducted in each of the selected CHOICE centres to collect the information from the citizens directly. The participants for these focused group discussions were chosen from the list of names and addresses of the citizens collected from the CHOICE centres and from the records of concerned government offices. Participants were invited on the basis of whosoever was available and willing to participate. Yet care was taken that citizens availing various services were duly represented. The criteria for the selection of citizens for the survey were the type of services being accessed by them.

The following points were covered during the focused group discussions with citizens availing e-services:

1. awareness about the services offered and the process involved
2. the reasons for opting for e-governance
3. problems faced in availing e-governance services
4. perceived benefits of e-governance
5. measures to improve the services

The following points were covered in the group discussions with the citizens availing the traditional/manual delivery of services:

1. awareness about e-governance schemes and the manual delivery system and the process involved
2. reasons for not opting for e-governance system
3. problems encountered in the traditional/manual system

Further, owners of the all three CHOICE centres were interviewed and information was obtained on their experience of administering e-services and suggestions, if any.

In addition, five personal interviews of the concerned government officers were conducted: two from the Chhattisgarh CHIPS, the implementing agency and three from the *tahsil* (local government unit) office, where the citizens avail the government services in the traditional/manual mode. A semi structured interview schedule was used for this on general points of discussion for ascertaining the doubts, questions, problems, suggestions indicated by the citizens, and the CHOICE centre agents.

E-GOVERNANCE IN INDIA THROUGH IT ENABLED GOVERNMENT SERVICES (E-GOVERNMENT)

The Existing Manual System in India

In India, the existing manual system, rooted in the colonial mould of public administration historically, is driven by a spirit of authority and control over citizens rather than on a spirit of service to them. It is a system where information is considered to be a privilege rather than a citizen's right. In this mould, the process for access to many government services and schemes is quite cumbersome in operational terms involving negotiating long winding procedures and inconvenient steps involved (Gupta, 2006). This has encouraged patronage and corrupt practices in administration. It is a system ridden with inefficiency, lack of coordination among different departments, complete lack of transparency, and hardly citizen friendly. The common citizens are at the receiving end of a cumbersome, iniquitous, and unjust service delivery system rather than their being included in participatory good governance processes (Bandyopadhyay, 2007; Chakrabarty & Bhattacharya, 2003; Chandra & Mukherjee, 2000; Prasad, 2006).

IT Enabled Government Services in India

The emergence of e-governance in India can be traced back to the 1970s when the National Informatics Centre (NIC) started networking government departments to harness their knowledge repository as necessary steps towards ensuring good governance. In the more recent times e-governance has taken deep roots in India. Every state has an IT policy in place and a huge budget for e governance as well. It is claimed and expected that e-governance would help in improving the lives of the citizens by curbing corruption in administration through increased transparency in the functioning of various departments, and also by providing citizens speedy, easy, and better access to various government services be it through simple applications such as online form filling, bill sourcing and payments, or complex applications like distance education or telemedicine. During the last decade IT/ITES policies have been in the priority list of development agendas of national and state governments. Even a brief review of the IT/ITES policies and e-governance documents of the national and state governments of India give the impression that the thrust is on providing tangible solutions to their day to day problems. There is a consensus at policy level that the value of e-governance is not truly realized unless it touches and improves the lives of masses and is specially targeted at improving the livelihood of the poor and vulnerable.

E-GOVERNANCE IN CHHATTISGARH: POLICY AND IMPLEMENTATION

The Policy

Chhattisgarh (http://chhattisgarh.nic.in/) is a comparatively new state of India that came into existence in the year 2000. In spite of its rich natural resources and hard working population, Chhattisgarh is marked with severe poverty, backwardness, and illiteracy. More than 79% of the population of the state lives in rural or forest areas and the majority of them are poor without access to basic services such as clean drinking water and sanitation, basic healthcare services, primary education, and agricultural extension services, and so forth.

Right from its inception, in preparing the road map for the development of the state, the state of Chhattisgarh has recognized the importance of information and communication technology as a key enabler in its economic development and in improving the quality of life of its citizens. The state position paper (PriceWaterhouseCoopers, 2001) prepared as a roadmap just after the emergence of the state has a separate comprehensive chapter on information communication technology. The state government has an information communication technology minister and there is an autonomous society named Chhattisgarh information technology promotion society (http://chips.gov.in/) to formulate and implement ICT related policies and programmes in the state.

All policy documents related to ICT reflect that in a state where 45% of population is living below poverty line the value of IT will not be truly realized unless it touches and improves the lives of the masses. The IT/ITES policy (IT/ITES Policy, 2005) of the state declares that IT will be used in reaching out to the masses and improving their livelihoods, especially for its overwhelming scheduled caste and scheduled tribe (SC & ST) population across 44% forest area, which has largely remained untouched by modern development. The 'scheduled castes' (SC) is the socially disadvantaged section of the Indian society on the basis of the caste system, identified for affirmative action by the Indian constitution. The scheduled tribes (ST) are the indigenous people of India, the forest dwellers commonly known as tribes, identified for affirmative action by the Indian constitution.

The IT policy aims at reaching out to the masses by removing the bottlenecks such as limited access to market related information, information about government schemes, modern farming practices, and rainfall forecasts, and so forth. The stated purpose in this policy document is to set benchmarks for quality and excellence in state government services to citizens, state transactions with citizens and businesses, internal state governmental operations through the strategic deployment of information technologies, and a concentrated focus on the opportunities provided by the information and communication technologies.

Implementation

At the operational level, for implementation there are three agencies providing different types of services related to e-governance in the state:

1. **National Informatics Centre (NIC):** The NIC (http://home.nic.in/) is responsible for preparing and maintaining the Web sites for the state and for districts. These Web sites generally contain basic geographical, economic, social, and cultural information about the districts and sometimes information related to the government's schemes and programmes. The Web sites provide information in English. However, the common language of the state is Hindi. Only 7% of people in India can understand English (Census India, 1991) and Chhattisgarh is considered to be one of the most backward states of India where the literacy rate is only 65.18% (Literacy Rate In India, 2001) and 79% of the rural population has a literacy rate of only 61.2%. Hence, there is a possibility of language barrier with information being available in English where a majority understands Hindi. However, those who are in need of help either due to illiteracy or language are provided assistance in accessing services by the CHOICE service agents.
2. **Chhattisgarh information technology promotion society (CHIPS):** An intensive review of the official Web sites of the Chhattisgarh state (http://www.chhattisgarh.nic.in) and the official Web sites of the 16 districts of the state, links to which are available at the official Web site of the state developed and managed by NIC, shows that the nodal agency and prime mover for propelling IT growth and implementation of IT plans in the state is CHIPS (http://chips.gov.in/chips.htm), a registered society promoted by the government. The chief minister, who heads the state, also heads the high powered governing council of CHIPS. It includes the minister for finance & commercial taxes, minister for commerce & industry (including IT), minister for education, and minister for panchayat (rural local government) & rural development, the chief secretary of the state, eminent persons from IT industry, and a representative from the ministry of information technology of the central government of India. CHIPS is involved in implementation of some mega IT projects like Chhattisgarh online information system for citizen empowerment (CHOICE), e-gram Suraj (e-local governance), e-procurement, state wide area network (SWAN), e-treasury,

Bhuiyan (e-land records), and geographical information system (GIS).

3. In addition, there is the e-governance division of an IT solutions company (named 'Neev' meaning 'foundation' in Hindi language) called Cyber Infodev Pvt. Ltd., based in New Delhi. NEEV (http://www.e-governanceindia.com/) provides a range of products and services to assist the government in using the ICT tools to their advantage. Currently they are running 24 e-governance centres known as 'E–Sangawari Kendras' in Chhattisgarh. The following government services are provided by these E –Sangawari Kendras (Centres):
   - caste certificate for schedule casts and scheduled tribes
   - caste certificate for other backward classes (OBC)
   - income certificate
   - certificate of residence
   - birth certificate
   - death certificate
   - temporary driving license

THE CHHATTISGARH ONLINE INFORMATION SYSTEM FOR CITIZEN EMPOWERMENT (CHOICE)

The public services under e-governance are provided through a special scheme known as the Chhattisgarh online information system for citizen empowerment (CHOICE) which is the focus of this study. This scheme is implemented by CHIPS and seeks to provide a one stop solution for anywhere-anytime based government. The CHOICE project works on public private partnership model with the help of private operators appointed as CHOICE agents. Initially the project has been rolled out in the state capital city of Raipur. A total of 145 services are proposed to be provided under e governance. The Web site claims to have 30 government to customers (G2C) and numerous government to business (G2B) services, but at the ground level currently only a few services are available.

Services Provided under CHOICE

1. caste certificate for schedule casts and scheduled tribes
2. caste certificate for other backward classes (OBC)
3. income certificate
4. certificate of residence
5. birth certificate
6. correction in birth certificates
7. inclusion of child's name in ration card
8. death certificate
9. public complaints
10. payment of electricity bills

Out of the prospective 145 services listed for electronic implementation, currently only a few services as indicated are provided through e-governance.

E-Governance through CHOICE

The e-governance under CHOICE is provided through private agents who are authorized by the government to provide the listed services. These CHOICE agents are located in various parts of the city. The customer can obtain the hard copy of the prescribed form to be filled up to avail each service from these CHOICE centres. This is the same old form used by non e-governance service delivery system. There is no change in the contents of the forms. The customer has to attach hard copies of all necessary documents. There is no facility for online receiving/filling of forms. Before submitting the hard copies of the documents, a customer has to get it certified by some public authority as in the manual system to authenticate the documents. After submission of the form the CHOICE agent scans the form along with all attached documents and sends it through Internet to all the concerned officers in various departments. The CHOICE agent issues a receipt to the citizen mentioning the date on which he will be able to get the required certificate. A customer has to pay government fees for accessing the service and in addition pay the charges for scanning and getting them sent to the authorities through Internet by the CHOICE agent. Generally to avail one service, a customer has to pay roughly an amount between 70-100 Rupees (one Indian Rupee = 0.0227428 U.S.$ and one U.S.$ = 43.9700 INR approximately, depending on prevailing exchange rate). The status of the application can also be tracked online or on mobile phone. In the existing manual system there was no such facility. The concerned authorities check the forms and documents online and if any changes are needed or any other information or clarification is required they send back the form to the CHOICE agent. When the customer reaches the centre again on the given date to collect the document, in most of the cases, s/he is asked to submit a revised form or complete some missing information. No prior information regarding the deficiencies is given to the citizens. After the documents are submitted/completed the same process is repeated. The concerned officer, after checking the form to his/her satisfaction, sends it to the competent authority to digitally sign the computer generated certificate. This certificate is sent back to the CHOICE agent online and the citizen can get a print out of the certificate only from the CHOICE agent. The government has fixed a time limit for delivery of the requested document. This time limit varies from certificate to certificate and ranges from between 10-15 days. This system has an inbuilt mechanism to ensure that all submitted forms can only be processed in the sequence they are submitted. Unless the earlier applications are processed, the new ones can not be processed. This has definitely impeded the practice of bribing officials for getting work done on preferential basis and jumping the queue.

E-GOVERNANCE IN CHHATTISGARH: AN ASSESSMENT AND EVALUATION

Assessment

In the foregoing survey it was found that in the limited areas where e services are operative in Chhattisgarh, it is perceived to have improved service delivery and citizen satisfaction. Citizens availing the services find service delivery through e-governance better than the old system of governance on the whole. The survey also yielded these further findings.

Hassle Free Services to Citizen

At the CHOICE centres, while the common man is treated as a customer wanting to access the service at a cost, he is also a source of income to the agent. Hence s/he gets due and good attention as a customer. Whereas in the government departments the common man is an ordinary citizen requesting the concerned staff to get his/her work done. As the CHOICE centres are open from 9 a.m. to 10 p.m. on all working days and holidays and are situated in various locations of the city, citizens are free to visit them according to their convenience of time and place. The government offices are open only between 10.30 a.m. to 5.30 p.m. and are closed on all holidays, forcing citizens to visit them during their own working days and hours, causing inconvenience. Moreover, citizens can track the status of their application through Internet or on mobile phone, unlike in the existing manual system.

E-governance through IT enabled services wherever in operation, has thus brought about a subtle paradigm shift from the erstwhile control oriented colonial and condescending attitude of Indian administration to the market framework of operation based on speed, efficiency and service oriented government process, and mechanism where services are products offered against payment of the marked price.

Table 1. Number of citizens availing the public services through e-governance and old manual system. A comparative sample from Chhattisgarh based on survey conducted in October-December 2006

Sl no	Name of the service	E-governance*	Old system of governance**
1.	Caste certificate(SC/ST)	135	16
2.	Caste certificate(OBC)	506	167
3.	Income certificate	137	49
4.	Certificate of residence	728	252
5.	Birth certificate	2245	318
6.	Correction in birth certificate	28	Nil
7.	Inclusion of child name	173	Nil
8.	Death certificate	169	56
9.	Public complaints	4	Nil
10.	Payment of electricity bills	Data not available	Data not available
	Total	4,210	858

*Data collected from: * CHOICE centres ** Government offices*

Curb on Corruption

It is perceived that there is no need to bribe the government official to get the work done under the e-government as there is no direct transaction with the government officials. Due to a computerized process there is no scope left for non submission of documents, manipulation of information, or tampering with the information given. There is also no scope of preferential treatment in the processing of applications which follows an electronic queue system which cannot be jumped by those with power and capacity to pay.

However, during the survey it was also found that those who do not have all completed documents or information for getting a service, or those who want to get the work done on a preferential basis, can still adopt this method through gratification of corrupt officials as the manual system is still in parallel operation. In fact, some people even went to the extent of suggesting that the old system is more suitable as it was open to manipulation if they did not have complete documentation. For example, one student needed a cast certificate within one day but under the e-governance system he would have been able to get it only after 15 days as it is a computerized system and the applications are processed according to the sequence in which they are submitted and there was little chance of jumping the queue. But he got the job done by paying a bribe and got his certificate within a day under the manual system. So there is a perception among some that in a way even today the old system could deliver speedily if only one could pay a bribe.

Restriction on Malpractices

As the whole process is computerized in the e governance process, there is no scope of submitting false/incomplete documents and information. Nor can records or data be manipulated or tampered with once the information obtained is computerized. Easy and convenient data retrieval helps in authentic information storage and retrieval for administrative use.

Reduced Scope for Traditional Administrative Arrogance

Since the services are being provided by the private agents and citizens are paying for the services, the dependence on government officials has drastically reduced and their traditional monopoly in providing these services has got eroded. This has also struck at the feeling of administrative arrogance and superiority of governmental officials over the citizens. Moreover, citizens are free to avail the services from any one of the 14 service providing centers. With a decentralized service delivery system with services as products being sold at a price, the citizen as the consumer of these services/ products has the scope of expecting quality service with speed, efficiency, and accuracy for the cost paid.

Equity Dimensions

In an automatic electronic system where the applications are processed in the sequence of their submission the earlier patronage based iniquitous practices, such as the processing the applications of the favorites on a priority basis, are completely eliminated. Each citizen is equal to the other in digital presence and gets treated equally in the service delivery.

New Employment Opportunities

Since most of the e-governance services in the state are outsourced to, and are provided by private agents, it has led to the expansion of employment opportunities in this new sector.

Citizen Empowerment through the E-governance Mechanism and Process of the Right to Information

The newly implemented Right to Information Act (RTI, 2005) in India is an important step towards citizen empowerment through transparency in governance mechanisms and processes as the right to information has equipped the common citizen to get ay information from any government office within a time frame. Penalties are attached to the denial of such information asked for by citizens spelling out the mandatory nature of the implementation of the RTI. Computerized processing of information and service delivery has facilitated the actual implementation of e governance and RTI mutually.

Cost and Time Effective

Citizens using e-governance schemes have felt that due to online working it saves the time spent in the files moving from table to table within a department or between departments in the hierarchy of administration thus cutting down what is called 'red tapism.' Online government processing is also increasingly paperless, saving considerable expenditure on paper. Computerized data base of all records is easier and cheaper for government in terms of maintenance, retrieval, and cost.

Increased Revenue to State Government

The e-services are available only against payment of charges, which was not the case in the manual system formally. In the old system though the services are free of charge, the respondent citizens reiterated in the current survey that they are generally forced to pay the same or more amount in cash as bribe in government offices to get their work done in time failing which unnecessary delays and harassment could be caused to them. Though the citizen may be spending the same amount but the money was not going into the government coffers but into the pockets of corrupt officials. As such transaction between the government official and citizen is unofficial and no receipt is issued, the government does not gain in revenue.

Under the e-governance services the citizens have to pay a service fees ranging from 20-40 Rupees to the government for accessing the e-governance schemes. In the electronic system the fees are paid to the CHOICE agent who issues a computer generated receipt to the customer. Unless a receipt is generated, the computer will not accept the application of the citizen. Hence there is no chance of getting the service done without paying the prescribed fees. There is a centralized monitoring system through which at the end of the day the collection from all CHOICE centres is calculated. The amount of the money thus collected is distributed between the government and the service providers again through a centralized computerized system adding to the revenue of the government as well as to the declared official income of the agents.

EVALUATION

Not Fully Operative Yet

Out of 145 services proposed to be covered under the e governance, only seven are fully in operation so far. This is resulting in decreasing interest of CHOICE agents in continuing partnering the services as lesser number of services to be offered means lesser income and more cost of running the services. It is therefore not cost effective if it is not fully operative. The sample data show that during October 2006 to December 2006 only 4210 citizens have accessed e-governance schemes in 14 CHOICE centres which means that the monetary inflow is not very encouraging. Such a low turnover is not found to be sufficient to run the CHOICE centres and is therefore not an attractive proposition from the business angle which could make it unsustainable.

The Old System Still Continues

The services that are covered under the e-governance are also provided through the old system. Those who want a privileged position in having their case handled and do not mind paying a gratification for getting their work done on priority through patronage links have a scope to get their work done through the old system. Some may even prefer this channel for immediate attention and speedy disposal of their case instead of going through a more transparent but non patronage based e governance. A major part of the whole process is still dealt with through traditional hard copies and customers have to visit the CHOICE centres in person to obtain and submit the application as well as to receive the results.

The Service Delivery Sometimes Takes More than Stipulated Time in E-Governance

The official time limit set is around 10 to 15 days to deliver the service to the citizen but mostly it takes more than 25 days in practice. The reasons for this delay are found to relate to:

1. Submission of incomplete information: Generally the applications submitted by the customers are not complete with regard to information required due to various reasons. In the traditional system a person submitted the application to the concerned officer directly, who informed the applicant about any further information or document required if that was not submitted along with the application. As services in the e governance mode are delivered by the private agents who are a step removed from the official governance structure, most of the times they themselves are not aware about the information or documents required. Generally therefore, incomplete applications reach the concerned authority in incomplete form causing unnecessary delays. The problem is particularly severe with the customers who are illiterate as in Chhattisgarh where there are a large number of them.
2. The language is official and technical: Often it is difficult for customers or the agents to understand the technical terms used in the government parlance correctly and provide the right information accordingly.

3. Lack of time bound response from administration: No time line is followed by concerned government echelons to process the applications. Hence delays of the old kind persist. Added to this are infrastructural problems like power cuts and link failures for justifying delays. The lackadaisical attitude of administrative authorities is evident from the fact that even though the services may not be delivered to citizens within the prescribed time limit, in official records it is shown as having been delivered to them in time. Thus a most interesting fact is that the e-governance initiatives that are said to evolve a corruption free administration are themselves not corruption free when administered by operators who are not so scrupulous.

Elitist Bias: Accessible More to Those Who Can Pay

E-governance is more easily adopted by and steered towards purposes that are of interest to the privileged few who can pay for it. A customer who wants to avail any service through e-governance has to spend roughly between 70 to 100 Rupees which includes official fees for service delivery and charges for scanning the documents and forms and sending it to the concerned government office through e-mail by the CHOICE agent. Obviously a citizen who is living below the poverty line (earning less than one U.S. dollar per day) can hardly afford it as is the case with a large number in Chhattisgarh. In a state where 45% of the population is living below the poverty line, paid e-governance services are sure to benefit the elite section of society more. Hence, in such a highly unequal society, e-administration is fraught with the potential to congeal the divide between the rich and the poor.

Urban Bias

There is also a clear urban bias in implementation of e-governance in Chhattisgarh. There is a tension between the policy aims and its operational impact. Though the democratic commitment of the policy is clear in emphasizing the need of using ICT for reaching the last digital node in the society and aims to particularly include the rural population, all e-governance projects are implemented in primarily urban areas due to the compulsions of the market in operational terms since the delivery of the services/products at the cutting edge is in private hands. This contradiction between the stated intentions of the e-governance policies and schemes emanating from a modernizing democratic government on the one hand and the market compulsions at the operational level on the other may sharpen the stark inequalities of the society instead of reducing them. Apart from threatening to develop a divide between those who can pay and those who can not pay for e-governance schemes there is threat of another kind, that of an urban–rural digital divide.

Thus most e-governance initiatives of the state are implemented in urban areas. If e-governance means improved delivery of government services to all citizens, the present model of e-governance in the state seems to provide these services to urban elites only at present. In addition, implementation of e-governance initiatives through private vendors has yet to reach the rural areas which are already marked by poverty, lack of awareness, and literacy and lack of infrastructure.

Gender Gap

Added to the rural urban divide is a further question of whether or to what extent the e-governance schemes are accessible to women both in the urban and the rural areas. Not a single CHOICE centre was found to be run by a woman. The CHOICE centres sampled here are basically cyber cafés providing Internet services to customers, most of them male in urban areas and women found to be completely absent in the rural areas. The reasons for this are many, ranging from the socio cultural factors to the patriarchal and male centric features of the social milieu which impedes women from accessing the e-governance schemes.

BOTTLENECKS IN EFFECTIVE E-GOVERNANCE

Lack of Political Will

In democratic countries like India political will is the most decisive driving force to successfully initiate crucial changes like transforming conventional governance to e-governance. In Chhattisgarh however, while there is a comprehensive policy in place, a congruent enthusiasm for implementation of the policies effectively seems to be lacking and a strong political will seems yet to evolve due to various reasons. Political leaders are still prone to use their power and position for building and strengthening their affiliations among the electorate through the patron client relationships particularly in rural and remote regions like in Chhattisgarh. The modern e-governance mechanisms are not amenable to this as it takes away some of the power of patronage. Hence, it might take a little more time for the political leaders to realize and actualize the potential of e-governance in citizen empowerment and in addressing the issues such as poverty alleviation, employment generation, and speedy service delivery and so forth, considered important by both people and leaders alike.

Need for Change of Attitude and Colonial 'Mind Set' of the Administration

Concern about reforming administration in India is not something new and e-governance is only the latest in the series. But the success of any effort requires transcending old restrictive mind sets of those in administration and bureaucracy. It is widely perceived both by the political leaders as well as people at large that it is extremely difficult to change the congealed mindset of the bureaucracy to bring in effective governance reforms as it requires a stupendous task of transforming the colonial mindset into a service oriented, transparent, and democratic one. As stated by one of the ministers of an Indian state in the context of e-governance in India "It had proved "extremely difficult" to change the mindset of bureaucracy to bring in effective governance reforms"(Gowda, 2004). This particular mind set is responsible for a delay in computerization of various government departments that acts as the speed breaker against covering all government services under e-governance. Given the colonial legacy of public administration structures and processes in a society which still has feudalistic features, coupled with the top down administrative approach and attitude, information is still considered as power in the hands of those who administer and not as an entitlement of citizens. Any move towards transparency of government structures and processes are thus viewed with apprehension and therefore any measure that aims at changing the status quo of this power structure is resisted by the bureaucracy. E-governance which has a capacity to collapse administrative distances with its immense potential for information dissemination and its wide access, is one such measure which may be accepted technologically but viewed with apprehension where it means transparency in governance structures and processes. Added to this is the administrative arrogance and egoism sometimes especially among the senior administrators who are not very well adapted to the technological revolution but do suffer from the false ego that they know everything, coupled with the assumption that anything they do not know is worthless! This attitude is often a major hurdle in the implementation of the e-governance projects. Moreover, the potential of e-governance to lessen corruption has also made the lower administrative echelons especially wary of accepting e-governance mechanisms and processes as some of them consider it as a hurdle for their earning through informal and unaccounted for channels.

Lack of Infrastructure, Especially in Rural Areas

Chhattisgarh is one of the most backward states of India. This backwardness is also reflected in IT related infrastructure. A total of only 3.8 % of households are having telephone connections and the percentage in rural areas is only 1.8 (Census India, 2001). Chhattisgarh was ranked second last in the list of state wise tele density list with an urban tele density of only 5.6 and rural tele density of only 0.4 where as the all India average was 15.2 for urban areas and 1.5 for rural areas (Ministry of Information Communication Technology, 2003). Apart from this, Chhattisgarh has also ranked poor in other measures related to e-preparedness/e-readiness (Ministry of Information Communication Technology, 2005). In the scale for e-readiness—Indian states Chhattisgarh was ranked as only an average achiever. Apart from this there are some other technical problems of connectivity like slow speed of broadband. Due to slow speed and poor accessibility of the Internet, many times agents have to visit government offices or banks personally to complete the transactions which completely defeats the purpose of e-governance mechanisms.

General Neglect of Rural Areas in Development Planning of the State

There has been a clear urban bias in the development agenda of the state government in general. Seventy-nine percent of the state population resides in rural areas. Most of the rural areas are remote from industrial zones, port facilities, urban markets, and urban employment opportunities, thus hampering their opportunities for economic growth.

Poverty

Chhattisgarh is comparatively a poorer state of India. More than 45% of the state population is living below the officially declared poverty line. The average annual income per person in the state is only 19,000 Rupees (Front Line, 2006) below the national average of 23,222 Rupees per person, the highest in the list is Chandigarh that has an annual per capita income of 67,370 Rupees (Rajasekharan, 2006). The expansion of e-governance requires huge financial resources which the state is not able to generate. The only option is to provide e-governance services to the citizen through private partners. But private agencies are driven by profit motives and as Chandigarh is a poor state its people do not have the paying capacity, the private sector may not be interested in running the services at a loss to itself as its business interests are not served.

SOME SUGGESTIONS

1. All government services should be covered under the e-governance umbrella at the earliest. To facilitate this, a sensitization campaign emphasizing the merits of e-governance should be organized for political leaders and top bureaucrats.
2. The old system of providing government services should be eliminated at the earliest.
3. All related departments should be fully computerized.
4. A comprehensive orientation and training in the presence of concerned government officers should be imparted to the agents who run the centres, regarding the filling in of application form and submission of related documents.
5. The cost of availing e-governance schemes is very high. Subsidized options should be

available at least for those who are living below the poverty line.

6. Some centres should specifically be allotted to women agents to encourage women to use the services of e-governance themselves to end their dependence on men for such work.
7. In rural areas the e-governance services should be provided for some time at least by the existing government administrative machinery and not by the private agents in order to make e governance services accessible and affordable to rural population.
8. To ensure that the emerging information society does not serve to further isolate rural population but to mainstream them, first and foremost the rural sector should figure as the priority area within the whole development agenda of the government in general and in ICTs' agenda in particular. Otherwise only the urban populace would stand to benefit from e-governance.
9. Every step of public service delivery should be covered under e-governance.
10. Experiences about the good practices should be shared, and wherever necessary capacity building programmes for formulation and implementation of e-governance activities should be organized. In India, there has been no dearth of such activities organized by national and international agencies but the concentration has been in metro cities or in the cities where ICT is in a more developed stage. The need of the hour is to include remote areas which are lagging behind, as in Chhattisgarh, for such activities on priority basis.

CONCLUSION

E-governance through IT enabled government services, which is the thrust of the new ICT based initiatives in India, is aimed at addressing the problems which besiege the old manual system which still exists in a large measure. In India the IT enabled government services are offered through a public private partnership to provide one-stop services such as bill payment, issue of licenses, birth/death certificates, and so forth, to citizens through a digitalized system. The actual delivery of services is done through private franchisees compensated on the basis of the volume of transactions. The incentives are structured to provide service with courtesy and minimal delay. The digitalized system seeks to be more speedy, efficient, and transparent compared to the old manual system based on direct government citizen contact.

What is required however is to eliminate or transcend the existing manual, time consuming processes open to patronage and corruption. Particularly to eliminate corruption, which is the bane of the existing governmental processes in India, there is need to eliminate unnecessary government citizen interactions. Electronic interaction should replace face to face interaction as far as possible in order to reduce corruption. This would also help in checking private citizens from becoming a party to corrupt practices by using loopholes in an inefficient milieu.

Eventually it is not IT by itself but its use in government processes that will lead to innovative changes towards efficient service delivery. E-governance and IT enabled government services will entail changes of a fundamental nature in the mechanisms and processes of administration including perhaps a change in the congealed colonial mindset, attitude, and approach overrunning Indian administration.

There is of course the issue of the cost of IT enabled services. IT enabled services involves a huge investment in terms of finances. Creating information systems and maintaining them by itself is a huge expenditure. Within the public private partnership framework, the cost attached to the services cannot be avoided. However, a large fraction of the population which is poor, illiterate, or does not have access to interact electronically would pose a serious challenge to e-governance. It may end up in governments running and maintaining an expensive electronic system for the few who can afford to pay, and a parallel manual system which is expensive (in that it may involve payment of gratification to corrupt officials) but inefficient for the vast majority of the masses. This would fly in the face of the basic aim of e-governance in India which is to collapse the distance between administration and citizen and making government services accessible to the last digital node in the society with speed, efficiency, and transparency.

Chhattisgarh is a comparatively new state with priorities of addressing the basic needs of people like water, livelihood, health, and education. Though at a very rudimentary stage the efforts of introducing e-governance are appreciable, especially taking into consideration the bottlenecks indicated in the article. The sample data used here clearly shows that the public services covered under e-governance aim to become citizen friendly and perhaps also mean a less corrupt system and therefore are preferred by the citizens. But at the same time the findings of the present study clearly indicate a wide gap between the objectives stated in the IT/ITES policies and other documents of the state government about the use of information communication technologies in governance and the ground reality. The thrust of the policy is to use ICT for development, especially for improvement of the lives of the rural poor, but the present shape of the e-governance in the state is far from this goal. Unless the e-governance is accessible to all and touches the lowest digital node, there is a danger of accentuating and further widening the pre existing gap between the rural and urban and the rich and the poor.

REFERENCES

Bandyopadhyay, D. (2007). *Land, labour and governance*. Calcutta: Worldview.

Chakrabarty, B., & Bhattacharya, M. (2003). *Public administration: A reader*. New Delhi: Oxford University Press.

Chandra, B., Mukherjee, M., & Mukherjee, A. (2000). *India after independence: 1947-2000*. New Delhi: Penguin Books.

Front Line. (2006). Special feature on Chhattisgarh. *Front Line, November*. Retrieved September 23, 2007, from http://pay.hindu.com/ebook%20-%20ebfl20061103part6.pdf

Gupta, D.N. (2006). *Business process re-engineering and change management: Learning from e-governance projects*. In R. K. Mitra (Ed.), *E-government: Macro issues*. New Delhi: Gift Publishing.

Ministry of Information Communication Technologies. (2005). *E-preparedness of states of India*. Retrieved August 25, 2007, from http://www.mit.gov.in/download/e-ready/EX_sum.PDF

Prasad, K. (2006). *Indian administration: Politics, policies and prospects*. New Delhi: Dorling Kindersley.

PriceWaterhouseCoopers. (2001). *Position paper, Chhattisgarh, Chapter V*. Retrieved August 20, 2007, from http://chhattisgarh.nic.in/opportunities/Information%20Technology.pdf

This work was previously published in International Journal of Electronic Government Research, Vol. 4, Issue 2, edited by M. Khosrow-Pour, pp. 12-26, copyright 2008 by IGI Publishing (an imprint of IGI Global).

Chapter 9
E-Governance and ICT Enabled Rural Development in Developing Countries:
Critical Lessons from RASI Project in India

G. Kannabiran
National Insitute of Technology, India

M. J. Xavier
SRM University, India

T. Banumathi
Kongu Arts and Science College, India

ABSTRACT

Proactive economic policies combined with the ICT revolution of the past decade have brought about many changes in managing businesses and organizations in developing countries like India. The prowess achieved through this revolution has also led to exploitation of ICT for better governance and rural development. As a result, several ICT projects have been initiated to foster improved governance and facilitate rural development by appropriately linking public and private institutions. RASI (Rural Access to Services through Internet) is one such government-private initiative to promote e-governance and ICT enabled rural development. Our longitudinal research is to analyze the factors related to access to and usage of the services offered through this project in Erode district of the state of Tamilnadu in India. Data for this empirical research was collected through survey and interviews during two time periods (2004 and 2006). Our findings show that the project has largely deviated from its objectives due to lack of government support, non-scalable technology and ownership issues. Based on our findings, we provide a set of recommendations to policy makers and implementing agencies.

INTRODUCTION

Even after 50 years of independence and successive planning efforts, significant rural development in India is still a dream rather than reality. One of the distinguishing features of India is that the rural India constitutes 700 million people living in 600,000 villages. These villages contain 72 percent of India's labour force and they are primarily employed in agriculture, forestry, fishing, etc. Delivering basic services and offering scope for economic and social development for these rural masses have been the biggest challenges faced by the governments. However, ICT (Information and Communication Technology) revolution of the past decade and key economic policies of the government have facilitated a new way to bring about development. While viewing government as a service provider, citizen is a consumer of public goods and services. Today's broad exposure of the public to private sector products and services in the new economy has caused expectations of government services to rise. In this research paper, we have attempted to evaluate empirically the overall effectiveness of one such Internet-based service delivery network. Our longitudinal study relates to the project RASI, kiosk based service delivery network, which is implemented in the state of Tamilnadu in India. The paper is organized as follows: We present a review of relevant literature followed by research questions and methodology. We then present the summary of the project, data analysis and a detailed discussion of our findings. We conclude with a set of implications for policy makers and directions for future research.

REVIEW OF LITERATURE

We begin our literature review by defining the term 'e-governance'. ICT, especially the Internet technologies, has changed the way how core activities are carried out in organizations and institutions. It is obvious that governments around the world are also in the pursuit of deployment of ICT-based solutions for facilitating good governance. Role of ICT in government has two dimensions. The first dimension is the use of ICT to automate internal processes of government and establish linkages across various departments. This is commonly referred as "e-government" which relates to the processes and structures pertinent to the electronic delivery of government services to the public (Fraga, 2002; Saxena, 2005). Perhaps, the second dimension of ICT use in government referred as "e-governance" is the ultimate revolution in bringing together all the stakeholders (citizen, private organizations, NGOs, research community etc) to link with e-government systems. Therefore, e- governance is an evolutionary and ICT based model that seeks to realize processes and structures for harnessing the potentialities of ICT at various levels of government and others for the purpose of enhancing good governance (Bedi et al., 2001; Holmes, 2001; Okot-Uma, 2000, Saxena, 2005). Although, the terms e-government and e-governance are used interchangeably by researchers, for the purpose of our research, we follow a broader definition stated by Commonwealth centre for e-governance: "e-governance is the commitment to utilize appropriate technologies to enhance governmental relationships, both internal and external, in order to advance democratic expression, human dignity and autonomy, support economic development and encourage fair and efficient delivery of services (Riley, 2001). Many other authors have also defined e-governance in this broader perspective covering both internal and external linkages through use of ICT (Heeks, 2001; Marche & McNiven, 2003; Zwahr et al. 2005; Grant & Chau, 2005). Probably, the next stage in use of ICT will be the evolution of "e-democracy" which refers to the processes and structures that encompass all forms of electronic communication between government and the citizens, such as information sharing, voting, polling, or discussion, thereby enabling citizens to participate in the government's policy making (Gronlund, 2001; Kannabiran et al, 2005).

The ever increasing e-governance opportunities coupled with the challenges in exploiting such opportunities have led to the development of framework and models for e-governance. Gartner's model of e-government identifies four phases- presence, interaction, transaction, and transformation (Gartner, 2001). Finger and Pécoud (2003) have proposed a model by distinguishing three different types of actors involved (public sector, private sector, third sector), three different policy functions (global, national, local), and three different degrees of making use of the ICT (policy making, regulation, operations). Kannabiran et al (2005) have proposed a model for managing citizen relationship by identifying functionalities namely 'identify', 'design', 'serve' and 'protect'. Marche and McNiven (2003) have proposed a model based on what is called "focus' and 'centricity'. Their model covered both citizen-centric and government-centric applications in e-governance. European Commission (Europa, 2001) has proposed a four-stage methodology for assessing the level of availability and sophistication of e-government services, which included information, interaction and transaction. Xavier and Pillai (2003) have proposed framework for government-to-citizen service delivery which highlighted the need for partnership of government, industry and academia for e-governance effectiveness. Nath (2001) classified e-governance models in terms of broadcasting/wider-dissemination, critical flow, comparative analysis, e-advocacy/lobbying and interactive-service.

There are many benefits that e-governance can bring to the stakeholders, especially in developing countries. Previous researchers have captured a number of noticeable benefits through empirical studies. Such benefits included faster delivery of services (Palanisamy, 2004), transparency in government decision making (Singla, 2002; Prattipati, 2003), accountability (World Bank 2001; Singla, 2002), real-time access to up-to-date information (Verton, 2000; Deakins & Dillon, 2002), administrative efficiency (Zipf, 2001), access to Internet technology (Bhatnagar, 2002), revenue generation (Deakins & Dillon, 2002), empowering women (Madon, 2004), reduction of transaction cost (Tulip, 2000), citizen-centered services (Sealy, 2003, Radhakumari, 2006). Along with these benefits, several initiatives are attempting to shape up the capability of individuals, communities and organizations (Garnham, 2000; Mansell, 2001).

The progress in e-governance in industrialized countries was largely prompted by the availability of Internet technology and became possible due to the fact that their internal operations of the government were already using ICT-based systems (Saxena, 2005). In the case of many developing countries like India, ICT use in the public sector was very low for a long time and therefore they had poor ICT infrastructure (Bhatnagar and Bjorn-Andersen, 1990; Yong, 2003). For developing countries, achieving first stage of e-governance itself took long time. Therefore, for many governments in the developing economies, "e-governance" was a significant, expensive and transformational change (Saxena, 2005). Despite high level of technology penetration in some developing countries, the gaps between digital haves and have-nots are growing in an exponential manner (Palanisamy, 2004). Based on an empirical study of 40 e-governance initiatives in developing and transitional countries, Heeks (2002) found that 35% of the e-governance projects were considered as 'total failures', meaning either 'not implemented' or 'abandoned immediately', 50% were classified as 'partial failures' and only 15% were classified as 'success', meaning these projects attained their major goals. According to Heeks (2001) developing countries had to accommodate certain unique conditions, needs and obstacles due to poor infrastructure, corruption, weak educational systems, and unequal access to technology. The high failure rates of e-governance projects, especially in rural areas of developing countries, could be due to inadequate application of strategic management principles in the life cycle of e-governance projects (Suri, 2005). It is also advocated that e-governance initiatives need to be understood from strategic management perspective.

Key challenges faced while implementing e-governance projects have been identified as lack of e-readiness and design-reality gaps for steering e-governance projects from failure to success (Heeks, 2003). According to Singla (2002) the key factors preventing rural communities from reaping the benefits of ICT are lack of awareness of ICT, lack of access facilities, language barriers in using the Internet, lack of local language information products, non-availability of government information online and Internet connectivity. Gupta et al. (2004) have identified proactive government, commitment, literate computer savvy population, framework for security, IT architecture, administrative reforms, connectivity through liberalization, and abound IT skills of private sector as success factors of e-governance in developing countries. E-governance in developing countries is a new opportunity for re-organizing the approaches, instruments and the logic of governing. However, unclear objectives and insufficient planning have led to inadequately designed systems thus not delivering the desired services (Basu, 2004). Further, according to Suri (2005), the methodology of formulating plan proposals in India is not adequate for e-governance projects initiated from central government and implemented through state governments. Gaps in project planning, strategy formulation and strategy implementation are the major causes for failure of e-governance projects. Tan et al. (2005) have argued that there is a rising need to view strategic stakeholder management as an imperative to e-governance. In order to ensure the overall success of e-governance, effectiveness parameters of the programmes need to be pre-defined and factors of change need to be managed carefully to give the real benefits to different stakeholders (Kumar et al. 2004). Through a survey, Madon and Kiran (2002) have found citizen attitudes towards government are changing as a result of an increased sense of trust and reciprocity between citizen and the state. Other related problems concerning implementation of e-governance initiatives included connectivity (Heeks, 2001; Rao, 2004), policy constraints (Rao, 2004;), data sharing (Sethi & Sethi, 2006), re-engineering of government systems (Rao, 2003), project management (Sethi & Sethi, 2006) inadequacy of training (Radhakumari, 2006), political scenario (Singla, 2002), access difficulty due to local languages (Rao, 2004), national security (Reily, 2005), the ability of individuals and communities to avail the services of e-governance (Madon, 2004), background administrative reforms (Madon, 2004), technology infrastructure (Singla, 2002), resistance to change (Singla, 2002), institutionalization of systems (Singla, 2002) and allocation of funds (Singla, 2002).

In developing economies like India, common man was not able to acquire the home computers and communications facilities to access government services. Therefore, many of the e-governance initiatives in India have involved designing and deploying community-based technologies that can be accessed at lower cost (Riley, 2005). Further most of the e-governance projects are combined with economic development projects that use the e-governance infrastructure. As a part of the structure for delivering services, a number of countries like India have attempted to set up citizen interface centers that will enable the general public to access the government services. An important feature that can be added to this process is 'self service', where the citizens can configure the service initially while registering and get support throughout their lifetime. Self-service by the citizens help the governments achieve the dual purpose of reducing cost as well as improving service levels (Kannabiran et al, 2005). Kiosks are personal computers that have been modified to withstand long hours of usage and operation in extreme conditions (Sargent & McLvor, 1996; Corcoran, 1994). Such kiosks are being located in remote locations that are connected with service providing agencies via telephone lines or wireless networks. Some kiosks have additional devices and capabilities, such as a printer, a telephone, a credit card reader, and/or a bar code scanner. Some kiosks have potential to provide citizens convenient access to information and services and to bridge the digital gap in the society (Ni & Ho, 2005). According to Morris et al (1995), there are three general types of kiosk systems. First types of kiosks are used for information dissemination. Second types of kiosks are used for interactive requirements through which individuals seek and clarify information from a central location. Third types of kiosks are used to carry out business activities, including financial transactions. These kiosks may be designed for hard or soft financial information to be carried across the network. Appropriateness to application, ease of use, aesthetics and ergonomics, physical structure, security and deployment are some of the guideline for kiosk implementation (Tung & Tan, 1998). Suitable user interface is one of the important pre-requisites of successful kiosk based deliveries. Maguire (1999) advocates aspects such as defining user requirements, location and encouraging use, physical access, introduction and instructions, language selection, privacy, help, structure and navigation, and customization as key user interface features to be included in the kiosk design.

Apart from other issues of implementing e-governance, kiosk-based service delivery is faced with additional problems. Rural development through ICT- based initiatives suffer due to choice of service delivery personnel, level of usage of service by citizen, need for restructuring government process and institutionalization of support (Srinivasan, 2004). Since the applications related to the employment generation and livelihood did not get attention, poor rural citizens gradually withdrew from using the kiosks (Rao, 2003). The kiosk operators do not find it remunerative to run the services due to very low volume of transactions with the existing services (Srinivasan, 2004). Perhaps low volume services need to be augmented with revenue generating activities like job work (data entry or minor desktop publishing), training and Internet surfing (Rao, 2003). According to a recent study of a similar project, it is found that services such as e-governance and desktop publishing were largely used by the citizens (Toyama et al, 2005). The study further revealed that language courses, income-generating services, services to support agriculture, basic computer education, and e-government have ever increasing scope for exploitation. It has been found that sustainability of such projects are dependent upon the economic viability and motivation of the operators of the kiosks (Dhawan, 2004; Srinivasan, 2004; Toyama et al, 2005). Even in developing countries where problems of low connectivity and human resource development are severe, creativity and careful planning can develop specific applications, services and information that can be delivered to targeted audiences (Basu, 2004). The government as well as project champions need to pay attention to the sustenance problems faced by these projects. Proper planning is needed in working out revenue models, ensuring the full implementations through appropriate tenure appointments of project champions, ensuring effective monitoring and maintenance of systems (Rao, 2003).

Many public and private sector ICTs enabled initiatives have been undertaken in India in the last decade especially to cater to the needs of agricultural or overall rural sector development. Some of these initiatives include e-Choupals by Indian Tobacco Company (ITC), Hindustan Lever limited (HLL) Shakti, Drishti, AgMarknet, Gyandoot and Parry Kiosks by EID Parry. All these ICTs enabled governance systems share the common objective of empowering rural communities to make right decisions related to their day-to-day activities and thereby improve their performance. Since, rural economy in India or for that matter in any developing country, has very strong linkages with the agricultural economy, the major thrust of these initiatives has been on the agriculture and allied sectors (Xavier & Pillai, 2003). These initiatives are basically digital network of private and public institutions which has come together and they offer service through Internet kiosks. We present below few of the popular initiatives:

Gyandoot: It is jointly implemented and managed by public private partnership. Gyandoot, which literally means 'Knowledge Messenger' in local language, is an e-governance program to provide knowledge access to tribal citizens with minimum investment. There are three entities involved in this endeavor: Gyandoot Council, the district government and the kiosk manager. The Gyandoot Council is financially independent and the state government plays the role of a facilitator only. The kiosk manager is a private individual, mainly a local entrepreneur. The project identifies the concerns of the villagers in the poverty-stricken, tribal-dominated rural area of Madhya Pradesh. Tribal farmers are able to get better returns for their agriculture produce by utilizing the services offered through this program. This program has also brought computer literacy and IT awareness to the rural people. There were some services that were very well received like Mandi (market) rates, and subsequently lost its sheen due to increasing usage of mobile phones. Driving license applications had been well received, but a recent study has revealed that it has lost some popularity due to resistance from local officials.

e-Choupal: This initiative was set up by the International Business Division of International Tobacco Company (ITC) to establish a more efficient agriculture supply chain aimed at delivering sustainable value to its customers around the world. Launched in the year 2000, e-Choupal reaches more than 18,000 villages through 3000 kiosks across five states and more links are being added. ITC has set a target of covering 100,000 villages across 15 states. The model has been specifically designed to tackle the challenges posed by fragmented farms, weak infrastructure and involvement of numerous intermediaries. E-Choupal uses ICT to cluster all the value chain participants, remove intermediaries and provides information and market signals directly to farmers. Village kiosks are managed by farmers themselves and enable direct access to information in local language on weather, market prices, disseminate knowledge on scientific practices and risk management, and also facilitate the sale of farm inputs and purchase of farm produce from the farmer's doorsteps. This process greatly reduces transaction costs, resulting in benefits to the farmers as well as to the ITC. The problems encountered while setting up and managing these kiosks are mainly lack of infrastructure poor reliability of power supply, non-availability of telecom connectivity and bandwidth. The biggest challenge has been of imparting skills to first-time Internet users in remote and inaccessible villages.

AGMARKET: This initiative has been created to establish a sound Agricultural Marketing Information System in India. The project is part of the Central Sector Scheme "Marketing Research and Information Network". The portal (http://agmarket.nic.in), developed as a part of the project, aims at providing "single window" service to cater to the diversified demands of market information. Important categories of portal contents are commodity prices and arrivals (daily market prices and arrivals, weekly/monthly price trends, future prices from national commodity exchanges, international prices, and so on), grades and standards, commodity profiles, mandi (market) profiles and market reforms related initiatives and schemes.

E-Seva: It is a G2C initiative of the state government of Andhra Pradesh. The aim is to provide a one stop, under a single-roof contact point for availing a wide spectrum of services from a number of different departments. E-Seva offers a host of services like payment of utility bills for water, electricity, telephone, submission of passport applications, booking tickets, etc. The website offers information on issues of interest and also provides downloadable forms. The services facilitate the following benefits to the citizens: flexibility in payment, increased working hours and facility of direct debit system. Though e-Seva centers collectively have processed more than 10 million transactions since inception, the total number of e-payments is still at four thousand transactions, highlighting that there is still some apprehension about the safety in online transaction, coupled with the usual low penetration of credit and debit cards and low computer literacy.

The Government of India is investing heavily in e-governance with each passing year registering an increase of almost 23% in e-governance spending. But with 70% of Indians living in its 600,000 villages and 95 percent not speaking English, models which do not support the rural delivery system will not contribute much to good governance (Ghosh & Banerjee, 2006). A number of e-governance initiatives are currently operational in rural India (Xavier & Pillai, 2003; Ghosh & Banerjee, 2006). Central government has launched ambitious projects like the National e-governance project at a cost of $1.3 billion to connect 600,000 villages through participation from various states, government agencies and corporate entities. The 100,000 multipurpose kiosks are likely to set up for enabling services like e-learning, e-training, e-teaching, e-health, telemedicine, e-farming, e-tourism, e-entertainment and e-commerce for the village entrepreneurs (Ghosh & Banerjee, 2006).

However, a clear understanding of effectiveness of the existing large projects has not been researched through longitudinal studies. Most of the literature has so far been based on anecdotal evidence rather than a systematic evaluation of the e-governance projects in the field. Much of what is written on this subject comprises practitioner reports, government documents and white papers (Grant, 2005). The present longitudinal research offers a critical analysis of a large e-governance and ICT based rural development initiative.

THE PROJECT-RASI

RASI (Rural Access to Services through Internet) is a project conceived by TeNeT, Indian Institute of Technology, Madras and n-Logue Communications, a private company located in Chennai, with the primary objective of delivering essential services such as education, healthcare and e-governance by setting up a network of village Internet centers called 'Chiraag' (means enlightenment) Internet kiosks. Chiraag, the connectivity project of n-Logue, has been initiated to eliminate the remoteness and backwardness, and to provide a sense of enlightenment to those who are deprived. The project currently functions in 40 districts and 200 centers in various Indian states. These kiosks work on the self-sustainable rural entrepreneurship model. The entrepreneurs in Tamilnadu get some funding support from the government in the form of subsidy.

The main features of the project are (Kanungo & Umashankar, 2006):

- Providing access to essential services like education, healthcare, agricultural advice and governance.
- Enabling rural livelihood through access to information, finance, market and insurance.
- Delivering government services at doorsteps in local language in an operator assisted environment.
- Providing services such as e-mail, chat and web browsing besides tele-administration and e-governance.
- Creating a middle tier of Local service provider (LSP), located within a distance of 30 km from any kiosk to ensure smooth connectivity.

Entrepreneurs, who are typically native men or women, manage these Chiraag kiosks. These individuals have at least high school education and demonstrated ability and motivation to run their own business. Each kiosk costs approximately $1200 to set up which includes (i) a set that receives the wireless corDECT signal (ii) branded PC with 15" color monitor with peripherals including speaker, microphone, CD-ROM, digital camera, inkjet printer and a sound card (iii) UPS (Uninterruptible Power Supply) with battery providing 4 hours of back-up power and (iv) an application suite consisting of word processing, browsing and e-mail software with support for the local language. The price also includes 6-months of unlimited Internet access, a marketing kit, and an introductory training provided by n-Logue. In order to facilitate smooth functioning of this model and ensure sustainability, a three-tier model consisting of a parent company, a middle tier operator and the kiosk owners was deployed.

At the top tier, n-Logue is responsible for overall management of the network. It facilitates relationships between service providers such as banks, governments and its business franchises. Second tier are the Local Service Providers (LSPs), responsible for managing the project at the local level. In coordination with n-Logue, the LSP has set up 'access centers' that provide last-mile access to the Chiraag kiosks. On the third tier of n-Logue's business model are the local entrepreneurs who are recruited by the LSP to invest in and set up Internet kiosks in their villages. These locally owned Internet kiosks offer a variety of Internet and computer-based services aimed at the rural market. iSee, a multiparty video conferencing application was developed due to collaborative efforts to meet the video communication needs in the project.

Several services have already been developed and deployed. Some of the important services offered through Chiraag Kiosks include: on-line education (English, Mathematics and Science subjects), healthcare service (in collaboration with private hospitals), agriculture information and support (in collaboration with research institutes and e-governance) to provide government forms and hustle the application process. Kiosk operators are encouraged to provide additional services, if they are financially viable and self sustainable.

N-Logue provides training to kiosk operators once the kiosks are set up. Guidance on marketing and managing the kiosk is also provided. Following the training, the owner completes an online evaluation of kiosk performance. Kiosk owners get added support through monthly meetings. Organized with the help of n-Logue, the meetings allow operators to share experience and advice one another. They also give n-Logue the opportunity to introduce new services and promotions, or conduct supplementary trainings. Each meeting features a guest speaker, usually a business professional or service provider, who provides additional teaching aimed at increasing the kiosk's earnings.

The project was implemented in Erode district in the state of Tamilnadu during 2003 with a promising scope to enable rural development. Erode district is one among the industrially developing districts of Tamilnadu. Industry and trade occupy a place of prominence in the economy of the district. Industries that flourished in early days in Erode district were handloom weaving and carpet manufacturing. The advent of modern era has changed these industries to some extent and the power loom weaving is slowly replacing it. Major industries include textile, engineering industries, sugar, oil extraction, leather, gem-cutting etc. The population of 2,600,000 is equally distributed with 50 % of the people living in rural areas. The Tamilnadu government patronized the project by providing a subsidy of up to 50% of investment for building up another 2000 centers in the state. Therefore, n-Logue is also planning to introduce low cost ATM machines, suited for village environment. Many other agencies were also invited by government of Tamilnadu to assist the implementation of RASI centers in collaboration with n-Logue communications.

Initial aims of the project included providing e-governance, but the absence of adequate digitized content such as downloadable certificates turned out to be a limiting factor for the full-scale deployment of e-governance services. It was also planned to provide many informational services such as school admissions, sports and entertainment news, etc. E-governance by providing information on government programs, online registrations for enterprises and government programs and issue of land records and government certificates were also planned by them (Dossani et al, 2005).

RESEARCH QUESTIONS AND METHODOLOGY

It is generally understood that n-Logue has developed a viable and scaleable model for delivering information-based services to rural areas. It was also believed that through its three-tiered franchisee business model based on corDECT technology, the company is able to quickly and cheaply scale its network. Significant opportunities also prevailed for the creation of new partnerships with corporations, governments, and NGOs whose use of n-Logue's networks bring further benefits and development in rural areas. However, sustainability and growth of this project is dependent upon the quality and quantity of benefits at the present level. Critical evaluation will enable right efforts of the governments and agencies for their aggressive expansion, more particularly in configuring, training and supporting the right personnel for replicating successful implementation of the projects in Tamilnadu. Moreover, it is important for the stakeholders to critically analyze the overall model before embarking it on a national scale. Therefore, our objectives of the research are:

i. to assess the level of awareness of the various types of services that are being offered
ii. to find out the factors that influence the extent of utilization of services
iii. to identify the level of satisfaction of citizens towards the services and
iv. to find out the problems faced by the end-users (citizens) and kiosk operators

We adopted a longitudinal approach for our research through data collected in two distinct time periods. Data was collected in 2004 and again in 2006 on some of the key aspects of services through survey of citizens from the target district of Tamilnadu. The survey questionnaire was designed based on initial discussions with citizen users, kiosk operators and government officials and was pilot tested before administering to a large number of respondents. The questionnaire was designed to gather demographic data such as age, education, income, occupation and gender and also awareness of services, usage of services, satisfaction with the services and attitude towards the Chiraag Internet kiosks. The level of satisfaction with the services was measured using a five point scale (1- highly dissatisfied, 2- dissatisfied, 3-neutral, 4-satisfied and 5-highly satisfied). Attitude towards the Internet center was measured by getting the respondents to rate the operators, fee, location, Internet speed etc. on a five point scale described earlier. Respondents were also asked to highlight the problems faced by them and give their suggestions for improvement. Two surveys were conducted among the users of Chiraag kiosks during 2004 and again in 2006. We obtained a total of 200 and 182 valid responses in 2004 and 2006 respectively. The sample size was arbitrarily fixed at 200 for the first survey. However for the second survey based on estimates from the first survey (at 95% confidence level and 10% allowable error) the sample size required was estimated as 176. We had actually collected 182 valid responses that were used for further analysis. Sampling of respondents was carried out in two stages. In the first stage, 20 kiosks were selected at random. In the second stage 10 respondents were selected from each kiosk using a systematic random sampling. We also interviewed 20 kiosk operators and asked them to comment on the changing characteristics of the project over the period of two years. The data collected from citizens and operators were supplemented through interviews with a few officials of the project. Data collected from operators through interviews are used as part of discussion.

DATA ANALYSIS AND INTERPRETATION

The data obtained from the citizen users was coded and analyzed using the statistical software SPSS. The data pertaining to 2004 and 2006 were initially analyzed separately. As our primary objective is to understand the changes over the two year period, we then prepared combined tables for both the surveys for demographics, awareness, usage and attitudes that are presented below.

Profile of Users

The two samples are comparable to each other on age and gender as can be seen from the profile of respondents in Tables 1 and 2. Age profile is pretty much the same while we see an increase in the percentage of women respondents in 2006. It is found that the percentage of female population using the services has increased marginally. However the z-value of 0.493 obtained using the binomial test of equality of two proportions indicates that the increase is not statistically significant.

Tables 3 and 4 give the educational and occupational profiles. These two profiles have undergone a lot of changes in the intervening period. The increase in the college graduates and professionals visiting Chiraag kiosk are not statistically significant (z values of 1.76 and 1.23 respectively). As regards occupation, the private sector employees have increased to 44 percent of the sample in 2006 as opposed to 9 percent in 2004 and the difference is statistically significant ($z = 7.67$ and $p=0.000$). The drop in the number of agriculturists visiting the kiosks is not statistically significant ($z=0.738$).

Factors that Influence the Usage

Importance ranking of the factors that influence the choice of Chiraag kiosks both during 2004 as well as 2006 surveys remain the same and they

Table 1. Age distribution

Category	2004		2006	
	Frequency	Percent	Frequency	Percent
Less than 25	134	67.0	117	64.6
25 and above	66	33.0	65	35.4
Total	200	100	182	100

Table 2. Gender distribution

Gender	2004		2006	
	Frequency	Percent	Frequency	Percent
Male	147	73.5	128	70.3
Female	53	26.5	54	29.7
Total	200	100	182	100

Table 3. Educational qualification

Category	2004		2006	
	Frequency	Percent	Frequency	Percent
No formal qualification	36	18.0	8	4.4
School Level	39	19.5	37	20.3
Collegiate	107	54.5	115	63.2
Professional	16	8.0	22	12.1
Total	200	100	182	100

Table 4. Occupation

Category	2004		2006	
	Frequency	Percent	Frequency	Percent
Agriculturist	33	17.9	12	15.0
Business person	77	41.8	23	28.8
Government Employee	57	31.0	10	12.5
Private Employee	17	9.2	35	43.8
Total	184	100	80	100

Table 5. Factors that influence the usage

Factor	2004		2006	
	Mean Score*	Rank	Mean Score	Rank
Variety of services offered	2.50	3	3.0	3
Location of the kiosks	2.14	1	1.7	1
Low fees	2.46	2	2.9	2
Citizen support	3.63	4	3.6	4
Availability of other resources	4.15	5	3.7	5
Base	200		182	

** Minimum – 1 and Maximum – 5*

have the same rank ordering as shown in Table-5. Location of the kiosks continues to be the number one factor, followed by low fees and the variety of services offered. Citizen support and availability of other resources continue to be the least important factors in both the surveys.

Usage of Services and the Level of Satisfaction

Most of the services have experienced a substantial decrease in usage during 2004 to 2006 as shown in Table 6. It included: Internet service, e-governance, health services, agricultural services, e-commerce, e-banking and telephony. Secondary services have gained usage during the

Table 6. Usage and level of satisfaction with Chiraag services

Service	Usage (Percent)			Level of Satisfaction**		
	2004	2006	z-value*	2004	2006	t-value
Internet services	100	87.9	-5.067†	4.3	3.7	9.272†
E-governance	42.3	6.6	-8.000†	3.4	2.4	4.665†
Health services	37.3	6.0	-7.314†	3.5	2.8	2.509†
Agriculture services	37.3	7.1	-7.000†	3.5	2.8	3.219†
Astrology	49.3	20.9	-5.774†	3.5	3.2	1.533‡
Matrimony services	38.7	9.3	-6.642†	3.5	3	2.431‡
E- Commerce	23.7	13.7	-2.487†	2.7	1.4	4.465†
E- Banking	16	2.2	-4.600†	2.9	1.3	5.846†
Chiraag education	39.3	24.7	-3.042†	3.9	3.9	0.013‡
Online services like bus, train and air ticket booking	42.7	9.3	-7.348†	3.2	3.2	0.166‡
Offline services (DTP, Project work)	48.7	54.4	1.112‡	3.3	3.9	-6.899†
Telephony and Photos	76.7	43.4	-6.651†	4.3	3.6	7.502†
* z-value from the binominal test for equality of proportions						
† Significant; ‡ Not Significant						
** Measured on a 5-point scale with 5 as highly satisfied						

period of study. People are found to be using the kiosks mostly for net browsing, off-line services such as DTP (Desk Top Publishing) and telephony though the marginal increase in the use of off-line services is not statistically significant.

As regards satisfaction with services, there is consistent decline from 2004 to 2006. Primary services, such as Internet services, e-governance, health services and agricultural services show a marked decline in the level of satisfaction. Only offline services have witnessed a statistically significant rise in the level of satisfaction. The difference in the level of satisfaction for the services such as astrology, matrimony, e-Commerce, e-Banking, Chiraag education and online services turned to be statistically not significant over the period of two years.

Problems with Chiraag Kiosks

The percentage of people experiencing problems with Chiraag kiosks has considerably reduced from 2004 to 2006. However, the kiosks do need to improve as more than half the respondents say that they have experienced problems with Chiraag kiosks. Additionally the severity ranking of problems in 2006 seem to be different from that in 2004 as can be seen in Table 7. Low speed has emerged as the most important problem in 2006 while it received only the third rank in 2004. Lack of privacy has not changed places in both 2004 and 2006. Lack of infrastructure is turning out to be critical (3rd rank) in 2006 as compared to 2004 (6th rank). Working hours seem to have improved in the last two years. Fee charged has remained least important in both the years as the amount charged continues to remain low.

Additional Services through Chiraag Kiosks

There is a considerable rise in the demand for more e-governance through the Chiraag kiosks in 2006 as compared to 2004 (See Table 8). However the interest in rural ATM has considerably reduced in 2006 as compared to 2004. The interest in

Table 7. Severity ranking of problems

Problem	2004		2006	
	Mean Score	**Severity Rank**	**Mean Score**	**Severity Rank**
Non availability	2.6	1	4.5	4
Lack of privacy	3.2	2	3.2	2
Regulation	5.0	4	4.7	5
Working hours	5.6	5	6.9	8
Lack of infrastructure	5.7	6	4.0	3
Lack guidance	6.4	8	6.2	7
Lack resources	6.3	7	5.4	6
Fees	6.5	9	8.1	9
Low speed	3.8	3	1.5	1

Table 8. Additional services through Chiraag kiosks

	2004		2006	
Additional Services	**Frequency**	**Percent**	**Frequency**	**Percent**
Rural ATM	42	34.6	6	9.1
Tele diagnostic Kit	26	21.4	24	33.7
Improved e-Banking & E-Commerce Services	44	36.3	22	30.5
More e-governance services	9	7.7	19	26.7
Total	121	100	71	100

tele-diagnostic kits has marginally gone up and e-banking and e-commerce services have marginally gone down.

DISCUSSION

E-governance and rural development through ICT is a boon for developing countries like India. The long felt need for serving people living in rural areas and emerging countrywide ICT capability together with infrastructure, provide a unique opportunity for exploitation. Our analysis and findings reveal many critical lessons for policy makers and other stakeholders in ICT implementations.

Considering the nature and type of services, it is found that only four of the whole set of services are being offered with some impact. First, the Chiraag education service is targeted towards a cross section of users. The services included: e-books for school children, technical books to students of polytechnics and a few handbooks for developing specific skills. The diffusion of these services in many locations is less. "Using proper technology and aligning with appropriate institutions, it will be possible to offer certificate and diploma courses through Chiraag," said an official of the project. The second service planned was healthcare delivery. Eye care service is one of the two services offered in this domain. This is offered in collaboration with Arvind Hospitals in Madurai through a bi-weekly live video discussion with patients. The other service planned was animal healthcare maintenance through video conferencing with veterinary hospital on weekly basis. The third service was agricultural advice through the Agricultural Research Institute located in Madurai. According to an operator, questions raised by farmers concerning cultivation of crops were collected at the kiosk and a weekly videoconference was used to get the advices from the institute. Fourth service was browsing facility to all cross sections of the users. DTP & telephony are the other services offered through kiosks, which is aimed at providing scope for additional revenue generation.

The very fact that 35 out of 60 kiosks are either closed or non-functional shows that there are many areas of concern for policy makers and service deliverers. Firstly, the profile of users of Chiraag kiosks appears to be changing over a period of time. There is a considerable shift in the user profile in terms of literacy and nature of employment. As presented in Table 3 and 4, the usage of the kiosks by people with no formal qualification and business people has reduced. The usage by agriculturist has also reduced over a period of two years. There is a gradual change towards up-market users. People at the bottom of the pyramid do not seem to be benefiting by these centers.

The project was supposedly set up to enable e-governance and support rural development by providing necessary information and transaction support. On the contrary, our research shows that the kiosks are primarily used for browsing and DTP work and therefore more and more of educated people and employees of private organizations tend to use the kiosks. Rao (2003) suggested that browsing and DTP may be made available to generate additional revenues through the kiosks. In the case of RASI, such services have become primary. "The primary services needed for rural population are not offered and our kiosks are used for secondary services", said an operator. While considering the factors that affect the usage of the kiosks, location of the kiosks and low fees have been ranked high. As presented in Table-5, the factor, 'variety of services', has been ranked as the third important factor. This further shows that the citizens visit the kiosks for browsing, which is available close to their place at low cost.

The services originally meant to be delivered through these kiosks, such as e-governance, e-commerce, e-banking etc. have not caught on with the users. The level of satisfaction with regard to services, there is a decline from 2004 to 2006 (Table-6). Primary services, such as e-governance, health services and agricultural services show a marked decline in the level of satisfaction. But, offline services have witnessed a statistically significant rise in the level of satisfaction. This further shows that the RASI project is not able to provide the desired services and therefore the satisfaction levels of such services have declined. The ranking of problems faced by the kiosks users have changed from non-availability to low speed over a period of two years (Table-7). According to the operators, the users were keen to come to kiosks and look for the desired services. Such services became increasingly non- available and the kiosks were mostly used for browsing. When it comes to browsing, the technology used for the connectivity has a limited bandwidth as compared to normal cybercafés. Therefore, it is obvious that the highest ranking of problems has moved to low speed.

Another interesting finding is that (Table -8) citizens expect provision of e-governance services and tele-diagnostic kit as additional services through the kiosks. These two are the essential services needed for the rural masses. The tele-diagnostic kit addresses the health and agriculture related problems. Additional emphasize to e-governance would help citizens to access government services. According to an operator, the necessary data sharing was not established with appropriate government departments, especially with local governments.

While the project has failed to meet the desired objectives, present kiosk operators too are not keen to continue with their operations. Income generated out of such a minimum number of visits of citizen would not be adequate for sustaining the service. The nature and quality of the service offering and the resulting poor scope for revenue generation have led to lack of commitment and motivation among operators. Browsing, the primary source of revenue is under competitive pressure due to introduction of competing facilities and services that are coming up in these areas. Strategies have to be evolved to retain the present operators by providing opportunities for growth.

Low speed has been identified as one of the critical problems faced by the citizens and operators. According to an operator, the speed of connectivity is poor because of corDECT wireless technology. This technology was found to be relevant during the initial time periods because of few services and low volume of usage. However, when other services such as agricultural advice and healthcare delivery were introduced, the bandwidth became a bottleneck in the overall service quality. The project may be migrated to higher levels of service delivery by reviving the committed services and launching activities in e-commerce, on-line education etc. Perhaps, bandwidth is the first technology area to be addressed in case new services are planned. It is worthwhile to consider other technology options that are provided by private players.

Lack of privacy, especially for women, is identified as one of the critical problems that are faced by the citizen (Madon, 2004). It is an important issue as women in the rural areas are normally confined to their homes and not encouraged to visit places such as Internet kiosks. Therefore, additional care needs to be taken to provide comfortable working environment. It may be a good idea to encourage more women operators. This will not only enable more women to come to the kiosks but also act as a non-deterrent to men. Lack of infrastructure, which has resulted due to inadequate revenue generation, is also identified as one of the problems faced by the users.

Our analysis shows that types and quality of services have moved away targeted users from the project. The project objectives and the required services have been diluted over these two years and thereby the entire profile of users has changed now. Our interviews with operators reveal that the primary reasons for the absence of e-governance is due to absence of integration with e-government systems. As found in the previous research, strategic management approach (Suri, 2005) and stakeholder analysis (Tan et al 2005) is an important prerequisite for a public-private partnership in e-governance projects. Our findings confirm the earlier findings that the projects in the area of e-governance and rural development suffer due to connectivity (Heeks, 2001; Rao, 2004) and data sharing (Sethi & Sethi, 2006). It is understood from the kiosk operators and officials that the change in policies of the state and poor back-end connectivity are some of the key reasons for the deterioration of services. Despite the exclusive focus on one aspect viz. computerization of government records and automating the back end processes (Xavier & Pillai, 2003), it is understood that some government departments are not ready to share data with e-governance applications. The project was supported by the previous government at the planning stage. By the time the project came into operation, there was a change in the government and the new government was not keen to support the initiative. Therefore, political context (Singla, 2002; Gupta et al, 2004) plays an important role in the success of e-governance and ICT based rural development.

With the present declining trend in usage and less motivated service delivery personnel, it is likely to be difficult to regain the mindshare of the rural masses, even if committed services are offered (Toyama, 2005). Therefore, it is always important to provide a set of comprehensive services with continuity to ensure enduring commitment to citizens. The policy makers have not attempted to look at the entire objective and implementation from the citizens' view point.

Therefore, success of service networks like Chiraag is based on 'what are delivered' and 'how they are delivered' through them. A citizen-centric approach to e-governance requires shifting the focus on the delivery of desired government services to citizens. Our longitudinal study covering the end-users (citizens) and operators reveals that many factors influence the overall success of the Chiraag network.

The level of satisfaction has been consistently declining for most of the services. There are two dimensions to the declining satisfaction. Firstly, not all the promised key services are being offered to the citizens. According to both officials of the project and operators, e-governance is the primary service that is expected out of the kiosks. Inability to offer these services has really affected the level of satisfaction. Secondly, the overall quality of the services that are presently offered has not made an impact. Inadequate coordination with agencies, financial viability of running the kiosks, non-scalable technology and decreasing levels of motivation of operators are some of the reasons for the poor quality of services.

IMPLICATIONS

Our research shows that RASI network is used more for browsing and secondary services like education, DTP and telephony. More and more of educated youth are using these kiosks for browsing and education. The main purpose for which the kiosks were introduced appears to be lost. The real benefit of providing e-governance and services that will engine rural development falls short of expectations. The services originally meant to be delivered through these kiosks, such as e-governance, e-commerce, e-banking etc. have not caught on with the users. Low speed, lack of privacy and lack of infrastructure are seen as critical problems that need to be addressed on a priority basis. The level of satisfaction has been consistently declining for most of the services. Further, care should be taken to make the operators motivated and professionally capable to carry out the activities of the center. The positive side of the story is that centers are not doing badly given the service levels. This is evidenced from the fact that 80 percent of present users are willing to recommend the center to other potential users.

It is leant that Chiraag kiosks located in a few other districts have ventured into online education and e-commerce services. However, these services are sporadic and likely to have less impact on the overall growth. We strongly feel that initiatives such as Chiraag will have to provide a comprehensive service both in depth and breadth on a sustainable basis. We notice the deviation from offering core services (such as e-governance, healthcare, support to core economic activities) to peripheral services (such as browsing, DTP and Telephony). Such a deviation will have its negative influence in the success of reviving the projects and also for implementing similar projects in other locations. Further research may be directed to compare this project with similar projects implemented in other states. Such efforts will reveal problems /opportunities and strategies adopted to manage them.

REFERENCES

Allen, B. A., Juillet, J., Paquet, G. & Roy, J. (2001) E-Governance & government on-line in Canada: Partnerships, people & prospects, Government Information Quarterly 18 93–104.

Backus, M. (2001) E-governance in Developing Countries, IICD Research Brief-No1, March, Available at www.ftpiicd.org/files/research/briefs/brief1.pdf.

Basu, S. (2004) E-Government and Developing Countries, International Review of Law Computers and Technology, Vol. 18, No. 1, pp. 109-132.

Basu, S. (2004) E-Government and Developing Countries: An Overview, International Review of Law computers, Vol. 18, No, 1, 109-132.

Bedi, K., Singh, P.J. and Srivastava, S. (2001), Government@net: New Governance opportunities for India, Sage Publications, New Delhi.

Bhatnagar, S.C. (2002) E-Government Case Studies in India, Online, Rev. 15th September, http://www1.worldbank.org/publicsector/egov/

Bhatnagar, S.C. and Bjorn-Andersen, N. (1990), Information Technology in Developing Countries, Elsevier Science, Amsterdam.

Burn, J. and Robins, G. (2003), "Moving towards e-government: a case study of organizational change processes", Logistics Information Management, Vol. 16 No. 1, pp. 25-35.

Cecchini S. and Raina M.(2003) Electronic Government and the Rural Poor: The Case of Gyandoot, Information Technology in Developing Countries, A Newsletter of IFIP Working Group 9.4 and Centre for Electronic Governance, Indian Institute of Management, Ahmedabad, 13(2), November.

Corcoran, C. T. (1994) Employment agency gets a grip on its workload, Infoworld, 16(46), 122.

Deakins, E. and Dillon, S.M. (2002) 'E-government in New Zealand: the local authority perspective', The International Journal of Public Sector Management, Bradford, Vol. 15, Nos. 4–5, pp.375–399.

Dhawan, V. (2004) Critical Success Factors for Rural ICT Projects in India: A study of n-Logue projects at Pabal and Baramati. Masters Thesis, Mehta School of Management, Indian Institute of Technology, Bombay.

Dossani, R., Misra, D. C. & Jhaveri, R. (2005) Enabling ICT for Rural India, Asia-Pacific Research Center, Stanford University, accessed through http://iis-db.stanford.edu/pubs/20972/ICT_full_Oct05.pdf.

Finger, M. and Pecoud, G. (2003) 'From e-government to e-governance? towards a model of e-governance', 3rd European Conference on E-government, Trinity College Dublin, 3–4 July, Ireland.

Fraga, E. (2002) "Trends in e-government: how to plan, design, and measure e-government", paper presented at the Government Management Information Sciences (GMIS) Conference, Santa Fe, NM, 17 June.

Garnham, N. (2000) Amartya Sen's "Capabilities" Approach to the Evaluation of Welfare and its Application to Communications, in Beyond Competition: Broadening the scope of telecommunications policy, Cammaerts, B. and Burgelmans, J.C (Eds.), VUB University Press, 25-37.

Ghosh, A. and Banerjee, G. (2006) A Study of E-governance in Rural India, Fourth International Conference on Electronic Governance.

Grant G. (2005) Realizing the Promise of Electronic Government, Editorial Preface, Journal of Global Information Management, 13(1), January-March.

Grant G. and Chau D. (2005) Developing a Generic Framework for E-Government, Journal of Global Information Management, 13(1), 1-30, Jan - March, Idea Group Publishing.

Gronlund, A. (2001) "Democracy in an IT-framed society", Communications of the ACM, Vol. 44 No. 1, pp. 23-6.

Gupta M.P., Kumar. P. and Jaijit B. (2004) Government Online, Opportunities and Challenges, Tata McGraw-Hill, New Delhi.

Heeks R. (2003) Most e-Government–for-Development Projects Fail: How can Risks be Reduced? i-Government Working Paper Series Paper No. 14, Available at www.sed.manchester. ac.uk/ idpm/publications/wp/igov/igov-wp14.pdf.

Heeks, R. (2001) "Understanding e-governance for development", paper no. 11, i-Government Working Paper Series, Institute for Development Policy and Management, University of Manchester, Manchester.

Heeks, R. (2002) E-government for Development, Institute for Development Policy and Management (IIPM), University of Manchester, UK.

Holmes, D. (2001) eGov: eBusiness Strategies for Government, Nicholas Brealey, London.

Kannabiran, G., Xavier, M. J., & Anantharaaj, A. (2004) Enabling e-governance through Citizen Relationship Management - concept, model and applications, Journal of Services Research, Vol. 4-2, 2004 223-240.

Kanungo, V. & Umashankar, C. (2006) RASI Project- E-Democracy, The Society for promotion of eGovernance, New Delhi, 2005.

Kumar P., Sushil and Gupta M.P. (2004) Towards E-Government, Management Challenges, Tata McGraw-Hill, New Delhi.

Madon S (2004) Evaluating the Developmental Impact of E-Governance Initiatives, Vol. 20, No. 5, pp. 1-13.

Maguire, M. C., (1999) A review of user-interface design guidelines for public information Kiosk systems, Int. J. Human-Computer Studies, 50, 263–286.

Madon, S. and Kiran, G. (2002) Information Technology for Citizen-Government Interface: A study of FRIENDS project in Kerala. World Bank Global Knowledge Sharing Program(GKSP). http://www1.worldbank.org/publicsector/bnpp/egovupdate.htm.

Mansell, R. (2001) New Media and the Power of Networks. First Dixons Public Lecture. The London School of Economics and Political Science, 23rd October.

Marche, S. and McNiven, J.D. (2003) "E-government and e-governance: the future isn't what it used to be", Canadian Journal of Administrative Science, Vol. 20 No. 1, pp. 74-86.

Morris et al, Kiosks: A technological overview. Available: http:// www.visi.com/~keefner/pdfs/Kiosk_paper.html#PTFToC2, 1995, accessed April 14, 2004.

Nath, V. (2006) Building and Sustaining Democratic and Accountable Governance Institutions using ICT- Models of Digital Governance, http://www.cddc.vt.edu/digitalgov/gov-models.html, accessed in March 2007

Ni, Y. N. & Ho, A. T. (2005) Challenges in e-government development: Lessons from two information Kiosk projects, Government Information Quarterly, 22, 58–74.

Nicholas, D., Huntington, P. & Williams, P. (2003) Three years of digital consumer health information: a longitudinal study of the touch screen health Kiosk, Information Processing and Management, 39, 479–502.

Okot-Uma, R.W. (2000) Electronic Governance: Re-Inventing Good Governance, Commonwealth Secretariat, London.

Okot-Uma, R.W. (2001) "Electronic governance: (leading to good government)", Electronic Governance and Electronic Democracy: Living and Working in the Connected World, The Commonwealth Centre for Electronic Governance, Ottawa, available at: www.electronegov.net (accessed 7 August 2003).

Palanisamy, R. (2004) 'Issues and challenges in e-governance planning', Electronic Government, Vol. 1, No. 3, pp.253–272.

Pannekoek, F., Bernard, P., Mitchell, D., Martin, C. and Dickin, J. (2002) 'The internet as a site of citizenship: the final report (Information Deficit Canadian Solutions 2001)', Canadian Journal of Communication, Toronto, Vol. 27, No. 4, pp.509–527.

Radhakumari (2006) Akshaya – A Grass Root Level IT Project in Kerala – An Unique Experiment with Broadband, Fourth International Conference on Electronic Governance.

Rao, S. S. (2004) Role of ICTs in India's rural community information systems, Vol. 6, No. 4, pp. 261-269.

Riley (2005) E-Governanace Comes of Age in the Commonwealth, pp. 207-211.

Riley, T.B. (2001) "Electronic governance in context", Electronic Governance and Electronic Democracy: Living and Working in the Connected World, The Commonwealth Centre for Electronic Governance, Ottawa, available at: www.electronegov.net (accessed 7 August 2003).

Sargent, G. & McLvor, J. (1996) Public access information: A prototype web Kiosk, Managing Information, 3(4), 32-35.

Saxena, K. B. C. (2005) Towards excellence in e-governance, International Journal of Public Sector Management, Vol. 18 No. 6, pp. 498-513.

Sealy, W.U. (2003) 'Empowering development through e-governance: creating smart communities in small island states', International Information & Library Review, Vol. 35, No. 2, pp.335–358.

Sethi, N. and Sethi, V. (2006) Public-Private-People Partnerships in E-government: A case study of Singapore Tracks, Fourth International Conference on Electronic Governance.

Singla, M. L. (2002) E-Governance- Transforming the National Bone Marrow, Journal of Management Research, Vol. 2, No. 3, 165-175

Srinivasan, J (2004) Sustainable Access in Rural India (SARI) project-Madurai, Tamilnadu, www.iiitb.ac.in/ICTforD/SARI%20final.pdf accessed during October 2005.

Suri P.K. (2005) NICNET based Agricultural Marketing Information Network - A Farmers Centric Portal on Agricultural Marketing in India and a Step towards Globalizing Indian Agriculture, Agricultural Marketing Journal, XLV(4) January-March.

Symonds, M. (2000) "A survey of government and the internet", The Economist, Vol. 355 No. 8176, pp. S3-S5.

Tan C.W., Shan L., Pan S.L. and Lim E.T.K. (2005) Managing Stakeholder Interests in e-Government Implementation: Lessons Learned from a Singapore e-Government Project, Journal of Global Information Management 13(1), 1-30, Jan-March.

Toyama, K., K. Kiri, M. Lakshmi Ratan, A. Nileshwar, R. Vedashree, R. F. MacGregor. (2005) Rural Kiosks in India, Microsoft Research Technical Report, MSR-TR-2004-146.

Tulip, S. (2000) 'Local launch pad', Supply Management, Vol. 5, No. 16, pp.34, 35.

Tung, L. L. & Tan, J. H., (1998) Model for the classification of Information Kiosks in Singapore, International Journal of Information Systems, Vol. 18, No. 4, 255-264.

United Nations Department of Economic and Social Affairs Report, World public sector report 2003: E-Government at the crossroads. New York, United Nations Publication, 2003.

World Bank (2001) Working Group on e-Governance, Discussion Forum, The World Bank, Washington, DC.

Xavier, M. J. & Pillai, R. P. (2003) Indian Experience in G2C Service Delivery Models: Select Case Studies and Lessons for Future Developments, International Conference on Electronic governance, New Delhi, 32-41.

Young J.S.L (2003) E-Government in Asia: Enabling Public Service Innovation in the 21st Century, Times Media, Singapore.

Zipf, M. (2001) 'E-government', Deutschland, Vol. 3, pp.62–65.

Zwahr T., Finger M. and Mueller P. (2005) More than Digitization-The Transformative Potential of E-Governance: An Exploratory Case Study, Proceedings of the 38th Hawaii International Conference on System Sciences, Available at www.computer.org.

This work was previously published in International Journal of Electronic Government Research, Vol. 4, Issue 3, edited by M. Khosrow-Pour, pp.1-19, copyright 2008 by IGI Publishing (an imprint of IGI Global).

Chapter 10
E-Government Organizational Performance Framework:
Case Study of Haryana State in India —A Log Linear Regression Analysis

Susheel Chhabra
Lal Bahadur Shastri Institute of Management, India

Mahadeo Jaiswal
Management Development Institute, India

ABSTRACT

The objective of this chapter is to design an e-government organizational performance framework and to suggest ICTs solutions through a case study of Haryana state government in India so as to enhance efficiency and effectiveness of services provided to citizens. The framework is suggested using responses collected from 150 government departments. The ICTs solutions were validated by data collected from 90 e-government experts. A log linear regression analysis is used to develop the framework. The framework with minor modifications can be developed for similar other e-government settings.

INTRODUCTION

In this society where performance has become basic requirement for development, investments alone can not guarantee the success for an organization. The key to get success is through optimal utilization and effective management of available resources. Along with public awareness and Internet usage, the demand for real-time transactions along with simplified, standardized ways to access government information has been increased. Governments all over the world are recognizing e-government as a strategic option to enhance efficiency and fine-tune their internal and external operations. In this competitive environment, only the projects that have been designed on the basis of best performance benchmarks will be successful. The important concern for the Indian government is that most of the e-government projects in the state governments are keeping their focus on imitating the success models and ignoring the adaptability to a particular region (Singh, 2005).

DOI: 10.4018/978-1-60566-918-2.ch010

There is an immediate need to suggest an e-government framework for a particular region to improve service effectiveness. The e-government organizational performance framework is suggested for the government departments of Haryana state in India.

The chapter is organized as follows. First, the literature review to develop the framework is presented. Using the literature review, the research methodology adopted, the hypothesis tested and the framework developed is set forth. Finally, recommendations and conclusions of the chapter are presented.

LITERATURE REVIEW

E-Government Initiatives: Government of Haryana, India

Haryana is one of the pioneering states in India. It has an area of 44,212 Sq Kms. For administrative purposes the state is divided into four divisions - Ambala, Rohtak, Gurgaon, and Hisar. The state government has 20 districts, 47 sub-divisions, 67 tehsils, 45 sub-tehsils, and 116 blocks. (http://en.wikipedia.org/wiki/Haryana). More than 70% of its population is dependent on agriculture for its livelihood. People speak several similar sounding dialects of Hindi.

The state government departments are playing a key role for the overall development of Haryana. The major Haryana government Departments include Agriculture Department, Employment Department, Excise and Taxation Department, Finance Department, Fisheries Department, Food and Supplies Department, Health Department, Home Guards and Civil Defense Department, Information Technology Department, Irrigation Department, Police Department, Public Health Department, Public Works Department, Rural Development Department, Sports and Youth Welfare Department, Technical Education Department, Transport and Civil Aviation Department, and Women and Child Development Department.

The mission of Haryana for proliferation of e-government is to achieve efficiency, transparency, and accountability by providing Information and Communication Technologies (ICTs) enabled access and opportunities for all, anytime, and anywhere. The Secretariat of Information Technology (SIT), Haryana State Electronic Development Corporation (HARTRON) (http://www.hartron.org/), and National Informatics Centre (NIC) (http://home.nic.in/) are playing a vital role in implementing various e-government projects in the state.

The government has framed policies, guidelines, and standards to facilitate e-government in the state government departments. Some of the prominent policies include - IT Policy, Web Policy, Right of Way (ROW) Policy, and IT-Plan Guidelines etc. (http://haryanait.nic.in/). The government has also conceptualized guide-lines for systematic approvals of e-government projects in the State.

The government, in collaboration with NIC, HARTRON, and SIT has implemented various e-government projects for Haryana government departments. Some of the major projects include House Tax Assessment and Collection Information System (HACIS), Online Treasuries Information System (OTIS), Haryana Registration Information System (HARIS), Haryana Land Records Information System (HALRIS), Food Network, Labour Courts Cases Justice Delivery and Tracking System, Automated Employment Exchange System, and Haryana government Employee Portal, etc.(http://haryanait.nic.in/New%20htmls/egov.htm).

Haryana government has established e-government citizen service centers in 8 out of 20 districts of Haryana (http://haryanait.nic.in/e-disha.htm) under the preview of New Agent of Information - district Level Integrated e-government Service of Haryana for All (NAIDISHA). The objectives of these centers are to provide hassle-free access to government services at the doorstep, improved quality of service, transparent, efficient and effective delivery, reliable real-time services, effective dissemination under single roof, reduced delivery and opportunity costs, elimination of 'touts' and exploitation, citizen friendly environment and quick redressal of citizen grievances.

These service centers have been established as front-end interface of Haryana government departments to provide e-government services to its citizens.

The back-end for these e-government citizen service centres is the services received from government departments. To provide effective citizen-centric services, there is a need to monitor the performance of the back-end (Departments). Keeping in view the need to strengthen the organizational performance of these departments and to suggest ICTs solutions, the research study was undertaken.

E-Government Organizational Performance Attributes

The attributes of organizational performance varies all over the world depending upon various geographical, demographical, and cultural dimensions. Since, the chapter deals with organizational performance of a state government in India, it is pertinent to study the organizational performance attributes of the Indian government.

Understanding why organizations fail can be a good start to formulate e-government organizational performance attributes. Government's problems are rooted in bureaucratic structures designed in the past simply do not function well in the rapidly changing, information-rich, knowledge intensive society and economy. There is a need to have a paradigm shift to ensure continued service in a world of budget reductions, increasing diversity and social challenges.

Especially in the context of developing countries, the pressure is mounting on the governments to reduce operating cost; service delivery mechanisms are undergoing fundamental changes and moving toward citizen-centric governments. Lack of vision and cultural issues are hindering the progress. There is a need to reengineer the government structures. This calls for a fundamental change to the government model.

According to Vittal (n.d.), the biggest challenge, which government faces in India, is the mindset of the public servants. This mindset needs to be changed radically. Sharma & Palvia (2004) identified various issues for implementing e-government in India. Some of the major issues identified include resistance to change, negative attitude towards the history of government technology adoption, non-citizen and business centric view of the government, and communication approach to offer government services which has been same with only difference that few files are available in electronic format.

According to Saxena & Wadhwa (2004), lack of infrastructure, political determination, leadership, skepticism, awareness, inadequate funding, budgetary resources, and economic climate for accepting and realizing the e - government are major issues of adaptation of Information and Communication Technologies (ICTs). A research study conducted by NASSCOM & Netscribes in ten states of India has also brought forward various e-government issues. Some of the major issues highlighted by the study include lack of reengineering efforts and seamless integration of various government departments. There is a question mark on sustainability of existing e-government projects, Intellectual Property Right (IPR) issues, low Personal Computer (PC) penetration in the government and state, and financial constraints.

The major attributes of organizational performance summarized include organization culture, and structures, regulatory environment, ICTs infrastructure, human resource management, reengineering, transparency, and citizen centric services.

Based on these attributes, a questionnaire for Haryana government departments was developed to assess the organizational performance of Haryana government departments (see Appendix A).

Research Hypotheses and Proposed Model

The government departments in Haryana are involved in providing back-end support to front-end e-government citizen service centers. The practice that measure organizational performance is termed as performance determinant. The organizational performance serves as the criterion variable that contributes to overall performance of the organization. The dependent variable on the other hand is the organizational performance of Haryana government departments. The performance of Haryana government departments has been measured using attributes as listed in the questionnaire (Appendix A). A factor analysis was performed to identify major dimensions of organizational performance (Table 1). The performance dimensions identified using factor analysis includes transparency, organization culture, ICTs infrastructure, regulatory environment, and citizen centricity. The dimensions are consistent with the parameters identified in the literature review section.

For testing the existing organizational performance of Haryana government departments, the following null hypothesis were proposed:

H1: *Organizational performance of Haryana government departments is satisfactory → organization culture*

H2: *Organizational performance of Haryana government departments is satisfactory → regulatory environment*

H3: *Organizational performance of Haryana government departments is satisfactory → ICTs infrastructure*

H4: *Organizational performance of Haryana government departments is satisfactory → Transparency*

H5: *Organizational performance of Haryana government departments is satisfactory → citizen centricity*

To design the organizational performance framework, a log-linear regression analysis was used to design the framework (Table 3 and 4).

The following null hypothesis were suggested to design the framework:

H6: *Organizational performance of Haryana government departments → is not related to organization culture*

H7: *Organizational performance of Haryana government departments → is not related to regulatory environment*

H8: *Organizational performance of Haryana government departments → is not related to ICTs infrastructure*

H9: *Organizational performance of Haryana government departments → is not related to transparency*

H10: *Organizational performance of Haryana government departments → is not related to citizen centricity*

Information and Communication Technologies (ICTs) are playing a significant role in enhancing the performance of organizations all over the world. Various items related to information technology were identified using secondary literature review consisting of unstructured interviews, onsite observations, etc. as listed in the questionnaire (see Appendix B). Factor analysis was conducted to identify the dimension structure for these items. The attributes of ICTs identified include (1) Process improvement, GUI, video conferencing and e-CRM; (2) Process reengineering, change management & ICTs infrastructure; (3) HRIS, RTI, Intranet, & E-Mail; (4) e-CRM, intranet & video conferencing; and (5) Electricity Generator & UPS.

To suggest ICTs solutions, the following null hypothesis were proposed:

H11: *ICTs solutions suggested for e-government organizational performance framework are significantly differing from expert opinions → Process improvement, GUI, video conferencing & e-CRM*

H12: *ICTs solutions suggested for e-government organizational performance framework are significantly differing from expert opinions → Process reengineering, change management & ICTs infrastructure*

H13: *ICTs solutions suggested for e-government organizational performance framework are significantly differing from expert opinions → HRIS, RTI, Intranet, & E-Mail*

H14: *ICTs solutions suggested for e-government organizational performance framework are significantly differing from expert opinions → e-CRM, intranet & video conferencing*

H15: *ICTs solutions suggested for e-government organizational performance framework are significantly differing from expert opinions → Electricity Generator & UPS*

To design the ICTs solutions framework, the following null hypotheses were proposed:

H16: *ICTs solutions → are not related to Process improvement, GUI, video conferencing & e-CRM*

H17: *ICTs solutions → are not related to Process reengineering, change management & ICTs infrastructure*

H18: *ICTs solutions → are not related to HR IS, RTI, Intranet, & e-mail*

H19: *ICTs solutions → are not related to e - CRM, intranet & video conferencing*

H20: *ICTs solutions → are not related to Electricity Generator & UPS*

Research Methodology

The research objectives of the study include:

1. To suggest e-government organizational performance framework for Haryana government departments involved in providing back-end support to front-end citizen service centers,
2. To suggest ICTs solutions framework for the organizational performance dimensions to enhance efficiency and effectiveness of e-government services provided to citizens.

Two questionnaires were designed, first was for officers of Haryana government departments, and second for e-government experts. Haryana government departments involved in providing back-end support to citizen service centers called 'government departments' for the purpose of the study and academicians, consultants, and industry experts, involved in practicing e-government were called 'e-government Experts' for the purpose of the study.(See Figures 1-4).

At the time of conducting the survey eight (8) e-government citizen service centers were operational out of 20 districts in Haryana. These districts were Panipat, Gurgaon, Karnal, Kaithal, Ambala, Hisar, Jind, and Panchkula. Based on geographic and demographic attributes, five (5) districts namely Panipat, Gurgaon, Karnal, Kaithal, and Ambala were selected for the study.

Various government departments are involved directly or indirectly providing back-end support to these service centers. Thirty (30) government departments were selected based on random sampling from those five (5) districts where these selected citizen service centers were operational. The sample size was 30 X 5 = 150. The respondents involved were above or equivalent to the rank of officers.

Several experts are involved in providing e-government solutions. The sample size to get experts was Ninety (90). The English draft of government department's questionnaire was translated into Hindi language as most of the officers preferred local language in answering the questions. The questionnaire to get response from

Figure 1. E-government organization performance framework

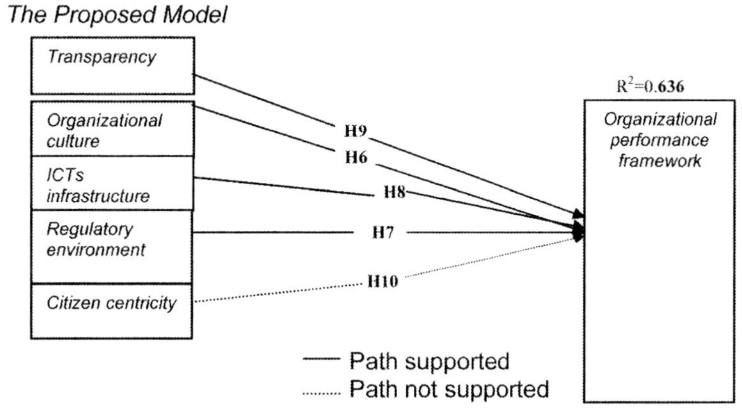

Figure 2. E-government organization performance framework: A conceptual diagram

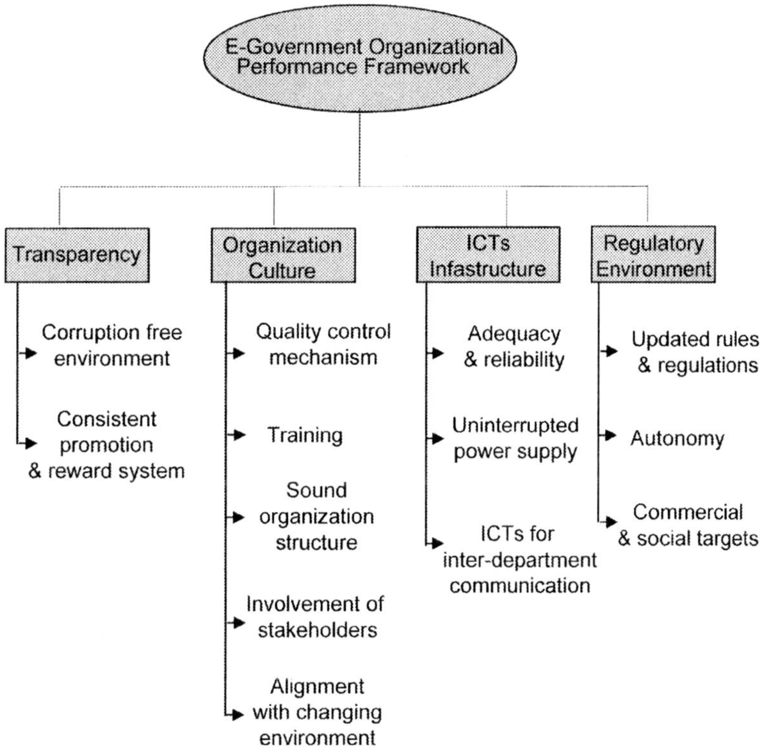

e-government experts was formulated in English language only. The responses for these questionnaires were obtained on a seven point Likert scale, 1 being strongly disagree, and 7 strongly agree (1-Strongly Disagree, 2-Disagree, 3-Somewhat Disagree, 4-Neutral, 5-Somewhat Agree, 6-Agree, and 7-Strongly Agree).

The officers of Haryana government departments were reluctant to divulge information on organizational performance of their respective departments. So, specific attributes about their

Figure 3. ICTs solutions framework

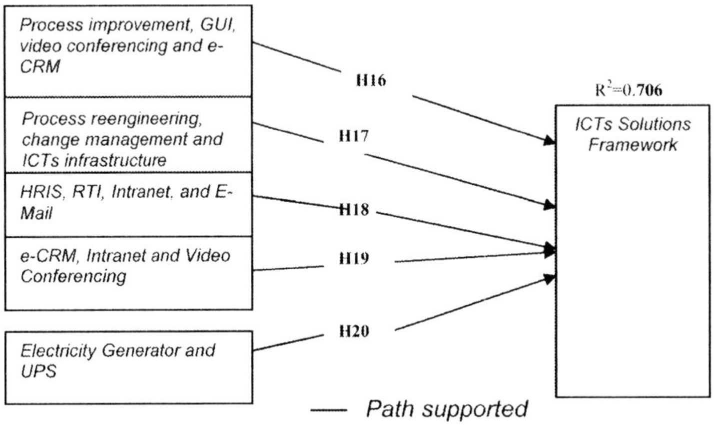

Figure 4. Conceptual diagram of ICTs solutions framework

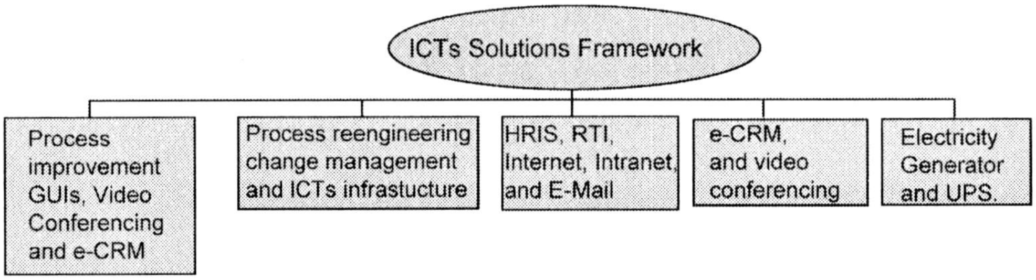

qualification, age, and other demo-graphic information were not asked in the questionnaire.

Statistical Analysis Processing

In order to analyze the data accrued from this research, t-test, factor analysis, and log linear regression analysis techniques were used. The log linear regression analysis was used to design the model. Factor analysis is a statistical data reduction technique used to explain variability among observed random variables in terms of fewer unobserved random variables called factors. Log-linear regression is a kind of regression aimed at finding the best fit between the data and a log-linear model. The major assumption of log-linear regression is that a linear relationship exists between the log of the dependent variable and the independent variables.

The application software SPSS was used for data tabulation and analysis.

E-Government Organizational Performance Framework

Factor Analysis

A factor analysis was conducted to identify factors (dimensions) of organizational performance using a sample size of 150. Factor analyzed a set of 14 items from the questionnaire of government departments (Q.4—Q.17, Appendix A) to test priori assumptions about the underlying factor structure. As a result, 5 factors were obtained. Keeping in view the nature of items, factors were logically grouped as transparency, organization culture, ICTs infrastructure, regulatory environment, and citizen centricity (Table 1).

Reliability of Instruments and Testing of Hypothesis

Before suggesting e-government organizational performance framework, it is pertinent to test existing organizational performance of Haryana government departments. Reliability of instruments and testing of hypothesis is given in Table 2.

The reliability of instruments (Reliability Alpha) for most of the dimensions is accept-able for this type of research ranging from .50 to .99. The t-values (*) as given in the Table shows significance of hypotheses ($H1_0$-$H4_0$) at 5% level. Hence, null hypothesis ($H1_0$-$H4_0$) was rejected. The hypothesis related to citizen centric services ($H5_0$) was accepted which shows that government

Table 1. Result of factor analysis

Dimension (s) along with and items	Factor-1	Factor-2	Factor-3	Factor-4	Factor-5
Factor 1: Organization culture					
Q.6 *There exists a quality control mechanism to improve services of the department.*	0.83	0.08	-0.07	0.00	0.12
Q.11 *Department provides adequate training to its employees.*	0.73	-0.03	0.25	0.30	-0.27
Q.4 *There exists a sound organization structure to facilitate departmental activities.*	0.72	0.49	0.20	0.06	0.03
Q.5 *Department solicit suggestions from its stake-holders in formulating goals and objectives of the department.*	0.67	0.19	-0.03	-0.17	0.52
Q.12 *Employees are able to align themselves with the changing environment.*	0.62	0.40	0.20	0.02	0.13
Factor 2: Regulatory environment					
Q.10 *Obsolete rules and regulations do not hinder the activities of the department.*	0.05	0.86	0.10	0.19	0.01
Q.9 *Department has given full autonomy to to its employees to discharge duties.*	0.19	0.66	0.09	0.21	0.49
Q.7 *Department has set commercial & social targets for its employees.*	0.44	0.63	-0.06	-0.04	-0.06
Factor 3: ICTs infrastructure					
Q.16 *There exists a reliable Information and Communication Technologies (ICTs) Infrastructure in the department.*	0.12	0.13	0.81	-0.23	0.09
Q.15 *Uninterrupted power supply is available from the Electricity Department for consistent usage of PCs.*	-0.08	-0.14	0.71	0.49	0.01
Q.14 *ICT infrastructure is available to facilitate inter-departmental communication.*	0.38	0.40	0.52	0.19	0.08
Factor 4: Transparency					
Q.13 *Department has set consistent promotion and reward system.*	0.43	0.36	-0.12	0.57	0.07
Q.17 *There exists a corruption free environment in the department.*	-0.01	0.16	0.06	0.79	0.21
Factor 5: Citizen centricity					
Q.8 *There is a proper feedback to enhance services provided to citizens.*	0.02	0.00	0.11	0.24	0.89

Note:
a. Extraction Method: Principal Component Analysis
b. Rotation Method: Varimax with Kaiser Normalization.
c. Rotation converged in 9 iterations.

departments are having sufficient monitoring and control mechanism to provide citizen centric services. However, acceptance of hypothesis at test value (5) does not mean that it does not require ICTs solution to enhance its efficiency. The mean value (4.79) for citizen centric services is still below 5 (Some What Agree), which is not adequate for exclusion for further analysis.

Framework Summary

A log linear regression analysis was used to design the organizational performance framework based on five attributes. Table 3 summarizes the framework.

The F value is significant at 1% level at (5/144) degree of freedom. The R square value (.636) indicates the overall contribution of organizational performance (63.6%) is significant to design the framework.

Relationship of Individual Factors to the Overall Organizational Performance

Table 4 illustrates the relationship among factors to the overall organizational performance. 'Critical Ratio' was calculated for each relation along with the findings. Most of the hypotheses were rejected, except $H10_0$ (citizen centricity). 'Critical Ratio' (t-values) calculated are greater than 1.96 and 2.32 which are known to be significant at 0.05 and 0.01 levels, respectively.

Hypothesis from $H6_0$-$H9_0$ are rejected at .01 and .05 level of significance. Hence, null hypothesis $H10_0$ was not found to be significant at .01 and

Table 2. Instruments reliability and testing of hypothesis

Test Value = 5 (Some What Agree)									
						Mean Difference	**95% Confidence Interval of the Difference**		
Null hypothesis	**#**	**Reliability Alpha**	**t value**	**Mean**	**Sig. (2-tailed)**		**Lower**	**Upper**	**Decision**
Organizational performance of Haryana government departments is satisfactory → organization culture	H10	.83	-5.50*	4.50	0.00	-0.50	-0.68	-0.32	Rejected
Organizational performance of Haryana government departments is satisfactory → regulatory environment	H20	.70	-4.33*	4.59	0.00	-0.41	-0.59	-0.22	Rejected
Organizational performance of Haryana government depart ments is satisfactory → ICTs infrastructure	H30	.58	-9.81*	4.13	0.00	-0.87	-1.05	-0.70	Rejected
Organizational performance of Haryana government departments is satisfactory → Transparency	H40	.50	-9.38*	4.04	0.00	-0.96	-1.17	-0.76	Rejected
Organizational performance of Haryana government departments is satisfactory → citizen centricity	H50	.99	-1.69	4.79	0.09	-0.21	-0.46	0.04	Accepted

Note: df= 149, * Significant at 5% level

Table 3. Framework summary

R	R Square	Adjusted R Square	Std. Error of the Estimate	Change Statistics				
				R Square Change	F Change	df1	df2	Sig. F Change
.798	.636	.624	.1743	.636	50.359*	5	144	.000

Note: Predictors variables / attributes:(Constant), organization culture, regulatory environment, ICTs infrastructure, transparency, and citizen centricity.

.05 levels. Hence, relationship of citizen centricity to the overall organizational performance was not established in this case.

Factor Contributions

The contribution of each factor to the organizational performance is summarized in Table 5.

The overall organizational performance explained by external factors is 0.636 (63.6%). The transparency has gained highest contribution (0.3 12) to the performance of Haryana government departments, followed by organization culture (0.306), ICTs infrastructure (0.237), regulatory environment (0.168), and citizen centricity (0.028).

E-Government Organizational Performance Framework

E-government organizational performance framework is shown in Figure 5 along with path coefficient; Figure 6 presents a conceptual diagram of this framework.

The study has suggested an empirically validated e-government organizational frame-work for Haryana government departments—organizational performance is totally explained 63.6% by the external attributes, which include transparency, organization culture, ICTs infra-structure, regulatory environment, and citizen centricity.

Table 4. Testing of hypothesis (path coefficients)

Null hypothesis		Un-standardized		Critical Ratio (t)	Sig.	Findings
		B	Std. Error			
(Constant)	#	0.026	0.103	0.249*	0.804	
Organizational performance framework of Haryana government departments → is not related to organization culture	H60	0.3 06	0.064	4.750*	0.000	Rejected
Organizational performance framework of Haryana government departments → is not related to regulatory environment	H70	0.168	0.070	2.405**	0.017	Rejected
Organizational performance framework of Haryana government departments → is not related to ICTs infrastructure	H80	0.237	0.053	4.459*	0.000	Rejected
Organizational performance framework of Haryana government departments → is not related to Transparency	H90	0.312	0.055	5.698*	0.000	Rejected
Organizational performance framework of Haryana government departments → is not related to citizen centricity	$H10_0$	0.028	0.03 6	0.780	0.437	Accepted

Note: Dependent Variable: Q18(Overall performance), Questionnaire, Appendix A * Significant at p< 0.01 level
** Significant at p< 0.05 level

Table 5. Contribution of factors to the organizational performance

Construct	No. of Items	B values
Overall contribution to organizational performance (R Square)		0.63 6
Transparency	2	0.3 12
Organization culture	5	0.3 06
ICTs infrastructure	3	0.237
Regulatory environment	3	0.168
Citizen centricity	1	0.028

ICTS SOLUTIONS FRAMEWORK

Keeping in view the organizational performance dimensions as validated in the framework (Figure 6), another questionnaire was designed for e-government experts to get their opinions and to recommend ICTs solutions.

Factor Analysis

A factor analysis was conducted to identify dimensions (factors) using a sample size of Ninety (90). Factor analyzed a set of 16 items from the e-government experts' questionnaire (Q5-Q20, Appendix B). As a result, 5 factors were obtained. As per their logical conclusions, factors grouped were (1) process improvement, Graphical User Interfaces (GUIs), video conferencing and Electronic Customer Relationship Management (e-CRM); (2) process reengineering, change management & ICTs infrastructure; (3) Human Resource Information Systems (HRIS), Right to Information Act (RTI), Internet, Intranet, and E-Mail; (4) Electronic Customer Relationship Management (e-CRM), intranet & video conferencing; and (5) Electricity Generator & Uninterrupted Power Supply (UPS). Dimensions along with factor loadings are given in Table 6 (factors are placed in descending order of their factor loadings).

Reliability of Instruments and Testing of Hypothesis

The five (5) factors (dimensions) as given in Table 6 were tested for their statistical significance. The hypothesis proposed, reliability of instruments, testing is given in Table 7.

The reliability of instruments for all dimensions is quite satisfactory. Which range from .63 to .97. Table shows significance of most of the hypothesis ($H11_0$-$H14_0$) at 5% level. The hypothesis related to electricity Generator & UPS was not found to be significant which shows that e-government experts do not agree on Electricity Generator and UPS as the permanent solution to solve the problem of consistent us-age of PCs. Very high mean values (5.23-6.17) were observed for these hypothesis ($H11_0$-$H14_0$) which indicates e-government experts are agree with the suggested ICTs solutions.

Framework Summary

A log linear regression analysis was conducted to design the framework based on predictor's variables. Table 8 given below summarizes the framework.

F value shows significant at 1% level at (5/84) degree of freedom. The R square value .706 (70.60%) indicates the overall contribution of ICTs solutions in this framework, which is very much accepted.

Figure 5. E-government organization performance framework with path

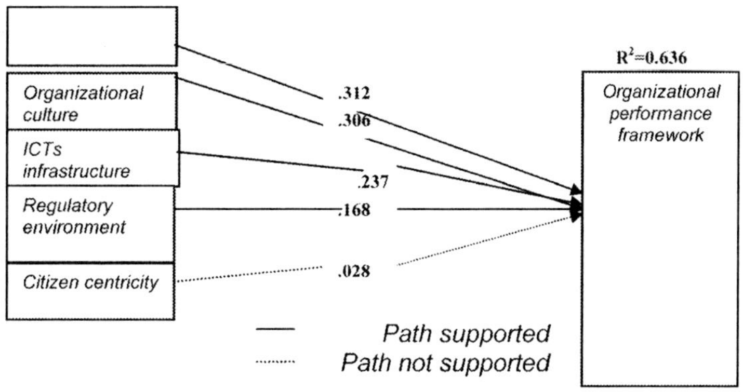

Figure 6. E-government organization performance framework: A conceptual diagram

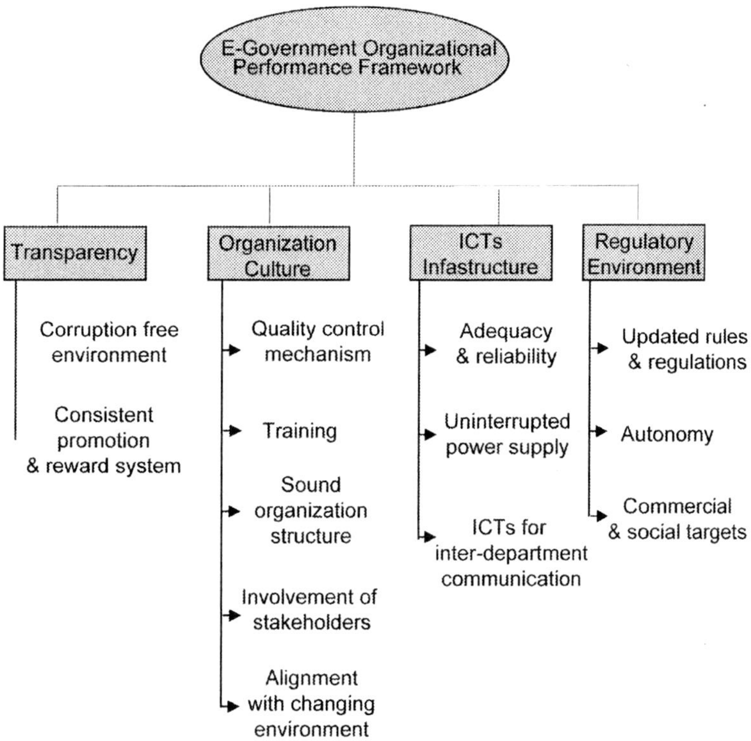

Relationship of individual dimensions (factors) to the overall ICTs Solutions Framework

Table 9 illustrates the relationships among the various factors studied to the ICTs solutions. 'Critical Ratio' (t-value) is calculated for each relation along with the findings.

The values of critical ratio (t) greater than 1.96 and 2.32 are known to be statistically significant at 0.05 and 0.01 levels, respectively. The critical ratios are consistently higher. All Hypothesis from $H11_0$-$R15_0$ is rejected at .01 and .05 level of significance. Hence the relationship of all the predictor variables with the overall ICTs solutions is established.

Table 6. Result of factor analysis

Factor (s)	Factor 1	Factor 2	Factor 3	Factor 4	Factor 5
Factor 1: Process improvement, GUI, video conferencing and e-CRM					
Q.14 *The response time to provide services can be improved using improved processes and integrating services.*	0.93	0.05	0. 12	-0.04	0.11
Q.9 *Open communication, training & extensive usage of Graphical User Interfaces (GUIs) can help to align employees according to dynamic changing global environment.*	0.86	0.23	0.03	-0.04	0.27
Q.16 *Video conferencing*	0.83	-0.02	0.06	0.28	0.02
Q.19 *Electronic Customer Relationship Management (e-CRM)*	0.76	0.39	0.11	0.26	-0.12
Factor 2: Process reengineering, change management and ICTs infrastructure					
Q.18 *Process Reengineering*	0.12	0.89	0.11	0.09	-0.05
Q.5 *Adequate & reliable Information and Communication Technologies (ICTs) infrastructure is required for meeting desired service levels.*	0.17	0.87	0.06	0.06	0.11
Q.10 *Process reengineering can minimize problem of bureaucracy and reduce problem of obsolete procedures and processes.*	0.06	0.81	0.13	0.17	-0.16
Q.17 *Change Management Processes*	0.42	0.54	0.44	0.20	0.29
Factor 3: HRIS, RTI, Intranet, & E-Mail					
Q.12 *Consistency & continuous improvement in employee appraisal, promotion and reward system can be ensured using Human Resource Information Systems (HRIS)*	-0.10	0.22	0.83	-0.04	0.23
Q.13 *Right to Information Act,(RTI) availability of updated information can help to bring transparency & hence reducing corruption in government departments.*	0.24	-0.09	0.71	-0.07	-0.04
Q.20 *Human Resource Information Systems (HRIS)*	0.10	0.41	0.64	0.30	-0.14
Q.8 *Internet, Intranet & E-Mail can enhance stakeholders' participation in e-government*	-0.06	0.36	0.63	0.50	-0.06
Factor 4: *e-CRM, intranet && video conferencing*					
Q.11 *Electronic Customer Relationship Management (e-CRM), audit, review & control mechanisms can ensure effective feedback.*	-0.05	0.17	0.08	0.83	0.26
Q.15 *Integrating government services using Intranet*	0.38	0.23	-0.16	0.71	-0.13
Q.7 *Communication and coordination among government departments can be improved by using Intranet and video conferencing tools.*	0.29	-0.07	0.53	0.66	-0.02
Factor 5: *Electricity Generator & UPS*					
Q.6 *Electricity generator, Uninterrupted Power Supply (UPS) can provide uninterrupted usage of PCs.*	0.20	-0.09	0.04	0.10	0.92

Factor Contributions

The contribution of each factor to the ICTs solutions is given in Table 10.

The overall contribution of ICTs solutions explained by external variables is 0.706(70.60%). Process improvement, GUIs, video conferencing and e-CRM has higher contribution (0.724) followed by process reengineering, change management and ICTs infrastructure (0.676); HRIS, RTI, Intranet, and E-Mail (0.216); and Electricity Generator and UPS (-0.137).

Table 7. Reliability of instruments and testing of hypothesis

Test Value = 5 (Some What Agree)								95% Confidence Interval of the Difference		
Null Hypothesis	#	Instruments Reliability Alpha	t value	Mean	Sig. (2-tailed)	Mean Difference	Lower	Upper	Decision
ICTs solutions suggested for e-government organizational framework are differing from expert opinions → Process improvement, GUIs, video conferencing & e-CRM	$H11_0$	.90	3.21*	5.45	0.00	**0.45**	0.17	0.73	Rejected
ICTs solutions suggested for e-government organizational framework are differing from expert opinions → Process reengineering, change management & ICTs infrastructure	$H12_0$	.86	8.06*	5.87	0.00	**0.87**	0.65	1.08	Rejected
ICTs solutions suggested for e-government organizational framework are differing from expert opinions → HRIS, RTI, Internet, Intranet, & E-Mail	$H13_0$	.77	15.74*	6.17	0.00	**1.17**	1.02	1.31	Rejected
ICTs solutions sug- gested for e-govern- ment organizational framework are differing from expert opinions → e-CRM, intranet & video conferencing	$H14_0$	.63	8.49*	5.80	0.00	**0.80**	0.61	0.99	Rejected
ICTs solutions suggested for e-government organizational framework are differing from expert opinions → Electricity Generator & UPS	$H15_0$	.97	.23	5.23	0.22	**0.23**	-0.14	0.61	Accepted

Note: df=89, * Significant at 5% level

Table 8. Framework summary

R	R Square	Adjusted R Square	Std. Error of the Estimate	Change Statistics				
				R Square Change	F Change	df1	df2	Sig. F Change
0.840	0.706	0.688	0.132	0.706	40.321	5	84	0.000

Note: Predictors variables:(Constant), (1) process improvement, GUI, video conferencing & e-CRM; (2) process reengineering, change management & ICTs infrastructure; (3) HRIS, RTI, Intranet, & E-Mail; (4) e-CRM, intranet & video conferencing; and (5) Electricity Generator & UPS.

ICTS SOLUTIONS FRAMEWORK

A framework for ICTs solutions is shown in Figure 7 along with the path co-efficient and Figure 8 presents a conceptual diagram of this framework.

The ICTs solution framework empirically validates the ICTs solution suggested to improve the effectiveness of items proposed in e-government organizational performance framework.

Table 9. Testing of hypothesis (path)

Null hypothesis		Un-standardized B	Un-standardized Std. Error	Critical Ratio (t)	Sig.	Findings
(Constant)	#	**-1.069**	**0.225**	**-4.758**	**0.000**	
ICTs solutions framework → is not related to Process improvement, GUI, video conferencing & e-CRM	$H16_0$	-0.137	0.045	-3.022*	0.003	Rejected
ICTs solutions frame work → is not related to Process reengineering, change management & ICTs infrastructure	$H16_0$	0.216	0.088	2.446**	0.017	Rejected
ICTs solutions frame work → is not related to HRIS, RTI, Internet, Intranet, & E-Mail	$H18_0$	0.676	0.146	4.639*	0.000	Rejected
ICTs solutions frame work → is not related to e-CRM, intranet & video conferencing	$H19_0$	0.724	0.095	7.616*	0.000	Rejected
ICTs solutions frame work → is not related to Electricity Generator & UPS	$H20_0$	0.112	0.034	3.319*	0.001	Rejected

Note: Dependent Variable: Q21 (Overall ICTs solutions), (Questionnaire, Appendix B) * Significant at p< 0.01 level
** Signifi cant at p< 0.05 level

CONCLUSION AND RECOMMENDATIONS

Government of Haryana after examining the need to fine-tune processes of its departments has taken various ICT initiatives. The major initiative of the state government has been the establishment of e-government citizen service centers in eight (8) out of twenty (20) districts. These citizen service centers have been established for providing various e-government services keeping in view the success achieved by other state governments.

Citizen Service Centre initiative has been found to be a one-sided view of the government. Currently, citizen service centers are functioning as front-end in terms of access to various e-government services. This front-end is getting support from the back-end (the Haryana government departments) to provide various services to citizens. Through focused interviews with selected officials of Haryana government departments and users of e-government services, it has been found that without strengthening the back-end; the e-government objectives can not be achieved.

Table 10. Factor contributions

Construct	No. of Items	B values
Overall contribution to ICTs solution (R Square)		0.706
Process improvement, GUI, video conferencing & e-CRM	4	0.724
Process reengineering, change management & ICTs infrastructure	4	0.676
HRIS, RTI, Internet Intranet, & E-Mail	4	0.2 16
e-CRM, Intranet & video conferencing	3	0.112
Electricity Generator & UPS	1	-0.137

Figure 7. ICTs solutions framework with path coefficients

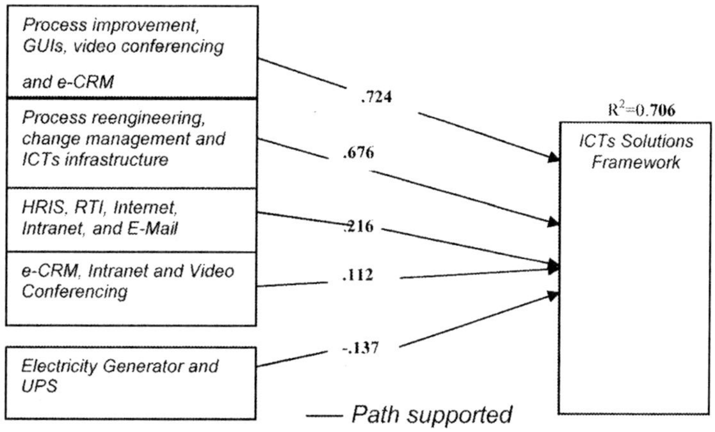

Figure 8. Conceptual diagram of ICTs solutions framework

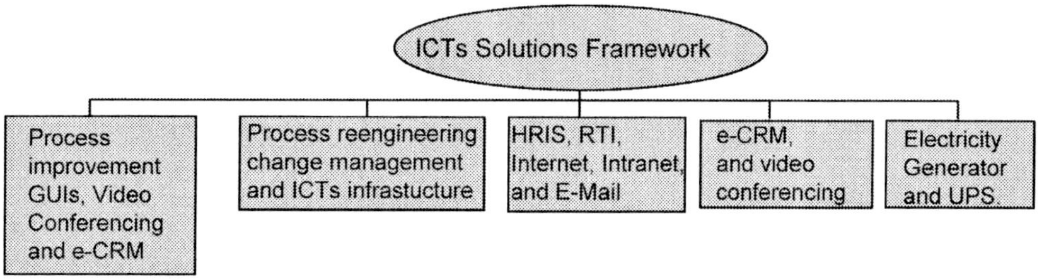

Hence, the chapter focused on identifying the organizational performance attributes; measuring their performance in Haryana government departments (back-end), and thereafter recommending ICTs solutions. A factor analysis was conducted on the performance attributes as identified from the literature. The major attributes of organizational performance identified include transparency, organizational culture, ICTs infrastructure, regulatory environment, and citizen centricity. Based on these five (5) attributes null hypothesis were proposed (H1-H5) assuming that existing organizational performance of Haryana government departments is satisfactory? A t-test was performed on these attributes to test the hypothesis. The results (Table 2) rejected most of the null hypothesis except citizen centricity.

The conclusions and recommendations to design an organizational performance framework (Figures 5 and 6) and ICTs solutions framework (Figures 7 and 8) are given as under:

Transparency

Transparency is the major catalyst for improving trust among citizens in accessing e-government services. The consistent promotion and reward system for departmental employees can help to bring transparency in the departmental functioning and hence enhancing morale of employees. There is a need to strengthen efforts to provide corruption free environment to improve fair access to e-government services by the citizens.

Right to Information Act, ready availability of updated information to the citizens can also help to bring transparency and hence reducing corruption in government departments. Bhatnagar, 2003 has demonstrated the potential impact of transparency in reducing corruption in government departments. Also, Cho et al., 2005 established that transparency and accountability is the core of the management system. The citizens and the city officials tend to have favorable opinions on the impact of its corruption control and its effect on transparency.

Organizational Culture

Another prominent attribute, organizational culture needs immediate attention in terms of enhancing effectiveness by setting up quality control mechanisms in e-government services. Sound organizational structure is required to facilitate departmental activities. Training of government officials has been identified as very crucial component in enhancing the quality of services. The involvement of citizens in formulating goals and objectives of the departments can help the government to incorporate citizens' views. There is an emergent need to align departmental employees to the fast changing environment.

Change management and process reengineering has found to be the major ICTs initiative to improve organizational culture, structure, quality, and provide necessary training to depart-mental employees. According to Gulledge, et al., 2002, public organizations by changing their organization structures can resolve the problem of obsolete procedures and processes. Hughes et al., 2006 in their research to investigate the role of business process redesign in creating citizen-centric e-government in Ireland has validated the importance of improving processes and successful deployment of e-government services.

Internet, Intranet, e-mail, and video conferencing can enhance stakeholders' participation in government departments. Tan et al., 2003 proposed a model for understanding into how organization-stakeholder relationships can be efficiently managed to bring about an effective overhaul of business processes. According to Shackleton et al., 2006, for the local government sector, Internet offers significant potential for the delivery of government services.

Open communication, training and Graphical User Interfaces (GUIs) can improve organizational culture in government departments. Lonti et al., 2003 after analyzing the adoption of work design and employee involvement practices in Canadian government workplaces has found that there is a high incidence of both flexible work design and employee involvement practices along with training found in government departments.

ICTs Infrastructure

ICTs infrastructure needs improvement in terms of providing adequate power backup for the consistent usage of PCs. The inter-department communication needs improvement for better coordination among departments. E-government experts' suggested that by proving adequate and reliable Information and Communication Technologies (ICTs) infrastructure the government can meet desired service levels in e-government services.

Regulatory Environment

The existing regulatory environment in Haryana government departments needs overhauling by updating existing rules and regulations. There is an emergent need to provide full autonomy to officers in discharging their duties. It has also been felt that by setting social and commercial targets for the departments, a competitive environment can be established to enhance e-government services.

Electronic Customer Relationship Management (e-CRM), audit, review and control mechanism can ensure effective feedback and control mechanism in providing e-government services. The feedback given by stockholder's can be used to provide autonomy to departments and hence setting commercial and social targets. King, 2006 in his research study has established that CRM-enabling call centers and the provision of routine transactions can help in understanding stakeholders better in terms of providing efficient regulatory environment in e-government services.

Contributions of the Study

The study has suggested e-government organizational performance framework and ICTs solutions framework to enhance efficiency and effectiveness e-government services provided to citizens for the Government of Haryana. The structure of this framework can be used as a reference point to suggest similar other models for the government.

REFERENCES

Bhatnagar, S. (2003).Administrative Corruption: How Does e-government Help? In *Proceedings of Global Corruption Report 2003, Transparency International*. Retrieved November, 15, 2008 from http://www.gipi.az/ssi_eng/egov/20030324.pdf

Cho, Y. H., & Choi, B.-D. (2005). E-government to combat corruption: The case of Seoul metropolitan government. *International Journal of Public Administration, 27*(10), 719–735. doi:10.1081/PAD-200029114

Gulledge, R. R., & Sommer, R. A. (2002). Business process management: Public sector implications. *Business Process Management Journal, 8*(4), 364–376. doi:10.1108/14637150210435017

Hughes, M., Scott, M., & Golden, W. (2006). The role of business process redesign in Ireland. *Business Process Management Journal, 12*(1), 76–87. doi:10.1108/14637150610643779

King, S. F. (2007). Citizens as customers: Exploring the future of CRM in UK local government. *Government Information Quarterly, 24*(1), 47–63. doi:10.1016/j.giq.2006.02.012

Lonti, Z., & Verma, A. (2003). The determinants of flexibility and innovation in the government workplace: Recent evidence from Canada. *Journal of Public Administration: Research and Theory, 13*(3), 283–309. doi:10.1093/jopart/mug025

Saxena, A., & Wadhwa, S. (2004). E-business perspective of e-governance. In M. P. Gupta (Ed.), *Promise of e-governance*. New Delhi: Tata McGraw Hill.

Shackleton, P., Fisher, J., & Dawson, L. (2006). E-government services in the local government context: An Australian case study. *Business Process Management Journal, 12*(1), 88–100. doi:10.1108/14637150610643788

Sharma, K. S., & Palvia, S. (2004). Organizational and cultural barriers to e-governance implementation in India. In M. P. Gupta (Ed.). *Towards e-governance*. New Delhi: Tata McGraw Hill.

Singh, A. (2005). Sidestepping pitfalls. DataQuest, May 21, 2005. Retrieved August 29, 2008 from http://www.dqindia.com/content/egovernance/2005/105052101.asp

Tan, C. W., & Pan, S.L. (2003). Managing e-transformation in the public sector: An e-government study of the inland revenue authority of Singapore (IRAS). *European Journal of Information Systems archive, 12*(4), 269-281.

Vittal, N. (n.d.). *Change management and process reengineering*. Paper presented in the CII e-governance summit, September 21, 2001, New Delhi. Retrieved May 30, 2006 from http://cvc.nic.in/vscvc/cvcspeeches/sp6sep01.pdf.

APPENDIX A

Questionnaire: Haryana Government departments

District:________________

The objective of this questionnaire is to know performance of your Department. The information provided by you will be kept confidential and will be used for academic purposes only.

I. Respondent's Profile

1. Officer's Name (Optional)
2. Designation
3. Department

II. Organizational Performance

Please give your ranking out of 7 (see Table 11):

1	2	3	4	5	6	7
Strongly Disagree	Disagree	Some What Disagree	Neutral	Some What Agree	Agree	Agree Strongly

4. There exists a sound organizational structure to facilitate Departmental activities.

   1 2 3 4 5 6 7
5. Department solicits suggestions from stakeholders in formulating goals and objectives of the department.

   1 2 3 4 5 6 7
6. There exists a quality control mechanism to improve services of the Department.

   1 2 3 4 5 6 7
7. Department has set commercial & social target for its employees.

   1 2 3 4 5 6 7
8. There is a proper feedback & control mechanism to monitor services provided to citizens.

   1 2 3 4 5 6 7
9. Department has given full autonomy to its employees to discharge responsibilities.

   1 2 3 4 5 6 7
10. Obsolete rules and regulations do not hinder the activities of the Department.

    1 2 3 4 5 6 7
11. Department provides adequate training to its employees.

    1 2 3 4 5 6 7
12. Employees are able to align themselves with the changing global environment.

1 2 3 4 5 6 7

13. Department has set consistent promotion and reward system.

1 2 3 4 5 6 7

14. ICT infrastructure is available to facilitate inter-department communication.

1 2 3 4 5 6 7

15. Uninterrupted power supply is available from the Electricity Department for consistent usage of PCs.

1 2 3 4 5 6 7

16. There exists a reliable Information and Communication Technologies (ICT) Infrastructure in the Department.

1 2 3 4 5 6 7

17. There exists a corruption free environment in the Department.

1 2 3 4 5 6 7

18. I am satisfied with the performance of the Department.

1 2 3 4 5 6 7

III. Suggestions

Thanks for your cooperation

APPENDIX 2

Questionnaire: E-Government Experts

Location:

The objective of this questionnaire is to obtain your opinion for possible Information and Communication Technologies (ICT) solutions to design an e-government framework for Haryana Government. The information provided by you will be kept confidential and will be used for academic purposes only.

Respondent's Profile

1. Expert's Name
2. Specialization
3. Designation
4. Affiliation

II. Information & Communication Technologies Solutions

Please give your ranking out of 7 (see Table 12):

1	2	3	4	5	6	7
Strongly Disagree	Disagree	Some What Disagree	Neutral	Some What Agree	Agree	Agree Strongly

5. Adequate & reliable Information and Communication Technologies (ICT) infrastructure is required for meeting desired service levels.

   1 2 3 4 5 6 7

6. Electricity generator, Uninterrupted Power Supply (UPS) can provide uninterrupted usage of PCs.

   1 2 3 4 5 6 7

7. Communication and coordination among government departments can be improved using Intranet and video conferencing tools.

   1 2 3 4 5 6 7

8. Intranet & e-mail can enhance stakeholders' participation in e-government

   1 2 3 4 5 6 7

9. Open communication, training & extensive usage of Graphical User Interfaces (GUI) can help to align employees according to dynamic changing global environment.

   1 2 3 4 5 6 7

10. Process reengineering can minimize problem of bureaucracy and reduce the problem of obsolete procedures and processes.

    1 2 3 4 5 6 7

11. Electronic Customer Relationship Management (e-CRM), audit, review & control mechanisms can ensure effective feedback.

    1 2 3 4 5 6 7

12. Consistency & continuous improvement in employee appraisal, promotion and reward system can be ensured using Human Resource Information Systems (HRIS)

    1 2 3 4 5 6 7

13. Right to Information Act, ready availability of updated information can help to bring transparency & hence reducing corruption in government departments.

    1 2 3 4 5 6 7

14. The response time to provide can be improved using improved processes and integrating Government services.

    1 2 3 4 5 6 7

Do you recommend e-government integrated platform using following ICT tools?:

15. Integrating government services using Intranet

    1 2 3 4 5 6 7

16. Video Conferencing

    1 2 3 4 5 6 7

17. Change Management

    1 2 3 4 5 6 7

18. Process Reengineering

    1 2 3 4 5 6 7

19. Electronic Customer Relationship Management (e-CRM)

    1 2 3 4 5 6 7

20. Human Resource Information Systems (HRIS)

    1 2 3 4 5 6 7

21. I am satisfied with the solution recommended as above to solve problems in providing e-government services to citizens by the government Departments

    1 2 3 4 5 6 7

Thanks for your cooperation

Chapter 11
E-Government in Saudi Arabia: Between Promise and Reality

Maher O. Al-Fakhri
Ministry of Civil Service, Saudi Arabia

Robert A. Cropf
Saint Louis University, USA

Gary Higgs
Saint Louis University, USA

Patrick Kelly
Saint Louis University, USA

ABSTRACT

Saudi Arabia is in the process of transitioning to e-government. Many of the Saudi government agencies have their own web sites; however, most are ineffective. Based on the findings of this study, the Saudis should consider several reforms, chief among which include the following: Increasing the awareness of its e-government program among its employees and the public at-large; making Internet access more available across the full spectrum of society; equipping public facilities for Internet usage; developing a legal framework for secure e-transactions; adopting a flexible approach to technological change and the IT environment more generally; providing IT training to government employees; partnering with the private sector to establish electronic fund transfers; and, finally, fostering 2-way communication between government agencies and between the government and the public.

INTRODUCTION

The private sector has made significant strides toward using electronic business, known as e-business, as a technological tool to provide services to their customers faster and better. E-business assists businesses in making faster decisions and helping to improve efficiency and productivity. Also many governments have taken steps toward implementing electronic government, or e-government, but their progress must be considered more deliberate and slow compared with the private sector. In fact, progress varies from one government to another (even within the U.S.). Some governments such as Sweden, the United States, and Singapore have made tremendous strides forward using e-government. According to Holmes (2001), the business sector is more eager to invest in technology than the public sector since companies must compete with each other to provide better services and attract customers. However, governments do not need to attract customers, and making a right decision is more important than making a fast decision. In the private sector, a quick decision is often important to remain competitive in the market place.

In theory, e-government provides opportunities for government agencies to do their jobs better in a less costly manner. Holmes (2001) says that e-government is being led by the need for government to improve services, reduce expenditures, meet public anticipations and improve relationships with citizens, and assist with economic development. Furthermore, e-government can play a significant role in building trust between governments and citizens by providing an opportunity for them to participate in the policy process (OECD 2003). E-government can create networks of information flow among the different parts of the government to facilitate access to services, and also to transform the working environment for public employees at all levels. According to the Organization for Economic Co-Operation and Development, or OECD, (2003) "[g]overnments will have to follow suite [sic] and adopt information society tools and working practices if they [want] to remain responsive to their citizens needs."

Recently, governments in the Middle East have started using e-government as a means to achieve a high level of performance while providing cost effective outcomes. However, many of these governments are still in the beginning of that process. Saudi Arabia, the biggest country in the middle east, is on course for a transition to e-government. Today, most of the Saudi government agencies have their own Web sites; however, most of these Web sites are inefficient in that they just provide basic and general information about the organizations and often the data are not up to date. While some of these Web sites offer better services, such as interactive services and the ability to submit a form, it is hard to find a government Web site where you can apply for a job, arrange an appointment, or renew a license.

According to Denslow (2005), there are some issues facing the adoption of e-government in the region. One of the largest challenges is the low levels of computer literacy rates and poor IT skills in the region. The United Arab Emirates hosted a conference entitled "e-government forum" that was organized by Datamatix group in May, 2005. The main goal of that conference was to address the problems and challenges facing e-government implementation in the region (Stensgaard, 2005).

REVIEW OF THE LITERATURE

There have been a number of studies that focus on the e-government experiences from several developing countries around the world. Many of these studies examine the effects, impacts, challenges, and issues of implementing e-government from the perspective of a developing nation. However, there have been relatively few studies on e-government in Saudi Arabia or the rest of the Arab world. Studies conducted by OECD (2003) provided depth examinations of several countries' experiences with implementing e-government including Australia, Canada, Denmark, Mexico, the United States, and Germany. The studied compared and evaluated the differences of implementing e-government among these selected OECD countries. Also, they focused on the challenges and obstacles that should be overcome in order for e-governments to flourish. The results showed the most important challenges facing governments today and in the future include lack of funds, shortage of skills, overall costs, lack of accountability, and difficulties of monitoring and evaluating e-government programs.

A study conducted by Heeks (2003) examined the failure and success rates of e-government in developing or transitional countries. Results indicated more than one-third of e-government projects in developing or transitional countries are total failures; half are partial failures; and roughly one-seventh are successes. The study showed no evidence that e-government failure rates are higher or lower in developing countries than in industrialized countries because of limitations in the methods used in that study.

Few studies have investigated the condition of e-government in Saudi Arabia or the rest of the Arab world. One of these studies was conducted by Al-Mashet (2005) and indicated the importance of non-technical factors, such as human, administrative, and economic, to implement e-government. The study found that there is plenty of research on the technical aspects of e-government implementation and IT while there is inadequate research done on the non-technical aspect. The study showed that there is recognition among specialists and practitioners of e-government to the importance of non-technical factors. However, that study only focused on factors of the success of implementing e-government in academic fields in Saudi Arabia, and it did not include support by particular examples of Saudi Arabia agencies.

Another study completed by Sandy (2002) addressed some obstacles facing implementation of e-government in the Arab world such as lack of funds, expense of costs, resistance of change, and the English language. The study found that there are a few examples of successful e-government in the Arab world such as Dubai. Additionally, comparison was done between the technology markets in the Arab world. It found that Saudi Arabia's technology market is the biggest market in the Arab world consisting of nearly 40% of technology consumptions in the region. Sandy supported his study by providing some examples of successful e-government projects in the world such as Canada, Singapore, the USA, and Switzerland.

Meso, Checchi, Sevcik, Loch, and Straub (2006) investigate how national information and communication technology (ICT) policies are disseminated in Egypt and why there is a differential awareness of policies among various sectors and/or professions. The findings suggest that a critical element for the implementation of national ICT strategies involves the correct positioning of ICT policies. This is especially true for developing countries, where the effects of ICTs in leveraging economic and social development are viewed as crucial.

Joshua Teitelbaum (2002) examines the effects of introducing the Internet to Saudi Arabia and the country's attempt to strike a balance between the communications, business, and economic changes wrought by the Web with the country's conservative form of Islam. He also discusses the Saudi opposition's use of the Internet and the Saudi government's efforts to block these sites and other sites deemed objectionable by the government.

Similarly, Fandy (1999) asserts that nowhere has the impact of globalization of the information society been felt more intensely than in the Middle East. His study indicates that in the Gulf states, the understanding of resistance, national boundaries, and territoriality as well as other social science concepts such as sovereignty, the nation state, and citizenship are becoming increasingly blurred by the reality of global ICT.

The World Summit on the Information Society

The World Summit on the Information Society (WSIS) was an effort by the United Nations to draw attention to the significance of information and communication problems, particularly in developing countries. The WSIS can be seen as an expansion and continuation of the European Union initiative on the information society, enlarging this initiative to encompass the greater "world community" and focusing on ICTs and IT infrastructure growth (Kenney & Valauskas, 2005). The WSIS has had two phases, the first phase took place in Geneva in December 2003, and the second phase took place in Tunis in November 2005. WSIS can be viewed as an effort on the part of the international community to move away from a concentration on "communication" to a focus on "information." As part of the WSIS, a number of case studies were done on the experience of IT development in Arab countries, which are summarized.

A number of different e-government initiatives have been launched in the Arab countries with the goal of achieving a high level of performance while providing cost-effective outcomes. According to the WSIS, most Arab countries developed strategic plans to improve their usage of technology to deliver services to their citizens. Those strategic plans depend for their success on the characteristics of each country, including the cultural ones.

Saudi Arabia, in particular, has recognized the essential role of e-government and IT. The Saudi government created a plan that includes a clear vision of the role of ICT in Saudi society. Saudi Arabia has been closely involved in the WSIS process including taking part in a regional conference hosted in Damascus 2004. In spite of the existence of national policies and strategies to foster the growth of ICT in Saudi Arabia, outside observers and Saudi officials believe that there is resistance to the Internet among some community leaders, therefore slowing down the pace to progress (United Nations, 2005).

Moreover, according to WSIS, Arab nations, in general, should pay more attention to development of the human capacity. Taking into consideration the increasing role of new services like e-health, e-government, e-learning and others, the Arab countries have to guarantee that information society remains inclusive for all. It should prevent creation of new divides (United Nations, 2005)

METHODOLOGY

In this article, both the number and types of the Saudi government's online services are examined using a survey that was sent to a number of government agencies. Furthermore, a comparison of the Saudi e-government program with two successful examples of e-government programs elsewhere is carried out. Additionally, issues regarding the awareness of Saudi government employees of the e-government initiatives and the problems and challenges that face Saudi government as it tries to implement its e-government program are examined. Thus, an exploratory survey was conducted using a questionnaire designed to measure the awareness of Saudi government employees regarding the e-government program as well as examining the challenges and problems facing the implementation of e-government program in Saudi public agencies.

Research Questions

The questions this research addresses can be divided into three parts. The first question focuses on the types of e-government initiatives that are being undertaken in public sector organizations in Saudi Arabia. The second question focuses on the awareness of Saudi governmental employees of implementation of e-government. The third question focuses on the problems and challenges that face the Saudi government as it tries to implement an e-government program.

Data Collection

Data for this research are collected primarily from two sources: government Web sites and mailed questionnaires. The researchers analyzed a variety of government Web sites to find out what services are available to the Saudi public. This research examined the content of current Web sites. Government Web sites are evaluated based on a variety features such as: online database, office address and phone number, technical assistance, disability access services, digital signatures, and credit card payment. The second data source is a questionnaire. The questionnaire was used to find out about the obstacles and issues facing the implementation of the e-government program in Saudi Arabia.

Each questionnaire was accompanied by cover letters which explained the purpose of the survey and directions for filling out the questionnaire. The questionnaires were answered confidentially and returned. The questionnaires were mailed to Saudi government's employees selected at random. The first section of the questionnaire is designed to obtain the subjects' personal information such as age, work experience, and educational background. The second section is designed to obtain information on their capabilities of using computer and Internet networks particularly in work and to measure their understanding of the concept of e-government. The third section is designed to obtain information about the types of e-government which are currently available in the Saudi public sector. The fourth section is designed to determine possible challenges and issues facing implementing e-government in Saudi Arabia today. The last section is designed to determine the types of available services to the public by agencies' Web sites and to evaluate the performance of these Web sites from the perspective of subjects.

RESEARCH ANALYSIS

E-Government in Saudi Arabia Compared to Other Countries

The first area of research has been to make a comparison of implementation of e-government program in Saudi Arabia with two countries, the United Arab Emirate and the United States. The reason for this selection is because both these countries have advanced online governments. The United Arab Emirate has been recognized as the top performer in e-government readiness in the Arab world and it is located in the same region, the middle east. Also, both Saudi Arabia and the United Arab Emirate share many similarities such as culture, political system, and economic status, while the United States has the highest rank in the world for implementing e-government in 2005 according to the study conducted by the United Nations Online Public Network and Finance (UNPAN) in 2005 (United Nations, 2005).

Saudi Arabia's E-Government Compared to United Arab Emirate's E-Government

The United Arab Emirate (UAE) is one of the six Gulf States. It lies to the east of Saudi Arabia. The UAE is the first Arab government to launch an e-government portal. According to the study conducted by UNPAN in 2005, the UAE has posted one of the most remarkable year-over-year gains among all the countries of the world in 2005. It is the ahead of all other Arab countries in implementing an e-government program successfully. Its ranking has risen from 60th place in 2004 to 42nd in 2005, while Saudi Arabia's ranking has improved from 90th place in 2004 to 80th in 2005 (United Nations, 2005).

Comparing Saudi Arabia's e-government initiative with UAE's e-government initiative requires evaluating both portals: First, the Saudi portal http://www.saudi.gov.sa only provides general and basic information and services such as information about e-government initiative in Saudi Arabia.[1] Some basic features offered by the portal such as e-mail address contact, search and comments, latest news and updating, online publications, foreign language, related links, and Saudi government links. While the UAE portal http://

www.government.ae/gov/en/index.jsp consists of four sections which are: residents, business, visitors, and government. Each one of these sections offers many services, including access to government departments and services and information on businesses and facilities for traders, investors, and companies. It is also possible for users to pay fines or renew credits cards and driving licenses. Other impressive features on the site itself include up-to-date information, as well as registration and e-tenders, which incorporate online bidding for public tenders. Also, the visitors' section offers varied services which would assist visitors to the UAE, such as information about culture, tours, weather, shopping, museums, and hotels. In addition, the UAE portal provides clear access to two excellent portals, one of which is e-dirham portal, http://www.e-dirham.gov.ae, for transactions, and the e-forms portal, http://www.uaesmartforms.com , for online forms advancing its interactive presence.[2] According to UNPAN, the e-dirham portal and the e-service which are part of UAE portal classified among the best practice models in the world in 2005 (United Nations, 2005).

Riyadh E-Government Portal Compared to Dubai E-Government Portal

Riyadh is the capital and largest city of Saudi Arabia. It is the political, administrative, and financial center of Saudi Arabia. The Riyadh e-government site http://www.arriyadh.com/index.asp established in 2002, offers a variety of information, news, weather, maps, as well as cultural, health, tourist, and shopping information, and other pages that are useful to the population of Riyadh as well as visitors.[3] The site aims to provide official online services for citizens and visitors through one single site.The site provides citizens and visitors with a modern and advanced database covering city activities and services, and economic, cultural, health, and scientific information. However, regarding e-government program, the site only provides information about the e-government initiative in Saudi Arabia and some basic services, such as access to Saudi public agencies, besides other related links.

On the other hand, Dubai, one of the United Arab Emirate cities and one of the most famous cities in the middle east, has made outstanding progress over the past couple of years in implementing an e-government program and becoming one of the world's most advanced online governments. The Dubai portal http://www.dubai.ae/ was established in 2001. The Dubai e-government project, representing 24 government departments, aims to offer official online services for citizens and visitors via one single site. The Dubai portal pledges that "citizens won't be required to go to different departments to apply for one single service," and that they "will have to be able to get access through different channels, Internet, mail, phone and front-desk operators, and through English and Arabic" (Dubai portal). The Dubai e-government portal is divided into six sections: citizens, residents, visitors, local business, foreign companies, and investment in Dubai. One of its strengths lies in its ease of use. For instance, the visitors' section provides updated information on activities in Dubai, a variety of information about hotels, transportation, entertainment, the latest immigration laws of the UAE, and information about obtaining visit visas. In addition, the site offers online flight booking via Emirate airline. The citizens' and residents' sections give citizens and residents of Dubai access to government departments and services, allowing people to pay fines, apply for a job, and renew driving licenses. Furthermore, the investment section offers a variety of information on businesses and facilities for traders, investors and companies. "Dubai citizens can make online payments for public services at no additional cost, using the ePay facility on the Dubai E-Government's payment gateway. E-Pay is a secure online payment method that lets users pay for public utilities or fines using credit card or the e-Dirham card under approval of the UAE

Ministry of Finance and Industry" (egovernment-United Arab Emirates, 2004).

Saudi Arabia's E-Government Compared To United States' E-Government

The UN global e-government readiness index 2005 presents the state of e-government readiness of many countries around the world. The measurement used by the United Nations is based on the capacity and willingness of countries to use e-government. According to the 2005 global e-government readiness report, which was conducted by the United Nations, the United States was the world leader in e-government readiness rankings from 2003 to 2005 (see Table 1) (United Nations, 2005). Also, another study conducted by Darrell M. West, director of the Taubman Center for Public Policy at Brown University, ranked the United States as the second highest ranked in the world for implementation of e-government in 2005, after Taiwan (2005).

The USA has had considerable success in launching governmental Internet-portals, which transform traditional communication between government agencies and citizens, optimizing the request procedure, and promoting better transparency of government institutions.

The FirstGov Project (www.firstgov.gov) is a single governmental Internet portal that was launched in September 2000. Its goal was to implement a national program to help U.S. government institutions transition to new information technologies. FirstGov.gov is the official U.S. gateway to all government information. The

Table 1. E-government readiness index rank changes 2003-2005 (Source: Global E-government Readiness Report 2005. Retrieved May 15, 2007, from http://unpan1.un.org/intradoc/groups/public/documents/un/unpan021888.pdf)

Country	2005	2004	2003	Change 2005-2004	Change 2005-2003
United States	1	1	1	0	0
Denmark	2	2	4	0	2
Sweden	3	4	2	1	-1
United Kingdom	4	3	5	-1	1
Republic of Korea	5	5	13	0	8
Australia	6	6	3	0	-3
Singapore	7	8	12	1	5
Canada	8	7	6	-1	-2
Finland	9	9	10	0	1
Norway	10	10	7	0	-3
Germany	11	12	9	1	-2
Netherlands	12	11	11	-1	-1
New Zealand	13	13	14	0	1
Japan	14	18	18	4	4
Iceland	15	14	15	-1	0
Austria	16	17	21	1	5
Switzerland	17	15	8	-2	-9
Belgium	18	16	23	-2	5
Estonia	19	20	16	1	-3
Ireland	20	19	17	-1	-3
Malta	21	21	27	0	6
Chile	22	22	22	0	0
France	23	24	25	1	2
Israel	24	23	24	-1	0
Italy	25	26	17	1	-8

strength of the United States online government presence is fundamentally driven by two major elements. First, it provides a tremendously useful Web portal http://www.firstgov.gov, which provides massive amounts of information and services in one place. The second strength, and the keystone of the United States' approach to e-government, is the reliance on integrated portals, which gather and consolidate information in one place, thus making it easier for users to find topic-specific information in an efficient way. According to the U.S. Department of Education site "On FirstGov.gov, you can search millions of Web pages from federal and state governments, the District of Columbia and U.S. territories. Most of these pages are not available on commercial Web sites. FirstGov has the most comprehensive search of government facilities anywhere on the Internet" (EDGAR, 2005). Also, it offers links to the frequent asked questions (FAQs) sections of a variety of government agencies. The FAQ feature also contains a response timeframe for submitted questions about the U.S. government. According to FirstGov, http://www.firstgov.gov/feedback/FeedbackForm.jsp, an answer will be provided for each submission within two business days, which is comparable to the practices in the private sector. Few countries offer a formal online consultation facility; however, the U.S. not only provides one but has implemented complete consultation portal (referred to as public comment/input in the U.S.)—a one stop site to comment on federal regulations, http://www.regulations.gov. For an overview, see http://www.whitehouse.gov/omb/egov/downloads/e-gov_initiatives.htm. Additionally, the U.S. is engaged in numerous interesting initiatives. For instance, the Department of Education, http://www.ed.gov, provides a distinctive feature, the "Teachers Ask the Secretary" section, http://www.ed.gov/teachers/how/reform/teachersask/index.html, where a person can ask the U.S. Secretary of Education a question and receive a reply posted on the site. According to UNPAN, the FirstGov portal and the U.S. Department of Education are the best practice models in the world in 200 (United Nations, 2005).The United States is far in advance of Saudi Arabia and many countries around the world in use and application of an e-government program.

In summary, there are some differences in the way countries around the world implement e-government. The Saudi public sector needs a strategic plan for implementing e-government projects in order to assure appropriate coordination between different organizations. It should also learn from the experience of other countries, such as the United Arab Emirate and the United States, in order to avoid any pitfalls that may be encountered. Saudi Arabia does not have a true national government site or portal, but there are some available government sites which have been expanded and improved dramatically since 2005. Whereas, its overall e-government development is still in the initial stages, the e-government portal provides a means through which citizens, companies, and residents can all attain government services in a fast and efficient way.

The portal would act as an entry way through which government organizations can offer their information and services, thus decreasing the number of required visits by citizens or residents to government agencies. In addition, the portal would ensure the integration and precision of the information provided to the public. Despite the fact that Saudi Arabia is lagging behind many other countries in implementing e-government applications, several attempts and initiatives have been ongoing.

SURVEY RESULTS AND ANALYSIS

The findings of this survey are based on 57 respondents to the questionnaire. The survey used snowball sampling and cannot ensure that participants are representative of Saudi government employees as a whole. However, the survey was distributed among a variety of Saudi government employees in term of government agency, position, age, length of service, and education. The observations and inferences the researchers draw from the survey results can therefore arguably apply to a large proportion of Saudi government employees. The questionnaire survey was designed for completion within 25-30 minutes. It consists of multiple choice questions and statements to which the employees could respond by marking several categories which range from "Strongly agree" to "Strongly disagree."[4]

The information from the survey can be divided into four areas: 1) demographic information, 2) the Saudi public sector's use of IT, 3) Saudi public employees' awareness of e-government, and 4) the challenges and issues facing e-government in Saudi Arabia. Each of the four sections is devoted to one of these areas with a discussion of the implications of the findings at the end of each section.

Demographic Information

The survey collected a broad range of demographic data from trial users. These data included the respondents' age, position, education, and length of their services.

The pie chart in this section provides an introductory snapshot of the distribution of the age of the respondents in this study. Half of the participants (50%) are between 40-50 years, 21 % of the respondents are between 30-40 years, while only 14 % of the participants are over 50 years, and 14% are between 20-30 years (Figure 1).

Most of the respondents in this study have been working in the public sector between 21-30 years, which is expected since the age of the majority of participants is between 40-50 years, followed by 30% having been working between 11-20 years (Figure 2).

Over 56% of the respondents are employees, followed by managers, 23%, general managers, 16%, and only around 4% of the participants are supervisors (Figure 3). The education level of respondents was quite high, 53% have a bachelor degree, and an additional 30% have master or Ph.D. degree, and only 16% have less than a bachelor degree (Figure 4).

Use of IT in the Public Sector in Saudi Arabia

This section measures what types of technology tools are available in the Saudi public sector, such as computers and Internet networks. The results were as follows:

Fully 88% of the respondents have computers compared to only 11% who do not have them. Of those who have computers, 26% rated their dependence on a computer network for achieving tasks as high or very high, 15% considered their dependence as average, while 5% said it is low (Figures 5 and 6).

Despite the growth of Internet use in Saudi Arabia, using the Internet to accomplish government tasks appears rarely. Over half of participants said that their departments do not have Internet connections at all (Figure 7). In addition, only 18% of those who have Internet connections at

Figure 1. The age of respondents

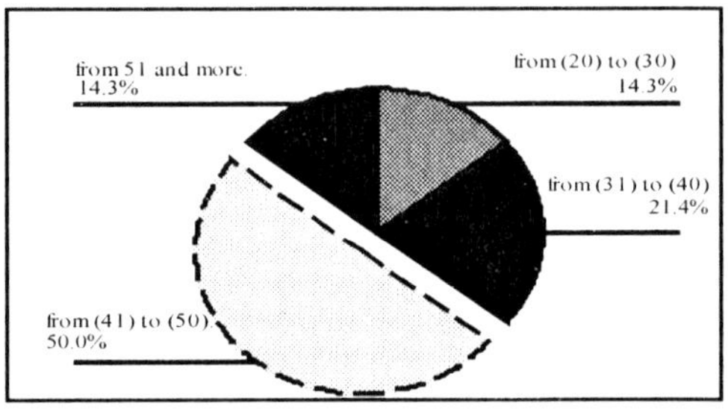

Figure 2. The length of respondents' service

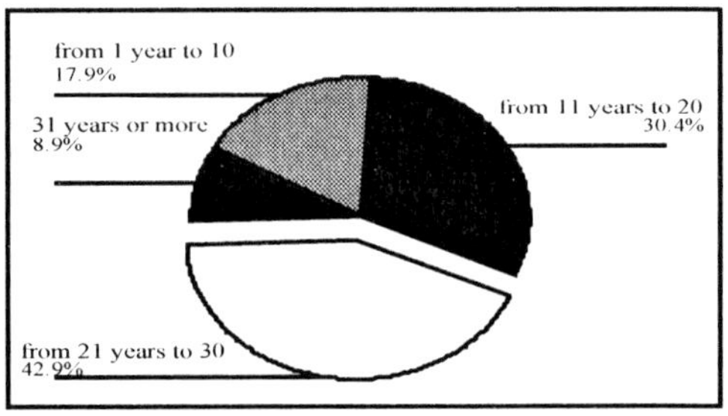

Figure 3. Job position of respondents

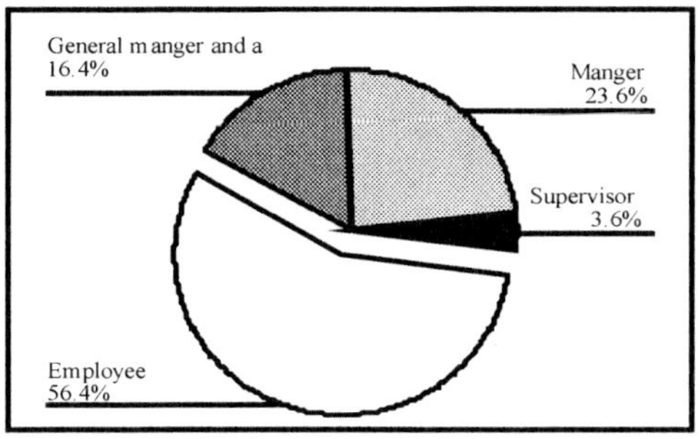

Figure 4. Education level of respondents

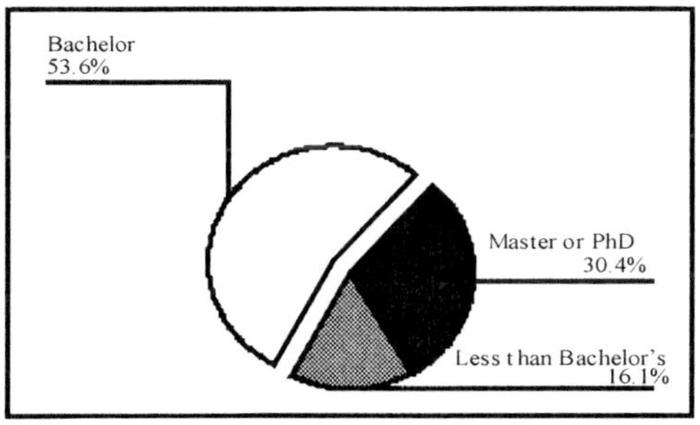

Figure 5. Agency connection to computer network

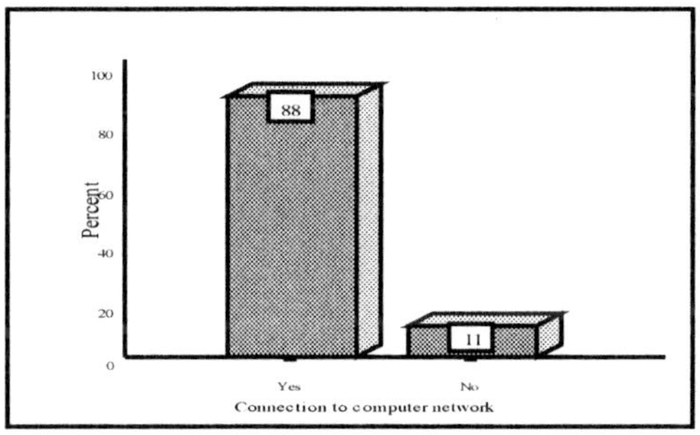

Figure 6. Computer usage for accomplishing tasks

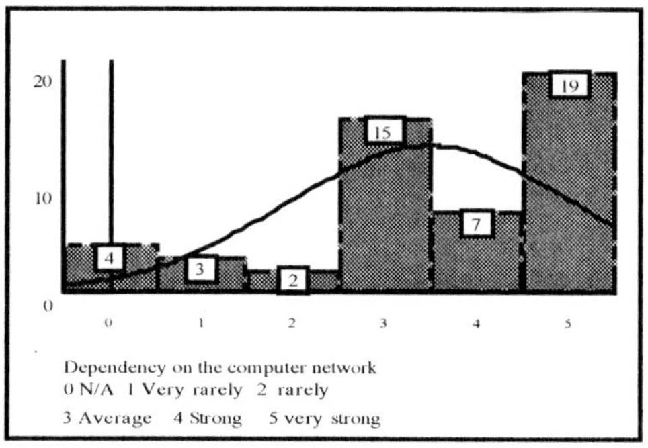

Figure 7. Employee dependence on the Internet

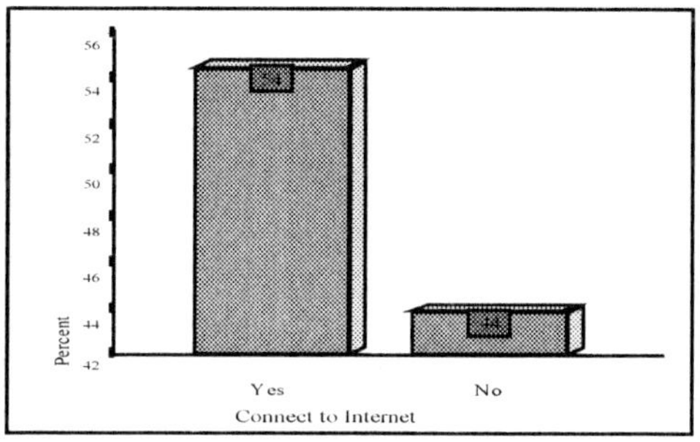

Figure 8. Using Internet for accomplishing tasks

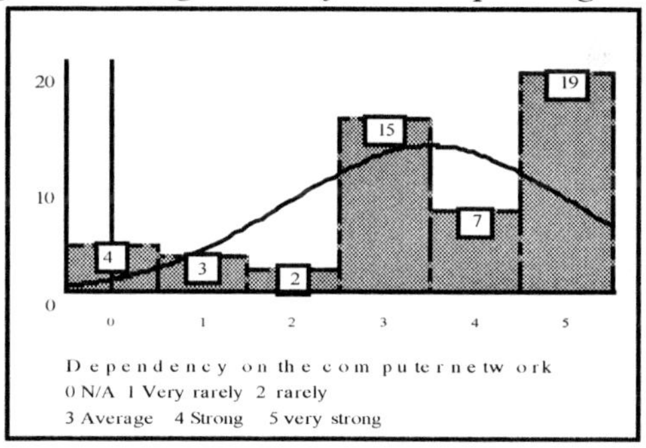

work are using the Internet to accomplish government tasks (Figure 8). Finally, only 25% of the government employees have access to Internet from work and 61% from home (Figure 9).

Employees's Awarness of E-Government

This section examines the level of awareness of Saudi government employees regarding the e-government program in the Saudi public sector. The key findings were as follows:

More than half of the respondents do not know whether or not their agencies are working on a timeframe to implement e-government successfully (Figure 10).

Thirty-seven percent of all participants do not know if the senior management supports the process of transitioning to e-government or not,

Figure 9. Accessing the Internet

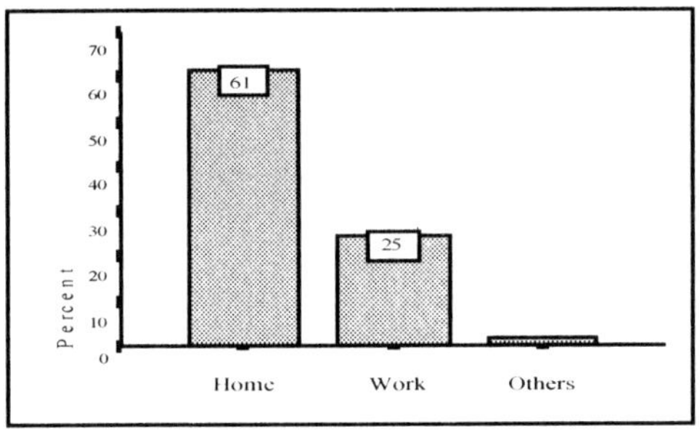

Figure 10. The agency has a timeframe to transition to e-government

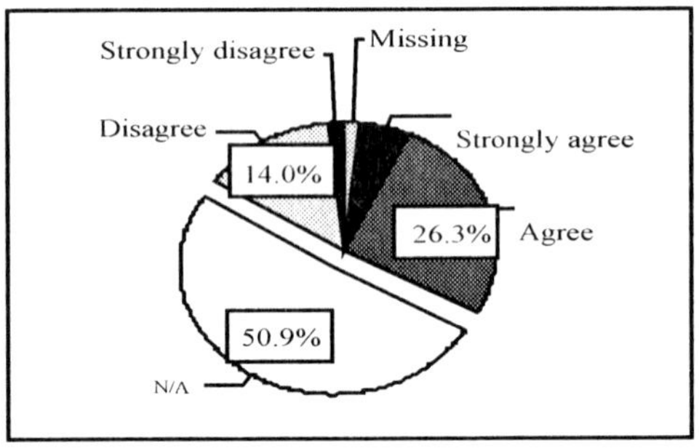

while 54% either agree or strongly agree that the senior management supports the transition to e-government (Figure 11).

Over half of the respondents do not know whether the information of users in their agencies' sites is secured or not (Figure 12).

Thirty-three percent of all respondents disagree that they have an opportunity to participate in their agency's plan for implementing an e-government program, while 35% do not know if they could participate or not. While 19% believe that their agencies allow them to contribute to an e-government plan, most of those who believe they have the chance to participate in the agency plan are general managers or at least at the managerial level (Figure 13).

Forty percent of the total participants believe that there is a Saudi portal of e-government, while 33% of the respondents do not know whether it exists or not (Figure 14).

Forty-two percent of the total respondents do not know if there is a collaboration between

Figure 11. Senior management supports the transition to e-government

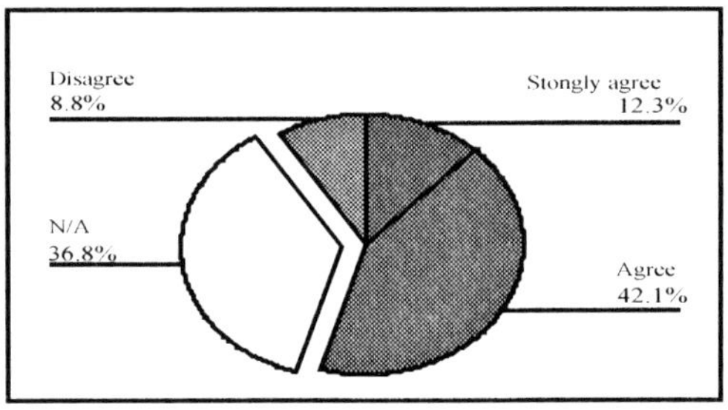

Figure 12. The information on the agency Web site is secure

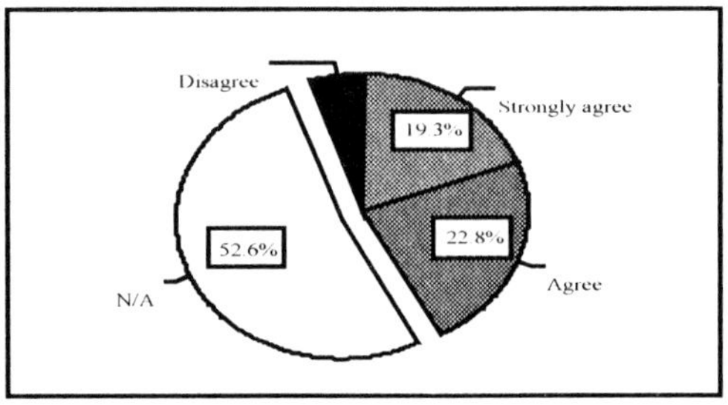

Figure 13. The agency allows its employees to participate in its plan to implement e-government

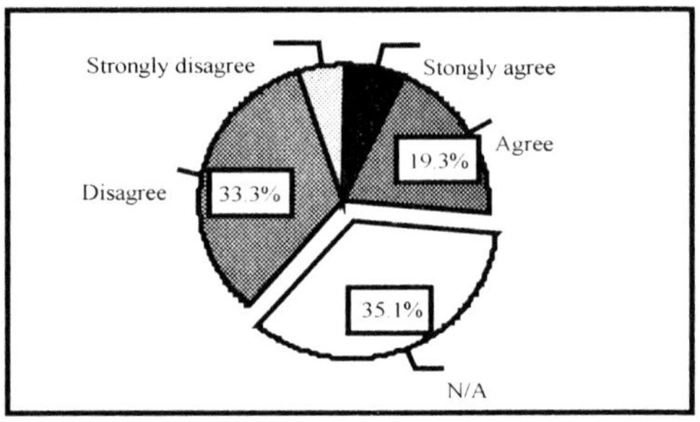

their agencies and other Saudi public agencies for implementing an e-government program or not. Another 21% believe that there is no collaboration, and 36% think that the Saudi government organizations collaborate with each other to implement an e-government program (Figure 15).

Over 50% of all respondents either disagree or strongly disagree with the statement that "employees could share information online to perform some government tasks," while 17% do not know if

Figure 14. There is a Saudi e-government program

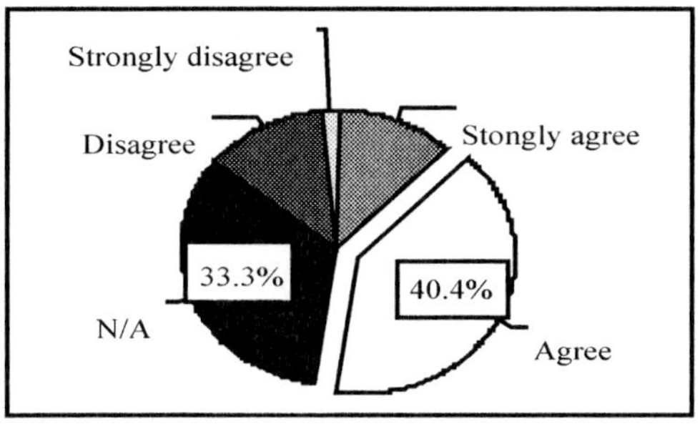

Figure 15. The agency collaborates with other agencies

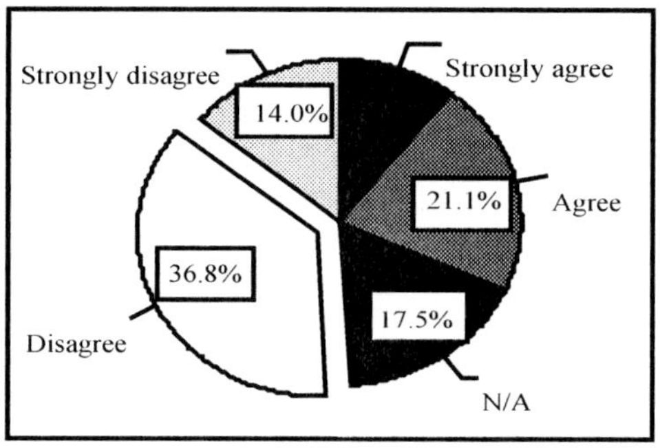

Figure 16 a. Employees share information online to perform tasks

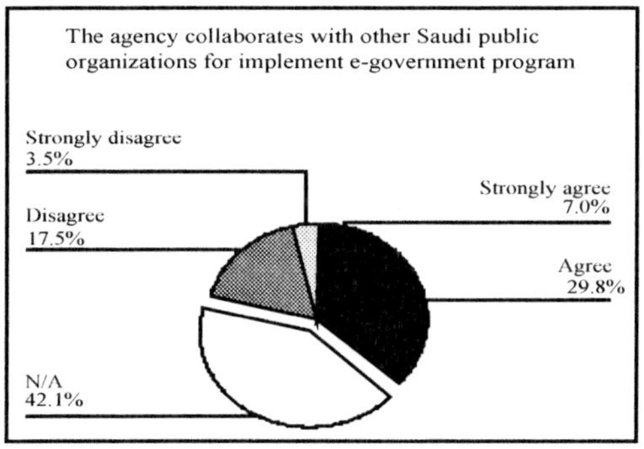

Figure 16b. Employee can share information with other saudi agencies through the agency's

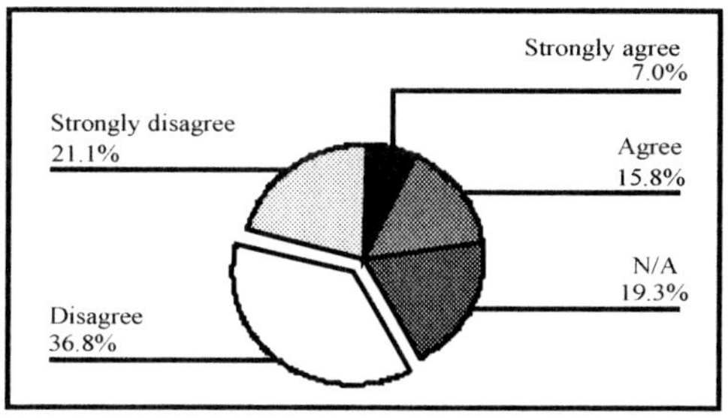

it is possible or not (Figure 16a). In addition, 58% disagree or strongly disagree with the possibility of sharing the information online between Saudi government agencies (Figure 16b).

Almost 39% of participants do not know if their agencies update information on their Web sites consistently or not (Figure 17). While 35% of all participants do not know whether their agencies' sites offer some essential services, such as submitting forms online or not, while 28% said that feature does not exist on their agencies' site; and 24% said it is available (Figure 18).

Almost 39% of the respondents disagree with the statement that, "the agency site allows users to make personal changes to their information or at least request the agency to make this change online," while 35% do not know if users could make changes or not (Figure 19).

Over 59% of all respondents agree or strongly agree with the statement that "the agency Web site provides just introductory information about the agency," while 28% disagree (Figure 20).

Thirty-three percent of all participants do not know whether information and services are offered in both Arabic and English on their agencies' sites or not, while 28% said that feature is not available and 23% said it is available (Figure 21).

Twenty-six percent of the total respondents do not know if their agencies' departments connect

Figure 17. The agency updates its information on its site frequently

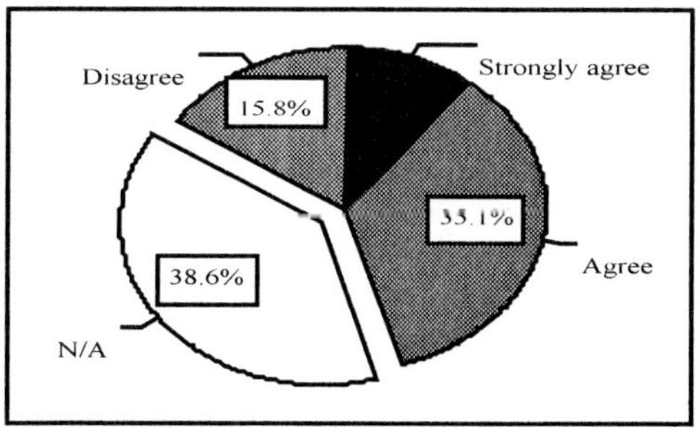

Figure 18. The agency site provides some essential services such as submitting forms online

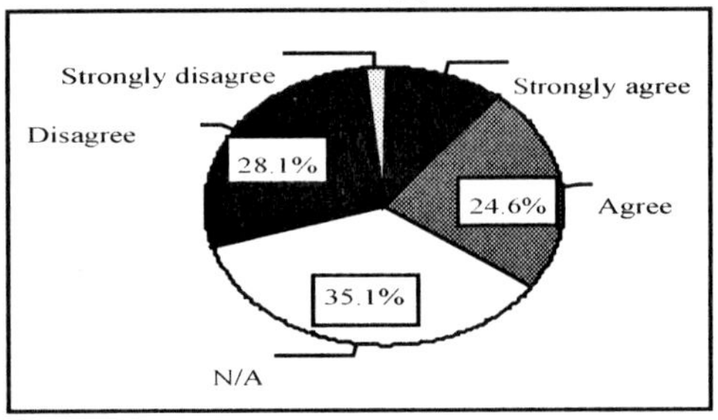

Figure 19. Agencies allow users to make personal changes online on their information

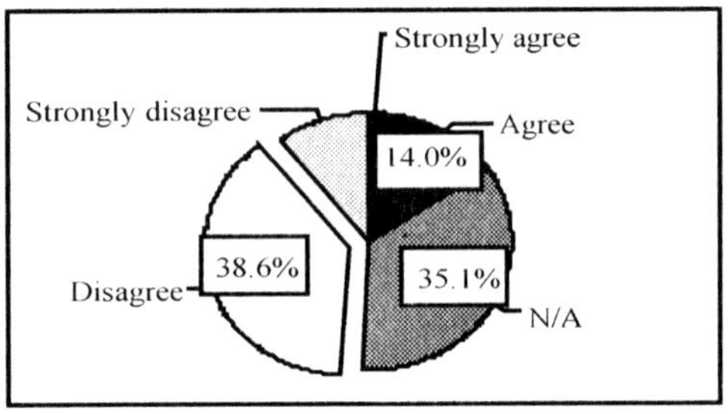

Figure 20. The Agency site provides just basic information about the agency

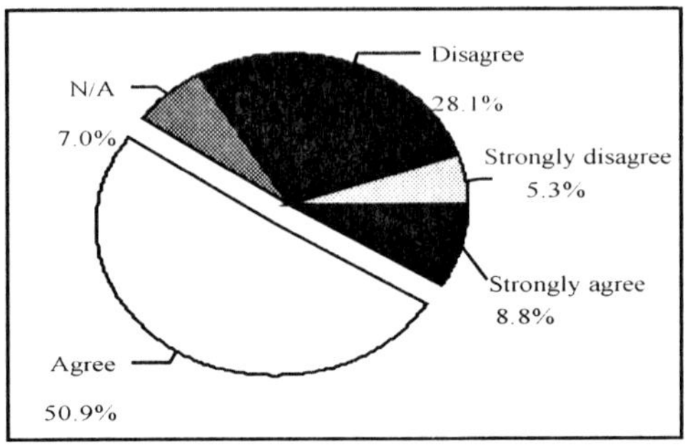

Figure 21. The agency's Web site provides all information and services in Arabic & English

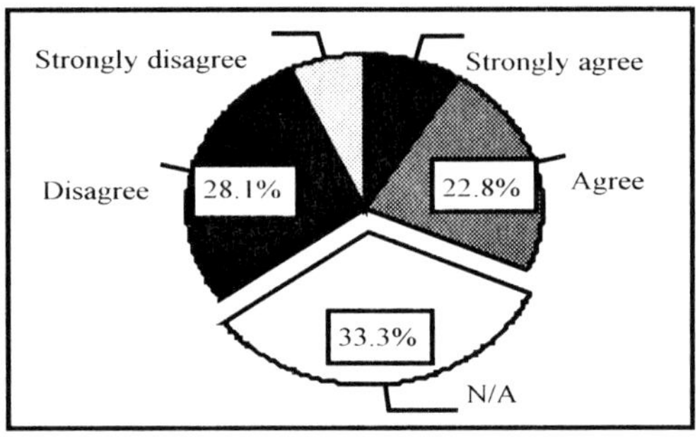

Figure 22. The agency departments connect

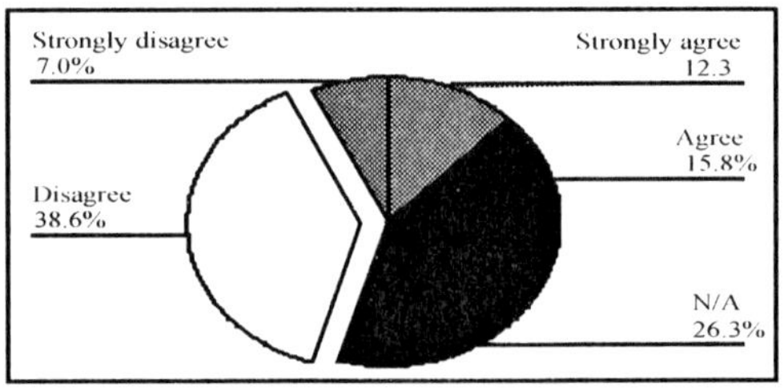

Figure 23. The agency site provides electronic signature

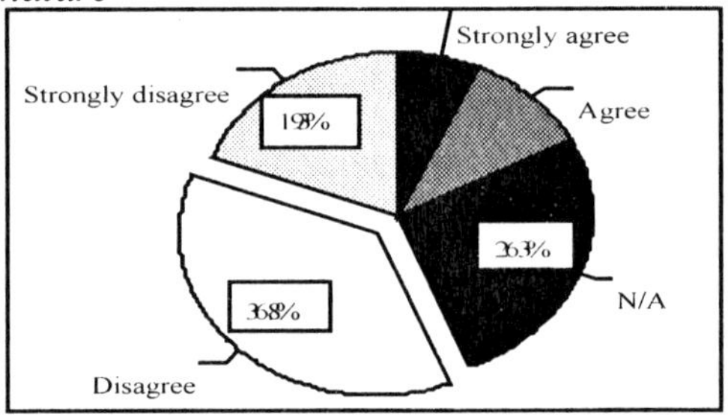

with each other online or not, while 45% disagree or strongly disagree that there is a connection between their agencies departments (Figure 22).

Fifty-six percent of all respondents either disagree or strongly disagree that their organizations have digital signatures feature, while 26% do not know if this feature is available or not (Figure 23).

Sixty-nine percent of all respondents either disagreed or strongly disagreed with the statement "the Internet is available for the entire agency's employees," while only 15% do not know if it Internet is available to all employees in their agencies or not (Figure 24).

The results in this section show that most of the participants do not have adequate knowledge and information regarding the process of implementing e-government in their organizations. The "do not know" selection is high in most of their responses, which indicates that their awareness of the process of implementing e-government is too low, or they do not access their agencies' sites

Figure 24. The internet is available for all the agency's employees

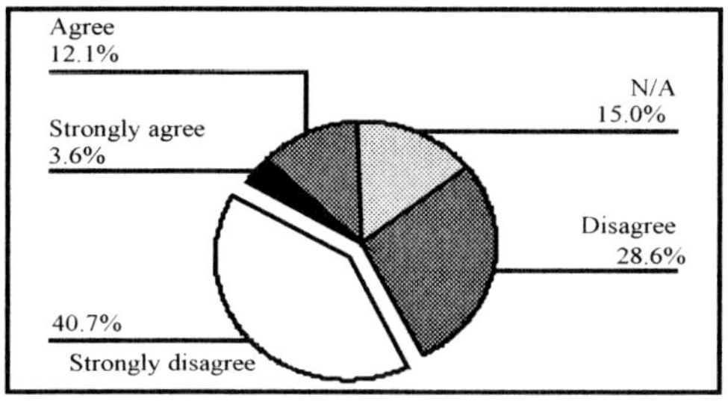

Figure 25. There is lack of e-government education among government employees

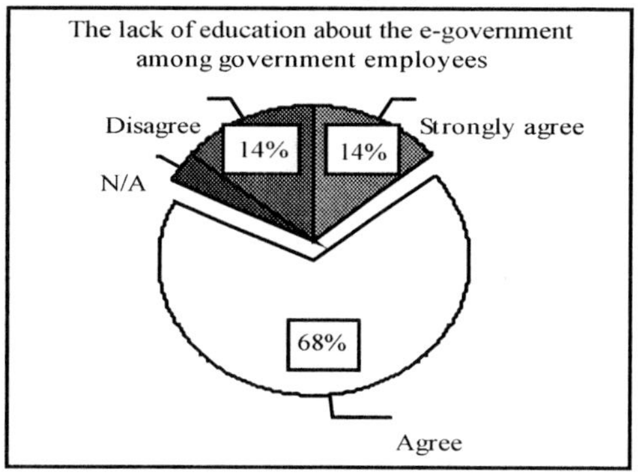

because they do not find them useful. Employees need to be aware of the e-government strategy and understand what it means to them as public employees. One of the crucial reasons for the lack of awareness has been the exclusion of employees from participation in the process of implementing an e-government program. As shown in Figure 13, only 19% said that they have an opportunity to participate in the e-government process. The participation process would most likely lead to an increase in employees' awareness and knowledge about an e-government program. Successful coordination between government and private organizations is also needed to build awareness about e-government and to help employees and leaders use technology. Additionally, the general finding in this section matches the result of analyzing the status of e-government in Saudi government Web sites. Both results indicate that the progress of e-government initiative in the public sector in Saudi Arabia has been modest at best.

Challenges and Issues Facing E-Government

The main reason for conducting the survey, as mentioned in the methodology section, is to answer the question "What are the challenges and issues facing implementing e-government in Saudi Arabia?" To answer this question the researchers placed 20 potential challenges and issues as statements in the survey and asked the participants to give their views on each of them.

What the researchers believe to be the most important findings are listed. In addition, 82% of the respondents either agree or strongly agree that there is lack of education about e-government among government employees, while 14% disagree (Figure 25).

Sixty-seven percent of all the respondents either agree or strongly agree with the statement "there is a lack of studies and research in Saudi Arabia regarding e-government," while only 18% disagree (Figure 26).

The survey shows that 68% of all respondents either agree or strongly agree with the statement that "the current agency structure is not appropriate to implement an e-government program," while 16% disagree or strongly disagree (Figure 27).

A high percentage—72%—of all survey respondents either agree or strongly agree with the statement that "the current regulations of the agency are not appropriate to the requirements

Figure 26. There is shortage of e-government research in Saudi Arabia

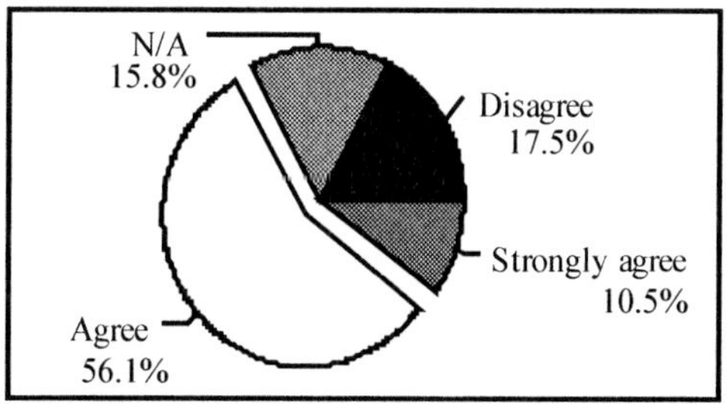

Figure 27. The agency structure is not conducive to e-government program

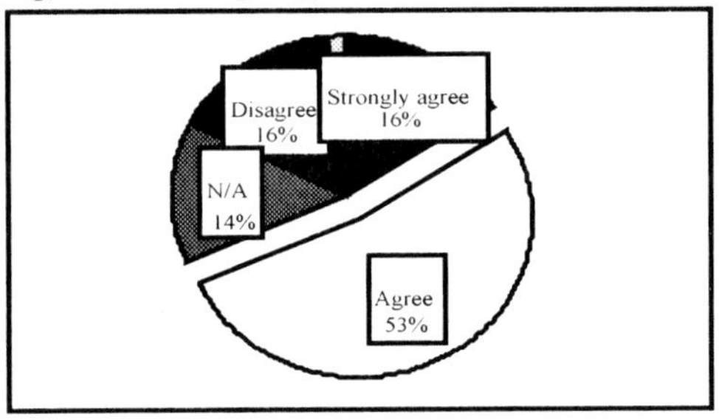

Figure 28. The agency's regulations is not conducive to e-government program

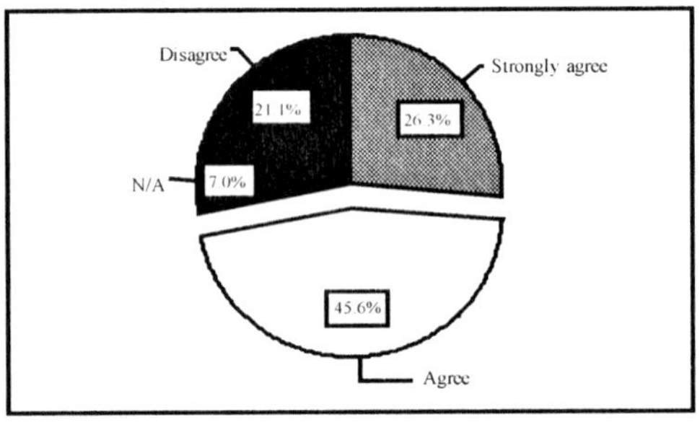

of implementing e-government," while only 21% disagree with that statement (Figure 28).

Half of the total participants either agree or strongly agree that senior management resists any change in the way an agency accomplishes work, while 23% disagree, and 27% do not know (Figure 29). However, 32% of the respondents disagree that employees resist any change in perform work, while 47% either agree or strongly agree that the employees' resistance to changing the way they perform work is an obstacle for implementing e-government (Figure 30).

Fully 65% of all respondents agreed with the statement that "fear of consequences and results of the process of transition to e-government" is one of the obstacles to implementing e-government, while 23% disagree with this statement, and 12% do not know (Figure 31).

Forty-seven percent of respondents consider providing the same services among the government agencies as an obstacle to implementing e-government successfully, whereas 26% do not

Figure 29. Senior management resists change

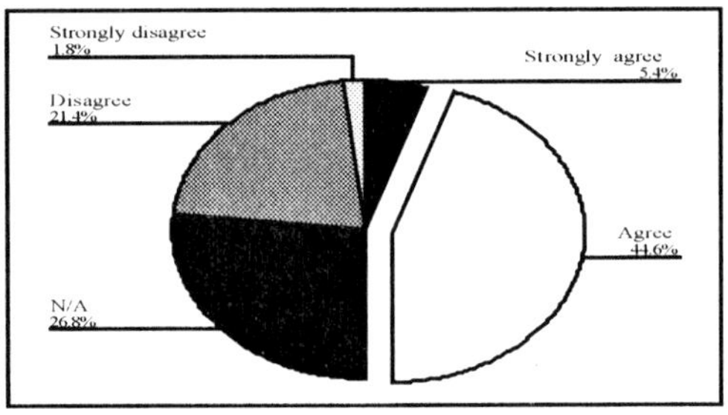

Figure 30. Employees resist change

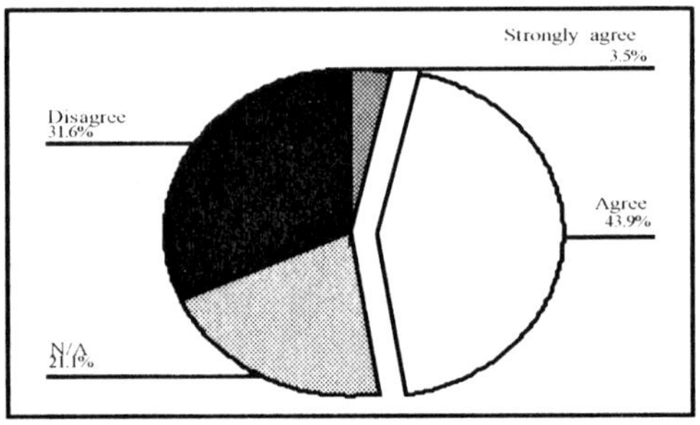

see that meddling is an issue, and 26% do not have an opinion about that (Figure 32).

The respondents divided almost equally on whether the small number of people using the Internet in Saudi Arabia is an issue of implementing e-government in the public sector or not. Forty-four percent believe this is an issue, while 39% did not see it as an obstacle (Figure 33).

Forty-eight percent of the total participants believe that the absence of a supervisory agency to oversee the implementation of an e-government

Figure 31. Fear of the process of transition to e-government

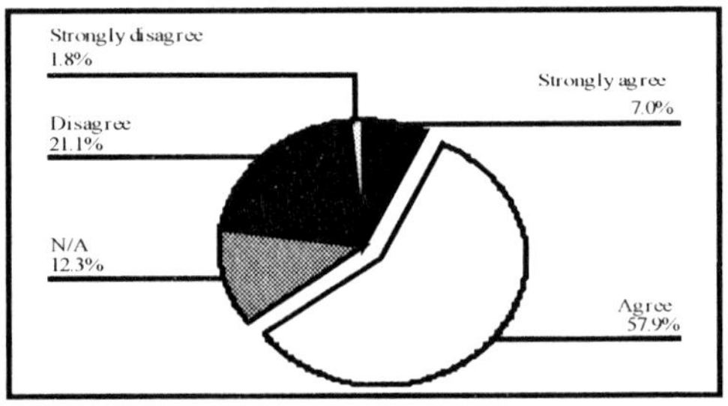

Figure 32. There is interference in providing the same services

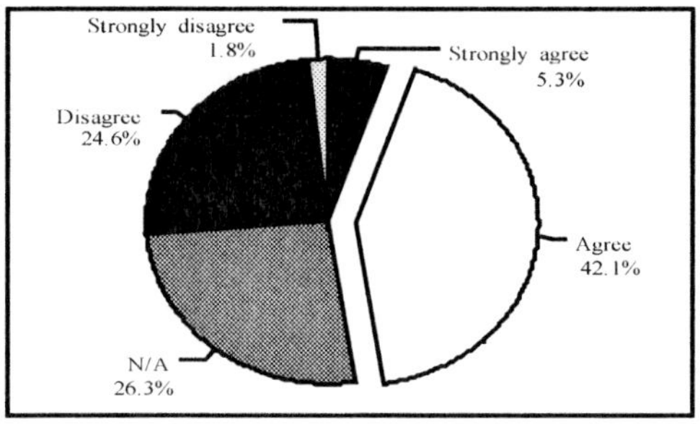

Figure 33. There is a small number of internet users in Saudi Arabia

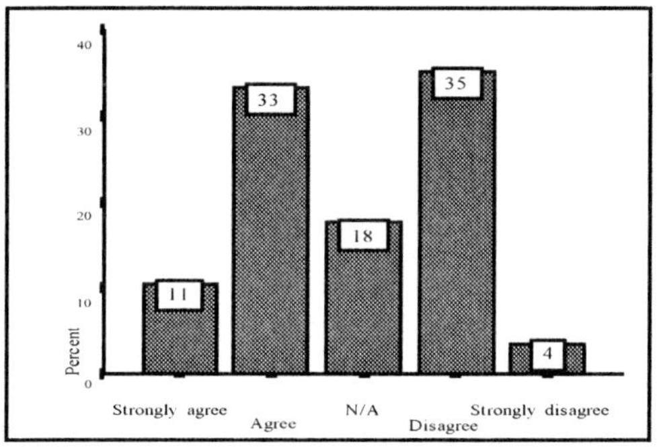

Figure 34. Absence of an agency to oversee e-government program

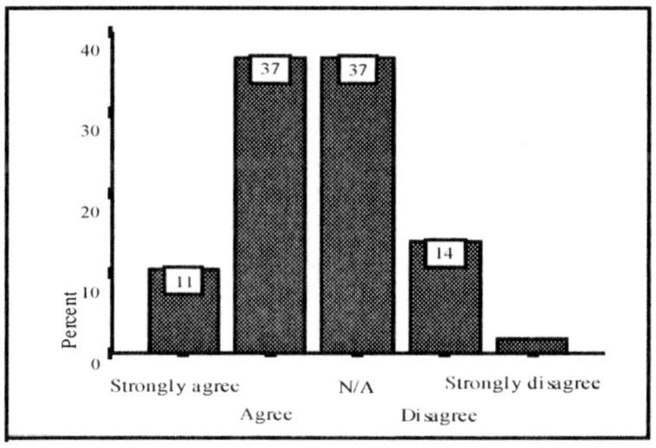

program in the Saudi public sector is slowing the pace of the process, while 14% do not consider that an issue, and 37% do not know (Figure 34).

Fully 64% of the total respondents agreed with the statement that "the lack of security and safety of information is considered one of the challenges facing implementing e-government

Figure 35. Security and safety of information is a challenge for e-government

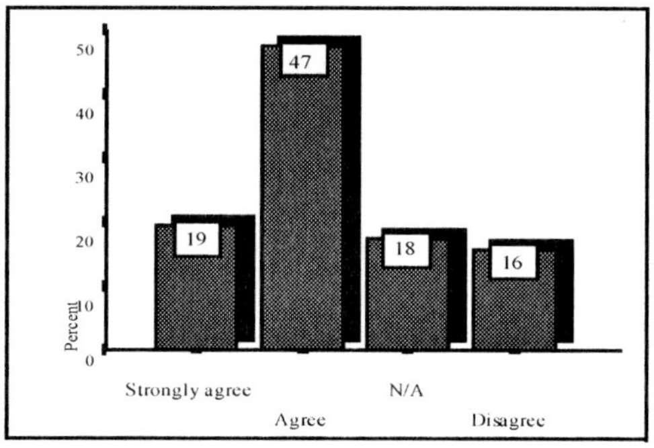

Figure 36. Dominance of English language online is an issue

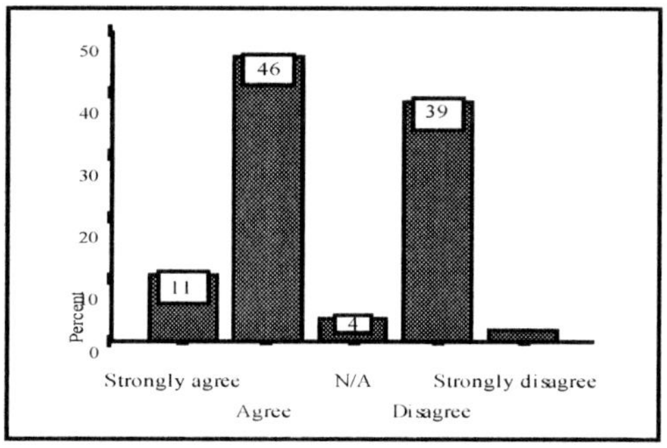

programs in Saudi government," while 16% disagree (Figure 35).

More than half—57%—of the participants agreed with the statement "the dominance of English language in the computer is one of the challenges facing the process of implementing e-government program in Saudi Arabia," while 39% believe that is not an issue (Figure 36).

A high percentage—72%—of all respondents agreed with the statement that "there is lack of trust in accomplishing tasks online among Saudi government employees," whereas 17% disagree with that statement (Figure 37).

Sixty-one percent of the total of the participants disagree or strongly disagree that a shortage of financial resources for implementing e-government in the Saudi public sector is an issue, while only 32% believe that it is a problem (Figure 38).

Figure 37. Lack of trust online

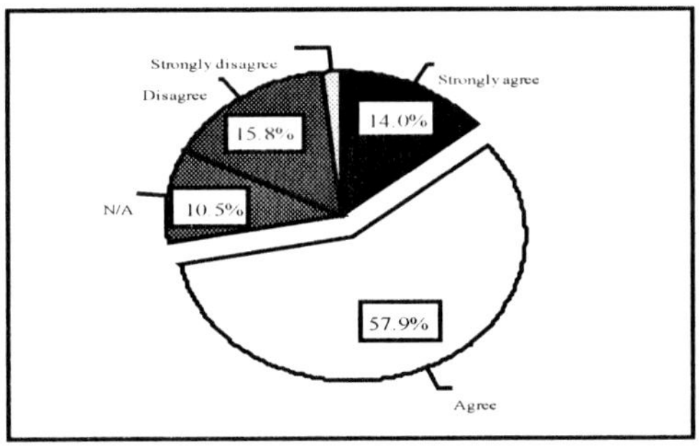

Figure 38. Shortage of financial resources to implement e-government

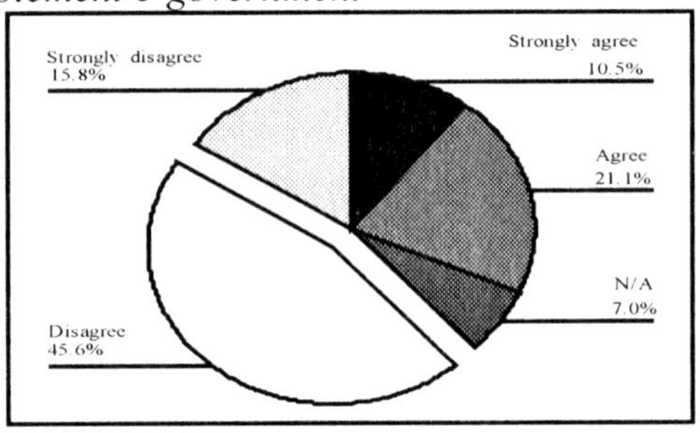

Sixty-three percent of all the respondents agreed that there is a shortage of qualified employees in dealing with IT, while only 30% disagree (Figure 39).

Sixty-five percent of the total respondents believe that there is a lack of training programs regarding the use of computers and the Internet, while 30% disagree (Figure 40).

The survey shows that 54% of the participants agree with the statement that "implementing e-government will reduce the role of employees in accomplishing work," while 39% disagree with that (Figure 41). In addition, 47% of the respondents believe that the e-government program will lead to elimination of some government jobs, while 38% disagree (Figure 42). Fifty-eight percent of the total respondents agreed with the statement "the implementation of an e-government program will lead to a decrease of the role of intercession which spreads in the society,"[5] while 21% disagree and 21% are not sure (Figure 43).[5]

Figure 39. Shortage of qualified employees in dealing with IT

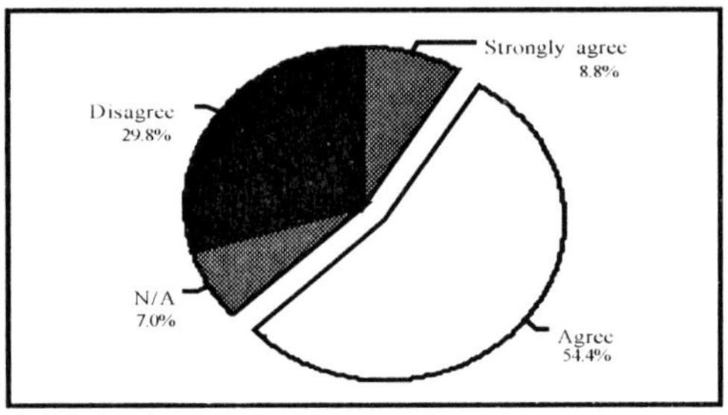

Figure 40. Lack of training programs regarding use of computers & Internet

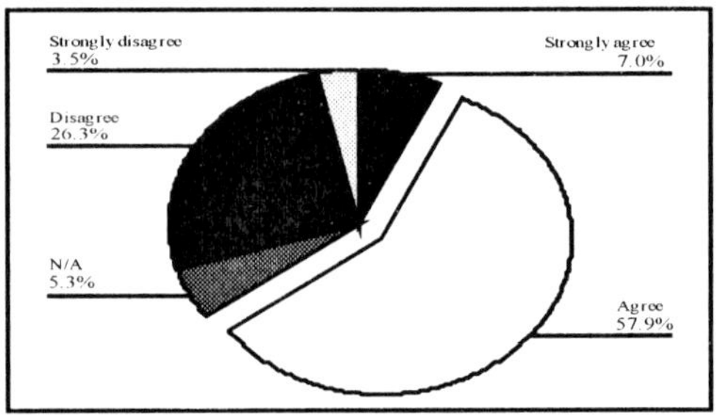

In light of the variety of challenges and issues facing the e-government program in the Saudi public sector, the researchers have classified the results of challenges and issues into two types. The first type is common issues and challenges, which most participants agree on. The second type is issues and challenges which half or less than half of the respondents agree on (Table 2).

Also, the researchers classified those challenges and issues to five categories:

Figure 41. E-government will reduce employee role

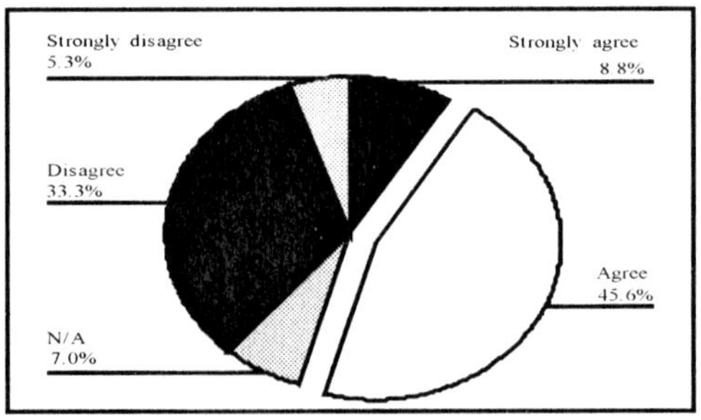

Figure 42. E-government program will lead to elimination of some government jobs

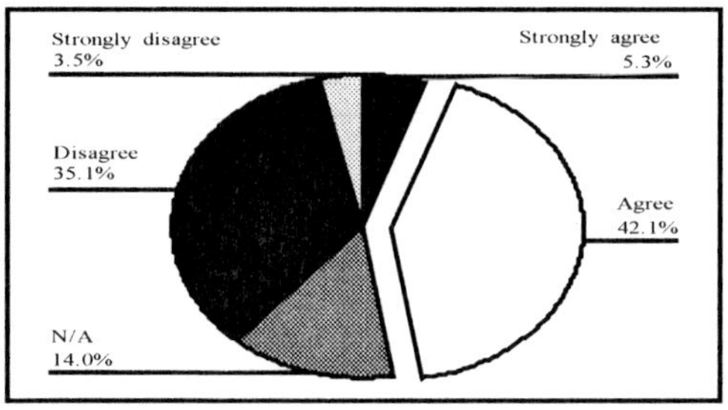

Figure 43. E-government program will lead to decrease of the role of intercession

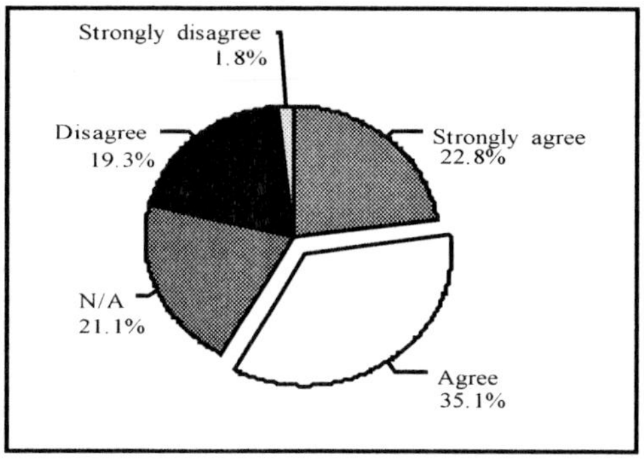

The first category (lacking of knowledge regarding e-government program) consists of the following items:

- the lack of knowledge about e-government in Saudi society
- the lack of knowledge about e-government among public organizations' employees
- the lack of trust in accomplishing tasks online amongst Saudi government employees

Table 2. The challenges and issues facing e-government program in Saudi Arabia

Rank	Common Challenges and Issues	Percentage
1	The lack of knowledge about the e-government in Saudi society	89%
2	The lack of knowledge about the e-government among public organizations' employees	82%
3	The current regulations of the agency are not appropriate to the requirements of implementing e-government	72%
3	The lack of trust in accomplishing tasks online amongst Saudi government employees	72%
4	The current agency structure is not appropriate to implementing e-government program	68%
5	The lack of studies and research in Saudi Arabia regarding e-government	67%
6	The fear of consequences and results of the process of transition to e-government	65%
6	The lack of training programs regarding use of computer and Internet	65%
7	The lack of security of information	64%
8	The shortage of qualified employees in dealing with IT	63%
9	The feeling that e-government program will lead to a decrease in the role of intercession	58%
10	The dominance of English as a computer language	57%
11	e-government will reduce the role of employees in accomplishing work	54%
	Less Common Challenges and Issues	
12	The senior management resists any change in the way an agency accomplishes work	50%
13	The absence of a supervisory agency to oversee the implementation of e-government program	48%
14	E-government program will lead to elimination of some government jobs	47%
14	The interference in providing the same services among the government agencies	47%
14	The resistance to change in the way that work is performed	47%
15	The small number of people using Internet in Saudi Arabia	44%
16	The shortage of financial resources	32%

- the lack of studies and research in Saudi Arabia regarding e-government

Over 80% of the respondents believe that a lack of knowledge about the government initiative in Saudi society and among the government's employees is an issue hindering the progress of implementing e-government in Saudi Arabia. This result matches the outcome in the previous section, which showed the knowledge about the e-government program among government employees is low. Moreover, few studies have been conducted about e-government in Saudi Arabia, as mentioned in the literature review. There seems to be a correlation between the low levels of awareness about e-government in Saudi society and the lack of research. The importance of more studies regarding e-government would help to enhance the awareness of an e-government program in the country. Furthermore, the lack of trust in accomplishing tasks online among Saudi government employees is caused by the lack of knowledge about the e-government program. The second category (regulation and structure of the Saudi public organizations) includes the following topic:

- The current regulations of the agency are not appropriate with the requirements of implementing e-government.

The current agency structure is not appropriate to implement an e-government program. Those challenges are the most crucial obstacles facing the implementation of e-government in the Saudi public sector. One of these challenges facing the Saudi public sector for implementing e-government is the implementation of responsive and effective law-enforcement systems. A large majority of the participants (72%) believe that the current regulation of Saudi organizations is not suitable to the requirements of implementing e-government. The success of the e-government program is greatly dependant on government's role in ensuring an appropriate legal framework for the process. The implementation of the e-government program will remain nominal in the Saudi public sector without a legal equivalence between digital and paper processes. In addition, 68% of the respondents believe that their agencies' structures are not appropriate to implement an e-government program. Organizational structure is one of the main elements which can contribute to either success or failure in adapting and reacting with the organizational environment. All the public agencies in the Saudi government are dominated by a heavily centralized bureaucracy. The environment in most Saudi organizations is stable and the nature of the tasks is routine and sequential. Furthermore, the jobs are rather simple and repetitive in nature. For instance, all employees in the Saudi public sector must know who their boss is, and each person should always respect the chain of command; that is, people should give orders only to their own subordinates and receive orders only through their own immediate superior. In this way, the people at the top can be sure that directives arrive where they are meant to go and know where responsibilities lie. Too much centralization hinders the Saudi government's capacity to adjust to subtle environment changes or new technologies. In this environment, the Saudis, however, do not have the drive to adapt and change with their environment. The Saudi bureaucracy lacks flexibility and adaptability.

The third category includes items relating to negative attitudes about e-government including the following:

- the fear of consequences and results of the process of transition to e-government
- The e-government program will lead to a decrease in the role of intercession which spread in the society.
- E-government will reduce the role of employees in accomplishing work.
- The e-government program will lead to the elimination of some government jobs.

Over half of the participants have a negative attitude regarding the e-government program, which is generated by the lack of knowledge of the program. An example of a fear of the consequences of the transition to e-government is the worry of losing some government records during transition from manual system to electronic system. To avoid that risk, the organizations could maintain a manual backup until the complete electronic system is assured. Furthermore, the feeling that an e-government program will lead to a loss of social connections in society was shared among the majority of the respondents. While that conclusion should be seen as a positive aspect of implementing e-government program, most of the participants see it as a disadvantage because they would lose part of their power. However, while e-government will play an essential role in decreasing employees' connections among those who do not understand the new technology, it might open up new ways for those who understand the new system enough to manipulate them.

The fourth category consists of items that relate to the non-technical barriers that impede implementation of e-government, including the following:

- the lack of training programs regarding computer use and Internet
- the shortage of qualified employees in dealing with IT
- the senior management resists any change in the way an agency accomplishes work.
- the absence of a supervisory agency to oversee the implementation of the e-government program
- the resisting change of the way that works is performed
- the small number using the Internet in Saudi Arabia
- the shortage of financial resources

According to Walker (2001): "People are the source of all knowledge in the knowledge age—and we have transitioned now from the industrial age to the knowledge age. Having enough of the right people with the right skills will make *the* difference between success and failure—particularly in the area of technology." The process of implementing the e-government program will not be effective unless appropriate skills and HR systems are developed by the Saudi government. The Saudi government needs to

Figure 44. The distribution of Saudi population in 2000

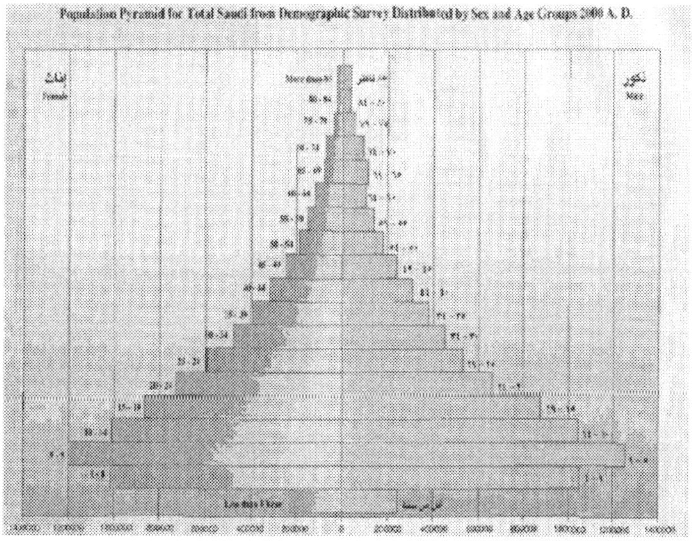

overcome a fundamental obstacle related to *human resources,* a shortage of skilled and qualified employees to deal with IT. The Saudi employees must have the training and tools they need to do their jobs. Also, another barrier to successful implementation of e-government in Saudi Arabia is the resistance of employees to change. The Saudi public agencies have a strong conservative streak. Fear of change is largely the result of ignorance, in addition to the normal emotional response associated with imagining the harm that could result to organization by something they can not control. Success will depend on breaking down the resistance to change. The e-government program does not only imply a series of changes of a purely technical character; it also suggests changes that are related to the structure of the administration and the bureaucratic procedures. E-government will change the way all levels of Saudi organizations communicate, disseminate information, and deliver services to public. That change would offer great potential in helping build better relationships between organizations and the public. The provision of online services via Web sites, which is considered the number one priority objective of many e-government programs, may not require complicated supporting changes. However, the development of Web sites will require far-reaching organizational change, especially as Web sites begin to offer deeper, more complex services. The Saudi government needs to change their operational practices to transfer from a traditional government to one using IT to deliver more services. However, to do that, Saudi public organizations need to be able to better adapt to change.

Moreover, there is no independent e-government agency or unit which is responsible for implementing an e-government program in Saudi Arabia. Such an agency would play an essential role in development and implementation of framework policies, laws and regulations, standards and guidelines, promote e-government infrastructure and applications, act as a body to educate Saudi employees as well as Saudi society about e-government, and provide support to individual e-government projects. However, the barriers to widespread knowledge include as the small number using the Internet in Saudi Arabia, and the shortage of financial resources. In fact, the number of Internet users in Saudi Arabia has been increasing rapidly in recent years. According to the study conducted by the U.S.-Saudi Arabian Business Council, Saudi Arabia is the largest market in the middle east, accounting for 40% of all regional IT spending and worth $4.6 billion (2005). Like most countries in the world, young people in Saudi Arabia are more likely to use the Internet than the old. According to the Saudi census conducted in 2000, over half of the Saudi population is under 15 years.[6] It can be inferred from this statistic that Internet usage among Saudis will grow dramatically in the near future. In addition, one of the common issues facing implementing e-government around the world is the shortage of financial resources; however, this is not considered to be an issue in the Saudi public organizations by the majority of the respondents.

Finally, the fifth category includes the following technical issues and challenges:

- the lack of security of information
- the domination of English in the computer

In general, the lack of security of information is an important issue in any new technology system. Saudi governmental organizations need to work together to set up an adequate security and privacy system in their Web sites. A successful e-government strategy should set up effective security controls in government processes and systems. Although the language dominating computer and Internet today is English, the ability to convert computer software from English to Arabic is becoming more common. This problem is not related to the Saudi organizations' Web sites, since those Web sites are provided in Arabic, but an obstacle does exist in dealing with basic computer and Internet language, such as writing a Web site name in English.

CONCLUSION AND RECOMMENDATIONS

In general, the Saudi government needs to understand the challenges facing the process of implementing an e-government program and should adopt the appropriate solutions to improve them. Based on the research described in this study, the following recommendations can be made:

- The Saudi government should spread the awareness of an e-government program among its employees and in the society. To increase awareness, Saudi government's organizations need to engage its employees in the e-government process. With a more participatory organization, employees can have input about the challenges of implementing the e-government within their organizations. One way to increase the participation process throughout Saudi public organizations would be to have monthly meetings for all employees. This would open communication and allow more opportunity to bring up suggestions and concerns between all levels of the hierarchy within the organizations. Saudi government organizations should seek maximum participation by encouraging all their employees to participate. Allowing and encouraging employees to provide their own solutions, instead of solutions provided by their managers or top level positions, would enhance the awareness of e-government. The Saudis need to change their way of thinking before changing the way of doing their works. Encouragement of the process of participation among government's employees in all levels would help to overcome many e-government's challenges and issues.
- In addition, computers and the Internet should be made available in every school, university, library, and in all public facilities.
- Moreover, the Saudi government needs to install a proper legal framework to provide for enforceable electronic transactions. For instance, the legal recognition of digital signatures is essential if they are to be used in e-government for the submission of electronic forms containing sensitive personal or financial information.
- Also, Saudi public organizations need to adopt a more flexible approach as represented by the organism metaphor, which suggests that successful organizations are fluid and adaptable to change.[7] This metaphor suggests that the environment and the organization are interdependent and the organization needs to be particularly sensitive to what is occurring in the environment (Morgan 1997). The Saudi public agencies need to move towards a restructuring where flexibility and openness to the surrounding technological environment and adaptability to constant change are given priority over the traditional rigidity of the Saudi bureaucratic structure.
- The Saudi public agencies need to provide adequate IT training and development to their employees.
- Saudi governments should help to make access to Internet available to the less fortunate in society as well as offer computer literacy education, particularly to the young and elderly people.
- The Saudi public sector should also work in partnership with the private sector to establish secure electronic fund transfer systems, which are important to the successful implementation of electronic government.

- Saudi Arabia needs to create an effective Web portal which can integrate information and services from different government agencies to assist the public to get seamless service without needing to know about the responsible government organization.
- More important, the Saudi agencies should not work separately from one another, they should allow two-way communication between government agencies with each other and with the public.
- Government sites should attempt to provide clear and simple language that is easily understood by the public.
- Services should be easily clustered together on the homepage rather than spread all over the Web site.
- Government sites should be organized in order to assist people in accessing the services and information they want to access.
- A future study could look at the major risks of e-government adoption and recommend some suggestions to avoid those risks.

REFERENCES

Al Mashet, O. (2005). *The Factors of success: Implementation of e-government in Saudi Universities*. Jeddah: King Abdulaziz University. Retrieved August 20, 2007, from http://www.kau.edu.sa/dvworkshop-Mon2.1.10.ppt

Denslow, C. (2005). ICDL seek to build Up computer skills. *IT Weekly*.

Fandy, M. (1999). CyberResistance: Saudi opposition between globalization and localization. *Comparative Studies in Society and History, 41*, 124-147.

eGovernment - United Arab Emirates - Archive - 1 November 2001 - 20 October 2004. "eGovernment introduces free online payment facility".

Heeks, R. (2003). *E-government for development: Success and failure rates of e-government in developing/transitional countries: Overview*. Manchester: University of Manchester.

Holmes, D. (2001). *E-government: E-business strategies for government*. London: Nicholas Brealey Publishing.

Meso, P., Checchi, R., Sevcik, G., Loch, K., & Straub, D. (2006). Knowledge spheres and the diffusion of national IT policies. *The Electronic Journal of Information Systems in Developing Countries, 23*.

Morgan, G. (1997). *Images of organization*. California: Sage Publications.

Organization for Economic Co-operation and Development. (2003). *The e-government imperative*. Paris: OCDE.

Pyati, A. (2005). WSIS: Whose vision of an information society? *First Monday, 10*(5). Retrieved May 1, 2007, from http://firstmonday.org/issues/issue10_5/pyati/index.html

Sandy, H. (2002). E-*government in the Arab world: Between reality and ambition*. Retrieved May 3, 2007, from http://unpan1.un.org/intradoc/groups/public/documents/ARADO/UNPAN005603.pps

Stensgaard, A. (2005). *International case studies*. In *Proceedings of the 11th GCC e-Government Forumin Dubai*.

Teitelbaum, J. (2002). Dueling for Da'wa: State vs. society on the Saudi Internet. *Middle East Journal*.

United Nations. (2005). *National profile for the information society in Saudi Arabia*. New York: United Nations Economic and Social Commission for Western Asia (ESCWA). Retrieved August 2, 2007, from http://www.escwa.org.lb/wsis/reports/docs/SaudiArabia_2005-E.pdf

U.S. Department of Education. (2005). *EDGAR version*. Retrieved June 23, 2005, from http://www.ed.gov/index.jhtml?src=a

Walker, D. M. (2001). *E-government in the information age: The long view*. Retrieved May 3, 2007, from http://www.gao.gov/cghome/ia/sld008.htm

West, D. (2005). *Global e-government 2005*. Providence, RI: Brown University.

ENDNOTES

1. Available in English at http://www.saudi.gov.sa/english/
2. Available in English at http://www.uaesmartforms.com/index.aspx
3. Available in English at http://www.arriyadh.com/En/index.as
4. All data analyses were performed using SPSS version 11.5.
5. Intercession or a social connection is favoritism shown to people who are either relatives or friends, it is spread in Saudi society and some see it as a positive aspect.
6. Source: Institute of Public Administration in Saudi Arabia (http://www.ipa.edu.sa/en/index.asp).
7. An organism metaphor is a term used by sociologist Gareth Morgan to describe an organization.

This work was previously published in International Journal of Electronic Government Research, Vol. 4, Issue 2, edited by M. Khosrow-Pour, pp. 59-85, copyright 2008 by IGI Publishing (an imprint of IGI Global).

Chapter 12
Institutions, Organizations, and Interorganizational IT Projects in the Mexican Federal Government

Luis F. Luna-Reyes
Universidad de las Americas-Puebla, Mexico

J. Ramon Gil-Garcia
Centro de Investigación y Docencia Económicas, Mexico

ABSTRACT

Electronic government has the potential of transforming the way government works and interacts with citizens. However, recent research has found that the promised benefits are rarely completely achieved. Some of these studies highlight the importance of institutions in shaping the development, implementation, and use of information technologies in government settings. Based on a survey and a set of interviews with Mexican federal government managers, this chapter explores the relationships between institutional arrangements, organizational forms, information technologies, and the outcomes of Mexican IT initiatives. Overall, the authors found that there are important interactions among these variables and important similarities exist between developed countries and other realities, such as Latin America. The research presented here contributes to the field by testing causal relationships often cited in the digital government literature, but with little empirical quantitative exploration. Moreover, understanding those relationships offers guidance in the implementation of interorganizational IT applications in government, potentially increasing their probability of success as well as the benefits for citizens and other stakeholders.

INTRODUCTION

According to Fountain (2001, 2004), information and communication technologies (ICTs) are one of the most important advances in this century and have the potential to significantly transform government. In fact, some government structures and processes have changed due to the incorporation of technological innovations such as the personal computer

DOI: 10.4018/978-1-60566-918-2.ch012

and the Internet (Fountain, 2004). Information technologies create interesting possibilities for government. They are used not only to improve the quality of services, but also to reduce costs and make policies and programs more effective (Gil-Garcia, 2006; Gil-Garcia & Helbig, 2006; Lim & Tang, 2008; OECD, 2003; Roy, 2007). Information and communication technologies are used as a catalyst for organizational change (Dawes, 2002; Holmes, 2001; Rocheleau, 2003; Welch & Pandey, 2007). They are also considered a tool to improve democratic participation in a variety of political topics (Carbo & Williams, 2004; Gil-Garcia, 2005; Hiller & Bélanger, 2001).

The term "electronic government" or "digital government" emerged within this context, and is still evolving (Gil-García & Luna-Reyes, 2006; Schelin, 2003; Yildiz, 2007). OECD defines e-government as the use of information and communication technologies for a better government or to improve the quality of its services, especially through the use of the Internet and Web technologies (OECD, 2003). Some general characteristics of e-government are: (1) the use of information and communication technologies, (2) supporting government actions, (3) improving the relationships between government and citizens, and (4) following a strategy to add value for participants in the process (Gil-García & Luna-Reyes, 2006). In contrast to electronic commerce, electronic government does not include only the transactional aspects, but also takes into consideration the democratic relationships between governments and citizens (6, 2001; Gil-Garcia, 2005; Scholl, 2002).

The implementation of these technological innovations has been challenging. In Mexico, information and communications technologies were first used widely in government in the '90s. However, it was only in 2001 when the Secretary of Communications and Transportation created the e-Mexico project. The e-Mexico initiative fosters innovation in government through the use of information technologies and also promotes the use of the Internet by certain sectors of Mexican society. New laws and regulations regarding electronic government in Mexico have supported this initiative. One important example is the Law for Transparency and Access to Government Public Information. The objective of this law is to establish the necessary mechanisms to guarantee any person the access to information from the different branches of government, autonomous constitutional organizations, and any federal agency (Poder Ejecutivo, 2002). The main objective of electronic government in Mexico is to use information and communication technologies to innovate and improve government and its relationships with citizens (OECD, 2005).

Therefore, the implementation of electronic government in Mexico needs to consider different factors such as laws and regulations, organizational structures, and the characteristics of the technologies themselves. This study proposes and empirically tests a model to explore the relationships between some of the factors that have an impact on information and communication technology projects in government. Institutional theory and Fountain's technology enactment framework provide the conceptual basis for this study.

After this brief introduction, the chapter is organized into five more sections. The following section presents a brief literature review of institutional theory and the technology enactment framework, as well as some of their applications to government settings. The third section describes the research model and hypotheses, and the fourth section includes a description of the research methods and procedures. Finally, the last two sections consist of a discussion of the main results and conclusions.

Institutional Theory and Government IT Projects

Institutional theory, particularly Fountain's technology enactment framework (Fountain, 1995, 2001), is central to this study. According to North,

"Institutions are the rules of the game in a society, or more formally, they are humanly conceived obligations, which configure human interaction" (North, 1999, p. 3). Another definition says that institutions are the joint group of rules, application mechanisms, and organizations that reinforce each other (Scheela & Van Dinh, 2004). Barley and Tolbert (1997) state that institutions represent obligations created by the options that individuals and groups have, but these obligations are subject to change over time. They define institutions as shared and typified rules with identified categories of social actors, as well as their appropriate activities and relations (Barley & Tolbert, 1997). Institutions can also be seen as guidelines that have been created by society and the individuals who are part of that society (Giddens, 1979, 1984). These guidelines or rules are generated and maintained over time through the micro-activity of social actors. In contrast, for Bansal (2005), institutions include macro-level structures like governments, professional associations, public opinion, and the media. Current institutional approaches recognize the interplay between social structures (macro) and the actions and interactions among individual actors (micro). Therefore, the basic principle of institutional theory is that individual actions and organizations are shaped by institutions, which, at the same time, are either reproduced or modified through the collective action of individuals and organizations (Brinton & Nee, 1998; Giddens, 1984; Scott, 2001).

Institutional approaches have been used to understand a great variety of phenomena in multiple disciplines including economics (North, 1999; Rutherford, 1999), political science (Peters, 2001), and sociology (Brinton & Nee, 1998). Within organizational research, institutional theory emphasizes the social context in which organizations are embedded and highlights the influence of culture or laws on decision making and formal structures (Bansal, 2005; Powell & DiMaggio, 1991; Scott, 2001). It also recognizes the importance of external pressures generated by actors in the social and economic environments and their influence on organizational characteristics and performance (Khadaroo, 2005). Institutional theory has been useful to understand organizational change by identifying relevant aspects of the context in which information technologies are designed and implemented (Bennett, Bouma, & Ciccozzi, 2004; Fountain, 2008; Hassan & Gil-Garcia, 2008; Schellong, 2007).

This theory argues that organizations and individuals are constrained by a series of rules, values, norms, and assumptions, which are created by them through their actions and interactions (Barley & Tolbert, 1997; Giddens, 1979, 1984). These rules and values greatly influence how things should be done, but they do not totally determine human action (Barley & Tolbert, 1997). Therefore, institutionalization is a continuous process that can only be observed over time. It is also a cultural and political process related to legitimacy and power – and not necessarily with efficiency (Powell & DiMaggio, 1991). Organizations adopt business practices that are perceived as legitimate in society as a result of coercive, normative, or imitation pressures (Khadaroo, 2005). Accordingly, there are different mechanisms that influence organizational change – in particular, competition, normative isomorphism, coercive isomorphism, and mimic isomorphism (Bennett et al., 2004; Powell & DiMaggio, 1991). Due to its main focus on institutions, some scholars argue that institutional approaches have not adequately included the material properties of technological artifacts in their analyses (Garson, 2003). Other researchers consider that most studies using institutional theory need to explicitly and clearly explain how they are incorporating the role of human agency and the reciprocal relationships between institutions and individual actions (Yang, 2003).

Based on the institutional tradition and as an attempt to explicitly include the role of technology in a comprehensive approach, Fountain (1995, 2001) develops a framework that "pays attention to the relation among information technologies, organizations, embeddedness, and institutions" (p. 83). Using empirical evidence from government information technology initiatives in the U.S. federal government, Fountain (2001) proposes a new way to conceptualize technology within an institutional theoretical tradition: the technology enactment framework.

The technology enactment theory attempts to explain the effects of organizational forms and institutional arrangements on the technology used by government agencies (Fountain, 1995, 2001; Gil-Garcia, 2006). According to this theory, the "technology is enacted in political, social, economic, and organizational contexts" (Fountain, 2004, p. 2). Fountain (2004) explains that "two of the most important influences on the enacted technology are organizations and networks" (p. 6), and provides examples of information technologies implemented in comparable organizational contexts but with very different results. The interactions among organizational characteristics, networks, and institutions may explain some of these differences. Based on the institutional tradition (Brinton & Nee, 1998; Powell & DiMaggio, 1991; Scott, 2001), she argues that the embeddedness of actors in social, cultural, cognitive, and institutional structures influences the design, perception, implementation, and use of information technologies. Each project is embedded in a certain organizational environment and is affected by specific institutional arrangements. As a result, each organization uses technology differently and obtains different performance, costs, and results (Dawes, 2002; Fountain, 2001). Therefore, organizational characteristics and institutional arrangements have an impact on the enacted technology (Fountain, 2001; Gil-Garcia, 2006; Luna-Reyes, Gil-García, & Cruz, 2006). These institutions could be seen as guides for action, but also limitations to those actions (Brinton & Nee, 1998; Fountain, 2001; Scott, 2001).

Fountain (2001) proposes an analytical distinction between objective technology and enacted technology. Objective technology is described in terms of its capacity and functionality – that is, hardware, software, telecommunications, and other material characteristics, independently of how people use them (Fountain, 2004). In contrast, enacted technology refers to how users perceive and act upon objective technologies. In this instance, the enacted technology could be conceived as a subset of the objective technology (Puron Cid & Gil-Garcia, 2004). However, social actors can also enact new uses that were not included as part of the original design and functionality (Fountain, 2001; Orlikowski, 2000). Therefore, the technology enactment is flexible and fluid and can be observed as it develops over time through interactions among social actors and between actors and technologies (Gil-Garcia, 2006; Orlikowski, 2000). Thus, the enacted technology is affected by social, cultural, cognitive, structural, and political factors, but it also affects these factors in a recursive relationship (Fountain, 2001, 2004). Social actors draw upon institutional arrangements and, therefore, the enacted technology is affected by institutions, organizational characteristics, and environmental conditions (Fountain, 2004; Luna-Reyes et al., 2006).

Fountain's analytical framework explains how social actors enact information technologies in order to adapt them to the existing organizational rules, routines, and relations (Fountain, 2001). These modifications are not necessarily optimal and make clear the influence of organizational and institutional arrangements on the selection, design, implementation, and use of information technologies (Fountain, 2004). In addition, organizational actors tend to enact technologies that preserve the current social order, networks, and structures (Fountain, 2001; Kraemer, King, Dunkle, & Lane, 1989).

In summary, Fountain's technology enactment framework argues that information technologies are embedded in organizational and institutional environments and it is very important to understand these environments (Fountain, 2004). Information technologies have the potential to

Figure 1. Research model

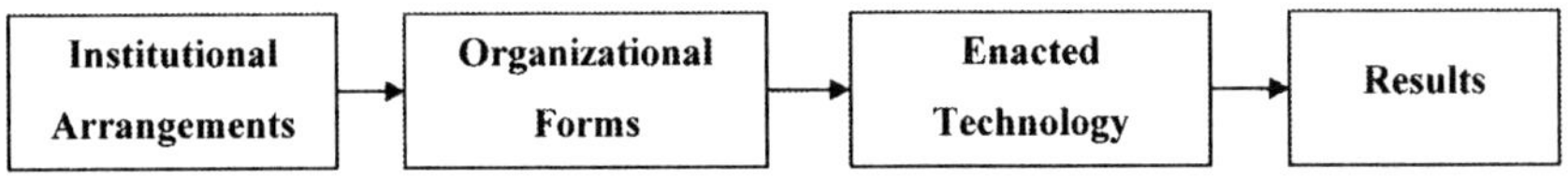

change business processes, communication patterns, coordination mechanisms, hierarchical structures, and other organizational characteristics. However, information technologies are also affected by organizational and institutional factors (Fountain, 2001, 2004; Gil-Garcia, 2006). The technology enactment framework recognizes this bi-directional and dynamic relationship and suggests alternatives to incorporate relevant variables into analytical models.

RESEARCH MODEL AND HYPOTHESES

As mentioned before, the research model used in this research is based on institutional theory, drawing specifically on the Technology Enactment Framework (Fountain, 2001) and extending it through a review of current literature on IT in organizations. According to the Technology Enactment Framework, institutional arrangements and organizational forms have an impact on the selection, implementation, and use of information technologies in government.

Institutional theory proposes that the context in which organizations develop has an influence on them (Bansal, 2005). Technology enactment refers to the relationships among institutions (legal, cognitive, cultural, and social), objective information technologies (hardware, software, and networks), organizational forms (bureaucracy, relationships, etc.), and the activities of actors through the selection, design, implementation, and use of information technologies in government settings (Dawes, 2002; Fountain, 2001; Gil-Garcia, 2006).

On the basis of these ideas, *Figure 1* shows the research model proposed in this chapter. In this model, institutional arrangements affect organizational forms and indirectly affect actors' choices about the conceptualization, design, and use of objective technologies, constituting a particular technology enactment. Then, the enacted technology influences organizational results such as efficiency or effectiveness.

In Figure 1, institutional arrangements are represented by procedures, habits, patterns, and regulations that serve as guidelines and constraints for action (Fountain, 2001; Gil-Garcia, 2006). In the particular case of information technology and digital government, we are also considering as institutional factors the institutional support to IT initiatives and institutional support to a specific project. Some of the projects included in the survey are systems mandated by law (such as the law regulating access to government information) or presidential initiatives (like some interorganizational projects conducted by the Ministry of Communications and Transportation). Other projects are also important from a single-agency perspective, but in most cases, decisions about technology not only depend on a single agency, but on several stakeholders, committees, bureaucratic rules, and the relevance of the project itself (Gil-Garcia, 2006). Institutional arrangements guide decisions about IT projects, such as size, goals, objectives, resources, and indicators of success (Fountain, 2001; Gil-Garcia, 2006). Goals, objectives, and resources are important organizational characteristics for a particular project. In this way, the first hypothesis of this research relates to the impact of institutional arrangements (laws, regulations, institutional support, etc.) on organizational forms, including goal setting, recognition, or the adequacy of resources to accomplish the goals.

H1: *Institutional arrangements have an influence on organizational forms in interorganizational IT projects.*

As mentioned before, enacted technology refers to specific choices about design and use of objective technologies, choices that can be observed through characteristics of the project's technology products (Puron Cid & Gil-Garcia, 2004). Enacted technology also refers to the use that different users decide to give to some objective technology (Fountain, 2001). Organizational forms directly influence these choices on design and use, and institutional arrangements also have an impact on the enacted technology, indirectly, through the influence that institutions have on organizational forms (Gil-Garcia, 2006). In this way, systems of goals, recognition, or the adequacy of resources (organizational forms) have a direct impact on specific choices or uses of technology (enacted technology) in a specific project. According to the enactment framework (Fountain, 2001), laws, regulations, institutional support, or other cultural factors (institutional arrangements) do not affect directly the technology choices (enacted technology), but indirectly through their influence on goals, objectives, and other organizational elements. These relationships are reflected in hypotheses 2 and 3.

H2: *Organizational forms affect the way in which technology is understood, designed, and used (enacted) in a particular interorganizational project.*

H3: *Institutional arrangements have an indirect effect on the technology application and use (enacted technology) in an interorganizational project through its influence on the organizational forms.*

Particular technology enactments, reflected in the usefulness or how easy it is to use a particular technical solution, are developed and subsequently used in order to have an impact on organizational performance and results. Better systems are designed to improve productivity, service quality, or efficiency (Fountain, 2001). Moreover, the context where a particular enactment takes place is the organization and, therefore, organizational forms also have an influence on the results of using information technologies. That is to say, the specific context (organization) has an influence on IT design, development, and use, but the technology itself also has an effect on performance (Fountain, 2004). In this way, specific enactments of technology have a direct effect on the expected results. The impacts of the organizational forms on the expected results are mediated by the enacted technology according to the enactment framework. Hypotheses 4 and 5 summarize these effects.

H4: *The enacted technology, which is the way technology is interpreted and used, has an effect on organizational results and performance.*

H5: *Organizational forms affect indirectly organizational results and performance through their direct effect on the enacted technology.*

RESEARCH DESIGN AND METHODS

The research reported here is part of a multi-method project developed in three stages. The first stage involved a series of interviews with project managers of interorganizational projects in the Mexican federal government. The second stage encompassed a survey applied to participants in the projects identified during the first stage. The third stage consisted of conducting three case studies, including additional interviews with participants in some projects and document research. This chapter reports on the results of the survey conducted during the summer of 2006. Data from the interviews developed in the first and third stages of the project is used to triangulate results and enrich the results from the quantitative analysis (Creswell, 1994). This section of the chapter then includes a brief description of the subjects, the data collection instruments, and the procedures followed in the research to gather empirical evidence for the relations in the hypotheses described in the previous section. We start by describing the population and the sampling methods, and then we describe the survey instrument and the procedures followed to apply the survey. The section ends with a brief description of the qualitative component of the study.

Sample

As mentioned before, our interest was to explore the effects of institutional arrangements and organizational forms on IT projects involving interorganizational collaboration. An initial sample of projects was identified during the first stage of the research. The projects were identified using the Internet as a search tool, and asking the project managers interviewed for additional projects to be included, following a snow ball sampling approach. In this way, 13 government agencies were identified as involved in interorganizational projects at the federal level (National Bank for Savings and Financial Services, Ministry of Public Administration, Ministry of Transportation, Ministry of Health, Federal Institute for Access to Information, Mexican Institute for Social Security, INFOTEC, Ministry of Justice, Internal Revenue Service, Ministry of Education, President's Internet Office, Ministry of Economy, and Ministry of Finance). The survey database was put together by compiling names and e-mail addresses of project participants from the agencies Web pages or from lists provided by the project managers interviewed. The database included 1,216 people from federal agencies who participate in 13 interorganizational projects. Therefore, the study uses a purposive sample of public managers involved in well-known interorganizational IT projects. Although the population is unknown, which may limit the generalizability of the results, this approach allows establishing a robust sampling framework for this research.

An electronic survey was developed[1] and the usable response rate was 23.2% (n = 282). Forty percent of respondents reported having more than 10 years of working experience in the federal government, and 81% reported having more than 10 years of working experience in general. Fifty-five percent of respondents have experience in the area of informatics, 31% in policy making, and 25% in program development. Most respondents have a college education (97%), while 40% have a graduate-level education.

Survey Instrument

A survey instrument was adapted and re-designed from Fountain's original instrument (Fountain, McKinnon, & Park, 2003). The instrument included questions that sought to understand the effects of institutional arrangements and organizational forms on interorganizational IT projects. The original instrument was first translated into Spanish and adapted to the Mexican context by the researchers. Then, to ensure content validity and comparability, the instrument was reviewed by two expert translators and four government officials in a two-stage process. Following their recommendations, the research team made adjustments and changes to the survey instrument for both content and format.

The final instrument had 35 questions;[2] five questions were associated with institutional arrangements, six with organizational forms, eight with enacted technology, and 10 with results. The questions related to institutional arrangements include perceptions about influences of government culture, legislation, support from congress, and institutional support for the use of IT. The questions in this scale showed a Cronbach-alpha value of 0.770 (see Table 1).

Organizational scale questions included aspects related to the definition of goals and performance indicators, adequacy of financial and human resources, and adequacy of recognition from managers. The alpha value for this scale was 0.733. Enacted technology was operationalized in the survey as a series of questions related to the quality of particular technology characteristics enacted in each project. Some of the main characteristics included were ease of use, usefulness, information quality, functionality, personalization, security, and privacy. The alpha coefficient for this scale was 0.932. Finally, results were measured as the level of project success in terms of productivity, cost reduction, transparency, citizen participation, effectiveness of government policies and programs, and quality of service. The alpha value for this scale was 0.905.

Procedures

As mentioned above, the survey was administered electronically using a commercial service called SurveyMonkey. Potential respondents (1,216 people) were sent an initial e-mail invitation to participate in the survey during the summer of 2006, giving them the option of declining the invitation. We sent a second e-mail providing the Web address of the survey to complete. We sent a total of three reminders. The first reminder was sent a week after the Web address was sent. The second reminder was sent one week later, and the last reminder was sent a day before the survey was closed.

After the initial e-mail with the survey the Web address was sent, we got 137 answers (11.3% response). The first reminder increased the responses to 221 (18.2% response). After the second reminder, the number of responses increased to 273 (22.5% response). With the last reminder, responses increased to 330 (27.1%). Unfortunately, 48 responses were blank with the exception of the first two questions, reducing the valid responses to 282. These usable responses correspond to a response rate of 23.2%, which is generally considered acceptable for a Web-based survey. Once the survey was closed, the database was cleaned and analyzed.

Table 1. Cronbach-Alpha values for main constructs in the model

Construct	Items in scale	Alpha value
Institutional Arrangements	5	0.770
Organizational Forms	6	0.733
Enacted Technology	8	0.932
Results	10	0.905

Interviews with Project Managers and Project Participants

As mentioned above, interviews conducted during the first and third stages of the project were used to triangulate and enrich the findings from the survey. During the first stage—which took place during the Fall 2005 and the Spring 2006—we interviewed 19 project managers from the 13 IT initiatives identified. The second round of interviews, involved 26 project participants of three highly collaborative projects in the areas of digital economy, education, and health. This second set of interviews took place during the Fall 2006 and the Spring 2007.

Interviewees were asked about the characteristics of their projects, the institutional environment, projects' cost and benefits, and their perceptions about project success, collaboration, and networking. The research team analyzed the interviews, using a coding scheme that included as its four main categories institutional arrangements, organizational forms, enacted technology, and results.[3] We looked for specific examples and counterexamples related to the relationships among the variables included in the research model and hypotheses of this study. We also looked for explanations of some of the relationships found in the statistical analysis. The following section summarizes and discusses the main results.

RESULTS AND DISCUSSION

In this section of the chapter, we present and discuss the results of the quantitative and qualitative analyses developed as part of the project. The section begins with the main results from the survey, and finishes with comments and additional information from the qualitative analysis of the interview data.

Survey Results and Discussion

The e-government projects included in the survey are considered successful by respondents (respondents were either participants in the e-government projects or users of the e-government systems associated with the projects). The number of agencies involved in the projects surveyed varied greatly. Many projects involved collaboration between 10 or fewer agencies; three projects involved more than 50 agencies working together. Overall, 88% of respondents believe their project has well-defined goals, 84% believe it is feasible that their project will reach these defined goals, and 75% believe there are clear indicators for success. Most respondents consider that their project is important for the country.

Although respondents consider their projects to be successful and to offer high-quality results, they also mention some problems. Problems are often associated with the lack of human and financial resources and mismatches between project goals and agencies regulations. In addition, respondents consider a variety of political factors, resistance to change, red-tape, and the influence of individual interests as important issues to consider when developing IT projects in government. Only half of the respondents believe the current laws support interorganizational digital government initiatives, and about one-third (35%) believe legislators support these kinds of projects.

Table 2 includes descriptive statistics for the main constructs in the proposed model. Maximum values in the table coincide with the maximum values of each scale. The relative positions of the means in each scale with respect to the maximum value are in the range from 76% to 86%. The lowest relative mean corresponds to Organizational Forms, and the highest to Enacted Technology. Translating the mean values to a 10-point scale to better understand their meaning, respondents assigned an 8.0 to the adequacy of laws, government culture, congress support, and institutional support (Institutional Arrangements), a 7.6 to the definition of goals and performance indicators, combined with the adequacy of human and financial resources and systems of recognition (Organizational Forms). They assigned an 8.6 to the current design of the interorganizational technologies in terms of ease of use, utility, quality, functionality, customization, security, and privacy (Enacted Technology), and an 8.3 to the success of the projects in terms of success measures such as cost reduction, effectiveness, increased productivity, or improved citizen participation (Results).

Table 2. Descriptive statistics for the main constructs

Construct	n	Min	Max	Mean	Std Dev
Institutional Arrangements	215[1]	10.0	35.0	28.08	4.05
Organizational Forms	228	10.0	30.0	22.99	4.19
Enacted Technology	242	24.0	80.0	69.22	8.68
Results	233	26.0	100.0	83.28	12.83

Table 3. Pearson correlations coefficients for main constructs in the model

Construct	Instituti. Arrangmt.	Organiz. Forms	Enacted Tech.	Results
Instituti. Arrangmt.	1			
Organiz. Forms	0.33 **	1		
Enacted Tech.	0.45 **	0.43 **	1	
Results	0.46 **	0.42 **	0.71 **	1

** $p<0.01$

Pearson correlation coefficients were calculated for all constructs (see Table 3). As shown in the table, the model constructs are moderately correlated. All correlations are significant at a $p<0.01$ level. The highest correlation exists between the enacted technology and the results, while the smallest correlation occurs between institutional arrangements and organizational forms.

In order to test the hypotheses posed by the proposed model, we used multiple linear regression. Equations 1 through 7 show the main regression equations used in this research. Regressions 1, 2, and 3 are used to test hypotheses 1, 2, and 4. To test indirect effects in hypotheses 3 and 5, we followed an approach proposed by Baron and Kenny (1986).

$$ORG = \beta_1 \; INST + \varepsilon \quad (1)$$

$$TECH = \beta_2 \; ORG + \varepsilon \quad (2)$$

$$RES = \beta_3 \; TECH + \varepsilon \quad (3)$$

$$TECH = \beta_4 \; INST + \varepsilon \quad (4)$$

$$RES = \beta_5 \; ORG + \varepsilon \quad (5)$$

$$TECH = \beta_6 \; ORG + \beta_7 \; INST + \varepsilon \quad (6)$$

$$RES = \beta_8 \; TECH + \beta_9 \; ORG + \varepsilon \quad (7)$$

where,

ORG = Organizational Forms

INST = Institutional Arrangements

TECH = Enacted Technology

RES = Results

The approach consists of four steps that involve estimating independent regression coefficients to establish mediation. Consider for example the case of hypothesis 3, in which the effect of institutional arrangements on the enacted technology is mediated by organizational forms (see *Figure 2*). The first stage when testing this hypothesis involves testing relation "c" in *Figure 2*, showing that the institutional arrangements have an impact on the enacted technology. The second step consists of testing the relationship between institutional arrangements and the mediator, organizational forms (relation "a" in the figure). If any of these two relations are not statistically significant, then the data does not provide evidence of mediation. The third step involves testing the effect of the mediator (organizational forms) on the final variable (enacted technology), controlling for institutional arrangements (the initial variable). If this last relation is statistically significant, and the path "c" becomes zero when controlled by the mediator, then there exists full mediation. If both paths are statistically significant ("b" and "c"), there is partial mediation.

In this way, to test hypothesis 3, we will use regressions (1), (4), and (6), testing the relation between institutional arrangements and the enacted technology, mediated by organizational

Figure 2. Relations for testing indirect relationships (Baron & Kenny, 1986)

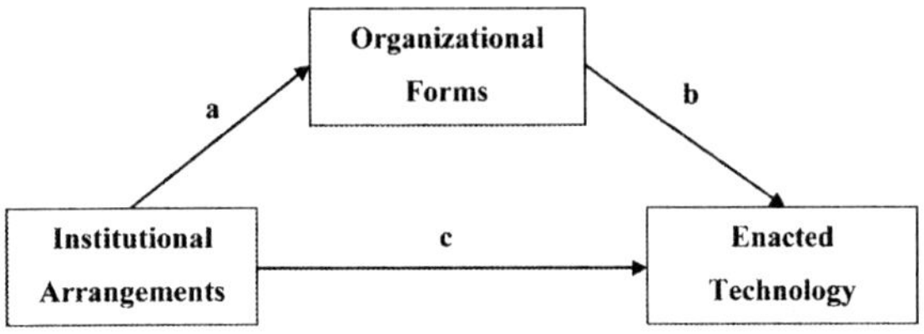

forms. Regressions (1) and (4) must be statistically significant. In regression (6), β_6 needs to be statistically significant, and β_7 must be zero to show full mediation. If both coefficients β_6 and β_7 are significant, there will be only partial mediation. To test the relation between organizational forms and results, mediated by enacted technology, we will use regressions (2), (5), and (7).

Table 4 summarizes the results of the seven regression models described above. The first column in the table contains the regression equation number. The second and third columns represent the dependent and independent variables in each regression equation. Column 4 in the table presents the standardized regression coefficients for each model. The last two columns show the R-square value, and the F-test for each model.

Looking at the values in regressions 1, 2, and 3, we can conclude that the survey data supports hypotheses 1, 2, and 4, finding significant direct relations between institutional arrangements and organizational forms, between organizational forms and the enacted technology, and also between the enacted technology and the results. It is important to notice that enacted technology explains more than 50% of the variance in Results.

In the case of hypothesis 3, there is a significant relationship between institutional arrangements and organizational forms, and also between institutional arrangements and enacted technology (regressions 1 and 4). Moreover, the relation between organizational forms and enacted technology is significant when controlling for institutional arrangements (regression 6). However, the relation between institutional arrangements and enacted technology is also significant when controlling for organizational forms. Therefore, the survey data supports a partial mediation of organizational forms on the effect of institutional arrangements on the enacted technology. It is important to note that for this dataset the impact of institutional arrangements on enacted technology is greater than the impact of organizational forms on the same variable.

In the case of hypothesis 5, there is a significant relation between organizational forms and results (regression 5), and between organizational forms and the enacted technology (regression 2). Again, looking at the coefficients of regression 7, we

Table 4. Summary of regression results

Dep. Var.	Indep. Var.	β	R^2	F
Organiz. Forms	Institut. Arrang.	0.33***	0.108	24.97***
Enacted Tech.	Organiz. Forms	0.43***	0.183	49.05***
Results	Enacted Tech.	0.71***	0.506	229.8***
Enacted Tech.	Institut. Arrang.	0.45***	0.201	51.97***
Results	Organiz. Forms	0.42***	0.180	46.54***
Enacted Tech.	Organiz. Forms Institut. Arrang.	0.30*** 0.35***	0.278	39.70***
Results	Enacted Tech Organiz. Forms	0.63*** 0.18**	0.528	114.7***

** p<0.01
*** p<0.001

observe that survey data supports the existence of partial mediation of enacted technology over the relationship between organizational forms and results.

In summary, the regression analyses presented in Table 4 fully support hypotheses 1, 2, and 4, and partially support hypotheses 3 and 5, given that there is no full mediation, but only partial mediation of the relationships in those hypotheses and, therefore, direct effects also exist.

Interview Results and Discussion

As a complementary approach to explore the relationships among institutional arrangements, organizational forms, enacted technology and results, we analyzed a set of interviews looking for instances both supporting and not supporting the causal relationships presented in our research model (see Figure 1). In general, we found much more instances of interviewees' comments supporting the existence of the four relationships, thus the interview data also supports the existence of these causal relationships. However, the quantitative analysis did not support the hypothesis of full mediation of organizational forms and enacted technology, and we wanted to further explore the direct relationship between Institutional Arrangements and Enacted Technology, and also the direct relationship between organizational forms and results.

Consistent with the findings of the quantitative analysis, interviews are also rich on data supporting those direct relationships. Interviewees clearly stated that institutional arrangements have an important impact on technology enactments. Particularly, interviewees made reference to the legal and cultural aspects of institutions and the way they affect particular technology characteristics or uses. Many interviewees mentioned the importance of legal frameworks and regulations as significant constraints in the use of technology. For example, one of the interviewees mentioned "the legal framework is very important for electronic service delivery. Once you convince an agency to provide an electronic service, you need to coordinate with the Federal Commission for Regulatory Improvements. If your service is not registered, you just can't go live with it."

Another interviewee was even more compelling in his argument "this is not only a technological discussion, or a discussion of making web pages or using the phone. All that [making web pages, etc] is very good and part of our business, but we need to have legal basis for everything we do so the citizen can be certain that it is allowed by law. All our systems have a legal basis. You can have the best technical solution, but without the legal basis you can't publish it." Moreover, there was also evidence of a bidirectional influence between particular technology enactments and the regulatory frameworks. One of the interviewees commented, "yes, we have changed the laws, and we still need to change more laws in order to be able to do more things, I am thinking about the digital signature, for example. We have also made agreements, on the basis of the current legal framework, to give certainty to the projects, so the next president can continue with them."

Cultural aspects are also institutional aspects influencing technology enactments, particularly technology adoption and resistance to change. One of the interviewees commented, "there are many issues involved beyond the technical concept, you have to deal with culture and trust. On this basis you will find organizations that will not want to adopt the system because they don't know how people are going to react or even because they don't like the idea of having an antenna on top of their offices." Others mentioned more specific problems such as certainty and trust in the Mexican culture, "people has their own perceptions… some for example do not trust the system without a receipt with a stamp. It gives certainty for any further claim." Therefore, qualitative data also supports the existence of a direct impact of institutional arrangements, particularly legal and cultural aspects, on how people understand and use the technology.

In terms of the relationship between organizational forms and results, we also found several important instances in the interview. For example, the lack of financial resources in the organizations was identified by many interviewees as an important factor affecting the results. One of them commented, "financial resources are very limited. We have many programs that have not given the best results or grow because we do not have the resources to promote them." Although this comment was repeated by many interviewees, many of them also stressed the importance of working in collaboration with other agencies to counterbalance this limitation. Another interviewee said, "We have developed a partnership with the ministry of labor. They have both the need and expertise to provide training, and we have the technical platform to provide such training. This is an important partnership because they provide the contents, the people, and we give them the technical platform and the tools for on-line training. We have with them a very successful pilot project."

These partnerships and networks are sometimes the only way to push forward a project and achieve the proposed results. As one of the project managers argued, "we do not have the capacity for such developments, we look for partnerships with public and private organizations as well as NGOs. We put together all our knowledge to create value." Therefore, the qualitative data also supports a direct impact of several organizational factors on the project results.

CONCLUSION

Given the importance of information and communication technologies in government, it is also essential to understand key factors affecting its use and implementation. We proposed five hypotheses based upon the Technology Enactment Framework, in order to empirically test the theory, but also to get a better understanding of the relationships among institutional arrangements, organizational forms, enacted technology, and results. In order to test the hypotheses, we administered a survey to public managers participating in interorganizational e-government projects in the Mexican federal government, and conducted a series of interviews with project managers. Research results allow us to derive implications for both theory and practice.

Survey results suggest that the Technology Enactment Framework (Fountain, 2001) can be potentially enriched with two additional causal relationships (see *Figure 3*). Although the original enactment framework suggests that the effects of institutional arrangements on the enacted technology are mediated by organizational forms, data from our survey also support a direct effect of institutional arrangements on the enacted technology. In fact, the effect of institutional arrangements is stronger than the effect of organizational forms. Qualitative data from the survey and the interviews to project managers support this additional causal relationship.

The whole Mexican IT strategy from 2000 to 2006 was driven by a presidential mandate. Moreover, particular technology enactments can be traced to mimetic mechanisms. For instance, many IT-related decisions are driven by best-practices research, or by current practices of a leading agency such as the Ministry of Finance, and sometimes it is difficult to trace IT-related

Figure 3. Revised model as suggested by survey and interview data

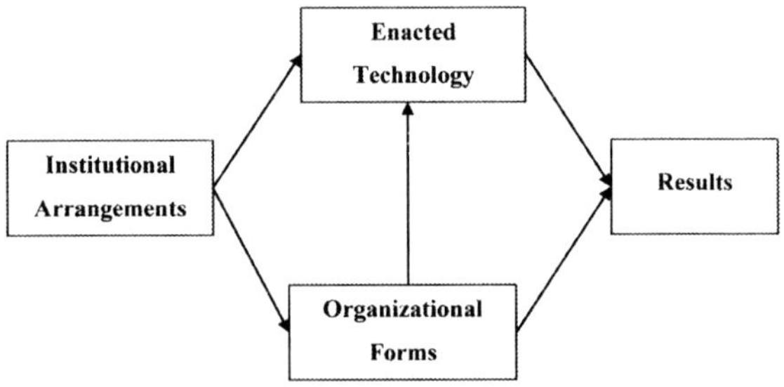

decisions to specific problems or needs. As in many other countries, technology decisions and designs are either constrained or enabled by the legal framework and regulations. Budget cycles, for example, constrain the size of the IT project, which in many cases cannot extend for more than a year.

The second causal relationship suggested by the survey data establishes a significant relationship between organizational forms and results. More concretely, decisions on organizational structures, goals, and performance indicators not only affect a particular technology enactment (characteristics and uses of the technology), but also affect directly the results of the project. As suggested by the interviews, partnerships and networks have been a key factor influencing project results. The e-Mexico program, for example, has as a strategic activity the development of telecenters in the whole country. Accomplishing this task involves collaboration of the Ministry of Transportation, the Ministry of Education, the Ministry of Health, and the Ministry of Social Development, among others. Different organizational forms of these ministries have not only affected the particular characteristics and actual uses of the telecenters sponsored by each of them, but also constrained or enabled the impact of the telecenters on the community. Therefore, it is clear that organizational characteristics not only affect the characteristics of the technology in use, but also the ultimate results of the project as a whole.

Additionally, survey and interview data provides support for the direct effects of institutional arrangements on organizational forms, organizational forms on the enacted technology, and enacted technology on organizational results. Thus, culture, laws, regulations, and institutional support have an important effect on organizational forms as they are reflected in goals, defining indicators, or during human and financial resource allocation. Moreover, these organizational forms have an impact on the characteristics of particular enactments of technology. For instance, adequacy of human and financial resources, as well as well-defined goals and performance indicators, have an impact on technological characteristics such as utility, quality of information, or ease of use. Finally, characteristics of a particular enactment have an effect on the results of using technology in government. That is to say, system functionality and quality have a positive impact on the expected results of the IT project in terms of efficiency, policy effectiveness, and service quality, among others.

Although organizational forms and enactments are under the control of project managers, they usually have more difficulty influencing institutional arrangements in which the project takes place. However, those institutional arrangements effect and constrain the project manager's work. Thus, to be able to manage an effective project, every manager should use at least part of his or her time looking for strategies to promote institutional change or take advantage of the current institutional arrangments. In the case of Mexico and the projects included in this research, these institutional arrangements are especially important, considering that almost half of the respondents recognized that laws and regulations need to be improved. Moreover, intensive lobbying may be an important strategy, given the perception of inadequate support for e-government projects and interorganizational collaboration from legislators.

Survey results also support the idea that effective technology enactments will deliver results for government organizations. There is a strong and significant relationship between these two variables. Therefore, given adequate institutional arrangements, project managers can make organizational and technology choices to deliver good results. However, the overall results depend on a careful and systematic identification of technical requirements and the use of adequate project management techniques.

Finally, this work contributes to the field by testing empirical evidence for important causal relationships often cited in the literature, but with little empirical quantitative exploration. Furthermore, it provides empirical evidence of the existence of such relationships in a context different from the context in which the theory was created, providing evidence of the applicability of the theory to different government contexts, particularly to Latin American countries such as Mexico.

ACKNOWLEDGMENT

This study was supported by the National Council of Science and Technology (CONACYT-Mexico) under grant SEP-2004-C01-46507 and by the National Science Foundation (NSF) under Grant No. 0131923. The views and conclusions expressed in this chapter are those of the authors alone and do not necessarily reflect the views of CONACYT or NSF. This chapter is based on work contributed by Mireya Estrada-Marroquín, Víctor M. Morán-Rodríguez, Bárbara Aguilera-Alcántara, and Cinthia B. Cruz. The authors particularly acknowledge the contributions of Mireya Estrada-Marroquín, who was a co-author in a previous version of this chapter.

REFERENCES

Bansal, P. (2005). Evolving sustainably: a longitudinal study of corporate sustainable development. *Strategic Management Journal*, *26*(3), 197–218. doi:10.1002/smj.441

Barley, S. R., & Tolbert, P. S. (1997). Institutionalization and structuration: studying the links between action and institution. *Organization Studies*, *18*(1), 93–117. doi:10.1177/017084069701800106

Baron, R. M., & Kenny, D. A. (1986). The moderator-mediator variable distinction in social psychological research: Conceptual, strategic and statistical considerations. *Journal of Personality and Social Psychology*, *51*, 1173–1182. doi:10.1037/0022-3514.51.6.1173

Bennett, M., Bouma, J. J., & Ciccozzi, E. (2004). An institutional perspective on the transfer of accounting knowledge: a case study. *Accounting Education*, *13*(3), 329–346. doi:10.1080/0963928042000273807

Brinton, M. C., & Nee, V. (1998). *The New Institutionalism in Sociology*. Stanford, CA: Stanford University Press.

Carbo, T., & Williams, J. G. (2004). Models and metrics for evaluating local electronic government systems and services. *Electronic . Journal of E-Government*, *2*(2), 95–104.

Creswell, J. W. (1994). *Research Design: Qualitative and Quantitative Approaches*. Thousand Oaks, CA: Sage Publications.

Dawes, S. (2002). Government and technology: User, not regulator. *Journal of Public Administration: Research and Theory*, *12*(4), 627–631.

Fountain, J. E. (1995). *Enacting Technology: An Institutional Perspective*. Cambridge, MA: John F. Kennedy School of Government, Harvard University.

Fountain, J. E. (2001). *Building the Virtual State. Information Technology and Institutional Change*. Washington, D.C.: Brookings Institution Press.

Fountain, J. E. (2004). *Prospects for the Virtual State*. Working papers. Retrieved May, 2006, from http://www.j.u-tokyo.ac.jp/coeps/pdf/040710.pdf

Fountain, J. E. (2008). Bureaucratic Reform and E-Government in the United States: An Institutional Perspective. In A. Chadwick & P. N. Howard (Eds.), *The Handbook of Internet Politics*. New York: Routledge.

Fountain, J. E., McKinnon, R., & Park, E. (2003). *E-Government Cross-Agency and Intergovernmental Initiatives Research Project: Web Survey Results*. Boston, MA: Working Papers Series, National Center for Digital Government, John F. Kennedy School of Government, Harvard University.

Garson, G. D. (2003). Technological telelogy and the theory of technology enactment. *Social Science Computer Review, 21*(4), 425–431. doi:10.1177/0894439303256371

Giddens, A. (1979). *Central Problems in Social Theory. Action, Structure and Contradiction in Social Analysis*. Berkeley and Los Angeles, CA: University of California Press.

Giddens, A. (1984). *The Constitution of Society*. Berkeley and Los Angeles, CA: University of California Press.

Gil-Garcia, J. R. (2005, September 1-4). *Do Citizens' Expectations Matter for E-Government? Exploring the Determinants of the Functionality of State Web Sites*. Paper presented at the 2005 APSA Annual Meeting, Washington, DC.

Gil-Garcia, J. R. (2006, January 4-7, 2006). *Enacting State Websites: A Mixed Method Study Exploring E-Government Success in Multi-Organizational Settings*. Paper presented at the 39th Hawaii International Conference on System Sciences (HICSS).

Gil-Garcia, J. R., & Helbig, N. (2006). Exploring e-government benefits and success factors. In A.-V. Anttiroiko & M. Malkia (Eds.), *Encyclopedia of digital government*. Hershey, PA: Idea Group Inc.

Gil-García, J. R., & Luna-Reyes, L. F. (2006). Integrating Conceptual Approaches to E-Government. In M. Khosrow-Pour (Ed.), *Encyclopedia of E-Commerce, E-Government, and Mobile Commerce* (pp. 636-643). Hershey, PA: Idea Group Reference.

Hassan, S., & Gil-Garcia, J. R. (2008). Institutional Theory and E-Government Research. In G. D. Garson & M. Khosrow-Pour (Eds.), *Handbook of Research on Public Information Technology*. Hershey, PA: IGI Global.

Hiller, J. S., & Bélanger, F. (2001). Privacy Strategies for Electronic Government. In M. A. Abramson & G. E. Means (Eds.), *E-Government 2001* (pp. 162-198). Lanham, Maryland: Rowman & Littlefield Publishers.

Holmes, D. (2001). *e.gov. e-business Strategies for Government*. London: Nicholas Brealey Publishing.

Khadaroo, M. I. (2005). An institutional theory perspective on the UK's Private Finance Initiative (PFI) accounting standard setting process. *Public Management Review, 7*(1), 69–94. doi:10.1080/1471903042000339428

Kraemer, K. L., King, J. L., Dunkle, D. E., & Lane, J. P. (1989). *Managing Information Systems. Change and Control in Organizational Computing*. San Francisco, CA: Jossey-Bass.

Lim, J. H., & Tang, S.-Y. (2008). Urban e-government initiatives and environmental decision performance in Korea. *Journal of Public Administration: Research and Theory, 18*(1), 109–138. doi:10.1093/jopart/mum005

Luna-Reyes, L. F., Gil-García, J. R., & Cruz, C. B. (2006, August 4-6). *Collaborative Digital Government in Mexico: Some Lessons from Federal Web-Based Inter-Organizational Information Integration Initiatives*. Paper presented at the 12th Americas Conference on Information Systems, Acapulco, Mexico.

North, D. C. (1999). *Institutions, Institutional Change, and Economic Performance*. New York: Cambridge University Press.

OECD. (2003). *OECD e-Government Studies: The E-Government Imperative*. Paris, France: OECD Publishing.

OECD. (2005). *OECD e-Government Studies: Mexico*. Paris, France: OECD Publishing.

Orlikowski, W. (2000). Using Technology and Constituting Structures: A practice lens for studying technology in organizations. *Organization Science, 11*(4), 404–428. doi:10.1287/orsc.11.4.404.14600

6P. (2001). E-governance. Do Digital Aids Make a Difference in Policy Making? In J. E. J. Prins (Ed.), *Designing E-Government. On the Crossroads of Technological Innovation and Institutional Change* (pp. 7-27). The Hague, Netherlands: Kluwer Law International.

Peters, B. G. (2001). *Institutional theory in political science. The 'new' institutionalism*. London: Continuum.

Poder Ejecutivo. (2002). *Ley Federal de Transparencia y Acceso a la Información Pública Gubernamental*. Retrieved September, 2006, from http://www.elaw.org/resources/text.asp?id=1544

Powell, W. W., & DiMaggio, P. J. (1991). *The New Institutionalism in organizational analysis*. Chicago, IL: University of Chicago Press.

Puron Cid, G., & Gil-Garcia, J. R. (2004). Enacting E-Budgeting in Mexico. *Public Finance and Management, 4*(2), 182–217.

Rocheleau, B. (2003). Politics, Accountability, and Governmental Information Systems. In G. D. Garson (Ed.), *Public Information Technology: Policy and Management Issues* (pp. 20-52). Hershey, PA: Idea Group Publishing.

Roy, J. (2007). E-Government in Canada: Transition or Transformation? In D. F. Norris (Ed.), *Current Issues and Trends in E-Government Research* (pp. 44-67). Hershey, PA: CyberTech Publishing.

Rutherford, M. (1999). *Institutions in economics. The old and the new institutionalism*. New York: Cambridge University Press.

Scheela, W., & Van Dinh, N. (2004). Venture capital in a transition economy: the case of Vietnam. *Venture Capital - An international journal of entrepreneurial finance, 6*(4), 333-350.

Schelin, S. H. (2003). E-Government: An Overview. In G. D. Garson (Ed.), *Public Information Technology: Policy and Management Issues* (pp. 120-137). Hershey, PA: Idea Group Publishing.

Schellong, A. (2007). *Extending the Technology Enactment Framework*. Boston, MA: Harvard University, Kennedy School of Government, Program on Networked Governance, Working Paper No. PNG07-003.

Scholl, H. J. (2002). *Executive Briefing on Electronic Government and Business Process Change*. Albany, NY: Center for Technology in Government.

Scott, W. R. (2001). *Institutions and organizations* (2nd ed.). Thousand Oaks, CA: Sage.

Welch, E. W., & Pandey, S. K. (2007). E-government and bureaucracy: Toward a better understanding of intranet implementation and its effects on red tape. *Journal of Public Administration: Research and Theory, 17*(3), 379–404. doi:10.1093/jopart/mul013

Yang, K. (2003). Neoinstitutionalism and e-government. *Social Science Computer Review, 21*(4), 432–442. doi:10.1177/0894439303256508

Yildiz, M. (2007). E-government research: reviewing the literature, limitations, and ways forward. *Government Information Quarterly*, *24*(3), 646–665. doi:10.1016/j.giq.2007.01.002

ENDNOTES

1 For the descriptive results of the survey see Luna-Reyes, L. F. and Gil-Garcia, J. R. (2008). *E-Government and Inter-Organizational Collaboration in Mexico: Survey Results*. NCDG Working Paper #08-003. National Center for Digital Government: University of Massachusetts at Amherst: Amherst, MA. Available at: http://www.umass.edu/digitalcenter/research/working_papers/08_003LReyesEgovMexico.pdf

2 Spanish version of the survey can be obtained from the authors. Other questions in the survey are related to respondents' demographics, and other factors not reported in this chapter. Questions used in each construct are listed in the appendix.

3 Spanish version of the interview protocol and the coding scheme can be obtained from the authors. The interview protocol was also a translation and adaptation from Fountain original study.

4 Number of observations is smaller than valid response rate because we are not making any imputation to missing values.

APPENDIX: SURVEY QUESTIONS IN EACH CONSTRUCT (TABLE 5)

Table 5.

Construct	Questions in the Survey
Organizational Forms	Definition of goals
	Definition of performance indicators
	Feasibility of goals
	Adequacy of human resources
	Adequacy of financial resources
	Recognition
Institutional Arrangements	Government culture
	Adequacy of laws
	Support from Congress
	Institutional support to IT
	Institutional support to project
Enacted Technology	Ease of use
	Utility
	Quality of information
	Functionality
	Personalization
	Security
	Privacy
	Quality of the system
Results	Success in general
	Productivity
	Cost reduction
	More effective policies and programs
	Transparency
	Quality of service
	Citizen participation
	IT infrastructure
	Improvements to the legal framework
	Project relevance

Chapter 13
Translucent States:
Political Mediation of E-Transparency[1]

María Frick
Organization of the American States and United Nations Educational, Scientific, and Cultural Organization (UNESCO)

ABSTRACT

This work focuses on online state communication through the analysis of Latin-American presidential portals. It postulates that even though governmental websites contribute to the dynamics of democracy in terms of greater transparency and participation in government processes, online government communication is neither completely symmetric nor transparent, since the ways of constructing, presenting and accessing the information are linked to cultural schemes. In this sense, the work argues that the search for transparency in Internet communication can expect -at best- clear and even translucent States, where transparency limits are determined by the sets of values and symbolic representations already existent in each society's political culture.

INTRODUCTION

Together with state's modernization process, government communication has acquired new relevance. In this context, new information and communication technologies (ICTs)—especially Internet—have achieved wide recognition. This is mainly due to the fact that an innovative capacity is attributed to them, as a contribution towards increasing public officials' decision transparency and supporting new ways of communication between government and civil society. As a result, Government portals and websites are then seen as being synonymous with State modernization. Furthermore, they appear to have an informative function free from any determining influence and their very presence is regarded as a contribution to transparency in public management and as an access door to citizen's participation in governmental processes.

The purpose of this work is to demonstrate that, since ways for building and displaying information as well as preparing means to access it are linked to cultural schemes, the conception of completely symmetric and transparent online government communications is not strictly speaking possible. On the contrary, it is suggested that the search for transparency in web communication can expect—at best—clear and even translucent States, where the transmission of messages and their meanings, are tinged with the political culture characteristics of each society.

The work is divided into four parts: The first one (point 2) explains the fallacy in the assumption of neutral communication imposed by the ideology accompanying the diffusion of new technologies. The second one (point 3) deals with communications' cultural mediation and introduces the possibility of hybridization and glocalization processes in the production of discursive practices on the Internet. The third, (point 4) deals with the relationship of communication, culture and hybridization from the point of view of political communication, and the systems of meaning and online representation within the political culture of each society. And the fourth one (point 5) analyzes empirically the political plot of virtual discourses in Latin-American States.

THE IDEOLOGY OF INFORMATION

In the late 80's, Latin American States began modernization processes focused on the notion of governance. In order to achieve equitable and democratic growths, these processes centered on the capacity of government institutions in terms of legitimacy and transparency. Thus, governmental communication acquired crucial significance, and problems related to diffusion, transmission and access to information became key elements in state management (Vega, 2002).

The notion of transparency is then associated to the free flow of, and access to, information regarding public actions and decisions, and this is considered a main link towards institutional strengthening and democratization (Heeks, 2004). The underlying hypothesis suggests that, if people can understand and be aware of government's management, they will participate more regularly in decision making, thus generating in officials and representatives a greater sense of responsibility in public affairs, and consequently contributing to the establishment of a better government (Balkin, 1998; Heeks, 2004).

Under these premises, when ICTs started, they were widely recognized, and their identification with transparency became omnipresent in the speeches of politicians, mass media and social elites (CEPAL, 2000; Wolton, 2000; Tapscott, 2004). There is no doubt that, under certain circumstances, their impact is beneficial to social and political development and welfare. However, in general, their incorporation has been associated with emphatically positive, neutral, and transforming discourses promising the eradication of almost every problem affecting society (Wiesner, n.d).

In this sense, there is a technological ideology according to which a change in technologies necessarily brings about a change in social relationships. This ideology arises from a classical definition of information, which considers that the communication act is a symmetric process between a sender and a receiver, and corresponds to a technical view of the social world that denies every principle of purpose and influence in social exchanges, and also rejects the influence of the effect of enunciation in communicative acts (Moragás, 1985; Wolton, 2000; Charaudeau, 2003).

This ideology has concrete consequences in the political sphere in particular. On one hand, by negating the possible existence of a purpose in exchanges, it does not take into account the possibility of officials and politicians simulating transparency virtues through rhetoric and media manipulation. Thus, it prevents the Internet from being understood as a tool of political action (Balkin, 1998). On the other hand, by stating that the Internet and the World Wide Web (WWW) are culturally neutral tools which permit transparent communication, it assumes that these technologies homogenize the design and contents of websites, detaching them from their cultural roots and consequently facilitating universal understanding (Ess and Sudweeks, 1998; Zhao, 2003).

As pointed out by Wolton (2000), the danger of this standpoint is forgetting that, beyond its utopian nature, the essential point in communication technology is the existing link between this technology, the cultural model of relationships between individuals, and the project this technology is concerned with. The ICTs are related to an integrated information system, the purpose of which is involved with the ambition of an "economy-world", and are also marked by the characteristics of the business model, insisting on a functional communication focused on results and speed of transmission (Wiesner, n.d; Moragás, 1985; Wolton, 2000). On the political sphere in particular, ICTs are related to the individualistic, liberal ideal. This is expressed in a technocratic liberalism in the following way:

- we do not have enough access to information;
- information is knowledge and knowledge is power, and,
- the access to information is the extension of democracy and the achievement of social equality (Winner, 1987).

Nevertheless, this line of reasoning has a number of fallacies. One of them—the one on which this work is based—is that the emphasis on the easiness of consulting and accessing information does not take into account cultural issues (Winner, 1987). The problem with online communication is not the access to information—as pointed out by technocratic liberalism but the division and hierarchy of knowledge, both before and after information is accessed, and in the information itself. Information is not simply the piece of data introduced, but is also the organization of data carried out in order to produce meaning or to make sense, ie.: what is called discourse, and this accounts for the way in which the different value systems organize the circulation of signs in order to produce meaning (Barón Porrás, n.d; Wolton, 2000; Charaudeau, 2003).

This means that, unlike the principles of the ideology of information, the way to construct and show information and establish the means to access it, is not universal but is related to cultural schemes (Brunner, 1988). In communicative actions among individuals, culture interposes symbolic mediations, i.e. organized sets of rules, values and meanings that function as implicit orders in every communicative act, establishing preferences with regard to the way individuals relate to themselves and others (Maturana, 1991). Thus, messages turn into discourses, i.e. sets of symbols invested with meaning within a time-space framework (Verón, 2004).

From this point of view, the fallacy in the assumption of transparency upheld by the information ideology arises from reducing communication to supports and techniques when—even though they are necessary—these conditions are not in themselves enough to deal with the issue. Apart from ignoring the purpose of communicative acts, its model overlooks the main cultural factor which goes beyond the technical aspect of information, referring to the processes of meaning inherent in communication (Bartoli, 1991).

Therefore, after this acknowledgement, the "technological revolution" becomes denaturalized. Even though the WWW and the Internet may be considered neutral tools, communication is inseparable from culture, so the setting looses its neutrality in the hands of the person using it and it becomes mediated by his culture (Martín-Barbero, 2003). Technology then appears to be insufficiently capable of changing society and its appraisal in terms of benefits and impacts stops being undeniably positive and becomes subject to the considerations of each different social context (Wiesner, n.d). Culture is fundamentally interwoven with communication, technology seems to be full of values, and the setting and its messages cease to be undeniably transparent as they become, at best, translucent.

INTERNET COMMUNICATION AND CULTURE

In online communication, the relationship between communication and culture can be seen in a website's design and content. This relationship has been studied in depth in the area of the Marketing studies oriented to e-commerce, advertising, and social Information Technology studies. In these fields, researchers oppose a standardization of navigation interfaces and web contents with a globalized consumer profile to their adaptation to regionally and culturally localized markets (Singh et Alt., 2005).

Although of a much more specific nature, this search parallels the one carried out by Social Sciences centered on the diffusion of new technologies, their consequences on the transnationalization of information flows and diversification of communication channels, and the emergence of new crossings between global and local spheres of information reception and production (Moragás, 1985). In both fields, there is a polarization among those who view these changes as a homogenizing process with consequences in terms of the acculturation and erosion of significant spaces in communication, and those who see them as an opportunity for local identity vindications (Vizer, 2003).

At the beginning, specifically in the marketing field, it was believed that as the Internet was a technology developed mainly by the U.S.A. and Europe, its contents and that its designs would tend to represent developed industrial countries values (Sackmary and Scalia, 1999). A similar argument stated that because of the user's predominant profile—most of them belonging to Western middle and upper classes—the Internet would tend to show some homogeneity in its sites' design, organization and contents (Simon, 1999). Some authors even predicted the existence of an "Internet imperialism" that would destabilize online's representation of different cultures in favor of a universal and deterritorialized cultural matrix associated with consumption and interactivity values.

In the analysis of this possibility, Sackmary and Scalia (1999) compared the portals of some Mexican and American companies and confirmed that, even though the sites had different designs, the content tended to be "neutral" towards differences of their cultural origins. This finding led authors to identify the emergence of a transnational web communication style avoiding specific visual or linguistic references. Similar conclusions were reached by Stengers, Troyers, Baetensi and Mushtaha (2004), who stated that the Web promotes the emergence of a cosmopolitan online culture, neutral to traditional cultural differences.

However, the increasing spread of the Internet revived the discussion, making way for a new kind of literature which emphasizes the persistence of local values in web communication. This perspective argues that, since websites are developed in different places around the world, their designs are influenced by the characteristics of the cultures in which they originate (Stengers et alt., 2004). Generally speaking, this standpoint agrees with the perspective held by Social Sciences stating that homogenization caused by communicative globalization may be accompanied by differentiation processes based on unchangeable cultural and identity vindications (Bayardo and Lacarrieu, 1997). The marketing field in particular, agrees with those who assert that in order to attract or retain users, it is necessary to adapt the websites to their characteristics, localizing; texts, visuals elements and contents so that they become "culturally appropriate".

A similar study was carried out by Del Galdo and Nielsen (1996), demonstrating the existence of variations in the use of color and web design in different cultures. Barber and Brade (1998) have also concluded that elements such as colors, texts, graphics and the space orientation of a website change according to different contexts, determining the navigation capacity of the users. Fink and Laupase (2000), on the other hand, showed Australian and Malaysian websites to people of these nationalities and found that, in general, Australians evaluated positively Australian websites, whereas Malaysians preferred those originating in their own country.

Finally, as a third position of this debate, the work of Zhao, Massey, Murphy and Fang (2003) established that the Internet is neither completely neutral—in the sense of a universal cultural matrix—nor is it specific to local values. On the contrary, they state that there is a hybridization phenomenon in the web characterized by the coexistence of changes and permanencies. On one hand, there are differences in the design and content of websites according to their cultural origin, and on the other hand, there are some similarities in design that may be attributed to the generalization of a neutral or non-specified cultural model.

This argument is compatible with the concepts of hybridization and "glocalization". In the area of cultural and anthropologic studies on identity, these concepts question the modern-traditional dichotomies in the processes of political and social development, suggesting possible crossings between these dualities (De Grandis, 1995; López de la Roche, 2000). From this perspective, hybridization is a process by which social actors take certain benefits from modernity, combining discrete structures or practices which exist separately in order to generate new structures, objects and practices (García Canclini, 2003).

Such a phenomenon may be understood as the result of a double movement: a "globalized localism" that involves a process by which a given local phenomenon is successfully globalized and a "localized globalism" that involves a specific impact of transnational practices or imperatives on local conditions, which must be structured and restructured in order to respond to such imperatives (Lozada, 2004). The result is then a process of "glocalization" in which globalization, established as monolithic and universal, is adapted to local conditions: Local communities adopt global values appropriating and incorporating them into their own way of doing things (Lull, 1995; Fernández Parrat, 2002).

As described by Martínez (2004), in the specific case of the production of discursive practices, this process occurs as a result of a balance of tension between global and local representations. In this relationship/tension, global representations do not "destroy" local ones; but instead, social actors try to cope with universalistic institutions—globalizing practices of other actors—in order to retake some control of their practices and representations, either individually or collectively.

From this angle, differences between websites from different countries may be seen in terms of a relationship/tension between hybridization and glocalization. From an intermediate position, it can be asserted that countries carry out design and content adaptations during the process of the adoption of a globalized technology and communication; but, even within this framework, there are pre-existing differences that correspond to domestic cultural patterns (Zhao et alt., 2003).

From this point of view, Internet does not necessarily force the importation of globalized values, but instead local communities retain their systems of values and preferences, adapting the use of the web to them, and generating an interaction between the global and the local (Hongladarom, 1998; Ess and Sudweeks, 1998). Thus, Internet contents and designs may fulfill the material, syntactic and even aesthetic characteristics which are typical of globalized formats but, at the same time, they maintain their own semantic characteristics which are related to local, social and cultural institutions (Wiesner, n.d). In this sense, the Internet is culturally mediated, and the relationship between online communication and culture may be understood as an ongoing transformation of identity processes in which new and old representations coexist and integrate in a variety of socio-cultural contexts (Lozada, 2004).

POLITICAL CULTURE IN THE STATE DISCOURSE

Generally speaking, political communication refers to the type of messages circulating within the political system and those essential for its functioning insofar as they determine its activity (Panebianco, 1982). Online state communication in particular, reflects that aspect of political communication concerned with communication as a non-propagandistic organizational instrument of the political and administrative activity.

Along similar lines, it can be stated that, since online communication is mediated by culture, political communication—within its own specific area of social communication—is mediated by political culture. It can also be stated that, in the specific sphere of politics, it also duplicates the conceptual relationship between communication and culture in the Internet, thus generating the possibility of hybridization and glocalization processes. The only difference is, in this case, the phenomenon refers to the conflict of values centered on society's power-relationships.

Political culture can be understood as a set of elements which compose the subjective perception of power and authority on the relationships held by a population, as well as tendencies and attitudes towards the political system (Peschard, 1996). In this sense, the relationship between political culture and communication is inherent to their nature: communication creates a political space and politics produce legitimizing symbols and signs understood through political culture (Colomé, 1994).

Hybridization processes have already been confirmed in other political communication spheres (Plasser, 2004); therefore, they may also exist in the area of state Internet communication. The emerging interrogation deals with establishing to what extent online representation systems respond to a globally legitimized political-communicative paradigm or whether they are rooted in local political culture. In other words: can we expect a transparent, globalized online communication detached from local political culture?

Assuming the existence of a dominant scheme determining the premises of a communications cultural construction, it might be expected that technological mechanisms controlled by democratic States transmit meanings and condense values associated with an articulated political culture centered on the democratic-liberal notion of citizenship. Specifically, a cultural identity inspired by liberal principles, sustaining the idea of a society with large autonomy from the State, and a democratic political culture viewing citizens as rational, free and equal individuals, subjects par excellence for participation in public affairs and power legitimization (Peschard, 1996). Moreover, it is precisely in this political conception, centered on individuals and democracy, where the use of new technologies for transparency is promoted (Wolton, 2000).

However, the permanence of heterogeneous cultural identities—even anti-values—mixed with this global discourse but also rooted in the local political system might be expected behind the veil of these values (Perina, 2002:6). Political culture is a composition of values and perceptions that, as such, does not include orientations of just one kind but usually combines democratic and/or modern perceptions and convictions with more or less authoritarian and/or traditional behavior patterns (Peschard, 1996; Perina, 2002). Therefore, it is possible to think that, beyond the similarity among political-communicative forms, local political culture may prevail and even alter forms and meanings of the leading political discourse.

So that despite the predominance of a specific model, communication is not universal but linked to the cultural schemes that determine it.

In the political-virtual sphere, the right path in the debate over communication and culture is abandoning the idea of a global and transparent political communication which is composed of all countries and cultures, and adopting a position supporting the existence of the phenomenon of hybridization of communication practices, which implies a complementation of national traditions and specific globalized cultures with components connected to Western liberal democracy. In other words: a point of view that considers the possibility of processes both of permanence and negotiation or merging of political identities, values, democratic practices and anti-value or non-democratic practices.

However, the possibility of this standpoint is connected to the theoretical perspective which is adopted on the concept of political culture. Specifically, to the set of perspectives which, with a multidisciplinary approach (anthropological, sociological, political) shapes what is known as "interpretative current". In opposition to the behaviorist school, this current approaches political culture as a part of typical cultural meanings in a community. Thus, political culture is not a sphere independent of general culture or civic culture (considered in relation to democratic values), but part of a sedimentation of representations, symbols and institutions giving meaning to a set of social actions. It is basically a configuration of meaning regarding the organization and hierarchy of power in some spheres (famlily, school, institutions, communities, nationalities, etc.) which eventually acquires, as main point of reference, codes built around the political order and the political system constituted and legitimized in society (Sánchez, 2000; Heras Gómez, 2002).

Only from this theoretical perspective, is it possible to consider political communication processes from a viewpoint that questions democratic discourse as an established reality and recovers the possibility of value mixtures and heterogeneous permanencies of meanings in societies´ political discourses (Cruces Villalobos and Díaz de Rada, 1995; Heras Gómez, 2002).

The particular richness in the view of political culture as a "hybrid mentality" lies, in this sense, in the fact that it possible to understand the communication processes in political systems taking into account the construction processes of modernity that are typical of each society (Brunner, 1998; López de la Roche, 2000). Then, from this point of view, it is possible to analyze the relationship between communication and culture in Latin-American States' online communication, and to answer to which extent political culture—with its systems of values, symbolic representations and social imaginary—permeates online messages, imposing a local language on the intended global transparency.

POLITICAL MEDIATION OF COMMUNICATION

In general, websites can be analyzed from both a functional and a symbolic dimension. The functional dimension refers to the way in which information is published on the sites; i.e. architectures of the texts (subdivisions and navigation bars or tools). Their analysis reflects a classification system that divides the social universe the site is informing about.

The symbolic dimension refers to meanings of site elements (visual images, symbols, signs, colors, textures and forms of the sites) and their relationship with mental guidelines or models that guide their organization of information (hierarchy, distribution, composition, disposition and differentiation). Their analysis crystallizes characteristics of national identity (shared images about the historical past and its relevance to collective projects and institutional loyalties of the present) and, through them, reflects society's political culture (Buchrucker, 1994).

Each of these dimensions can be approached with a specific method and show, at the same time, complementary results. Their analysis is explained below, considering as universe the presidential portals of the Spanish speakers of Latin America and the Caribbean (see Table 1). First, sites are analyzed according to a functional and quantitative measurement of their transparency; subsequently a symbolic, interpretative analysis is made on two of the most transparent sites of the region.

The functional dimension can be analyzed by gathering information on the site's main characteristics, according to the e-transparency indicators suggested by the "E-Government for Development" of the University of Manchester (United Kingdom) (Heeks, 2004). For the purposes of this work, these indicators were adapted in order to elaborate a questionnaire of 65 variables later applied in the 15 functioning presidential websites in September, 2006 (see Table 2).

According to information gathered, it can be observed that, in general, regional sites present a 21 percentage point average; the Mexican presidential site being the one that most stands out with 62.3 points. With a lower score, but still higher than average, Chilean and Nicaraguan sites also stand out with 40 points each. The sites with lower values are the Uruguayan (18.4 points) and the Venezuelan (14 points) ones (see Graph 1).

When results are broken down according to index categories, it can be observed that in general the most developed aspect of sites is the provision of information, with dimensions of "report" and "openness" following in importance. "Transaction" and "responsibility" are below the average. This means that, in the region, sites are being used mainly to spread information, whereas the possibilities offered by the web for interaction with citizens and democratic control are aspects which are poorly exploited (see Graph 2).

If these results are analyzed in dimensions, a closer approach is possible. Regarding the "infor-

Table 1. Websites sample (Hispanic countries, Latin America. N = 17)

Argentina	http://www.presidencia.gov.ar
Bolivia	http://www.presidencia.gov.bo
Chile	http://www.presidencia.cl
Colombia	http://www.presidencia.gov.co
Costa Rica	http://www.casapres.go.cr
El Salvador	http://www.casapres.gpb.sv
Guatemala	http://www.guatemala.gob.gt
Honduras	http://www.presidencia.gob.hn
México	http://www.presidencia.gob.mx
Nicaragua	http://www.presidencia.gob.ni
Panamá	http://www.presidencia.gob.pa
Paraguay	http://www.presidencia.gov.py
Uruguay	http://www.presidencia.gub.uy
Venezuela	http://www.venezuela.gov.ve
Ecuador *	http://www.presidencia.gov.ec
República Dominicana *	http://www.presidencia.gov.do
Perú **	http://www.presidencia.gob.pe

*Notes: * Not available site. ** Not available: maintenance. September, 2006.*

Table 2. Online transparency dimensions and indicators

1. Information	Provides detailed information about government´ functions and staff.
2. Participation	Provides online tools for citizens' consultation and participation.
3. Report	Provides detailed information or statistics about government performance.
4. Openness	Provides comparative information about government´ performance during different administrations.
5. Accountability	Provides mechanisms to punish or to award public servants.

Graph 1. Online transparency index (Presidential Sites; Mean: 21)

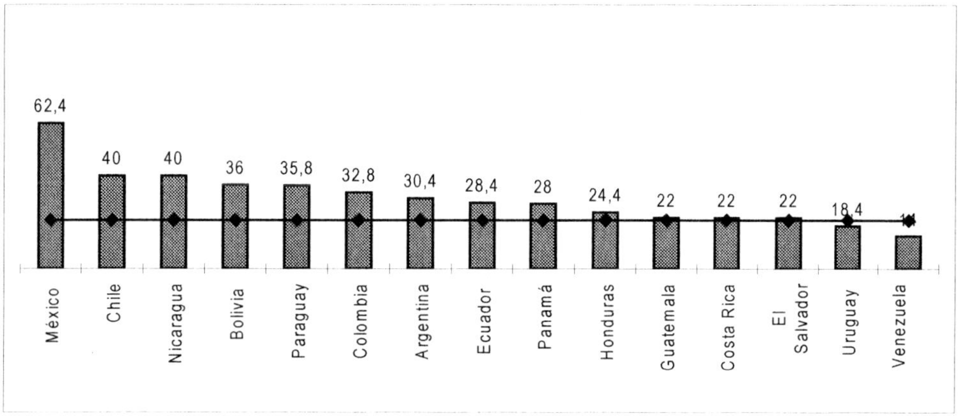

Graph 2. Online transparency index, by transparency dimensions

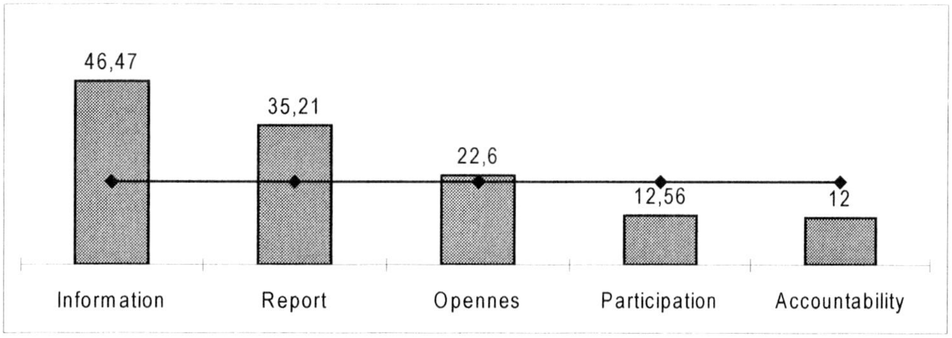

mation" dimension, it can be observed that—on a regional average of 46.47 points and with Mexico and Chile still leading—Bolivia reaches an important third place, whereas Venezuela, Guatemala and Costa Rica show the lowest development.

This dimension can be broken down into sub-dimensions of "general information" and "contact information". The "general information" sub-dimension takes into account access to the following information: general introduction to power, Presidential Palace presentation, general information about the country and its national symbols, information about the President, First Lady, Vice-President and Cabinet and its members. In this category, on a 51.18-point average, presidencies that score most points are the ones from Mexico (90.91), Chile (72.73), El Salvador (72.73), Bolivia and Honduras (63.64 points each) (see Table 3).

Table 3. Transparency values and user friendliness per country and dimensions

Transparency dimension		Argentina	Bolivia	Chile	Colombia
1	Information	52,94	64,71	70,59	47,06
	General information	54,55	63,64	72,73	54,55
	Contact information	50,00	66,67	66,67	33,33
2	Participation	11,11	11,11	11,11	11,11
3	Report	28,57	35,71	42,86	35,71
4	Openness	20,00	20,00	20,00	40,00
5	Accountability	20,00	0,00	0,00	40,00
6	User friendliness	6,67	6,67	46,67	13,33
Transparency dimension		Costa Rica	Ecuador	El Salvador	Guatemala
1	Information	23,53	47,06	47,06	23,53
	General information	27,27	54,55	72,73	27,27
	Contact information	16,67	33,33	0,00	16,67
2	Participation	11,11	11,11	0,00	0,00
3	Report	35,71	28,57	21,43	28,57
4	Openness	20,00	20,00	0,00	60,00
5	Accountability	0,00	20,00	0,00	0,00
6	User friendliness	13,33	20,00	0,00	13,33
Transparency dimension		Honduras	México	Nicaragua	Panamá
1	Information	47,06	88,24	52,94	35,29
	General information	63,64	90,91	45,45	27,27
	Contact information	16,67	83,33	66,67	50,00
2	Participation	11,11	33,33	11,11	11,11
3	Report	21,43	71,43	57,14	42,86
4	Openness	0,00	60,00	40,00	20,00
5	Accountability	20,00	20,00	0,00	0,00
6	User friendliness	13,33	46,67	6,67	0,00
Transparency dimension		Paraguay	Uruguay	Venezuela	Regional mean
1	Information	44,12	29,41	23,53	46,47
	General information	50,00	27,27	36,36	51,18
	Contact information	33,33	33,33	0,00	37,83
2	Participation	11,11	22,22	22,22	12.56
3	Report	57,14	14,29	7,14	35,21
4	Openness	20,00	0,00	0,00	22,60
5	Accountability	40,00	20,00	0,00	12,00
6	User friendliness	13,33	26,67	6,67	15,53

On the other hand, the "contact information" sub-dimension refers to publication of information allowing users to contact—either electronically or in a traditional way—the President, First Lady, Vice-President, Cabinet and its members, the remaining government powers and organisms dependent on the Executive Power. On a 37.83 point average—apart from Mexican and Chilean sites–, developments in Bolivia and Nicaragua stand out with 66.67 points each (see Table 3).

The second dimension of analysis in the index is "report". This refers to the publication of information about: President's agenda, First Lady, Vice-President and the Cabinet, presidential speeches (text and multimedia), the government plan, performance indicators and management statistics, access to government publications, laws and documents, existence of a press or novelty section and the possibility of subscribing to an e-bulletin. In the region, on a 35.21-point average and behind the Mexican leadership, Paraguayan (57.14) and Nicaraguan (57.14) sites stand out. These sites are the most transparent in terms of providing specific details or indicators about public administration decisions and actions (see Table 3).

The third dimension in order of importance in the region is "openness", and it refers to providing information allowing website users to access management indicators and documents for tracking public issues over a period of time. Specifically: archives of presidential discourses, comparative indicators, indicators about the government's plan and its specific goals over time. This dimension presents a 22.6-point average. The Guatemalan presidential site stands out in it with the same values as the Mexican one. 60 points (see Table 3).

The "participation" and "responsibility" dimensions of the region are below the average. "Participation" dimension refers to providing online consultation and participation mechanisms, and presents a poor evolution in the region. Only Mexico, Uruguay and Venezuela exceed the 12.56 point average; nevertheless some analytical remarks must be made about each case.

The Mexican site stands out because it provides a link to a general consultation office, presents a guide to the consultation procedure, and makes them available online; but it does not provide participation mechanisms. The Uruguayan site does not provide information about consultations; but on 2005 it provided an online survey mechanism. Although nowadays it is not available, up to 3,500 people participated in this proposal. Finally, the Venezuelan site—just like the Mexican one—provides general consultation mechanisms, but does not offer participation mechanisms. Following this tendency, regional presidential sites present a 25-point average with regard to provision of consultation mechanisms, and an 8-point average in the provision of participation mechanisms (see Table 3).

On the other hand, "responsibility" dimension refers to the amount of information, the contents of published mechanisms for contacting those in charge of sites, and the possibility of complaining or commenting on government employees' performance, as well as the presence of contact links or information with an Ombudsman. Despite its importance in terms of public management transparency, this is the dimension that is the least developed in regional presidential sites. It reaches an average of 12 points, exceeded only by half of the cases; whereas the other half presents values equivalent of zero (see Table 3).

Finally, apart from the 50 variables of the transparency index, values obtained by sites in an analysis of "user-friendliness" should be emphasized. This small gathering of information (15 variables) takes into account web tools provided by sites in order to make it easier for citizens to navigate. Included among them are: the FAQ section, site map, content index, absence of dead links, help menu, services for specific groups, etc.

The relevance of this analysis consists in showing that it is reasonable to think that a site which is difficult to navigate is less transparent than one that is easier for citizens to use; therefore, those sites with low levels of user-friendliness have less transparency degrees. However, it is noted that, while 11 out of 15 sites analyzed are below average, Uruguay -for example- which has a very low transparency level, is among the most user-friendly sites. Consequently, the question about the relationship between design, navigability and transparency, is still open.

In general, results revealed by the index suggest that there is a varied range of e-transparency in the region and, therefore, it is not possible to assert that the construction and publication of websites in public administration guarantee homogeneous levels of transparency. Moreover, when comparing the e-transparency index with offline transparency indicators, it was confirmed that in some cases online transparency is even lower than the institutions' real transparency. Or, conversely, that certain countries reach higher levels of online transparency than of offline transparency. Although it is difficult to measure the transparency of governmental institutions, both the "Corruption Perceptions Index" of Transparency International (TI, 2004) and the "Budget Transparency Index" of *International Budget Project* show these differences (IBP, 2003) (see Table 4).

In principle, it could be assumed that development of an Information Society on a local level is not enough to promote an advanced portal development in those cases in which offline transparency is lower than online transparency. However, correlation between e-transparency and e-government development indicators (UNDP, 2005) is not significant (r = 0,29, s = 0,25). Thus, it can be confirmed that, even in countries with higher offline transparency levels, a mere presence in the Internet does not guarantee that citizens will have transparent and accessible information allowing them to participate pro-actively in formal structures and within democratic boundaries. That is, that the Internet does not necessarily promote a free flow of, and access to, public decisions and actions. Even though the web can potentially expand and accelerate information exchanges between government and civil society, so far, this possibility has not increased transparency and participation in government issues.

Table 4. Online vs. offline transparency (Source: International Budget Project, 2003; International Transparency, 2004)

	Online Transparency	Offline Transparency (IT)	Offline Transparency (IBP)
México	0,62	0,36	0,5
Chile	0,4	0,74	0,62
Nicaragua	0,4	0,27	0,46
Colombia	0,33	0,38	0,44
Argentina	0,3	0,25	0,44
Costa Rica	0,22	0,49	0,49
El Salvador	0,22	0,42	0,4
Bolivia	0,36	0,22	...
Paraguay	0,36	0,19	...
Panamá	0,26	0,37	...
Guatemala	0,22	0,22	...
Uruguay	0,18	0,62	...
Venezuela	0,14	0,23	...

On the other hand, in those cases in which online institutional presence is more transparent than the real one, the irrelevance of e-government development in transparency levels reached, may indicate that these initiatives could have come from isolated projects made by computer technicians or professionals from the press and communication sectors rather than from governments' efforts to enhance management and relationships with citizens. In this sense, web communication would be product of an ability to manipulate the setting in order to fulfill requirements of globalized communication—exceeding, in many cases, indexes of real transparency about government, as is the case in Mexico.

This observation also contradicts the hypothesis of the ideology of information, according to which a change in technologies means a change in social relationships: the existence of a good portal in the Internet does not necessarily mean a more transparent institution. On the contrary, just as the idea of hybridization in online communication implies, traditional social patterns or dynamics coexist with orders and devices of the globalization process; in this case, regarding the production of discursive practices in the Internet (see Graph 3).

SYMBOLIC DIMENSION OF STATE COMMUNICATION

Analysis of the functional dimension of sites reveals that, far from being inevitably neutral and transforming, online communication can be interpreted as a political action tool which may be used to stimulate transparency virtues. It also reveals that, for the time being, and in opposition to, the thesis of the ideology of information, the Internet has not excelled as a tool for promoting political change. Nevertheless, can this form of communication be free from every cultural determination?

When observing the sites, we can say that they have a common, generalized format, and a series of common elements. In their home pages, for example, a series of common elements can be identified. Among them: URL address, a left navigation bar, a top header of the site, a central content body, and -in some cases- a right content bar. On the other hand, colors tend to be similar (light blue, white, red, blue), showing lack of textures—except in the case of Uruguay. Fonts also tend to be similar (arial, verdana), just like the basic navigation logos. In general, although there are technical conditions typical of the

Graph 3. Online transparency vs. offline transparency

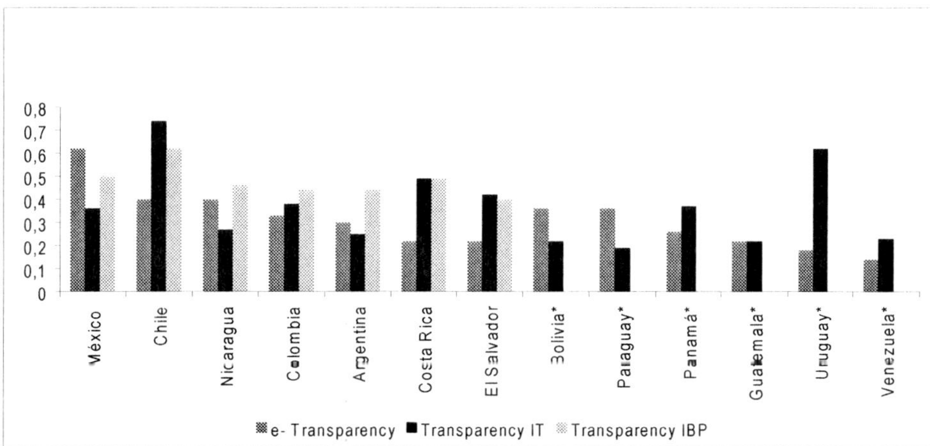

environment, it can be said that there is a basic, globalized pattern in these kinds of discursive practices.

However, inside this homogeneous format, there are specific cultural anchors that localize discourses; value systems that organize site details and elements which have particular meanings. This mediation does not impede transparency -in the sense of access to information- it superimposes a layer of locally codified meanings on the discourse that embeds the meaning in a geographical way and weakens the idea of transparent communication—in the sense of homogeneity and globality—of universal understanding. This mediation can be analyzed through the symbolic dimension of sites. That is, through meanings of the system's elements and their relation with mental guidelines and models which guide the organization of information. For that purpose, semiotic thought is a potential tool of analysis.

For Semiotics, message senders are restricted and subject to historical and cultural conditions and, in consequence, their messages are structured in semantic codes, or in fields which integrate and make up all their parts, both regarding the use of certain cultural units (meanings) and their possible position combinations or values. Departing from the text up to its creation conditions, Semiotics compares textual surfaces in search for discursive disparities that make production properties and conditions of each text visible, revealing their identities (Becerra, n.d; Eco, 1968; Verón, 2004).

For the purposes of this work, two groups of variables can be taken into account as a guide for comparing such disparities. Firstly, those corresponding to the historical, political and contextual characteristics of each society. As Joaquín Brunner (1988) states, the whole national community has a communicative pattern which, through symbolic universes, organizes interpretations, grants the identity principle, and at the same time expresses each community's historical, political and cultural experience (Brunner, 1988). These characteristics, cannot be left aside as they make the case unique. They must be integrated into the analysis for a better understanding of online communication.

Secondly; those cultural variables that explain differences between nations, and shape—among others—values constituted around the political system and power relationships within society. For that, I suggest taking the dimensions proposed by Dutch anthropologist Geert Hofstede (1999). In "Culture and Organizations: The mental software", Hofstede suggested 4 cultural categories which allow visualization—by means of ideal types—of the axis of mental structures and models articulating the way in which individuals shape social thought; particularly: beliefs, mental ideas about, and representations of, social and political order and the place citizens occupy in it.

Although this model has provoked many comments and debates (Søndergaard, n.d; McSweeney, 2002), its main virtue is that, from an interpretative point of view, its categories allow the discovery of different subjectivities as regards power relationships and their permanence in online discourses. Moreover, it is one of the few cultural studies about Latin American countries with updated, comparative and available data. And it is probably the only model of this type with precedents in web studies - Simon (1999), Sighn (2000), Markus and Gould (2000), Zahedi, van Pelt and Song (2001), Dormann and Chisalita (2002), Zahir, Doping and Hunter (2002), and Pavlou and Chai (2002), among others.

From these groups of variables, I suggest exploring the main page of the Mexican presidential portal—the most advanced one in the region. I specifically suggest looking for traces or evidence of local political culture through comparison with other regional portals; i.e. the political frame which mediates online communication. Departing from the assumption that sites are part of a globally legitimated political and communicative paradigm, I will analyze both the presence of elements typical of national historical political situation and experience, and the presence of meanings embedded in local political culture.

MEXICAN PRESIDENTIAL PORTAL

In general, in the top header of sites, a pattern common to all cases can be observed: a closed semantic balance, made up of an image that displays the meaning determined by the text. These images are visual stereotypes culturally associated with the "Presidency" semantic field, such as: the national flag or coat of arms and the presidential office or palace. However, apart from these general characteristics, very noteworthy peculiarities can be observed in the Mexican site (see Appendix).

The image of a flag that flutters and exceeds the limits of the navigation bar itself stands out in this site. On the left can be observed the federal government logo introduced during the process of state modernization. In the middle, in a space destined to an event schedule, is the Red Cross emblem in commemoration of its international day.

From a semiotic perspective, it can be said that the peculiarity of this composition is that the text reading "Presidency of the Republic" refers not only to the image of a government but also to the image of a nation (represented by the flag), appealing to a very concrete historical-political experience. In Mexican culture, ritual references continuously maintain and recreate nationalism (Alonso and Rodríguez, 1990). The flag in particular is a strong symbol that transmits identity through the historical union of the nation (González Chávez, 2004). This nationalism also generates another basic cultural feature - anti-imperialism in all its forms. In México, the process of forging a national identity did not stop during the course of the 19th century but instead it kept on updating (Rojas, 2003).

The noteworthy presence of the flag in the composition of the top bar denotes, in this sense, the existence of a strong nationalism inside and outside the country, re-affirming the nation to both itself and to neighboring countries. However, it is neither isolating nor excluding, as is demonstrated by the space left in the top bar and dedicated to the celebration of international days: in this specific instance, publishing the Red Cross logo for its anniversary.

Another possible connotative turn of this composition refers to tensions between Region-Nation and Region-State couples (Alonso and Rodríguez, 1990). Unlike the case of Chile (with a coat of arms and the presidential palace), for example, we can observe a predominance of the idea of the nation (represented by the flag) over the idea of the State and its political organization (represented by the federal government's logo). This has an even stronger nature than the State institutions, represented in a smaller size logo and central location.

Like Argentina, Mexico is a federal State. But unlike the former, there are no symbolic references to territory or local government powers. That is because, although the government in power has tried identifying the Sate with the nation, the country's consolidation and modernization implied a higher power concentration in federal government exacerbating regional feelings, causing fractures and the rejection of the State's capital. Thus, the symbolic appeal to national unity and international strength is based on the region-nation notion, as way to present the region-State notion based on it. This has a real, homogeneous and unified identity of a less controversial nature than the one based on society's bonds and political organization (Alonso and Rodríguez, 1990; Merino, 2003).

As regards the central body of contents, President Vicente Fox's portrait is especially noticeable. Although photographs of this kind can also be found - among others - in Chilean and Argentine sites, this case is even more notable: the President is alone in front of a microphone, formally dressed, with a serious and calm look, his eyes fixed on a distant point, apparently assuming the responsibility of his job in the presence of public opinion.

From a contextual point of view, this image agrees with efforts made by the President near the end of his administration and July 2006 presidential elections. Although during political campaign for his candidature Vicente Fox Quesada fought against the solemn political stereotype as he tried to present a cheerful and self-confident personality (González, 2002), the 2006 electoral struggle forced him to account for and make public the results of his administration. Furthermore, he had to provide positive results in order to strengthen his political party's position during the electoral dispute.

A second connotation; -of a historical rather than a contextual nature - refers to power centralization typical of the Mexican political system. The fundamental standard of the Mexican political system is presidential centralization; a central symbol of Mexican political culture is the Presidency of the Republic as the center of political power, from which all of the people's benefits or the lack thereof, emanates. (Alonso and Rodríguez, 1990:357).

This characteristic of Mexican political culture is also evident if the dimension and location of the image are related to the other photographs published on the page. Unlike the case of Chile, for example, the only photographs published—besides the President's—are those of five Government employees responsible for government projects. These are considerably smaller and located situated on site's second page, on the left content bar. The prominence of the President is also backed by the left navigation bar. The three first links of this bar refer to the President, followed by the Cabinet and First Lady. The remaining links refer to news about government action ("Good News" and "Approach to change"), the government palace ("Los Pinos"), Mexico and citizen services.

These observations refer to a cultural characteristic of Mexican society, which, of all the Latin American countries, has the highest degree of hierarchical distance. Just as Hofstede defines it, "hierarchical distance" is the extent to which members of a society expect and accept that power is unequally distributed (Hofstede, 1999). In his ideal type, countries with high hierarchical distance are characterized by the fact that, in them, hierarchy reflects inequality between people, centralization is common, and the leader's power prevails over institutions (Hofstede, 1999).

Mexico in particular has a hierarchical society similar to a caste-system, in which the patriarchal family exerts control over its members. These primary institutions—the basis of sociability and social control—are politically translated into a State and a political culture associated to a corporate, vertical, authoritarian and very presidential system (Alonso and Rodríguez, 1990). Therefore, in Mexico there is a complex articulation between a democratic political system based on individualism and an image of society as an organic whole, made up of segments interrelated in a hierarchical way (Adler Lomitz, 1994:295).

As Zahedi, van Pelt, and Song (2001) explain, it is expected that sites of societies characterized by high levels of hierarchical distance tend to present references associated with authority, power and expertise values. Therefore, in the symbolic aspect, they become indicators of importance: 1) social or moral emphasis and its symbols, 2) emphasis on expertise or authority by official's or experts' logos, illustrations or certificates, and 3) prominence of social roles according to the importance given to citizens, leaders or officials (Markus and Gould, 2000).

These aspects are evident in the Mexican site as seen in different elements. Firstly, they can be seen in the emphasis on national symbols in the top bar—the only case of this kind among the sites analyzed. They are also evident in the fact that this is the only site which publishes an official recognition for its services (third page); in the overexposure of the President's portrait with regard to its size and location, compared to the officials 'portraits, and in relation to its location in the order established by the left navigation bar.

Finally, regarding the right navigation bar of the site, it can be seen that there are two particular characteristics that are consistent with other Mexican cultural characteristics. The first one is that there is a predominance of references to the achievements and statistics of Government action in the site. The links "Where are we and where do we go" (accompanied by a statistical graphic showing growth), "8 Big achievements of democracy" (with an image which highlights number 8), "The good news" (with a check mark of approval), "Talking of results" (with photographs of officials responsible for different programs), and "The best rated" (with best rated Government actions), denote the importance attributed to material success and progress, economic success and performance. The second characteristic is that the three images published do not refer to people but to actions referring to prisons, work and security.

And that is because—unlike the case of Chile, for example—images in this part of the site do not connote the importance of people but rather of governmental politics in areas of; security, work and housing—possibly the most important part of the public agenda. As happens in other sites, the right content bar reinforces connotations of the site's central field. However, in this case the difference lies in the fact that the values reaffirmed here do not correspond to the ones of a female-orientated society (as is the case with Chile) but of a male-orientated one. Along with Venezuela and Argentina, Mexico is one of the most male-orientated countries of Latin America (Hofstede, 1999).

According to Hofstede, dominant values in masculine societies are material success and progress, and great importance is given to money and material objects. Their ideal is performance and they give maximum priority to the maintenance of economic development. (Hofstede, 1999). As Zahedi, van Pelt, and Song (2001) explain in terms of web communication design, websites of a masculine society (as opposed to a feminine one) will transmit values associated with success, strength and personal reassurance.

CONCLUSION

This work deals with government communication on the Internet from a perspective that corrects dissociation between State and Society, revealing the political-cultural structures connecting them. Through comparative analysis of systems of meaning, it is possible to see the role of culture as mediation in a medium that boasts of being transparent.

Results obtained confirm that online communication cannot be understood exclusively from a technological perspective, since political, social and cultural conditions define intercourses and their aesthetics, symbolic and linguistic characteristics. However, at the same time as they enable the communication process, such conditions also veil aspired transparency.

Although the Internet is a revolutionary tool, it does not represent a radical change in society, political culture or the State, in the sense that it does not imply, in itself, either harmony or reciprocity and does not establish a realm of symmetric and transparent relationships. On the contrary, like any mass media, Internet adapts to power relationships and struggles, and to appropriations of meaning. From a political viewpoint, it is not possible to hope for a more translucent communication.

In a context where the material foundations of democracies are being developed on the basis of communication, knowledge and information, this assertion highlights the role of culture in politics as seen in the struggles and in the appropriations of meaning. It is also worth noticing the need for in-depth studies of the characteristics of virtual communication as well as the possibilities of articulating tensions between homogenization and heterogeneity into equations which are beneficial in terms of identity and power.

It is illusory to conceive of cyberspace as an entity generating by itself modern democratic communications, being as it is a symbolic field where identities struggle and are reinvented. Firstly, the insertion of the Internet neither produces nor changes the existing contents, but it certainly modifies the ways to access it. Nowadays, thanks to the web, many more people can access the government information. However, informative richness should be searched for, not only with this technological tool, but also in citizen's and institution's ways of using such information.

Furthermore, far from being symmetric and transparent, online political communication is crossed by complex symbolic plots derived from the hybridization of a common political paradigm and representations produced in local cultures. Internet allows faster and, in some cases, more direct communication. However, that feature is never a synonym for transparency—in the sense of the absence of value determinations. Online communication is filled with values.

REFRENCES

Adler Lomnitz, Larissa (1994). "Identidad nacional/ cultura política: los casos de Chile y México". In Adler Lomnitz, Larissa (ED), *Redes sociales, cultura y poder: Ensayos de antropología latinoamericana*. FLACSO, México.

Alonso, Jorge and Rodríguez Lapuente, Manuel (1990). "La cultura política y el poder en México". In Hugo Zemelman (ED), *Cultura y política en América Latina*. Siglo Veintiuno Editores, España.

Balkin, Jack (1998). "How Mass Media Simulate Political Transparency". Retrieved from: http://www.yale.edu/lawweb/jbalkin/articles/media01.htm

Barber, Wendy and Brade, Albert (1998). "Culturability: The Merging of Culture and Usability". Paper presented at the 1998 4th Conference on Human Factors and the Web (HFWeb '98). Retrieved from: http://www.research.att.com/conf/hfweb/proceedings/barber

Bartoli, Annie (1991). "Comunicación y organización: la organización comunicante y la comunicación organizada". Paidós, México.

Barón Porras, Luis (n.d.). "Los poderes en las culturas: comunicación, lenguaje y memoria". Centro de Investigación y Educación Popular, CINEP. Retrieved from: http://www.colnodo.apc.org/aa/img_upload/13e08f09d1591809155e45a9932c599f/PODERES.pdf

Bayardo, Rubens and Lacarrieu, Mónica (1997). *Globalización e identidad cultural* Ciccus Giunta, Buenos Aires.

Becerra, Aníbal (n.d.). "Umberto Eco y el análisis semiótico- estructural de los fenómenos socioculturales". *Nombre Falso*, Autumn 2004. Retrieved from: http://www.infoamerica.org/articulos/b/becerra_artieda.htm

Birdsall, William (1996). "The Internet and the Ideology of Information Technology". Paper presented at INET96 Proceedings 96. Retrieved from: http://www.isoc.org/inet96/proceedings/e3/e3_2.htm

Bourges-Waldegg, Paula and Scrivener, Stephen (1998). "Meaning: The central issue in cross-cultural HCI design". *Interacting with Computers Special Issue, 9* (3). Retrieved from: http://www.citeulike.org/user/archer/article/455060

Brunner, José J. (1988). *Un espejo trizado: Ensayos sobre cultura y políticas culturales*. Facultad Latinoamericana de Ciencias Sociales (FLACSO); Santiago de Chile. Retrieved from: http://mt.educarchile.cl/MT/jjbrunner/archives/libros/Un_Espejo_Trizado

Buchrucker, Cristian (1994). "Notas sobre la problemática histórico-ideológica de la identidad nacional argentina". In Rapoport, Mario (ed.), *Globalización, integración e identidad nacional.* GEL, Buenos Aires. Pp.311-312.

Castells, Manuel (2004). "La dimensión cultural de Internet". *Cultura, Sociedad y Tecnología*, November- December 2004. Retrieved from: http://www.aloj.us.es/gicomcult/revista/detalle.asp?Id=19&edicion=Comunicaci%F3n%2C+Tecnolog%EDas+y+Pr%E1cticas+culturales+en+la+Cibercultura%2E+Noviembre%2DDiciembre+2004

CEPAL (2000). *América Latina y el Caribe en la transición hacia una Sociedad del Conocimiento. Una agenda de políticas públicas.* Economic Commission for Latin America and the Caribbean (ECLAL), United Nations. Retrieved from: http://www.eclac.cl/publicaciones/SecretariaEjecutiva/3/lcl1383/lcl1383e.pdf

Chang Coupland, Jennifer; Tekchandaney, Jayesh R.; Rangaswamy, Arvind; and Simpson, Timothy W. (2003). "Websites as Personalities and Playgrounds: Their Effects on Brand Image" eBusiness Research Center Working Paper, Penn State University. Retrieved from: http://www.smeal.psu.edu/ebrc/publications/res_papers/2003_02.pdf

Charaudeau, Patrick (2003). *El discurso de la información: La construcción del espejo social.* Editorial Gedisa, Barcelona.

Choong, Yee-Yin and Salvendy, Gavriel (1999). "Implications for design of computer interfaces for Chinese users in mainland China". *International Journal of Human–Computer Interaction*, N° 11. Retrieved from: http://www.leaonline.com/doi/abs/10.1207/s15327590ijhc1101_2

Colomé, Gabriel (1994). "Política y medios de comunicación: una aproximación teórica". Working Paper N °91, Universitat Autònoma de Barcelona. Retrieved from: http://www.diba.es/innovacio/fitxers/colome.pdf

Cruces Villalobos, Francisco and Díaz de Rada, Ángel (1995). "La cultura política, ¿es parte de la política cultural, o es parte de la política, o es parte de la cultura?". *Política y Sociedad*, N° 18.

Cyr, Dianne; Ilsever, Joe; Bonanni, Carole; and Bowes, John (2004). "Website Design and Culture: An Empirical Investigation". Paper presented at 2004th International Workshop for the Internationalisation of Products and Systems, Vancouver. Retrieved from: http://www.diannecyr.com/docs/website_design_and_culture.pdf

De Grandis, Rita (1995). "Incursiones en torno a hibridación, Una propuesta para discusión: De la mediación lingüística de Bajtín a la mediación simbólica de Canclini". Latin American Studies Association: LASA95 Papers Pilot Project. Retrieved from: http://lanic.utexas.edu/project/lasa95/grandis.html

Del Galdo, Elisa and Nielsen, Jakob (Eds.) (1996). *International User Interfaces.* John Wiley & Sons, Nueva York.

Dormann, Claire and Chisalita, Cristina. (2002). "Cultural Values in Web Site Design". Paper presented at Eleventh European Conference on Cognitive Ergonomics (ECCE-11), 2002, Catania, Italy. Retrieved from: http://www.cs.vu.nl/~martijn/gta/docs/Hofstede-dormann.pdf

Eco, Umberto (1989). *La estructura ausente. Introducción a la semiótica.* Editorial Lumen, Barcelona.

Eco, Umberto (2000). *Tratado de Semiótica General.* Editorial Lumen, Barcelona.

Ess, Charles and Sudweeks, Fay (1998). "Computer-mediated communication or culturally-mediated computing? Challenging assumptions of the electronic global village". *The Electronic Journal of Communication / La Revue Electronique de Communication*, N° 8. Retrieved from: http://www.cios.org/getfile%5CEss_V8N398

Faiola, Anthony and Matei, Sorin (2005). "Cultural cognitive style and web design: Beyond a behavioral inquiry into computer-mediated communication". *Journal of Computer-Mediated Communication,* N° 11. Retrieved from: http://jcmc.indiana.edu/vol11/issue1/faiola.html

Fernández Parratt, Sonia (2002). "La glocalización de la comunicación". *Ámbitos, Revista Andaluza de Comunicación*, N° 7-8. Retrieved from: http://www.comunicacionymedios.com/Reflexion/teorias/glocalizacion.htm

Fink, Dieter and Laupase, Ricky (2000). "Perceptions of Web site design characteristics: a Malaysian/ Australian comparison". *Internet Research: Electronic Networking Applications and Policy*, N° 10. Retrieved from: http://www.emeraldinsight.com/Insight/ViewContentServlet?Filename=Published/EmeraldFullTextArticle/Articles/1720100104.html

García Canclini, Néstor (2003). "Noticias recientes sobre la hibridación". *Revista Transcultural de Música*, N° 7, 2003. Retrieved from: http://www.sibetrans.com/trans/trans7/canclini.htm

González Chávez, José Ramón (2004). "Simbolismo de la bandera nacional de México". *Derecho y Cultura*, N° 13. Retrieved from: http://www.juridicas.unam.mx/publica/librev/rev/derycul/cont/13/ens/ens7.pdf

González, Adriana (2002). "Análisis semiótico de las campañas electorales". *Razón y Palabra*, N° 25. Retrieved from: http://www.cem.itesm.mx/dacs/publicaciones/logos/anteriores/n25/agonzal.html

Halavais, Alexander (2000). "National borders on the World Wide Web". *New Media & Society*, N° 2.

Haseloff, Otto W. (1970). "Sobre las condiciones del efecto de la comunicación política y publicitaria". In Otto W. Haseloff (ED), *La comunicación*. Editorial Nuevo Tiempo, Venezuela.

Heeks, Richard (2004). "eGovernment for Development: Transparency Definitions Page". DoWire Democracies Online. Retrieved from: http://www.egov4dev.org/transpdefn.htm

Heras Gómez, Leticia (2002). "Cultura política: El estado del arte contemporáneo". *Convergencia*, N° 30. Retrieved from: http://editorial.unab.edu.co/revistas/reflexion/pdfs/dem_48_4_c.pdf

Hofstede, Geert (1999). *Culturas y Organizaciones: El Software Mental.* Alianza Editorial, Madrid.

Hongladarom, Soraj (1998). "Global culture, local cultures, and the Internet: The Thai example". *En "Proceedings Cultural Attitudes Towards Communication and Technology '98", University of Sydney, Australia.* Retrieved from: http://www.it.murdoch.edu.au/~sudweeks/catac98/pdf/19_hongladarom.pdf

IBP (2003). "Índice latinoamericano de transparencia presupuestaria". *International Budget Project* (IBP). Retrieved from: http://www.internationalbudget.org/themes/BudTrans/Spanish.pdf

IDD (2005). Índice de Desarrollo Democrático de América Latina 2005. Konrad Adenauer Foundation. Retrieved from: http://www.idd-lat.org

Ju-Pak, Kuen-Hee (1999). "Content dimensions of Web advertising: a cross-national comparison". *International Journal of Advertising*, N° 18.

Latinobarómetro (2004). Latinobarómetro 2004: una década de mediciones. Retrieved from: http://www.latinobarometro.org

López de la Roche, Fabio (2000). "Aproximaciones al concepto de cultura política". *Convergencia*, N° 22. Retrieved from: http://redalyc.uaemex.mx/redalyc/src/inicio/ArtPdfRed.jsp?iCve=10502205&iCveNum=17

Lozada, Mireya (2004). "El Ciberciudadano: Representaciones, redes y resistencias en Venezuela y América Latina". Colección Monografías, N° 10. Retrieved from: http://globalcult.org.ve/doc/Monografias/MonografiaLozada.doc

Lull, James (1995). *Medios, comunicación y cultura.* Amorrortu Editores, Buenos Aires.

Markus, Aaron y Gould, Emilie (2000). "Cross-currents: Cultural dimensions and global web user- interface design". *Interactions*, Vol. 7, Issue 4. Retrieved from: http://portal.acm.org/citation.cfm?id=345238

Markus, Aaron, Armitage, Joh, Volker, Frank and Guttman, Edward (1999). "Globalization of User Interface Design for the Web". Retrieved from: http://zing.ncsl.nist.gov/hfweb/proceedings/marcus

Martín- Barbero, Jesús (2003). *De los medios a las mediaciones.* Editorial Nomos-Convenio Andrés Bello, Santa Fe de Bogotá.

Martínez, Gildardo (2004) "Internet y ciudadanía global: procesos de producción de representaciones sociales de ciudadanía en tiempos de globalización". In Daniel Mato (ED), *Políticas de ciudadanía y sociedad civil en tiempos de globalización.* Caracas: FACES, Universidad Central de Venezuela. Retrieved from:: http://globalcult.org.ve/pub/Rocky/Libro2/Martinez.pdf

Maturana, León (1991). *Comunicación, Sistema y Cultura*; Editorial Almogesto, Buenos Aires.

McSweeney, Brendan (2002). "Hofstede's model of national cultural differences and their consequences: A triumph or faith – A failure of analysis". *Human Relations*, Vol. 55, N° 1, [January] 2002, pp. 89-118. Retrieved from: http://geert-hofstede.international-business-center.com/mcsweeney.shtml

Merino, Mauricio (2003). "La formación del Estado nacional mexicano. El pasado colonial, las ideas liberales y los gobiernos locales como elementos delineadores del Estado". Retrieved from: http://bv.gva.es/documentos/Merino.doc

Moragás, Miguel de (1985). "Transformación tecnológica y tipología de los medios. Importancia política de la noción de ámbito comunicativo" In Moragás, Miguel de (1985), *Sociología de la comunicación de masas, IV: Nuevos problemas y transformación tecnológica* Editorial Gustavo Gili, Barcelona.

Moragás, Miguel de (n.d.). "Internet: facilidades tecnológicas, dificultades de comunicación". Retrieved from: http://www.comminit.com/la/teoriasdecambio/teorias2004/teorias-24.html

Panebianco, Angelo (1982). "Comunicación política". En Bobbio y Mateuci (ED), *Diccionario de Ciencia Política*, Editorial Siglo XXI, Madrid.

Pavlou, Paul y Chai, Lin (2002). «What drives electronic commerce across cultures? A cross-cultural empirical investigation of the theory of planned behavior», *Journal of Electronic Commerce Research*, Vol. 3 N° 4. Retrieved from: http://www.csulb.edu/web/journals/jecr/issues/20024/paper4.pdf

Plasser, Fritz (2004). "La comunicación política en los hemisferios Norte y Sur. ¿Qué intercambio reciproco puede esperarse?". *Diálogo Político*, N° 2, Marzo 2004, Argentina. Pp. 165-180.

Perina, Rubén (2002). "Gobernabilidad, cultura política y liderazgo: Esbozo para una teoría". Retrieved from: http://www.upd.oas.org/cursos/documentos/aspSmartUpload/files/Gobernabilidad%20Cult%20Pol%20y%20%20Liderazgo%20%20Sept%2005%20nuevo.doc

Peschard, Jaqueline (1996). *La cultura política democrática. Cuadernos de Divulgación de la Cultura Democrática*, N° 2; Instituto Federal Electoral, México. Retrieved from: http://www.ife.org.mx/InternetCDA/estaticos/DECEYEC/la_cultura_politica_democratica.htm

Rojas Mix, Miguel (2003). "El imaginario nacional en las repúblicas latinoamericanas del siglo XIX". Retrieved from: http://bv.gva.es/documentos/Rojas.doc

Sackmary, Benjamin y Scalia, Lynne (1999). "Cultural patterns of WWW business sites: A comparison of Mexican and USA companies". Retrieved from: http://marketing.byu.edu/htmlpages/ccrs/proceedings99/sackmary.htm

Sánchez Ruiz., Enrique (2000). "Televisión, cultura política, autoritarismo y violencia: La formación ciudadana de todos los días". *Razón y Palabra*, 17, Febrero- Abril. Retrieved from: http://www.cem.itesm.mx/dacs/publicaciones/logos/anteriores/n17/17ssanchez.html

Sears, Andrew; Jacko, Julie; y Dubach, Erica (2000). "International aspects of World Wide Web usability and the role of high-end graphical enhancements". *International Journal of Human-Computer Interaction,* Vol. 12, Issue 2. Retrieved from: http://www.leaonline.com/doi/abs/10.1207%2FS15327590IJHC1202_5

Sheppard, Charles y Scholtz, Jean (1999). "The Effects of Cultural Markers on Web Site" Paper presented at Proceedings of the Fifth Conference on Human Factors & the Web, Gaithesburg, Maryland. Retrieved from: http://zing.ncsl.nist.gov/hfweb/proceedings/sheppard/index

Simon, Steven J. (1999). "A Cross Cultural Analysis of Web Site Design: An Empirical Study of Global Web Users" Paper Presented at the Seventh Cross-Cultural Consumer Business Studies Research Conference, Cancun, Mexico. Retrieved from: http://marketing.byu.edu/htmlpages/ccrs/proceedings99/simon.htm

Singh, Nitish (2000). "Analyzing Cultural Sensitivity of Websites: A Normative Framework". Journal of Practical Global Business. Retrieved from: http://iiei.edu/journal/Jour_2/journalvl_p32.pdf

Singh, Nitish; Kumar, Vikas; y Baack, Daniel (2005). "Adaptation of cultural content: evidence from B2C ecommerce firms". *European Journal of Marketing*, Vol. 39, Issue 1/2. Emerald Group Publishing Limited. Retrieved from: http://www.emeraldinsight.com/Insight/viewPDF.jsp?Filename=html/Output/Published/EmeraldFullTextArticle/Pdf/0070390105.pdf

Søndergaard, Mikael (n.d.). "In my opinion". Opinion Article, European Business Forum. Retrieved from: http://geert-hofstede.international-business-center.com/Sondergaard.shtml

Stengers, Hélene ; De Troyer, Olga ; Mushtaha, Abdalghani; Baetens, Martine ; y Boers, Frank. (2004). "Localization of Web Sites: Is there still a need for it?". Retrieved from: http://www.ht04.org/workshops/WebEngineering/HT04WE_Stengers.pdf

Sun, Huatong (2001). "Building a Culturally Competent Corporate Web Site: An Exploratory Study of Cultural Markers in Multilingual Web Design". Paper presented at Proceedings of SIGDOC 2001. Retrieved from: http://faculty.gvsu.edu/sunh/resch/acm01.pdf

Tapscott, Mark (2004). "Internet Revolution is Forcing Transparency". Center for Media and Public Policy, Heritage Foundation. Retrieved from: http://www.developmentgateway.org/egovernment/rc/ItemDetail.do~1024669

TI (2004). "Índice de percepción de la corrupción". Transparencia Internacional América Latina y el Caribe (TILAC), Transparencia Internacional (TI). Retrieved from: http://www.transparency.org/policy_research/surveys_indices/cpi/2004

Tsikriktsis, Nikos (2002). "Does culture influence web site quality expectations? An empirical study", *Journal of Service Research*, Vol. 5 No.2. Retrieved from: http://jsr.sagepub.com/cgi/content/abstract/5/2/101

UNDP (2005). *Global E-Government E-Readiness Report 2005: From E-Government to E-Inclusion*. Department of Economic and Social Affairs, United Nations. Retrieved from:: http://www.unpan.org/egovernment5.asp

van Dam, Nik; Evers, Nik; y Arts, Florann A. (2005). "Cultural User Experience Issues in E-Government: Designing for a Multi-Cultural Society". *Lecture Notes in Computer Science*, Vol. 3081. Retrieved from: http://hcs.science.uva.nl/usr/evers/DamEversArts.pdf

Vega, Hannia (2002). "La comunicación de gobierno en Internet". In *Estrategias de Comunicación para Gobiernos*, de Izurieta, Z., Perina, R., y Arteton, C. (Editores); La Crujía Ediciones, Buenos Aires.

Verón, Eliseo (1971). "Ideología y comunicación de masas: La semantización de la violencia política". Nueva Visión, Buenos Aires. Retrieved from: http://www.nombrefalso.com.ar/apuntes/pdf/veron.pdf

Verón, Eliseo (1985). "La palabra adversativa: Observaciones sobre la enunciación política". In *El discurso político: lenguajes y acontecimientos*. Editorial Hachette, Buenos Aires.

Verón, Eliseo (2004). *Fragmentos de un tejido*; Colección "El mamífero parlante". Editorial Gedisa, Barcelona.

Victor, Stephen P. (n.d.). "Information Architecture and the Construction of Ideology: A Proposal for a Qualitative Study of a School District's Web Pages". College of Education, University of Houston Houston. Retrieved from: http://itech1.coe.uga.edu/itforum/paper59/paper59.htm

Vizer, Eduardo A. (2003). *La trama (in)visible de la vida social. Comunicación, sentido y realidad*. Ediciones La Crujía, Buenos Aires.

Winner, Langdom (1987). *La ballena y el reactor* Editorial Gedisa, Barcelona.

Wiesner Salamanca, Santiago (n.d.). "Internet: ¿Cómo se dice / cómo se usa?". Research Paper, Project "Usos de las nuevas tecnologías de comunicación e información para la construcción de la paz en Colombia", Facultad de Comunicación Social para la Paz de la Universidad Santo Tomás-Facultad de Humanidades de la Pontificia Universidad Javeriana. Retrieved from: http://www.colnodo.apc.org/aa/img_upload/13e08f09d1591809155e45a9932c599f/WIESNER.pdf

Wolton, Dominique (2000). *Internet, ¿y después? Una teoría crítica de los nuevos medios de comunicación.* Editorial Gedisa, Barcelona.

Zahedi, Fatemeh; van Pelt, William; y Song, Jaeki (2001). "A conceptual framework for international web design". *IEEE Transactions on Professional Communication*, Vol. 44, Issue 2. Retrieved from: http://tc.primaryspaces.com/zahedi.pdf

Zahir, Sajjad; Dobing, Brian; y Hunter, Gordon (2002), "Cross-cultural dimensions of internet portals", *Internet Research: Electronic Networking Applications and Policy*, Vol. 12 N° 3. Retrieved from: http://www.emeraldinsight.com/Insight/ViewContentServlet?Filename=Published/EmeraldFullTextArticle/Articles/1720120301.html

Zhao, Wenyong; Massey, Brian L.; Murphy, Jamie; y Fang, Liu (2003). "Cultural Dimensions of Website Design and Content". *Prometheus*, Vol. 21, N° 21. Carfax Publishing, Taylor and Francis Ltd. Retrieved from: http://web.biz.uwa.edu.au/staff/jmurphy/Cultural_Dimensions.pdf

ENDNOTE

1 This article is an abstract from a postgraduate's thesis. The original version dwells in depth on the subject, analyzes other practical examples and brings up detailed information on the research process' methodology. This version is available online at http://www.mariafrick.com.ar

This work was previously published in International Journal of Electronic Government Research, Vol. 4, Issue 3, edited by M. Khosrow-Pour, pp. 81-102, copyright 2008 by IGI Publishing (an imprint of IGI Global).

Chapter 14
The Örebro City Citizen-Oriented E-Government Strategy

Andreas Ask
Örebro University, Sweden

Mathias Hatakka
Örebro University, Sweden

Åke Grönlund
Örebro University, Sweden

ABSTRACT

This article discusses practices, opportunities, and challenges in local e-government project management by means of a case study involving interviews, document studies, and an element of action research, over eight months. The analysis against e-government success factors finds seven "critical issues"; political timing, resource allocation, political mandate, distinction between administrative and political responsibilities, coordination of departments, dependence on providers, and use of standards. We found these issues open for local choice, influences of strong individuals and groups, and chance. This is a consequence of the prevailing strategic model for the public sector, New Public Management, which leaves these issues to be filled by negotiations among many actors with different roles, goals, and action space. The general lesson is that there is a need for practical ways of acting strategically to reduce the risk level and increase the ability to implement policy.

INTRODUCTION

Electronic government (e-government) is typically defined as a positive development concerning three main actors; government administrations; users of government services, i.e. citizens and companies; and the political system due to "better democracy" typically meaning more openness (Gore, 1993; Grant & Chau, 2005, Grönlund, 2002; 2005; OECD, 2003; UN, 2004; UNDESA, 2003). e-government definitions across the globe unanimously point to these three things, more efficient operations, better services and better democracy. An example is the EU definition:

Electronic Government is the use of Information and Communication Technologies in public administrations combined with organizational change and new skills in order to improve public services and democratic processes. [EU, 2004]

The value of e-government is supposed to come as (1) administrative rationalization, in particular government reorganization and integration across and within government agencies, and (2) increased value for citizens due to more openness, better integrated and hence better, quicker and more transparent services (Grönlund, 2002). Values of e-government are hence mainly conceived at system – whole-of-government – level. It is conventional wisdom that e-government benefits come from reorganization, not from ICT directly. Adding ICT to existing processes means added costs. Benefits have to come either by reduced production costs or better services, or both. The academic discussion of values is well summarized by Table 1 (adapted from Lau, 2007), and includes both tangible and non-tangible costs and benefits.

While these values can seem reasonable enough, achieving them is altogether a different challenge. Not only are intangible values just that, intangible and hard to measure, also, even if measured they are hard to balance against more tangible costs. Attempts have been made and measures devised (e.g. eGEP, 2006a; 2006b), but it has proven hard to implement such criteria in the incentives of individual government agencies, where the development is supposed to take place. Hence basic tangible economic measures so far prevail and grander plans for interoperability, better services to citizens, etc. come second. Also in terms of doability e-government implementation is a challenge because of the complexity of government organization, the complexity of demands, and the lack of general standards to follow.

Swedish government is organized in three tiers, national, regional and local, each politically governed. Many tasks cut across levels, e.g. health care which involves both local and regional levels as producers of health care and national government as providing health insurance and regulation, mainly for the medical part. The Swedish public sector has a strict new public management (NPM) management model, which means governance is by budget and goals, not detailed regulation. This means coordination and standardization are for the most part not issues for enforcement but up to negotiation among many actors with both political and economic agendas. The NPM mode of governance is at work not only at the organizational level, it also applies within cities and regional organizations.

E-government in Sweden, as in the industrialized world in general, is funded within the ordinary budgets. This means any investment will have to pay back within the budget of the involved organization. Guiding the development are general national plans, but details are largely left to individual government agencies. The development so far has seen the large national government agencies such as Taxation, Social Insurance, Labor Market Information, and Student Loans applying electronic service (e-service) models to substantial economic benefit and considerable service improvement using web sites with information and automated services and call centres

Table 1. Values pertinent to e-government (Lau, 2007)

	GOVERNMENTS	NONGOVERNMENT STAKEHOLDER
Direct financial costs and benefits	Reducing costs, increasing value of services	Better services, reduced administrative burden
Direct non-financial costs and benefits	Synergies across delivery channels, sharing and reusing data resources	Increased user satisfaction, increasing privacy
Indirect costs and benefits	"Good governance"; supporting legitimacy, supporting growth	

to replace staff. In municipalities the picture is different. Scale benefits are harder to find as many cities are small and because municipal organization is heavily departmentalized, borders drawn both by different legal frameworks regulating different tasks and by traditions, and professional competence areas.

The general view is that municipalities/local governments are lagging, and there is a call for them to implement e-services. This is for reasons of economy and modernity as well as management. e-services have shown to be efficient elsewhere, people tend to increasingly prefer e-services to traditional ones, and city management wants to have better tools for steering the organization and producing qualitative and measurable output.

This article will illustrate the complexity of achieving real change by means of a case study of a local e-government design and implementation project in a Swedish city. The research questions are

- How is e-government implementation projects managed?
- How are whole-system e-government success factors such as interoperability, standards, convergence incentives etc. handled in local development?

The purpose of the article is mainly to illustrate the complexity and point to particularly difficult challenges where the "butterfly syndrome" seems to apply: little differences in local conditions may entail very different decisions leading to vastly different results.

BACKGROUND: THE MOVIT PROJECT

Örebro City is considered big in a Swedish perspective. It has 11474 employees and a population of 127 733 at turn of the year 2005 (Örebro City executive board, 2006, p. 37). The development towards e-services had been going on for many years. It is impossible to set a fixed starting point as the target has moved. Starting from setting up webs in the mid-1990s, steps have been taken at several occasions. In 2001 the "24 hour agency" came up, after national government initiative. In 2004 the first project aiming at integrating the city IT-wise, the "e-Platform", was launched. In 2005, 0,8 MSEK were designated to coordinating e-services and in 2007 the responsibility this was transferred from the IT Advisory board to the MovIT project, to be described below. The purpose was to achieve more powerful coordination as control was moved from the IT people to the direct control of the CEO (Chief Executive Officer, a title increasingly used for the highest administrative official in Swedish cities).

After the 2006 election a new political majority expressed a need for City of Örebro to become more citizen oriented. In the budget for 2007 it was explicitly stated that the focus for the City's activities must be the citizens.

> *...Citizens and their choices in life are the primary goal of the City. Whether the citizen is a student, tenant, user, client or customer she should always be the centre of the municipal efforts. No department in the City exists as an end in itself; the citizens' are always the most important stakeholder. The aim must be to improve the quality of life for the citizens, by allowing them to take part in and engage in the decision-making processes at an early stage, which will create more well informed citizens and a stable democracy.* (Örebro City executive board, 2006, p. 4)

To implement this political wish, the City needed to improve the services towards businesses as well as citizens. The City needed to improve their efficiency and to become more easily accessible. The politicians wanted their citizens to see the City as a service provider and it should be clear what kind of services it provided. To accommodate this, the City launched a project called

FRAM with the primary goal of designing a new organizational plan for the entire administrative staff. The purpose was to reallocate resources amounting to 150 MSEK to achieve "services close to the citizens". This is a considerable number, roughly 3% of the total City budget and perhaps 20 % of the administrative costs, although these are not possible to directly trace in the budget as they are dispersed across departments. To achieve this, FRAM has two main focus areas.

1. Streamlining internal processes within the City, to implement automation, and self service where possible, to relocate staff to enable the City to respond to the needs of the citizens in a more direct and effective way (the bottom left box in Figure 1).
2. External processes, directly affecting the citizens; such as providing e-services, providing a unified and improved complaint management procedure so the citizen could give feedback on the services the City provides. This is the MovIT project (the bottom right box in Figure 1).

The projects are interrelated. FRAM is to free resources, MovIT is to design a citizen-centered approach to services. The bottom left box in Figure 1 illustrates not a project but the ongoing work with e-government to improve back-office administrative routines. Clearly development of e-services affect the internal organizational – and the other way around – so the development is conceived as moving forward in parallel with the two projects interacting. In this early phase, experiences are sought from implementation of a few services so as to be able to decide on the best organization before the large-scale implementation.

This article focuses on the MovIT[1] part, because that is most crucial for e-government imple-

Figure 1. Overall map of Örebro efforts for achieving citizen-oriented services (MovIT – Steering Committee, 2007)

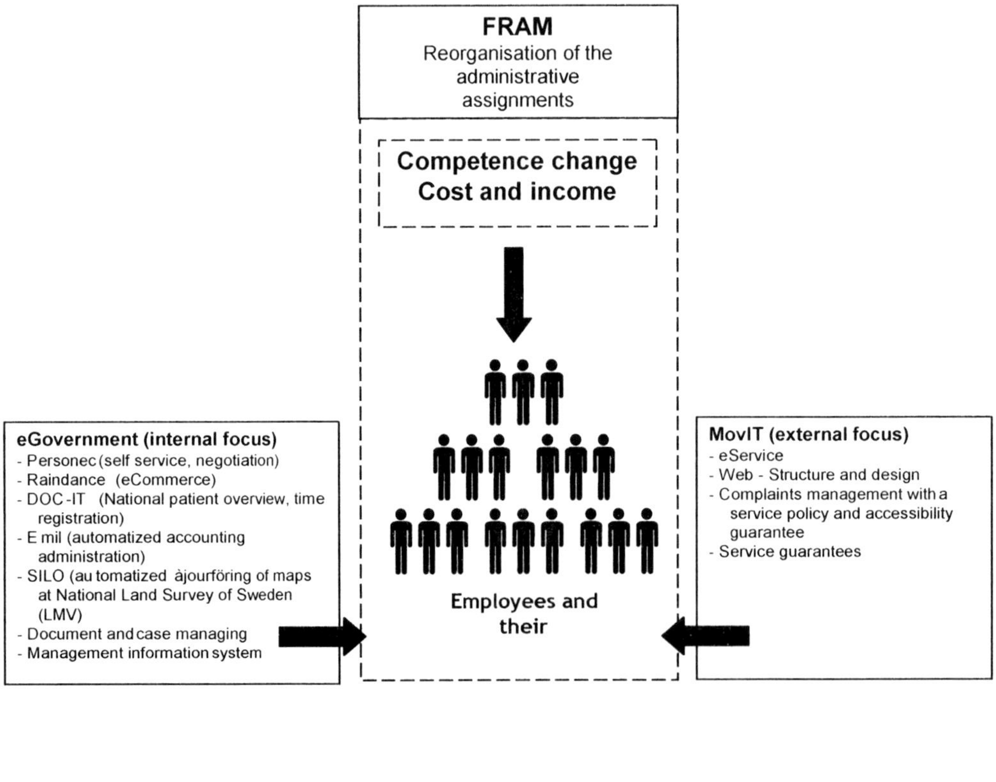

mentation. To be effective, both the reorganization of administrative work (FRAM) and the back-office administrative support ("e-government") must be designed to support the e-service model (Grönlund, 2004).

METHOD

The first and second authors have taken part in the MovIT project since it was launched in May 2007 as part of a large-scale cooperation between the City and the university aiming at both employing university resources to help in development and giving PhD students access to empirical data. The process therefore included an element of action research. However, the data for this article was specifically collected in early 2008, halfway into the MovIT project. Interviews were made (by authors 1 and 2) with key actors in the project, in total 10 people, and documents guiding the development in the City since the early 2000s were analyzed. Group interviews were conducted with the members of the steering committee. Individual interviews were held with the project managers and with representatives from the organizations that were affected by the changes. The authors also studied all the documentation produced during the project, such as project reports, project directives etc. Based on this information, the project history was described by the first author. The third author, who has not taken part in the project work in any way, then analyzed the story in the perspective of e-government development in general. Issues that were particularly interesting for either posing obstacles or facilitating development were then investigated further by additional interviews and information searching. This way we were reasonably able to distinguish between the role as advisors and participants in the project group and the analytical role. The findings were presented to the steering committee and the project managers to check accuracy of details and to get feedback on the conclusions drawn.

Although there may still be a risk of bias due to two of the authors having taken active part in discussions, if not formal decisions, it should be noted that we do not draw either specific or general conclusions about causal relations in the development. We use the case story to extract problematic situations which are key to a successful development process, as measured by generally agreed e-government success factors. These problematic situations are analyzed in terms of their antecedents so as to provide understanding of the situation in which decisions crucial to the future development are made. The purpose of this is to achieve a better understanding of local development processes. While this understanding can serve as guidance for others, and while we do believe that the situations we found in Örebro are quite common, we do not claim that our findings are complete or universally applicable. We see them as lessons learned, and our contribution is to highlight these lessons and to relate them to the discussion about e-government strategies in such a way as to be able to discuss (local) implementation of strategies, an area still in need of research.

The main quest for our investigation was to understand how transformational projects aiming at fundamental change are managed. Successful e-government amounts to reorganization and focus on citizens and this is precisely the goal of MovIT. More specifically, our research questions were:

1. How is project work organized, and resources allocated, so as to achieve the political goals of "citizen centred services?
2. How are issues of standards, cohesion and convergence—basic e-government success factors—handled so that interoperability and effectiveness are achieved not just in an internal perspective but also with respect to coordination and cooperation with other government organizations?

Figure 2. Components of the MovIT project

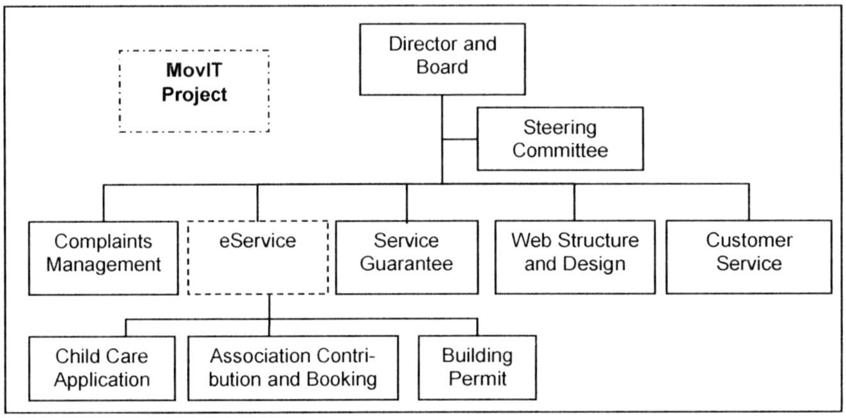

MAIN FOCUS OF THE ARTICLE: FINDINGS

This section describes the MovIT project in terms of its design and its different sub projects. The description is a narrative from which we have extracted "critical issues." These are, in this text, implicitly derived from the e-government literature which we do not here review. In the Conclusions part, these critical issues are more strictly reviewed by relation to some models from that literature.

PROJECT ORGANIZATION, THE MOVIT SETUP

The MovIT project was set up to implement a political decision. The City CEO has the overall and official responsibility of the project, however, as some of the changes may have political implications she needs to get approval from the City Executive Board, the political executive body. The project includes a Board representing all three program sectors (Children and Education, Civil Engineering and Social Welfare) and staff from the central City Administration Office. The CD and the Board are the formal decision makers of MovIT. The project also features a steering committee of six people; the project manager who is a development coordinator outside of MovIT and is part of the Board as well, the head of the Information Department, who is also part of the managerial body, one IT-strategist, one organization strategist, one organizational and IT coordinator and one PhD student from Örebro University. The steering committee has the operational responsibility to decide on the processes and activities in the projects owned by MovIT.

It was clear that politicians wanted quick action. As MovIT was not in the position to implement projects at individual city departments, it was important to set up the project in such a way that MovIT proposals could be quickly endorsed by the different sectors and aligned with already existing strategies for IT and organizational development. In order to achieve this, it was decided that the steering committee would consist of people that had adequate competence, such as development work, had an organisational rather than departmental perspective on development, and who had previously shown that they could handle the pressure that change involves. Steering committee members were solicited by the Board after discussion within the board on suitable staff members, they were chosen on the criterion of competence, not representativity.

Initially there were four sub-projects within MovIT: Complaints management, e-service, Service Guarantee, and Web structure and design, each with a separate project manager and a project group. The manager for each project would be responsible for adherence to the project directives, to brief the steering committee on progress, to ask for permission on activities, ideas etc. Later on, one more project was added: Customer Service. The steering committee realised that one of the key points where citizens would contact the City would be the central City Reception (called customer service), as opposed to at the individual departments, and due to this it was decided to incorporate it with MovIT.

This set of projects (Figure 2) was intended to cover the problem situation well enough to get started; a few test services, policies for the purpose of focusing more directly on citizens, and reorganization to implement these policies and at the same time accommodate the envisioned gradual transition towards e-services. As we shall see below, different approaches were taken for the different sub projects. Some were conducted top-down, such as the service guarantee and the customer service, while others were implemented in a bottom-up fashion, such as the web services.

Priorities

MovIT started to implement a political initiative, and meeting deadlines was important. Politicians wanted results quickly, the subprojects should be finished and the e-services implemented and operational when the steering committee handed in the final project report in August 2008. Although no formal date for delivery was politically decided, the steering committee considered quick action very important. As a result, all other criteria were designed to meet that critical limitation. One of the steering committee members expressed this problem during the group interview:

We see time as "sacred" as it is a political decree which ultimately implies compromises either with cost or quality, and in our case it will be the quality that will suffer first. If we would abide by the quality demands, it would at least take a year to deliver a functioning e-service. (S1, October 31, 2007)

As a consequence, the steering committee was very clear to explicitly pass this decision on in the different project directives; the schedule of each project was not to be deviated from.

Critical issue 1, political timing: Political directives often come with time limits. This is good in that it spurs action but it can also cause trouble as quality may be affected. In this case political wish was clearly given strong preference. Although we cannot today see distinct negative outcomes of this it certainly has affected the project process as we shall see below.

Financing and Resources

The MovIT budget was estimated to 1.5M SEK during 2007. This budget would cover common costs i.e. activities that were common for all areas of the City like the service guarantee, service policy etc. education of staff regarding the accessibility guarantees etc. The three e-service projects would not be covered by the MovIT budget. This was because the steering committee felt that the design and implementation of e-services should be seen as organizational improvements and hence be covered by the budgets for each department and for the IT department. The argument was that this would lead to the staff being more effective. However if the e-service implementation would require any additional cost due to usability and accessibility requirements imposed centrally departments could ask for financial support, subject to Steering Committee approval. Criteria for approval were not settled beforehand.

Furthermore, neither MovIT overall nor the individual projects had any clear guidelines on how to fund activities. It all came down to what the steering committee felt was reasonable.

We decide the budget; but the project managers can come up with activity suggestions and suggestion on how work. But it is the committee's responsibility to accept the idea as feasible and say ok run with it. (Steering committee member, October 31, 2007)

Salaries for people participating were paid by city departments, not by MovIT. Staff hence had to be recruited by voluntary agreements with departments. In total, around 50 people were recruited to work with MovIT, each contributing anything from 25 % to 100 % of their working time. This was done by means of informal arrangements which meant that each department had to bear the costs for staff working on MovIT. This meant that some staff had to work on the MovIT project as well as with there normal duties in the City without any time reduction. This conflict of interests led to negotiations between departments and MovIT management. While enough understanding was reached to keep the project running, this informal resource allocation was a constant trouble.

The informality was not just about the actual project, but also about the actual e-services to be implemented. This is something that the project managers were somewhat unclear about. Some of the project managers acknowledged that the organization he or she was worked for would cover the cost for the implementation of the e-service but one of the project managers saw it as "reasonable to assume" that the MovIT project would fund some parts of the implementation when the organization felt it became to expensive. The reason for this was due to the fact that it was requirements from the steering committee that had to be followed during negotiation with a supplier, and if the cost then became to high then the manager assumed that it would be funded by MovIT as it was their requirements. And in some ways this was also true as the steering committee had approved to cover some of additional costs when the negotiations through SAMBRUK (an informal cooperation with several other cities) was still an option, but when those negotiation broke down and the alternative found was the current system provider the steering committee backed down on their previous decision and took on the entire cost as it now was a matter of internal improvements of an existing system.

Critical issue 2, resource allocation: This story shows one of the critical points of NPM. As resources are distributed to individual departments resources for projects have to be negotiated, even in a case like this when political directives are strong. The result of the negotiations depends on individuals. It is basically the leadership skills of the project manager – and of course any political pressure s/he is able to put on departments – that makes the difference between failure and success. This pressure can come from other policies, and as we shall see below some such means were indeed used.

COMPLAINTS MANAGEMENT

The complaints management project, as it somewhat negatively was called, was the first to be launched by MovIT. It began in May 2007 and it was decided that the project would deliver a general service policy and an access guarantee proposal by the end of 2007. It was also charged with the task of generating a common complaints handling procedure for the entire City.

Prior to MovIT Örebro City did not have common complaints procedure so each department could handle the complaint as they saw fit. The only common procedure that existed was the registration of incoming and outgoing documents as mail and e-mail fall under the Swedish principle of Public Access and must be registered and saved for later access by the public. The lack of a common procedure however made it hard to follow up on any complaint or feedback centrally and rendered it almost impossible to do any form of statistical analysis on the complaints and the responses to these for the entire City. This was

Figure 3. The process model for the complaints procedure (Örebro City, 2007a)

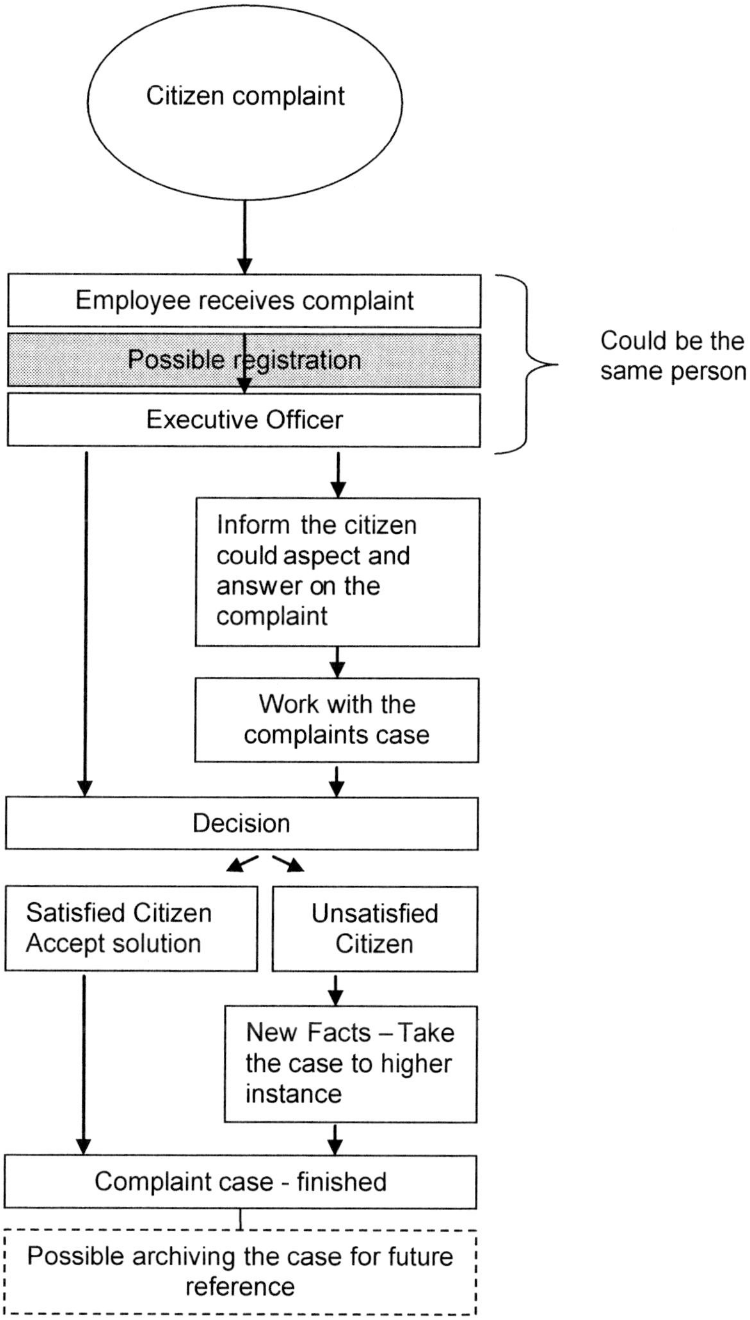

seen as ineffective and therefore a common procedure was developed. Adhering to this, every employee would know how to handle complaints and all complaints would be dealt with in the same way. Figure 3 shows the process model that was developed.

The project group decided on four categories of complaints (Children & Education, Health & Welfare, City Engineering and Other/unknown). This categorization made it possible to shorten the lead time of the complaints handling procedure as the responsible person receiving complaints would more quickly be able to pass them on in the correct direction. To help employees in handling incoming complaints the "gift principle" (meaning considering any input a "gift", something positive to be used for improvement of services) was formulated. This principle states explicitly how to handle the citizen and her complaint and it prevents the employee from becoming defensive when a citizen contacts the City to complain.

When speaking with a citizen regarding a complaint you should:

- Tell the citizen that you are sorry that the citizen has concerns and is dissatisfied;
- Promise that you will deal with the problem, if you can not solve it yourself then you will make sure the right person received the complaint;
- Ask for as much information as possible
- Thank the citizen for contacting you with her concern or issue;
- Explain that the reason why you are grateful is because it is important for the City to get feedback because it allows the City to handle or solve the issue. (Örebro City Administrations Office, 2007)

In addition to creating a common complaints procedure the MovIT project would also create a service policy and an access guarantee. These two documents would assist employees in their communication with citizen. The service policy) would state how each employee should act towards citizens, the access guarantee would state how and when the City should be accessible for a citizen.

The service policy that was accepted by the Executive Board states that it is every employee's responsibility to:

- answer all citizens in a committed, affable and professional way,
- make sure that citizens get in touch with whoever they seek or need to find,
- handle any complaints, standpoint or proposal according to the common complaints procedure,
- contact the citizen as soon as there is an answer to a question or a decision,
- apologize when a mistake has been made,
- correct any mistakes, and
- inform when s/he is not available.

The common responsibilities for individual employees are to:

- always focus on the citizens' needs,
- give information in a way so it can be understood by all citizens,
- make sure that all important information is accessible for citizens,
- help each other and to collaborate to give the citizens' business and visitors good quality services,
- continuously learn from the work being done whether it be mistakes or good work in order to improved the processes continuously, and
- use the service guarantees that exist and make sure that citizens' get knowledge of its existence and make it easily accessible.

On top of the service policy there is the access guarantee. This states that all citizens should be able to get in contact with every department, organization etc. during weekdays. A citizen should only need to call once to get in touch with the employee s/he is seeking. If no employee responsible for the issue the citizen needs help with is immediately available, the citizen should be contacted within two days of the initial contact. Any decision, contact or answer of a question through mail or e-mail should be communicated to the citizen within five workdays. The access guarantee also states that citizens always should experience that employees in the City are addressing their issue in a sympathetic, helpful, and efficient way. Furthermore, citizens should recognize that the City and its employees correct any mistakes done. Citizens should also be aware of the City's goals to improve all things that need to be improved.

To be able to have a common procedure for complaints the project defines "complaint" as

when a citizen shows signs of, or expresses, a dissatisfaction of the service delivery, the quality of the service provided, or the lack of, or unavailability of, service. (Örebro City, 2007b)

Based on these common principles each department then has to define complaints specific for their area. This work falls outside of MovIT and the project group would only provide the general definition. Figure 4 shows the general complaints procedure as defined by MovIT and its relation to the service policy and the guarantees for access and service.

The service policy and access guarantee have been approved by the City executive committee and the service policy have been in effect since January 1st 2008, the access guarantee will be in effect from September 1st 2008. The complaints procedure has been approved and during 2008 and the work in creating the routine and connecting it to the customer service will continue throughout 2008. No issues or problems have been perceived that will cause any problems for the continuation of the subproject.

Critical issue 3, political mandate: The guarantees described above are critical instruments for convergence across city departments, both generally and in terms of forming a basis for developing standardized e-services. The guarantees are a direct result of political directives. Without such, important instruments will not be developed.

The service guarantee sub-project was responsible for designing and implementing local service guarantees at departments throughout the City, all based on the common guarantee discussed above. These guarantees would state clearly what a citizen can require from the City when they utilize a particular service from the City.

To move this work forward the steering committee decided that 24 employees were needed as

Figure 4. The relations between service policy, accessibility & service guarantees and complaints procedure.

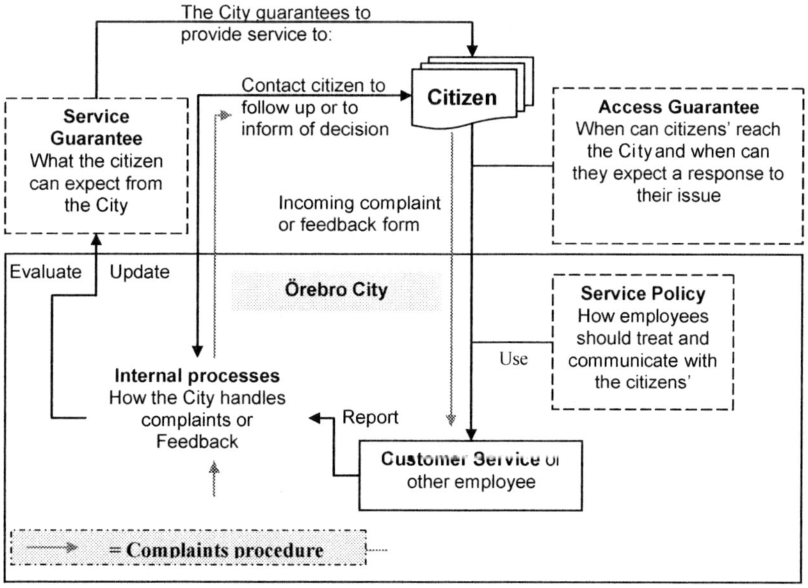

"development coaches". These coaches would be educated in designing (local) service guarantees, and would then each help one department with the design of their guarantees. Eventually only 14 people were found, but this seems not to have significantly slowed down the process. There were not as many focus groups (the method used) as planned, but guarantees were produced on time. A bigger problem was that the project manager could not influence who got assigned as coach, this was decided each department and not necessarily by the competence criteria on the project's wish list. This caused problems as the manager in some cases had to work as a supervisor to some of staff in the project group instead on only focusing on leading the project forward.

The service guarantees were developed on time. The basic content of a guarantee is the following:

1. Description of the service area.
2. Explicitly stated guarantee.
3. Contact information if the citizen wants to give feedback or complain.
4. What kind of service the City is offering in return in case of unsatisfactory delivery of service.
5. How the citizen could acquire more information regarding the service area.

The project group designed a total of 15 guarantees:

- Four within the School sector, focusing on what a citizens as parents and children can request regarding education.
- Seven within the Social Welfare sector focusing on financial aid, and aid to elderly and disabled citizens.
- Four in the Civil Engineering sector regarding environment and health protection, food control, building permits and water supply, snow removal and garbage disposal.

These guarantees address many issues including delivery time, assistance availability, information availability etc. Each guarantee is tailored for a specific service. While there is no general guarantee, several services might have the same guarantee specification. One of the issues that had to be solved was the service in return in case the City failed to deliver the service as the guarantee states. Guarantees in the public sector are complicated as there are many kinds of services and each comes with specific legal regulation. According to the Swedish Association of Local Authorities and Regions (SALAR) a city can only offer four types of responses when dealing with complaints and service guarantees:

- Being proactive: the City contacts a citizen and explains that s/he can not get the service s/he is supposed to, and explains why. The reason would likely be legal regulation.
- Free service: If the City for some reason can not provide the service when it should, in some cases the citizen can get the service free at a later time. This is something that is common occurrence in the welfare system if a citizen eligible for welfare does not get the check on time s/he could get cash so as to be able to buy groceries. And this would not lead to a reduction of welfare later on.
- Economic compensation can be given to individual citizens if the service delivery is unacceptable.
- Alternative service: If alternative services exist then a citizen could choose an alternative instead. For instance, if the home care service cannot make their food delivery the citizen could get the offer to visit a local restaurant at the City's expense.

In some cases financial guarantees are impossible, for example in education, because Swedish law prohibits cities to give economic compensations of any kind of services provided free of charge due to legislation. In such cases guarantees can only be about availability, access to information, venues for influencing services, and similar.

The 15 service guarantees in Örebro were accepted by the Executive Board and have been sent out to the city departments for an internal trial period between January and March 2008. The project group will continue to develop new guarantees in areas not yet addressed and make changes to the ones already designed based on the feedback they receive from the trial period. They will also start on creating tutorial information to be used to educate staff when the guarantees get implemented. One of the problems still to be solved is the lack of development coaches.

Critical issue 4, distinction between political and administrative responsibilities: As this story shows, clearly guarantees have to be both legal and meaningful, i.e. providing real value to citizens. Issues arise when e.g. "good education" cannot be guaranteed in terms of compensation. Is "information" and "availability" enough? This is where the distinction between politics and administration becomes clear. The administration can only guarantee access, anything to do with the quality of education beyond professionalism and legal actions are rather political issues.

E-Services

The City had been working towards implementing e-service for several years prior to the launch of MovIT, starting in 2002 when discussions on becoming a "24/7 agency" begun. At that time discussions involved mainly technical staff working on the possibilities of complying with the 24/7 agency guidelines. With no interest at strategic level in the city, progress was slow.

During 2003 the City launched a pilot project focusing on creating common definitions of concepts for the entire city and to create a knowledge bank for e-service issues. In the final report of this pilot it was argued that e-services will affect all parts of the city and that creating common definitions would allow efficiency in implementing e-service in the future. The pilot put together common definitions for concepts such as e-service, e-government, e-democracy, e-ID etc. The final report pointed out that "we have created the first (theoretical) version of the common definitions that the City will use, the definitions will however require revisions and updates as the City implements more e-services". This pilot is in a sense MovIT's pre-study as MovIT in many cases follows the recommendations and uses the definitions the pilot developed.

In 2005 the City allocated 800 000 SEK to coordination of e-services. One purpose was to prevent uncoordinated development of e-services at individual departments. Örebro also joined SAMBRUK, an organization involving many cities in establishing interoperable and shared technical solutions. Although the City had been working consistently on moving towards becoming a 24/7 agency for the past few years, at this point it became clear that designing universal—city-wide—formats for e-services required a more comprehensive analysis:

We had ideas of implementing an e-service earlier but then someone started to think and it turned out that we could not implement an e-service without doing a thorough analysis of our processes and organization because the added value to citizens could not only come from just providing the service online, we also needed to make our processes and our organization more efficient. (Steering committee member, November 28, 2007)

Under the MovIT project, in 2007 departments were invited to submit proposals for e-services to the IT Advisory Board (ITAB). Some proposals did not take issues like citizen value into consideration, and so the ITAB turned many proposals down. This standpoint was eventually altered so as to not exclude departments which might have led them to consider separate and potentially non-interoperable solutions. The Board started to accept proposals with a requirement clause:

in order for the IT-advisory board to add the service into the IT-plan — which is necessary for achieving central funding — the department had to arrange so the service provided would at least reach a certain minimum level with respect to the requirements set by the ITAB; it had to be compatible with the current software and it had to comply with the current security standards. For MovIT, another basic requirement was that the service would either improve the efficiency and effectiveness of the organization, provide added value to citizens, or both.

One reason for this change in attitude was that the ITAB felt that if they kept turning many proposals down then no or very few services would ever be provided as an e-service. Another reason was that there were problems with suppliers trying to circumvent the decision making hierarchy of the City;

What is happening is that suppliers circumvent the centralized IT-support and the production manager and the IT-advisory board and call directly to department managers and tell them "we have a great IT solution for you" and then persuade them to not contact our IT-support. The department manager becomes interested and checks his budget and figure it's better to spend the money before the financial year ends. (Steering committee member, October 31, 2007)

Clearly this is an important issue for interoperability. The ITAB move towards becoming more welcoming to e-service proposals from departments was designed to promote interoperability and convergence. By approving the proposals they would be able to prevent suppliers from circumventing the ITAB (and nowadays MovIT); the head of the organization would have to discuss any system accepted in the IT plan with the ITAB.

Critical issue 5, coordination of departments: Under the New Public Management (NPM) governance model, individual departments are in charge of their budget. Any attempt at coordination must be more by carrot than by stick. Carrots include central funding, in this case the IT plan and MovIT. Sticks are legal regulation, but such is typically not detailed enough to prevent problems like the ones here described, precisely because of the NPM model — it is supposed to encourage business thinking at department level and hence there must be real choices to be made at that level.

The entire re-organization of the administrative processes, the FRAM project, was planned to be completed during spring 2008. In parallel MovIT launched its e-service project with the goal of implementing a set of e-services which should be operational by January 2008. As time was tight, the steering committee wanted to speed up ongoing work with e-services rather than start new projects from scratch. Hence they reconsidered previous projects and looked into which e-services the IT advisory board had approved and added to the general IT-plan. Several departments had already begun moving from manual to electronic services and were at different stages in their implementation. Three e-services — out of some 40 proposals — were selected to initially be implemented as MovIT projects, all of which already existed in the general IT-plan:

1. Child care service to parents; application, information, registering of vacation etc.
2. Applications for building permits.
3. Service to civil society organizations, mainly sports clubs; booking and applications for financial support.

This choice of already approved projects was intended to make implementation quick. There were also other considerations. There is some confusion generally as to the definition of an e-service is. In the mid 1990s anything on the web would be considered a service, but gradually this has changed. Today, Verva (the Swedish national regulatory body for e-government) defines e-service as: Service that has been designed to be delivered electronically, using technology such as mobile phones, digital TV, Computers or through advanced telephone services. This is a wide, general, definition so to be able to make distinctions and monitor progress. Verva also defines four levels of e-services; information, interaction, transaction and integration. The information level consists of presenting the City and the services it provides on the Internet, which Örebro has done at orebro.se. The interaction level concerns providing simple services on the City website such as application forms, and other simple self service like searching for public documents. Örebro has reached this level to some extent. The transaction level is about allowing for citizens to acquire, set and edit private information by providing personalized e-service which requires special login such as e-ID. The City is doing pre-studies how they can achieve this level and the Work the e-service project does in MovIT is mainly about this level. The integration level is the final level where the city is integrated enough to become transparent. This is the 24/7 authority; the city has achieved convergence and interoperability between its departments so as to allow for citizens to be able to access everything the city provides on the Internet through one single contact point.

Örebro, quite naturally, has adopted Verva's definition. MovIT set focus on the third level, transaction, thus eliminating some of the proposals in the IT-plan as they could be categorized as being level one or two. Hence MovIT raised the general level of ambition somewhat. Next, time and costs had to be considered as well as benefits. The criteria chosen were:

- How much it would cost to implement.
- How long it would take to implement.
- How it would benefit the citizens.
- How popular it would be.

Because complete e-services, meaning level 3 or 4, were still new and demand was unknown it was considered beneficial to initially implement popular services so the very idea of e-service would not have to be marketed to the public.

Implementation

The services that were chosen turned out to be more problematic to implement that initially understood. Örebro City is part of SAMBRUK which is a joint project involving over 30 municipalities in Sweden. The idea is to collaborate when developing e-services, sharing software, definitions and process models. The project follows the ambitions and statements made by the Swedish government; to become a coordinated public sector with e-services (http://www.sambruk.se/). Participation is voluntary so cities decide themselves which e-service projects they will participate in. However, they do need to be ready to adjust to the common guidelines in some common fundamental issues. The large number of cities collaborating in SAMBRUK makes procurement procedures a daunting endeavor. First all must reach a common ground on specifications, suppliers, time frames, cost distribution etc. Then they need make deals with suppliers, which may not be easy as these may be more interested in dealing with cities individually. MovIT thought that collaborating with several other cities would allow them to put more pressure on the suppliers and to divide the development cost between many partners thus lowering the cost for Örebro. Hence two of the e-service projects (Service to civil society organizations and Child care service to parents) begun negotiations through SAMBRUK during fall 2006. For the Child care service to parents' project this cooperation proved unsuccessful:

We had begun the procurement procedure with SAMBRUK in the fall last year but it did not turn out well since the major suppliers where unwilling to open their system for an external e-service. This lead to postponement of the procurement and we had look for other solutions (Project manager, November 28, 2007)

This unwillingness made the negotiations require more time then anticipated. Indeed they would not reach the final stage until at the earliest in April/May 2008, that is, by the time the whole MovIT project was expected to be finished. Hence a new solution was needed. A new supplier was brought in, who had a product that needed some adjustment. This meant unanticipated costs, but it brought the plan reasonably back on schedule

The Civil society organizations support project also experienced problems with the SAMBRUK cooperation, however this time it was not due to the suppliers but the cities themselves. They could not come to an agreement on which suppliers to use since almost all of them advocated to use their own supplier. In the end the SAMBRUK negotiations were postponed and the project manager had to come up with an alternative solution. The alternative chosen was a module available for the current information system. However the module was not completely compatible with the system – despite it being a module of it – and hence needed some updating. From a quality point of view this was not deemed to be the perfect solution but the steering committee agreed to it since they wanted an e-service to become implemented. The first part of the e-service was launched in December 2007, and citizen can now book facilities owned by the City.

In conclusion, this subproject has not achieved all its goals. The building permit project is on hold until further notice pending results from evaluation of an external pilot involving five other cities regarding a common e-service for building permits. The project for Child care service is hoping to solve the technical issues during 2008 so the e-service can be launched although somewhat later then originally anticipated. The NGO support project has launched an e-service and to be able to develop it more, the project needs to do more analysis and to find a solution for the locking and passage system. This work will continue during 2008.

Verva has also agreed to fund the eID solution MovIT has agreed upon for three e-services, since the building permit project is on hold. MovIT decided to add another service. The third and new service is closely related to the Child care service to parents' project. It's a service for parents to allow them to get information on their children's attendance records. This service does not have its own project group as it is closely related to the Child care services.

Critical issue 6, dependence on providers: It is a long standing problem that cities are much in the hands of their suppliers. As this story shows, these do not necessarily want cities to join forces to get better deals from providers. Also, it is hard for cities to engage new providers. They often feel comfortable with the one they use, and handling many is generally more complicated.

WEB STRUCTURE AND DESIGN

In the project directive for the web structure and design project it stated that the project should focus on a few specified target groups when designing the web structure and design for the city's web site (www.orebro.se). To achieve this, the project group decided on a method that focuses on charting effects. The project group did extensive analyses of the organization's strategies and other both political and administrative steering documents to see what the City wanted to achieve strategically. Based on this information the project group had workshops with decision makers and strategic staff to come up with a set of main target groups. Although clearly the web is for all it would not be possible to focus on all possible target group that might exist. Hence the City followed Verva's methodological advice. Verva recommends prioritizing between the existing target groups and to acquire in-depth knowledge of the chosen target groups as it is a condition to "be able to choose between functions and solutions for the overarching design of the website, to create a logical information structure and a good graphic layout, and to realize the most benefits of the IT-investment" (Verva, 2007)

Eventually five target groups were selected as first priority. In-depth interviews with citizens' belonging to those target groups were held, based on which "personas", archetypical users, were designed with the assistance of a consultant company, InUse, experts in this field. The personas were intended to encompass five of the main target groups; the choice was Parents, Entrepreneurs, Relative, Recreational, and Culture. Clearly this solution is partial – how about elderly, for example? Immigrants? While it is possible that the web design can be improved this way, it is clear that new demands will follow as supply and use increase. However, this method is just one out of many to decide web design. This method focused on web design with the purpose of being close to certain user groups which are thought to have distinctly different needs. There are alternatives. One would be focusing on general usability for the purpose of making services "look and feel" as similar as possible. One argument for such thinking is that over a lifetime most people will use all services, parents help children, children help parents and so they become assistant users for some other target group. Hence, the argument goes, it is best to have a consistent and proven general design. For such design there are international guidelines. Yet another, compatible, alternative is focusing on clustering service supply according to "life situations". This approach groups services for "youth", "parents", "elderly" together so users not just find things they actually look for but also become aware of services relevant to them which they did not know about beforehand. Examples of this include many national web sites in e.g. Austria and Sweden. Whichever method chosen there is no single best solution. There are always trade-offs to be made.

Critical issue 7, use standards selectively: Standards are clearly useful as they facilitate design. As this story shows there are not only technical standards but also such that pertain to use and service organization. These standards are rather best practices than unequivocal standards, but best practices often become so familiar among users that changing them is hard. In this case there was no complete service supply to organize, but in a few years there will be. Then there will be need for another revision of the web. Timing is important, On the one hand, imposing an abundance of standards to a web with yet very few services may be overkill. On the other hand, making too special designs—non-standard—may prove expensive at next revision as services may have developed in different directions design wise and may require considerable changes.

FUTURE TRENDS

In this article we have told a story of an ongoing radical e-government case involving considerable reorganization and a clear, politically decided, citizen focus. Our findings can be summarized as a number of critical issues, critical because the choices made at these junctions may have profound effects on the outcomes. In this section we first summarize the challenges, and then go on to analyzing them in terms of future trends in the field. The changes and the importance of them are:

1. **Political timing:** Political directives often come with time limits. This is good in that it spurs action but it can also cause trouble as quality may be affected. In this case clearly political wish for quick results was given highest priority and all other criteria were adjusted accordingly.
2. **Resource allocation:** This story shows one of the critical points of NPM. As resources are distributed to individual departments resources for projects have to be negotiated, even in a case like this when political directives are strong. The result of the

negotiations depends on individuals. It is basically the charm of the project manager – and of course any political pressure s/he is able to put on departments – that makes the difference between failure and success. This pressure can come from other policies, and as we shall see below some such means were indeed used.

3. **Political mandate:** The guarantees described above are critical instruments for convergence across city departments, both generally and in terms of forming a basis for developing standardized e-services. The guarantees are a direct result of political directives. Without such, important instruments will not happen.
4. **Distinction between administrative and political responsibilities:** As this story shows, clearly guarantees have to be both legal and meaningful, i.e. providing real value to citizens. Issues arise when important things like "good education" cannot be guaranteed but rather elements of it such as access, information etc. Making service guarantees explicit also makes it explicit where administration ends and politics starts. This puts new pressure on politicians
5. **Coordination under NPM:** Under the NPM model, individual departments are in charge of their budget. Any attempt at coordination must be more by carrot than by stick. Carrots include central funding, in this case the IT plan and MovIT. Sticks are legal regulation, but such is typically not detailed enough to prevent issues like the ones here describes, precisely because of the NPM model – it is supposed to encourage business thinking at department level and hence there must be real choices to be made at that level.
6. **Dependence on providers:** It is a long standing problem that cities are much in the hands of their suppliers. As this story shows, these do not necessarily want cities to join forces to get better deals from providers. Also, it is hard for cities to engage new providers. They often feel comfortable with the one they use, and handling many is generally more complicated.
7. **Choosing among standards and best practices**. While standards are clearly useful they often com in the form of de facto standards or best practices and are therefore hard to discern. Timing is important. Over standardization at an early stage may prove both costly and cumbersome, but so will waiting too long to use established best practices.

At a more general level this case story can be considered in the perspective of strategic management model. The prevailing model today is New Public Management, a model where economic measurement at department level is the most prominent technique. We have seen in this case that many of the problems encountered have to do quite directly with this model. A common theme in this story is that lacking national plans local organizations are struggling to find development models that are both interoperable beyond the own organization and economical. This struggle involves both partnerships and makeshift solutions, here illustrated for example by the SAMBRUK problems and the ITAB's changes in strategy to prevent other actors – vendors and departments – to circumvent the City policy. While it is methodologically incorrect to generalize from a single case, it is clear that these problems are directly derived from the NPM governance model. Hence the case is illustrative also for other countries even if the details may be different depending on the exact implementation of NPM. The case shows that the economic model for governance, NPM, is conserving institutions rather than promoting change in several ways:

- It prevents development of national frameworks, such as enterprise architectures, which are necessary for the convergences processes that need to take place to make interaction across government organizations smoother. We saw in this case that such would have helped at several points, where now instead the City had to cook up local standards.
- It requires complicated cooperation's across both political and economic borders to not only implement shared services but also to finding economic advantages in procurement, service etc. This was clearly illustrated by the SAMBRUK debacle.

In summary this case exhibits a quite ambitious project where e-government ideals such as interoperability, single face to citizens, customer-oriented services etc. were clearly proclaimed at the political level and ambitiously implemented at the administrative level. While changes are still ongoing we can already see "inscriptions" in the form of policies for services and access, an increased set of standards at city level, and a started if not yet completed reorganization of the administration. We have highlighted some problems for local e-government development and pointed out that many of these have to do with lack of national coordination and a strategic model for government that is not conducive to such comprehensive changes that are necessary to make the best out of e-government. We believe that that a future trend is that this type of ambitious whole-of-government, albeit only local in this case, approaches will become ever more important, for economic as well as service reasons. We believe governments, including local, will over the next few years develop – indeed, will have to develop – skills in meeting these challenges. This involves strategic changes to the NPM governance model, not just little fixes to emergencies, as this case has demonstrated.

CONCLUSION

This article has studied a case where a city has attempted a politically decided strategic overhaul of service supply with a strong focus on citizen value. We found seven "critical issues" which are necessary to address in a coherent and determined manner in order to be able to pursue such a strategic management approach. The seven issues are political timing, resource allocation, political mandate, distinction between administrative and political responsibilities, coordination of departments, dependence on providers, and wise use of standards. These are issues where development is open for local choice, influences of strong individuals and groups, and indeed chance. Addressing them strategically amounts to a considerable change in the mainstream governance paradigm, New Public Management, as this is not sufficient to implement all the potential benefits of e-government. Indeed, this situation is in much a consequence of NPM. This model by design leaves these issues in a void which has to be filled by negotiations among many actors with different roles, goals, and action space.

While this case tells just one story of how these negotiations turned out, there are general lessons to learn in that there is such a void, that it has to be filled, and if it is not filled strategically it will be open for unexpected turns of events. Clearly one case is not enough to show how this should be done, but this case clearly illustrates some of the challenges to be met, as well as benefits and shortcomings of different approaches to problem solutions which are common today.

REFERENCES

Accenture (2005). *E-Government leadership in customer service: New expectations, new experiences*. Retrieved December 15, 2005, from www.accenture.com

Accenture (2004). *E-Government leadership: High performance, maximum value.* Accenture Consulting. Retrieved December 15, 2005, from http://www.accenture.com/xdoc/en/industries/government/gove_egov_value.pdf

Behn, R. D. (2006). The challenge of evaluating M-Government, E-Government, and P-Government. In Mayer-Schönbeger & Lazer (Eds.), *From Electronic Government to Information Government*, 213-238. Cambridge, Massachusetts: MIT Press

Boston, J., Martin, J., Pallot, J., & Walsh, P. (1996). *Public management: The New Zealand model.* Auckland: Oxford University Press.

CSN (2006). Annual Report. http://www.csn.se/polopoly_fs/1.2432!arsredovisning2006.pdf (visited Jan 27, 2008)

DGIM (2005). Online availability of public services: How is Europe progressing. Web based survey on Electronic Public Services. *Report of the fifth measurement, October 2004. Prepared by Capgemini for the European Commission Directorate General for Information.* Retrieved December 15, 2005, from http://europa.eu.int/information_society/soccul/egov/egov_benchmarking_2005.pdf

Dunleavy, P., Margetts, H., Bastow, S., & Tinkler, J. (2007). *Digital era governance: IT corporations, the state, and E-Government.* Oxford: Oxford University Press, 2006. ISBN 0 19 929619 7

eGEP (2006a). *Measurement framework final version*, eGov Economics Project, European Commission, Brussels. http://217.59.60.50/eGEP/Static/Contents/final/D.2.4_Measurement_Framework_final_version.pdf (visited Jan 20, 2008)

eGEP (2006b). *Compendium to the measurement framework*, eGov Economics Project, European Commission, Brussels. http://217.59.60.50/eGEP/Static/Contents/final/Measurement_Framework%20_Compendium.pdf (visited Jan 20, 2008)

EU (2004). *eGov Research in Europe. European Commission.* . Retrieved December 15, 2005, from http://europa.eu.int/information_society/programmes/egov_rd/text_en.htm

Gore, A. (1993). Reengineering through liformation technology. Accompanying *Report of the National Performance Review.* Washington: Office of the Vice President.

Grant, G., & Chau, D. (2005, January-March). Developing a generic framework for E-Government. *Journal of Global Information Management, 13*(1), 1-30.

Grönlund, Å. (2002). *Electronic government – Design, applications, and management.* Hershey, PA: Idea Group.

Grönlund, Å. (2004). The E-Service model - As implemented at Swedish National Labour Market Administration. In K Mark Weaver (ed), *Proceedings of Academy of Mangement*, New Orleans August 11-13, 2004. www.aomonline.org

Grönlund, Å. (2005). Introducing W-Gov: History, definitions, and issues. *Communications of AIS, 15*(electronic journal, www.cais.org).

Jervall, L., & Persson, T. (2006). *IT-stöd inom landstingen i Sverige.*

Lau, Edwin (2006). Electronic government and the drive for growth and equity. In Mayer-Schönbeger & Lazer (Eds.), *From Electronic Government to Information Government*, 39-58. Cambridge, Massachusetts: MIT Press

Malmer, G. (2007). *IT-strategi för vård och omsorg.* http://www.skl.se/artikel.asp?C=5235&A=48864, visited Jan 15, 2008.

OECD (2003). *The E-Government imperative.* Paris: OECD E-Government Studies. ISBN 92-64-10117-9

Örebro City executive board. (2006). *Budget 2007 med prioriterade mål (Budget with priorities).* Örebro kommun.

Örebro City Administration Office. (2007). *Servicepolicy och Tillgänglighetsgaranti för Örebro Kommun.*

Örebro City. (2007a). *Dialogen kring Klagomål*

Örebro City. (2007b). *Klagomålshantering i Örebro Kommun*

MovIT – Steering Committee. (2007). *Medborgarorienterad verksamhetsutvecking med stöd av IT*

UN (2004). *Towards access for opportunity. Global E-Government Readiness Report 2004.* New York: United Nations, Department for Economic and Social Affairs, Division for Public Administration and Development Management. Retrieved December 29, 2005, from www.unpan.org/eGov4.asp

UNDESA (2003) *e-Government at the Crossroads. World Public Sector Report 2003.* United Nations Department of Economic and Social Affairs. United Nations, New York. Retrieved December 29, 2005, from www.un.org/esa/desa/desaNews/desa94.html

Verva (2007) *Utgå från målgruppernas behov.* Retrieved February 1, 2008, from http://www.verva.se/verksamhetsstod/webb/vl24/2006/2/1/3/

West, D. M. (2003). *Global E-Government*, http://www.insidepolitics.org/egovt03int.pdf; (visited August December 29, 2005)

World Bank (2004) *World Bank E-Government.* Retrieved December 29, 2005, from http://www1.worldbank.org/ publicsector/egov/

ENDNOTE

1 MovIT is Swedish acronym for *Citizen oriented development with ICT support.*

This work was previously published in International Journal of Electronic Government Research, Vol. 4, Issue 4, edited by M. Khosrow-Pour, pp. 69-88, copyright 2008 by IGI Publishing (an imprint of IGI Global).

Chapter 15
Assessing Local Readiness for City E-Governance in Europe

Krassimira Paskaleva
Institute for Technology Assessment and Systems Analysis, Germany, and University of Manchester, UK

ABSTRACT

This article shares experience on aspects related to the methodology and modeling of a framework of City E-Governance Readiness. We discuss Europe's progress in this domain using an "e-readiness" assessment methodology: the Integrated City E-Governance Policy Model of the IntelCities Research Project (2004-2007). Practices and trends in 12 European cities are analyzed, drawing on the results of a comprehensive digital city governance survey. A set of propositions are explored about the future of city e-governance. This article suggests that urban governments need to refine their most relevant definition of "e-governance readiness" and the underlying goals and assumptions which shape e-governance outcomes. Cities also need to adapt their approaches strategically and in the light of the increasing demand for "good governance" in an increasingly complex and networked urban knowledge society.

INTRODUCTION

In the last decade, "governance" has emerged as a guiding principle of modern European democracies. In the public sector domain, it has been generally referred to as a system of rules, processes and behaviors that affect the way in which government powers are exercised on different levels, particularly as regards openness, participation, accountability, effectiveness and coherence (Barzelay, 2001; Blanke & Lopez-Clarosa, 2004; European Commission, 2003; Harding, 1998; Kolsaker, 2007; McNeil, et al., 2003; OECD 2003a,b,c; Pierre, 1999; Rhodes, 1996; Stoker, 2000; Tat-Kei Ho, 2002; Timmers, 2004). The latter constructs are in fact the main principles of "good governance", the urban projection of which is known to lead to the more sustainable city (Castells & Hall,

Eds., 1994; European Commission 2002; Van Den Berg & Van Winden, 2002). In the pursuit of the "sustainable city" in the electronic age, a recent IntelCities Integrated Project[1] developed the notion of "city e-governance" that is principally viewed as "good governance" in which urban government uses advanced Information and Communication Technologies (ICT) to exercise its powers given by the citizens based on a new organization and relationships with the stakeholders and the local community, towards achieving common urban development goals (Paskaleva-Shapira, 2005; Van Der Meer & Van Winden, 2003). This approach is radically different from other existing approaches to local e-governance. It emphasizes the broader urban aspects of ICT adoption in city governing and provides for integrated development and strategic policy-making.

During 2004-2007, the IntelCities Project brought together eighteen cities, twenty ICT companies and thirty three research groups from Europe to pool advanced knowledge and experience of electronic government, urban planning and knowledge systems and citizens participation and create a new and innovative interoperable e-government platform and services to meet the needs of both residents and businesses. To assist the architecture, evaluation and implementation of the Integrated Open System City Platform (e-City Platform), the City e-Governance Framework was developed as a novel approach to urban policy-making in the electronic age. An integrated system of policies and actions was designed to establish the basis for the necessary transformation in urban e-governance (Paskaleva-Shapira, 2005).

But, as the study has shown, the latter can be seriously hindered if initiatives are disjointed and uncoordinated by an overall framework and strategy. Although many urban governments are creating variety of electronic services and the debate on how ICT are changing our cities is in the same way growing, the work on city e-governance and its assessment of readiness remains strikingly poor. Some crucial issues of framework development are barely discussed in the literature and guidance for implementation is missing. So with this article, we intend to contribute to this debate by conceptualizing a framework that could guide the preparedness of the City toward an e-governance model. This emphasis fits in the recent strands of technology research in social sciences that focus on the context-dependency of the uptake of technologies (Van Der Meer & Van Winden, 2003). In our approach, we move away from the predominantly ICT-focused idea of city e-readiness, but instead stress complexity and integrated approach of e-governance on the local level. Our starting point is that, for a number of reasons, in cities the ICT adoption and application is embedded in the specific economic, institutional, social and spatial structures and processes. What is more, and as Zimmermann (2005) suggested too, in the wake of resolving complex problems by means of holistic approaches and integrated management and policies, complex strategies, nurtured with local knowledge and participation are urgently required. Accordingly, we chose this "integrated approach"[2] to developing a city e-governance readiness framework to analyze Europe's recent progress in this domain. To reveal this complexity and cohesiveness, in the first part of the article we preset a conceptual framework that helps us to unravel the local aspects of e-governance readiness. We introduce the concept of "city e-governance" to describe local policies and the role of government and the various stakeholders in it. We make a distinction between five key policy dimensions of city e-governance: general framework and conditions, e-services and ICT advance, government modernization, stakeholder participation, and policy innovation. We suggest a hypothesis on the interaction between the five dimensions as engine for the dynamics of the urban e-governance. We also pin point other urban policies that may influence these dynamics. The second part of the article is about actual city e-governance policies and practice in European cities. We illustrate this with a comparative analysis of a twelve city survey study from eight countries in Europe, representing a diversity of political, socio-economic and cultural conditions. The article is organized as follows: In section 2, we present the conceptual framework to analyze urban e-governance. In section 3, the concept of city e-readiness is introduced and elaborated. In sections 4-5, we describe actual urban practices and make propositions about the future of city e-governance in Europe. Section 6 concludes with the main findings and the implications for boosting the e-governance readiness of European cities.

CITY E-GOVERNANCE: A CONCEPTUAL FRAMEWORK

This section falls into two parts: the first looks at overreaching issues of e-governance in cities, while the second outlines the characteristics and qualities of the Integrated City e-Governance Policy Model that is suitable for the countries of the European Union (EU).

Resulting from a combination of swift ICT and policy developments during the last several years, electronic government in Europe have shown a dramatic shift from information diffusion towards community-based interactive models of services, participation and innovation. In parallel, the construct of "e-governance" is emerging as a novel platform for governing in the 21st Century's Europe. As a result, within both central and local governments of the Union, the effort to transform the delivery of public services through the adoption of advanced ICT has been constantly on the rise. Likewise, as information technologies increasingly penetrate the public sphere, societies and governments are bound to contemplate the use of these tools to remodel democratic practices and transform relations between citizens and public services. As a result, electronic government is emerging as an issue of not solely technology but as a new tool to reinvent the way in which service providers and customers interact and transform government processes, provide leadership, enable economic and democratic development, and reinvent the role of government itself in society (European Commission 2004, 2005, 2007). Accordingly, integrated public services and innovative organizational change in government-to-citizens relationships, including citizen-centric services, participation and open interoperable frameworks are emerging as the main prerequisites to dealing with the challenges of the digital era in the transition to participatory democracies in the EU member states.

Yet, despite the wide popularity of electronic government in all spheres in life, there seems to be an ambiguity about its content and structure, particularly at the local level. In the literature to day, two main terms have been used to describe electronic government – "e-government" and "e-governance". These have often been used indiscriminately and there is a genuine confusion about their differences and the underlying principles and implications. In this section we attempt to bring some clarity about the nature and goals of e-governance at the local level as pursued and applied by the countries of the European Union. Specifically, we seek to highlight the strategic elements that are based on research and experience related to the urban level of e-governance.

What is E-Governance in Cities?

Governance is a widely used concept in Europe and around the world. Most commonly, it regards government but other private and non-governmental organization and social entities as well. Mainly, it deals with reasoning and decision-making in the sphere of how societies, communities, families, as well as the political, administrative and economic systems, govern the different areas of life, at all levels of society (Stoker, 1998). In the light of the institutional economic literature and according to Zimmermann (2005) electronic governance in particular deals, in its broader context, with "the challenges of modern information technologies, especially in the form of ICT (TV, Radio, telephones, computers and networks) and the direction and application they should take in the different areas of life, the public sector included" (p.19). What should be kept in mind, however, is that e-governance in the public sector should play a key role in the modernization of state, community and society by including alternative negotiating mechanism among the stakeholders, potentially empowering local government itself (Le Galés, 1998). This means that governance should not be regarded as an administrative category, or the rational administration of a local entity. Rather, it should refer to the complexity of social relations in society (Moulaert & Delladetsima, 2002). In cities, where an increasing number of cultural and socio-economic identities complicate democratic policy and administration, governance should coordinate the relationships and the actors within the different spheres of life, meaning that the relations between institutions, agents and society should become the empowering vehicle behind the urban development agenda (Paskaleva-Shapira, 2008).

Much importantly, considering that ICT are attributed a major role in the delivery of EU's policies for sustainable development, and particularly at the regional and local level, it is difficult to discuss the importance of successful exploitation of ICT without accounting for the broader urban pursuits for sustainability and prosperity (Cooper, Hamilton & Bentivegna, 2005; European Commission, 2002). Sustainable urban development basically implies that cities need to become economically efficient, socially integrated and environmentally friendly in order to provide and improve the quality of life of their citizens; therefore corporations and urban authorities have to come to agreements, aimed at integrating citizens' demands for environmental protection, economic competitiveness and social cohesion. This new approach, however calls for a radical shift from government-led urban development to urban governance of decision and policy-making based on interactions between the stakeholders in the city (the *participatory society* paradigm). In light of this "stakeholder approach" to sustainable urban development and the impacts of ICT on society and community, the concept of "city e-governance" can be introduced, which can generally be defined as the *capacity and ability of local government to deploy ICT to enhance social prosperity, facilitate effective decision making and improved public policies in the urban community by transforming relations with citizens, businesses, and other organizations in the pursuit of strategic sustainable development goals* (OECD, 2003a; Paskaleva-Shapira, 2005; Zimmermann, 2005).

So whilst e-government is generally taken as the use of ICT for delivery of government services (Moon, 2002), and is hence strongly associated with administrative governing of a single actor, in our approach to e-governance we move away from the directive capacities of the city towards its ability to engage in networks with the urban stakeholders and other organizations so as to pursue common urban policy goals. This approach is consistent and integrates the ideas of several other authors to e-governance such as Mistri (1999), who defined governance as "the capacity of local administrations, in a dialectic exchange with social organizations and firms, to guide the growth process" (p.133); Jessop (1997), who described it as "the complex art of steering multiple agencies, institutions and systems which are both operationally autonomous from another and structurally coupled through various forms of reciprocal interdependence" (p.95), and Van Der Meer and Van Winden (2003) who concluded that the success of e-governance in Europe basically depends on the capacity of urban management to engage in local networks with local companies, citizens and intermediary organizations, as well as their ability to mobilize external resources.

There are multiple opportunities arising from our conceptual approach to city e-governance. The most important implication is that it offers the potential of a common framework of open government, advanced democracy and inclusive decision-making in the urban communities where ICT can serve a variety of different ends: better delivery of government services to citizens, improved interactions with business and industry, citizens' empowerment through access to information and opportunities, or more efficient government management. What's more, it facilitates the information, communication and transactions with a wide variety of urban stakeholders based on their specifics and demands. This in turn entails interactions and consultations between government, businesses and citizens resulting in the stakeholder participation in local governing. As such, e-governance is intrinsically linked to e-democracy, which to many represents greater and more effective citizen participation enabled by the internet, mobile communications, and other technologies in representative democracies as well as through more participatory or direct forms of citizen involvement in addressing public challenges (Kolsaker, 2006; Office of the e-Envoy, 2002; Rydin & Pennington, 2000). The latter attribute is particularly important in our approach, one that bears the true difference between the more conventional understandings of e-government and the inclusive and transforming nature of e-governance. And lastly but not least, e-governance success also lies in reorganizing the workings within and between government agencies for increasing efficiency and in integrating front/mid and back office systems and service delivery channels for improving effectiveness of government operations and integrating services across organizational boundaries and across layers of government (Millard & Iversen, 2004). This way e-governance can make the interaction between government and society and the inter-agency relationships more friendly, convenient, and transparent (Riley, 2007; The World Bank, 2007).

Clearly, the mission of e-governance nowadays expands and the expectations of European societies rise, especially at the local level, where policies really matter. From a tool to deliver services, e-governance emerges as a yardstick of the capacity and ability of government to reform and improve to better serve its citizens. It also means engaging with the stakeholders to share the risks, opportunities and benefits of collaboration in steering the affairs of the community. It too can offer potential solutions to leaders to better assume their responsibilities. Finally, it invites people to participate in making the decisions of the communities they live, work and enjoy. But to fulfill its missions, e-governance has to reflect the principles and objectives of sustainable urban development which has only been subject to research for about half a decade and is still unexplored in many aspects (Sannarnes, Henriksen & Andersen, 2006). Establishing an integrated framework of city e-governance is thus necessary to help urban authorities link polices and actions that reflect its logic and improve overall urban development. The model developed next is a demonstration of one such integrated and strategic approach to city e-governance.

An Integrated City E-Governance Model

For reasons of space, we reduce the summary of the conceptualization of e-governance to several key lines that are most relevant to the present study (Paskaleva, 2005). The most important facts about understanding city e-governance by policy makers but researcher as well are the following: First, city e-governance should be understood not as a means itself but as instrumental to achieving goals, in other words it is a means to an end and includes both the results of the actions and their impacts on the sector, the city and the overall urban community. External and internal factors alike determine the success of the process, but the local condintions are driving. Second, the innovation in the ICT sector is one of the main drivers of success, as cities who are more serious about ICT are generally better

Figure 1. IntelCities city e-governance policy model (Source: Paskaleva-Shapira, 2007. "© Copyright 2007 IEEE – All rights reserved")

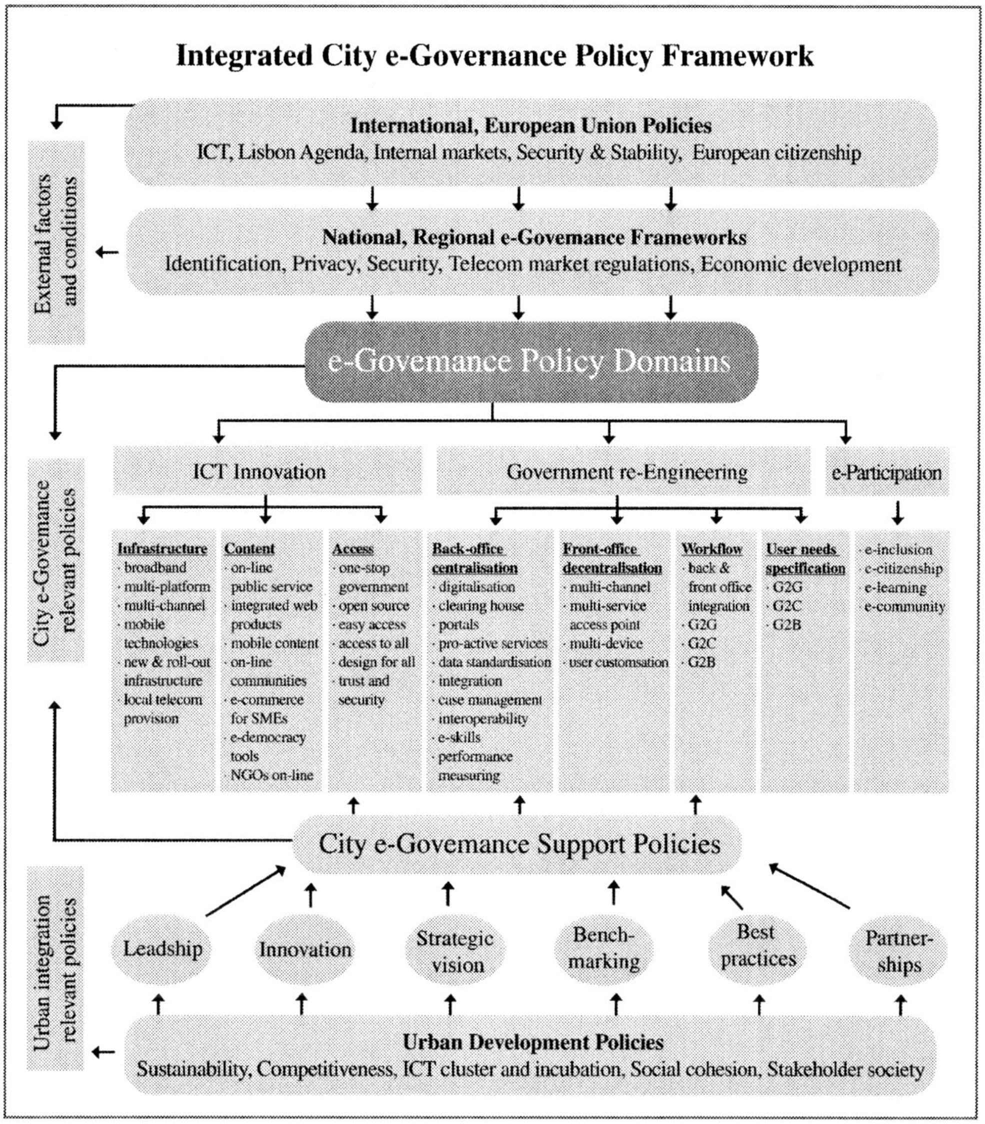

off. There is a prior need for improving services but technology follows the model of participatory e-governance. Third, if e-governance should help restore and increase the legitimacy of the public sphere as well as of local politics, then there is a need for the transformation of government at the very bottom. Therefore, city e-governance should be viewed as an essential instrument to government modernization and innovation (OECD, 2003c) through successful business process re-engineering [3], allowing it to work in radically different ways; making it also possible to break old "rules" and create entirely new processes; and supporting decentralization by means of increased flexibility and customization, among others. In effect, the source of e-governance success lies in reorganizing the working processes within and between government agencies for integrating the back/mid and front office systems and the service delivery channels (Millard & Iversen, 2004). In the complex urban context, however, perhaps even more important is the fourth dimension of e-governance – one that emphasizes the collaborative and inclusive nature and relationships between government, businesses, citizens and community organizations aimed at maximizing the benefits of strategic partnering, networking and coalition building for achiving common urban policy goals. So in e-governance, the relational capital of cities is not only a means to work out things with the stakeholders, but can also be a powerful tool to influence the external factors that influence it. Fifth, it should be stress out too that city e-governance is after all a policy option of urban making where continuously increasing and strengthening the public value should be a guiding benchmark of government success. The political leadership is to bring about the integration and cooperation of the public actors. Stakeholder involvement in policy and particularly the private sector, bottom-up decisions aligned with general visions and strategies on the urban level, and cooperation of public agencies on different level in various ICT-related policies can lead to institutional reform and innovation (Goodin, 1996). Finally, we can also suggest that our city e-governance model, presented in the figure above, is in fact a system innovation model that is dependant on other urban development policies, such as sustainability, competitiveness, social inclusion and so forth (Paskaleva-Shapira, 2007). Therefore, existing ideas, practices and relations should be always questioned and reviewed so as to improve and endure (Castells & Hall, 1994; Snellen & Van Der Donk, 1998; Van Den Berg, Van Der Meer & Pol, 2004; Van Den Berg & Van Winden, 2002).

Put in a nutshell, our model deals with the technological advance and the resulting quality of e-services, socio-economic, legal and inclusion issues of city e-governance development and identifies ways to innovation, particularly with regard to the integration of front-and back-offices and government modernization. It also defines the strategies in key e-governance policies as well as the themes central to implementation in relevance to building and developing the technical and knowledge infrastructure that is able to link together the city e-governance with strategic development and participatory urban processes. The outcomes should be an increased and strengthened public value geared toward building sustainable and prosperous communities.

In terms of the main users, it is important to underline that city e-governance has three main components: government (public institutions

Figure 2. E-governance and stakeholder interactions

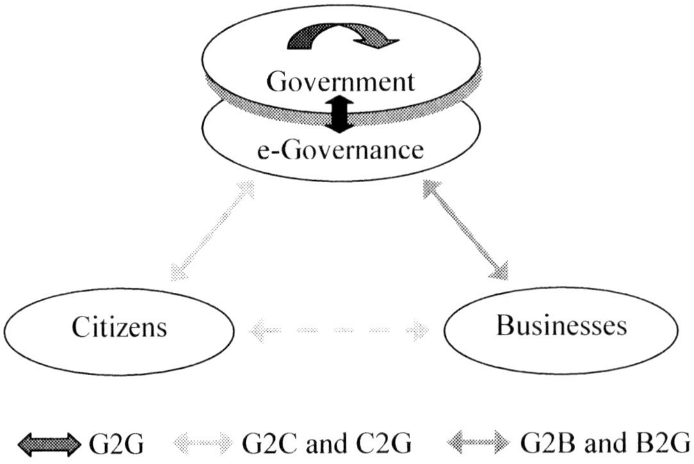

and politicians) to citizens (G2C); government to government (G2G); and government to businesses (G2B). In all three cases, the relationship is twofold between the parties with government steering the cooperation, as shown in Figure 2:

DEFINING LOCAL READINESS FOR CITY E-GOVERNANCE

Based on these clearly defined goals and priorities, we propose a methodological approach to assessing the readiness of cities to e-governance by discussing the concept of e-readiness first and then developing our own framework that is relevant to the adopted conceptual model of city e-governance.

The Concept of E-Readiness

With the importance of e-governance continually increasing and the greater role it is assuming in public management and policies in the European democracies (Traunmüller, 2004; Van Den Berg & van Der Meer, 2004), demands for assessing the "readiness" of cities and localities are, understandingly on the rise too. The attention for e-readiness is justified by the fact that positive and sustainable policy programs and initiatives oriented to ICT diffusion and use within and across countries and cities is considered a fundamental requisite for economic and social growth at the local and national level. In this sense, ICT's sustainable adoption is now seen as part of the competitiveness of regions, localities, and countries. Accordingly, various "e-readiness" indexes have been in use during the last few years to assess the progress of nations and economies, and more recently, of cities across the world as well. The differences between the indexes, however, are wide. Approaches, definitions, structures, and goals vary as do the corresponding results. For example, the Computer Systems Policy Project's (CSPP) e-Readiness Guide for Living in a Networked World (Technology CEO Council, 2002) defines an "e-ready community" as one that has high-speed access in a competitive market; with constant access and application of ICT in schools, government offices, businesses, healthcare facilities and homes; user privacy and online security; and government policies which are favorable to promoting connectedness and use of the Network, i.e. the focus is on the technology and level of use by the users. The World Economic Forum Consultation Report describes "e-readiness" as the ability of the ICT networks to effectively adapt to the social and economic advancement, hence links technology use to overall growth and prosperity (World Economic Forum, 2007). The Global e-Policy e-Government Institute at Harvard University (2003), one of the most acclaimed institution in "e-readiness" research defines an "e-ready society" as the one that has the necessary physical infrastructure and integrated ICT throughout businesses, communities, and the government, strong telecommunications competition, independent regulation with a commitment to universal access, and no limits on trade or foreign investment, in a word, interconnectedness, independence and competitiveness are considered key drivers of success. On the European level, the Kable and Government Computing Report on Europe's Readiness for E-government (http://www.kablenet.com/) claims that government becomes "e-government" or "e-ready" when the public sector digitizes its processes and interactions, whether internal or external with business or with the public, in our view, a rather narrow approach to the deployment of ICT by government which ignores a number of critical issues - such as strategic goals, stakeholder participation, and scales - among others.

On the local urban level, whilst various methods and tools exist to measure the readiness of cities with regard to the adoption of technology, cohesive assessment frameworks for e-governance and its implementation are practically missing. Existing approaches and results largely vary as well. For example, the first assessment of digital governance carried out by the Global e-Policy e-Government Institute in 2003, focused on the municipal web sites (front office) throughout the world from the perspective of e-democracy. The Rutgers-SKKU E-Governance Performance Index (http://i-policy.typepad.com/information-policy/2006/06/rutgersskku_ego.html) chose a tool that reflects the user's goals from the perspectives of five core areas: (i) security and privacy, (ii) usability, (iii) content, (iv) services, and (v) citizen participation. The 2002 e-Forum survey (http://www.ist-world.org/) studied the level of penetration with PCs and use of emails across the administration of EU member countries on average. Finally, the European E-city Award (http://www.eec-award.com/) performs an annual ranking of the best cities in e-government practices – starting from 2002 – based on an analysis of the information and services offered by cities' Internet portals (supply side perspective) from the viewpoint of different user groups such as citizens, tourists and companies. But can these one-sided frameworks capture the different dimensions of the much more complex e-governance phenomenon? The lack of debate of this kind shows that e-governance readiness on local level is an exploited terrain. Just recently, two studies have tackled the issue of determinants of cities' readiness for e-government. The first one by Van Der Meer and Van Winden (2003) proposed that the analysis of the way European urban policy-makers guide their city into the information age should be based on three key manifestations of ICT adoption - content, infrastructure and access - whilst Zimmermann's work (2005) suggested that the implementation of e-government should be guided by a framework based on a future oriented "strategic approach". So the issue of the dimensions in our opinion is fundamental in the discussions on the progress of city e-governance, both in scientific and political context.

This however requires a methodical reasoning. Clearly tools and methods for measuring e-readiness of cities can vary depending on the definitions and assessments tools are diverse depending on their goals, strategies and results. It should be underlined however, that an e-readiness assessment, when properly applied in a larger framework of evaluation is a first step toward converting good intentions into planned actions that bring real changes to the urban community. Therefore, an e-readiness assessment framework has to be cohesive and strategic – it should guide development efforts and gauge progress, determining the current situation, in order to plan for the future and advocate specific changes. Moreover, e-readiness should also be considered a vital tool for judging the impacts of ICT on the urban development. This is not an easy job as there are many dimensions and factors associated with what it means to achieve a level of preparedness in the modern interconnected city.

As recent debates on cities in the digital era centre on the notion of building sustainable cities through strategic and integrated development, it gradually becomes clear that e-governance can not only measure the level of readiness of the city administrations to deploy ICT in delivering quality public services aiming broader goals of urban sustainability but can also reflect the government's own ability and capacity to use ICT and the extent to which it equips its people to do the same for policy innovation and building the inclusive community. To do so, however "e-readiness" must integrate e-governance approaches and tools with those of the "e-government" and "e-democracy" (Global e-Policy e-Government Institute, 2003), so as to reflect the ability of the overall society to benefit from ICT cohesively and strategically (Paskaleva-Shapira, 2007). Figure 3 represents our vision of understanding readiness in city e-governance.

In this light, we propose a city e-governance assessment approach that can measure what we are looking for—an "e-governance ready city"—and we select a set of key dimensions and assessment categories that fit best to our conceptual model. It

Figure 3. Model for city e-governance readiness (Source: Paskaleva-Shapira, 2007. "© Copyright 2007 IEEE – All rights reserved")

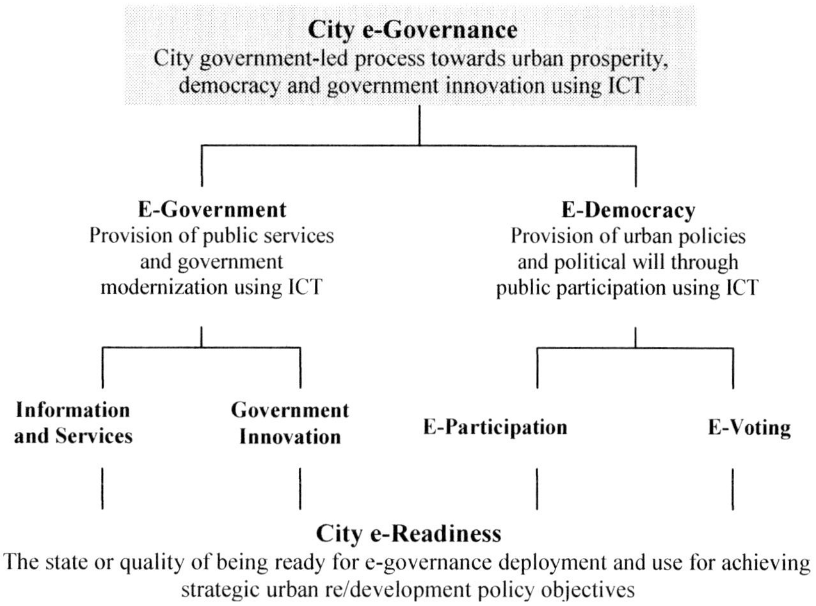

is important to underline again that our approach reinforces two key premises: One, suggesting that ICT deployment requires a general city- and actor-wider integrated urban development and regulatory environment in which the stakeholder concerns are included in the decision-making process; and two, that the level of usage and impact of ICT on the three stakeholder groups (individuals, businesses, and governments) is linked to their level of preparedness (or capability) to participate in the development, use and benefit from ICT (stakeholder empowerment).

Here is a description of our assessment approach. We distinguish *five key dimensions* of *readiness* for city e-governance and their main categories: 1) the *e-governance integrated framework dimension* focusing on the strategic vision, concept and definition, legislative framework, learning and diffusion of "best practices", stakeholder participation, integration, implementation, monitoring, evaluation, review, and innovation, 2) the *e-service dimension* which includes all types of e-services that meet the needs and requirements of citizens and businesses making information available and providing interactive public services on-line accessible for all using multi-platform access to create connections and interaction between citizens, enterprises and administrations and the IT systems that supports their delivery based on broadband connection, interoperability frameworks, open standards, and secure and reliable information infrastructure; 3) the *public management dimension,* which includes developing instruments of data management and knowledge management that incorporate "good governance" practices in the operations of the local government, back office centralization, front office decentralization, back-front office integration, human development, networking, and so forth; 4) the *citizens' participation dimension*, focusing on the continuous interaction between government and the citizens in the making of urban governing and accounting for key attributes such as users, tools, services, functions, usage, inclusion, and empowerment; and 5) *Policy innovation* as the fifth key dimension, dealing with the continuous review and enhancement of policies that are directly relevant to e-governance (e-services, government modernization, e-participation), urban integration policies (social cohesion, inclusive society, curb of digital divide[4], stakeholder collaboration, participation in decision making, livable community), the competitive city (sustainable economy, society and environment) and other relevant regional, national, European Union and international policies.

From a policy-making point of view, it seems important to understand that the drive for building the e-ready city should result in the consideration of all of these dimensions and categories in a coherent, achievable framework and strategy which is tailored to meet the needs of a particular urban community. This means that positive sustainable results concerning e-governance at the local level can be obtained through a synergic assessment of all five categories accounting for the specific context, priorities and strategies. In the next section, we demonstrate how they interact in some European cities through a selected set of nine qualitative indicators[5].

CITY E-GOVERNANCE EUROPE

This section consists of three parts: the first describes the study methodology, the second focuses on the state of play and the third offers propositions about the future trends and opportunities to city e-governance.

Study Methodology

According to the adopted approach of assessing readiness for city e-governance, below we attempt to present the recent progress of twelve IntelCities partner cities: Athens (Greece), Reykjavik (Iceland), Venice (Italy), Linz (Austria), Karlsruhe (Germany), Barcelona (Spain), Siena (Italy), Marseille (France), Nice (France), Manchester (Unite Kingdom) Florence (Italy) and Camden (London, United Kingdom). For our purpose, this is a good sample of cities. They are located in different countries, which could reveal some general trends and differences of the urban context. They also differ in size, economic structure and overall performance in e-governance. We focused mainly on large and mid-size European cities as previous research and studies on e-governance related issues confirm the positive relationship between the size of cities and the level of e-governance policies and initiatives promoted in those cities (Van Der Meer & Van Der Winden, 2003). And as previous rankings have shown, each of the cities has its particular focus in e-governance policy. For example in the global ranking of digital governance (Global e-Policy e-Government Institute, 2003) that looked at city portals from the point of e-democracy, Reykjavik scored 31, Athens 51, and London 55. At the same time, in the European evaluation of cities of the e-City Award, which assesses readiness based on e-services and their users, Barcelona ranked 10, Florence 21, Linz 31, London, 57, Marseille 58, Nice 63, Manchester 70, Venice 74 and Athens 118. Though evaluations were rooted on city portals, the differences and the inconsistencies of the results from the two rankings are more than apparent. In our case, based on a comprehensive study approach, the feedback offered by the cities described a complex process of technology development and use at the local level, with ICT development and e-services representing the core of the e-governance strategy of the local administrations.

The present analysis is based on the results of an electronic survey applied in 2005. Multiple choice and closed and open-ended questions were used to probe a wide range of information and insights on the cities' practice and policies in urban e-governance. A comprehensive set of indicators was applied to examine issues such as general framework conditions, enables and drivers, e-services, technology, organizations, citizens' participation and integration with national and regional processes and policies that were further linked to future technologies, government modernization, new business models, impacts, priorities, investment strategies, decision- and policy-making processes, and user demands. The survey was directed to the ICT-responsible officials in the local administrations that were previously contacted and agreed with to participate in the study. But as the scope of the survey was wide and going beyond the domain of the IT departments, representatives from other units were asked to participate as well, for example from the urban planning department and the Mayor's office. Thus the results that were yielded were considered representative of the broader city management perspective on e-governance.

Furthermore, as e-governance is an articulate and rich concept, which cannot be described only by the answers of government officials, research was based also on:

- Review of best practices of city e-governance in Europe (with support of evidence from the United States, Canada, Australia, New Zealand and elsewhere) (Thorleifsdottir et al., 2004).
- Review of city policies (Di Maria, Vergani & Paskaleva-Shapira, 2005).
- Secondary reports and documentation

The next section looks at what the study cities have achieved so far and analyzes the level implementation of e-governance in their urban affairs.

State of Play

We chose to present nine assessment categories for the purpose of the study. The latter are considered representative of the main research premises in assessing readiness for city e-governance noted in the previous section.

Definition of concept and framework: In our city e-governance readiness model, the context and the definition of e-governance have a special importance. Current practice shows that information provision and e-services are the main focus of city e-governance in Europe and the level of progress in defining and deploying a cohesive concept and framework is different between cities. Amongst the study cases, the first, most advanced group, included Reykjavik (Iceland) Camden (United Kingdom), Linz (Austria), Barcelona (Spain), Siena (Italy), and Venice (Italy). These cities have already developed a relatively comprehensive and consistent approach to e-governance based on leading national or international programs and initiatives and they are heavily investing in ICT. Open source and standards are commonly used in the local administrations for the provision of a wide range of generally sophisticated on-line services to citizens and businesses, often aiming broader public benefits. Interactive service applications are common and citizens are frequently encouraged to participate in local bottom-up decision-making processes. State-of-the-art data and knowledge management systems are used in the back-offices and innovation appears a driving factor in the process. The second, less advanced group of cities – such as Athens, Nice, Marseille and Manchester – came out moderately ready for the e-governance, offering less complex e-solutions and including a modest level of participation of their users. The last and least progressed type of cities, as Karlsruhe in Germany for example, are still at the onset of strategizing and planning for e-governance which is evolving primarily around information provision activities. Besides differences in the cultural and political approaches, urban economics is also an important factor in the level of progress achieved so far – while urban regeneration is a driver in e-Manchester, tourism is key to e-Venice and in Reykjavik – "my e-community" motivates progress and innovation in the city e-governance. In general, the case of Reykjavik is exemplar as a model of an "e-ready" city, as it could be expected for geographical and territorial reasons. The city explicitly declares to look at e-governance as the readiness of its institutions and inhabitants for using ICT in governmental processes and services. Reykjavik is considered to have full citizens' readiness as computer literacy. The legislation of the Icelandic Government represents the legal instrument to make of Reykjavik the most e-ready city. It places emphasis on eliminating legal hindrances to electronic commerce, while maintaining strong consumer protection as well as the protection of individuals with regard to the processing of personal data.

Online Services: Provision of e-services is in the centre of city e-governance in Europe today (Thorleifsdottir et al., 2004). Developing on-line applications and services by request is a main priority, followed by e-consultation. The more advanced cities tend to use more sophisticated services for content management and security (i.e. GIS, payment system or CRM). These have also made substantial investments in creating multiple points of access, based on ICT, most often motivated by the need to improve public awareness of the network technologies and build a closer relationship between government and citizens by reducing physical distances and barriers. Through multimedia or widely diffused technology solutions (mobile phones, TV) these cities typically seek to foster the use of ICT among the citizens and increase the use of the on-line public services. Yet, learning and training programs and multiple channels are of a lesser priority and more cohesive, integrated approaches to technology platforms are generally rare. Moreover, building citizen's capacity appears of no significant relevance to improving the quality of online services and their use.

E-Participation: The level of readiness of cities in e-participation was assessed in regard to three main areas — citizens' access to opportunities, ICT and capacity building, and strategic development priorities. The study revealed that e-governance by and large provides a limited and unequal access of citizens to the social and economic opportunities that are available in the urban communities. Only one forth of the cities offer such opportunities online, yet only to half of the local population. Whilst e-mail usage and access to the Internet is well above ninety per cent, majority of cities are yet to make a real progress in this area. At the same time, when asked about the importance of the issue, all cities demonstrate a strong interest in supporting the wider involvement of citizens and users as a relevant and necessary step to enriching and extending the quality and objectives of e-governance in their communities. Some are already developing the infrastructure necessary for online offering through interactive solutions, others are still to up-grade theirs. All, however, insist on the need to improve government's internal processes before moving toward multiple channels for connecting with the users that will increase access and use of urban e-governance.

It was also revealed that existing ICT systems and capacity building programmes primarily focus on web content management and less on urban development and management issues. Tools such as e-forums, e-discussions and e-boards for suggestions and comments from the citizens are generally widely used by the city administrations to promote public involvement in the urban affairs. Yet, only half of the cities think that they have made a real progress in this area. Other e-participation tools such as online polls and e-surveys, e-voting and e-referendum in spite of everything remain of little use whilst more deliberative platforms such as institutions' or citizens' e-panel or local e-parliament are almost not present. Similarly, citizens' capacity building e-tools that produce user-generated content still remain broadly unpopular.

Finally, with regard to the future priorities of e-participation, these are focusing primarily on consultations on city development programs, development of tools that promote transparency (information access) and solicitation of peoples' opinion and suggestions on handling the urban affairs. Online polling and voting is more of a long-term objective and enhancing social cohesion and people's interest in their place of living is a least thought about option.

Government transformation: Increasing the efficiency by reducing costs and time is a priority concern of most cities. However, issues such as streamlining internal processes and improving information flow and delivery of services evoke less motivation. Least acknowledged remain goals such as enhancing the quality and effectiveness of decision-making and improving the transparency of the public sector in its workings. Reykjavik again is a noteworthy example of a good progress. ICT is widely used in all government actions, including education, childcare, social services, culture, finance, planning and building, utilities and other technical matters, environmental issues, public transport, and so forth. Several of the ICT systems are common for all institutions, offices and departments, e.g. ERP and HRM systems, whilst others serve a group of institutions or a single one, according to the scope of their activities. Over ninety five per cent of the businesses in the city use ICT systems and tax and custom declarations are mostly submitted by ICT. Back-office functions (document management, case management, etc.) are ninety five per cent digitalized. For citizens an e-mail response is equivalent to a letter response and in many cases applications and service requests are handled electronically too (Thorleifsdottir, et al., 2004).

Driving actors: ICT providers appear central to the delivery of city e-governance in Europe, hence the private sector is often in the front line of defining the e-city platforms, tools and activities. At the same time, city administrations widely recognize that key to the success of e-governance should be the driving role of the city departments and their political systems. Indeed, in our more advanced cases, the role of the Mayors and the City Councils has proven pivotal to their success, yet there is much more to be done among the many others. As far as the future is concerned, investment priorities more or less reflect the previously mentioned trends, demonstrating a generally moderate level of interest in back-office reorganization, urban technology networks and even less in human development, knowledge networks and training.

Urban impacts: Social integration and inclusion and curbing the digital divide are among the best-recognized impacts of e-governance on sustainable urban development. Increasing the efficiency of the relationships and processes between the citizens and government are rated in the second place along with the need to improve the functions of the local e-administration. The increase of public participation in the decision-making (influence/contribution to community well-being) is a concern of only half of the cities. On the far end remains the appreciation of other urban benefits such as achieving livable communities, higher transparency of public administrations, streamlining back-office systems and processes, government monitoring and public feedback, and socio-economic sustainability.

Impediments to implementation: The main obstacles to city e-governance are the lack of financial resources and adequate human skills and competencies, followed by the lack of organizational flexibility due to legal restrictions, low political support, technology interoperability, limited access and lack of technological infrastructures. Legislation ranks at the bottom of the list. But the first and most fundament issue is the lack of strong and strategic vision of e-governance with regard to the overall welfare of the city and its citizens.

Vertical integration: Despite the self-evident need for local e-governance to coordinate with other levels of governance, few cities appear to have achieved a sufficient level of integration with regional and national e-government systems. One third of them claim a moderate success whilst another third reports an insignificant advance. The rest, to their disadvantage, have in effect failed to link with other levels of digital government, both regionally and on the national level.

Propositions for E-Readiness

Based on these results, a number of useful propositions can be made for the state of play and future progress of city e-governance in Europe, and namely:

Proposition 1: *An integrated and systematic approach to city e-governance is still missing. Implementation is single-sided, focusing extensively on service provision. E-governance, as a participatory and transformational process, structure and organization, is not an explicit goal of the European cities. And it is yet to be used as a competitive tool in the urban affairs.*

Proposition 2: *The level of citizens' inclusion in city e-governance is relatively moderate. Providing access is a priority strategy, yet half of the urban population does not use the potentials and benefits of e-governance, hence remains marginalized in the larger urban society.*

Proposition 3: *The broad potentials of ICT applications remain insufficiently used by urban administrations. Whilst on-line forums have widely taken off, other e-participation tools and applications are still in their infancy with progress in collaborative knowledge management platforms remaining rather modest; hence, a direct and deliberative participation in the urban decision making and planning is basically still missing.*

Proposition 4: *Future investment priorities of city e-governance mirror today's focal points. Though access is given a more weight, e-consultation remains the single participatory mode whilst deliberative applications remain largely unused. Government-led active participation is practically a wish, whilst a citizens-led participation process is yet to be discovered.*

Proposition 5: *The broader and complex urban scope of the city e-governance impacts is generally unknown. Whilst the benefits for social integration, inclusion and digital divide are generally well recognized and the participation of citizens in decision-making is somewhat valued, the potentials of city e-governance for urban re/development and long-term urban competitiveness and sustainability remain largely unappreciated.*

Proposition 6: *The full benefits of city e-governance for government innovation and modernization are yet to be discovered. Whilst the effects on improving the effectiveness of urban government are well known, the potential impacts on back-office modernization, community knowledge networks, strategic urban development and democratic governing remain much undervalued.*

Proposition 7: *Some key city e-governance actors remain still marginalized. ICT companies are mostly driving the implementation of the process. Urban administrations are the main promoters but technical expertise influences decisions the most. Political back up is insufficient, despite proving highly beneficial in the "good case" examples. And only rarely citizens' entities are involved and/or play an important role in the e-governance decision-making.*

Proposition 8: *Existing investment priorities do not trigger the emerging needs of e-governance strategic development. Back-office modernization, technology and networking initiatives will likely utilize most of the expected funding whilst building human capacity remains a low priority. The development of community knowledge platforms is yet to rise to the interest of urban administrations.*

Proposition 9: *Current efforts to overcome the obstacles to city e-governance do not match existing strategies for investments. Despite recognizing the need for more human development, the latter is not given an adequate weight in the investment strategies. Interoperability is a small concern for* *the technology, despite existing evidence of limitations. The digital divide is of no greater importance too, though half of the urban population remains digitally marginalized, hence not sharing the wide spectrum of benefits.*

CONCLUSION: SEIZING THE OPPORTUNITY OF LOCAL READINESS FOR BOOSTING E-GOVERNANCE

This study has shown that in the New Century the mission of e-governance in Europe expands and the expectations of society are continuously rising. Especially at the local level, where policies truly matter, along with the quest for better services to citizens, other aspirations of local prosperity and harmony (the *sustainability* paradigm) are making the agenda too. Such as, among others achieving a more effective government, enhanced local democracy, inclusive decision-making and participatory policy processes. But embracing these in real life practice imposes a great many challenges not only to government but to the overall society as well.

Cities indeed can be important drivers of e-governance. In the process, the leadership role of the local government is undisputed as regard to setting the right framework, defining and engaging the stakeholders, modernizing itself, and innovating policy that accounts for the broader urban impacts, the potential obstacles and future challenges on the road to implementation and integration. From a tool to deliver services, e-governance becomes a yard stick of the capacity and ability of government to reform and improve to better serve its citizens and community not only today but strategically as well. This means that e-governance in fact can become a competitive tool of urban governing. So the issues of mission and scale here impose themselves dramatically.

There are many factors that promote cities to be ready for e-governance. It is important however that the assessment approaches are integrated and strategically developed focusing on the ongoing changes, future plans, policy priorities and investment opportunities that are linked to strategic development trends, governance challenges, institutional modernization, and policy innovation so as to reflect the specific cohesive nature of e-governance and account for the benefits of evaluation at the local urban level.

Our study has demonstrated that measuring readiness for e-governance offers a way to understanding of the preparedness of the municipalities, together with individuals and businesses toward integrated urban development for building the sustainable city in competitive way. An e-readiness assessment methodology can be used not just as an information-gathering mechanism for governments as they plan their strategies for ICT integration in urban development but it can also help them focus their efforts from within, and identify areas where external support or aid is required. Nevertheless they are useful tools for key policy decision makers charting the city's strategic direction in order to enhance overall urban competitiveness. Our proposed e-readiness approach is a summary measure of the city's ability to participate in and benefit from e-governance developments. In particular, urban governments and policy makers can exploit those results to model the evaluation of their performance and the policies supporting and promoting ICT in their economy and society.

Currently, urban governments in Europe are investing heavily both politically and financially in e-governance as a route to economic growth and inclusive communities. Yet, it is evident from this research that progress is overall relatively slow and is not delivering the efficiency or the impacts promised. This depends on a variety of factors but most importantly is the lack of comprehensive and strategic vision of the role and workings of city e-governance in relation to the overall urban development and policies. Nevertheless, one of the key conclusions is that urban policy makers can have a substantial influence on the shaping of the local e-governance if it is defined in a way that best fits the local conditions and the goals of urban sustainability and societal prosperity. Moreover, they can help define the strategies and engage with the stakeholders to pursue the urban strategic objectives. So what is mostly required is a public sector leadership that creates the enabling environment for increased public and private sector participation in e-governance interactions. But to enable participation, increase the legitimacy and to implement e-governance, the right strategies have to be developed first. Yet, depending on the "maturity" of local e-governance, these can be involved on a different level and scale.

In light of this new understanding of the mission and scope of e-governance, we proposed a five-dimensional approach to measuring the readiness of cities that includes assessment of the e-governance framework, diversity and quality of the e-service, modernization of public management, citizens' participation in decision-making and a continuous policy innovation. As we have shown, there are strong indications that these five main dimensions of city e-governance readiness are mutually reinforcing. Taking them in relation can have broad-based beneficial impacts for a city. A question that comes to mind however is how local is the readiness for city e-governance. Clearly, it's a process not solely fuelled by local factors, as our integrated model reveals, but the latter indeed matters a great deal. Because, after all city e-governance is a subject of policy option of urban making where continuously increasing and strengthening the public value should be a guiding benchmark of government success. But to be really effective, policies promoting e-governance must be based on acceptance and promotion of the guiding principles of "good governance" adjusted to the local specifics and in view of promoting urban innovation, competitiveness, and sustainability.

So despite the sufficient progress made, city e-governance is still to become a means of engaging citizens directly in the decision-making process. The discourse of integrated urban development for sustainability also requires a robust and enabling role of government. In conceptualizing e-governance as a facilitator of the sustainable city via ICT, governments need to play out stronger the significance of the governance approach to urban development and assessment. In this article we argued that it is only by factoring in such complexities that those governments can truly understand e-governance in the networked urban society and have proposed the adoption of e-readiness evaluation to provide for the implementation of the integrated city e-governance model.

But we also found substantial differences in the policy approaches of the European cities to e-governance. Some are providing variety of interactive services based on citizens' participation, others offer less complex solutions and limited stakeholder involvement, whilst third are just on the onset of developing e-governance approaches and practices. Unsurprisingly however, whilst the more advanced cases are somewhat aware of the potentials and the benefits of e-governance, the less progressive ones remain generally 'ignorant' about the issue.

Finally, by drawing the attention on assessing readiness for city e-governance and sharing our approaches and experience in this field, we have tried to provide a baseline and a starting point to policy-makers and researchers who want to use e-readiness assessment to plan for the integration of technologies in urban making and governing, and to organizations that are considering new assessments. We also hope that the study can push governments and society at large to work and improve their efforts in increasing the quality of their city situation and enhancing their policy making. This, however, calls for a whole new mind of handling by the urban decision-makers, administrators and politicians – to move from the sporadic and uncoordinated actions in e-governance to ICT integration, effective management, organizational and policy innovation and change. This radical shift should be driven by all the stakeholders in collaboration and strategically, towards building the sustainable and competitive city. The benefits that accrue to the wider urban community justify this.

ACKNOWLEDGMENT

This research was partially funded by the European Commission, DG/RTD Information Society Technology, Six Framework Programme, IntelCities Integrated Project (IST-2002-37373).

REFERENCES

Barzelay, M. (Ed.). (2001). *The new public management: Improving research and policy dialogue*. Berkeley: University of California Press.

Blanke, J., & Lopez-Clarosa, A. (2004). *The Lisbon review 2004: An assessment of policies and reforms in Europe*. Geneva, Switzerland: World Economic Forum. Retrieved April 24, 2008, from http://www.weforum.org/pdf/Gcr/LisbonReview/Lisbon_Review_2004.pdf

Castells, M., & Hall, P. (Eds.). (1994). *Technopolies of the world*. London: Routledge.

Cooper, I., Hamilton, A., & Bentivegna, V. (2005). Sustainable urban development: Networked communities, virtual organizations and the production of knowledge. In S. Curwell, M. Deakin and M. Symes (Eds.), *Sustainable urban development: The framework, protocols and environmental assessment methods* (pp. 211-231). Oxon, PA: Routledge.

Di Maria, E., Vergani, S., & Paskaleva-Shapira, K. (2005). *E-Governance practices, strategies and polices of European cities: State-of-the-art* ('IntelCities' Project Report D11.1.2). Retrieved from 'IntelCities' Project official web site: http://www.intelcitiesproject.com

European Commission. (2002). *Vision and roadmaps for sustainable development in a networked knowledge society* (Report from the Information Society Directorate-General on new methods of work and electronic commerce). Retrieved April 24, 2008, from ftp://ftp.cordis.europa.eu/pub/ist/docs/ka2/visionsandroadmapsfinal20020131.pdf

European Commission. (2003). *European Governance: A White Article*. Retrieved June 10, 2007, from http://europa.eu.int/eur-lex/en/com/cnc/2001/com2001_0428en01.pdf

European Commission. (2004). *4th European Conference on eGovernment, ECEG Dublin, Ireland, 17-18 June*. Retrieved June 10, 2007, from http://www.academic-conferences.org/eceg2004/eceg2004-home.htm

European Commission. (2005). *E-Government Communication*. Retrieved April 24, 2008, from http://europa.eu.int/information_society/eeurope/2005/

European Commission. (2007). *Fourth Ministerial eGovernment Conference: Reaping the benefits of e-government, 20-21 September 2007 in Lisbon*. Retrieved April 24, 2008, from http://ec.europa.eu/idabc/en/document/7196

Global e-Policy eGovernment Institute. (2003). *Digital governance in municipalities worldwide: An assessment of municipal web sites throughout the world*. Retrieved April 10, 2008, from http://unpan1.un.org/intradoc/groups/public/documents/aspa/unpan012905.pdf

Goodin, R. (Ed.) (1996). *The theory of institutional design*. Cambridge: Cambridge University Press.

Hammer, M., & Champy, J. (1993). *Reengineering the corporation: A manifesto for business revolution*. New York: Harper Business.

Harding, A. (1998). Regime formation in Manchester and Edinburgh. In G. Stoker (Ed.), *The new politics of British local governance*. London: Macmillan.

Information Technologies Group. (2000). *Readiness for the networked world: A guide for developing countries* (Online Guide on Assessing Readiness). Bethesda, MD: Harvard University, Centre for International Development.

Jessop, B. (1997). Capitalism and its future: Remarks on regulation, government and governance. *Review of International Political Economy, 4*(3), 561-581.

Kolsaker, A. (2006). Reconceptualising e-government as a tool of governance: The UK case. *International Journal of Electronic Government, 3*(4), 347-355.

Kolsaker, A. (2007). Understanding e-government (G2C) in the knowledge society. *International Journal of Information Technology and Management, 6*(2-4), 138-147.

Le Gales, P. (1998). Regulation and governance in European cities. *International Journal of Urban and Regional Research, 22*(3), 482-506.

McNeil, R. S., Tolbert, C. J., Mossberger, K., & Dotterweich, L. J. (2003). Innovating in digital government in the American states. *Social Science Quarterly, 84*(1), 52-70.

Millard, J., & Iversen, J. (2004). *Reorganization of government back offices for better electronic public services – European good practices*. Final report to the European Commission, January.

Mistri, M. (1999). Industrial districts and local governance in the Italian experience. *Human Systems Management, 18*(2), 131-139.

Moon, M. J. (2002). The evolution of e-government among municipalities: Rhetoric or reality. *Public Administration Review, 62*(4), 424-433.

Moulaert, F., & Delladetsima, P. (2002). *Globalisation and integrated area development in European cities*. Oxford: Oxford University Press.

OECD. (2003a). *Checklist for e-government leaders* (OCDE Policy Brief on September 2003). Paris: OECD Observer. Retrieved June 10, 2007, from http://www.oecd.org/dataoecd/62/58/11923037.pdf

OECD. (2003b). *Engaging citizens online for better policy-making* (OCDE Policy Brief on March, 2003). Paris: OECD Observer. Retrieved June 10, 2007, from http://www.oecd.org/dataoecd/62/23/2501856.pdf

OECD. (2003c). *The E-Government imperative: Main findings* (OCDE Policy Brief on March, 2003). Paris: OECD Observer. Retrieved June 11, 2007, from http://www.oecd.org/dataoecd/60/60/2502539.pdf

Office of the e-Envoy. (2002). UK online Annual Report 2002. Retrieved April 24, 2008, from http://archive.cabinetoffice.gov.uk/e-envoy/reports-annrep-2002/$file/04-01.htm

Paskaleva-Shapira, K. (2005). City E-Governance as an innovative urban public policy framework. In M. Böhlen, J. Gamper, W. Polasek and M. Wimmer (Eds.), *Proceedings of the TED Conference on e-Government: Electronic Democracy: The Challenges Ahead*. IFIP, 3-11.

Paskaleva-Shapira, (2007). E-City Europe: Status, propositions and opportunities. *Proceedings of the 3rd IET International Conference on Intelligent Environments, IE 07*, IEEE, 510-516.

Paskaleva-Shapira, K. (2008). Urban sustainability and governance: Challenges of the knowledge society. In Vreeker, R., Deakin, M. & Curwell, S. (Eds.). *Sustainable Urban Development*, Routledge, London (Forthcoming).

Pierre, J. (1999). Models of urban governance: The institutional dimensions of urban politics. *Urban Affairs Review, 34*(3), 372-96.

Rhodes, R. (1996). The new governance: Governing without government. *Political Studies, 44*(4), 652-667.

Riley, T. B. (2007). Strategies for the effective implementation of E-Government projects. *Journal of Business and Public Policy, 1*(1), 1-11.

Rutgers-SKKU. (2005). *E-Governance Performance Report.* Retrieved April 23, 2008, from http://andromeda.rutgers.edu/~egovinst/Website/press2005.htm

Rydin, Y., & Pennington, M. (2000). Public participation and local environmental planning: The collective action problem and the potential of social capital. *Local Environment, 5*(2), 153-169.

Sannarnes, M. K., Henriksen, H. Z., & Andersen, K.V. (2006). The E-Government melting pot: Lacking new public management and innovation flavor? In M.A. Wimer, H.J. Scholl, A. Gröndlund, and K.V. Andersend (Eds.), *Proceedings of Electronic Government: 5th International Conference, EGOV 2006, Krakow, Poland, September 4-8, 2006* (pp.25-36). Heidelberg: Springer Berlin.

Snellen, I. TH. M., & Van Der Donk, W. B. H. J. (Eds.). (1998). *Public administration in an information age, a handbook.* Amsterdam: IOS Press.

Stoker, G. (1998). Governance as a theory: Five propositions. *International Social Science Journal, 50*(155), 17-28.

Stoker, G. (2000). Urban political science and the challenge of urban governance. In J. Pierre (Ed.), *Debating governance: Authority, steering and democracy.* Oxford: Oxford University Press.

Tat-Kei Ho, A. (2002). Reinventing local governments and the E-Government initiative. *Public Administration Review, 62*(4), 410-420.

Technology CEO Council. (2002). The CSPP readiness guide: For living in the networked world. Retrieved April 24, 2008, from http://www.techceocouncil.org/documents/NW_Readiness_Guide.pdf

Thorleifsdottir, A., Paskaleva-Shapira, K., Forseback, L., Tzovaras, D., Christodoulou, E., & Schnepf, D. (2004). *Best practices in e-governance.* ('IntelCities' Project Report D15.2.2). Retrieved from 'IntelCities' Project official web site: http://www.intelcitiesproject.com

Timmers, P. (2004). *European Commission perspectives on E-Government* [PowerPoint slides]. Presentation at IntelCities project kickoff meeting, 12 March, Brussels. Retrieved from 'IntelCities' Project official web site: http://www.intelcitiesproject.com

Traunmüller, R. (Ed.). (2004). *Electronic government: Third International Conference, EGOV 2004, Zaragoza, Spain, August 30-September 3, 2004, Proceedings.* Linz: Sprinter.

Van Den Berg, L., Van Der Meer, I., & Pol, P. (2004). *Social challenges and organizing capacities in cities: Experiences in eight European cities.* Aldershot: Ashgate Publishing Ltd.

Van Den Berg, L., & Van Winden, W. (2002). *Information and communication technology as potential catalysis for sustainable urban development: Experiences in Eindhoven, Helsinki, Manchester, Marseilles and The Hage.* Aldershot: Ashgate Publishing Ltd.

Van Der Meer, L., & Van Winden, W. (2003). E-governance in cities: A comparison of urban ICT policies. *Regional Studies, 37*(4), 407-419.

Wilhelm, A. (2005). *Digital nation: Towards an inclusive information society.* MIT Press, 133-134.

The World Bank. (2007). *Definition of e-government.* Retrieved May 24, 2007, from http://go.worldbank.org/M1JHE0Z280

World Economic Forum. (2007). *Global competitiveness report 2007-2008*. Houndmills, Baingstoke, Hampshire: Macmillan Publishers Limited.

Zimmermann, W. (2005). 'eStrategy' for E-Government in cities: An introduction. *UMP-Asia Occasional* (Article No. 62). Retrieved April 24, 2008, from http://www.serd.ait.ac.th/ump/OP%20Dr.%20Willie%20ed%20vers%202005%20from%20GS.pdf

ENDNOTES

1. IntelCities Integrated Project: Intelligent Cities, European Commission, DG/RTD Information Society Technology, Six Framework Programme (IST-2002-37373), http://www.intelcitiesproject.com.
2. Strategic policy approach promoting ICT diffusion and use within and across cities as a fundamental requisite for economic and social prosperity in which the sustainable adoption and use of ICT is considered part of building the sustainable urban communities. In this spirit, the revitalization of urban settlements in European cities combines different dimensions calling for political mobilization based on public participation and social dynamics (Moulaert & Delladetsima, 2002).
3. Described in business literature by the originators of the concept Hammer & Champy (1993) as "the fundamental rethinking of and radical redesign of business processes to achieve dramatic improvements in critical, contemporary measures of performance, such as cost, quality, service and speed".
4. A term referring to the gap between those people with effective access to digital and information technology and those without access to it. It includes the imbalances in physical access to technology as well as the imbalances in resources and skills needed to effectively participate as a digital citizen (Wilhelm, 2004, p. 133-134).
5. A total of fifty indicators were used in the IntelCities study. The detailed survey and results of the analysis can be found in the Research Report "*E-Governance practices, strategies and polices of European cities: State-of-the art*" (Di Maria, Vergani & Paskaleva-Shapira, 2005). In this article, we present a selection of indicators that account for the most important factors that are impacting e-readiness in the context of integrated city e-governance.

This work was previously published in International Journal of Electronic Government Research, Vol. 4, Issue 4, edited by M. Khosrow-Pour, pp. 17-36, copyright 2008 by IGI Publishing (an imprint of IGI Global).

Chapter 16
Linking Local E-Government Development Stages to Collaboration Strategy

Hyun Joon Kim
Korea University, Republic of Korea

Jooho Lee
University of Idaho, USA

Soonhee Kim
Syracuse University, USA

ABSTRACT

The purpose of this study is to explore the connection between the stages of e-government development and collaboration demands in local government. Specifically, this study analyzes the demand for intergovernmental, interagency, and intersectoral collaborations during the three stages of local e-government development, including e-government initiation, application development, and integration. Based on an in-depth case study, this paper identifies specific collaboration types demanded during local e-government development in the Gangnam district government in Seoul, Korea. In each stage of e-government development, the local government encountered varying degrees and types of resource dependence upon internal and external organizational units. A particular type of collaboration became dominant in each stage as the relative importance of each collaboration type changed.

INTRODUCTION

All levels of government organizations have adopted electronic government (e-government) as a strategic tool for enhancing the quality of external services as well as streamlining internal operations (Ho, 2002; Holden *et al.*, 2003; Norris *et al.*, 2001; West, 2004). E-government development requires collaboration among government agencies to ensure interoperability, avoid duplication, ensure coherent action in a range of crucial areas such as security and privacy, and provide the framework and capacity for seamless services (Organization for Economic Co-Operation and Development [OECD], 2003). Allen, Juillet, Paquet, and Roy (2005) note that e-government must be built on a fluid, constantly adapting collaborative governance system that responds to several challenges in the public sector: 1) new opportunities to link agencies through online applications; 2) policy challenges demanding a growing level of coordination across all levels of government and sectors; and 3) an emphasis on performance requiring external alignment and internal integration and cooperation.

In order to develop e-government, customer-centric government agencies that traditionally focus on their own missions and narrowly defined publics must now communicate, share information, and cooperate to enhance services across government agencies and levels (McDaniel, 2003). E-government leaders in local governments particularly need to both identify potential barriers in central government legislative and regulatory frameworks, and make sure that the necessary collaboration strategies are in place to facilitate and promote e-government development (GSA, 2002; OECD, 2003).

Studies of local e-government development found that collaboration and partnership are essential to the implementation of local e-government (Center for Technology in Government [CTG], 2004; Improvement and Development Agency [IdeA] and Society of Information Technology Management [Socitm], 2002). These studies emphasize that collaboration is essential to focus on e-government services and to integrate the processes necessary to address the issues faced by citizens and customers of locally-delivered e-government services. While prior research studied specific cases and best practices of collaborations and partnerships, there is limited discussion about the connection between local e-government development stages and collaboration strategy.

The objective of this paper is to explore the relationship between the stages of e-government development and collaboration demands, and to propose a framework outlining the particular types of collaboration that are critical for achieving the goals of each e-government development stage. The paper analyzes how and why particular types of collaboration become important at different stages of e-government development in the context of local e-government. Based on an in-depth case study, this paper examines specific collaboration types demanded during local e-government development in South Korea. Specifically, this study analyzes the demand for intergovernmental, interagency, and intersectoral collaborations during the three stages of local e-government development, including e-government initiation, application development, and integration.

The local government selected for this study is the Gangnam district ("Gangnam-gu"), located in Seoul Metropolitan Government, South Korea. Gangnam-gu has been acknowledged for innovative local e-government services (Intelligence Community Forum, 2006). For example, the National Committee of E-Government Development in South Korea recognized the development of e-government in Gangnam-gu as the best e-government practice in the country for three consecutive years, starting in 2001.

This paper first reviews the current literature on e-government development stages and the types of e-government collaboration. The second section describes the research setting and research method. The following section presents the findings about the linkage between e-government development stages and three types of collaboration demands. Finally, implications and lessons of this study for effective local e-government development and managerial leadership are discussed.

THREE STAGES OF E-GOVERNMENT DEVELOPMENT IN LOCAL GOVERNMENT

E-government can be broadly defined as the electronic provision of government services through electronic means, especially e-government applications (e-applications) (Holden et al., 2003; Norris et al., 2001; West, 2004). E-applications are the web-based information systems that perform e-government transactions between government and citizens and businesses. They provide transaction services including information processing (e.g., online retrieval of parking ticket information or online tax filing) and monetary transactions (e.g., online parking fine payment or online vehicle registration renewal), as well as one-way information delivery (i.e., tourist information). Therefore, the end-users of e-applications are citizens and businesses, not bureaucrats.

Previous studies on e-government suggest that e-government grows through several developmental stages (Charih & Robert, 2004; Hiller & Belanger, 2001; Layne & Lee, 2001; Reddick, 2004; UN/ASPA, 2002). Existing e-government development stage frameworks are primarily focused on assessing government websites and suggesting a set of indicators to measure technical sophistication and functionalities (Anderson & Henriksen, 2006; Moon, 2002). These frameworks provide some benchmarks for e-government policy makers, but researchers have paid little attention to defining e-government development stages beyond technical functionality of e-government.

Anderson and Henriksen (2006)'s Public Sector Process Rebuilding (PPR) model is an approach to overcome the limitations of technology oriented e-government development frameworks. They propose a four stage maturity model focusing on the key organizational activities in each stage and the scope of stakeholders to be affected by each stage's development. Drawing on the PPR model, we conceptualize that e-government development into three stages: initiation, application development, and integration. Each stage delineates the major goals of e-government initiatives and the types of organizational entities to be involved.1 Even though the development of e-government does not always evolve stage by stage, three stages of e-application development can provide a useful framework to understand the general pattern of development processes among heterogeneous e-government applications.

The E-government Initiation Stage

The general goal of the initiation stage of e-government development is to create a vision for e-government services that complements to traditional modes of government service delivery to citizens and businesses, and to make those government services available online at local government websites. Specifically, this phase involves the identification of government services that are feasible to implement online and the procurement of technologies that enable the provision of those services.

As local governments explore potential e-government services during this early stage of e-government development, it is crucial for them to assess how existing law, regulations and policies influence the employment of e-government services. The failure to identify potential problems due to ignorance of current constraints can lead to incorrect e-government application development and wasted resources. During the initiation stage, local governments also tend to purchase off-the-shelf packages to implement immediate utilization without incurring procurement and maintenance costs.

The E-Government Application Development Stage

At the application development stage, local governments move beyond merely putting relatively simple and general government services online to developing e-applications capable of performing complicated and specialized transactions. Since the off-the-shelf applications typically adopted at the initiation stage do not fully satisfy the demands for unique functionalities of e-applications, local governments in the second stage focus on developing customized e-applications.

Specifically, at this stage, local governments adopt advanced e-government services that perform advanced monetary and information transactions. As these transactions transmit personal and financial data of end-users (i.e., citizens and businesses), local governments are often required to develop e-applications with more secure technologies that ensure safe transactions.

The E-Government Integration Stage

The goal of the e-government integration stage is to connect different e-applications to share complete, real-time and transparent information within a local government and across different levels of government. Throughout the initiation and application development stages, e-applications are often deployed and customized under the responsibility of different program units within a local government without involving peer units (including internal IT experts). These independently developed e-applications tend to create information silos across functional units within a local government as well as across different levels of government. Those "islands of e-applications" prohibit seamless flow of information from one application to the other. To resolve this problem, two types of integration efforts can be made at this stage. Horizontal integration involves connecting the various e-applications operated by different functional units within a local government. Vertical integration binds the e-applications developed by local governments to the e-applications used by higher levels of government.

COLLABORATION TYPES IN LOCAL E-GOVERNMENT DEVELOPMENT

The emphasis on performance and results-oriented reform has led researchers to emphasize the need for government agencies to collaborate and enable integration, sharing, and transfer of information and knowledge within agencies and in governmental networks (Fountain, 2001; Holzer & Callahan, 1998; Huxham & Vangen, 2000; Linden, 2002). Collaboration is generally conceptualized with special attention to the value that cannot be created by a single organization. Huxham focuses on the benefits or advantages of collaboration and defines it as "a positive form of working in association with others for some form of mutual benefit" (Huxham, 1996, 7). Similarly, Bardach views collaboration as "any joint activity by two or more agencies that is intended to increase public values by their working together rather than separately" (Bardach, 1998, 8). Based on that definition, we may identify a set of elements comprising collaboration: mutual relationships, common goals, exchange of resources and shared rewards and responsibilities (Mattessich *et al.*, 2001; Sagawa & Segal, 2000; Wood & Gray, 1991).

Scholars and practitioners identify several interorganizational collaborations that contribute to the establishment of successful e-government development and innovations (Craig & Schriar, 2001; CTG, 2004; IdeA & Socitm, 2002; Reddick & Frank, 2006). Three types of collaboration related to local e-government development analyzed in this paper are intergovernmental collaboration, interagency collaboration within a government, and intersectoral collaboration.

Intergovernmental Collaboration

Intergovernmental collaboration refers to a vertical agreement or intergovernmental alliance among different levels of government (i.e., federal, state, and local governments) (CTG, 2004). In recent years, the importance of intergovernmental collaboration has been increasingly recognized in public sector organizations related to e-government development (CTG, 2004; Fountain, 2001; GSA, 2002). The following types of support may be provided by intergovernmental collaboration: modifying existing rules and regulations or creating new ones to legalize electronic administrative procedures and service delivery mechanisms; setting a technology standard for e-government application; and providing financial assistance for purchasing and developing information systems for e-government transformation.

In order to establish customer-focused local e-government, e-government leaders pay attention to managing e-government systems within a common framework to ensure interoperability, develop a sustainable e-government funding program, maximize implementation efficiency and avoid duplication across different levels of government (IdeA & Socitm, 2002). Infrastructure needs and legal requirements should be assessed against the background of requirements for and desired results of planned e-government development (CTG, 2004; Fountain, 2001; GSA, 2002).

In reality, central government and local governments implementing e-applications struggle with structural and systematic issues, particularly a lack of standards and legal permissions to combine local information and services between agencies and levels of government (IdeA & Socitm, 2002). Related to the development of interoperable government systems, Landsbergen and Wolken (1998) state that it is necessary not only to eliminate legal and policy barriers, but also to achieve the correct balance between central directives and local needs. Furthermore, the lack of common infrastructure, privacy protection, and security concerns necessitates intergovernmental support, coordination and collaboration in local e-government development (IdeA & Socitm, 2002).[2]

Interagency Collaboration within a Government

E-government development also requires growing coordination and collaboration across functional units within a government. Interagency collaboration concerns information and knowledge sharing across functional units as well as data sharing across heterogeneous information systems within the government in order to foster citizen-focused e-government applications. Interagency collaboration within a government is also important for supporting government operations, integrating processes, facilitating management, streamlining workflow, and improving service quality, accountability, and efficiency (CTG, 2004).

With respect to interagency collaboration for e-government development, scholars and practitioners have paid attention to the relationship between program (or business) units and IT units within a government (Bugler & Bretschneider, 1993; Kraemer *et al.*, 1989). Whether IT units are centralized or decentralized has been identified as a crucial issue because IT governance structure shapes interagency collaboration (Ross *et al.*, 1998; Ward & Peppard, 2002). Several challenges related to interagency collaboration that influence the level of integration and efficiency in e-government innovation should be noted: managing culture change across government; creating new business arrangements and revamping technical infrastructure in the public sector; and developing common protocols for web use, security, data exchange and system design management (CTG 2004; IDeA and Socitm 2002).

Intersectoral Collaboration

Another important type of collaboration that has been emphasized in e-government literature is intersectoral collaboration (i.e., nonprofit, private, and government). A report from the National Association of State Chief Information Officers (NASCIO, 2005) emphasizes that a rapidly changing technological environment requires new thinking and innovative approaches to strengthen cooperation and collaboration between government and the private sector. Special attention has been paid to public-private collaboration due to the increased outsourcing of e-government projects, including back office applications, web applications, integration/networks, IT datacenters, and desktop support (Chen & Perry, 2003; CTG, 2004).

A collaboration study conducted by CTG (2004) found that public-private partnerships go beyond traditional contracting and outsourcing to include a more equal sharing of resources, risks and benefits associated with e-government projects. Chen and Perry (2003) note that trust and cooperation is important to the creation of partnerships. As a result, longer-term outsourcing contracts are increasingly developed.3 Meanwhile, some scholars emphasize a control-based approach that sees a need for short-term, not long-term, contracts and a need for a mix of in-house work and selective external outsourcing (Barrett & Greene, 2001).

METHODOLOGY

Research Setting

Gangnam-gu is one of 25 district governments located in Seoul Metropolitan Area, and it employs approximately 1,400 civil servants. Approximately 530,000 residents reside within the jurisdiction of the Gangnam-gu, and most of them are highly educated and occupy high-income brackets. According to a recent survey conducted by Seoul Metropolitan Government (Seoul city, 2005), most households in the Gangnam-gu area utilize computers (91.05%) and high-speed internet (95.09%) in their homes. Gangnam-gu is also a central business district where high-profile industries have their headquarters or branches. In particular, the Gangnam-gu embraces high-tech companies such as IT and Internet-related companies along the Gangnam-gu's "Teheran Valley," known as the Silicon Valley of Korea. Those lucrative community characteristics serve as a crucial source of support for Gangnam-gu's innovative e-government transformation.

In 1988 the National Assembly of Korea broke with the political tradition of centralized authority by passing the Self-Governance Act, which encouraged local governance and grassroots democracy. Elections for local legislative council seats began in 1991; elections for city mayors and provincial governors began in 1995. The advent of the Self-Governing Local Government era has played a critical role in the emergence of e-government initiated by local governments.

The history of e-government in Korea reveals that the central government has guided local governments as well as central government agencies in developing nation-wide e-government strategies. The presence of centralized e-government initiatives in Korea is indicated by a series of legislation, such as the Framework Act on Informatization Promotion (1995), the Master Plan for Informatization Promotion (1996), and Cyber Korea 21 (1999), that promote computerization and informatization in Korea (Special Committee for E-government, 2003). While the central government still exerts great influence on lower level governments as shown in E-government Vision 2006, the elected mayor has facilitated various forms of innovation efforts in local governments.

Under the current mayor's leadership, Gangnam-gu has implemented 71 e-government applications since 1995 as part of its innovative Smart Gangnam - Cyber City Project. Through e-government innovations, Gangnam-gu is leading local government reform efforts, making great strides to significantly enhance the public value of its democratic processes and government services. Its achievement has been also recognized globally. Gangnam-gu has been recognized as one of the top municipalities in the world in advancing e-government. For instance, the Intelligence Community Forum has ranked Gangnam-gu as one of the 2006 Top Seven Intelligent communities (Intelligence Community Forum, 2006). Seoul, the umbrella city where Gangnam-gu is located, has also been selected as one of the leading e-government municipalities (Holzer & Kim, 2005).

Research Method

The case study method is particularly suitable for "capturing the knowledge of practitioners and developing theories from it" (Benbasat, Goldstein, & Mead, 1987, p. 370). This paper uses an in-depth case study method as an instrument to explore and trace how and why particular types of collaboration become important at different stages of e-government development (Stake, 2000). The data for this study was collected from the e-government research project conducted by the Center for Information and Technology of Syracuse University and Korea University, with support from the Gangnam-gu government. We collected both qualitative and quantitative data for this case study. Data collected from two distinctive methods can provide different types of information. Patterns emerging from the in-depth analysis of interviews with Gangnam-gu employees and key e-government policy documents provide insights that advance our understanding of the association between varying e-government goals and corresponding collaboration types. The survey method is employed to complement the analysis of qualitative data. The analysis of the survey data is descriptive, because this study is not intended to test a set of theoretical propositions. It is rather aimed at exploring the potential theoretical implications. Therefore, the survey data analysis is used to provide supplementary information to support findings from the case study.

The first phase of the e-government research project was launched in Gangnam-gu in December 2003. We conducted 40 semi-structured interviews, including project leaders, sponsors, initiators, and executive champions as well as staff responsible for different aspects of the project such as technology infrastructure, marketing strategy, legal affairs and human resources. Table 1 shows the description of interviewees of Gangnam-gu.

The research team utilized an interview protocol containing questions related to e-government project initiation (history, scope, management) and the collaboration process (participants, negotiation, objectives, conflicts etc.) (see Appendix 1 for the interview questions). For this study, we analyzed the interview data pertaining to collaboration to examine how a local government managed intergovernmental, intersectoral and interagency collaborations according to the e-government development stage. For efficient and consistent coding, we used Atlas/ti software package for qualitative analysis.

Employee surveys were conducted in July 2004. The sample size was 492 employees from 15 departments. Our research team did pretested a survey instrument with the Social Welfare Department before distributing it to our sample. We received feedback from those who participated in this pretest and rectified some vague questions. Our research team implemented a survey at two departments: Computerized Information Department (CID) and the Parking Department. The Policy and Planning Department implemented the survey at the remaining 13 departments. As a result, the response rate was 58.13% (286/492). Table 2 shows the demographic characteristics of survey respondents.

FINDINGS

Intergovernmental Collaboration

The E-government Initiation Stage: This study found that Gangnam-gu encountered high-demands for intergovernmental collaboration due to the lack of shared vision and organizational culture for local e-government development, and the constraints of existing institutional arrangements for the delivery of e-applications. Since

Table 1. Description of interviewees

Demographic Variables	Characteristics	Number of Interviewees
Organizational Tenure	1 – 9 years	5
	10 – 19 years	17
	Over 20 years	18
Organizational Rank	Rank 2 (Vice Mayor)	1
	Rank 4 (Director)	6
	Rank 5 (Manager)	5
	Rank 6 (Team leader)	13
	Rank 7	9
	Rank 8	4
	Rank 9	2
Organizational Affiliation	Vice Mayor	1
	Bureau Director	6
	IT Department	8
	Parking Department	7
	General Affairs Department	3
	Policy Planning Department	4
	Land Registry Department	4
	Social Welfare Department	2
	Tax Department	3
	Culture and Public Relations Department	1
	Civil Affairs Department	1

Gangnam-gu was an early adopter of innovative e-applications, they often faced challenges such as institutional and legal approvals from upper level governments which were directly and indirectly engaged in local e-government services.

Many interviewees in Gangnam-gu indicated that Gangnam-gu and upper level governments, such as central government agencies and Seoul Metropolitan Government, did not have a shared vision for e-government development, vertical and horizontal integration, and privacy and security concerns at the stage of e-government initiation. Furthermore, they mentioned that Gangnam-gu and upper level governments both faced the challenge of understanding different organizational cultures in government agencies. For example, one of interviewees confessed:

Seoul metropolitan government thinks they are the higher organization than Gangnam district. So they think top-down instruction. When we initiate innovation, they interrupt us. …… Venture firms cannot make proposals to Seoul metropolitan government because the public officials in Seoul metropolitan government are not changed. …… For new programs, we need budget. Seoul metropolitan government doesn't approve new programs saying that we can do new programs offline. …… we created ideas and expanded the programs. At first, we had a lot of objections and obstacles. The central government asked why a district government tried to do new programs spending hundreds of millions won. …… For several cases, Seoul metropolitan government asked us to bring new programs if citizens want and accept them.

Table 2. Demographic characteristics of employee survey respondents

Demographic Variables	Characteristics	Survey Respondents
Organizational Tenure	1 – 9 years	58
	10 – 19 years	154
	Over 20 years	53
Organizational Rank	Rank 4 (Director)	1
	Rank 5 (Manager)	4
	Rank 6 (Team leader)	35
	Rank 7	68
	Rank 8	83
	Rank 9	55
	Rank 10	11
Department	IT	18
	Parking	84
	General Affairs	17
	Land Registry	16
	Tax	12
	Culture and Public Relations	9
	Civil Affairs	10
	Family Welfare	5
	Park and Green Zone	6
	Transportation Administration	7
	Health Sanitation	11
	Self-governing Administration	14
	Financial Administration	15
	Construction Management	18
	Environmental Cleaning	20

This study also found that at the stage of e-government initiation, there was no formal structure to support all jurisdictions in the collaborative effort to develop infrastructure, standards, and information integration among different levels of government. Moreover, this study found that limited support from central government agencies and duplicated projects, laws, and a lack of coordination with other divisions were significant barriers to e government development at the initiation stage. Poor understanding of the importance of intergovernmental partnership and collaboration for local e-government development caused one-way communication initiated by Gangnam-gu related to innovative e-government projects. The one-way communication was also a way to comply with current laws requiring the central government's approval for new e-government development initiated by local governments. The study results furthermore indicate that a hierarchical intergovernmental relationship causes conflicts between local government and central government agencies when there is a demand for collaboration during local e-government development.

Local government laws in South Korea also caused for Gangnam-gu to face high demands for collaboration with upper level governments while initiating innovative local e-applications. For example, when Gangnam-gu was developing the idea for online local tax reporting, the district faced a legal challenge. As the local tax law states that local business must submit local tax reports through regular mail, Gangnam-gu had to ask for the central government's support and assistance on changing the local tax law. However, the central government informed Gangnam-gu that the local tax law could not be changed just to suit Gangnam-gu's need. One of interviewees who worked for online taxation services said:

Yes, there is the process managed by Ministry of Government Administration and Home Affairs [MOGAHA]. Local governments need to obtain the approval from MOGAHA to develop a certain system. The purpose of the regulation is preventing the duplication of the work related to E-government and setting up the standard for local governments. Once the standard is established, it should be customized for the integration of DB and creation of sharing system of DB considering the characters of each district. Basic 21 tax services [that Gangnam was initiating] are crucial services for all district governments. So it was also desirable for MOGAHA that someone else took the responsibility for it. However, in the process of negotiating with MOGAHA, we experienced difficulties of getting the approval.

Table 3 shows the employee survey results on barriers to e-government initiation. Like the interview data, the results reveal that employees in Gangnam-gu perceived intergovernmental collaboration as the most difficult barrier for e-government development at the initiation stage. Specifically, nearly 41 percent of the survey respondents reported a lack of collaboration among different levels of government as a barrier to e-government development.

In summary, at the initiation stage of e-government development, the lack of mutual understanding and the constraints of existing institutional arrangements caused Gangnam-gu to face high demands for intergovernmental collaboration.

E-government Application Development and Integration Stages: Due to the accumulated ex-

Table 3. Barriers of e-government initiation

Survey Items	Mean (s.d.)	Strongly Disagree (%)	Disagree (%)	Neutral (%)	Agree (%)	Strongly Agree (%)
1. Lack of collaboration among departments within Gangnam-gu has been a barrier to e-government initiatives	3.16 (0.88)	11 (3.9)	42 (14.9)	135 (48)	77 (27.4)	16 (5.7)
2. Lack of support from Gangnam-gu Council (elected council members) has been a barrier to e-government initiatives	2.89 (0.83)	13 (4.7)	64 (23.1)	147 (53.1)	44 (15.9)	9 (3.2)
3. Lack of collaboration among different levels of government (national government, metropolitan government, and other local governments) has been a barrier to e-government initiatives	3.25 (0.91)	9 (3.2)	44 (15.7)	113 (40.4)	94 (33.6)	20 (7.1)
4. Issues regarding privacy have been barriers to e-government initiatives	3.04 (0.85)	15 (5.2)	40 (14.4)	150 (54.2)	62 (22.4)	10 (3.6)
5. Issues regarding security have been barriers to e-government initiatives	3.10 (0.82)	8 (2.9)	47 (16.8)	145 (51.8)	69 (24.6)	11 (3.9)

N=287

periences of intergovernmental interaction during the initiation stage, Gangnam-gu requested less intergovernmental collaboration at the application development stage. Furthermore, by this stage of development central government agencies had a better understanding of Gangnam-gu e-government projects; this helped build two-way communications. However, Gangnam-gu still had to negotiate with the central government regarding privacy protection and security concerns that were not addressed at the initiation stage. One interviewee indicates as follows:

At that time, if we had access to the resident registration network of the Ministry of Government Administration and Home Affairs or vehicle registration of the Ministry of Construction and Transportation, we could get personal information. But, the central government did not want that kind of information to be disclosed, so they prevented our access, because even hackers can go and get the information. So, they did not allow us to use their network. However, many local governments refuted that we can make a firewall to prevent such a thing. And there is no problem now.

Through continuous communication and persuasion initiated by Gangnam-gu, both the district and the central government developed a higher level of trust, support, and collaboration at the application development stage. This study also found that higher demand for intergovernmental collaboration continues to exist at the integration stage due to the need for resolving privacy and security concerns for data and information sharing across different levels of governments. As one manager said:

Legally and institutionally, we have security concerns and issues of protecting personal information. For example, we try to open as much information as we can to the public but the central government holds the regulation that it needs to be judged because of security matters.

Interagency Collaboration in Gangnam-Gu

The E-government Initiation Stage: We found that interagency collaboration was not in great demand at the initiation stage due to the lack of motivation for program departments to collaborate with other peer units within the local government. Once Gangnam-gu determined the types of government services to be put online, they allocated their resources to the program departments to provide e-government services. Given that e-government services were closely tied to particular program domains, the program departments were responsible for the deployment of e-applications at this phase. For instance, collaboration with peer units could have been a significant issue if the Parking Department had relied on peer units (in particular, the IT department) for developing and running parking applications. However, the Parking Department instead relied on an external IT vendor for the provision of online parking services at this stage. Since the Parking Department controlled computing resources (e.g., web servers), they independently employed the off-the-shelf parking applications in their department. The off-the-shelf parking applications involved simple technology with standardized data structures and modules. Therefore, they had little influence on the government-wide technological infrastructure that was controlled by the CID of Gangnam-gu. Furthermore, the fact that the off-the-shelf parking applications were free or cheap allowed the Parking Department to be less dependent on peer units such as the Finance Administration Division, which is responsible for government contracts with private IT vendors.

The E-government Application Development Stage: This study also found that interagency collaboration remained insignificant during the customization of e-applications because program departments continued to collaborate with external IT vendors during the development stage. This was especially the case among program departments that involved external vendors during the e-application initiation stage because program departments and their IT vendors had established shared technological and programmatic knowledge about existing e-applications.

The process of customizing e-applications sometimes requires technological support from internal IT experts responsible for managing government-wide information systems that support local government management (including intra networks, back-office application systems, databases etc.) because of the potential changes from the customized e-applications. However, customizing e-applications doesn't require the involvement of internal IT experts because customized e-applications are usually operated interdependently by the collaboration between program departments and IT contractors.

For instance, since parking ticket fines are one of the critical sources of local revenue in Korea, the Parking Department of Gangnam-gu has paid special attention to improving existing parking applications that allow parking ticket-receivers to pay parking fines online. While it customized the parking applications, the Parking Department continued to collaborate with the existing IT vendor and also collaborated with private organizations such as bank and credit card companies in order to provide online payment services. However, the Parking Department did not consider it necessary to collaborate with the CID because the CID lacked local knowledge about the complicated parking services delivery system and had insufficient experience related to the various external needs of online parking services.

The E-government Integration Stage: This study found that the importance of and demand for interagency collaborations, particularly collaboration between peer units within Gangnam-gu (e.g., parking department and IT department), increased at the stage of e-government integration. Demand increased as Gangnam-gu's internal units started recognizing the need to commit greater effort to interagency collaboration in order to successfully integrate e-government applications. This study also found that the CID aligned various program needs with the supply of external IT services in terms of organization-wide e-government development and sustainability at the integration stage.

For instance, local governments are often responsible for providing government services on behalf of upper levels of government. Imposing and collecting fines is one of the services Gangnam-gu is required to conduct on behalf of the Seoul Metropolitan Government. In order to effectively manage some fines (e.g., Environment Improvement Fine, Traffic-induced Fine), Seoul Metropolitan Government developed back-office application systems called Non-tax Revenue systems and distributed them to 25 local governments in the Seoul Metropolitan area. Prior to e-application development, Gangnam-gu used these Non-tax Revenue Systems in different functional departments (e.g., Environment Cleaning Department, Transportation Administration Department, Construction Management Department) that were responsible for collecting various fines. To effectively integrate those related services, the CID of Gangnam-Gu initiated the development of e-applications called Online Non-tax systems. Using Online Non-tax systems, citizens and firms pay those fines online through a single window. During the development of this integrated system, the CID was needed to collaborate with other program departments because the CID had insufficient local knowledge about the non-tax services and lacked experience with the various external needs of those services. Meanwhile, program departments that had previously been responsible for collecting those fines were less motivated to outsource services to private vendors because non-tax fines are directly deposited to the account of Seoul city government. As a result, both IT and program needs led to collaborate between the CID and the program departments.

The CID of Gangnam-gu has been actively involved in orchestrating all the e-application activities within peer departments since it established a strategic e-government plan, called the Information Systems Plan (ISP). As e-government matures, local governments often make comprehensive IT plans for the effective management of isolated e-applications. According to the ISP in Gangnam-gu, the CID implemented two large integration projects (called STAR projects 1 and 2). In order for the CID to effectively achieve the goals of those projects, it was imperative to actively involve all e-government related activities (e.g., e-application planning, implementation, vendor selection, etc.) that each program unit had been responsible for. The demand for interagency collaboration also led Gangnam-gu to establish a Special IT Project Committee, through which the vice mayor and division directors facilitate interagency coordination and collaboration among different divisions of local government. One of interviewees said:

If we intend to develop [new e-applications], we consult with the Computerization & Information Division, and the Division appoints a developer or when it decided to develop its own, it will develop [it]. The issue is the process of consultation..... Well, interchanges are made between the Divisions, and things will be carried out this way.

In addition, an interview with the IT vendor who maintains online parking systems reveals that the IT vendor regularly visited the Gangnam-gu office to check out the status of parking applications. However, the IT vendor must gain the approval from the CID in order to access online parking systems which are embedded within the government-wide information system, the so-called Enterprise Information Portal (EIP), of Gangnam-gu. In order for this IT vendor to gain this approval, the Parking Department needed the cooperation of the CID. In other words, the IT vendor couldn't gain access to the EIP to maintain parking applications effectively without coordination between the Parking Department and the CID.

Intersectoral Collaboration

The E-government Initiation Stage: Intersectoral collaboration in Gangnam-gu's e-government transformation is mostly related to forming collaborative outsourcing relationships with IT vendors. One noteworthy finding is that business relationships with outsourcing vendors have evolved over time. In the initiation stage, Gangnam-gu's relationships with vendors were merely a simple contractual relationship to purchase off-the-shelf-computer packages or to develop brochure-type web sites. Gangnam-gu focused on selecting vendors whose reputation was proven in the market. Therefore, intersectoral collaboration in this stage was not considered a significant issue.

The E-government Application Development Stage: Collaboration with vendors emerged as an important subject during the application development stage. E-applications tailored to implement particular government services on the web were not readily available as off-the-shelf products. To develop e-applications customized for specific tasks, vendors needed to collect a broad array of information about the business process. Intimate, frequent, and seamless communication between vendor and government became a salient issue for sharing the information and building a common understanding of the final product.

E-application development also involves a high level of technical complexity because the developer has to make considerable adaptations to ready-made applications in order to satisfy the government's needs. Sometimes a brand new e-application must be developed. Due to these technical challenges, outsourcing for e-application development is less likely than off-the-shelf packages to successfully deliver the final product the government envisioned. Gangnam-gu tried to build a collaborative working relationship with outsourcing partners to minimize the barriers to application development such as inadequate information sharing, lack of trust, and unnecessary conflicts. One project manager who was in charge of developing parking applications stated that:

For us, this project was very new. In the beginning, we didn't have a clear picture for this application. We continually met and discussed with the vendor throughout the project implementation period. If we had let them do whatever they could do without building a close relationship, the output would be horrible. The quality of output depends on the [collaborative] relationship between the vendor and the government.

Sometimes vendors were willing to collaborate with Gangnam-gu to build a strategic partnership. For instance, Gangnam-gu developed several e-applications without spending taxpayers' money. Vendors invested their resources in the development of new applications without charge, and in exchange Gangnam-gu allowed the vendors to access the information about the targeted government services and gave the vendors opportunities to test the feasibility of the new applications. If the new applications worked successfully, the vendors could make formal contracts with Gangnam-gu to further develop the applications or use the proven success for marketing the applications to other local governments.

The E-government Integration Stage: This study also found that at the e-government integration stage there is a higher demand for intergovernmental collaboration due to the need for horizontal as well as vertical information sharing. One strategy that enabled the smooth flow of horizontal integration initiatives included an ISP implementation contract between Gangnam-gu and the same vendors who initially developed the ISP. The continued relationship benefited both Gangnam-gu and the vendors insofar as it allowed both parties to accumulate and utilize the enormous amount of shared information, knowledge and trust. Vertical integration of e-applications led to a new form of intersectoral collaboration between Gangnam-gu and vendors. As the central and the Seoul Metropolitan governments encouraged the vertical integration of e-government services, Gangnam-gu's e-applications were frequently cited as a best practice. Therefore it is not surprising that the vendors that developed Gangnam-gu's e-applications were favored during vertical integration. Being the best practice in the field was also advantageous to Gangnam-gu. Had the central agencies or the metropolitan government adopted a totally new standard, Gangnam-gu would have had to pay additional customization costs to modify their existing systems. Therefore, the finding indicates that both Gangnam-gu and vendors benefit from intersectoral collaboration.

DISCUSSION

The analysis of the three types of collaboration in three stages of e-government development shows that Gangnam-gu experienced various collaboration challenges as it continued to develop e-government applications. In each stage of e-government development, Gangnam-gu encountered varying degrees and types of resource dependence upon internal and external organizational units. A particular type of collaboration became dominant in each stage as the relative importance of each collaboration type changed. Based upon our analysis of the Gangnam-gu case, we categorized the types of collaboration demanded in each stage of development as either "high," "medium," or "low" (Figure 1).

The E-government Initiation Stage: In the first stage, a local government launching e-government transformation needs to acquire approval for the new initiatives from upper-level governments. This study shows that building a collaborative

Figure 1. Local e-government development stage and collaboration demand

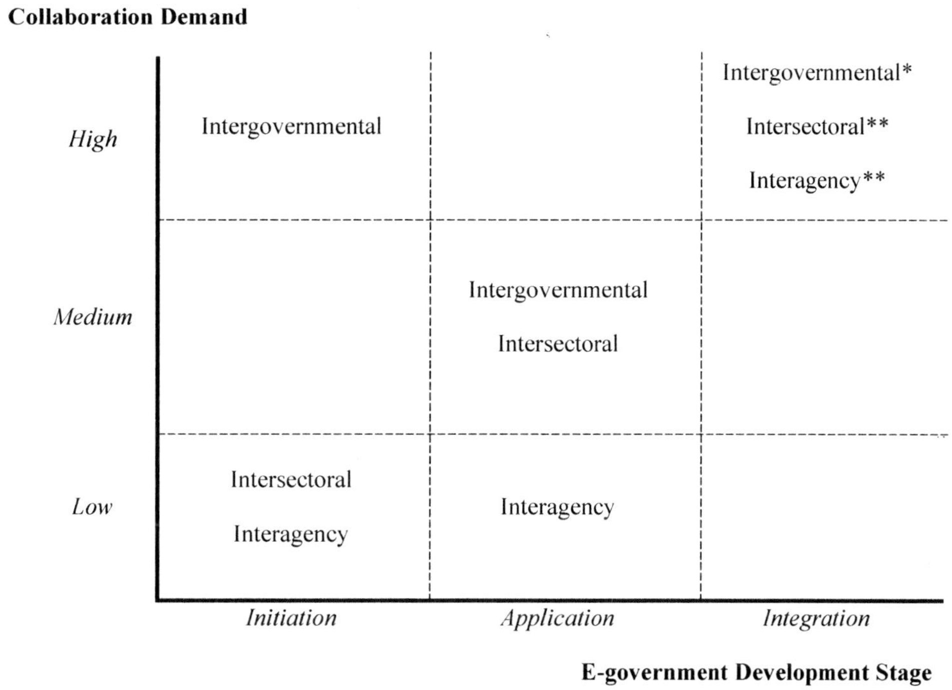

* *indicates the level of collaboration demand for vertical integration between different levels of governments*

** *indicates the level of collaboration demand for horizontal integration within a government*

relationship with authorizing external government organizations is often critical for acquiring legal and institutional endorsement for e-government transformation, and for acquiring financial resources from upper-level governments. This kind of collaboration is especially critical for those local governments that are among the first to adopt e-government. In order to secure prompt and seamless support from external government organizations, the local government initiating e-government transformation ought to build a close and collaborative relationship with upper-level governments.[4]

The E-government Application Development Stage: During the second stage, where a local government starts developing e-applications customized for particular functions, building a business relationship with private vendors becomes a primary collaboration task. When a government organization does not have the advanced in-house technological capacity to develop and maintain e-applications, private vendors play crucial roles on behalf of the government client. The abilities to share information about the business process of the targeted services or management tasks, develop a clear understanding of the functional expectations of the e-application, and build trust between the government and the vendor become the critical success factors in this type of collaboration. Intergovernmental collaboration is still important for defining the legal conditions (e.g. privacy and security) under which data owned by the upper-level government can be accessed. If the basic institutional arrangement for e-government has already been set up in the first stage, new demand for intergovernmental collaboration in this stage will be limited to areas where new technologies are emerging (e.g. mobile services).[5]

The E-government Integration Stage: At the final stage, integrating e-government applications, the demand for interagency and intersectoral collaboration increases to its peak as the local government seeks to integrate e-government applications horizontally. A series of fragmented e-government development initiatives in the first two stages may result in the inefficient use of organizational resources for duplicate systems, the lack of data sharing, and the absence of knowledge sharing between functional units. A central IT unit capable of leading organization-wide e-government integration may play a key role in fostering interagency collaboration. Because of the complexity of the integration process, it is necessary for local governments to make tremendous efforts toward combining the strengths of collaborating partners.

Integration also demands intergovernmental collaboration, especially between upper and lower level governments. According to this study, if a lower level government makes significant early progress in e-government transformation, it has a chance to influence upper level government's policy decisions for vertical integration by setting the standards for integration. One may expect that an upper level government will utilize those local governments that adopt e-government first as examples for other lower level governments. Regardless of how the standard is chosen, collaboration between different levels of government is a necessary condition to successful vertical integration as well as effective privacy and security policy implementation.

Management matters: How did Gangnam-gu overcome the challenge of collaboration through the local e-government development stages? The studied case shows several efforts at intergovernmental coordination and collaboration initiated by Gangnam-gu, including a committee for e-government coordination, formal and informal communications, persuasion, and knowledge sharing. Since establishing a partnership with several private corporations in 2002, Gangnam-gu has also developed a 2-week intensive management training program for employees that covers subjects including managing changes, emphasizing customer focus, developing leadership skills, changing organizational culture, improving communication skills, and creating excellent workplace quality.

While there is no centralized formal system for guiding intergovernmental collaboration, each e-government project team leader made a commitment to communicate effectively and continuously with agencies in different levels of government. Sometimes the mayor, vice mayor, and department directors contacted central government and local council members to explain the proposed e-government project. Furthermore, through the creation of a Special IT Project Committee, managerial leaders in Gangnam-gu discussed efforts for interagency coordination and intergovernmental collaboration. The following comments further indicate how leadership from the vice mayor, senior managers and middle managers contributed to intergovernmental and interagency collaboration in Gangnam-gu:

Division managers and bureau directors have made great efforts to promote e-government innovations in the process of negotiation with central government agencies or Seoul Metropolitan Government.

The vice mayor convened division managers and asked them to actively cooperate for the projects promoted by the IT Division. As a result, a Special IT Project Committee has been formed. When tough things emerge, concerned team managers and staffs in charge are called and their opinions are submitted; then, things are coordinated.

This study also found that the mayor actively utilizes incentive systems to motivate and to recognize employees' commitment to e-government innovations. Employees who generated innovative ideas for e-government development and implementation were given cash rewards as well as promotions. As IT vendors became increasingly aware of Gangnam-gu's willingness to innovate, private vendors began contacting Gangnam-gu officials with new ideas and products that could enhance the quality of services. This trend has produced many joint venture projects between Gangnam-gu and businesses, which have resulted in numerous inventive e-government services.

CONCLUSION

This study found that local e-government leadership faces continuous but varying degrees of challenges related to intergovernmental collaboration, interagency coordination, and intersectoral partnership building. The suggested matrix of collaboration demand experienced by Gangnam-gu during each of the various e-government development stages can provide a guide for local governments to advance e-government transformation by using appropriate collaboration strategies in stage of development. However, while this matrix can be applicable to other local governments that are conducting e-government projects, due caution is necessary. Since this matrix has been developed based upon the findings from Gangnam-gu, which was one of the first local governments to adopt e-government in Korea, it could have limited applicability in a different environment. The fact that Seoul has a highly advanced information technology infrastructure and that Korea has numerous IT vendors providing a variety of IT services and products throughout the country can be another factor that limits the applicability of the proposed matrix in regions where such external resources are not available. In addition, local governments that are slower to adopt e-government do not necessarily follow the three stages. Rather, some of them start from either the second or third stage of e-government development, skipping one or both of the first two stages.

However, the main collaboration challenges identified for each stage can still emerge as long as the local governments a) depend on external organizations to acquire institutional and technical resources for e-government transformation, and b) seek collaboration among internal government units to meet horizontal integration needs. We presume that the matrix can be generalized among local governments where the following conditions are met: a local government is an early adopter of e-government in the area; technologies necessary for e-government transformation are accessible; financial resources are readily available for e-government investment; and upper-level governments exert strong control over local governments. Future researchers may also want to focus on a) collaboration between e-application end-users (i.e., citizens, non-profit organizations, associations, and business) and local governments, b) collaboration between local council members and local e-government leaders, and c) knowledge-transfer collaboration among local governments from various nations.

In order for e-government leadership to emphasize collaboration, the following practices can be applied. First, e-government leaders must focus on creating an organizational culture where employees consistently share information about e-government initiatives, collaboration, and best practices through ongoing project updates with staff, division leaders, department heads, and officials. Second, e-government leaders must make efforts to create a culture of organizational learning by encouraging employees to analyze past e-government collaboration attempts, both successful and failed, and to suggest how the organization can apply those lessons to further improve collaboration practices. Third, e-government leaders should make sure that employees clearly understand the importance of intergovernmental, interagency, and intersectoral collaboration in achieving e-government performance and organizational effectiveness. Finally, the study findings strongly imply that central governments and local governments should work together to establish an appropriate organizational structure for facilitating collaboration; and to develop a shared framework for e-government policies and rules, information sharing, and privacy and security.

ACKNOWLEDGMENT

Support for this research by the Division of Policy Planning at Gangnam-gu is gratefully acknowledged. We also thank the Gangnam-gu project team members, including Stuart Bretschneider, Jon Gant, Heungsuk Choi, and Michael Ahn. An earlier version of this paper was presented at the Collaborative Public Management Conference held in Washington D.C. in 2006.

REFERENCES

Allen, B., Juillet, L., Paquet, G., & Roy, J. (2005). E-government as collaborative governance: Structural, accountability and cultural reform. In M. Khosrow-Pour (Ed.), *Practicing e-government: A global perspective* (pp. 1-15). New York: Idea Group Publishing.

Anderson, K. V., & Henriksen, H. Z. (2006). E-government maturity models: Extension of the Layne and Lee model. *Government Information Quarterly, 23*(2), 236-248.

Bardach, E. (1998). *Getting agencies work together: The practice and theory of managerial craftsmanship.* Washington, D.C: Brookings Institution Press.

Barrett, K., & Greene, R. (2001). *Powering up: How public managers can take control of information technology.* Washington, D.C: CQ Press.

Benbasat, I., Goldstein, D. K., & Mead, M. (1987). The case research strategy in studies of information systems. *MIS Quarterly, 11*(3), 369-386.

Bugler, D. T., & Bretschneider, S. (1993). Technology push or program pull: Interest in new information technologies within public organizations. In B. Bozeman (Ed.), *Public management: The state of the art* (pp. 275-293). San Francisco: Jossey-Bass.

Charih, M., & Robert, J. (2004). Government on-line in the federal government of Canada: The organizational issues. *International Review of Administrative Sciences, 70*(2), 373-384.

Chen, Y.-C., & Perry, J. L. (2003). *IT outsourcing: A primer for public managers.* Washington, D.C: IBM Endowment for the Business of Government.

Craig, A., & Schriar, S. (2001). The find-it! Illinois controlled vocabulary: Improving access to government information through the Jessica subject tree. *Government Information Quarterly, 18*(3), 195-208.

Center for Technology in Government. (2004). New models of collaboration: An overview. Retrieved August 15, 2006, from http://www.ctg.albany.edu/publications/reports/new_models_exec/new_models_exec.pdf

Fountain, J. E. (2001). *Building the virtual state: Information technology and institutional change.* Washington, D.C: Brookings Institution Press.

GSA. (2002). *Government without boundaries: A management approach to inter-governmental programs.* Washington, D.C: Office of Intergovernmental Solutions.

Hiller, J., & Belanger, F. (2001). *Privacy strategies for electronic government*: The PricewaterhouseCoopers Endowment for the Business of Government.

Ho, A. T. (2002). Reinventing local governments and the e-government initiative. *Public Administration Review, 62*(4), 434-441.

Holden, S. H., Norris, D., & Fletcher, P. (2003). Electronic government at the local level. *Public Performance and Management Review, 26*(4), 325-344.

Holzer, M., & Callahan, K. (1998). *Governments at work: Best practice and model programs*. London: Sage.

Holzer, M., & Kim, S.T. (2005). Digital governance in municipalities worldwide (2005): UN/ASPA.

Huxham, C. (1996). Collaboration and collaborative advantage. In C. Huxham (Ed.), *Creating collaborative advantage* (pp. 1-18). Thousand Oaks, C.A: Sage Publications, Inc.

Huxham, C., & Vangen, S. (2000). Leadership in the shaping and implementation of collaboration agendas: How things happen in a (not quite) joined-up world. *Academy of Management Journal, 43*(6), 1159-1166.

IdeA, & Socitm. (2002). Local e-government now: A worldwide view. Retrieved August 15, 2006, from http://www.locregis.net/aaa/LEGNUK.PDF

Intelligence Community Forum. (2006). The top seven intelligent communities of 2006. Retrieved September 20, 2006, from http://www.intelligentcommunity.org/associations/5315/files/TopSevenIC-2006.pdf

Kraemer, K. L., King, J. L., Dunkle, D. E., & Lane., J. P. (1989). *Managing information systems: Change and control in organizational computing* (1st ed.). San Francisco: Jossey-Bass Publishers.

Landsbergen, D., & Wolken, G. (1998). *Eliminating legal and policy barriers to interoperable government systems*.

Layne, K., & Lee, J. (2001). Developing fully functional e-government: A four stage model. *Government Information Quarterly, 18*(2), 122-136.

Linden, R. M. (2002). *Working across boundaries: Making collaboration work in government and nonprofit organizations*. San Francisco: Jossey-Bass.

Mattessich, P. W., Murray-Close, M., & Monsey, B. R. (2001). *Collaboration: What makes it work* (2 ed.). St. Paul, Minnesota: Amherst H. Wilder Foundation.

McDaniel, E. A. (2003). *Facilitating cross-boundary leadership in emerging e-government leaders*. Paper presented at the Informing Science + IT Education Conference, Fori, Finland.

Moon, M. J. (2002). The evolution of e-government among municipalities: Rhetoric or reality? *Public Administration Review, 62*(4), 424-433.

NASCIO. (2005). Connecting the silos: Using governance models to achieve data integration. Retrieved July 10, 2006, from www.nscio.org

Norris, D., Holden, S. H., & Fletcher, P. D. (2001). *E-government: Web sites and web access*. Washington, D.C: International City/County Management Association.

Organization of Economic Co-Operation and Development (2003). Checklist for e-government leaders. Retrieved October 10, 2005, from http://www.oecd.org/publications/Pol_brief

Reddick, C. G. (2004). A two-stage model of e-government growth: Theories and empirical evidence for U.S. Cities. *Government Information Quarterly, 21*(1), 51-64.

Reddick, C. G., & Frank, H. A. (2006). The perceived impacts of e-government on U.S. Cities: A survey of Florida and Texas city managers. *Government Information Quarterly, Corrected Proof, 23*(2), 249-266.

Ross, J. W., Beath, C. M., & Goodhue, D. L. (1998). Develop long-term competitiveness through it assets. *Sloan Management Review, 38*(1), 31-43.

Sagawa, S., & Segal, E. (2000). *Common interest common good: Creating value through business and social sector partnerships*. Boston, M.A: Harvard Business School Press.

Special Committee for E-government. (2003). Korea's e-government: Completion of e-government framework: Special Committee for E-government, Republic of Korea.

Stake, R. E. (2000). *The art of case study research*. Thousand Oaks, CA: Sage Publications.

United Nations and American Society for Public Administration (2002), Benchmarking E-Government: A Global Perspective, UN/ASPA, New York, NY.

Ward, J., & Peppard, J. (2002). *Strategic planning for information systems*. New York: John Wiley & Sons, LTD.

West, D. M. (2004). E-government and the transformation of service delivery and citizen attitudes. *Public Administration Review, 64*(1), 15-27.

Wood, D., & Gray., B. (1991). Toward a comprehensive theory of collaboration. *Journal of Applied Behavioral Science, 27*(1), 139-162.

ENDNOTES

1 Unlike the PPR model which adopts four stages, our model is composed of three stages. One of the crucial differences between stage two (extension) and stage three (maturity) in the PPR model is whether the organization abandons intranet or not. Since our study conceptualizes E-government focusing on e-government applications, we do not see any compelling reason to follow the PPR model's division of the second and third stages.

2 Various challenges for intergovernmental collaborations should be noted: inadequate resources to replace technologically obsolescent hardware and software, the various political issues and budgetary cycles that repeatedly disrupt the long-run planning and implementation of projects, and turf battles between agencies to secure resources and avoid costs and risks (IDeA and Socitm 2002).

3 A good example of intersectoral collaboration is the Indiana state website. Access Indiana, the official information and transaction portal for the state of Indiana, has become a leading example of intersectoral partnerships. Access Indiana has become known for operating a self-supporting, public-private enterprise model, which has allowed the entire network to be built and maintained without spending tax dollars (CTG, 2004).

4 We have deduced that the technical complexity and novelty of e-government transformation is not a major challenge for governments at the e-government initiation stage because the type of technology used tends to be off-the-shelf packages rather than e-applications tailored for the government's unique needs. Interagency collaboration among functional units within an organization remains minimal because this stage does not pursue integration across different functions. Rather than close consultation and collaboration with other units, each unit is likely to pursue its own independent e-government transformation without seeking the coordination of multiple e-government initiatives.

5 The demand for interagency collaboration at this stage remains at a low level because this stage is not intended for integrative e-government operation of multiple organizational units. Instead of pursuing enterprise-wide integration, the unit implementing e-government development focuses on advancing the functionality of a particular e-application to enhance the performance of its own task.

APPENDIX 1

Interview Questions

Q1. In your opinion, what is E-government in Gangnam-gu?
Q2. Can you describe briefly the history of E-government development in Gangnam-gu?
Q3. Please describe the E-government planning process in Gangnam-gu.
Q4. How do you finance designing and implementing E-government projects and operating E-government services?
Q5. What is your understanding of how technologies related to E-government services are managed?
Q6. What aspects of E-government services are outsourced and what are the reasons of such decisions?
Q7. How is E-government in Gangnam-gu related to other levels of government (such as central government, Seoul metropolitan government, and any other district governments), Gangnam-gu legislature, private companies, and civil organizations?
Q8. How has E-government changed the delivery of local government services in Gangnam-gu?
Q9. How do you evaluate the performance of the E-government services in Gangnam-gu?
Q10. What factors have enabled a smooth flow of the E-government projects?
Q11. What factors have impaired the smooth flow of the E-government projects?
Q12. In your opinion, what are the critical success factors of the E-government in Gangnam-gu?
Q13. What are the barriers to the E-government?
Q14. If you could start the E-government in Gangnam-gu again, how would you do it differently?
Q15. Is there any body else we may have to talk to about E-government?

This work was previously published in International Journal of Electronic Government Research, Vol. 4, Issue 3, edited by M. Khosrow-Pour, pp. 36-56, copyright 2009 by IGI Publishing (an imprint of IGI Global).

Chapter 17
E-Democracy from the Perspective of Local Elected Members

Zahid Parvez
University of Wolverhampton, UK

ABSTRACT

Although efforts for developing e-democracy have been underway for over a decade, recent literature indicates that its uptake by citizens and Elected Members (EMs) is still very low. This paper explores the underlying reasons for why this is so from the perspective of local EMs in the context of UK local authorities. It draws on findings reported in earlier works supplemented with primary case study data. Findings are interpreted through the lens of Giddens structuration theory, which assists in drawing out issues related to three dimensions of human agency: communication of meaning, exercising power and sanctioning behaviour. The paper abstracts categories of agency from the findings and uses these to formulate eight propositions for creating an e-friendly democratic culture and enhancing EMs uptake of e-democracy. These propositions provide an indication for future e-democracy research direction.

INTRODUCTION

Efforts for developing e-democracy (or electronic democracy) have been underway in many developed countries across the world, particularly since the early 1990's (ever since the Internet based technologies became widely available to people). Over this period, literature in the field notes many innovations in e-democracy tools (e.g. Abrahamson, Arterton & Orren, 1988; Van de Donk, Snellen & Tops, 1995; Tsagarousianou, Tambini & Byran, 1998; Bellamy & Taylor, 1998; Hague & Loader, 1999; Hacker & Van Dijk, 2000; Hoff, Horrocks & Tops, 2000; Kearns, Bend & Stern, 2002; Clift 2003; Macintosh, Coleman & Lalljee, 2005; Mahrer & Krimmer, 2005; Coleman & Norris, 2005; Robinson 2005; Norris, 2005; Maria and Micelli, 2005; Pratchett, Wingfield &

Polat, 2005, 2006; Mackintosh and Whyte, 2006). These innovations include: e-discussion forums, e-consultations, e-petitioning, e-voting, weblogs, webcasts, e-panels, e-groups, and websites providing information on Elected Members and for accessing remote democratic political information. However, despite many years of efforts in this direction, very few local Elected Members (EMs) and citizens are actually choosing to engage in the democratic process through e-democracy (e.g. Coleman & Gøtze, 2001; Pratchett, Wingfield & Polat, 2005; Robinson 2005; Cross 2006; Evans 2006; Parvez 2006b). This article explores the underlying reasons for why this is so from the perspective of local EMs.

Recent literature explains this low uptake by drawing attention to structural factors and barriers surrounding e-democracy. The agency of actors (i.e. the purposive actions, why and how actors engage through e-democracy) has not received the same attention and, thus, been insufficiently researched. Pratchett, Wingfield and Polat (2005), for example, highlight four barriers that affect the design and implementation of e-democracy tools: the particular democratic understanding held by e-democracy designers and implementers, organisational constraints (resources and conceptual), structural limitations (i.e. external factors that shape or constrain opportunities for developing e-democracy), and citizen restraint (demand for e-democracy). Coleman and Norris (2005) identify four similar barriers: political, participatory, organizational and technological. Others have pointed to the digital divide (e.g. Norris 2001; Chadwick 2006) as another key barrier in the low uptake of ICT enabled practices. Likewise, Parvez (2006b) highlights two structural factors that shape e-democracy tools as well as facilitate and constrain actors in e-democracy engagement: institutional mediation structures and ICT mediation structures.

These insights into the barriers and social structures are useful in that they throw light on how e-democracy tools become shaped and how their use is framed within institutions. However, they do not aid in understanding how actors' perceptions about e-democracy are shaped, why they choose to engage or not engage through e-democracy tools, and what problems they encounter in their engagement. Structural factors are, therefore, only useful to the extent that they aid in understanding how actors are facilitated and constrained in their actual/possible engagement in democratic practices through ICT. They do not illuminate actors' agency; their propensity to engage or what encourages or deters their uptake of e-democracy tools. This article is an attempt towards filling this gap in the extant literature in the field.

The article applies Giddens (1984) Structuration Theory as a framework to build understanding of EMs' agency in local e-democracy. The theory focuses attention on social processes into which ICT are embedded. Its application brings to attention the agency of EMs and social structures that facilitate and constrain their actions in e-democracy. Agency is about action and the underlying intentions and motivations of actors. It includes an understanding of how actors make sense of and conceptualise e-democracy, the reasons for appropriating e-democracy tools, how they actually make use of e-democracy tools, what problems they encounter in their use of these tools, and whether engagement through e-democracy achieves the intended outcomes. The article argues that insights into these dimensions of EMs agency could assist in uncovering the underlying reasons for the low uptake of e-democracy.

This article draws upon recent works as well as on primary case study data to develop a deeper understanding on EMs agency. In particular, it makes the following three key contributions:

1. Drawing on recent works and supplementing them with primary data, it abstracts agency categories that influence EMs conceptualisation of e-democracy and their actual engagement through e-democracy tools.

2. In light of these agency categories, it advances eight propositions for enhancing EMs engagement through e-democracy tools for further inquiry and assessment.
3. It demonstrates the usefulness of Giddens structuration theory in explicating agency of actors in e-democracy and provides a new direction for future e-democracy research.

The next section of the article provides an overview of the theoretical perspective employed to uncover EMs agency surrounding e-democracy. This is followed by a brief discussion of the UK e-democracy context and the role of EMs in local democracy. On these foundations, the methodology adopted for the case study research is outlined. This is followed by a discussion on agency categories that are abstracted under each of the three dimensions of agency. Finally, the abstracted agency categories are employed to formulate eight propositions for enhancing e-democracy uptake. The article concludes by presenting policy and theoretical implications of the insights developed in this article.

STRUCTURATION LENS FOR EXAMINING AGENCY FACTORS

The extant literature offers a range of theoretical perspectives through which the relationship between ICT and social processes can be examined (e.g. Bijkr, Hughes & Pinch, 1987; Zuboff, 1988; Weick 1990; Kraemer & King, 1994; Walsham, 1997; Callon, 1999; Dutton, 1999; Feenburg, 1999; Fountain, 2001; Orlikowski, 1992, 2000; Chadwick 2006). This body of literature provides insights into how ICTs are adopted and adapted in different institutional contexts, and how social processes and human agency moderate their impact.

E-democracy, like other emerging electronically mediated social/business practices such as e-commerce, e-business and e-government, can be conceptualised and studied through many lenses. These include technological determinism, social constructivism, social shaping, informatization, critical theory and structuration theory amongst others. Different lenses are underpinned by different assumptions and bring into focus different set of socio-economic drivers behind e-democracy. They also assist in illuminating different agency issues and social structures surrounding it. Thus, each lens frames the way e-democracy is interpreted and how its role is conceptualised in local democracy. The structuration theory (Giddens 1984) is particularly useful as it assists in illuminating both social structures and agency factors in e-democracy practices and hence has the potential of providing a more rounded understanding of the role e-democracy could play in local democracy (Orlikowski 1992, 2000; Parvez & Ahmed, 2006; Parvez 2006a; Parvez 2006b).

Drawing on structuration theory, Orlikowski (1992, 2000) argues that ICT are equivocal in that different actors can interpret them in different ways. She contends that just by making ICT available to actors, does not imply that they will necessarily use them. Actors do not merely accommodate a new ICT, but they interpret it and hence conceptualise it in different ways. These different conceptualisations in turn influence actors' choice to draw on the new technology and how they appropriate it. Accordingly, to understand the role of new technology, researchers need to explore the context into which both the technology and actors are embedded. Thus, besides technological factors, it is also important to understand, in an integrated way, the institutional and agency factors surrounding e-democracy within the context of democratic political governance (Orlikowski 2000; Parvez 2006a). Structuration theory provides three dimensions of structure (structures of signification, domination and legitimation) and three corresponding dimensions of agency (communication of meaning, facilities and sanctioning behaviour). Taken together, these dimensions provide a fresh perspective and a useful framework for building insights into social structures and agency issues surrounding e-democracy. These insights could assist in understanding the reasons for the low uptake of e-democracy.

In structuration theory, the unit of analysis is social practices (i.e. meaningful activities) that actors engage in through ICT. According to Giddens (1984) social practices can be decomposed into their components of social structures and agency factors. Social structures are the rules and resources that come into play in social action, which enable as well as constrain actors. They are both the medium and the product of human action (Giddens 1984). Actors draw on social structures to engage in social practices and in so doing they produce and reproduce social structures. In social action, actors draw on modalities to produce and reproduce structures of signification (structures of meaning), domination (structures of power) and legitimation (structures of sanctions). This is shown in Figure 1. Rose and Lewis (2001) adapted Giddens original interaction analysis tool and placed the enacted role of technology at the 'modality' level. They argue that the enacted role of ICT provides the modalities (i.e. means by which structures are translated into action) that actors draw upon when appropriating ICT in social action to reproduce social structures.

Agency in the structuration theory refers to the purposive actions of social actors. It is not simply an ability to intend, but is tied with action (or intervention). An understanding of human agency can assist in uncovering the subjective reality constructed by EMs in their use (or lack of use) of e-democracy tools in the democratic political process. Giddens (1984) draws attention to three interrelated and interdependent dimensions of human agency in social practices: communication of meaning, exercising power and sanctioning behaviour. EMs draw on ICT as a medium to interact in democratic practices to communicate meaning, exercise power and/or to sanction behaviour.

This suggests that when EMs' interact to communicate meaning they draw on interpretative schemes to make sense of their own and others' interpretations and attitudes towards e-democracy. Interpretive schemes include stocks of knowledge that actors' posses, the enacted role of ICT, or their personal interests that they draw upon in making sense of ICT role, and in so doing they produce and reproduce structures of signification.

When EMs interact for exercising power, they draw on facilities to carry out their everyday work, to authorise other actors or to allocate resources. Facilities such as technological artefacts can be granted or withheld (e.g. by ICT managers or policymakers) in e-democracy practices, and in so doing actors produce and reproduce structures of domination. However, if other actors challenge these structures they create dialectics of control,

Figure 1. Interaction analysis tool based on structuration theory (reproduced from Rose and Lewis, 2001, p.154)

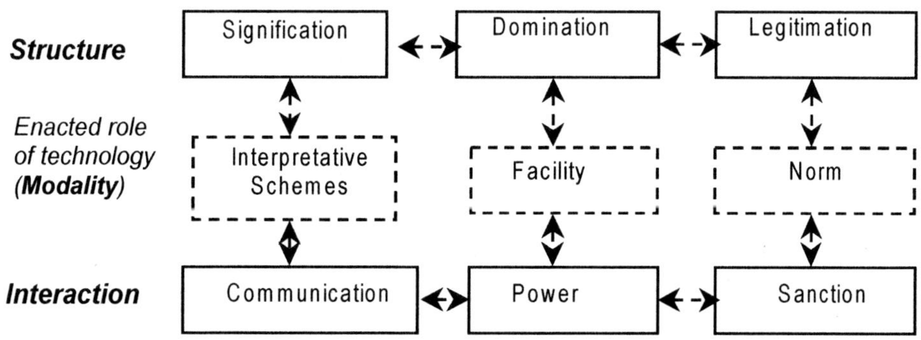

which becomes resolved through a process of time, leading to new structures of domination.

When EMs sanction (or justify) their own or other actors' behaviour in ICT use, they draw on established or perceived norms. Norms influence whether the use of ICT in a social practice is appropriate or not, or the way ICT are expected to be used. Actors draw upon the norms they perceive to sanction behaviour, and in doing so they produce and reproduce structures of legitimation.

Thus, structuration theory as a framework suggests that EMs are facilitated and constrained in e-democracy practices by a number of factors. These include EMs knowledge and skills of ICT, how they conceptualise e-democracy, by the wider policies and institutional rules surrounding e-democracy practices (which determines the level of control EMs have over ICT facilities), by the influence of other actors in the way they use ICT resources, by the influence of their own personal reflections/thinking in the way they use ICT, and by the influence of the wider discourse shaping their everyday democratic activities. These factors influence the strategies EMs bring to bear in their appropriation of e-democracy. This concept of agency suggests that human actors are not (always) passive receivers of the impact of ICT and hence rejects technological determinism. On the contrary, actors play a role in shaping technological artefacts and in moderating their effects in social processes. Actors can comply with the rules for ICT use, modify, or even change the way they appropriate ICT. The structuration theory also suggests that human actions have consequences and these can be either intended (i.e. according to intentions or what was planned) or unintended. These consequences can also lead to a change in social structures.

These ideas are applied in the subsequent sections of the article to explicate the agency of EMs so as to build insights into how they make sense of e-democracy tools, why they choose to engage through these tools, to what extent they utilise them and how they are facilitated and constrained in the process. Insights into these questions can assist in uncovering the underlying reasons for why there is low uptake of e-democracy.

UK E-DEMOCRACY CONTEXT AND ROLE OF ELECTED MEMBERS

The 'New Labour' Government in the UK, since coming to office in 1997, has undertaken initiatives to tackle the culture of democratic political apathy, low turnout at polls and the general issues of democratic disengagement. These initiatives have aimed at invigorating democratic renewal in local government. To enhance local democracy, the Government brought forward a number of guiding documents such as DETR (1998), DTLR (2001), and Cabinet Office (2002, 2004). In these documents, e-democracy is broadly understood as the use ICT in democratic governance processes.

The Modernisation agenda of the New Labour Government aimed at improving and modernising local government. According to Sullivan (2002) this agenda is contained under three main headings: modern public services, democratic renewal and community leadership. The agenda proposes a number of reforms including new models of political structure, frequent consultation with local people, the use of referenda and ways of making it easier to vote (e.g. postal voting and e-voting). In addition, for improving public services and administration, the reform agenda draws the attention of local governments to providing community leadership, best value performance reviews and e-government. As part of this comprehensive agenda, consideration was given to a number of innovative practices (both off-line and on-line) for engaging citizens and EMs. These included citizens' juries, standing citizens' panels, deliberative opinion polls, consultative forums, focus groups, visioning, round-tables, community planning conferences and regular referenda (Stewart 1997). E- Democracy was proposed as an important means along with, or integrated within these other innovations for enhancing local democracy.

The UK has an established representative model of democracy. In this model, citizens elect their representatives who are then empowered to make decisions on their behalf. Thus, the democratically Elected Members (EMs) are central to local democracy as they are the representatives of citizens. As representatives, they play a number of important roles. According to Goss and Corrigan (1999) EMs act as advisors and information providers to local citizens, they play the role of listeners, advocates (represent the interests of constituents), ring-holders (hold together diverse interests and voices), facilitators (provides leadership and support efforts for community development) and empowering citizens to address issues that concern them. Kawalek and Wastell (2001) add two other roles to this list that have emerged in light of the recent changes in political management in UK local authorities; namely executive and scrutiny roles (i.e. investigate and audit the policies of the executive).

Thus, to perform these complex roles efficiently and effectively, it is vital for EMs to build strong communication with local communities with e-democracy tools. These tools could enhance their representative roles, enable EMs to communicate easily with each other, as well as keep their constituents informed of local developments, provide them with an opportunity to respond to local authority issues and raise issues of their own. ICTs could assist them in managing casework, develop personal blogs, enable online surgeries, consultation and petitions, and engage hard to reach communities and groups.

Recent works (e.g. Pratchett, Wingfield & Polat, 2005; Robinson 2005) indicate that most local authorities in the UK provide EMs with an e-mail address and access to personal computers. Many EMs also have a personal web page, which provides relevant personal details, contact information, details of surgery hours, and news about their wards. In addition, EMs have access to the Internet and to their local authority's Intranet. They also have access to ICT support and training to assist them in using e-democracy tools.

A synthesis of recent e-democracy literature (e.g. Chen 2002; Kernaghan, Riehle, & Lo, 2003; Filzmaier, Stainer-H¨ammerle & Snellen, 2004; Hoff 2004; Jarvis & Wilkerson 2005; Coleman & Norris 2005; Pratchett, Wingfield & Polat, 2005; Robinson 2005; Evans 2006; Parvez 2006b) reveals that the following general uses of e-democracy tools are made by different EMs:

- *Access to remote Information*: ICT facilitate online access to official papers, reports, letters, ward information, database of constituents, other corporate data, agenda and minutes of committee meetings, casework and messages. The Internet is employed by some EMs to publicise information on their activities, to access remote websites for background information on government policies or on issues to be discussed at committee meetings, and also for news, media reports, etc.
- *Production of documents and presentations*: Many EMs use ICT systems for production of letters, reports, presentations, leaflets, and placing personal details on websites, etc.
- *Processing and analysing information*: ICT are powerful tools for analysing data, and thus, they are employed by some EMs for analysing crime data, voting data, ward information, age profiles of constituents, or for analysing data on other areas of interest and concern.
- *Internal and external communication*: Some EMs use ICT for communicating with constituents, officers, other EMs, residents and voluntary bodies. In addition, some EMs use ICT to establish one-to-many or many-to-many interactive communications channels – e.g. set up e-groups with local citizens, and establish online consultations and discussion

forums with a range of individuals, groups and public agencies.

- *Conduct online surveys or request online feedback:* Some EMs also use ICT for conducting e-surveys and e-polls to identify service users and constituents' views on services and/or policy issues.

However, despite the availability of a range of ICT resources and systems, and the variety of ways some EMs are beginning to make use of these, very few are actually utilising these technologies to support their diverse representative roles. Many elected representatives still prefer personal contact, the press, and radio and television to some extent, as opposed to the Internet and ICT in general, and thus, the uptake of e-democracy is slow as a number of studies observe (e.g. as quoted below)

In Canada: '...significant minority of MPs choose to make little or no use of ICTs' (Kernaghan, Riehle & Lo, 2003, p.25)

In the UK: "Paul Evans, head of the Councillor.info scheme to provide elected members with a web presence, says only a tiny percentage of councillors use their sites to do anything more than list contact details". (Cross 2006)

Despite the hopes and rhetoric of many e-democracy champions, however, there is little evidence that contemporary initiatives are galvanising public engagement and revolutionising political participation... experiments with electronic voting have not greatly increased electoral turnout... while other forms of electronic participation, such as online discussion forums, political blogs and so on, have enjoyed only patchy success. (Pratchett, 2007)

In view of this background, efforts towards developing understanding as to why the uptake of e-democracy is low amongst EMs would make an important contribution to the existing literature in the field.

ELECTED MEMBERS AGENCY CATEGORIES

Due to lack of insights on EMs agency in the extant e-democracy literature, the following discussion draws on primary case study data that provides further insights into EMs agency surrounding e-democracy.

In-depth case study research in three local authorities within the West Midlands Region of the UK (Birmingham City Council, Wolverhampton City Council and Telford & Wrekin Council) was undertaken between February and August 2003. Efforts to develop e-government were well underway in all these three local authorities at that time. This was because the national UK Government had set a target for local governments to ensure 100% of services that could be provided electronically should be online by 2005. Basic ICT facilitated were available to EMs in all the three local authorities for over three years prior to this research. These included desktop computers, basic Microsoft suite or Lotus Notes (for word processing, spreadsheet, database, etc.), e-mail and Internet facilities. Whereas with Birmingham and Wolverhampton City Councils, EMs had to share personal computers that were located in each of the political party's group offices, Telford & Wrekin offered personal desktop computers or laptops to each EM.

The key difficulty encountered in the research process was to identify EMs who actually made some regular use of ICT to support their everyday work. In the final sample, a total of twelve EMs (who actually used e-democracy tools in some aspects of their everyday work) were selected from the three local authorities (i.e. four EMs from each local authority; one from each of the three major political parties and one EM who was the Head of ICT policy).

This small scale research, in line with Giddens (1984) theory, adopted a qualitative research strategy. Semi-structured interviews were used as they enabled the elicitation of subjective data related to the meanings, purposes and experiences of EMs in e-democracy. The interviews explored agency issues under each of the three dimensions of agency identified in structuration theory: communication of meaning, exercising power and sanctioning behaviour. The issues explored included the following: how EMs made sense of e-democracy, the purposes they used e-democracy tools for, the extent of their engagement in e-democracy, how they are facilitated or constrained in their use of e-democracy tools, issues of power and dialectics of control, and how their use of e-democracy tools is legitimated.

Evidence collected from each EM was first compared with other EMs within the same local authority, and then with EMs from other local authorities. The emerging patterns and themes in the evidence were noted. This process was facilitated through making contrasts/comparisons and abstracting by subsuming particular details into general categories (Miles & Hubermann, 1995). Through this process the emerging agency categories were noted.

This evidence from the interviews was also corroborated with documents published by each local authority such as: Best value performance, E-government statement, ICT development priorities and policies in general, budget details, Corporate Policy, Community Strategy, and ICT use policy (acceptable use policy). These published documents provided an official view of the issues that each local authority was trying to address, their institutional objectives, as well as priorities and plans for ICT development and use in local government and local democracy. They also provided formal contextual information on the local authorities in which this research was located.

The abstracted agency categories for EMs are shown in Figure 2 (Giddens interaction analysis tool - at the modality level) and discussed in the proceeding sections of this article. These are then

Figure 2. Giddens (1984) interaction analysis tool highlighting modalities EMs draw upon to enact structures for e-democracy uptake

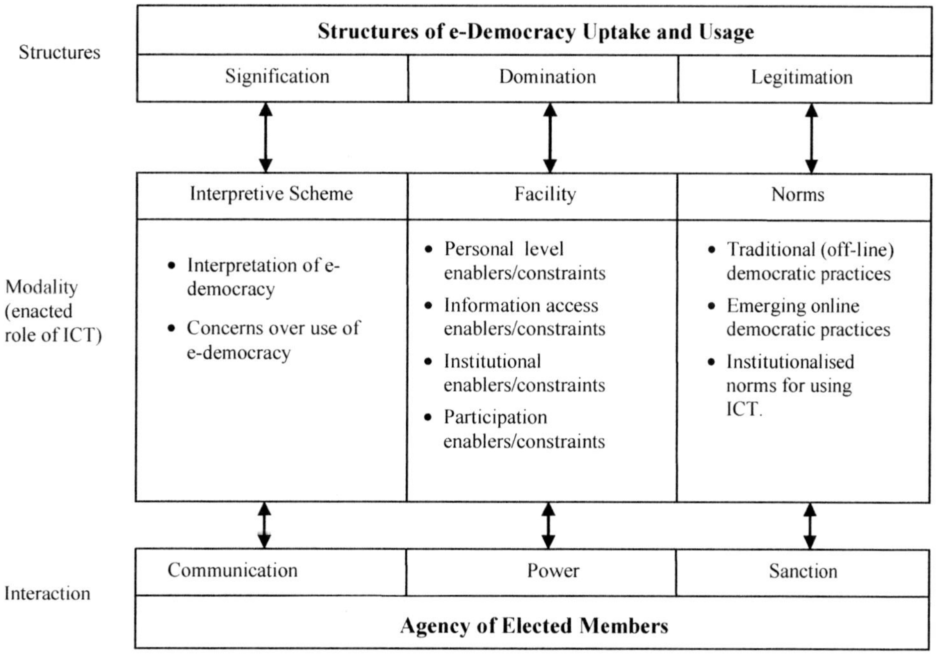

employed to formulate propositions for enhancing EMs engagement in e-democracy.

COMMUNICATION OF MEANING

This section focuses on the interpretive schemes that EMs in the case study drew upon to make sense of their own and others use of e-democracy tools. Interpretive schemes can assist in understanding how actors think about ICT and the purposes they attach to them in local democracy. From an analysis of case study findings, the following two key categories of interpretive schemes emerged: *interpretations* and *concerns* regarding ICT role in local democracy. These are elaborated below.

Interpretations: the findings suggest that EMs constructed their interpretations of ICTs from their stocks of knowledge in two ways: by considering how useful these technologies would be in supporting their representative role, and the impact their use will have on their role as representative and more generally on local democracy. Due to their possessing different stocks of knowledge and experiences with ICT, different EMs interpreted ICT use and role in local democracy in different ways, and this influenced how they conceptualised ICT and their attitudes towards e-democracy.

Evidence indicated a lack of shared understanding amongst EMs regarding the role of e-democracy in local democracy. This was true within EMs of the same political party and across political parties. The following were some of the ways different EMs perceived ICT uses: as administration tools; as tools for accessing remote information; as communications tools; as tools for facilitating the posting of basic information about themselves on Web pages; as tools for on-line consultations and deliberation of local political issues with citizens.

Those who did employ ICT were mostly young IT literate EMs. Some of these EMs employed ICT to assist in the production of letters, reports and leaflets. Others used ICT to access timely information such as official papers, reports, council meeting agenda and minutes. A few EMs used the Internet to access remote websites for wider information on government policies, media reports, or on issues to be discussed at committee meetings.

Regarding a deeper use of ICT, only one EM from the sample interviewed had set up an e-group to communicate with some of his constituents, and one other showed interest in online discussion forums. Another two EMs were beginning to use ICT for enhancing their effectiveness and reaching out to citizens. Examples in this direction included the following: an EM accessing remote information directly via the Internet in order to learn about developments related to local authorities (at Telford & Wrekin Council); an EM communicating with officers and citizens through e-mail (at Telford & Wrekin Council); an EM building direct access to citizens through establishing community e-groups (at Wolverhampton City Council). There was no evidence of EMs using ICT to interact with each other. Moreover, the traditional ways of communication (e.g. face-to-face, meetings, memos, etc.) were still dominant. The dominant communication methods employed were letters, telephone and face-to-face interactions through meetings and surgeries. This gives an indication of the peripheral role of ICT in democratic engagement between actors at the time of data collection in all three case local authorities.

There were also different opinions regarding which model of democracy could be strengthened through e-democracy applications. It appeared that all of the EMs interviewed took the representative model of democracy as the accepted norm. Three EMs raised concerns over a direct democracy model or plebiscitary model of democracy, as this could undermine their role and make them somewhat redundant in local democracy. However, within the umbrella of this representative model of democracy, two EMs indicated a preference for a participatory model of democracy that would enhance the participation of different actors groups in democratic governance.

Concerns: Besides their interpretations of ICT, actors also appeared to draw on their concerns regarding the negative aspects of ICT in local democracy to make sense of e-democracy. The findings revealed that some EMs were concerned about an increase in workload, the potential centrality and increasing power of officers in e-democracy, monitoring and surveillance of ICT usage, computer hacking and viruses, increasing transparency of their personal details through web pages, and issues of social exclusion and biased opinions dominating on-line consultations and discussions. Fears about the adoption of plebiscites were also expressed by two EMs.

In light of the above discussion, together with insights provided by earlier studies and knowledge of ICT capabilities, the following different conceptualisations that EMs constructed for ICT role in local democracy can be distinguished:

- ICTs as administrative/supportive tools: for data management and analysis, document production and management, and accessing remote information (e.g. minutes of committee meetings, policy documents, budget details, etc.)
- ICTs as tools for publicity: for disseminating information, having a web presence, use of weblogs to share views and commentary on issues with constituents.
- ICTs as communication tools: for communication between different actor groups through e-mails, websites, online discussion forums and on-line petitioning.
- ICTs as polling and e-voting tools: for employing ICT for online surveys, e-polling, e-consultations and e-voting.
- ICT as tools for monitoring, surveillance, changing flows of information, manipulation and hence affecting the balance of power and for reinforcing social exclusion.

These different conceptualisations, constructed through EMs *interpretations* and *concerns* over ICT usage, appeared to shape their attitudes towards e-democracy and hence the extent of their uptake of e-democracy tools.

EXERCISING POWER

Power is generally understood as the 'ability to act' and Giddens defines power as 'the capacity to achieve outcomes' (1984: 257). Structures of domination (or structures of power) both enable as well as constrain actors in social practices. Actors exercise power through their everyday work and this often requires an ability to influence change in how and to what extent they are authorized to operate in their roles, or in how resources are allocated. EMs draw on ICT facilities to access information or engage in communication with other actors. They are facilitated or constrained in this process by the authority they have to access institutional resources or by their own abilities, skills and knowledge (i.e. personal resources) to use these facilities.

From the case study data the following four agency categories of enablers/constraints emerged related to how EMs drew on ICT facilities to engage in e-democracy: personal, information, institutional and participation constraints.

Personal level constraints: the personal issues in appropriating e-democracy tools raised by EMs included the following:

- Lack of ICT skills; a few EMs were also put off by the jargon used
- A perceived increase in their workload through use of ICT; e.g. the need to respond to e-mails, updating of web pages, etc.
- Having apprehensions regarding how they used ICT, which they thought were being monitored by officers.

Information access constraints: EMs perceived a number of constraints in their access to information resources through ICT. Some of these included:

- Being denied access to a number of local authority's information systems (e.g. Housing information system)
- Need for authorisation from content managers to upload information onto local authority's website.
- Not having ICT facilities where they need them (e.g. in their homes).

Institutional level constraints: A few EMs expressed the view that the rules outlined in the ICT Acceptable Use Policies (AUP) hindered them in their broader roles as representatives of citizens in local democracy. These AUPs were perceived as placing restrictions on them in using ICT for their party political work. This policy was based on UK Law that prohibits the use of the local authorities' ICT facilities for party political work. In all three local authorities, EMs had to sign an agreement for complying to the AUP before they were given authorisation to use ICT. However, one EM, at one local authority, refused to sign the agreement as he felt that he would be greatly restricted in his use of e-mail and the Internet. This reveals the dialectic of control in operation, and demonstrates actors' capacity to resist rules and influence change in policy through a process of negotiation/conflict.

Moreover, EMs had not been consulted in identifying their ICT needs to support their diverse roles. This was true across all the three case local authorities at the time of data collection. This suggests that whatever ICT facilities the ICT department felt appropriate for EMs were provided. This could perhaps explain, to some extent, the reasons for some of the constraints EMs were experiencing.

Participation constraints: Some EMs did not feel the need to participate in online discussions as the issues opened up by the local authority were not very meaningful/relevant to them or were very limited in range.

SANCTIONING BEHAVIOUR

This section discusses the categories of norms EMs drew upon to sanction (justify) their use (or lack of use) of e-democracy tools. From the case study findings, three categories perceived by EMs for ICT usage were identified: traditional (off-line) information exchange and communications methods; emerging online information exchange and communications methods; institutionalised norms for using ICT.

Traditional (off-line) information exchange and communications methods: Those EMs who did not use e-democracy tools justified their lack of use through comments such as the following: "Computers are too much of a hassle", "I don't see the point of computers in my role as a representative", "I can't be bothered to switch on the computer", "Most of my work is through face-to-face interactions and meetings – I really don't need computers". It appears that these EMs drew on established off-line norms of the status quo to justify not using e-democracy tools. Traditional communication practices such as face-to-face meetings, surgeries and so on are still dominant in local democracy. Robinson (2005) also states that 73% of EMs in her research indicated that most of their time is spent in meetings. Thus, these EMs did not feel the need for using ICT in supporting their work

Emerging online information exchange and communications methods: Those who did employ ICT, justified their use through comments such as the following: "ICT are the future", "Everyone is using them, so why not Councillors", "ICT will help to change things around here"; "They could help me in keeping in touch with my constituents - get feedback from them, and make me more efficient in my work". Thus, this group of EMs justified their use of e-democracy tools by drawing on the changing situation in local democracy, which in their view was the emerging norm on conducting democratic affairs. They also justified their use by arguing that these technologies offer alternative communications channels to communicate with their constituents and are useful tools to enhance their efficiency. Thus, through time, as more EMs begin to use ICT in supporting their diverse roles, new structures of legitimation surrounding e-democracy could be produced.

Institutionalised norms for using ICT: Those EMs who did employ ICT were influenced by the norms for ICT usage and the established model of democracy. EMs appeared to exploit ICT in a facilitating/supporting role rather than in a substantive/innovative role. Only a very few innovative uses of ICT were identified and these included an e-mail group set up by an EM to communicate with some of his constituents; an EM cross-checking information provided by his local authority on the Internet, and another EM employing ICT to obtain ward information and analysing age profiles of constituents. There was insufficient evidence to indicate any radical changes that challenged traditional off-line democratic practices. This suggests that ICT use was facilitating established activities and procedures of local democratic governance and not really bringing forward any radical changes to these. Examples of many-to-many interactive democratic practices were lacking from the data. However, a few EMs indicated that they would prefer a greater participation of citizens and EMs in local democracy, which is clearly an indication of a desire to change the norms of democratic practice. The ICT Acceptable Use Policy (AUP) in each local authority in the study also appeared to influence how EMs employed ICT. The AUPs spelt out what the norms were for ICT use and what sanctions would be applied against improper use of these resources. For a vibrant democratic engagement, a more flexible policy framework might perhaps be required that enables EMs access to information that they require in fulfilling their complex roles.

CONCLUSION

The article has drawn on insights offered by earlier works in the field as well as on primary case study data to build insights into EMs attitudes and use of e-democracy tools. The findings, interpreted through the Structuration theory, have drawn out the modalities (i.e. the interpretive schemes, facilities and norms) that EMs draw upon to enact structures (i.e. the rules and resources that frame their views and actions) for e-democracy uptake and usage.

An holistic view of these insights, assisted in formulating eight propositions for enhancing EMs uptake of e-democracy. These are presented in Table 1 and put forward for further inquiry and assessment.

In conclusion, the following policy and theoretical implications of this study are put forward.

E-Democracy Policy Implications: Currently e-democracy policy appears to be driven from the top-down. Policy makers and ICT management exert considerable influence on the design of e-democracy tools and how they are expected to be employed in local democracy. However, consultation with EMs regarding their views on e-democracy and their ICT needs appears not to be taken into account in the process of policy formulation. Therefore, in light of the eight propositions offered in this article, it is suggested that e-democracy policy needs to consider three important issues. First, it needs to move away from a top-down approach to policy. EMs need to be engaged in the e-democracy policy formulation process. Their interpretations of e-democracy tools need to be understood and their information and communications needs for democratic engagement identified through consultations with them. Moreover, a deeper understanding of EMs complex and multifaceted roles would assist in

Table 1. Propositions for enhancing Elected Members uptake of e-democracy derived from agency categories

Dimensions of Agency	Agency categories	Propositions for enhancing EMs engagement in e-democracy
Communication of meaning	• Narrow conceptualisations of e-democracy • Concerns over use of e-democracy tools	***Proposition #1***: The broader the interpretation EMs have of ICT role in local democracy, the more positive will be their propensity to use e-democracy tools. ***Proposition #2***: The greater the perceived benefits EMs have of ICT in their everyday roles, the more positive will be their propensity to use e-democracy tools. ***Proposition #3:*** The weaker the concern over the negative impacts of ICT, the more positive will be EMs propensity to appropriate e-democracy tools.
Exercising power	• Personal level enablers/constraints • Information access enablers/constraints • Institutional level enablers/constraints • Participation enablers/constraints	***Proposition #4***: A more unhindered online access to information resources required to fulfil EMs roles will be positively related to their propensity to engage in e-democracy. ***Proposition #5***: Having the required skills to use ICT will be positively related to EMs propensity to use e-democracy tools. ***Proposition #6***: An ICT use policy that is flexible enough to cater for the new and emerging information exchange and communication needs of EMs will be positively related to EMs propensity to engage in e-democracy. ***Proposition #7***: Issues opened up for e-participation that EMs find interesting and relevant will be positively related to their propensity to engage in e-democracy.
Sanctioning behaviour	• Traditional (off-line) democratic practices • Emerging online democratic practices • Institutionalised norms for using ICT.	***Proposition #8***: A more e-ready democratic political culture will be positively related to EMs propensity to engage in e-democracy.

providing more effective e-tools for supporting them. Also, e-democracy policy needs to give consideration to other agency issues such as computer literacy and training, user-friendly computer interfaces, and on-line costs that could constrain EMs in their interactions mediated by ICT.

Second, parallel efforts are required to create a more ICT conducive and e-ready democratic political culture. This requires attention to both technology and people issues. There is a need for an effective ICT infrastructure, user-friendly e-democracy tools, e-enabled communications structures that supports online interactivity (as opposed to broadcast structures), and a review of ICT Acceptable Use Policy that caters for the new and changing information exchange and communication needs of EMs and citizens. In addition, there is a need for re-examining the way democracy is conducted. In particular, the mode of democratic engagement needs to be conducive to an on-line environment. This suggests a need for integrating on-line environments with traditional off-line democratic practices. Also, wider ranges of online discussion topics need to be opened up that are relevant and meaningful to EMs. This e-friendly democratic political culture would assist in enhancing EMs propensity to use e-democracy tools.

Theoretical implications: According to the theory of structuration, technology is only a material resource and on its own has own no social meaning. It is what actors choose to do or not do with technology that is of social significance. Thus, merely providing EMs with e-tools does not in itself signify an enhancement of e-democracy. It is how EMs interpret e-democracy and what they choose to do with ICT under the surrounding social structures that would assist in understanding the role of e-democracy in the wider democratic political process.

The above discussion demonstrates the usefulness of the structuration theory. It provides a useful lens to draw out the underlying social structures and agency factors that come into play in social action. Regarding the agency of EMs, this article has focused on drawing out how EMs communicate meaning, exercise power and sanction behaviour. It has done so through interpreting EMs attitudes and uses of ICT in local democracy. Structuration theory assisted in explaining why, in the absence of a shared understanding, different actors interpreted and conceptualised e-democracy in different ways. The findings also lent support to Giddens view that actors are not passive recipients of the impact of structures. With ICTs, they could choose to reproduce or even challenge these structures and hence open up the possibilities of introducing change in the way democracy is practiced in society. Moreover, the theory assists in moving us away from narrow technical aspects of e-democracy and brings to the fore social, organisational and ethical aspects. In contrast to the traditional accounts of technology, which tend to characterize IT as a mere tool, structuration theory portrays ICT as a material resource embedded in a complex socio-technical network, where technological effects are indirect and moderated by the interplay of human agency and social structures.

In conclusion, from a structuration perspective, a low uptake of e-democracy from the perspective of EMs can be explained by the following three key reasons:

- Narrow and/or negative interpretive schemes drawn on by EMs in making sense of e-democracy.
- Personal, information access, institutional and participation constraints sensed by EMs when drawing on ICT facilities to engage in e-democracy.
- Conflicting norms sensed by EMs in the local democratic political culture related to how information is to be exchanged and communication methods to be used.

E-democracy has the potential to play a more important role in democratic renewal. However, for realising this potential, a more e-friendly and open democratic political culture is required. Addressing EMs' and citizens' agency issues surrounding e-democracy tools would contribute towards creating such a culture and assist in increasing the uptake of e-democracy.

REFERENCES

Abramson, J, B, Arterton, F, C, & Orren, G, R (1988). *The Electronic Commonwealth: The Impact of New Media Technologies on Democratic Politics.* New York: Basic Books.

Bellamy, C. & Taylor, J.A. (1998). *Governing in the Information Age.* London: Open University Press.

Bijkr, W., Hughes, T. & Pinch, T. (eds.). (1987) *Social Construction of Technological Systems: New Directions in the Sociology and History of Technology.* Cambridge, MA: MIT Press.

Cabinet Office (2002). *In the Service of Democracy: A Consultation Paper on a Policy for Electronic Democracy.* London: Cabinet Office.

Cabinet Office (2004). *E-Democracy Briefing.* London: Cabinet Office.

Callon, M. (1999). Actor-network theory – the market test. In J. Law & J. Hassard (eds.), *Actor Network Theory and After.* Oxford: Blackwell Publishers.

Chadwick, A. (2006). *Internet Politics: States, Citizens, and New Communication Technologies.* New York: Oxford University Press.

Chen, P. (2002). *Australian Elected Representatives use of New Media Technologies*. Research Report, Centre for Public Policy University of Melbourne.

Clift, S (2003). *E-Government and Democracy: Representation and citizen engagement in the information age*. United Nations- DESA.

Coleman, S. & Norris, D.F. (2005). *A New Agenda for E-democracy*. Oxford Internet Institute, Forum Discussion Paper No. 4, January.

Cross, M. (2006). E-democracy: tied up in red tape. *The Guardian*. Retrieved February 22, from http://politics.guardian.co.uk/egovernment/story/0,,1714670,00.html

DETR (1998). *Modern Local Government: In Touch with the People*. London: DETR

DTLR (2001). *Strong local leadership, quality public services*. London: The Stationery Office

Dutton, W. H. (1999). *Society On the Line: Information Politics in the Digital Age*. Oxford: Oxford University Press.

Evans, P. (2006). How Local Authorities can motivate Councillors to update their websites – and how they can be promoted to the public. *The Councillor.info project*. Retrieve March 8, 2007, from http://www.popteltechnology.coop/Shared_ASP_Files/GFSR.asp?NodeID=89255&AttributeName=FileName

Feenburg, A. (1999). *Questioning Technology*. London: Routledge.

Filzmaier, P., Stainer-H¨ammerle, K., & Snellen, I. (2004). Information management of MPs: Experiences from Austria, Denmark and the Netherlands. *Information Polity*, 9(1/2), 17–28

Fountain, J.E. (2001). *Building the Virtual State: Information Technology and Institutional Change*. Brookings Institution Press: Washington, DC.

Giddens, A. (1984). *The Constitution of Society: Outline of the Theory of Structuration*. Cambridge: Polity.

Goss, S. & Corrigan, P. (1999). *Starting to Modernise: Developing New Roles for Council Members*. London: New Local Government Network.

Hacker, K.L. & Van Dijk, J. (Eds.) (2000). *Digital Democracy, Issues of Theory and Practice*. London: Sage Publications.

Hague, B.N. & Loader, B.D. (Eds.) (1999). *Digital Democracy: Discourse and Decision Making in the Information Age*. London: Routledge.

Hoff, J. (2004). The Democractic Potentials of Information Technology: Attitudes of European MPs towards new technology. *Information Polity*, 9(1/2), 55-66.

Hoff, J., Horrocks, I. & Tops, P. (Eds.) (2000). *Democratic Governance and New Technology, Technologically Mediated Innovations in Political Practices in Western Europe*. London: Routledge.

Jarvis, S., & Wilkerson, K. (2005). Congress on the Internet: Messages on the homepages of the U.S. House of Representatives, 1996 and 2001. *Journal of Computer-Mediated Communication, 10* (2), article 9. Retrieve March 8, 2007, from http://jcmc.indiana.edu/vol10/issue2/jarvis.html

Kawalek, P., & Wastell, D. (2001). The Informed Representative: The Information Needs of Local Elected Decision Makers. In Remenyi, D., & Bannister, F., *European Conference on e-Government*. Reading: MCIL:

Kearns, I., Bend, J. & Stern, B. (2002). *e-Participation in Local Government*. London: Institute for Public Policy Research.

Kernaghan K., Riehle, N. & Lo, J. (2003). Politicians's use of ICTs: a Survey of Federal Parliamentarians. *Crossing Boundaries*. Retrieved March 8, from www.publicsectorit.ca/publications/CBStudy.pdf

Kraemer, K.L. & King, J.L. (1994). Social analysis of information systems: the Irvine School, 1970–1994. *Informatization and the Public Sector*, 3(2), 163–182.

Macintosh, A., Coleman, S. & Lalljee, M. (2005). E-Methods for Public Engagement: Helping Local Authorities Communicate with Citizens. *Local e-Democracy National Project*. Retrieved March 8, from http://itc.napier.ac.uk/ITC/Documents/eMethods_guide2005.pdf

Macintosh, A. & Whyte, A. (2006). Evaluating how Participation Changes Local Democracy. *eGovernment Workshop '06 (eGOV06)*. September 11 2006, Brunel University, West London

Mahrer, H. & Krimmer, R. (2005). Towards the enhancement of e-democracy: identifying the notion of the 'Middleman Paradox'. *Information Systems Journal*, 15, 27–42.

Maria, E. D. & Micelli, S. (eds.) (2005). *On Line Citizenship. Emerging Technologies for European Cities*. New York: Springer.

Miles, M. B. and Huberman, A. M. (1994). *An Expanded Sourcebook: Qualitative Data Analysis,* 2nd edition. London: Sage Publications.

Norris, P. (2005). The Impact of the Internet on Political Activism: Evidence from Europe. *International Journal of Electronic Government Research*, 1(1), 20-39.

Orlikowski, W.J. (1992). The duality of technology: rethinking the concept of technology in organizations. *Organisational Science*, 3(3), 398–427.

Orlikowski, W.J. (2000). Using technology and constituting structures: a practice lens for studying technology in organizations. *Organizational Science*, 11(4), 404–428.

Parvez, Z. & Ahmed, P. (2006). Towards Building An Integrated Perspective of e-Democracy in Practice. *Information, Communication & Society*, 9(5), 612–632.

Parvez, Z. (2006a). Examining e-Democracy Through A Double Structuration Loop. *Electronic Government*, 3(3), 329–346.

Parvez, Z. (2006b). Informatization of Local Democracy: A Structuration Perspective. *Information Polity*, 11(1), 67-83.

Pratchett, L., Wingfield M. & Polat, R. K.(2005). Barriers to e-Democracy: Local Government Experiences and Responses. *Local e-Democracy National Project*, Retrieved March 8, from http://www.icele.org/downloads/Researchreport.pdf

Pratchett, L.; Wingfield, M. & Polat, R. K. (2006). Local Democracy Online: An Analysis of Local Government Web Sites in England and Wales. *International Journal of Electronic Government Research*, 2(3), 75-92.

Pratchett, L (2007). *Local e-Democracy in Europe: Democratic X-ray as the Basis for Comparative Analysis*. International Conference Direct Democracy in Latin America. 14-15 March, Buenos Aires, Argentina. Retrieved March 8, from http://www.dd-la.ch/download/Pratchett_Lawrence.pdf

Robinson, E. (2005). *Councillors' Websites: an analysis. Local e-Democracy National Project*. Retrieved, March 8, from, http://www.icele.org/downloads/Councillorswebsitesedit.pdf

Rose, J. & Lewis, P. (2001). Structuration theory, action research, and information systems development. In L. Russo, B. Fitzgerald & J.I. DeGross (Eds.). *Realigning Research and Practice in Information Systems Development: The Social and Organizational Perspective*. Boston: Kluwer Academic Publishers.

Tsagarousianou, R., Tambini, D. & Bryan, C. (1998). *Cyberdemocracy: Technology, Cities and Civic Networks*. London: Routledge.

Van de Donk, W.B.H.J., Snellen, I.M. & Tops, P.W. (1995). *Orwell in Athens: A Perspective on Informatization and Democracy*. Netherlands: IOS Press.

Walsham, G. (1997). Actor-network theory and IS research: current status and future prospects. In Lee, A., S., Liebenau, J., and DeGross, J., I. (eds.). *Information Systems and Qualitative Research*. London: Chapman & Hall.

Zuboff, S. (1988). *In the Age of the Smart Machine*. New York: Basic Books.

This work was previously published in International Journal of Electronic Government Research, Vol. 4, Issue 3, edited by M. Khosrow-Pour, pp. 20-35, copyright 2008 by IGI Publishing (an imprint of IGI Global).

Chapter 18
Administrative Leadership and the Electronic City: Challenges and Opportunities

Greg Streib
Georgia State University, USA

Ignacio Navarro
Georgia State University, USA

ABSTRACT

Much has been written about the benefits of e-government, but far less has been written about how the e-government revolution will be staffed. Many questions remain about whether we have the capacity to develop and provide new e-government services. This chapter seeks to add to our knowledge in this area by examining three perspectives on the readiness of administrative leaders for effective development of e-government systems and strategies. The authors examine the lingering division of policy and administration, present an assessment of the technology knowledge of city managers, and finish with an examination of the leadership strategies available to administrative leaders in city government for achieving the kind of comprehensive changes that many e-government initiatives require. The authors find challenges in each of these important areas and also opportunities. The chapter concludes with recommendations for administrative leaders to break free from these different barriers to success.

INTRODUCTION

Technology has changed the world over the past few decades in far more ways that we probably realize and cities are no exception, but this is not to say that the pressures, costs, and benefits are the same across all parts of modern society or that the capacities for change and the degree of flexibility are the same. Cities arise across generations, and our governmental systems developed more as bulwarks against rapid change than conduits for progress. The challenge may be especially great in United States where we have struggled with the relationship between politics and administration. Genuine disagreements exist about when and how this distinction developed (Lynn, 2001), but the affects are quite real. E-government implementation requires both policy leadership and administrative skill, and this is certain to hinder the development of electronic cities. Among other things, such

DOI: 10.4018/978-1-60566-918-2.ch018

efforts require insight, initiative, substantial administrative changes, and reasonable efforts to assess progress, and dividing these needs between political and administrative spheres is not really plausible. Making e-government work challenges governmental systems in ways that are exceptional. Our perspectives on local governance in the United States have been changing (Nalbandian, 2005), but at nothing like the pace of technological change.

E-government is not something that we can push aside and ignore, however, and this is especially true for local governments, which offer a mix of service and communication intensive activities that can and do mesh well with Internet technology. A first step is to acknowledge that Internet technologies are changing the parameters of local government in important ways. Then we must find ways to work around the existing barriers to progress.

The goal of this chapter is to begin sorting out the different kinds of administrative leadership responsibilities that effective e-government requires. Our focus is on city managers in the United States in large part due to data availability, but our analysis is certainly relevant to cities using other governmental forms wherever they are located. Collaborative relationships between elected officials and appointed administrators are not uncommon in local governments, and the struggle to develop e-government infrastructure is a global challenge (UN, 2005). The issues we examine include the difficult nature of the relationship between political leaders and appointed professionals in local government, the technical skills and knowledge possessed by local public managers, and the leadership strategies that could help to produce successful outcomes. We are breaking some new ground here, but also building on a rapidly growing body of research. The role of technology in local government has not been totally overlooked at this point, but we are far from thinking about e-government progress as an essential local government responsibility. We will start with a brief look at the e-government landscape from a local government management perspective.

E-GOVERNMENT IN A LOCAL CONTEXT

E-Government Defined

E-government can be described as encompassing all things electronic (UN and ASPA, 2001), but this is not going to serve us well. Nor can we allow e-government to become synonymous with IT (information technology). As Moon (2002) noted, e-government may *use* IT; the IT should be viewed as a means to an end. Local governments already do use a wide range of specialized knowledge and tools to assess their financial status, to hire and fire employees, provide clean water, etc. E-government does present some unique challenges, but the local government management perspective needs to be that e-government is just one of many services. The IT and geek connection has helped to make e-government a responsibility that is easy to marginalize and leave for someone else to do. If e-government is rocket science, then only rocket scientists will have e-government. Using technology to better serve citizens is a management responsibility, and we need to approach e-government from a public management perspective (Zouridis and Thaens, 2003).

The nature of e-government was aptly described by Alfred Ho (2002) when he linked it to the "reinventing government" movement (Osborne and Gaebler, 1992). Key goals are better service delivery, a focus on citizen needs, and community ownership. As Ho points out, Internet technologies provide ways to achieve these goals in cost effective ways. This is not to say that E-government and reinventing government are linked seamlessly, but they do share a similar heritage and many similar goals. Both emerged during roughly the same time period and both have been driven by similar impulses to break down bureaucratic barriers and transform government.

E-Government Supply and Demand

There are different perspectives on the pace of e-government development in local governments that do not seem relevant here. The bottom line is that e-government is widely used in cities and at increasing levels of sophistication. The ICMA surveys from 2000 and 2002 are the best sources for assessing the current status of local e-government in the United States. These data show that as of 2002, nearly 90 percent of general purpose governments now have Web sites (Norris and Moon, 2005). Further, the findings suggest that as of now (2008), most city government Web sites would be no more than 10 years old; a smaller minority could have been around as long as 13 years (Norris and Moon, 2005). Web sites and Web services are relatively new, and they have become substantial local government responsibilities. Nearly half of the respondents to the 2002 ICMA survey indicated that there were staff and financial barriers to e-government, and over a third indicated that a lack of Web expertise was a barrier (Norris and Moon, 2005). It is an arguable claim, but there may well be a bolder vision for e-government in the European Union (European Commission, 2005), and there is also evidence of substantial implementation progress (DGIM, 2005). On the whole, however, it appears that even innovative governments around the world are struggling to make full use of e-government applications (UN, 2005).

The ICMA studies have received considerable use, and they have certainly increased our understanding of e-government implementation, but they do not tell us much about e-government benefits. When local government officials were asked about possible e-government benefits in 2002, only 17% of the ICMA respondents indicated that their business processes were more efficient and just 15% of the respondents felt that they had reduced time demands on their staff. Findings from a more focused study of city managers in Texas and Florida found more positive results, such as improved productivity and improved city manager effectiveness (Reddick and Frank, 2007). This study appeared to show distinct e-government management benefits, though "agree" was the modal category in the responses. Roughly the same number disagreed with the management items as strongly agreed. On the whole, findings indicate some potential for e-government, if we accept the argument that we are looking at early assessments that foretell greater future impacts. From the ICMA study in 2002 we also know that many jurisdictions have a wide range of financial and nonfinancial e-government services in development.

E-Government Demand

The progress in developing local government Internet capacity only hints at the existence of a demand for these services. Is there pressure to provide more e-government than citizens want or do citizens want more e-government than they have? While we may never know the ideal balance between e-government demand and supply, there is some data available on current citizen preferences.

A polling study conducted by Thomas and Streib (2003) found that e-government users were generally satisfied with government Web sites. This study also found that Internet research was the most common reason why citizens visited these sites, and a poll by the Pew Internet and American Life Project produced similar findings (Reddick, 2005). We also know that most local government Web sites are focused on providing information (Holden, Norris, and Fletcher, 2003; Reddick 2004).

The research to date does not show strong demand for more sophisticated Internet applications. Thomas and Streib (2005) found that most citizens were not using the Internet as a way to communicate with government officials, for example. One recent study compared polling data from citizens and government officials and found greater knowledge and excitement about the future prospects of e-government among the officials and greater concerns about online threats among the citizens (Moon and Welch, 2005). Of particular concern were citizen responses indicating that e-government might reduce service quality (by making government less personal and making it difficult to get answers). Of course, demand issues are not confined to the United States. Researchers in Europe have documented this same sort of gap between the capabilities of e-government technology and the actual online activities of citizens (van Deursen, 2006).

At present, it certainly does appear that there is a definite preference for traditional means of communication among the general population of Internet users. Reddick (2005) found that citizens preferred the telephone for two-way communications, and a polling study by Streib and Navarro (2006) produced similar findings. A report by the Council for Excellence in Government (2003) did ask a wide range of e-government demand questions, and the findings showed some interest in conducting government transactions online. Overall, the findings confirmed that few citizens are conducting e-government transactions at the present time and that in-person communications were the preferred method of contact, but there was a slight preference for e-government transactions among e-government users and respondents that lived in best practice areas (where more e-government services were available).

Implementation Challenges

It has been argued that e-government will bring changes that are more incremental than transformational (West, 2004), but others still foresee more dramatic changes (Eggers, 2005) or at least withhold judgment until more time has passed (Jaeger, 2003). Whatever trajectory that e-government takes, there is no question that success will require applying traditional assessment and control tools (Steyaert, 2004; Stowers, 2004) and effective leadership. Following the leadership definition of Bennis (1992), good management is needed to make sure that work is getting done correctly, and leadership is needed to help identify the right things to do.

Even basic information sharing can be done in ways that range from dreadful to exemplary. The thorny details involved in even basic e-government applications include selecting and organizing the material to be provided; assigning Web site responsibilities; assigning resources to departments and individuals (Web storage, staff time, graphics, etc.); maintaining the accuracy of information (new entries and periodic reviews for accuracy); assuring consistency in style, and assuring privacy (Layne and Lee, 2001).

Even e-government efforts focused mostly on providing information require involvement from all levels of an organization, and top officials must play an important role (McClure, 2000). Not surprisingly, a management reform orientation has been found related to the establishment of comprehensive e-government initiatives (Moon and Norris, 2005). Implementing e-government initiatives is not business as usual, and there is evidence that all local governments may not be up to the challenge. In a survey of local government officials on the implementation of performance measurement, Poister and Streib (1999) found weaknesses at the employee level. Over half of the respondents indicated that their employees at least sometimes lacked the necessary analytical skills, and over 60% of the respondents agreed that they at least sometimes had trouble getting lower level employees to support their performance measurement system. There are strong similarities between the organizational demands presented by e-government and performance measurement, and these findings are reason for concern.

Assessments of actual local government Web sites are already revealing weaknesses. Research by Justice, Melitski, and Smith (2006) found that even large jurisdictions in the United States did not fully adhere to the recommended practices that were published by the Government Finance Officers Association in 2003--pertaining to Web access for budget documents and financial reports. Similarly, Scott (2006) found "...very little evidence that U.S. municipal government Web sites support significant public involvement" (p. 349). Scott did find much information and a range of communication options available on municipal Web sites, but the bottom line conclusion was that municipal governments did not seem to understand or acknowledge the potential that the Internet can do.

We might speculate that government officials wisely sense a limited public interest in financial documents and Internet communications, but it seems far too early for definitive conclusions on this matters. An interesting study by Tolbert and Mossberger (2006) found that use of local government Web sites seemed related to increased trust under certain circumstances. Web site users who believed that local government Web sites could improve responsiveness had higher levels of trust. If we take this to heart, then providing basic financial documents would seem like something that local governments would find a way to do. Questions remain about how to develop the best Web sites (that balance cost efficiencies with citizen satisfaction), of course, and leaders with knowledge, vision, and appropriate leadership skills are needed to help sort this out.

POLITICS AND ADMINISTRATION

Government with a Divided Purpose

Our experience with e-government to date shows steady forward progress and also demonstrates that the development of sophisticated applications will require a focused effort. This could be difficult when achieving this level of focus requires spanning both policy and administration. Developing effective e-government applications requires translating often abstract ideas into administrative realities. It is not always clear who has this job in US local governments. The call for a politics and administration dichotomy is often traced to Woodrow Wilson (1887) who advocated what he called a "business of government." While many now believe that Wilson's arguments were misunderstood (Svara, 1998), there is no question that many came to believe that effective public administration could best be achieved by steering clear of policy making.

In the case of local government, there is currently widespread agreement among researchers that the role of city managers includes both administration and policy. Nalbandian (1990) arrived at this conclusion after interviews and discussions with practicing managers, and the 1996 Council-Manager Plan Task Force survey that was sponsored by the International City/County Management Association (ICMA) found that the majority of city managers, "are involved extensively in the initiation and development of policy" (Selden, Brewer, & Brudney, 1999). Svara (1999) presented similar findings. It could be said that city managers are now viewed as important policy actors (Nalbandian, 1991; Morgan and Watson, 1992).

However, many questions remain about the level of policy leadership that city managers are willing to provide. Authors such as Banovetz (1994) have argued that city managers may well view opportunities for policy leadership as threatening. Others have argued that there are aspects of the politics and administration dichotomy that should actually be retained (Montjoy and Watson, 1995). Even if city managers are active participants in policymaking, this does not assure that they would be willing to take personal responsibility for major initiatives. Without a doubt, city managers can certainly influence the development of electronic cities, but it is unlikely that they will become e-government champions without strong political backing from elected officials.

An additional possibility to consider is that city managers may indeed have the capacity to implement substantial e-government reforms but choose not to do it—or at least choose to do it in ways that best suit their own interests, which would be consistent with the conclusions reached in an analysis of e-government research presented by Kraemer and King (2003). They concluded, for example, that information technology in government has actually been used to strengthen existing (hierarchical) organizational structures rather than reform them. Their take on this was that hierarchy suits the interest of those in power. Overall, they argued that the benefits of technology have been handled like political favors, and the primary beneficiaries have been those in favor with dominant coalitions. Those left out include middle managers, staff, and ordinary citizens.

Thus far, it can be said that Kraemer and King do not present a majority view, but they may strike a nerve or two. E-government offers some fantastic ways to bring citizens into decision making processes (Bevarly and Ulma, 2007-08), and we know that progress in this area has actually been quite mixed. It is certainly a possible explanation that this happens because government officials are seeking to limit citizen involvement.

THE TECHNOLOGY LITERACY OF CITY MANAGERS

As discussed above, e-government implementation places a great reliance on local government administrative leaders and it is not clear that they are up to the task. At a basic level, we need to wonder about basic technology literacy. Research does show that leader credibility is an important component of successful local government innovations (Ihrke, Proctor, and Gabris, 2003). In this context, technological literacy needs to address both a familiarity with different technologies and an understanding of how they might function within a local government context. E-government is not going to arrive in a box. Software will improve, and venders will continue to present cities with interesting tools and solutions, but meaningful progress will certainly require knowledgeable public leaders. This sort of knowledge can be considered a first step toward providing the level of leadership that is required.

The Technology Knowledge of City Managers

There is some information available about the technology knowledge of city managers that comes from the Applied Knowledge Assessment (AKA) that was developed by a team that included faculty from Georgia State University (GSU), ICMA staff, and involved city and county managers from across the nation. The AKA is a 116 item assessment instrument that addresses 18 practices for effective local government managers that were identified through an ICMA sponsored, two-year Dialogue on the Profession that began in 1992. One of these practices assesses technology literacy. The development of the instrument was presented in detail by Streib (1995).

When it comes to technology literacy, the AKA responses provide data on assessment items that managers themselves identified as important using items that managers helped to write. The AKA scoring was validated by using the responses from hundreds of managers who completed the instrument during the development phase. A short survey was also used to assess the value of the AKA when it was still in draft form. As reported by Streib (2005), 74% of the survey respondents agreed that the items were realistic, and 86% agreed that the content covered what managers needed to know.

The first printing of the Applied Knowledge Assessment was in the spring of 1999, and thousands of public officials have completed it since this time. Taking the AKA has also become a requirement for becoming an ICMA Credentialed Manager, and there are currently over 1000 credentialed managers. We report the responses of the 1195 practicing city managers who completed the AKA between 1999 and the spring of 2007.

The Technology Literacy Practice

The AKA contains seven items intended to measure each respondent's technology literacy, relative to the needs city governments. Some of these items addressed the management aspects of technology more than others, but all of the items addressed issues that were likely to arise in a local government context—as judged by the city managers who helped to craft and/or who reviewed the items. The topics addressed fell into two broad categories: (A) knowledge about electronic (primarily Internet) technologies, and (B) knowledge about how to implement and/or use technology effectively within a municipal government.

Table 1 shows how 1195 city managers performed on the technological literacy practice and the entire ICMA Applied Knowledge Assessment. The first column depicts the average score on the 7 technology items, and the second column shows the total raw score in all areas of the AKA. Scores are divided by age, geographic region, years of experience in government, and years in current position.

The results in Table 1 are encouraging in that the responding managers did better on the technology literacy practice than on the AKA as a whole. That is, the scores on the technology practice are higher than the scores on some of the 17 other practices covered on the assessment. Overall, the responding managers received an average score of 82 percent on the AKA; in contrast, the average score of the technology practice was 88 percent. This finding was statistically significant across all groups of city managers.

Even though city mangers as a whole performed impressively on the AKA technology literacy practice, some groups did perform better than others. As Table 1 shows, we did find some modest regional differences. City mangers in the north-eastern region of the country received a higher average than their counterparts in the north-central and southern regions.[1]

Another interesting finding was the relation between performance on the technology literacy practice and the age of the city manager respondents. City managers between 56 and 65 years old did very well on the entire AKA, but they did not score as well as younger managers on the technology practice—on average.[2] It seems plausible that younger managers might have some advantages when it comes to technology, though we also found that youth alone does also bring some limitations. The effect of age in Table 1 is most pronounced for those few AKA city manager respondents at age 66 or above—who received fairly low scores on the technology practice items.

The negative relationship between age and technology literacy scores in the AKA does not mean that simply being younger leads to higher scores on the technology practice. We also found a positive relationship between performance on the technology literacy practice and the number of years of experience in government.[3] Managers with less than 3 years of experience in government answered an average of 84% of the technology items correctly, and city managers with 13–17 years of experience in government answered 89% of the technology items correctly. It is certainly good news that city managers who were in the profession when the Internet first emerged are receiving the highest scores on the ICMA technology literacy practice. It is also worth noting that these findings do not allow for any solid conclusions about the managers with 18 or more years of service. Unfortunately, this category is too broad to be of much use since it could include managers that were 40 just as well as those who were 70. (There are 700 respondents in this category 18 years and above category.)

Table 1.City manager scores on the ICMA applied knowledge assessment: practice seven/technology literacy and overall

City Manager Scores on the ICMA Applied Knowledge Assessment:Practice Seven/Technology Literacy and Overall			
	% Correct Answers on Technology Items	% Correct Answers on All AKA Items	All Valid Respondents
Age Group			
25 or less	100.00%	68.10%	1
26 to 35	87.33%	80.23%	124
36 to 45	89.02%	81.49%	311
46 to 55	88.44%	82.64%	571
56 to 65	85.40%	81.61%	181
66 or more	81.63%	76.11%	7
Total	87.99%	81.89%	1195
Geographic Region			
Northeast	90.20%	81.91%	191
North Central	87.45%	81.62%	386
South	87.39%	81.31%	375
West	88.01%	83.19%	243
Total	87.99%	81.89%	1195
Years/Government			
Under 3 years	84.52%	75.29%	24
3 to 7	87.12%	78.77%	112
8 to 12	86.86%	79.66%	162
13 to 17	89.10%	81.70%	173
18 or more	88.19%	83.17%	709
Total	87.97%	81.90%	1180
Years/Current Job			
Under 3 years	87.52%	80.70%	404
3 to 7	87.61%	82.15%	414
8 to 12	89.49%	83.43%	174
13 to 17	87.82%	82.45%	102
18 or more	88.70%	83.56%	67
Total	87.94%	81.95%	1161

Table 2 displays the results for the individual technology items, which we have classified as addressing tech knowledge or tech management. As the name implies, the tech knowledge items were more directed at whether managers were knowledgeable about the kinds of technologies that were encountered in a city government. One question asked about how to best protect networked computers from viruses, for example. Management questions addressed staffing issues and the likely impacts of technology on city operations. One of these questions asked about the appropriateness of placing certain types of employee information on the Internet and another

Table 2. City manager performance on individual technology practice items

City Manager Performance on Individual Technology Practice Items							
	Item 1	Item 2	Item 3	Item 4	Item 5	Item 6	Item 7
	Tech Knowledge	Tech Knowledge	Tech Knowledge	Tech Knowledge	Managing Tech	Managing Tech	Managing Tech
Age Group							
25 or less	100.00%	100.00%	100.00%	100.00%	100.00%	100.00%	100.00%
26 to 35	91.94%	100.00%	94.35%	96.77%	84.68%	64.52%	79.03%
36 to 45	91.00%	99.68%	89.39%	98.07%	87.46%	74.60%	82.96%
46 to 55	91.77%	99.12%	89.84%	98.42%	86.51%	77.58%	75.83%
56 to 65	83.98%	99.45%	88.40%	97.79%	81.77%	76.80%	69.61%
66 or more	85.71%	100.00%	71.43%	85.71%	85.71%	85.71%	57.14%
Total	90.38%	99.41%	89.87%	97.99%	85.86%	75.40%	76.99%
Geographic Region							
Northeast	91.10%	99.48%	94.76%	98.95%	87.96%	76.44%	82.72%
North Central	91.71%	99.22%	90.67%	96.89%	84.97%	71.24%	77.46%
South	88.53%	100.00%	85.07%	98.13%	85.87%	78.13%	76.00%
West	90.53%	98.77%	92.18%	98.77%	85.60%	76.95%	73.25%
Total	90.38%	99.41%	89.87%	97.99%	85.86%	75.40%	76.99%
Years/Government							
Under 3 years	91.67%	100.00%	91.67%	100.00%	75.00%	58.33%	75.00%
3 to 7	91.07%	100.00%	89.29%	98.21%	90.18%	66.07%	75.00%
8 to 12	90.12%	99.38%	90.12%	97.53%	86.42%	66.67%	77.78%
13 to 17	90.75%	99.42%	89.60%	98.27%	89.60%	74.57%	81.50%
18 or more	90.13%	99.29%	89.84%	97.88%	84.34%	79.83%	76.02%
Total	90.34%	99.41%	89.83%	97.97%	85.76%	75.51%	76.95%
Years/Current Job							
Under 3 years	90.35%	99.75%	89.11%	98.27%	84.65%	75.25%	75.25%
3 to 7	91.79%	99.03%	90.82%	97.34%	85.99%	71.74%	76.57%
8 to 12	90.23%	100.00%	89.08%	97.70%	89.66%	81.03%	78.74%
13 to 17	87.25%	99.02%	89.22%	100.00%	83.33%	77.45%	78.43%
18 or more	85.07%	98.51%	91.04%	97.01%	88.06%	80.60%	80.60%
Total	90.27%	99.40%	89.84%	97.93%	85.96%	75.37%	76.83%

addressed the possibilities of cost savings from investments in new technologies.

As Table 2 shows, respondents in the lower age groupings did tend to do better on the tech knowledge items, though this tendency was only really striking on items one and three. Clearly, youth often produced a greater familiarity with the technology applications addressed by those items. However, what is most interesting about this table is that the advantages of youth had obvious limitations—the advantage was limited to the items focused on tech knowledge and did not extend to managing technology. In contrast, manager groupings with higher ages and/or more experience tended to score better on the items more focused on the managerial or implementation aspects of technology.

Age, Experience, and Technological Literacy

So far, the differing contributions of age and experience are somewhat elusive. The previous tables suggest that age and experience play different roles, but it is hard to draw any firm conclusions. One reason is that some younger managers may already have quite a bit of experience, and some older managers may actually be newer members of the field. The age and experience categories do not do a perfect job of separating the effects of age and experience. It turns out that this mixing of age and experience does hide some interesting findings.

To explore this further, we first created new versions of our age and experience variables. The updated age variable has just two categories, 46 years or older and 45 years or younger, and the updated experience variable also has just two categories, 13 years of experience or more and 12 years of experience or less. These changes allow us to produce more distinct groups and make maximum use of the data available.

These modified variables reveal four distinct groups. The lowest scores on all of the technology items (on average) went to the two groupings of managers with 12 years of experience or less, regardless of their age. This is in contrast to the two groupings of managers with 13 years of experience or more. Within the grouping of managers with less experience, those 45 years old or less did receive slightly higher scores, which reaffirms the role of age in technology literacy. Youth conferred a slight benefit, but only among those managers with less experience.

While we found some advantages to youth among the less experienced managers, there was a sharp contrast between the scores of the less experienced and those with more experience. The total scores on the technology literacy practice were best for the groupings of managers with higher experience levels regardless of their age. These findings suggest that youth is associated with greater knowledge about technology, as common sense would suggest, but that experience in government also plays an important role. These findings are displayed in Table 3, and the scores on all the technology items combined can be found in the left-most column.

A close look at Table 3 clearly shows both the advantages that younger managers bring to technology issues and the advantage of experience. The younger group of managers with less experience received the highest scores on the technology knowledge items (in the middle column), though the scores only ranged from a high of 96 percent to a low of 92 percent. The younger/less experience group was even ahead of the younger group of managers with 13 or more years of experience. A likely explanation is that the managers in the younger/less experience group are not as old as

Table 3. Age, experience and technology literacy

Age, Experience, and Technological Literacy			
Age/Experience Group	**Total Score (all Items)**	**Total Score Tech Knowledge**	**Total Score Managing Tech**
Age 45 Years (and Less) & Experience 12 Years (or Less)	79%	96%	77%
Age 45 Years (and Less) & Experience 13 Years (or More)	83%	94%	84%
Age 46 Years (and More) & Experience 12 Years (or Less)	78%	92%	75%
Age 46 Years (and More & Experience 13 Years (or More)	83%	94%	79%

those managers in the younger/more experienced group. There is a 12 year range in the lowest age category that does allow some variation. The grouping of younger/less experienced managers and younger/more experienced managers probably contain somewhat different age mixes.

The findings in the middle column did also affirm the value of experience because the higher experience groups dominated the second tier of scores--with average scores of 94%, regardless of age. Both the younger/more experienced group and the older/more experienced group received the same score. The lowest scores in the middle column went to the grouping of managers that were older and who also had less experience.

The scores on the technology management items in the right-hand column were the most dramatic. The younger managers with more experience did considerably better than the other groups. Also, the grouping of older managers with more experience received higher scores than the grouping younger managers with less experience that had received the highest scores on the tech knowledge items. Once again, the lowest scores on the managing technology items went to the grouping of managers with higher ages and less experience.

E-GOVERNMENT LEADERSHIP STRATEGIES

City managers with technological literacy are an essential pre-condition for the development and enhancement of e-government in U.S. council-manager governments, but matching this knowledge with yesterday's management approaches and standards is probably not the route to success. This is especially true due to the unique role that city managers and other administrators play in local governments. It is possible to imagine that a highly politicized, incremental process could lead to e-government progress, but, at best, this would only precede a lengthy implementation process that most likely outlasts the coalition that started it off. Political leaders may also serve as advocates or champions, but, again, this leaves a substantial role for administrators—possibly extending to actual coalition building. From almost any perspective, new technology initiatives will require administrators to take on roles that depart from their typical responsibilities.

Success will require focused policy leadership that is applied through the use of effective management processes. Responsibilities could be shared across a management team, but ground-breaking e-government initiatives will require someone to take on the role of champion, and the city manager may be a logical choice in council–manager governments. The political aspects of this role are clearly a downside, but the city manager is the one best able to provide linkages between city administrative structures and processes to policy goals and action plans. The necessary leadership involves establishing a process that will produce a viable action plan (finding the right things to do), in cooperation with elected officials, and guiding the implementation process in effective ways.

Strategic Management as a Foundation

A good starting point is to recognize that many or most e-government initiatives represent important strategic decisions. They should be congruent with the values and mission of the organization, and they should be supported by a well articulated vision. Strategic management offers a process that can be used to develop e-government initiatives that would include these steps: assessing organizational strengths and weaknesses, identification of stakeholder concerns, development of a vision and appropriate goals and objectives, feasibility analysis, and development of a strategic agenda and action plans (Poister and Streib, 2005). This type of a process is a method for identifying the right things to do, and it can be applied city-wide or used in a more selective way. The research by Poister and Streib did find that only a small proportion of city governments are using all elements of the strategic management process, which does raise some questions about the e-government capacity of cities.

It should also be noted that the strategic management process can be enhanced in ways that can help to maximize the community benefits. Moore (1995) recommends a focus on the creation of public value by assessing fit with mission and purpose, managing outward to establish legitimacy and build support, and managing downward to improve organizational capabilities. These different components of Moore's approach certainly emphasize what is needed to successfully implement e-government initiatives. This is especially true because of the prominence given to visionary leadership in recent years. As was wonderfully described by Westley and Mintzberg (1989), visionaries are found in all walks of life and they possess a wide range of motives. The arguments presented by Moore are a reminder to city managers to stay focused on appropriate objectives such as community building.

Leadership Objectives

As noted above, strategic management can be considered as incorporating a form of visionary leadership, but proceeding in this way tells us little about the kinds of methods that need to be used. A vision is needed—best focused on increasing public value, but simply pronouncing this vision will not be enough. A unique aspect of e-government is that it cannot be easily placed into a traditional administrative hierarchy. It requires integrative channels within organizations that traditional hierarchical forms do not provide (Kieley, et al., 2002; Ho, 2002). There needs to be substantial pulling from the top of the organization and active involvement down to the very bottom. This will not be easy, but it is hard to get around the fact that all members of an organization have something to contribute to an e-government effort. Consider how a city Web page might help citizens involved in repairing a water leak to their property, for example. The city inspectors have information that they can use and this needs to be accessed and shared. City government employees possess useful information of all kinds and e-government that flows from the top of the organization is stripped of this content.

Given the organizational challenge that e-government presents, integration should be an important objective of city manager leadership efforts. Integrative leadership involves actions that build and improve upon organizational abilities and management systems (Ingraham, 2001). Leadership is a driver that pushes changes through organizations that already have a results oriented structure, critical information needed to make good decisions, and an appropriate level of capacity. Integrative leadership is an important component of virtually any comprehensive initiative, and it has been shown to produce results (Moynihan and Ingraham, 2004).

While integration can occur within a city, managers may also find themselves dealing with shared-power relationships (Bryson and Crosby, 1992) that extend beyond the doors of city hall. As Svara (1994) noted, power in council-manager governments is fragmented, and not along the familiar lines created by separation of powers. In his view, facilitative leadership has become an important objective of city managers. This is a form of leadership that is collaborative and focused on the achievement of common goals. Knowledge of technology is not equally distributed and someone with the ability to build effective collaborative groups and partnerships must develop and champion a vision that can develop broad community support and be successfully implemented.

City managers should be aware that experience is showing that effective collaboration requires high levels of trust (Guffey, 2003). Integrity is a key ingredient in successful collaborations because mutual accountability must be assured (Whitaker, Henderson, Altman-Sauer, 2004).

City managers have commented on the rising demand for involvement and power sharing in policymaking and problem-solving (Nalbandian, 1999). Effective leadership should empower all participants (Guffey, 2006). Building collaborative relationships is also an essential component of integrative leadership within a city government; the same rules apply, though intensive communication from top leadership is an additional need (Trahant, 2007).

FUTURE TRENDS

The analysis we presented in this chapter builds from the assumption that e-government success requires integration into existing professional administrative structures. Certainly in local governments in the United States, appointed administrators play a critical leadership role, due to their tenure in office, their level of knowledge, their leadership skills and their professional commitment to good government. If our assumption is correct, then we may have discovered an important reason why e-government implementation has not have moved as briskly as enthusiasts would like.

We found that city managers who had taken the ICMA Applied Knowledge Assessment did actually possess some relevant knowledge, but we also discovered some interesting complexities. For example, we found a generational quality to e-government related knowledge suggesting that that there are subgroups of managers who view (and use) Internet technologies in fundamentally different ways. We also concluded that specialized leadership skills may be needed. We do not address the prevalence of these skills in this chapter, but they are unlikely to be equally distributed among government managers.

These findings suggest a lack of capacity that will keep the trajectory of e-government development relatively flat for the foreseeable future. There will be exceptions, of course--instances where a group of individuals unite around a common vision and/or leader and find the resources they need to sustain an e-government initiative of some kind, but these fortuitous situations are not likely to be the norm. Broader initiatives by central governments are also a possible path to success. We noted activity along these lines earlier in our chapter. Projects such as INTELCITY simply do not exist in the United States (INTELCITY, 2004-2006). The broad visioning and consensus building piece has never happened.

Organizational Strategies

While a positive external environment would provide benefits, all e-government initiatives will eventually get down to individual organizations, and there are some strategies that they could follow to increase their chances of success, for example:

1. Leaders should carefully monitor the flow of information in their organizations. E-government at this stage of development is about information sharing. Information hording may actually be the norm. Many management tools and processes have stressed better communication and control across levels of an organization, and progress has been slow. This type of weakness may take on new meaning as e-government expectations grow.
2. Strategic management offers leaders an effective process that can provide the kind of infrastructure needed for e-government success, but the current evidence suggests that few city governments in the United States are using strategic management to its full potential, and this is probably also true of other government organizations. This raises questions about the ability of governments to get full use out of e-government. Greater investment in strategic management is likely to also improve e-government capacity.

3. New and future entrants to government service should realize that there are probably more aspects to their jobs that they can only learn on the job than they thought. Conventional wisdom suggests that certain aspects of the budget cycle might be best learned in a job setting, for example, but technology skills might come as surprise. Again, the evidence discussed in this chapter applied to the United States specifically, though there is no reason to think that these needs only exist in this one country.

E-government has given idealists much to think about, but it has become increasingly clear that bold ideas cannot be easily translated into either citizen excitement or actual services. Progress has been quicker in some countries than others, but it is certainly correct to say that the vast majority of governments in the world today do not make full use of the technology tools that are available to them. Anything is possible over the very long term, but the short term does not appear to offer more than gradual, incremental change. This is not a very effective way to engage technologies that are developing exponentially.

REFERENCES

Banovetz, J. M. (1994). City managers: Will they reject policy leadership? *Public Productivity & Management Review*, *17*(4), 313–324. doi:10.2307/3380830

Bennis, W. (1984). Where have all the leaders gone? In W. Rosenbach & R. Taylor (Eds.), *Contemporary Issues in Leadership* (2nd ed., pp. 2-23). Boulder, Colorado: Westview Press.

Bevarly, D., & Ulma, J. (2007-08). Citizen involvement in the digital age. *Public Management*, *6*(4), 3–7.

Bryson, J., & Crosby, B. (1992). *Leadership for the common good: Tackling public problems in a shared-power world.* San Francisco: Jossey Bass.

Council for Excellence in Government. (2003). *The new e-government equation: ease, engagement, privacy and protection.* Washington, DC: Prepared by Hart–Teeter for the Council for Excellence in Government.

DGIM. (2005). Online availability of public services: How is Europe progressing. Web based survey on Electronic Public Services. Report of the fifth measurement, October 2004. Prepared by Capgemini for the European Commission Directorate General for Information. Retrieved December 15, 2007, from http://ec.europa.eu/information_society/soccul/egov/egov_benchmarking_2005.pdf

Eggers, W. (2005). *Government 2.0: Using technology to improve education, cut red tape, reduce gridlock, and enhance democracy.* Lanham, MD: Roman and Littlefield Publishers.

European Commission. (2005). *i2010 – A European information society for growth and Employment.* Brussels, Belgium: European Commission.

Fairholm, M. R. (2004). Different perspectives on the practice of leadership. *Public Administration Review*, *64*(5), 577–590. doi:10.1111/j.1540-6210.2004.00405.x

Guffey, K. M. (2003). Collaborative networks: the initial design strongly influences the outcome. *Public Management*, *32*(2), 42.

Guffey, K. M. (2006). Empowering collaborations in the hollow state. *International Journal of Public Administration*, *29*(8), 561–575. doi:10.1080/01900690500455271

Ho, A. (2002). Reinventing local governments and the e-government initiative. *Public Administration Review*, *62*(4), 434–444. doi:10.1111/0033-3352.00197

Holden, S. H., Norris, D. F., & Fletcher, P. (2003). Electronic government at the local level: progress to date and future issues. *Public Performance & Management Review*, *26*(4), 325–344. doi:10.1177/1530957603026004002

Ihrke, D., Proctor, R., & Gabris, J. (2003). Understanding innovation in municipal government: city council member perspectives. *Journal of Urban Affairs*, *25*(1), 79–90. doi:10.1111/1467-9906.t01-1-00006

Ingraham, P. (2001). *Linking leadership to performance in public organizations*. Paris: Organization for Economic Co-Operation and Development.

INTELCITIES. (2004-2006). *Intelligent Cities project* (N°: IST.2002-507860). EU VI Framework, Information Society Technologies, http://www.intelcitiesproject.com

Jaeger, P. (2003). The endless wire: E-government as global phenomenon. *Government Information Quarterly*, *20*(4), 323–331. doi:10.1016/j.giq.2003.08.003

Justice, J.,, & Melitski, J., & Smith, Daniel L. (2006). E-government as an instrument of fiscal accountability and responsiveness: Do the best practitioners employ the best practices? *American Review of Public Administration*, *36*(3), 301–322. doi:10.1177/0275074005283797

Kaylor, C., Deshazo, R., & Van Eck, D. (2001). Gauging e-government: A report on implementing services among American cities. *Government Information Quarterly*, *18*(4), 293–307. doi:10.1016/S0740-624X(01)00089-2

Kieley, B., Lane, G., Paquet, G., & Roy, J. (2002). E-government in Canada: Services online or public service renewal? In Å. Grönlund (Ed.), *Electronic government: design, applications, and management* (pp. 340-355). Hershey, PA: Idea Group Publishing.

Kraemer, K., & King, J. (2003). Information technology and administrative reform: Will the time after e-government be different? *Center for Research on Information Technology and Organizations. IT in Government*. Paper 337.

Layne, K., & Lee, J. (2001). Developing fully functional e-government: A four stage model. *Government Information Quarterly*, *18*(2), 122–136. doi:10.1016/S0740-624X(01)00066-1

Lynn, L. E. Jr. (2001). The myth of the bureaucratic paradigm: what traditional public administration really stood for. *Public Administration Review*, *61*(2), 144–160. doi:10.1111/0033-3352.00016

McClure, D. (2000). *Statement of David L. McClure, U.S. General Accounting Office, before the Subcommittee on Government Management, Information and Technology.* Committee on Government Reform, House of Representatives. Retrieved December 15, 2007 from http://www.gao.gov

Milward, H. B., & Snyder, L. O. (1996). Electronic government: linking citizens to public organizations through technology. *Journal of Public Administration: Research and Theory*, *6*(2), 261–276.

Montjoy, R. S., & Watson, D. J. (1995). A case for reinterpreted dichotomy of politics and administration as a professional standard in council-manager government. *Public Administration Review*, *55*(3), 231–239. doi:10.2307/3110241

Moon, J. (2002). The evolution of e-government among municipalities: Rhetoric or reality? *Public Administration Review*, *62*(4), 424–433. doi:10.1111/0033-3352.00196

Moon, J., & Welch, E. (2005). Same bed, different dreams? A comparative analysis of citizen and bureaucrat perspectives on e-government. *Review of Public Personnel Administration*, *25*(3), 243–264. doi:10.1177/0734371X05275508

Moore, M. (1995). *Creating public value: Strategic management in government*. Harvard University Press: Cambridge, MA, 1995.

Morgan, D. R., & Watson, S. S. (1992). Policy Leadership in council-manager cities: comparing mayors and managers. *Public Administration Review*, *52*(5), 438–446. doi:10.2307/976803

Moynihan, Donald P., & Ingraham, P. (2004). Integrative leadership in the public sector: A model of performance-information use. *Administration & Society*, *36*(4), 427–453. doi:10.1177/0095399704266748

Nalbandian, J. (1989). The contemporary role of city managers. *American Review of Public Administration*, *19*(4), 261–279. doi:10.1177/027507408901900401

Nalbandian, J. (1991). Professionalism in local government. San Francisco: Jossey-Bass.

Nalbandian, J. (1999). Facilitating community, enabling democracy: new roles for local government managers. *Public Administration Review*, *59*(3), 187–197. doi:10.2307/3109948

Nalbandian, J. (2005). Professionals and the conflicting forces of administrative modernization and civic engagement. *American Review of Public Administration*, *35*(4), 311–326. doi:10.1177/0275074005279897

Newland, C. A. (1989). The future of council-manager government, In H. George Frederickson (Ed.), *Ideal and Practice in Council-Manager Government.* Washington, DC: International City Management Association.

Norris, D., & Jae Moon, J. (2005). Advancing e-government at the grassroots: tortoise or hare? *Public Administration Review*, *65*(1), 64–75. doi:10.1111/j.1540-6210.2005.00431.x

Norris, D., & Jae Moon, J. (2005). Does managerial orientation matter? The adoption of reinventing government and e-government at the municipal level. *Information Systems Journal*, *15*(1), 43–60. doi:10.1111/j.1365-2575.2005.00185.x

Osborne, D., & Gaebler, T. (1993). *Reinventing government: how the entrepreneurial spirit is transforming the public sector*. New York: Plume.

Poister, T., & Streib, G. (1994). Municipal management tools from 1976 to 1993: An overview and update. *Public Productivity & Management Review*, *18*(2), 115–125. doi:10.2307/3380641

Poister, T., & Streib, G. (1999). Performance measurement in municipal government: Assessing the state of the practice. *Public Administration Review*, *59*(4), 325–335. doi:10.2307/3110115

Poister, T., & Streib, G. (2005). Elements of strategic planning and management in municipal government: status after two decades. *Public Administration Review*, *65*(1), 45–56. doi:10.1111/j.1540-6210.2005.00429.x

Poister, T. H., & Streib, G. (1999). Strategic management in the public sector: concepts, models, and processes. *Public Productivity and Management Review*, *22*(3), 308–325. doi:10.2307/3380706

Reddick, C. (2004). A two-stage model of e-government growth: Theories and empirical evidence for U.S. cities. *Government Information Quarterly*, *21*(1), 51–64. doi:10.1016/j.giq.2003.11.004

Reddick, C. (2005). Citizen-initiated contacts with government comparing phones and websites. *Journal of E-Government*, *2*(1), 27–53. doi:10.1300/J399v02n01_03

Reddick, C., & Frank, H. (2007). E-government and its influence on managerial effectiveness: A survey of Florida and Texas city managers. *Financial Accountability & Management, 23*(1), 1–26. doi:10.1111/j.1468-0408.2007.00417.x

Schneider, M., & Teske, P. (1994). The bureaucratic entrepreneur: The case of city managers. *Public Administration Review, 54*(4), 331–340. doi:10.2307/977380

Scott, J. (2006). "E" the people: Do U.S. municipal government web sites support public involvement? *Public Administration Review, 66*(3), 341–353. doi:10.1111/j.1540-6210.2006.00593.x

Selden, C. S., Brewer, G., & Brudney, J. (1999). The role of city managers: Are they principals, agents, or both? *American Review of Public Administration, 29*(2), 124–148. doi:10.1177/02750749922064319

Steyaert, J. C. (2004). Measuring the performance of electronic government services. *Information & Management, 41*(3), 369–375. doi:10.1016/S0378-7206(03)00025-9

Stowers, G. (2004). *Measuring the Performance in E-Government.* Washington, DC: IBM Center for the Business of Government.

Streib, G. (2005). Quantifying the knowledge of public management professionals: Developing an assessment tool for local government managers. *Public Performance & Management Review, 28*(3), 418–436.

Streib, G., & Navarro, I. A. (2006). Citizen demand for interactive e-government: The case of Georgia consumer services. *American Review of Public Administration, 36*(3), 288–300. doi:10.1177/0275074005283371

Svara, J. (1998). The politics-administration dichotomy model as aberration. *Public Administration Review, 58*(1), 51–58. doi:10.2307/976889

Svara, J. (2003). Effective mayoral leadership in council-manager cities: Reassessing the facilitative model. *National Civic Review, 92*(2), 157–172. doi:10.1002/ncr.14

Svara, J., et al. (1994). *Facilitative leadership in local government: Lessons from successful mayors and chairpersons.* San Francisco: Jossey-Bass Publishers.

Thomas, J., & Streib, G. (2003). The new face of government: Citizen-initiated contacts in the era of e-government. *Journal of Public Administration: Research and Theory, 13*(1), 83–102. doi:10.1093/jpart/mug010

Thomas, J., & Streib, G. (2005). E-democracy, e-commerce, and e-research: Examining the electronic ties between citizens and governments. *Administration & Society, 37*(3), 259–280. doi:10.1177/0095399704273212

Tolbert, C., & Mossberger, K. (2003). The effects of e-government on trust and confidence in government. *Public Administration Review, 66*(3), 354–369. doi:10.1111/j.1540-6210.2006.00594.x

Trahant, B. (2007). Debunking five myths concerning employee engagement. *Public Management, 36*(1), 53–59.

UN. (2005). Global e-government readiness report 2005. Towards access for opportunity. New York: United Nations, Department for Economic and Social Affairs, Division for Public Administration and Development Management. Retrieved December 29, 2007, from http://www.unpan.org/egovernment4.asp

United Nations/American Society for Public Administration (UN/ASPA). (2002). *Benchmarking e-government: a global perspective.* New York: United Nations/American Society for Public Administration.

van Deursen, A., van Dijk, J., & Ebbers, W. (2006). *Why e-government usage lags behind: Explaining the gap between potential and actual usage of electronic public services in the Netherlands* (LNCS, pp. 269-280). Berlin: Springer, Heidelberg.

West, D. (2004). E-government and the transformation of service delivery and citizen attitudes. *Public Administration Review, 64*(1), 15–27. doi:10.1111/j.1540-6210.2004.00343.x

Westley F., & Mintzberg, H. (1989). Visionary leadership and strategic management, Strategic Management Journal, 10(summer), 17-32

Whitaker, G., Henderson, M., & Altman-Sauer, L. (2004). Collaboration: Calls for mutual accountability. *Public Management, 86*(11), 16–20.

Wilson, W. (1887). The study of an administration. *Political Science Quarterly, 2*(2), 197–222. doi:10.2307/2139277

Zouridis, S., & Thaens, M. (2003). E-government: Towards a public administration approach. *The Asian Journal of Public Administration, 25*(2), 159–183.

KEY TERMS AND DEFINITIONS

Applied Knowledge Assessment (AKA): A 116 item multiple-choice assessment developed by the International City/County Management Association and the Andrew Young School of Policy Studies at Georgia State University. It contains questions that tap knowledge of local government principles and practices and the ability to apply them to management situations. Taking the AKA is required to become an ICMA credentialed local government manager.

City Manager: An appointed administrator in a local government with the council-manager form of government. This is a common structure for local governments in the United States and also in the Republic of Ireland. An elected council (generally ranging in size from 5-11) has a predominant policy role while the city manager works primarily on administration. The manager functions as a chief executive officer under the direction of the council. City managers usually have a contractual relationship with a city, specifying their duties and responsibilities, and they can be removed by a council vote.

Facilitative Leadership: Leadership without controlling that stresses empowerment, collaboration, and the identification and achievement of common goals.

Integrative Leadership: A form of government leadership that stresses the importance of actions that enhance the utility and function of management systems as a way of improving the capacity of an organization.

International City/County Management Credentialed Manager: A member of the International City/County Management Association who has completed the Applied Knowledge Assessment who also has significant experience as a senior management executive in local government, has earned a degree, preferably in public administration or a related field, and who has demonstrated a commitment to high standards of integrity and to lifelong learning and professional development.

Practices for Effective Local Government Management: In 1991, the ICMA assigned their Task Force on Continuing Education and Professional Development to identify the competencies and skills required of an effective local government manager. During a process facilitated by the task force, ICMA members agreed on a list of Practices that were essential to effective local government management. The 18 Practices that were identified provided a framework for the development of the ICMA Applied Knowledge Assessment.

Strategic Management: A variation of strategic planning that seeks to link long-term strategies and goals with short-term actions. Strategy is focused on assessing the internal and external environments of an organization, and strategic management seeks to interject this knowledge into management decisions in an effective and lasting way.

ENDNOTES

1 This difference was statistically significant even when controlling for age, experience in government, and years in current job in a multiple regression framework.

2 This difference was statistically significant even when controlling for regional differences, experience in government and years in current job in a multiple regression framework.

3 This relation was statistically significant even when controlling for regional differences, and age group in a multiple regression framework.

Chapter 19
Reflections and Proposals on Public Officials Training and Promotion of E-Government[1]

Graciela M. Falivene
National Institute of Public Administration, Argentina

Graciela M. Silva
National Institute of Public Administration, Argentina

ABSTRACT

Argentina is a country characterized by successive discontinuities and heavily conditioned by a troubled political-institutional history. This article will argue that only the interaction and coherence between training and management systems created simultaneously as the dynamic expression of change can result in public organizations in tune with the characteristics of the knowledge society. Only those projects that have incorporated from their inception self-regulation, interaction, and readjustment mechanisms may provide answers in times that are difficult to compare with other periods in public administrations. The nation's problems have never been as complex as they are today, nor did we have tools as powerful as the ICTs to solve them. From a complexity approach, it explores the synergic bonds between the promotion of e-government (EG) and the training and learning processes of public officials.

INTRODUCTION: HYPOTHESIS, OBJECTIVES, AND METHODOLOGY

Argentina is a country characterized by successive discontinuities (CLAD-SIARE, 2005) and heavily conditioned by a troubled political-institutional history (Tesoro, 2004). This article will argue that only the interaction and coherence between training and management systems created simultaneously as the dynamic expression of change can result in public organizations in tune with the characteristics of the knowledge society. Only those projects that have incorporated from their inception self-regulation, interaction, and readjustment mechanisms may provide answers in times that are difficult to compare with other periods in public administrations. The nation's problems have never been as complex as they are today, nor did we have tools as powerful as the ICTs to solve them. Therefore, focusing on current public administration in Argentina is to focus on complexity.

This article is intended as a reflective essay and an implementation proposal. From a complexity approach, it explores the synergic bonds between the promotion of e-government (EG) and the training and learning processes of public officials. By EG "the use of information and communication technology in public administrations combined with organizational change and new competencies in order to improve public services and democratic processes, and strengthen support to public policies" (EU E-Government Commission, 2003) is meant.

The study's methodology implies a dialectical approach to the interaction of all e-government goals, as stated in the current *Plan Nacional,*2 particularly as regards: improvement of citizen services with the use of ICTs; ICTs characteristics, especially learning the Internet as a new language; and identification of strategies that will facilitate the mobilization of available resources and make means and goals consistent, in the least possible time. Thus, the goal is to make public officials training strategies consistent with the open and participatory processes that the Argentine public administration is calling for in its relationship with the citizenry.

The key aspects of the conceptual model adopted, and the premises to conceiving public officials training strategies that will promote EG are developed in the second section. The third section focuses on a series of proposals that seek to generate skills to deal with EG processes, based on the potentiality of the intranets and the available technological resources in public administration, particularly the emergence of the so-called Web 2.0 or social Web. Lastly, the fourth section identifies resistances to the inclusion of new ICTs in public administration, and proposes a series of recommendations in its concluding remarks.

CONCEPTUAL DIMENSIONS

Main Conceptual Dimensions

Ethical-Valuation of GE's Training

Respect for an individual's dignity, loyalty, solidarity, ethical correctness, and mutual trust are fundamental pillars of humanist thought—which is believed to be essential to conceptualize the relationship between public administration and citizens, and the relationships inside the actual public sector. Far from conceiving the organization as a "heavenly" model, it is argued that the environments that are most likely to solve coexistence dilemmas are those in which reflection, expression, and communication are encouraged. Numerous research studies have surveyed citizens' low levels of trust in public institutions. There is a need to constantly renew legitimacy, reassuring the quality of public services in order to guarantee a positive "social assessment," that is, a high degree of satisfaction in the social environment where public organizations perform their activities. This notion in turn casts new lights on how professional ethics are understood. When moving from an ethical-valuation framework to a pragmatic dimension and analyzing EG's results in detail, the only "good results" or "quality" results considered are those that include a social dimension. EG will only be effective if it is capable of achieving the ends, goals, and objectives that society expects of it. In the current knowledge and information society, administrative efficiency is one of the core aspects of notions of equity or equal opportunity. EG's management will "work well" not just by virtue of the amount of computer equipment installed or the number of visits to a government Web site. Rather it will work to the extent that it contributes to a more equitable distribution of the social product, and to improved and more transparent regulatory and monitoring actions. In countries like Argentina, with high poverty and exclusion levels, if EG is not effective for those who are most in need it will not be capable either of providing equity, and thus it will be ethically incompetent.

Epistemological Dimension: An Approach from Complexity Theory

According to Edgar Morin, one of the most renowned complexity theorists, the challenge is how to approach complexity in a non-simplifying way, since the simplifying modes of knowledge mutilate the realities or phenomena they intend to explain. It is actually about training ourselves in ways of thinking that attempt to engage in dialogues, to negotiate with what is real. For Morin, we need to ignore the programs; we must invent strategies in order to get out of the crises.3 It is frequently necessary to ignore the solutions that solve old-type crises and come up with new solutions. Complex thinking is not only useful for organizational, social, or political problems. A thinking that challenges uncertainty may cast new light on the strategies of our uncertain world. A thinking that unites may illuminate an ethics of unity and solidarity. To direct our action towards solving complex situations, Morin provides a set of supplementary and interdependent principles. These in turn have served as guidelines for the creation of the strategies and proposals advanced in this article.

The systemic or organizing principle: it integrates knowledge of the parts to knowledge of the whole. The hologramatic principle: each point contains almost the entire information of the object it represents and reveals the apparent paradox of complex systems, in which not only the parts are in the whole, but the whole is inscribed in the parts. The retroactive circle principle: it enables the system's autonomy. The retroactive circle (or feedback) allows, in a negative form, to reduce the detours and stabilize the system, while in its positive form feedback becomes an amplifying mechanism. The recursive circle principle: it goes beyond the notion of regulation to self-reproduction and self-organization. It is a generating circle in which products and effects are in turn themselves producers, the causes of that which produced them. The self-eco-organization principle (autonomy/dependency): live beings are self-organizers that self-produce themselves endlessly and spend energy to protect their autonomy. As they need to take energy, information, and organization from their environment, their autonomy is inseparable from their dependency. The dialogical principle: it enables the rational assumption of associating contradictory notions to regard the same complex phenomenon. The principle that reintroduces the subject of knowledge in all knowledge: it restores the subject and unveils the main cognitive problem. Every knowledge is a reconstruction/translation by a subject operating within a given culture and time.

Institutional Dimension: EG and the Challenges of Training Institutions

In keeping with the required changes and in order to effect those changes, state agencies—particularly those whose specific mission is the training of public officials—should revisit their dominant practices and thus undergo the same empowerment processes that the state experiences as regards its citizens when it applies an EG strategy. In the same way that EG enables citizens to manage a great number of services unassisted, training designs should prioritize collaborative work mechanisms in the context of communities of practice, facilitate and legitimize self-training and the self-evaluation of acquired learning, and promote processes of reflection and accountability for all intervening actors. Thus, it is understood that the EG/e-learning relationship should have a hologramatic behavior, as described. On the other hand—and to the extent that nobody can guarantee social, productive, and political scenarios that will remain consistent throughout the sometimes long terms required by the design and application of professional training—the way and the methods of conceptualizing organizational forms, as well as the teaching methodologies associated to this kind of training needs to be changed. The competencies that should be developed should not continue to be based on a strictly technical, formal, disciplinary knowledge as was the case in the past. Rather, they should include the practical and unpredictable knowledge of any work experience (Rojas, 1999). It is thus urgent to build strategies that would take the most advantage of already existing ICTs and information systems in public administration, and to promote strategies to identify and support social spaces in which to generate agreements for action. An even greater challenge when training in EG environments is approached, is to secure the commitment of the organizational actors involved: technicians, professionals, politicians, bureaucrats, both those who directly service citizens' claims—either face to face or in other mediated ways—those who are in charge of processing and monitoring information, or the decision-makers who generate administrative actions which assign resources. It also has to be ensured that these actors communicate effectively, overcoming the differences of their respective subcultures and including themselves in the shared utopia of bringing the administration closer to citizens. There may be multiple mechanisms, but the inescapable condition is that they should promote the right collective innovation processes in spirals of "adaptive planning."[4] Their reformulation should consider public officials and users as actors who perform these readjustments during the design and development of the study plan, turning them into allies or partners of planning thus defined.

Some Premises to Conceive Public Officials Training Strategies that Will Promote EG

Consider How Innovation Is Achieved: Pay Attention to the Spiral of Organizational Knowledge Creation (Nonaka & Takeuchi, 1999)

One of the most renowned theorists of the organizational creation of knowledge, Dr. Ikujiro Nonaka, synthesizes his theory as follows: "Drawing especially on Polanyi, I conceptualized knowledge in terms of two types, tacit knowledge and explicit knowledge. Tacit knowledge is personal, context-specific, and therefore hard to formalize and communicate. Explicit knowledge, on the other hand, is transmittable in formal and systematic language. Tacit and explicit knowledge are not separated but are mutually supplementary. Without experience we cannot really understand. But, unless we try to convert tacit knowledge into explicit knowledge we cannot reflect upon it, nor share it in the organization" (Scharmer, 1996).

For Nonaka, the spiral of organizational knowledge creation is based on a double spiral movement between tacit and explicit knowledge (Figure 1). Socialization is the process by which tacit common knowledge is created through the sharing of experience. For socialization, an interaction space in which people simultaneously exchange experiences, space, and time must be built, so that they create a common body of beliefs and competencies. Externalization is the process by which tacit knowledge is articulated in explicit knowledge,

Figure 1. Spiral of organizational knowledge creation (Nonaka - Takeuchi) (Source: Scharmer, 1996)

	To tacit knowledge	To explicit knowledge
From tacit knowledge	Socialization	Externalization
From explicit knowledge	Internalization	Combination

such as concepts and/or diagrams, using metaphors, analogies, and/or charts. Combination is the process by which new explicit knowledge is assembled with the existing knowledge within a systematic knowledge. Internalization is the process by which explicit knowledge is transformed and incorporated, making it tacit, converting it into operative knowledge, that is, in know-how. Explicit documented knowledge in text, video, or other formats facilitates the internalization process. For example, handbooks—the ultimate externalization—are widely used for internalization purposes.

Stimulate the Dialogue between Peers Geared towards Management

The approach of the learning processes reached a turning point with the works of Jean Lave and Etienne Wenger (Lave & Wenger, 1991; Wenger, 1998). These authors privilege collective experience in the work place and they assign new value to social learning, situated learning, and community learning. As we have frequently verified in our own practice (Falivene, Gurmendi & Silva, 2003; Falivene & Kaufman, 2005), social learning in communities of practice5 is a valuable tool for furthering knowledge management, continuing education, and innovation in public organizations. It has often been confirmed that it is precisely in the "field"—that is, in the dialogue among peers, in the explanation between colleagues—where high impact learning for the organization is accomplished. It is in the field that concepts are situated, their importance is validated, and their legitimacy is ensured in a much more significant way than in most classroom situations. The quality of learning is directly associated to the quality of the dialogue that participants are able to create. You may get information from your colleagues at work, in a book, or through computer based training (CBT); but it is in the work place that you learn, where identity is forged, opinions are validated, values are mediated, beliefs are shaped, suppositions are verified, and prejudices are modified. Social mediation is the key. And it is precisely here where work groups and officials networks, united in communities of practice, help give meaning to what is learned and further the comprehension of phenomena exponentially. Developing excellent and closed "in-class" theoretical models is of little use if they cannot coexist, or are contradictory with the real practices of public administration. Groups and communities need to be identified in order to build a shared repertoire of key concepts, develop the tools and a common language, share stories, and shed light on sensitivities. This is where the true learning that EG's cultural change entails stands. In order to achieve it, one of the main challenges is to keep a community of practice active (Wenger, McDermott, & Snyder, 2002).

Generate Spaces to Share Meanings and Senses

Sharing meanings emphasizes the main difference between personal knowledge and the social knowledge that implies understanding and building collective competencies. This shared meaning is the power that underlies language and communication. Sharing critiques, participative diagnoses, action agreements, and post-action reflections play a key role in the learning process in order to achieve these shared meanings. The common perception of signs, symptoms, and patterns is what enables the creation of alternative courses of action, because when you name these new results you create the possibility to intervene in change. This takes place mostly as a result of conversations within groups, and it may be recognized in the topics discussed, the agreed agenda, in beliefs, and in the language of the community of practice. Many times, a closed and codified language segregates a certain community. It is then that the capacity to participate in collaborative learning processes is considered a key competence (Digenti, 1998).

Privilege Deep and Generative Knowledge

Knowledge is more a life process than the acquisition of an object. It is associated to who we are, it surfaces in dialogue and through the social transmission of practices. Knowing is a participative act. Deep knowledge is more than just contents. It is the capacity to act according to the situation: competence understood as an articulated system (Le Boterf, 1991). Deep and generative knowledge is based on maintaining the tension and balance between the habitual practices and dissemination of the community's technical core, and the fostering of flexibility provided by working between communities and promoting inter-area approaches. The underlying, tacit beliefs are difficult, if not impossible to modify in traditional, expository, and unidirectional practices. The most stimulating spaces for creativity are those that encourage work between the borders of communities of practice; only there can innovations that transcend the fragmentary dimension be designed and agreed upon. It is there that the true meaning of networking may be built. To provide an example, in the inventory of competencies used by the Human Resources Department of British Columbia, Canada, the highest competence level for continuing learning is defined as that in which an individual explores the knowledge of a wide variety of resources to create a vision of the future and its subsequent implications (www.hrtoolkit.gov.bc.ca/staffing/staffing_steps/job_requirements/overview.htm). The individual thus uses knowledge arising from his/her own or other areas of expertise, and has a deep understanding of the organization and its environment to create a vision of how work may be improved by applying new emergent approaches and new tools, methods, and technologies.

Consider Both Training for EG Management and EG Management for Training as Simultaneous

The rapid development of ICTs puts them at the core of a rich debate as regards their role and possible applications in the training challenges that have been explained. One of the poles that strain this debate considers ICTs as an end in themselves. Its advocates presume that the very presence of this resource will bring forth the goals of job training. ICTs' fetishization in the development and organization of (Internet) distance learning frequently shifts the focus away from one of the main issues in current debates: the quality of training (www.adeit.uv.es/mecaodl). From these standpoints, it is often realized that most of e-learning developments focus on individual learning, where the relationship between the PC and the learner is a metaphor of the secular teacher-student relationship. A proof of that is the almost exclusive focus on contents, application programs, or technical support in online training, vis-à-vis the rare references to the true protagonists of this environment—the learners. By placing the individual at the center, both socially and collectively, it is seen that technological literacy to operate in the Web is essential to training and cannot be considered just one content more. The Internet is a language in itself (Logan, 2005). The Web has its own and unique semantics of Web sites, Web pages, Internets, intranets, and extranets, with its own syntax, that is, hypertexts and hyperlinks. Each platform has its message, and the Internet's and the Web's message has five essential features: two-way communication, easy access to information, continuing learning, alignment and integration, and community. It is all about displaying the potential for articulating technology as a way of carrying out the agreed upon reforms on network management models, where different communities of practice are identified and interface. These communities serve to strengthen daily management and to trigger inter-institutional coordination strategies in public administration (Falivene & Kaufman, 2005). The role of training agencies at the inter-institutional crossroads is remarkable in the construction of "bridges" between these communities of practice. These bridges allow us to experience the cognitive dissonance produced in border interactions, which stimulates creativity and deep learning, facilitates change, and fosters innovation.

Consider the Crisis of Contents

If it it is considered that half of our school knowledge turns obsolete every 20 years, that the same happens with academic knowledge every 10 years, with professional knowledge every 5 years, with technological knowledge every 3 years, and with information technology every year (Breinstein & Wendt, 2005), the conclusion that throughout an individual's life learning has become a defining trait of professional activity in the knowledge society is arrived at quickly. Those who learn in professional contexts require every time to broaden their knowledge based on a repertoire of competencies achieved at work and on demand. On the other hand, the methods to generate teaching/learning materials are very expensive and labor-intensive, but the problems emerge when contents cannot be accessed easily from other systems (interoperability), or upgraded and adapted for different purposes. In order to overcome these restrictions, learning materials should have a modular design, they should be stocked in a format that is independent of the platform and allows for dynamic access through interconnected knowledge reservoirs. Both the forms and the contents and presentation methods should be interchangeable, combinable, re-combinable, and re-usable, independently of their environmental systems, authorization systems, and contextual applications. This facilitates the transportation of contents between different learning management systems, and reduces development, distribution, and maintenance costs. Thus, individuals, communities, and organizations may actually choose a learning path rather than a curricular-based course.

Prioritize the Collaborative Building of Conceptual Maps

Because contents have an expiration date, new approaches of open learning are focusing the debate regarding the design of training activities on the creation and identification of the so called "reusable learning objects" (Abaitua, Barrutieta, Díaz, Jacob, & Quintana, 2003), accessible through the combinable architecture of meta-data reservoirs and technologies. This issue has called a great deal of attention to the value of the communities of practice—as communities of learning—in building conceptual maps that facilitate the design of e-learning activities based on these learning objects. In previous works the potential of communities of practice as sites of knowledge management in critical contexts (Falivene, 2004) have been enlarged on, and as socialization, innovation, and learning environments in public organizations (Falivene, Silva, & Gurmendi, 2003). Here, to emphasize the center role these communities have in building conceptual maps (Cmap Tools, 2004) is wanted, a fundamental tool both for the creation and identification of "learning objects," and for the establishment of knowledge reservoirs that will facilitate their reutilization and promote the innovative spiral. The National Learning Infrastructure Initiative is an example of this (http://www.educause.edu/nlii/), which between October 2002 and December 2003 organized pilot communities of practice who mapped their own learning space (Cañas et al, 2004). Another example is Merlot, the Multimedia Educational Resource for Learning and Online Teaching (http://www.merlot.org/Home.po), a knowledge reservoir and a community of people associated to higher education, which in turn works as a directory of experts who share materials and create reviews and comments. These cases allow us to identify the value of building a conceptual map in the midst of a community of practice in order to recover materials and have access to open learning environments.

PROPOSALS TO PROMOTE E-GOVERNMENT BASED ON TRAINING STRATEGIES FOR PUBLIC OFFICIALS

In previous works the advantages of applying a strategy of knowledge management in the training of public officials has been referred to. In this article the working proposal is focused on the potentialities of the intranets and other emergent technological resources in public administration, in order to generate capacities to deal with EG processes.

Taking the Most Advantage of Public Administration Agencies' Intranets as a Continuing Education Resource for EG

The intranets are to public officials and employees what EG is to citizens: both require digital inclusion and the acquisition of the so called "sixth language" or Internet language (Logan, 2004). Most public organizations have intranets with different degrees of development. An intranet is an excellent reservoir of available information, a communication platform, and a space to develop internal paperwork. Institutional intranets may become a dynamic environment for multiple collaborative activities and key elements to execute knowledge management initiatives and EG promotion instead of being static reservoirs of documents. However, this supposes a much more intense use of the resource, especially by staff training and development areas. The proposal is to think of knowledge management through institutional intranets following three mutually including scales:

Organizational

This level includes the knowledge that everybody needs. It is the typical standard content of the corporate or institutional intranet that includes policies, regulations, and general procedures in the shape of guidelines or handbooks. However, in knowledge management communities, interpersonal communication plays a significant and critical role in building agreements for action and as a stimulus for reflection and creativity. An essential step to promote the emergence and sustainability of these communities is to make it easy for people to contact each other fluidly, a key aspect in large organizations such as public agencies. A simple and effective way is to include the staff directory in the intranet.

Units, Teams, and Communities of Practice

The information that will be shared by units or teams is not of general interest for the entire organization. At this intermediate organizational scale—work groups, project teams, communities of practice, or competence area—collaborative environments may have a great influence by capturing and sharing knowledge. The issue of communities of practice and intranets in public administration merits a separate mention. The communities of practice approach introduced by Lave and Wenger (1991), and then enlarged by Wenger (1998) and Snyder and Wenger (2003) for public sector agencies, has served to acknowledge the importance of the less formal processes of sharing and socializing knowledge that take place among peers and within small groups with similar interests, in order to promote change and publicize innovation inside organizations. This has proved its value within knowledge management communities and the professional forums fostered by the INAP (National Institute of Public Administration). The Computer systems head staff and the information & data centers head staff (Falivene, 2004) are good examples. The intranet may play a valuable role providing support to the development of communities of practice activities, through the construction of a homepage or collaborative virtual environment that enables members' interaction, especially those who do not share a physical space. Thus it is possible to publicize the communities of practice results and products to the rest of the organization. The design of training activities—agreeing upon agendas based on conceptual maps—includes different learning objects available in the intranet and the Internet, as well as the directory of experts for specific advice. These activities often have face to face interaction spaces associated to the corresponding community of practice forum (Trouvé & García Acosta, 2004). In these online formats it is essential to consider the principles of adult education outlined by Knowles (Knowles, 1980) and nowadays revalued in light of the emergence of ICTs.6 One of the key elements of a community of practice is that the group is responsible for the "update" of knowledge in their domain. This often requires the creation of knowledge database or content reservoirs. Once this knowledge is uploaded, it may be shared with others who are dealing with similar challenges. These knowledge databases can be built by applying different technological solutions (Cobos & Esquivel, 2002). But beyond the tools applied, what is most important is to establish criteria to share knowledge based on the needs of the actual community of practice. While the community of practice focuses on human interaction and building agreements towards a commitment schedule, it should be supported by a suitable technological infrastructure platform (Chart 1). As the community grows, it is also necessary to build a knowledge resource that will eventually strengthen and add value to it. In both cases, the intranet plays a significant role enabling the community of practice to grow. On the other hand, the actual intranet is strengthened when its significant community roles is acknowledged.

Chart 1. Flow chart in a community of practice

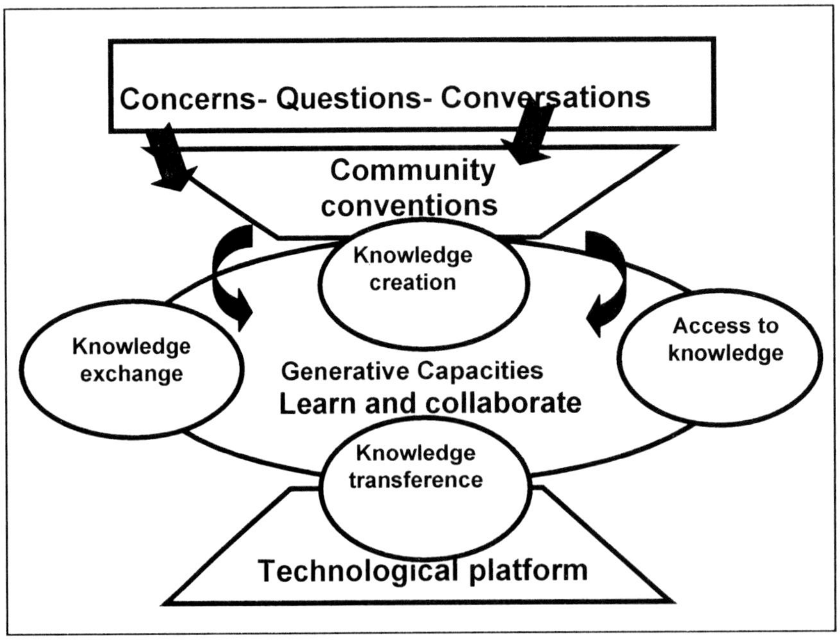

Personal

In technical terms: an individual's personal knowledge, necessary competencies, and expertise. This knowledge is often shared via e-mail, while personal competencies are developed through assisted self-learning, with the help of trainers, coachers, facilitators, and/or mentors. The risk is that individuals may encapsulate information inside their areas in a semi-structured format inaccessible to others. Due to the changes in organizational structures that periodically affect public administration agencies, typically very valuable knowledge resources remain inaccessible because the documents are not clearly labeled. When this happens, the knowledge is very difficult to recover. Sometimes extreme solutions involve erasing all the information because there is no one with the necessary knowledge to reuse it. On the contrary, when there is a list of specific competencies, expertise, and knowledge of every individual in the organization, it facilitates the search of knowledge resources, even when people do not know each other personally. If each person in the staff directory is linked to the diagram of its unit, it is then easier to share knowledge between the areas. Online self-learning formats are greatly empowered because they enable the experts' search to solve problems with the help of others, thus contributing to build bonds that go back and forth between people and the projects they participate in. On the other hand, the promotion of human and intellectual capital increases employees' self-esteem and re-legitimates public service. The challenge is to actually make people list their expertise instead of hiding it, so that they are willing to be consulted and keep their knowledge updated.[7] To be able to accomplish this, incentives mechanisms are essential to keeping the information updated.

These scales should be visualized in the intranet environment as a whole and classified according to a common taxonomy.

APPRECIATE EMERGENT TECHNOLOGICAL RESOURCES FOR THE CREATION OF SITUATED KNOWLEDGE, DECISION MAKING, AND PUBLIC OFFICIALS TRAINING

The Internet has become the most visible face of the integration of large scale, easy-access information systems (Saorín Pérez, 2002). Its exponential growth in the last years allows access to information that is valuable and updated for public officials. From legal, economic, demographic, or geographic databases available at national and international government Web sites, to scientific and dissemination papers available in full and endorsed by prestigious academic institutions. The large amount of information compiled in the systems generated by the actual agency where public officials work can also be added. But this large amount of information generated by the development of technological resources can only be justified if it is used to create valuable knowledge that will improve the process in which it was created, and thus the citizens' quality of life. The degree to which every individual responsible for a process keeps the information updated, the way in which workflow systems are established, how people agree on building meta-databases to generate knowledge reservoirs, the methods used to recognize relevant patterns or discover and create situated knowledge to build scenarios, and the governmental decision-making, are all steps that assist in the effective implementation of EG. The development of tools such as data warehouses and data mining is a good example. A data warehouse allows organizations to handle large volumes of information, based on a process of physical separation between production of daily operations and the operations that support the organization's decisions (Gurmendi, 2005). Being a dynamic project, it evolves and is nurtured with use. It should be flexible and scalable, since it must provide a computer-based infrastructure able to sustain all the changes the organization undergoes. It cannot be bought. What can be bought is the work tool, but the data warehouse is built with a single architecture that supports the organization's requirements. It simplifies decision-making processes because it provides integrated data images. It facilitates the comparative and future vision process, and enables the relation with other data, indicators samples, and consolidated information. Quick and easy data access allows users to make their own searches.8 Additionally, data mining involves the process of discovering current and significant patterns, profiles, and trends through data analysis. For example, to analyze a government Web site using pattern-recognition technologies, such as neuronal networks, learning machines, and genetic algorithms. It is an iterative process of pattern extraction derived of online transactions (clicking on a link or banner, requesting information via e-mail, completing a form) in order to improve the services offered by the organization's Web site (Sánchez Ovcharóv, 2005).

To these a large repertoire of new technological tools associated to the emergence of the Web 2.0 or social Web may be added. The Web 2.0 is a way of understanding the Internet whereby the organization and flow of information depend on the behavior of the individual accessing the Web, allowing a much easier and centralized access to contents. It also encourages participation through simple tools, such as Web logs and wikis (Santamaría Glez, 2006). They are characterized by low cost, widespread use and collective creation since they are typically open source developments resulting from the real need to exchange knowledge. They are not large knowledge management systems, but rather initiatives that, like free e-mail and browsers, are very popular. Web logs (http://newsletter.nitle.org/v2_n1_winter2003/features_weblogs.php) have become widespread since 2003 and 2004 and continue to increase exponentially. In their simplest form, a web log—generally called blog—is an online journal created by one or more reporters. They represent a new class of publishing tool that some people see as disruptive of traditional forms. A Web log provides a simple interface to generate entries, typically with an online form. Being published on a Web site, a standard page design and format is added to it. The number of Web logs on the Internet is increasing exponentially and they cover almost every topic. From a knowledge management standpoint, Web logs have the value of narrative to transform messages in a powerful communication tool. Web logs are being increasingly used by individuals, communities, and companies to share knowledge crossing traditional borders and they may become quite interesting tools when used within an organization. In the latter case, they are known as 'knowledge logs' or 'k-logs.' Those in favor of this resource see it as a way of breaking down intra-organizational barriers and facilitating a more efficient flow of information and knowledge. For example, key individuals may record the progress of strategic projects. Or they may refer to critical topics in the institutional agenda. Resting on the prestige and reputation of the writer, Web logs share the well known benefits of "story tellers," that is, reporters. Project teams may also use Web logs to communicate with the larger organization and keep information updated on who is doing what in the team. Thus, the team's Web log acts as the project's spokesperson, and as a file of past decisions.

Wikis (http://wiki.org/wiki.cgi?WhatIsWiki) offer a new approach to online content management and publishing. They are self-regulated virtual communities that generate contents freely. They are published in web pages that allow users to edit, erase, and add information. Essentially, they are ultra-light content management systems, developed in the open source environment. Wikis allow for the collective creation of hypertextual documents, using a simple diagram of labels and markers. The autonomy to modify or add information is endless. A paradigmatic example is Wikipedia (http://www.wikipedia.org), an online encyclopedia where millions of users contribute their knowledge on several topics. It undergoes constant change due to the community that constantly feeds its contents. Wiki sites are monitored by the more active participants, as in any community of practice. The authors of each modification may sign or remain anonymous, but they must quote their sources. An interesting way of using wikis in public administration's institutional intranets is to keep procedure manuals permanently updated. From a knowledge management and public administration training standpoint, how wikis handle themselves vis-à-vis the absence of restrictions and controls is found to be very interesting. In fact, control resides mainly in the actual dynamics of the community that feeds and uses them, and despite being too open, vandalism is almost non-existent (Japas, 2005). When aggressions do occur, it is the actual participants who take care of repairing the damage. Classic security systems also contribute to this self-regulation, such as blocking addresses or creating a users record with their corresponding passwords. Due to easy editing, wikis have become a very popular platform for collaborative work, and thus an ideal tool for communities of practice or knowledge sharing teams.

CONCLUSION

Today, a wide spectrum of technological resources allows public officials to rely on a wealth of updated and accessible information as never before. Moreover, they have mechanisms to create or discover valuable knowledge for institutional analysis, scenario building, and decision making.

Given the layered dissemination of ICTs, the possibility of applying energies and resources becomes real at all levels and stages. We advance towards open and interactive organizational morphologies, and today very few people question the fact that ICTs are inherent to public administration and essential in the swift process of going from one organizational stage to the next. This situation is particularly relevant in current public administration, characterized by increasing complexity both as regards its development and also the possibilities that citizens and even officials themselves have of grasping that complexity. These concerns lead to the incorporation of a conceptual framework that is based on non-simplifying ways of dealing with very complex and highly uncertain situations. Citizens see the state both as being close and distant at the same time. Close because in one way or another they need it; distant because they cannot understand its structure or how it works. This complexity is inborn to the actual political-administrative system which, in dynamic interaction with social and economic change, results in permanent transformations in public administration. These changes concern essential features such as the organization's functional and hierarchical chart, multiple strategies of staff recruitment, and a large number of regulations, among others.

On the other hand, the increased ability to articulate public and private resources as well as the access to new information and communication technologies (ICTs) enables the transformation of organizations through complex operations which are in fact facilitated by these long range technologies.

Paradoxically, in our daily work (Falivene & Silva, 2005) we are witness to the underuse of these technological/information resources. Resistance to the incorporation of ICTs in public administration is detected, caused in almost every case by a strong under-assessment of their potentiality. Thus, it would be a mistake to suppose that ICTs will automatically optimize public administration unless the processes of technological inclusion are supplemented with training strategies for public officials suited to meet the challenges of the knowledge society.

Moreover, and as has been stated in the ethical dimensions of the study's conceptual approach, if action is not explicitly directed by values such as transparency, lawfulness, equity, loyalty, social justice, solidarity, and integrity together with the ability to focus on results in tune with citizens' claims and needs, and explicitly seeking the general wellbeing and the strengthening of democratic culture, ICTs contribution will be little relevant to public administration.

Neither will it be possible to make intelligent use of ICTs in this sector unless people are trained not only in ICT management, but also in "learning to learn" methods that aim at a continuous, situated knowledge of how to take advantage of the enormous potential of current information systems and emergent technological resources to create knowledge about state and society. It is believed that this is a top priority strategic competence in the training of public officials because it enables the relevant design, execution, and assessment of public policy, as well as scenario analysis and government decision-making at large.

Accordingly, a set of premises has been developed—included in the second section—that will allow for the creation of strategies basically aimed at creating and promoting collaborative learning environments focused on the exchange, creation, and preservation of situated knowledge.

Another key element for a successful incorporation of EG initiatives is to include technological dimensions in job profiling tools. Although this will be the topic of future works, it would like to be pointed out that the international experience (State Employment Public Service, 2004) reveals that new work forms—associated to new technologies—have a high impact in redefining job profiling.

Thus, as has already been argued in the proposal to improve EG initiatives with public officials training—discussed in the third section—it is believed that the curricula should necessarily include specific competencies referred to the conceptualization and management of new technological resources applied to public policy management, as well as those associated to new organizational morphologies necessary for EG. This should be also included in staff selection, development, and evaluation systems. Equally important is to bear in mind the great teaching potential of the intranets in their different scales: organizational individuals, groups, teams, and communities.

Finally, the value attributed to emergent technological resources—particularly those associated to the appearance of the so-called Web 2.0 or social Web—in designing combined strategies to create and promote EG in Argentina, signals a remarkable difference in the quality and efficacy of public policies in this field.

REFERENCES

Abaitua, J., Barrutieta, G., Díaz, J., Jacob, I., & Quintana, F. (2003). Contenidos y metacontenidos en la edición digital. *Letras de Deusto, July-September.* Retrieved March 15, 2007, from http://paginaspersonales.deusto.es/abaitua/konzeptu/htxt/letrasUD_03.pdf

Breinstein, E., & Wendt, A. (2003, July 15-18). Didactic modeling of learning objects: evolving *standards* and methods of evaluation in metadata-based course development. In *Proceedings of the Eden 2003 Annual Conference "The quality dialogue integrating quality cultures in flexible, distance and e-learning,"* Rhodes, Greece. Retrieved March 15, 2007, from http://www.eden-online.org/eden.php?menuId=133&contentId=153

British Columbia Human Resources Office. (n. d.). *Establish qualifications and competencies.* Retrieved March 15, 2007, from http://www.hr-toolkit.gov.bc.ca/staffing/staffing_steps/job_requirements/overview.htm

Cañas, A. J., Hill, G., Roser, C., Suri, F., Lot, J., Gómez, G., et al. (2004). Cmaptools: a knowledge modeling and sharing environment. Concept maps: Theory, methodology, technology. In *Proceedings of the 1st International Conference on Concept Mapping.* Pamplona, Spain: Universidad Pública de Navarra. Retrieved March 15, 2007, from http://cmc.ihmc.us/papers/cmc2004-283.pdf

CLAD-SIARE. (2005). *El gobierno electrónico como medio para acercar el Estado a la ciudadanía.* Retrieved March 15, 2007, from http://www.clad.org.ve/siare/innotend/gobelec/gobelec.html

Cobos, R., Esquivel, J. A., & Alaman, X. (2002). IT tools for knowledge management: a study of the current situation.*CEPIS, Up Grade, III*(1), February. Retrieved March 15, 2007, from. http://www.upgrade-cepis.org

Comisión *e-government* UE. (2003). El papel de la administración electrónica en el futuro de Europa. *Comunicación de la Comisión, de 26 septiembre 2003, al Consejo, al Parlamento Europeo, al Comité Económico y Social Europeo y al Comité de las Regiones.* Retrieved March 15, 2007, from http://europa.eu.int/scadplus/leg/es/lvb/l24226b.htm

Digenti, D. (1998). Collaborative learning: a core capability for organizations in the new economy. *Reflections, 1,* Retrieved March 15, 2007, from http://mitpress.mit.edu/journals/sols/digenti.pdf

Drake, D. B., Steckler, N. A., & Koch, M. J. (2004). Information sharing in and across government agencies: The role and influence of scientist, politician, and bureaucrat subcultures. *Social Science Computer Review, 22*(1), Retrieved March 15, 2007, from http://ssc.sagepub.com/cgi/reprint/22/1/67

Falivene, G. (2004). Reformas de las políticas de formación directiva para el fortalecimiento institucional en contextos de crisis: aprendizajes realizados. *Reforma y Democracia, Revista del CLAD, 29,* 95-130.

Falivene, G., Gurmendi, L., & Silva, G. (2003, October). El *e-learning* como mecanismo articulador de procesos de gestión del conocimiento y formación continua en las organizaciones públicas: el caso del Sistema de Información Universitaria (SIU). *1er. Premio del Concurso Internacional de Ensayos sobre Mecanismos de e-learning para Mejorar la Educación a Distancia de Funcionarios Públicos en Iberoamérica,* called by CLAD y co-sponsored by the government of Spain (MAP-AECI-FIIAPP). Panamá. Retrieved March 15, 2007, from http://www.clad.org.ve/fulltext/0048201.pdf

Falivene, G., & Kaufman, E. (2005). Training and articulating public agencies in Argentina. In E. Coakes & S. H. Clarke (Eds.), *Encyclopedia of communities of practice and knowledge management.* Idea Group. Retrieved March 15, 2007, from http://www.idea-group.com/encyclopedia/details.asp?ID=458

Falivene, G., & Silva, G. (2003). Formación directiva para la creación de una cultura del conocimiento y de la calidad en las organizaciones públicas. *I° Congreso de Gestión de la Calidad de la Ciudad de Buenos Aires. Gobierno de la Ciudad Autónoma de Buenos Aires.* Buenos Aires, 2003. Retrieved March 15, 2007, from http://cffp.sgp.gov.ar/contenidos/inap/capacitacion/docs/falivene-silva.pdf

Falivene, G., & Silva, G. (2005). Formas de aprendizaje de directivos públicos en la Argentina. Estudio de casos, Informe de avance de investigación, Documento interno, Programa de Innovación de la Capacitación. Buenos Aires: INAP.

Fundación Universidad Empresa de Valencia (sponsored by the European Commission within the framework of the Socrates-Minerva project). (n.d). MECA-ODL, Guía metodológica para el análisis de la calidad de la formación a distancia en Internet. Retrieved March 15, 2007, from www.adeit.uv.es/mecaodl

Gurmendi, L. (2005). SIU—data warehouse: herramientas para la toma de decisiones. *Info SIU, Sistema de Información Universitaria,* Monthly Bulletin, June 2005. Retrieved March 15, 2007, from http://www.siu.edu.ar/infosiu/nota.php?nw=5&nota=37

Jefatura de Gabinete de Ministros, Subsecretaría de la Gestión Pública, *Plan Nacional de Gobierno Electrónico,* Decree 378/2005.

Kaufman, E. (2005). Los modelos participativos de gobierno electrónico: Formación de funcionarios y constitución de redes interorganizacionales público - privadas. In S. Finkielevich (coord.), *TIC y desarrollo local. Municipios e Internet.* Buenos Aires: Ed. La Crujía.

Knowles, M. (1980). *The modern practice of adult education.* New York: Cambridge University Press.

Japas, D. (2005, July 10). Internet: wikimanía. *Revista La Nación,* Buenos Aires.

Lave, J., & Wenger, E. (1991). *Situated learning. Legitimate peripheral participation.* New York: Cambridge University Press.

Le Botertf, G. (1991). *Cómo invertir en formación.* Barcelona: EADA Gestión.

Logan, R. K. (2000). *The extended mind: Understanding language and thought in terms of complexity and chaos theory.* University of Toronto. Retrieved March 15, 2007, from http://www.upscale.utoronto.ca/GeneralInterest/Logan/Extended/Extended.html

Logan, R. K. (2004). *The sixth language: Learning a living in the internet age.* Caldwell: Blackburn Press.

Morin, E. (1996). *Introducción al pensamiento complejo.* Barcelona: Gedisa.

Nonaka, I., & Takeuchi, H. (1999a). *The knowledge-creating company.* New York: Oxford University Press.

Nonaka, I., & Takeuchi, H. (1999b). *La organización creadora de conocimiento: Cómo las compañías japonesas crean la dinámica de la innovación.* México City: Oxford Press.

Polanyi, M. (1958). *Personal knowledge.* Chicago: The University of Chicago Press.

Rojas, E. (1999, May-August). Las instituciones de formación profesional frente a desafíos teóricos inéditos. *Boletín CINTERFOR, 146,*

Saint-Onge, H., Wallace, D. (2003). *Leveraging communities of practice for strategic advantage.* Boston: Butterworth-Heinemann.

Sánchez Ovcharóv, S. (2004). *Qué es el data mining.* Data Mining Institute. Retrieved March 15, 2007, from http://www.estadistico.com/arts.html?20010219

Santamaría Glez, F. (2006). La Web 2.0: caracterísiticas, implicancias en el entorno educativo y algunas de sus herramientas, Seminario Internacional Virtual Educa Cono Sur, Buenos Aires. Retrieved March 15, 2007, from http://www.iesevevirtual.edu.ar/virtualeduca/ponencias2006/La%20Web20_Santamaria.pdf

Saorín Pérez, T. (2002). Modelo conceptual para la automatización de bibliotecas en el contexto digital (Doctoral dissertation, School of Information and Data Sciences, University of Murcia, 2002).

Scharmer, C. O. (1996, February 23). Knowledge has to do with truth, goodness, and beauty. Conversation with professor Ikujiro Nonaka. *Dialog on Leadership,* Tokyo, Japan. Retrieved March 15, 2007, from http://www.dialogonleadership.org/Nonaka-1996.pdf

Servicio Público de Empleo Estatal. *Servicio de Observatorio Ocupacional. (2004). Incidencia de la Sociedad de la Información en el mercado de trabajo. Ocupaciones afectadas por las nuevas formas de trabajo.* Madrid:

Snyder, W. M., & Wenger, E. (2003). *Communities of practice in government the case for sponsorship.* (Report to the CIO Council of the U.S. Federal Government). Retrieved March 15, 2007, from http://www.ewenger.com/pub/pubusfedciodownload.htm

Tesoro, J. L. (2003, February). La probidad, el civismo y la equidad como determinantes básicos del desempeño del gobierno electrónico. *Revista Probidad, 21*. Retrieved March 15, 2007, from http://www.revistaprobidad.info/021/002.html

Tesoro, J. L. (2004). *El gobierno electrónico en la argentina: indagación comparativa y apreciación estratégica*. Retrieved March 15, 2007, from http://www.infoleg.gov.ar/basehome/noticias/Tesoro_16-01-04.htm

Trouvé, A. T., & García Acosta, A. (2004, November 2-6). Proyecto Padrinazgo de Publicaciones Periódicas Argentinas (4P-AR): reconocimiento de las competencias desplegadas en el trabajo en redes. *IXº Congreso Internacional del CLAD sobre la Reforma del Estado y de la Administración Pública*, Madrid, Spain.

Wenger, E. (1998). *Communities of practice. learning, meaning and identity*. New York: Cambridge University Press.

Wenger, E. (2000). Communities of practice and social learning systems. *Organization Articles, 7*.

Wenger, E. (2001). Comunidades de práctica: aprendizaje, significado e identidad. *Cognición y Desarrollo Humano*, 38.

Wenger, E., McDermott, R., & Snyder, W. (2002). *Cultivating communities of practice*. Boston: Harvard Business School Publishing.

ENDNOTES

1 This article is a version of the paper presented at the CLAD X International Conference on State Reform and Public Administration, Santiago, Chile, October 18-21, 2005.

2 The *Plan Nacional de Gobierno Electrónico* (EG government plan) promotes the intensive use of ICTs with the following goals in mind: offer better citizen / inhabitant services, optimize public management, guarantee transparency in government actions, reduce cost of proceedings, create new spaces for citizen participation, include underprivileged individuals, companies, and communities, and foster the inclusion of Argentine production to the world market.

3 For Morin, action is strategy to the extent that, based on an initial decision, allows imagining a certain number of action scenarios. Thus, strategy is contrary to program, which it considers suited to a stable environment, since programs do not demand being alert, it does not demand innovation.

4 See *Libro blanco para la mejora de los servicios públicos* (Spain, 2000).

5 A community of practice is defined as a group of people who share an interest, sometimes a passion, for something they know how to do, and who interact regularly to learn how to do it better. See Lave and Wenger (1991).

6 These principles are: 1. adults conduct their own learning process; 2. adults need to know why they learn; 3. adults appreciate being involved in the establishment of their own learning goals; 4. adults prefer to learn in an environment of mutual trust, respect, and freedom of expression; 5. adults learn from their own experience and from the experience of others; 6. adults would rather that knowledge be immediately applied; 7. adults learn better when they are involved in the learning process; 8. adults wish to be involved in the evaluation of their own progress in the accomplishment of their goals.

7 For example, the competencies database designed to integrate human resources in the CGPs (Decentralized Government Agencies of the Government of the Autonomous City of Buenos Aires) has fallen into disuse. This database was supposed to be available online on the intranet. The database was generated through self-evaluation of the key admin-

istrative processes. Among other issues, it considered whether people could carry out the process with or without help; if they could teach it or if they needed to learn it. The database would also have a virtual library or knowledge reservoir where handbooks and guidelines of all the processes considered would be always updated.

8 For an application of these tools in public Argentine universities management, see the SIU (University Information System) documents at: http://www.siu.edu.ar/soluciones/data_warehouse

This work was previously published in International Journal of Electronic Government Research, Vol. 4, Issue 2, edited by M. Khosrow-Pour, pp. 43-58, copyright 2008 by IGI Publishing (an imprint of IGI Global).

Chapter 20
Moving from E-Government to T-Government:
A Study of Process Reengineering Challenges in a UK Local Authority Context

Vishanth Weerakkody
Brunel University, UK

Gurjit Dhillon
Brunel University, UK

ABSTRACT

The UK government is striving towards a vision for government-wide transformation, in which local authorities and central government departments are endeavouring to work with each other to deliver better services to citizens via a one-stop-shop environment for all services under the guise of electronic government (e-government). Having successfully e-enabled customer facing processes, the UK government is now working towards reengineering and e-enabling back office processes and information systems to facilitate more joined-up and citizen centric e-government services; these efforts are referred to as the transformational stage of e-government or T-Government. This paper seeks to explore what T-Government means to local authorities in the UK and what process related challenges have to be overcome to successfully implement transformational change in local government.

INTRODUCTION

Since the advent of the Internet some forty years ago (Ho, 2002), the number of Information and Communication Technology (ICT) driven services have quadrupled making today's society a technology and Internet savvy one. The Internet has enabled businesses to trade and offer services using ICT to respond to consumer needs around the clock and from any location. While the 1990s saw the internet enabled e-commerce revolution with private and multinational organizations, in the new millennium we have witnessed public sector organizations embracing the same principles of e-business through the introduction of national Electronic Government (e-government) initiatives. Since the mid 1990s ICT has played an important role in incrementally changing and shifting traditional and bureaucratic government models into the current e-government model where services are delivered according customers' needs (Wimmer, 2004). The drivers for e-government broadly include improving internal cost and management efficiencies, encouraging citizen participation, promoting economic development and improving overall governance (Schware *et al.,* 2003; Gandhi and Cross, 2001; Lee *et al.,* 2005). All developed countries have now implemented some form of e-government (Al-Kibsi et al. 2001; Palanisamy, 2004; Accenture 2005) – with most having implemented transactional level services (See for instance Layne and Lee, 2001; Weerakkody et al., 2007); and the majority of developing countries are beginning to follow suit (Karunanada and Weerakkody, 2006). E-government is seen as no longer an option but a necessity for all countries aiming for better and efficient governance (Gupta and Jana, 2003).

With the popularity of e-government growing, various researchers have offered different definitions to explain the concept (Seifert and Petersen, 2002; Holden et al., 2003). However, these definitions differ according to the varying e-government focus and are usually centered on technology, business, process, citizen, government or a functional perspective. For instance, Seifert and Petersen (2002) explains e-government with a functional focus; Burn and Robins (2003) defines it with a citizens focus; Zhiyuan (2002) views e-government with a technology focus; Wassenaar (2000) classifies it with a business focus; Wimmer and Traunmuller (2000) takes a more government centered view; and Bonham et al. (2001) defines it with a process focus. In essence therefore, e-government is about the transformation of internal and external processes of government using information and communication technologies to provide efficient and user focused services to citizens, businesses and other stakeholders (Lee and Hong, 2002; Gupta and Jana, 2003; Evans, 2003; Basu , 2004; Gandhi and Cross, 2001; Burn et al., 2003; Stoltzfus, 2004).

Many researchers have proposed various stages of e-government development (Layne and Lee, 2001; Siau and Long, 2005). These stages revolve mainly around four phases, which are web presence, interaction, transaction and transformation (Baum and Di Maio, 2001; Balutis, 2001; Layne and Lee, 2001). The transformational phase of e-government implementation (or T-Government) is the highest level of maturity for e-government programmes, thus it is also the most challenging phase to reach (Layne and Lee, 2001). The transformation phase encompasses redefining the delivery of government services by providing a single point of contact to citizens' that makes the government completely transparent to citizens and businesses (Affisco and Soliman, 2006). To realise the aforementioned and to provide citizens with seamless services, e-government will therefore need business processes that can be continuously optimized and expanded outside the enterprise and outside internal enterprise systems (Fagan, 2006; Fustes, 2003a; Champy, 2002). However, many researchers such as Lee *et al.,* 2005, Holden *et al.,* (2002), Layne and Lee (2001), and Sarikas and Weerakkody, (2007) identified that most e-government initiatives often stagnate at the transaction stage of development; only a few will succeed to offer sophisticated, value added and truly efficient and transparent online services using a single point of contact. The reason being that the transformation stage of e-government will only be achieved when the different participating agencies collaborate, streamline their business processes and integrate systems that have been historically fragmented (Hu *et al.,* 2006; Weerakkody et al., 2007). Therefore, in order for e-government to progress to a high level of information systems and technology (IS/IT) and process integration, governments will need to radically transform most public sector agencies.

In most countries the focus of the early stages of e-government has been to e-enable existing front office processes in their current state without significant improvements or efficiency gains. Consequently, many of these governments are now embarking on the final stage of e-government (i.e. transformation of internal back office and external inter organisational processes). In the UK for instance, the government is pursuing a far-reaching and ambitious programme of innovation and radical change in the public sector (Daniel and Ward, 2006; Beynon-Davies and Martin, 2004). The modernisation agenda of public services in the UK is termed "transformational government", which aims to place technology at the heart of agenda to improve services from technological investment through business process reengineering (BPR) and re-designs (Cabinet Office, 2006). In comparison, the American government has also proposed a transformational stage e-government project called "Reengineering through Information Technology" and the Canadian government launched the "Blueprint for Renewing Government Services Using IT" (Li, 2005). In the UK, the Transformational Government Strategy was introduced in 2005 and sets out a six-year improvement journey for public services in the UK (Cabinet Office, 2006). The UK target for reaching the transformational stage of e-government is 2011 (ibid). The overall emphasis of the transformational government strategy is therefore to increase the amount of data availability through digitisation and to allow data sharing between departments (Caldwell, 2005; McIvor *et al.*, 2002).

Transformational government is defined by Murphy (2005) as radically changing the way government conducts its business internally and externally. The transformational phase of e-government should primarily focus upon cost savings and service improvement through back-office process and IS/IT change. Ultimately, the objective of the transformational stage of e-government implies that process reengineering is needed to rethink the value propositions of the government and how they function in serving citizens more efficiently and effectively (Palanisamy, 2004).

In this article we seek to examine the true practical meaning of 'transformational government' (or what is popularly referred to in the UK as T-Government). The motivation for the research is therefore to examine whether 'transformation' really means radical change of public sector processes [as in the case of BPR (Hammer and Champy, 1993)] or is it merely incremental business process and IS/IT change. Therefore, the research questions guiding this article are: a) what does T-Government mean to local authorities in the UK; and b) what process related challenges do they need to overcome in order to implement T-Government. To explore these questions we undertook a case study in a large local authority in London, UK and this article analyses the initial empirical findings from this study. The case study examines a core public service process that is executed at local government level and highlights key process and information systems challenges and consequent realities of implementing transformational stage e-government in the UK.

The research is timely since currently most governments around the globe, in particular developed countries, have already e-enabled their key customer facing or front office processes (referred to as e-government) and are now preparing to transform their administrative and back office processes (under the guise of t-government). Therefore, we believe that our analysis will be useful to local government agencies and policy makers seeking to promote the 'transformational government strategy' in the UK. Researchers in the area of business process management can also benefit by obtaining insights into the application of ICT and the resulting influence it has on local government processes.

In order to explore the abovementioned issues, this article is structured as follows: the next section offers a contextual background of the transformational stage of e-government; this is followed by a summary of the empirical data collection strategy; thereafter the key empirical findings are presented; finally the article concludes by providing a discussion of the key findings and answering the research questions set out above.

T-GOVERNMENT: A CONTEXTUAL BACKGROUND

At present, technology has been the driving force behind e-government, but governments globally have finally realized that it is only one of the important components needed for successful transformation (Di Maio, 2006). Conversely, e-government implementation does not only mean developing well designed websites but also adapting the internal business processes to handle the input from online services (Mansar, 2006). Adapting business processes implies radically rethinking the way business processes work currently (Mansar, 2006; Hammer and Champy, 1993; Davenport, 1993). Researchers such as Mansar (2006) and Layne and Lee (2001) highlights that business process reengineering is particularly important when e-government projects reach the later stages of development such as the transformational stage where the majority of public services are centralised, integrated and are made available more efficiently and effectively from a single point of access (also referred to as a one-stop-shop) (Wimmer, 2004). In particular, it has been reported that 85% to 95% of public sector e-commerce websites are not linked up with their back office processes (Mansar, 2006). Therefore, it is clear that for the UK government to reach a high level of e-government development, process reengineering and process integration techniques are categorically needed. Moreover, from an e-government growth perspective [see for instance Layne and Lee (2001)] the UK is in its third wave of development; having already established the infrastructure and basic services (Daniel and Ward, 2006; Weerakkody *et al.*, 2006), the focus is now on ICT-enabled business transformation (Murphy, 2005). However, Murphy (2005) argues that the transformation stage of e-government (or T-Government as a buzzword) is about changing fundamentally the way government does what it does. Altghough many have argued that e-government implies dramatic organizational and institutional changes (Montagna, 2005; Murphey, 2005); few governments have reached the process integration or transformation stages (O'Donnell *et al.*, 2003). On the contrary, studies suggest that ICT has been used in the public sector most often to reinforce existing organizational arrangements and power distributions rather than to change them (Kraemer and King, 2005).

Many academics and practitioners have referred to the final stage of e-government systems by different names such as horizontal integration (Layne and Lee, 2001), transformation (Baum and Di Maio, 2001), transforming government (Murphy, 2005; Balutis, 2001) and fully integrated or single point of access (Layne and Lee, 2001; Irani *et al.*, 2006). However, many scholars have also agreed on the purpose of this final stage of e-government implementation, i.e. that it leads to integrated government services and information is accessible by citizens and businesses from a single point (one-stop-shop) (Irani *et al.*, 2006). In particular Murphy's (2005) interpretation of the evolution of e-government below (Figure 1) distinguishes from the classifications suggested by for instance Baum and Di Maio (2001) and Balutis (2001) who describe the final stage as 'transformation and transforming government'; and Layne and Lee (2001) who refine the 'transform' stage into two stages: 'vertical integration' and 'horizontal integration'. Figure 1 shows the evolution of e-government according to Murphy (2005) and relates particularly well to the UK's transformational government agenda.

Figure 1. The evolution of e-government [adapted from Murphy (2005)]

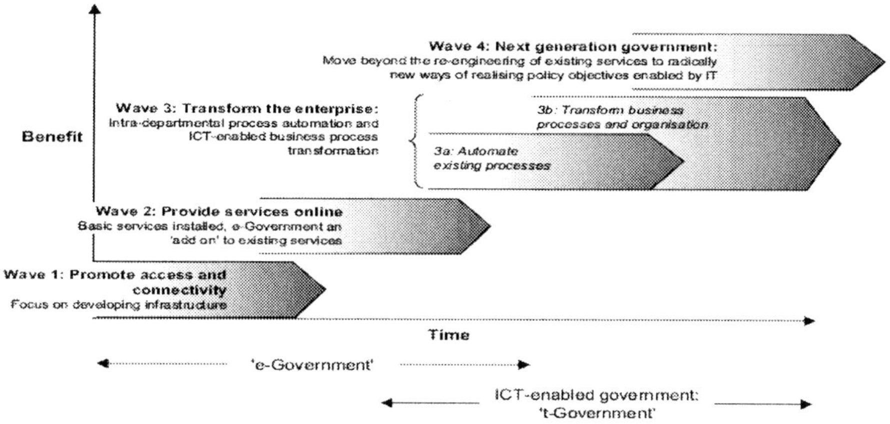

Where is the UK in terms of T-Government?

As identified before, the UK e-government initiative is in its third wave of development (as in figure 1, Murphy, 2005). In the third wave of development the increasing emphasis is upon the automation of existing back-office processes and integration both within and between services. In this context, the UK is promoting the development of closer horizontal and vertical integrations between different government services and departments. Furthermore, the emphasis is on the need to radically reengineer their business processes, and implement smarter, quicker processes which are enabled through ICT. Ultimately local authorities have to restructure their organisations to create a leaner organisation and move staff to more value adding roles to improve service delivery (Murphy, 2005). Thereafter, the fourth and final wave of development emphasizes next generation government, where most business processes are radically reengineered and IS/IT systems are collaborated vertically and horizontally throughout the entire organisation with relevant private sector organisations also linked together. This stage implies total transformation of government, where re-organisation is radical and across organisational boundaries and challenging traditional bureaucratic structures (Murphy, 2005; also see Champy, 2002).

The transformational government (t-government) strategy in the UK aims to place technology at the heart of the agenda to transform public service delivery and sets out a six-year improvement journey for public services in the UK (Cabinet Office report, 2007). The t-government phrase describes the process of improving services by leveraging the benefits from technological investment through business process reengineering and re-designs (www.improvementnetwork.gov.uk; Caldwell, 2005). Therefore, t-government is seen by many as the second phase of e-government, which focuses upon cost savings and service improvement through back-office process and IS/IT change. The t-government vision will require three key transformations, which firstly includes services enabled by ICT that are designed around the citizen and not the provider. Secondly, governments must move towards a shared services culture, thus eliminating data duplication and integrating and reengineering back-office processes. Thirdly, there must be broadening and deepening of government's professionalism in terms of planning delivery, management and governance of IT-enabled change (www.cio.gov.uk; Palanisamy,

2004). In this context, the UK government is attempting to fundamentally change the way in which information technology is used, in order to achieve joined up working between different parts of government and providing new, efficient and convenient ways for citizens and businesses to interact with government and to receive services (McIvor *et al.*, 2002; Beynon-Davies and Martin, 2004). Furthermore, the UK government has set an ambitious target for reaching the transformational stage of e-government, which aims to be fully complete by the end of 2011 (Cabinet Office report, 2007).

However, in order to achieve significant results in terms of phase 3 (transformation) in figure 1, research indicates that different government entities must work together by adopting processes that enable collecting data once for multiple uses and by streamlining redundant processes (Fagan, 2006; Weerakkody et al., 2007). Therefore, shallow e-commerce portals overlaid as a thin veneer on top of outdated organisational processes and aging IT systems will fail to transform the way of doing business or fail to deliver return on investment (Fagan, 2006). While the transformation stage of e-government proposes radical change in a manner that has not been seen before in the public sector, it is obvious that transformational change initiatives are also highly complex and challenging endeavours (Earl, 1994; West, 2004; Scholl, 2002). The bitter lessons that were learned in the private sector should serve as a stern reminder of this (Willcocks, 1995). Like BPR in the 1990's, some argue that more than 70% of e-government initiatives have failed to meet the initial transformation objectives in the early stages of e-government implementation (Gandhi and Cross, 2001; Beynon-Davies and Martin, 2004; Di Maio, 2006). Most of these failures have been attributed to the inability of governments to change business processes in response to the e-government model (ibid). Therefore, ultimately, these early failures have resulted in an even more pressing need to integrate the front-end and back-end systems and processes (West, 2004; Sarikas and Weerakkody, 2007) and changes to business processes in order to reap the full potential of e-government initiatives (Kim *et al.*, 2007). The most commonly encountered change barriers/factors affecting transformational efforts include limited implementation time (Tennant and Wu, 2005), poor information systems architecture (Edwards and Peppard, 1994; Willcocks, 1995), limited funds (Sutcliffe, 1999), lack of top managerial support and commitment (Hill and McNulty, 1998; Willcocks, 1995; Tennant and Wu, 2005; Attaran, 2004; Chan and Choi, 1997) and employee resistance (Mansar, 2006; West, 2004).

In this context, analysis of a variety of e-government efforts suggests that incorporating lessons learned from BPR can provide insight into what is needed to achieve the transformational stage of e-government (figure 1, 3rd and 4th phases) (Fagan, 2006; Weerakkody et al., 2006). Also, significant social, organisational and technical challenges will need to be understood well and overcome in those efforts that strive to achieve governmental transformation (Affisco and Soliman, 2006). Consequently, success will require the ability to rethink processes in a cross-functional way as championed by BPR approaches; while this has proven difficult in the private sector, research suggests that government entities face even greater challenges (Fagan, 2006; Weerakkody et al., 2006). The key transformational change challenges from an e-government literature perspective are summarised in table 1.

RESEARCH APPROACH

This study uses a qualitative research approach utilising semi structured interviews and document reviews in a case study setting (Myers, 1997; Kaplan and Duchon, 1988; Knott and Waites, 1998; Silverman, 2000; Walsham, 1995; Dix *et al.*, 2004; Gable, 1994). The advantages of using qualitative research are that it provides in-depth insight,

Table 1. Challenges affecting transformational change: an e-government literature perspective

Challenges Affecting Transformation Efforts in E-government	Source
Organisational Challenges	
Reluctance to embrace change	Mansar (2006); Beynon-Davies and Martin (2004)
Bureaucratic organisational structure	Hu *et al.*, (2006); Altameem *et al.*, (2006); Fang (2006); Kraemer and King (2005)
The lack of leadership in change efforts	Beynon-Davies and Martin (2004); O'Donnell *et al.*, (2003)
Process Change Challenges	
Confusing existing processes	Wimmer (2001); Gouscos *et al.*, (2006); Altameem *et al.*, (2006)
Information fragmentation	Gouscos *et al.*, (2006)
Incremental and modest change	Beynon-Davies and Martin (2004)
Cultural and Social Challenges	
Organisational culture	Montagna (2005); Ebrahim and Irani (2005);
Unwillingness to share IS/IT systems and processes	Ebrahim and Irani (2005); Murphy (2005); Conklin (2007)
Employee resistance to change and fear of change	Robinson and Griffiths (2005); Murphy (2005)
Data sharing and data protection laws	Murphy (2005)
IS/IT Integration Challenges	
Inflexible and incompatible legacy systems	BCS (2006); Gichoya (2005); McIvor (2002) ; Sarikas and Weerakkody, 2007)
Existing legacy systems increase costs	Dhillon et al., 2007); Ezz & Papazafeiropoulou (2006); Ebrahim and Irani (2005)
Lack of technology and BPR skills by IT staff	Holden *et al.*, (2006); Ramaswamy and Selian (2007)

provides flexibility and the results obtained are in real life like and rich with ideas (Ruyter and Scholl, 1998; Creswell, 2003). Furthermore, case studies are useful in providing a multidimensional picture of a situation (Whitman and Woszczynski, 2004). Case studies also offer the potential for generating alternative explanations from different stakeholder perspectives, thereby allowing the researcher to highlight contradictions and misunderstandings (Flick, 2006). Conversely, Yin (2003) suggests that case studies are appropriate where the purpose is to study current events, and where it is not necessary to control behavioural events or variables.

Open-ended semi-structured interviews were conducted with key figures involved in the e-government implementation programme in a large local authority in London UK (hereafter referred to as Council Y) during the period January to March 2006. The council was initially contacted using personal connections. Emails and telephone conversations were exchanged at the beginning which then led to the identification of relevant people to interview in the council. The actual interviews were then conducted by the researchers visiting the council premises during the aforementioned periods. A semi-structured interview approach was used in the research, as it was not necessary to ask questions in a specific order (Yin, 2003; Chen, 2004). The interviews were conducted with four local authority staff, including middle management, IT and operational level staff, and one representative from a partner organisation. All these interviewees were collectively responsible for delivering public services. This research was complemented with an interview with a citizen - who is the receiver of the service provided by government. Follow-up structured interviews were thereafter arranged with the same staff and citizen in order to confirm the results and clarify any unclear information (Yin, 2003). Since the focus of this research was to explore process management and integration aspects of e-government, the questions were fairly focused. Notes were taken during the interviews in a logbook and later transcribed into the computer.

The participants were given a consent form to read through regarding ethical considerations and their rights to withdraw from the study anytime without any prior notice or explanation. The formal interviews lasted approximately one to one and a half hours, and were undertaken in a meeting room of the council buildings. This allowed the researchers and respondents to build the necessary rapport and privacy for the required questions. Data triangulation was used by comparing and contrasting the interview findings with document reviews as it was necessary to validate and verify the findings of the primary data with secondary information (Saunders *et al.*, 2002; Mingers, 2003). This ensured that no bias emerged from either the participants or the researcher, thus the findings and conclusion made from the cases are valid (Yin, 2003).

PROCESS TRANSFORMATION: A UK LOCAL GOVERNMENT PERSPECTIVE

In section two a literature review identified numerous challenges that local government agencies may face when moving from a simple online information provisioning stage to the transformational stage of e-government. In this section we explore the impact of these issues in real life. As mentioned before we examine the execution of a key public service processes and related process management and integration issues in a large local council in the UK (identified as X). By examining these key processes we hope to answer the two research questions set out in the introduction section of this article: a) what does T-Government mean to local authorities in the UK; and b) what process related challenges do they need to overcome in order to implement T-Government.

Case Study: The Student Loan Application Process at Council X

The case that was studied involved investigating the execution of a key public service process and related process and systems integration issues in one of the largest local councils in the UK (identified as X). Located in northwest London, Council X employs over 7,800 staff and owns 79 buildings that are available to the public. The services provided by council X include central service departments (finance, law, administration and benefits services), housing services, library and community services, environment services and education. Council X's electronic government statement states that 'for council X, e-government is about using ICT's to support the delivery of community strategy targets by making services more accessible, improving efficiency and supporting strong commitment to social inclusion'.

Figure 2. Student loan application process – a use case model

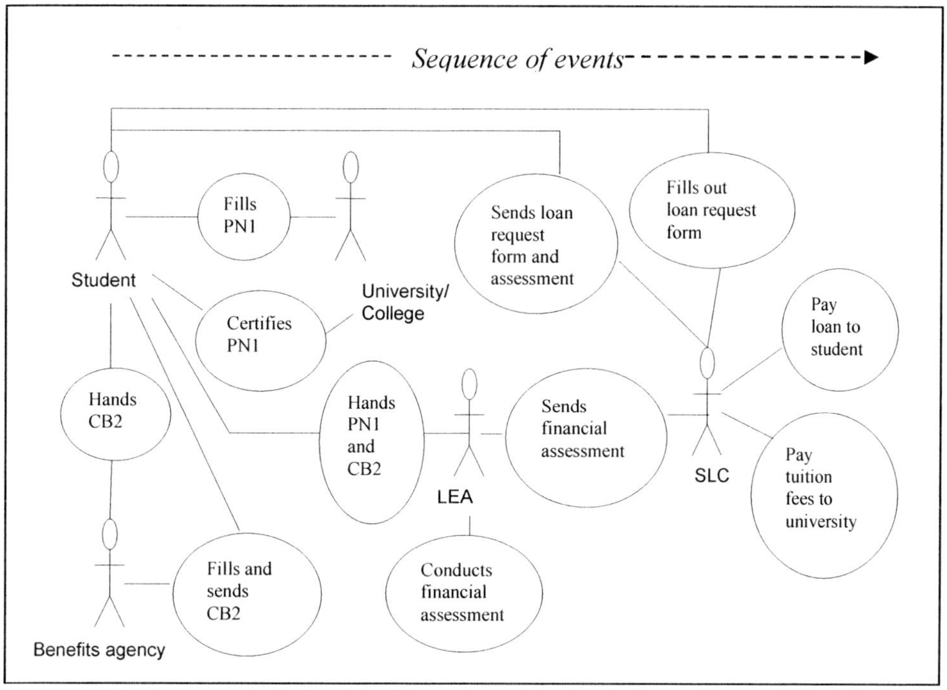

Since the aim of this research was to explore process and systems transformation aspects in local government, the researchers chose to focus on a key service provided by the council, the student loan application process (SLA). This process is typical of a core public service offered and relates to the loan applications made by prospective university students (citizens) to pay their tuition fees and subsistence during the course of their university studies. In particular this public service is unique in the UK as nearly three quarters of a million citizens (80% of the eligible students/citizens) take out financial assistance every year to finance their university studies (Student Loan Company, 2006). Therefore, this process is representative of a critical public service that handles millions of transactional data. Given this context, interviews were conducted primarily at council X's Local Education Authority (LEA). These interviews identified a scenario where lack of harmonization and integration between business processes and underlying IS/IT systems had resulted in inefficient and ineffective process execution and service delivery in local government (LG). Interviews with council X staff that were responsible for the student loan application process identified two key activities relating to the process, which primarily revolved around the handling of different documents. These include processing the different applications received from students for loans and tuition fees (identified as PN1 forms) and confirmation of benefits (identified as CB2 forms). The first form (PN1) contains general information on the student such as personal details, income, parent's income etc., while the second form (CB2) contains information about any benefits the student or their parents claim.

The following scenario describes the student loan application process. Once the student sends the completed forms (PN1 and CB2) to the LEA, an administrator manually enters the details onto the LEA Computer system. At the same time information provided on the CB2 form is checked against the benefits agency records. Using this information the systems generates a financial assessment on the student, which is sent manually (by post) to an organisation known as the Students Loans Company (SLC). To complement the investigation conducted at the LEA, interviews were conducted with staff at the SLC, council X's Benefits Agency and a student applying for the loan. The respective roles of these different entities and the sequence of activities that are executed to administer the student loan are outlined in Figure 2.

Council X's Benefits Agency: Council X's benefits agency is just one of the local functions at X. Their role is to provide benefits to citizens who are unemployed and are unable to work (such as income support and job seekers allowance). The LEA regularly needs information from the benefits agency to aid them in the process of making financial assessments for students. This is done using the confirmation of benefits-CB2 form. However, interviews with the benefits agency staff indicated that the LEA does not directly contact the benefits agency to obtain this information. Instead, the student is responsible to get part of the CB2 form completed by the benefits agency, which is then sent to the LEA by the student.

The Students Loan Company (SLC): The SLC is an organization set up to pay the tuition fees to the student's university. The SLC also pays the student an instalment of loans throughout the academic year. The SLC does this by using the assessment information from the LEA. As noted earlier, interviews with staff at the SLC showed that there is no harmonization of processes and integration of systems between the LEA and SLC with the assessment information for every student being sent by mail on a regular basis.

The Student: Interviews with a university student in possession of a student loan confirmed the ineffectiveness of the lengthy process involved in the loan application process. It was revealed that the student applying for a loan and tuition fee payments, has to go through the same process every academic year. The student needs to fill out the first form (PN1) and the first section of the CB2 form. The student is then in direct contact with all the entities in the process including the LEA, SLC and the benefits agency. The student interviewed reported, "this is a very time consuming and lengthy process".

Figure 2 shows that the SLA process begins with the student filling out two forms, which include the PN1, and CB2 form. The PN1 form goes to the college or university the student is currently attending. The CB2 form goes to the benefits agency, where one section of the form is filled out and given back to the student. Once the two forms are complete, these are handed over to the LEA. The LEA then uses this information to make an assessment on the student's eligibility for the loan using an IT system at council X's office. Once the assessment is made, the LEA passes this information manually to the SLC.

With the financial assessment received from the LEA, the SLC then enters this information into their computer system and sends the student a loan request form and the assessment information made by LEA. The loan request form is used by the student to indicate how much money they want to borrow. Once the SLC has received the completed loan request form, they are then able to start with instalment payments to the student along with the tuition fee payments made to the student's university.

The scenario above clearly contradicts council X's vision for e-government led change and highlights a number of process and IS integration problems in a key public service process. The first problem lies in the student handing the CB2 form to the benefits agency for them to complete one section of the form. If the student delays this process, this also delays the financial assessment process at the LEA in council X. This is further compounded by delays that occur when the benefits agency is slow to give back the CB2 form to the student.

A second problem occurs with the exchanging of information between the LEA and SLC. The

LEA receives a large number of requests from students, in particular during the period leading up to a new academic year, where each student loan application can take between 2-3 weeks to assess. Once these assessments are made they are then sent to the SLC by post. One LEA worker stated during the interviews that, "using this method of communication can be sometimes troublesome when there are postal problems or delays". This can cause delays and financial difficulties to the students receiving the loan as well as the university enlisting the student. Furthermore, delays in obtaining the financial assessment information can result in delays in the student's enrolment process at the university/collage.

The last problem occurs with the 'student loan request forms', which are sent to the students by the SLC. Delay can arise here again due to postal problems and lost or misplaced forms. This could mean that the student would need to contact the SLC and request a new form, which could take up to 1-2 weeks to arrive by post.

Given the above context, in order to realise the transformational stage of e-government the student loan application process needs to be significantly improved. It was clear from our investigation that the lengthy cycle time and resulting process inefficiencies were caused mainly due to lack of harmonization and integration of process and supporting IS/IT systems (see Champy, 2002) between various internal and external entities in the context of council X. Hence, it can be argued that there was scope for radical improvements to the process [as in BPR (Hammer and Champy, 1993)] that would not only transform the SLA process from a largely manual state to electronic, but reduce the cycle time by well over 50 percent. This would however require the integration and harmonization of processes and IS/IT systems between the LEA, SLC and Benefits Agency. With a new integrated system the following requirements need to be realized: a) the student should be able to hand both forms (PN1 and CB2) directly to the LEA; b) when the financial assessment has been made by LEA, the SLC should be able to access the information electronically through a direct link; c) the student should be able to access their financial assessment online, eliminating postal problems that can occur with hard copies; and d) the student should also be able to fill out the loan request form online.

DISCUSSION AND CONCLUSION

The two research questions this article set out to address were: a) what does t-government mean to local authorities in the UK; and b) what process related challenges do they need to overcome in order to implement t-government. If the first question is viewed from a literature perspective, research by Lee *et al.,* (2005), Norris and Moon (2006) and Sarikas and Weerakkody (2007) finds that local e-government remains mainly informational and seldom is it achieving joined up service delivery or the potential positive impacts claimed by its most ardent advocates. Authors such as Kraemer and King (2005) have also argued that e-government is not transformational, but is incremental. These authors further predict that the trajectory of local e-government that has been observed to date (i.e. incremental change) is likely to continue into the foreseeable future. Although many governmental entities have built one-stop shops to streamline the waiting, the basic article-based forms continue to rule the day (Conklin, 2007). It can be said that these forms are the items that enable the power base of significant numbers of bureaucrats, with careers to protect and they defend their turf fiercely through the application of complex and complicated rules and regulations, designed in part to maintain their status quo of power in the system (ibid).

When viewed from an empirical perspective, the case study described in the previous section illustrates that although the UK is considered to be in the 3rd wave of e-government (or t-government; figure 1) services are still delivered to citizens with major inherent process and IS/IT inefficiencies. Lack of synergy between local government, other public sector and private agencies' business processes and IS/IT systems prove that much more needs to be done in terms of fundamentally rethinking and radical reengineering of these processes if joint up services are to be delivered through a single point of access [i.e. the 3rd wave of e-government according to figure 1, Murphy (2005)]. However, in general, it is accepted that public sector agencies are slower in achieving transformational benefits from technology than private sector organisations (Montagna, 2005) mainly due to bureaucratic business practices, lack of skills and organisational structures that are not prepared to face radical change (Holmes, 2001; Weerakkody *at al.*, 2007). Furthermore, process and IS/IT related factors that influence 'radical change' have not been exhaustively researched to date in a public sector environment and therefore hitherto less well known. Given this context, there is much scope for local government agencies implementing t-government to learn from the lessons of organisational change in the private sector; certainly, before embarking on BPR type change they can identify factors that may challenge transformational change in the public sector (Wimmer, 2001; Fagan, 2006; Weerakkody *et al.*, 2007). However, there has been relatively little research conducted on transformational stage challenges in e-government, thus there is a need to research further in this area of study (Kim *et al.*, 2007). Some of the key high level challenges that organisations faced during the BPR movement when radically changing their processes and IS/IT systems included resistance from employees, legacy systems constraints, cultural and political constraints, lack of senior management commitment, negative employee attitude and resistance to change (Weerakkody and Currie, 2003; O'Donnell *et al.*, 2003; Weerakkody and Hinton, 1999; Willcocks, 1995; Mumford, 1994). Therefore, it is understandable that for the public sector these challenges will be even more severe in an environment that can be described as bureaucratic, functionally oriented, and legacy system driven (Weerakkody et al., 2007). Hence, understanding the key challenges will no doubt help facilitate the transformational stage of e-government better (Larsen and Klischewski, 2004).

In the context of the second research question (process related challenges impeding t-government), the case study described in this article shows that the transfer of the *student loan application* process from a largely manual to an automated, fully e-enabled state would require radical reengineering of these processes. However, as illustrated in figures 2, this will require a high level of process harmonisation and systems interoperability between different internal functions and external organisations to enable better online-real-time communication and information exchange [as in the case of Champy (2002)]. While this research has identified one example of process inefficiencies at local government level, yet we can argue that there will be many other local authorities that repeat the same inefficient processes. Therefore, to realise more customer-focused and joined up service delivery in the UK (vis-à-vis t-government), public sector agencies will require a substantial level of integration of back-end information systems such as, council tax systems, benefits systems, electoral registers, land and property systems etc. (Beynon-Davies and Martin, 2004). Given this context, local authorities will need to explore emerging technologies such as service oriented architecture and web services that can offer fast and cost effective solution to councils (like X) by helping to retain many existing (functional) legacy applications in the council, but instead of staying in relative isolation from each other, they can be integrated to create new services that are more attuned to the needs of the citizens (Fustes, 2003; Weerakkody et al., 2007). Yet, from an organizational perspective, the paradigm shift that need to be realised to change these processes would mean that local government will need to breakdown their departmental or silo culture and overcome resistance to change as seen in other forms of organizational change such as business process reengineering (Avgerou, 1993; Sahay and Walsham, 1997; Weerakkody and Hinton 1999). Nonetheless, on the positive side, improving key processes such as the aforementioned and consequently succeeding at a local level is imperative as empirical research in the UK strongly suggests that successful local best practices can be mirrored at national level (Hackney and Jones, 2002; www.kable.com).

REFERENCES

Avgerou, C. (1993). Information systems for development planning. *International Journal of Information Management, 13*, 260-273.

Fustes, M. (2003, July). The unconstrained business. *Insight, 3*, 15-17.

Accenture (2005). *Leadership in customer service: New expectations, new experiences*, www.accenture.com

Al-Kibsi, G., de Boer, K., Mourshed, M., & Rea, N. (2001). Putting citizens online not in line. *The McKinsley Quarterly, 2*, 65-73.

Affisco, J., & Soliman, K. (2006). E-government: A strategic operations management framework for service delivery. *Business Process Management Journal, 12*(1), 13-21.

Basu, Subhajit (2004). E-Government and developing countries: An overview. *International Review of Law Computers, 18*(1), 109-132.

Baum, C., & Di Maio, A. (2001). *Gartner's four phases of e-government model*, available at: http://gartner3.gartnerweb.com/public/static/hotc/00094235.html [Accessed on 25th May 2007]

Balutis, A. P. (2001). *E-government 2001. Part I: Understanding the challenge and evolving strategies. The Public Manager*, 33-7.

Bonham, G., Seifert, J., & Thorson, S (2001). *The transformational potential of E-Government: The role of political leadership. The 4th Pan European International Relations Conference of the European Consortium for Political Research*, the University of Kent, Canterbury, U.K.

Beynon-Davies, P., & Martin, S. (2004). Electronic local government and the modernisation agenda: Progress and prospects for public service improvement. *Local government studies, 30*(2), 214-229.

Boyatzis, R. (1998). *Transforming oualitative information*. USA: Sage Publications.

Burn, F., & Robins, G. (2003). Moving towards E-Government: A case study of organisational change processes. *Logistics Information Management, 16*(1), 25-35.

Cabinet Office (2006) available at: http://www.cio.gov.uk/documents/annual_report2006/trans_gov2006.doc [Accessed on 29th May 2007]

Champy, J. (2002). *X-Engineering the corporation: Reinventing your business in the digital age*. Warner Books

Crane, J. (2005). *Qualitative research methods*, available at: http://web.isp.cz [Accessed on 28th May 2007]

Creswell, J. (2003). Research design, qualitative, quantitative, and mixed methods approaches, Second Edition. Thousand Oaks, London: Sage Publications.

Davenport, T. H. (1993). *Process innovation: Reengineering work through information technology*. Harvard Business School Press

Deitel, H., Deitel, P., & Steinbuhler, K. (2001). *E-Business and E-commerce for managers*. Prentice Hall, NJ: New Jersey Press

Di Maio, A. (2006). Moving from E-Government to government transformation. *Business Issues*, 1-3, available at: http://www.gartner.com

Evans , G. (2003). *Implementing E-Government: An executive report for civil servants and their advisors*. Hampshire, England: Gower Publishing Limited.

Di Maio, A. (2006). *Moving from E-Government to government transformation. Business Issues*, 1-3, available at: http://www.gartner.com

Earl, M. J. (1994). The new & old of business process redesign. *Journal Of Strategic Information Systems, 3*(1), 5-22.

Fagan, M. (2006). *Exploring city, county and state E-Government initiatives: An east Texas perspective. Business Process Management Journal, 12*(1),101-112.

Flick, U. (2006). An introduction to qualitative research, Third Edition. Thousand Oaks, London: Sage Publications.

Fustes, M. (2003a, July). The unconstrained business. *Insight, 3*, 15-17.

Gandhi, S., & Cross, C. (2001, October). E-Government initiative at city of Orlando: Current trends and future directions. *Proceedings of the URISA conference*, 1-12.

Gupta, M. P., & Jana, D. (2003). E-Government evaluation: A framework and case study. *Government Information Quarterly, 20*, 365-387.

Hackney, R., & Jones, S. (2002, April). Towards E-Government in the Welsh (UK) Assembly: An Iiformation systems evaluation. *ISOneWorld Conference and Convention,* Las Vegas, USA.

Hammer, M., & Champy, J. (1993). Reengineering the corporation: A manifesto for business revolution. NY: Harper Collins Publishers Inc.

Holden, S. H., Norris, D. F., & Fletcher, P. D. (2003). Electronic government at the local level: Progress to date and future issues. *Public Performance and Management Review, 26*(4), 325-344.

Ho, A. (2002, July-August). Reinventing local governments and the 'E-Government' initiative. *Public Administration review, 62*(4), 434-444.

Hu, P., Cui, D., & Sherwood, A. (2006). Examining cross-agency collaborations in E-Government initiatives. *Proceedings of the 39th Hawaii International Conference on System Sciences,* pp.1-11

Irani, Z., Al-Sebie, M., & Elliman, T. (2006). Transaction stage of E-Government systems: Identification of its location & importance. *Proceedings of the 39th Hawaii International Conference on System Sciences, IEEE*, 1-9.

Jain, P. (2002). The catch-up state: E-Government in Japan. *Japanese Studies, 22*(3), 237-255.

Kaplan, B., & Duchon, D. (1988). Combining qualitative and quantitative methods in information systems research: A case study. *MIS Quarterly, 12*(4), 571-586.

Kim, H., Pan, G., & Pan, S. (2007). Managing IT-enabled transformation in the public sector: Case study on E-Government in South Korea. *Government Information Quarterly, 24*, 338-352.

Knott, G., & Waites, N. (1998). *Computer studies*, 4th Edition. Sunderland, England: Business Education Publishers Limited

Kraemer, K. L., & John, L. K. (2006). Information technology and administrative reform: Will E-Government be different? *International Journal of Electronic Government Research 2*(1), 1-20.

Layne, K., & Lee, J. (2001). Developing fully functional E-Government: A four-stage model. *Government Information Quarterly, 18*(2), 122-136.

Larsen, M., & Klischewski, R. (2004). Process ownership challenges in IT-enabled transformation of interorganizational business processes. *Proceedings of the 37th Hawaii International Conference on System Sciences, IEEE*, 1-11.

Lee, S. M., Tan, X., &Trimi, S. (2005). *Current practices of leading E-Government countries. Communications of the ACM, 48*(10), 99-104.

Li, B. (2005). *On the barriers to the development of E-Government in China. Communications of ACM,* 549-552

Mansar, S. (2006). E-Government implementation: Impact on business processes, *IEEE*, 1-5.

McGrath, K. (2002). The golden circle: A way of arguing and acting about technology in the London ambulance aervice. *European Journal of Information Systems, 11*(4). 251-266.

McIvor, R., McHugh, M., & Cadden, C. (2002). Internet technologies: Supporting transparency in the public sector. *The International Journal of Public Sector Management, 15* (3), 170-187.

Mingers, J. (2001). *Combining IS research methods: Towards a pluralist methodology. Information Systems Research, 12*(3), 240-259.

Murphy, J. (MP Parliamentary Secretary Cabinet Office Report) (2005). Beyond E-Government the world's most successful technology-enabled transformations. *Executive summary, INSEAD the business school for the world,* 1-124, available at: www.localtgov.org.uk

Myers, M. D. (1997). Qualitative research in information systems. *MIS Quarterly, 21*, 241-242.

Mumford, E. (1994). New treatments or old remedies: Is business process reengineering really Socio-technical design? *Journal of Strategic Information Systems, 3*(4), 313-326.

Student Loan Company (2006). Student support for higher education in England. *Academic Year 2006/07 (Provisional), Student Load Company,* ww.slc.co.uk/pdf/slcsfr032006.pdf

Norris, D. F., & Moon, M. J. (2005). Advancing E-Government at the grass roots: Tortoise or hare? *Public Administration Review, 65*(1), 64-75.

Palanisamy, R. (2004). Issues and challenges in e-governance planning. *Electronic government, 1*(3), 253-273.

Sahay, S., & Walsham, G. (1997). Social structures & management agency in India. *Organisation Studies, 18*, 415-444.

Scholl, H. (2002). *Current practices in E-Government-induced business process change (BPC): An empirical study of Current Practices,* 1(2), 27-49.

Scholl, H. (2005). Organizational transformation through E-Government: Myth or reality? *Lecture Notes in Computer Science, LNCS 3591/2005,* 1-11, Springer.

Sarikas, O. D., & Weerakkody, V. (2007). Realising integrated E-Government services: A UK local government perspective. *Transforming Government: People, Process and Policy, 1*(2). Emerald

Seifert, J., & Petersen, E. (2002). The promise of all things E: Expectations and challenges of emergent electronic government. *Perspectives on Global Development and Technology, 1*(2). 193-213.

Silverman, D. (2000). *Doing qualitative research: A practical handbook.* London: Sage Publications.

Saunders, M., Lewis, P., & Thornhill, A. (2002). Research methods for business students, 3rd Edition, London: Prentice Hall.

Ruyter, K. D., & Scholl, N. (1998). Positioning qualitative market research: Reflections from theory and practice. *Qualitative Market Research: An International Journal, 1*(1), 7-14.

UN (2005). *World public sector report: Global E-government Readiness: From E-Government to E-Inclusion.* United Nations, New York.

Wassenaar, A. (2000). E-Governmental value chain models. DEXA, IEEE Press, 289-293.

Weerakkody, V., Janssen, M., & Hjort-Madsen, K. (2007). Realising integrated E-Government services: A european perspective._*Journal of Cases in Electronic Commerce*, 3(2), 14-38. Idea Group, ISSN 1548-0623.

Weerakkody, V., Baire, S., & Choudrie, J. (2006, January). E-Government: A case for process improvement in the public sector. *Hawaii International Conference on Systems Sciences (Hicss-39).*

Weerakkody, V., & Currie, W. (2003). Integrating business process reengineering with information systems development: Issues & implications. *Lecture Notes in Computer Science, LNCS 2678*, 302-320. Springer.

Weerakkody, V. J. P., & Hinton, C. M. (1999). Exploiting information systems & technology through business process improvement. *Knowledge and Process Management: The Journal Of Corporate Transformation, 6*(1). UK: John Wiley & Sons, Ltd..

West, D. (2004). *E-Government and the transformation of service delivery and citizen attitudes. Public Administration Review, 64*(1), 15-27.

Wimmer, M., & Traunmuller, R. (2000). Trends in electronic government: Managing distributed knowledge. *Proceedings from 11th International Workshop on Database and Expert Systems Applications*, 340-345. New York: Springer.

Wimmer, M. (2004). A European perspective towards online one-stop government: The eGov project. *Electronic Commerce Research and Applications*, 92-103.

Willcocks, L. (1995). False promise or delivering the goods? Recent findings on the economics and impact of business process reengineering. *Proceedings of The 2nd European Conference On IT Investment Evaluation.* UK

Whitman, M., & Woszczynski, A. (2004). The handbook of information systems research. Hershey: Idea group publishing.

Yin, R. K. (2003). *Case study research: Design and methods*, 3rd Edition. London: Sage Publications.

Zhiyuan, F. (2002). E-Government in digital era: Concepts, practice and development. *International Journal of The Computer, The Internet and Management, 10*(2), 1-22.

This work was previously published in International Journal of Electronic Government Research, Vol. 4, Issue 4, edited by M. Khosrow-Pour, pp. 1-16, copyright 2008 by IGI Publishing (an imprint of IGI Global).

Chapter 21
Instititutional Opportunities and Challenges of the Wireless City

Sukumar Ganapati
Florida International University, USA

ABSTRACT

This chapter explores the institutional opportunities and challenges of adopting wireless communications for mobile government at the local level. The basic ingredients of wireless for m-government include the wireless devices and the wireless infrastructure. The proliferation of wireless devices provides opportunities for transforming field operations, coordinating emergency management, enhancing citizen services and participation, and narrowing the digital divide. Challenges, however, exist in terms of wireless security, interoperability, and infrastructure provision.

INTRODUCTION

Wireless communication is a core building block for the mobile government. The basic ingredients of the wireless communications include the wireless devices and the wireless infrastructure required for communications among the devices. Wireless devices have rapidly evolved and diffused world-wide. For example, mobile phones, which are common forms of wireless devices, have evolved from the traditional analog cellular phones to digital "smartphones" with internet and other capabilities (e.g. camera, location awareness). The growth of mobile phones is not limited to the developed world; they have become commonplace in the developing world, leap-frogging the landline phone connections. The wireless infrastructure for supporting communications between the devices has also advanced considerably. Several types of wireless infrastructure support have emerged in the recent years, including the Wi-Fi, WiMax, and Mesh Networks. The wireless infrastructure complements wired infrastructure in providing last mile solutions for data transmission as well as voice communications.

The purpose of this chapter is to outline some of these key institutional opportunities and challenges of adopting the evolving wireless technology for

DOI: 10.4018/978-1-60566-918-2.ch021

e-government at the local level. Wireless devices provide opportunities for both better government service delivery and citizen participation. The proliferation of wireless devices has enabled the mobile government (i.e. m-government), which refers to the provision of government services (government to government, government to business, and government to citizen services) using the various forms of wireless technologies (especially mobile phones). Wireless devices, for example, have been adopted for greater efficiency of field operations, emergency management, and to enable citizen participation. Wireless broadband offers opportunities for reducing the digital divide. Barack Obama's use of text messages and the Blackberry during the 2008 Presidential campaign also popularized the use of wireless devices.

Challenges, however, exist in terms of security of wireless communications, interoperability, and infrastructure provision. Despite encryption technologies, wireless networks (particularly open ones) are prone to security breaches through various means (e.g. spoofing). Confidentiality of sensitive information could be compromised in such networks. Interoperability, which broadly refers to the ability of devices to work together to exchange and use information, is a challenge due to the different technological standards and vendor preferences. Organizational, political, and legal issues could complicate the achievement of interoperability. Much debate has also centered on the institutional mechanisms of provision of the wireless infrastructure. Wireless accessibility in the field requires extensive wireless networks. Although wireless hotspots are available in several locations, such as coffee shops, fast food places, airports, and hotel lobbies, such wireless coverage is not available beyond these sites. In the face of private sector failure, municipalities stepped in to provide the wireless networks. However, municipal wireless networks have also hit snags recently in the United States, with a few major cities dropping their plans for implementing such networks.

The rest of the chapter is organized as follows. The subsequent section describes the evolution of the wireless communications, enabling the m-government. Next, the institutional opportunities of the wireless for m-government are examined. After this, the challenges of the wireless communications are identified. Finally, the chapter concludes with the major a summary of the major opportunities and challenges.

EVOLUTION OF WIRELESS COMMUNICATIONS

Wireless communications are not new. The telegraph network was invented by Samuel Morse in 1838. Guglielmo Marconi obtained the patent for wireless telegraph in 1897. Radio communications have been in use since the beginning of the 20th century. Mobile telephone services were introduced after World War II, with the Federal Communications Commission's (FCC) recognizing them as new class of services in 1949. However, the modern wireless communications technology has evolved significantly since then. The widespread growth of wireless across the globe is also a more recent phenomenon, since the late 1990s. The exponential growth of wireless communications is one of the key drivers enabling the mobile government (Kuscu, Kushchu, and Yu, 2007).

Wireless communications requires both the wireless devices and the wireless infrastructure to enable communications between the devices. Mobile phones are the common examples of wireless devices; however, the devices encompass a range of other gadgets such as remote control devices, Global Positioning System (GPS) units, remote garage door openers, satellite television, wireless computer peripherals and networks, and so on. Wireless communications are fundamentally based on the transmission and reception of radio wave signals. Unlike wired communications, wireless does not require a physical cable connection.

Rather, the wireless infrastructure comprises of antennas to transmit and receive radio signals. The evolution of the wireless devices and the infrastructure is explored below.

Wireless Devices

Mobile phones are the most ubiquitous among the wireless devices that are also of much importance to the m-government. Three generations of mobile phones are generally identified, although intermediate generations of phones also exist. The *first generation* phones introduced in the 1980s were the cellular phones that were based on the transmission and reception of analog signals. Analog systems refer to modulation (amplitude or frequency) of sinusoidal radio wave forms for communications delivery and reception. They typically have been based on circuit switching, which use a dedicated channel between nodes and terminals for communication; the channel is not available to other users until it is released. Initially designed for use inside vehicles mounted with antennas, the cellular phones have evolved into lightweight handheld mobile devices for use indoors and outdoors. The cellular concept is based on division of a coverage area into nonoverlapping cells, where specific channels are assigned to each cell. The cellular division allows cell phones to be mobile since the continuity of radio signals are maintained by the antenna in each cell (Goldsmith, 2005).

In the early 1990s, the *second generation* of mobile phones was deployed, which marked a shift from analog to digital signals, but still based on circuit switching (McNurlin and Sprague, 2006). Digital refers to binary (0 or 1) radio wave transmission and reception. Digital wireless offers more advantages over analog: it can accommodate more users, reduced background noise, better sound quality, and more security. Besides voice communications, the 2G mobile phones support data services such as text messaging, email, and internet access. However, the 2G phones conform to different incompatible standards, such as Code-Division Multiple Access (CDMA), Time-Division Multiple Access (TDMA), and Global System for Mobile communication (GSM). Hence, phones that work with one technology do not necessarily work on another network that supports a different technology.

More recent mobile phones are *third generation* phones, which provide broadband access with much higher data transmission rates and capacity. In contrast to the circuit switching of earlier generations, the 3G phones are based on Internet Protocol's packet switching, where data from the sending device is broken down into small packets and transmitted over the Internet using the best available route; the packets are then reassembled at the receiver's device. Packet switching provides benefits in terms of higher data rates and greater bandwidth. The 3G phones offer mobile Internet access and multimedia applications (e.g. video streaming and conferencing, internet browsing, navigational maps) (Camarillo and García-Martín, 2004). The phones were developed based on the International Mobile Telecommunications (IMT-2000) family of standards. Yet, similar to the 2G phones, incompatibilities exist between the 3G technologies, such as the Evolution Data Only (EVDO) and Universal Mobile Telecommunications System (UMTS). A further set of future *fourth generation* phones are still evolving, which are expected to provide data network connections at speeds that are faster than the 3G phones. However, debates surround the standards for the 4G technologies, with alternatives such as Long-Term Evolution (LTE), Worldwide Interoperability for Microwave Access (WiMAX) and Ultra Mobile Broadband (UMB).

The 3G phones reflect a convergence of cellular functions with the internet, facilitated by the IP Multimedia Subsystem (IMS) technology (Camarillo and García-Martín, 2006). The *smartphones* build on such convergence to provide additional capabilities, such as the personal digital assistant (PDA), location awareness (e.g. using Geographic

Information Systems, GIS), Voice over IP, and connecting to Wi-Fi networks for other web-based tasks (Ilyas and Ahson, 2006). Prominent smartphones include the Motorola's RAZR/RAZR2, Apple's iPhone, Resarch In Motion's (RIM) BlackBerry, and some models of Nokia. While these phones have traditionally featured proprietary operating systems (e.g. Symbian, Microsoft Mobile), the more recent moves toward open source (e.g. Google's Android) provide prospects for a new range of mobile applications. The software applications on the devices have also gained more significance as the smartphones begin to mimic computers and carry out multiple tasks besides web browsing. Smartphones feature many applications that are traditionally accessed through a computer (e.g. calendar, word processing, mapping, specialized applications such as customer relationship management). Mobile Web 2.0 applications are also emerging. While Short Message Service (SMS) has been the traditional form of text messaging, Twitter has increasingly gained prominence as a micro-blogging service where short messages could be relayed instantly to a mass of people over the mobile phones and the web. Other web applications for obtaining real time weather information, traffic updates, location of friends (e.g. Loopt), and for linking with social networking sites have also emerged.

The mobile phones proliferated across the world during the 21st century, driven by the technology improvements, lowering of costs of the mobile devices and airtime, and liberalization of government controls. Table 1 shows the growth of mobile phone subscribers worldwide between 1995 and 2007. As the table shows, the percentage of mobile phone subscribers grew exorbitantly from 1.6% in 1995 to over 50% by 2007 (comparably, urban population reached 50% in 2007). The growth has been especially significant between 2000 and 2007. However, there are regional variations. Europe leads the mobile phone penetration rate with 111.3% (i.e. one person could own more than one mobile phone) in 2007; Oceania and Americas follow at 79.2% and 72.2% respectively. Although Asia trails behind at 37.6%, China and India represent big markets for mobile phones due to their sheer population size. The growth of mobile phones has also been significant in Africa. Thus, despite regional variations, there is significant growth in the adoption of mobile phones across the world during the 2000s. Developing countries provide prospects for further growth of the phones, leapfrogging the obstacles of adopting landline phones (Sauter and Watson, 2008). In developed countries too, the percentage of mobile phone *only* subscribers has also been on the rise due to lower costs. Overall, mobile

Table 1. Growth of mobile subscribers, 1995-2007

	1995	2000	2007
Mobile subscribers (million)	90.77	737.92	3,352.77
World Population (million)	5,696.48	6,094.92	6,691.41
Percent mobile subscribers worldwide	1.6%	12.1%	50.1%
Mobile subscribers by world regions:			
Africa		1.9%	28.4%
Americas		21.7%	72.2%
Asia		6.6%	37.6%
Europe		36.9%	111.3%
Oceania		33.3%	79.2%

Source: International Telecommunications Union (2008)

constituted 72.3% of the telephone subscribers worldwide in 2007 (International Telecommunications Union, 2008).

Wireless Infrastructure

Wireless communications require the transmission of radio signals that are propagated through the space at a range of frequency spectrum. With the rapid growth of wireless devices, the frequency spectrum has become increasingly crowded with a number of competing devices. The management of the spectrum is thus a key issue for the wireless infrastructure. Although the International Telecommunication Union governs the broad rules of spectrum use, countries have taken different approaches to the management of the frequency spectrum. In the United States, the frequency spectrum is managed by the Federal Communications Commission (FCC) and the National Telecommunications and Information Administration (NTIA). Whereas FCC manages radio frequencies used by commercial providers (e.g radio and television broadcasters) and public safety and health officials (e.g., police and emergency medical technicians), NTIA manages the frequencies used by the federal government (e.g., air traffic control and national defense).

The frequency spectrum could be licensed or unlicensed. Licensed spectrum covers the range of frequencies that service providers have exclusive rights to transmit (e.g. TV and radio station frequencies) in a particular geographical area. Service providers obtain the rights through FCC auction or sublease from another provider having the rights to transmit over the spectrum. Unlicensed spectrum includes the range of frequencies that are not allocated to any service provider. Licensed and unlicensed frequencies have their strengths and weaknesses. Licensed frequencies are costly, but have little interference from other providers. Unlicensed frequencies do not involve any costs, but are limited in power, and are more prone to interference from competing devices using the same frequencies. Both licensed and unlicensed frequencies are used for the wireless broadband networks.

Ganapati and Schoepp (2008) argue that the wireless is the future of the broadband. With the convergence of mobile voice functions with internet applications, the demand for wireless broadband has grown. According to Coffman and Odlyzko (2002), internet data traffic almost doubles annually; the advent of 3G phones imposes even greater pressure on the wireless infrastructure for voice and data communications. Broadband refers to fast internet connections, although the standards differ across countries. The wired broadband infrastructure is based on a cable connection; examples include the Digital Subscriber Line (DSL) (which use telephone lines), Cable (which use cable television's co-axial lines), Fiber to the Home (FTTH) (which use fiber lines), and Broadband over Powerline (BPL) (which use power lines). Wireless broadband infrastructure includes wireless antenna and/or towers for internet connectivity.

Table 2 shows the growth of internet and broadband subscribers in the world from 2000 to 2007. As the table shows, the worldwide internet penetration was 20.89% in 2007; broadband was subscribed by only 5.41 percent. Worldwide, the internet and broadband penetration is relatively low as compared to that of the mobile devices. There are also regional variations in the internet and broadband subscription, with Oceania, Europe, and the Americas on the lead. Although Asia shows as lagging behind, countries like Japan, Singapore, and South Korea have very high degree of internet and broadband penetration. Japan and South Korea particularly boast high degree of penetration of the 3G phones that combine mobile telephony and internet.

Wireless broadband infrastructure could be classified into short-, medium-, and long-range networks based on the geographical coverage. *Short-range* Personal Area Networks (PANs) span about 30 feet (they comply with IEEE 802.15

Table 2. Growth of internet and broadband subscribers, 2000-2007

	Percent Internet Subscribers		Percent Broadband Subscribers	
	2000	2007	2000	2007
Africa	0.55	5.46	-	0.21
Americas	18.79	43.42	1.16	11.20
Asia	3.08	14.43	0.18	3.33
Europe	14.07	44.29	0.26	14.24
Oceania	35.58	52.77	0.12	17.15
World	6.51	20.89	0.35	5.41

Source: International Telecommunications Union (2008)

family of standards). For example, Bluetooth and Ultra Wide Band (UWB) are PAN technologies. Bluetooth equipment use the unlicensed frequency (2.4 GHz) and have speeds of upto 720 kbps; they could be used for home security, streaming audio, ad-hoc file sharing. UWB uses low-powered, pulse modulation (often exceeding 1 GHz) and can have much higher speeds upto 100 mbps; the higher speeds allow it to be used for wireless monitors and faster data transfer between various devices. The short range PANs are unsuitable for wireless broadband at a larger geographical scale such as the city level.

Medium range wireless is used for point-to-point communications upto 300 feet, and is generally utilized for local area networks. Wi-Fi (Wireless Fidelity) is the most common form of the medium range wireless. Wi-Fi hotspots are venues equipped with Wi-Fi antenna, enabling access to wireless broadband. Wi-Fi access points transmit radio signals in the unlicensed frequency spectrum. Wi-Fi devices comply with the IEEE 802.11 family of standards. The wireless access points installed in homes are typically Wi-Fi routers. Wired backhaul connections (e.g. DSL or fiber) generally link the hotspots to the service provider or the network core. Since the range of a Wi-Fi access point is limited, a network of such access points is required for an area wide coverage (e.g. citywide or neighborhood level). According to JiWire.com (2009), which tracks hotspots around the world, there were nearly 252,000 free and pay Wi-Fi locations in 139 countries by January 2009.

Long range wireless networks are point-to-point or point-to-multipoint connections that can span distances as far as 30 miles. Wireless Metropolitan Area Networks (WMANs) are such long-range networks. WMANs are vendor specific or comply with IEEE 802.16 standards. The basic 802.16 standard requires line of sight (i.e. no intermediate barriers). WiMax (World-wide Interoperability for Microwave Access), a more recent long-range technology, is based on improved 802.16 standards approved in 2005 for interoperability and data transfer. WiMax does not require line of sight and can penetrate through obstructions like buildings and trees. Under such non line of sight conditions, WiMax covers about 3 miles radius to provide a data speed upto 75 mbps; with line of sight, the range could go upto 31 miles and provide data speed upto 155 mbps. WiMax typically requires the installation of a base transmission tower for broadcasting the signal. WiMAX could operate on both on the licensed and unlicenced frequencies. Due to their longer range, WiMaX networks can produce a "wireless cloud" connectivity that covers an entire city using a few base stations. WiMax networks require one access point for about two square miles in urban areas, and one every six square miles for rural areas. In contrast, Wi-Fi networks require 24 to 40 access points per square mile (Opsahl, 2008). WiMax networks are also not as widely available as Wi-Fi, although a few cities have implemented WiMax networks. WiMax networks are frequently used for broadband access to mobile phones. WiMax also holds much potential for rural areas, where wired infrastructure may be deficient and there is longer line of sight.

The mesh networks are hybrid alternatives, which could be built on Wi-Fi networks. In this, each access point is a Wi-Fi device that acts as a node. The node is a self-standing relay (i.e. antenna) that can be powered by solar energy. The mesh consists of several nodes at short distances, enabling them to communicate with each other. There is no central tower required for transmission. When one node is down, another functioning node is used to transmit the data. As the prices of the nodes have fallen down over time, mesh networks have also become popular alternative for area wide coverage. Typically, the mesh networks use the unlicensed frequency. Mesh networking provides new opportunities for communities to provide wireless broadband (e.g., Wi-Fi cooperatives).

INSTITUTIONAL OPPORTUNITIES AND CHALLENGES

Institutions broadly refer to the "frameworks of norms, rules, and practices which structure action" (Healey, 2007, p. 64). They could be formal or informal (North, 1990). They shape as well as are shaped by the government organizations. Jane Fountain (2001) argued that institutions play a key factor in shaping the form of e-government. According to her, "the embeddedness of government actors in cognitive, cultural, social, and institutional structures influences the design, perceptions, and uses of the Internet" (p. 88). Although Fountain is cautious of the technological opportunities of the internet (and related technologies) for transforming government processes, as Yang (2003) argues, "the evolution of e-government is a process of institutionalization" (p. 437). The proliferation of the wireless is yet another technological development that holds both prospects as well as challenges for newer government practices. Undoubtedly, the institutionalization depends on the willingness and capacity of the government officials themselves to adapt to the wireless technology. Some of the key institutional opportunities and challenges of adopting wireless by local governments are considered below. In this context, m-government is not distinctive from e-government; rather, as Kuscu, Kuschu, and Yu (2007) argue, m-government is an extension of the e-government. Many of the m-government services build on e-government services. Although providing some advanced m-government services may depend on a local government's capacity for e-government services, m-government services could develop independently. For example, in African countries, internet penetration is low, but mobile phone subscription has grown significantly. SMS messages using mobile phones played a critical role to oversee fairness of the election process in several African countries (KatrinVerclas, 2008).

Institutional Opportunities

The main advantages of wireless over wired connections are flexibility and mobility. Wireless devices are portable and can be flexibly used in the field for real time data reading or data input. The devices' real time data capability provides institutional opportunities in three areas: transforming field operations; coordinating emergency management; and enhancing citizen services and participation. Moreover, the lower costs of the wireless infrastructure and devices offer opportunities for reducing the digital divide.

Transforming field operations. Examples of information provision in real-time by governments already abound. Such examples include information on: weather, government telephone directory, news, public health, traffic updates.

However, provision of such real time information is a "low-hanging fruit" for organizations. Wireless allows opportunities for efficiency gains in field operations. Field personnel with smartphones can access databases and documents without having to return to the office. The smartphones effectively extend the office to the field seamlessly. Combined with other technologies such as Geographic Information Systems (GIS), Geographic Positioning Systems (GPS), cameras, Radio Frequency Identification (RFID) devices, the wireless systems provide further capacity for field operations. For example, GPS and GIS enabled devices provide efficiency in terms of location, routing, and remote supervision. Wireless cameras provide remote monitoring capabilities. Scholl et. al. (2007) argue that wireless projects aim to automate fieldwork operations, improve field responsiveness, and to speed up the field processes, while using resources and assets more efficiently. In Hong Kong, for example, the Drainage Services department captures inspection results of drainage complaints and conditions in field sites using mobile phones (Government of Hong Kong Special Administrative Region, 2008).

Institutionally, just as internet technology provided opportunities for transformation of government organizations from a stove pipe model to a more horizontal organizational model and collaboration across agencies (Layne and Lee, 2001), the wireless technologies has the potential to blur the traditional boundaries between office and field operations. Organizations with extensive needs of field operations are likely to be transformed with the m-government. Rossel, Finger and Misuraca (2006) argue that the m-government emphasis should be on activities of those administrative agencies that have to be mobile to provide services efficiently. Such organizations include health and environmental agencies, hazard detection, social service agencies, traffic monitoring, cadastre related, on-site permitting, etc.

Coordinating emergency management. Real time communications are particularly needed for saving lives when disasters occur. Mobile communications (combined with the internet) provide new institutional opportunities for emergency management on this front. When a disaster occurs, first responders such as the police, fire, medical services, and search and rescue groups need to be coordinated. The first responders need to quickly gather, analyze, and disseminate information rapidly to deploy the emergency personnel. Residents in the disaster area could help alert the first responders and play a significant role in recovery. Emergency management research shows that informal networks of residents groups often undertake critical tasks during emergency response and rescue period, such as saving lives, providing food, and cleaning the debris (e.g., Dynes, Quarantelli, and Wenger, 1990; Rodriguez, Trainor and Quarantelli, 2006; Tierney and Trainor, 2004). Portability of mobile phones assists in maintaining communications among residents as well as with first responders to foster and strengthen the informal networks for enhancing rescue efforts. Moreover, mobile phones help maintain communications when other modes of communications may be inaccessible or damaged.

Moon (2004) argues that "m-government has improved emergency management by allowing faster, more dynamic, and more collaborative communication within and among agencies." According to him, law enforcement and emergency management reforms are two top areas of functional use of wireless technologies in the state governments in the United States. First responders and other agencies (e.g. Los Angeles Fire Department, Washington State Department of Transportation) have begun to send public safety and emergency notification through Twitter, which can be sent and received on Twitter.com, e-mails, smartphones, and social networking sites like Facebook (Williams, 2009). Community Response Grids (CRGs) provide another instance of the institutional potential of mobile phones for emergency management. According to Jaeger et. al. (2007), CRGs are web-based systems that integrate internet and mobile technologies to respond to emergency situations by enabling first responders to disseminate instructions and residents to report information and assist one another. CRGs use the wireless technology as a medium to enable coordination between first responders and residents.

Enhancing citizen services and participation. The proliferation of mobile phones among citizens offers institutional opportunities for the phones to be used as tools for enhancing citizen services and for citizen participation and empowerment in the m-government. Mobile phones have been used to enhance citizen services by local governments. For example, payments using mobile phones have been used for various purposes. Mobile phone payments for parking spots have been implemented in many cities. Singapore's Easi- Electronic Road Pricing (ERP), a mobile phone-based version of congestion price charging, allows charges to be paid through the monthly mobile bill. Other citizen services such as scheduling appointments in public agencies using mobile phones have also been enabled. For example, Hong Kong allows searching available timeslots for filing a marriage notice using 3G phones (Government of Hong Kong Special Administrative Region, 2008).

Although wireless provides technological opportunities for enhancing citizen services, the transformative institutional potential of the wireless lies in enabling citizen participation and empowerment. With the growth of portable wireless devices, citizens become sensors who can instantaneously relay information about the environment they are in. Wireless devices enable *sousveillance*, or surveillance of the surveillers (Mann, Nolan, and Wellman, 2003). Government authorities and processes could be monitored by ordinary people. For example, the police beating of Rodney King after he had been stopped for a traffic violation Los Angeles was videotaped; the videotape provided the case for trial against the police officers involved and to curtail police brutality. Mobile phones with cameras can similarly record incidents and off the cuff remarks by government authorities, which can then be posted quickly on Youtube and other video sharing sites.

Wireless devices such as pagers and mobile phones have enabled citizens to mobilize collective action and organize rallies and protests. Castells (2007, p. 251) argues that "the ability of network technology to distribute horizontally messages that resonate with the public consciousness in ways that are trustworthy" spurred social movements. Text and twitter messages get picked up by other citizens with similar interests and political views for organizing collective action. Rheingold (2001) identified the mass mobilization as *smart mobs*, who are *ad hoc*, self-organized citizen networks. Smart mobs use wireless devices, internet, and peer to peer networks to convey common social concerns and to coordinate collective action. Numerous social trends across the world indicate the coming together of citizens for political action: political mobilization using SMS messages to overthrow the Estrada government in Phillipines in 2001; spontaneous youth mobilization against Prime Minister Aznar in Spain prompting his defeat in the elections in 2004; youth demonstration mobilized by SMS messages in Ukraine to protest election fraud and demand a revote in 2004. Spontaneous networks have also been mobilized for development purposes, such as the "twestival" (Twitter's tweet festival) on February 12, 2009 organized in over 175 cities worldwide to network within local Twitter communities to raise funds for the nonprofit "charity: water" to install wells and and other water projects in developing countries. Text2Help is another mobile phone based initiative that was activated by American Red Cross and the Wireless Foundation in the United States to raise funding for the Red Cross after Hurricane Katrina; the initiative has since been activated a few times after major disasters. MobileActive.org is another nonprofit that capitalizes on the ubiquity of mobile phones as a means for increasing the effectiveness of grassroots for organizing, communications, and service and information delivery.

Narrowing digital divide. Digital divide refers to the differences in accessibility to information and computer technologies between different regions (developed vs developing countries; urban and rural areas) and socio-economic groups (e.g., race, income, gender, age, and skills). Based on their study of a panel of 161 countries, Chinn and Fairlie (2006) highlight the need for public investment in human capital, telecommunications infrastructure, and regulatory policies in order to reduce the global digital divide. Differences in internet access also exist between rural and urban areas within many countries, including the United States. In developing countries, the gap between rural and urban areas is exaggerated by the lack of wired infrastructure for landlines.

Wireless offers prospects for reducing the digital divide due to the better affordability of wireless devices and the wireless infrastructure. As discussed earlier, mobile phone devices have grown exponentially throughout the world, exceeding 50% penetration in 2007. Mobile phones have become vehicles for economic development. The Grameen Bank, which pioneered microfinancing in Bangladesh, also began providing cell phone services in the late 1990s for connecting poor people in villages with urban markets. Ntaliani, Costopoulou, and Karetsos (2008) highlight the use of SMS to provide cost-effective government to business services for agriculture in rural Greece. Different forms of mobile-banking have emerged in Africa. Mobile phone banking services, such as those provided by M-PESA in Kenya and WIZZIT in South Africa, have enabled mobile transactions where banking operations are not readily available and serve low-income groups (Basu, 2008; Ivatury and Pickens, 2006).

Wireless infrastructure provides cost advantages over the wired infrastructure (especially fiber) since an extensive network of cables does not have to be laid. Wi-Fi and WiMax networks offer cost advantages for rural areas (Zhang and Wolff, 2004). Proponents of "digital inclusion" have argued for providing wireless networks for broader internet accessibility (Camp, Knightly, and Reed, 2006). Yet, wireless internet access in rural areas of developing countries remains more complicated due to shortage or uncertain supply of electricity and unavailability of wired infrastructure for backhaul connections. Moreover, the issue of bridging the digital divide is not related to infrastructure costs only; it is also related to greater technological access and the technical abilities of the users (Mossberger, Tolbert, and Stansbury, 2003).

Institutional Challenges

Although the wireless offers several institutional opportunities for enabling the m-government, it poses challenges too. The primary challenges of adopting the wireless include: wireless security; interoperability; and infrastructure provision. These challenges are considered below. Concerns over the impact of radio frequencies on the health of users have also been raised; however, the evaluation of these impacts is beyond the scope of this chapter (for reviews, see Government Accounting Office, 2001; Sienkiewicz and Kowalczuk, 2004).

Wireless security. Wireless security is a major concern for m-government due to privacy and confidentiality considerations. Government agencies are typically large warehouses of private and sensitive information about the citizens. Information transmitted over government networks need to be secure. In this, although wired networks also pose security problems (e.g. hacking), wireless devices are more vulnerable than wired networks. Some of the security problems specific to wireless networks arise due to the intrinsic character of radio wave propagation—the radio signals could be intercepted. The U.S. Government Accounting Office (2005) reported that the signal leakage (i.e. broadcasting of signals beyond the periphery of government buildings) pose a potential security threat. With the convergence of telephony and web applications in the 3G mobile phones, the network security issues become critical for the mobile phones too. Leavitt (2005) highlights that internet problems like viruses, worms, and others are particularly significant for the smartphones. Other common forms of wireless network security problems include (Macumber and Cheung, 2007):

- Spoofing or masquerading, where an intruder impersonates an authorized user and exploits the user's privileges
- War-driving or eavesdropping, where an intruder monitors transmissions to gain access to confidential information
- Traffic analysis, where an intruder an intruder monitors patterns of communication
- Man in the middle, where the intruder intercepts transmissions
- Jamming, resulting in denial of service, where an intruder flood an access point by emitting excess radio signals at the same frequency spectrum to prevent authorized users from accessing it

Technological solutions toward containing the above security threats are mainly oriented towards maintaining the integrity of the network. Some of these solutions are similar to those implemented for wired networks. The technological solutions include:

- Encryption of communications to protect the confidentiality of information
- Authentication of users using smart cards or other means. Wired Equivalent Protocol (WEP) provides a static key to authenticate, but can be cracked into fairly easily. Systems using dynamic keys (Extensible Authentication Protocol (EAP), Robust Secure Network (RSN), Wireless Robust Authentication Protocol (WRAP)) provide better privacy of communications.
- Virtual Private Networks (VPN), which establish a secure tunnel with strong authentication and encryption mechanism (e.g. Public Key Infrastructure, PKI) over a shared public network to provide high degree of privacy
- Firewalls, which control the communications among networks or between a host and a network.

Technological solutions like EAP and VPN are well established to provide secure data transmission, comparable to those of wired networks (e.g., see Ashley, Hinton, and Vandenwauver, 2001). Yet, the technological solutions do not necessarily remove the security concerns of wireless networks. Organizational routines also need to be developed to routinely monitor intrusions and to minimize human errors in order to ensure security.

Interoperability. Although wireless technology has evolved rapidly, incompatibilities between the technologies underlying the devices and the infrastructure are barriers to exchanging information. As described earlier, the evolution of mobile phones over the generations has been accompanied by incompatible and diverse array of technologies and standards. Interoperability among different systems is particularly of high importance during emergency events. For example, different New York City organizations were unable to communicate in the immediate aftermath of the 9/11 incident due to incompatible radio systems (the Fire Department was still using analog radios that failed) (Kettl, 2004).

Further incompatibility within the wireless domain arises between the 3G mobile phone networks (that are based on IMT-2000 family of standards) and the wireless internet networks (such as Wi-Fi, which are based on IEEE standards). As Lehr and McKnight (2003) observe, "the two technologies reflect fundamentally different service, industry, and architectural design goals, origins, and philosophies." They argue that two technologies are both complementary as well as in competition with each other. Interoperability between two wireless systems requires devices to be able to work under both systems. For example, a computer with a Wi-Fi modem should be able to access cellular networks (e.g. CDMA); a mobile phone should be able to switch between the cellular network and the wireless available in Wi-Fi hotspots. Interoperability capitalizes the strengths of both cellular and Wi-Fi networks. Load balancing between the two different networks can increase the efficiency of the overall system (Joseph, Manoj, and Murthy, 2004).

Interoperability, however, is not only technological issue of compatibility between the wireless devices, but also an organizational issue with respect to the e-government. The failure to act in a timely and coordinated manner in New Orleans after Hurricane Katrina was partly due to communication failures among the different branches of federal, state, and local government agencies. In his examination of the Justice Information Network in Washington, Scholl (2005) argues that technological interoperability may be the less difficult to address than organizational, legal, political, and social aspects. Indeed, different organizations within the government have different priorities and processes. Interoperability, then, is an institutional challenge requiring high level of coordination among the entities to harmonize their models and processes with available wireless technologies (see Peristeras, Tarabanis, and Goudos (forthcoming), for a review and prescription of a model driven approach for standardization; the U.S. government's Federal Enterprise Architecture provides another model).

Provision of wireless networks. Institutional challenges exist in terms of who should provide the wireless infrastructure. While the demand for mobile phones has proliferated worldwide, and there have been opportunities for private sector to capitalize on the demand, the private sector provision of wireless networks for internet connectivity has not been as lustrous. Although Wi-Fi hotspots are available in libraries, coffee shops, hotels, and airports, citywide or area wide wireless coverage is much less developed. In the context of the private sector failure to provide wireless networks, many municipalities around the world have stepped in to provide free Wi-Fi networks to residents. Municipalities envisaged economic development benefits due to wireless broadband. Wireless broadband would enable retail and other trade benefiting local businesses, especially in economically depressed areas (Lehr, et. al., 2005). Municipal provision of the wireless broadband has also been justified for digital inclusion, bringing in such groups that were traditionally left out of internet usage due to digital divide. Lastly, the government itself is a consumer of the wireless broadband, and the infrastructure would help deliver the services to citizens more efficiently.

The municipal provision of wireless broadband networks is, however, quite controversial. Private telephone and cable service providers have been critical of the municipal provision. A few major municipalities in the United States such as Chicago, Houston, Miami-Dade dropped their plans. Private agencies such as Earthlink and Metro-Fi, which were initially enthusiastic in partnering for providing municipal wireless services, retreated from such projects (Urbina, 2008). Critics argue against the municipal provision of wireless broadband on several grounds (Balhoff and Rowe, 2005; Ellig, 2006; New Millennium Research Council, 2005). According to them, justification for government intervention due to market failure is not warranted; government intervention would not be as efficient as the private enterprise and induce anti-competitive practices by artificially lowering prices; municipal wireless networks will neither bridge the digital divide, nor will it hold economic development benefits.

Consequent to the critics and withdrawal of private agencies, municipalities have taken a renewed approach towards implementing wireless networks. Several models of wireless networks have emerged (Ganapati and Schoepp, 2008). These include: municipal ownership and development; community ownership and development; public-private partnerships; and private ownership and development. Municipalities have drawn away from the first alternative of full ownership and development. Recent models of wireless networks have begun to emerge in various forms of public-private partnerships, with the government as anchor tenants or users of the network infrastructure and charging residents for the use of network services (Lavallee, 2008). Prominent examples of municipal wireless networks include:

- "Wireless Minneapolis" in Minneapolis, United States, where the city pays a fixed annual fee too USI Wireless, a private agency, for its use of network for government purposes. Residents also pay a fee for their services. About 85 to 90% of the city is provided coverage (Lavallee, 2008).
- "HotCity" in Luxembourg, Belgium, where the city partnered with the P&T Luxembourg, which owns most of the fixed wireless network, in order to improve communications for the day-to-day operations of municipal workers. Residents are also offered paid as well as free access. About half of the city is provided coverage (Baritault, 2009).
- "WiFly" in Taipei, Taiwan, where the city partnered with Q-Ware, a local internet provider. Although the local government uses the network, the internet phone services are also provided to residents at nominal rates. In 2006, JiWire.com recognized Taipei as the city with largest public Wi-Fi network in the world, with 90% coverage. Yet, the network has attracted few users (Belson, 2006).

Local governments use wireless networks for public safety, emergency, transportation, public health, and field use by employees. Wi-Fi networks enable law enforcement officials to use their laptops or PDAs in their cars to search databases such as vehicle records, criminal offenses, and drivers' licenses, to file reports and write tickets from the field. Emergency vehicles such as fire and ambulance have also used wireless broadband. Wireless connections with remote sensors are used for Automated Meter Reading (i.e. ability to read utility meters on residential and commercial buildings remotely). Furthermore, expanding broadband access provides a means of increasing long distance education opportunities.

CONCLUSION

Wireless communications form the technological basis for m-government. This chapter outlined the major aspects of wireless technology, their opportunities, and challenges for m-government. Wireless encompasses both the wireless devices and the wireless infrastructure. Although wireless is not new, wireless devices (especially mobile phones) grew exponentially across the world during the 2000s. Smartphones with the 3G technology provide capabilities for both the traditional telephony services and web connectivity. Wireless infrastructure supporting internet services have also evolved during this century; alternatives include Wi-Fi, WiMax, and mesh networks.

The proliferation of the wireless devices and the wireless infrastructure hold much prospects for m-government at the local level. The chapter identified four such opportunities. First, wireless devices are likely to transform agencies with extensive field operations, with the ability to connect the office and field work seamlessly through field accessibility. Second, wireless provides opportunities for coordinating emergency management due to their portability and ability to maintain communication links between first responders and residents in times of disaster. Third, wireless devices could enhance citizen services and provide an additional tool for public participation and to mobilize collective action. Fourth, wireless holds prospects for reducing the digital divide.

Although the above prospects are promising, wireless also hold challenges for the m-government. First, wireless poses security threats as it is more prone to intrusion than wired connections. Second, interoperability of the wireless devices is a challenge, particularly as the mobile phones and the wireless networks conform to different families of standards. Organizational challenges of interoperability may also impede the functioning of m-government. Lastly, despite its advantages, the provision of wireless infrastructure is a challenge. While the private sector has been hesitant in providing the infrastructure, municipal wireless networks have also had a setback since major cities reneged on the plans to implement freely accessible city-wide internet networks. Newer models of the municipal wireless networks have begun to emerge, where the municipalities undertake various forms of public-private partnership with reduced expectations, adoption of wireless for government uses, and charging residents for wireless services.

REFERENCES

Ashley, P. Hinton, H., & Vandenwauver, M. (2001) Wired versus wireless security: the Internet, WAP and iMode for E-commerce. In *Proceedings of the 17th Annual Computer Security Applications Conference, 2001.* Washington, D.C.: IEEE.

Balhoff, M. J., & Rowe, R. C. (2005). Municipal broadband: Digging beneath the surface. Retrieved February 15, 2009, from http://www.balhoffrowe.com/pdf/Municipal%20Broadband--Digging%20Beneath%20the%20Surface.pdf.

Baritault, A. (2009). Luxembourg: Model of a successful muni Wi-Fi network. Retrieved February 15, 2009, from http://www.muniwireless.com/2009/02/15/luxembourg-model-muni-wifi-network.

Basu, I. (2008). Mobile phone payment system blossoms in Kenya. *Digital Communities*, Retrieved February 15, 2009, from http://www.govtech.com/dc/articles/240801.

Belson, K. (2006, June 26). What if they built an urban wireless network and hardly anyone used it? *New York Times*. Retrieved February 15, 2009, from http://www.nytimes.com/2006/06/26/technology/26taipei.html.

Camarillo, G., & García-Martín, M. A. (2004). *The 3G IP Multimedia Subsystem (IMS): Merging the Internet and the cellular worlds*. Chichester, UK: John Wiley and Sons, Ltd.

Camp, J. D., Knightly, E. W., & Reed, W. S. (2006). Developing and deploying multihop wireless networks for low-income communities. *Journal of Urban Technology, 13*, 129–137. doi:10.1080/10630730601146094

Chinn, M. D., & Fairliey, R. W. (2006). The determinants of the global digital divide: A cross-country analysis of computer and internet penetration. *Oxford Economic Papers, 59*, 16–44. doi:10.1093/oep/gpl024

Coffman, K. G., & Odlyzko, A. M. (2002). Internet growth: Is there a "Moore's Law" for data traffic? In J. M. Abello, P. M. Pardalos, & M. G. C. Resende (Eds.), *Handbook of Massive Data Sets*. Dordrecht and London: Kluwer Academic Publishers.

Dynes, R. R., Quarantelli, E. L., & Wenger, D. 1990. *Individual and organizational response to the 1985 earthquake in Mexico City, Mexico*. Newark: University of Delaware, Disaster Research Center.

Ellig, J. (2007). *A dynamic perspective on government broadband initiatives*. Policy Study 349. Los Angeles: Reason Foundation. Retrieved February 15, 2009, from http://www.reason.org/ps349polsum.pdf.

Fountain, J. (2001) *Building the virtual state: Information technology and institutional change*. Washington, D.C.: Brookings Institution Press.

Ganapati, S., & Schoepp, C. F. (2008). The wireless city. *International Journal of Electronic Government Research, 4*, 54–68.

Goldsmith, A. (2005). *Wireless communications*. UK: Cambridge University Press.

Government Accounting Office. (2001) *Telecommunications: Research and regulatory efforts on mobile phone health issues*. Retrieved February 15, 2009, http://www.gao.gov/new.items/d01545.pdf.

Government Accounting Office. (2005). *Information security: Federal agencies need to improve controls over wireless networks*. Retrieved February 15, 2009, http://www.gao.gov/new.items/d05383.pdf.

Government of Hong Kong Special Administrative Region. (2008). *M-government*. Retrieved February 15, 2009, from http://www.info.gov.hk/digital21/e-gov/eng/init/mgov.htm

Healey, P. (2007). The new institutionalism and the transformative goals of planning. In N. Verma (ed.), *Institutions and planning*. Amsterdam: The Elsevier.

Ilyas, M., & Ahson, S. A. (2006). *Smartphones: Research report*. Chicago: International Engineering Consortium.

International Telecommunications Union. (2008) *International Telecommunications Union/ ICT Indicators Database*. Retrieved February 15, 2009, from http://www.itu.int/ITU-D/ICTEYE/Indicators/Indicators.aspx#.

Ivatury, G., & Pickens, M. (2006). *Mobile phone banking and low-income customers: Evidence from South Africa*. Washington, DC: CGAP, United Nations Foundation, and Vodafone Group Foundation. Retrieved February 15, 2009, from http://go.worldbank.org/43SKY07120.

Jaeger, P. T., Shneiderman, B., Fleischmann, K. R., Preece, J., Qu, Y., & Wu, P. F. (2007). Community response grids: E-government, social networks, and effective emergency management. *Telecommunications Policy, 31*, 592–604. doi:10.1016/j.telpol.2007.07.008

JiWire.com. (2009) *Wi-Fi Finder*. Retrieved February 15, 2009, from http://www.jiwire.com/search-hotspot-locations.htm.

Joseph, D. A. Manoj, B. S., and Murthy, C. S. R. (2004) Interoperability of WiFi hotspots and cellular networks. WMASH '04: In *Proceedings of the 2nd ACM international workshop on Wireless mobile applications and services on WLAN hotspots*. New York: ACM.

KatrinVerclas. (2008). *SMS Critical in Election Monitoring in Ghana*. Retrieved February 15, 2009, from http://mobileactive.org/sms-critical-election-observation-ghana.

Kettl, D. F. (2004). *System under stress: Homeland security and American politics*. Washington: CQ.

Kuscu, M. H., Kuschu, I., & Yu, B. (2007) Introducing mobile government. In I. Kushcu (Ed.), *Mobile government: An emerging direction in e-government*. Hershey, PA: IGI Publishing.

Lavallee, A. (2008, December 8). A second look at citywide Wi-Fi. *Wall Street Journal*. Retrieved February 15, 2009, from http://online.wsj.com/article/SB122840941903779747.html.

Layne, K., & Lee, J. (2001). Developing fully functional e-government: A four stage model. *Government Information Quarterly, 18*, 122–136. doi:10.1016/S0740-624X(01)00066-1

Leavitt, N. (2005, April). Mobile phones: The next frontier for Hackers? *Computer*, 38(4), 20–23.

Lehr, W., & McKnight, L. W. (2003). Wireless Internet access: 3G vs. WiFi? *Telecommunications Policy, 27*, 351–370. doi:10.1016/S0308-5961(03)00004-1

Macumber, H., & Cheung, B. (2007). A secure wireless data access service for the government of Canada. In I. Kushcu (Ed.), *Mobile government: An emerging direction in e-government*. Hershey, PA: IGI Publishing.

Mann, S., Nolan, J., & Wellman, B. (2003). Sousveillance: Inventing and using wearable computing devices for data collection in surveillance environments. *Surveillance & Society, 1*, 331–355.

McNurlin, B. C., & Sprague, R. H. (2006) *Information systems management in practice* (6th ed.). Upper Saddle River, NJ: Prentice Hall.

Moon, M. J. (2004) *From e-government to m-government? Emerging practices in the use of mobile technology by state governments*. Washington, DC: IBM Center for the Business of Government.

Mossberger, K., Tolbert, C. J., & Stansbury, M. (2003). *Virtual inequality: Beyond the digital divide*. Washington, DC: Georgetown University Press.

New Millennium Research Council. (2005). *Not in the public interest – The myth of municipal Wi-Fi networks*. Washington, D.C. Retrieved February 15, 2009, from http://www.newmillenniumresearch.org/archive/wifireport2305.pdf.

North, D. (1990). *Institutions, institutional change and economic performance*. New York: University of Cambridge.

Ntaliani, M., & Costopoulou, C., C., Karetsos, S. (2008). Mobile government: A challenge for agriculture. *Government Information Quarterly, 25*(4),699–716. doi:10.1016/j.giq.2007.04.010

Opsahl, A. (2008). Cities use WiMAX to create municipal wireless networks. *Government Technology*. Retrieved February 15, 2009, from http://www.govtech.com/gt/241661?id=&story_pg=1

Peristeras, V., Tarabanis, K., & Goudos, S. K. (forthcoming). Model-driven eGovernment interoperability: A review of the state of the art. *Computer Standards & Interfaces*, 31(4), 613.

Rheingold, H. (2002). *Smart mobs: The next social revolution*. Cambridge, MA: Perseus Publishing.

Rodriguez, H., Trainor, J., & Quarantelli, E. L. (2006). Rising to the challenges of a catastrophe: the emergent and prosocial behavior following Hurricane Katrina. *The Annals of the American Academy of Political and Social Science, 604*(1), 82–101. doi:10.1177/0002716205284677

Rossel, P., Finger, M., & Misuraca, G. (2006). "Mobile" e-Government Options: Between Technology-driven and Usercentric. *The Electronic . Journal of E-Government, 4*, 79–86.

Sauter, R., & Watson, J. (2008) Technology leapfrogging: A review of the evidence. A report for DFID. Brighton, UK: Sussex Energy Group. Retrieved February 15, 2009, from http://www.dfid.gov.uk/pubs/files/DFIDLeapfroggingReportWeb.pdf.

Scholl, H. (2005) Interoperability in e-government: More than just smart middleware. In *Proceedings of the 38th Annual Hawaii International Conference on System Sciences (HICSS'05) - Track 5 - Volume 05*. Washington, DC: IEEE Computer Society. Retrieved February 15, 2009, from http://portal.acm.org

Scholl, H. J., Fidel, R., Liua, S., Paulsmeyer, M., & Unsworth, K. (2007). E-government field force automation: Promises, challenges, and stakeholders. In M. A.Wimmer, J. Scholl, & A. Grönlund (Eds.), *Electronic Government. 6th International Conference, EGOV 2007 Regensburg, Germany, September 3-7, 2007 Proceedings*. Berlin: Springer-Verlag.

Sienkiewicz, Z. J., & Kowalczuk, C. I. (2005). *A summary of recent reports on mobile phones and health (2000-2004)*. NRPB-W65. National Radiological Protection Board, U.K.

Tierney, K. J., & Trainor, J. (2004). *Networks and resilience in the World Trade Center disaster*. Buffalo, New York: Multidisciplinary Center for Earthquake Engineering Research.

Urbina, I. (2008, March 22). Hopes for wireless cities fade as Internet providers pull out. *The New York Times*, pp. A1, A10.

Williams, M. (2009). Governments use Twitter for emergency alerts, traffic notices and more. *Government Technology*. Retrieved February 15, 2009, from http://www.govtech.com/gt/579338?topic=117680.

Yang, K. (2003). Neoinstitutionalism and e-government: Beyond Jane Fountain. *Social Science Computer Review*, *21*(4),432–442. doi:10.1177/0894439303256508

Zhang, M., & Wolff, R. S. (2004, February). Crossing the digital divide: Cost-effective broadband wireless access for rural and remote areas. *IEEE Communications Magazine*, 99–105. doi:10.1109/MCOM.2003.1267107

Compilation of References

6P. (2001). E-governance. Do Digital Aids Make a Difference in Policy Making? In J. E. J. Prins (Ed.), *Designing E-Government. On the Crossroads of Technological Innovation and Institutional Change* (pp. 7-27). The Hague, Netherlands: Kluwer Law International.

Abaitua, J., Barrutieta, G., Díaz, J., Jacob, I., & Quintana, F. (2003). Contenidos y metacontenidos en la edición digital. *Letras de Deusto, July-September*. Retrieved March 15, 2007, from http://paginaspersonales.deusto.es/abaitua/konzeptu/htxt/letrasUD_03.pdf

Abramson, J, B, Arterton, F, C, & Orren, G, R (1988). *The Electronic Commonwealth: The Impact of New Media Technologies on Democratic Politics*. New York: Basic Books.

Accenture (2004). *E-Government leadership: High performance, maximum value*. Accenture Consulting. Retrieved December 15, 2005, from http://www.accenture.com/xdoc/en/industries/government/gove_egov_value.pdf

Accenture (2005). *E-Government leadership in customer service: New expectations, new experiences*. Retrieved December 15, 2005, from www.accenture.com

Accenture (2005). *Leadership in customer service: New expectations, new experiences*, www.accenture.com

Accenture, Markle, & UNDP (2001). *Creating a development dynamic: Final report of the digital opportunity initiative*. New York: UNDP. Retrieved January 21, 2006, from http://www.opt-init.org/framework/onepage/onepage.html

Adkins, R. (n.d.). *Air Force knowledge now*. Retrieved February 22, 2007, from http://www.e-gov.com/events/2005/km/downloads/KM05_2-3_Adkins.pdf

Adler Lomnitz, Larissa (1994). "Identidad nacional/cultura política: los casos de Chile y México". In Adler Lomnitz, Larissa (ED), *Redes sociales, cultura y poder: Ensayos de antropología latinoamericana*. FLACSO, México.

Affisco, J., & Soliman, K. (2006). E-government: A strategic operations management framework for service delivery. *Business Process Management Journal, 12*(1), 13-21.

Akbulut, A. (2203). *An investigation of the factors that influence electronic information sharing between state and local agencies*. PhD Dissertation Thesis. Louisiana State University.

Al Mashet, O. (2005). *The Factors of success: Implementation of e-government in Saudi Universities*. Jeddah: King Abdulaziz University. Retrieved August 20, 2007, from http://www.kau.edu.sa/dvworkshop-Mon2.1.10.ppt

Al-Kibsi, G., de Boer, K., Mourshed, M., & Rea, N. (2001). Putting citizens online not in line. *The McKinsley Quarterly, 2*, 65-73.

Allen, B. A., Juillet, J., Paquet, G. & Roy, J. (2001) E-Governance & government on-line in Canada: Partnerships, people & prospects, Government Information Quarterly 18 93–104.

Allen, B., Juillet, L., Paquet, G., & Roy, J. (2005). E-government as collaborative governance: Structural, accountability and cultural reform. In M. Khosrow-Pour (Ed.), *Practicing e-government: A global perspective* (pp. 1-15). New York: Idea Group Publishing.

Alonso, Jorge and Rodríguez Lapuente, Manuel (1990). "La cultura política y el poder en México". In Hugo

Zemelman (ED), *Cultura y política en América Latina*. Siglo Veintiuno Editores, España.

Andersen, D., & Dawes, S. (1991). *Government information management. A primer and casebook*. Englewood Cliffs, NJ: Prentice Hall.

Anderson, K. V., & Henriksen, H. Z. (2006). E-government maturity models: Extension of the Layne and Lee model. *Government Information Quarterly, 23*(2), 236-248.

Archmann, S., & Kudlacek, I. (2008). Interoperability and the exchange of good practice cases. European Journal of ePractice, 2(1), 3-12.

Ashley, P. Hinton, H., & Vandenwauver, M. (2001) Wired versus wireless security: the Internet, WAP and iMode for E-commerce. In *Proceedings of the 17th Annual Computer Security Applications Conference, 2001*. Washington, D.C.: IEEE.

Austin, J. L. (1962). *How to do things with words*. Cambridge, MA: Harvard University Press.

Avgerou, C. (1993). Information systems for development planning. *International Journal of Information Management, 13*, 260-273.

Backus, M. (2001) E-governance in Developing Countries, IICD Research Brief-No1, March, Available at www.ftpiicd.org/files/research/briefs/brief1.pdf.

Baehni, S., Eugster, P. Th., & Guerraoui, E. (2004, June). Data-aware multicast. In *Proceedings of the 5th IEEE International Conference on Dependable Systems and Networks (DSN '04)*.

Balhoff, M. J., & Rowe, R. C. (2005). Municipal broadband: Digging beneath the surface. Retrieved February 15, 2009, from http://www.balhoffrowe.com/pdf/Municipal%20Broadband--Digging%20Beneath%20the%20Surface.pdf.

Balkin, Jack (1998). "How Mass Media Simulate Political Transparency". Retrieved from: http://www.yale.edu/lawweb/jbalkin/articles/media01.htm

Balutis, A. P. (2001). *E-government 2001. Part I: Understanding the challenge and evolving strategies. The Public Manager*, 33-7.

Bandyopadhyay, D. (2007). *Land, labour and governance*. Calcutta: Worldview.

Banovetz, J. M. (1994). City managers: Will they reject policy leadership? *Public Productivity & Management Review, 17*(4), 313–324. doi:10.2307/3380830

Bansal, P. (2005). Evolving sustainably: a longitudinal study of corporate sustainable development. *Strategic Management Journal, 26*(3), 197–218. doi:10.1002/smj.441

Barber, Wendy and Brade, Albert (1998). Culturability: The Merging of Culture and Usability. Paper presented at the 1998 4th Conference on Human Factors and the Web (HFWeb '98). Retrieved from: http://www.research.att.com/conf/hfweb/proceedings/barber

Bardach, E. (1998). *Getting agencies work together: The practice and theory of managerial craftsmanship*. Washington, D.C: Brookings Institution Press.

Baritault, A. (2009). Luxembourg: Model of a successful muni Wi-Fi network. Retrieved February 15, 2009, from http://www.muniwireless.com/2009/02/15/luxembourg-model-muni-wifi-network.

Barley, S. R., & Tolbert, P. S. (1997). Institutionalization and structuration: studying the links between action and institution. *Organization Studies, 18*(1), 93–117. doi:10.1177/017084069701800106

Barón Porras, Luis (n.d.). "Los poderes en las culturas: comunicación, lenguaje y memoria". Centro de Investigación y Educación Popular, CINEP. Retrieved from: http://www.colnodo.apc.org/aa/img_upload/13e08f09d1591809155e45a9932c599f/PODERES.pdf

Baron, R. M., & Kenny, D. A. (1986). The moderator-mediator variable distinction in social psychological research: Conceptual, strategic and statistical considerations. *Journal of Personality and Social Psychology, 51*, 1173–1182. doi:10.1037/0022-3514.51.6.1173

Barrett, K., & Greene, R. (2001). *Powering up: How public managers can take control of information technology*. Washington, D.C: CQ Press.

Bartoli, Annie (1991). "Comunicación y organización: la organización comunicante y la comunicación organizada". Paidós, México.

Barzelay, M. (Ed.). (2001). *The new public management: Improving research and policy dialogue*. Berkeley: University of California Press.

Basu, I. (2008). Mobile phone payment system blossoms in Kenya. *Digital Communities*, Retrieved February 15, 2009, from http://www.govtech.com/dc/articles/240801.

Basu, S. (2004) E-Government and Developing Countries, International Review of Law Computers and Technology, Vol. 18, No. 1, pp. 109-132.

Basu, Subhajit (2004). E-Government and developing countries: An overview. *International Review of Law Computers, 18*(1), 109-132.

Baum, C., & Di Maio, A. (2001). *Gartner's four phases of e-government model*, available at: http://gartner3.gartnerweb.com/public/static/hotc/00094235.html [Accessed on 25th May 2007]

Bayardo, Rubens and Lacarrieu, Mónica (1997). *Globalización e identidad cultural* Ciccus Giunta, Buenos Aires.

Becerra, Aníbal (n.d.). "Umberto Eco y el análisis semiótico- estructural de los fenómenos socioculturales". *Nombre Falso*, Autumn 2004. Retrieved from: http://www.infoamerica.org/articulos/b/becerra_artieda.htm

Bechhofer, S., Moller, R., & Crowther, P. (2003). The DIG description logic interface. In *Proceedings of 2003 International Workshop on Description Logic (DL2003), Rome, Italy* (pp. 85-94).

Bedi, K., Singh, P.J. and Srivastava, S. (2001), Government@net: New Governance opportunities for India, Sage Publications, New Delhi.

Behn, R. D. (2006). The challenge of evaluating M-Government, E-Government, and P-Government. In Mayer-Schönbeger & Lazer (Eds.), *From Electronic Government to Information Government*, 213-238. Cambridge, Massachusetts: MIT Press

Bekkers, V. (2005). The governance of back office integration in e-government: some Dutch experiences. In M. Wimmer et al (Eds.), *EGOV 2005* (LNCS 3591, pp. 12-25).

Bellamy, C. & Taylor, J.A. (1998). *Governing in the Information Age*. London: Open University Press.

Belson, K. (2006, June 26). What if they built an urban wireless network and hardly anyone used it? *New York Times*. Retrieved February 15, 2009, from http://www.nytimes.com/2006/06/26/technology/26taipei.html.

Benamou, N., Busson, A., & Keravel, A. (2004). Impact of e-government interoperability in local governments. In R. Traunmüller (Ed.), *EGOV 2004* (LNCS 3183, pp. 82-87).

Benbasat, I., Goldstein, D. K., & Mead, M. (1987). The case research strategy in studies of information systems. *MIS Quarterly, 11*(3), 369-386.

Bennett, M., Bouma, J. J., & Ciccozzi, E. (2004). An institutional perspective on the transfer of accounting knowledge: a case study. *Accounting Education, 13*(3), 329–346. doi:10.1080/0963928042000273807

Bennis, W. (1984). Where have all the leaders gone? In W. Rosenbach & R. Taylor (Eds.), *Contemporary Issues in Leadership* (2nd ed., pp. 2-23). Boulder, Colorado: Westview Press.

Bevarly, D., & Ulma, J. (2007-08). Citizen involvement in the digital age. *Public Management, 6*(4), 3–7.

Beynon-Davies, P., & Martin, S. (2004). Electronic local government and the modernisation agenda: Progress and prospects for public service improvement. *Local government studies, 30*(2), 214-229.

Bhatnagar, A. (2006). *Paving the road towards pro-poor e-governance: Findings and observations from Asia-Pacific case studies*. Bangkok: UNDP, Asia Pacific Development Information Programme (APDIP). Available at http://www.apdip.net/projects/e-government/capblg/casestudies/Overview.pdf

Bhatnagar, S. (2003).Administrative Corruption: How Does e-government Help? In *Proceedings of Global Corruption Report 2003, Transparency International*. Retrieved November, 15, 2008 from http://www.gipi.az/ssi_eng/egov/20030324.pdf

Bhatnagar, S.C. (2002) E-Government Case Studies in India, Online, Rev. 15th September, http://www1.worldbank.org/publicsector/egov/

Bhatnagar, S.C. and Bjorn-Andersen, N. (1990), Information Technology in Developing Countries, Elsevier Science, Amsterdam.

Bijkr, W., Hughes, T. & Pinch, T. (eds.). (1987) *Social Construction of Technological Systems: New Directions in the Sociology and History of Technology*. Cambridge, MA: MIT Press.

Birdsall, William (1996). "The Internet and the Ideology of Information Technology". Paper presented at INET96 Proceedings 96. Retrieved from: http://www.isoc.org/inet96/proceedings/e3/e3_2.htm

Blanke, J., & Lopez-Clarosa, A. (2004). *The Lisbon review 2004: An assessment of policies and reforms in Europe*. Geneva, Switzerland: World Economic Forum. Retrieved April 24, 2008, from http://www.weforum.org/pdf/Gcr/LisbonReview/Lisbon_Review_2004.pdf

Blattman, C., Jensen, R., & Roman, R. (2003). Assessing the need and potential of community networking for development in rural India. *The Information Society, 19*, 349-364.

Bonham, G., Seifert, J., & Thorson, S (2001). *The transformational potential of E-Government: The role of political leadership. The 4th Pan European International Relations Conference of the European Consortium for Political Research*, the University of Kent, Canterbury, U.K.

Boston, J., Martin, J., Pallot, J., & Walsh, P. (1996). *Public management: The New Zealand model*. Auckland: Oxford University Press.

Bourges-Waldegg, Paula and Scrivener, Stephen (1998). "Meaning: The central issue in cross-cultural HCI design". *Interacting with Computers Special Issue, 9* (3). Retrieved from: http://www.citeulike.org/user/archer/article/455060

Boyan, J. A., & Littman, M. L. (1994). Packet routing in dynamically changing networks: A reinforcement learning approach. *Advances in Neural Information Processing Systems, 6.*

Boyatzis, R. (1998). *Transforming oualitative information*. USA: Sage Publications.

Brasil (2008). *e-PING: Padrões de interoperabilidade de governo eletrônico versão 4.0*. Brasília: Comitê Executivo de Governo Eletrônico.

Bray, T. (1998). *RDF and metadata*. Retrieved January 20, 2007, from http://www.xml.com/pub/a/98/06/rdf.html

Breinstein, E., & Wendt, A. (2003, July 15-18). Didactic modeling of learning objects: evolving *standards* and methods of evaluation in metadata-based course development. In *Proceedings of the Eden 2003 Annual Conference "The quality dialogue integrating quality cultures in flexible, distance and e-learning,"* Rhodes, Greece. Retrieved March 15, 2007, from http://www.eden-online.org/eden.php?menuId=133&contentId=153

Brinton, M. C., & Nee, V. (1998). *The New Institutionalism in Sociology*. Stanford, CA: Stanford University Press.

British Columbia Human Resources Office. (n. d.). *Establish qualifications and competencies*. Retrieved March 15, 2007, from http://www.hrtoolkit.gov.bc.ca/staffing/staffing_steps/job_requirements/overview.htm

Brunner, José J. (1988). *Un espejo trizado: Ensayos sobre cultura y políticas culturales*. Facultad Latinoamericana de Ciencias Sociales (FLACSO); Santiago de Chile. Retrieved from: http://mt.educarchile.cl/MT/jjbrunner/archives/libros/Un_Espejo_Trizado

Bryson, J., & Crosby, B. (1992). *Leadership for the common good: Tackling public problems in a shared-power world*. San Francisco: Jossey Bass.

Buchrucker, Cristian (1994). "Notas sobre la problemática histórico-ideológica de la identidad nacional argentina". In Rapoport, Mario (ed.), *Globalización, integración e identidad nacional*. GEL, Buenos Aires. Pp.311-312.

Bugler, D. T., & Bretschneider, S. (1993). Technology push or program pull: Interest in new information technologies within public organizations. In B. Bozeman (Ed.), *Public management: The state of the art* (pp. 275-293). San Francisco: Jossey-Bass.

Burn, F., & Robins, G. (2003). Moving towards E-Government: A case study of organisational change processes. *Logistics Information Management, 16*(1), 25-35.

Burn, J. and Robins, G. (2003), "Moving towards e-government: a case study of organizational change processes", Logistics Information Management, Vol. 16 No. 1, pp. 25-35.

Buyya, R., Stockinger, H., Giddy, J., & Abramson, D. (2001, August 20-24). Economic models for management of resources in peer-to-peer and grid computing. In *Proceedings of International Conference on Commercial Applications for High-Performance Computing,* Denver, CO. SPIE Press.

Cabinet Office (2002). *In the Service of Democracy: A Consultation Paper on a Policy for Electronic Democracy.* London: Cabinet Office.

Cabinet Office (2004). *E-Democracy Briefing.* London: Cabinet Office.

Cabinet Office (2006) available at: http://www.cio.gov.uk/documents/annual_report2006/trans_gov2006.doc [Accessed on 29th May 2007]

Caenen, G., & Pauwels, E. J. (2002). *Logistic regression models for relevance feedback in content-based image retrieval.* San Jose, CA: Storage and Retrieval for Media Databases.

Callon, M. (1999). Actor-network theory – the market test. In J. Law & J. Hassard (eds.), *Actor Network Theory and After.* Oxford: Blackwell Publishers.

Camarillo, G., & García-Martín, M. A. (2004). *The 3G IP Multimedia Subsystem (IMS): Merging the Internet and the cellular worlds.* Chichester, UK: John Wiley and Sons, Ltd.

Camp, J. D., Knightly, E. W., & Reed, W. S. (2006). Developing and deploying multihop wireless networks for low-income communities. *Journal of Urban Technology, 13,* 129–137. doi:10.1080/10630730601146094

Campbell, A. E. (1999). *Ontological mediation: Finding translation across dialects by asking questions.* Unpublished doctoral dissertation, University at Buffalo, The State University of New York, Department of Computer Science and Engineering.

Campbell, A. E., & Shapiro, S. C. (1998). *Algorithms for ontological mediation* (Tech. Rep. No. 98-2). University at Buffalo, The State University of New York, Department of Computer Science and Engineering, SNePS Research Group.

Cañas, A. J., Hill, G., Roser, C., Suri, F., Lot, J., Gómez, G., et al. (2004). Cmaptools: a knowledge modeling and sharing environment. Concept maps: Theory, methodology, technology. In *Proceedings of the 1st International Conference on Concept Mapping.* Pamplona, Spain: Universidad Pública de Navarra. Retrieved March 15, 2007, from http://cmc.ihmc.us/papers/cmc2004-283.pdf

Carbo, T., & Williams, J. G. (2004). Models and metrics for evaluating local electronic government systems and services. *Electronic. Journal of E-Government, 2*(2), 95–104.

Carson, C., Belongie, S., Greenspan, H., & Malik, J. (2002). Blobworld: Image segmentation using expectation-maximization and its application to image querying. *IEEE Transactions on Pattern Analysis and Machine Intelligence, 24*(8), 1026-1038.

Carvalho, M. (2006). *Distributed resource coordination strategies for mobile ad hoc networks.* Unpublished PhD dissertation, Tulane University, New Orleans, LA.

Carvalho, M., & Breedy, M. (2002, October). Supporting flexible data feeds in dynamic sensor grids through mobile agents. In *Proceedings of the 6th International Conference in Mobile Agents (MA 2002),* Barcelona, Spain.

Carvalho, M., Pechoucek, M., & Suri, N. (2005, July). A mobile agent-based middleware for opportunistic resource allocation and communications. In *Proceedings of the Fourth International Joint Conference on Autonomous Agents and Multiagent Systems; Defense Applications of Multi-Agent Systems (DAMAS).*

Castells, M., & Hall, P. (Eds.). (1994). *Technopolies of the world.* London: Routledge.

Castells, Manuel (2004). "La dimensión cultural de Internet". *Cultura, Sociedad y Tecnología,* November-December 2004. Retrieved from: http://www.aloj.us.es/gicomcult/revista/detalle.asp?Id=19&edicion=Comunicaci%F3n%2C+Tecnolog%EDas+y+Pr%E1cticas+culturales+en+la+Cibercultura%2E+Noviembre%2DDiciembre+2004

Cava, I., & Guijarro, L. (2003). Interoperability issues of shared infrastructures for e-government. In R. Traunmüller (Ed.), *EGOV 2003* (LNCS 2739, pp. 369-372).

Cecchini S. and Raina M.(2003) Electronic Government and the Rural Poor: The Case of Gyandoot, Information Technology in Developing Countries, A Newsletter of IFIP Working Group 9.4 and Centre for Electronic Governance, Indian Institute of Management, Ahmedabad, 13(2), November.

Cecchini, S., & Scott, C. (2003). Can information and communications technology applications contribute to poverty reduction? Lessons from rural India. *Information Technology for Development, 10*, 73-84.

Center for Technology in Government. (2004). New models of collaboration: An overview. Retrieved August 15, 2006, from http://www.ctg.albany.edu/publications/reports/new_models_exec/new_models_exec.pdf

CEPAL (2000). *América Latina y el Caribe en la transición hacia una Sociedad del Conocimiento. Una agenda de políticas públicas*. Economic Commission for Latin America and the Caribbean (ECLAL), United Nations. Retrieved from: http://www.eclac.cl/publicaciones/SecretariaEjecutiva/3/lcl1383/lcl1383e.pdf

Cerami, E. (2002). *Web services essentials*. CA: O Reilly & Associates.

Chadwick, A. (2006). *Internet Politics: States, Citizens, and New Communication Technologies*. New York: Oxford University Press.

Chakrabarty, B., & Bhattacharya, M. (2003). *Public administration: A reader*. New Delhi: Oxford University Press.

Champy, J. (2002). *X-Engineering the corporation: Reinventing your business in the digital age*. Warner Books

Chandra, B., Mukherjee, M., & Mukherjee, A. (2000). *India after independence: 1947-2000*. New Delhi: Penguin Books.

Chang Coupland, Jennifer; Tekchandaney, Jayesh R.; Rangaswamy, Arvind; and Simpson, Timothy W. (2003). "Websites as Personalities and Playgrounds: Their Effects on Brand Image" eBusiness Research Center Working Paper, Penn State University. Retrieved from: http://www.smeal.psu.edu/ebrc/publications/res_papers/2003_02.pdf

Chang, Y., Ho, T., & Kaelbling, L. (2004). Mobilized ad-hoc networks: A reinforcement learning approach. In *Proceedings of the First International Conference on Autonomic Computing (ICAC'04)* (pp. 240-247).

Charaudeau, Patrick (2003). *El discurso de la información: La construcción del espejo social*. Editorial Gedisa, Barcelona.

Charih, M., & Robert, J. (2004). Government on-line in the federal government of Canada: The organizational issues. *International Review of Administrative Sciences, 70*(2), 373-384.

Chen, P. (2002). *Australian Elected Representatives use of New Media Technologies*. Research Report, Centre for Public Policy University of Melbourne.

Chen, Y. N., Chen, H. M., Huang, W., & Ching, R. K. H. (2006). E-government strategies in developed and developing countries: An implementation framework and case study. *Journal of Global Information Management, 14*(1).

Chen, Y., & Schwan, K. (2005, November). Opportunistic overlays: Efficient content delivery in mobile ad hoc networks. In *Proceedings of the 6th ACM/IFIP/USENIX International Middleware Conference (Middleware 2005)*.

Chen, Y.-C., & Perry, J. L. (2003). *IT outsourcing: A primer for public managers*. Washington, D.C: IBM Endowment for the Business of Government.

Chinn, M. D., & Fairliey, R. W. (2006). The determinants of the global digital divide: A cross-country analysis of computer and internet penetration. *Oxford Economic Papers, 59*, 16–44. doi:10.1093/oep/gpl024

Cho, Y. H., & Choi, B.-D. (2005). E-government to combat corruption: The case of Seoul metropolitan government. *International Journal of Public Administration, 27*(10), 719–735. doi:10.1081/PAD-200029114

Choi, S. P. M., & Yeung, D. Y. (1996). Predictive q-routing: A memory-based reinforcement learning approach to adaptive traffic control. In *Proceedings of NIPS-8* (pp. 910-945).

Choong, Yee-Yin and Salvendy, Gavriel (1999). "Implications for design of computer interfaces for Chinese users in mainland China". *International Journal of Human–Computer Interaction*, N° 11. Retrieved from: http://www.leaonline.com/doi/abs/10.1207/s15327590ijhc1101_2

CLAD-SIARE. (2005). *El gobierno electrónico como medio para acercar el Estado a la ciudadanía*. Retrieved March 15, 2007, from http://www.clad.org.ve/siare/innotend/gobelec/gobelec.html

Clift, S (2003). *E-Government and Democracy: Representation and citizen engagement in the information age*. United Nations- DESA.

Cobos, R., Esquivel, J. A., & Alaman, X. (2002). IT tools for knowledge management: a study of the current situation.*CEPIS, Up Grade, III*(1), February. Retrieved March 15, 2007, from. http://www.upgrade-cepis.org

Coffman, K. G., & Odlyzko, A. M. (2002). Internet growth: Is there a "Moore's Law" for data traffic? In J. M. Abello, P. M. Pardalos, & M. G. C. Resende (Eds.), *Handbook of Massive Data Sets*. Dordrecht and London: Kluwer Academic Publishers.

Coleman, S. & Norris, D.F. (2005). *A New Agenda for E-democracy*. Oxford Internet Institute, Forum Discussion Paper No. 4, January.

Coleman, S. (2005). New mediation and direct representation: Representation in the digital age. *New Media & Society, 7*.

Colomé, Gabriel (1994). "Política y medios de comunicación: una aproximación teórica". Working Paper N °91, Universitat Autónoma de Barcelona. Retrieved from: http://www.diba.es/innovacio/fitxers/colome.pdf

Comisión *e-government* UE. (2003). El papel de la administración electrónica en el futuro de Europa. *Comunicación de la Comisión, de 26 septiembre 2003, al Consejo, al Parlamento Europeo, al Comité Económico y Social Europeo y al Comité de las Regiones*. Retrieved March 15, 2007, from http://europa.eu.int/scadplus/leg/es/lvb/l24226b.htm

Community Information Center, CIC. (2003). *E-setu: e-governance project in Jorhat*. East Jorhat, Assam, India: Nakachari. Retrieved August 15, 2007, from http://www.cic.nic.in/cicwebpages/Assam/jorhateast/About%20e-setu.htm

Connolly, D., Harmelen, F. V., Horrocks, I., McGuinness, D. L., Patel-Schneider, P. F. & Stein L. A. (2001). *DAML+OIL (March 2001) reference description*. Retrieved January 20, 2007, from http://www.w3.org/TR/daml+oil-reference

Cooper, I., Hamilton, A., & Bentivegna, V. (2005). Sustainable urban development: Networked communities, virtual organizations and the production of knowledge. In S. Curwell, M. Deakin and M. Symes (Eds.), *Sustainable urban development: The framework, protocols and environmental assessment methods* (pp. 211-231). Oxon, PA: Routledge.

Corcoran, C. T. (1994) Employment agency gets a grip on its workload, Infoworld, 16(46), 122.

Council for Excellence in Government. (2003). *The new e-government equation: ease, engagement, privacy and protection*. Washington, DC: Prepared by Hart–Teeter for the Council for Excellence in Government.

Craig, A., & Schriar, S. (2001). The find-it! Illinois controlled vocabulary: Improving access to government information through the Jessica subject tree. *Government Information Quarterly, 18*(3), 195-208.

Crane, J. (2005). *Qualitative research methods*, available at: http://web.isp.cz [Accessed on 28th May 2007]

Creswell, J. (2003). Research design, qualitative, quantitative, and mixed methods approaches, Second Edition. Thousand Oaks, London: Sage Publications.

Creswell, J. W. (1994). *Research Design: Qualitative and Quantitative Approaches*. Thousand Oaks, CA: Sage Publications.

Cross, M. (2006). E-democracy: tied up in red tape. *The Guardian*. Retrieved February 22, from http://politics.guardian.co.uk/egovernment/story/0,,1714670,00.html

Cruces Villalobos, Francisco and Díaz de Rada, Ángel (1995). "La cultura política, ¿es parte de la política cultural, o es parte de la política, o es parte de la cultura?". *Política y Sociedad*, N° 18.

CSN (2006). Annual Report. http://www.csn.se/polopoly_fs/1.2432!arsredovisning2006.pdf (visited Jan 27, 2008)

Curran, E. (2003). *Swarm: Cooperative reinforcement learning for routing in ad hoc networks*. Unpublished MSc thesis, Trinity College, Dublin, Ireland.

Cyr, Dianne; Ilsever, Joe; Bonanni, Carole; and Bowes, John (2004). "Website Design and Culture: An Empirical Investigation". Paper presented at 2004th International Workshop for the Internationalisation of Products and Systems, Vancouver. Retrieved from: http://www.diannecyr.com/docs/website_design_and_culture.pdf

Daubechies, I. (1992). *Ten lectures on wavelets.* Philadelphia: SIAM.

Davenport, T. H. (1993). *Process innovation: Reengineering work through information technology.* Harvard Business School Press

David, P., & Greenstein, S. (1990). The economics of compatibility standards: An introduction to recent research. *Economics of Innovation and New Technology, 1*(1-2), 3–41. doi:10.1080/10438599000000002

David, P., & Steinmueller, W. (1994). Economics of compatibility standards and competition in telecommunication networks. *Information Economics and Policy, 6*(3-4), 217–241. doi:10.1016/0167-6245(94)90003-5

Dawes, S. (1996). Interagency information sharing: expected benefits, manageable risks. *Journal of Policy Analysis and Management, 15*(3), 377–394. doi:10.1002/(SICI)1520-6688(199622)15:3<377::AID-PAM3>3.0.CO;2-F

Dawes, S. (2002). Government and technology: User, not regulator. *Journal of Public Administration: Research and Theory, 12*(4), 627–631.

Dawes, S., & Bloniarz, P. (2001). *Knowledge networking in the public sector.* New York: Center for Technology in Government, University at Albany/SUNY.

De Grandis, Rita (1995). "Incursiones en torno a hibridación, Una propuesta para discusión: De la mediación lingüística de Bajtín a la mediación simbólica de Canclini". Latin American Studies Association: LASA95 Papers Pilot Project. Retrieved from: http://lanic.utexas.edu/project/lasa95/grandis.html

De', R., & Sen, C. (2004). The complex nature of e-government projects: A case study of Bhoomi, an initiative in Karnataka, India. *Lecture Notes in Computer Science, 3183.*

Deakins, E. and Dillon, S.M. (2002) 'E-government in New Zealand: the local authority perspective', The International Journal of Public Sector Management, Bradford, Vol. 15, Nos. 4–5, pp.375–399.

Defense Information Systems Agency (DISA)—Net-Centric Enterprise Services. (2006, September 8). *Net-centric enterprise services user guide, Version 1.0/ECB 1.2.* Retrieved February 20, 2007, from http://www.disa.mil/nces/NCES_UG_Final_v1_0.pdf

Defense Information Systems Agency, Department of Defense (DISA). (2006, November 3). *Core services—Net-centric enterprise services.* Retrieved February 22, 2007, from http://www.disa.mil/main/prodsol/cs_nces.html

Deitel, H., Deitel, P., & Steinbuhler, K. (2001). *E-Business and E-commerce for managers.* Prentice Hall, NJ: New Jersey Press

Del Galdo, Elisa and Nielsen, Jakob (Eds.) (1996). *International User Interfaces.* John Wiley & Sons, Nueva York.

Denslow, C. (2005). ICDL seek to build Up computer skills. *IT Weekly.*

Department of Defense (DoD). (2000, March). *Organizational chart.* Retrieved April 20, 2007, from http://www.defenselink.mil/odam/omp/pubs/GuideBook/Pdf/DoD.PDF

Department of Homeland Security (DHS). (2006, June 26). *Special report | Component approach aiding IT infrastructure consolidation.* Retrieved January 31, 2007, from http://www.gcn.com/print/25_17/41104-1.html

Department of Homeland Security (DHS). (2006, June 26). *Special report | Forward motion, amid widely documented IT failures, security advances and infrastructure upgrades are gaining traction at DHS.* Retrieved January 31, 2007, from http://www.gcn.com/print/25_16/41076-1.html

Department of Homeland Security (DHS). (2006, September). *History: Who became part of the department?* Retrieved April 20, 2007, from http://www.dhs.gov/xabout/history/editorial_0133.shtm

Department of Homeland Security at Naval Post Graduate School. (n.d.). *Homeland security digital library.* Retrieved January 19, 2007, from https://www.hsdl.org/

DETR (1998). *Modern Local Government: In Touch with the People.* London: DETR

DGIM (2005). Online availability of public services: How is Europe progressing. Web based survey on Electronic Public Services. *Report of the fifth measurement,*

October 2004. Prepared by Capgemini for the European Commission Directorate General for Information. Retrieved December 15, 2005, from http://europa.eu.int/information_society/soccul/egov/egov_benchmarking_2005.pdf

Dhawan, V. (2004) Critical Success Factors for Rural ICT Projects in India: A study of n-Logue projects at Pabal and Baramati. Masters Thesis, Mehta School of Management, Indian Institute of Technology, Bombay.

Di Maio, A. (2006). *Moving from E-Government to government transformation. Business Issues*, 1-3, available at: http://www.gartner.com

Di Maria, E., Vergani, S., & Paskaleva-Shapira, K. (2005). *E-Governance practices, strategies and polices of European cities: State-of-the-art* ('IntelCities' Project Report D11.1.2). Retrieved from 'IntelCities' Project official web site: http://www.intelcitiesproject.com

Digenti, D. (1998). Collaborative learning: a core capability for organizations in the new economy. *Reflections*, *1*, Retrieved March 15, 2007, from http://mitpress.mit.edu/journals/sols/digenti.pdf

Ding, L., Kolari, P., Ding, Z., Avancha, S., Finin, T., & Joshi, A. (2005). *Using ontologies in the Semantic Web: A survey* (TR-CS-05-07). University of Maryland, Baltimore County, Ebiquity Research Group.

Dormann, Claire and Chisalita, Cristina. (2002). "Cultural Values in Web Site Design". Paper presented at Eleventh European Conference on Cognitive Ergonomics (ECCE-11), 2002, Catania, Italy. Retrieved from: http://www.cs.vu.nl/~martijn/gta/docs/Hofstede-dormann.pdf

Dos Santos, E., & Reinhard, N. (2007). Setting interoperability standards for e-government: An exploratory case study. Electronic Government, an International Journal, 4(4), 379-394.

Dossani, R., Misra, D. C. & Jhaveri, R. (2005) Enabling ICT for Rural India, Asia-Pacific Research Center, Stanford University, accessed through http://iis-db.stanford.edu/pubs/20972/ICT_full_Oct05.pdf.

Dowling, J., Curran, E., Cunningham, R., & Cahill, V. (2005, May). Using feedback in collaborative reinforcement learning to adaptively optimize MANET routing. *IEEE Transactions on Systems, Man, and Cybernetics—Part A: Systems and Humans, 35*(3).

Drake, D. B., Steckler, N. A., & Koch, M. J. (2004). Information sharing in and across government agencies: The role and influence of scientist, politician, and bureaucrat subcultures. *Social Science Computer Review*, *22*(1), Retrieved March 15, 2007, from http://ssc.sagepub.com/cgi/reprint/22/1/67

Drupal. (2007). Retrieved July 23, 2007, from http://www.drupal.org

DTLR (2001). *Strong local leadership, quality public services.* London: The Stationery Office

Dunleavy, P., Margetts, H., Bastow, S., & Tinkler, J. (2007). *Digital era governance: IT corporations, the state, and E-Government.* Oxford: Oxford University Press, 2006. ISBN 0 19 929619 7

Duran-Limon, et al. (2000). *Context-aware middleware for pervasive ad hoc environments.* (Tech. Rep.). Project CORTEX.

Dutton, W. H. (1999). *Society On the Line: Information Politics in the Digital Age*. Oxford: Oxford University Press.

Dynes, R. R., Quarantelli, E. L., & Wenger, D. 1990. *Individual and organizational response to the 1985 earthquake in Mexico City, Mexico.* Newark: University of Delaware, Disaster Research Center.

Earl, M. J. (1994). The new & old of business process redesign. *Journal Of Strategic Information Systems, 3*(1), 5-22.

Eco, Umberto (1989). *La estructura ausente. Introducción a la semiótica.* Editorial Lumen, Barcelona.

Eco, Umberto (2000). *Tratado de Semiótica General.* Editorial Lumen, Barcelona.

eGEP (2006a). *Measurement framework final version*, eGov Economics Project, European Commission, Brussels. http://217.59.60.50/eGEP/Static/Contents/final/D.2.4_Measurement_Framework_final_version.pdf (visited Jan 20, 2008)

eGEP (2006b). *Compendium to the measurement framework*, eGov Economics Project, European Commission, Brussels. http://217.59.60.50/eGEP/Static/Contents/final/Measurement_Framework%20_Compendium.pdf (visited Jan 20, 2008)

Eggers, W. (2005). *Government 2.0: Using technology to improve education, cut red tape, reduce gridlock, and enhance democracy.* Lanham, MD: Roman and Littlefield Publishers.

e-GIF (2004). *e-Government Interoperability Framework.* Office of the e-Envoy – Cabinet Office, UK.

eGovernment - United Arab Emirates - Archive - 1 November 2001 - 20 October 2004. "eGovernment introduces free online payment facility".

Ellig, J. (2007). *A dynamic perspective on government broadband initiatives.* Policy Study 349. Los Angeles: Reason Foundation. Retrieved February 15, 2009, from http://www.reason.org/ps349polsum.pdf.

Enser, P., & Sandom, C. (2003). Towards a comprehensive survey of the semantic gap in visual image retrieval. (LNCS 2728, pp. 279-287).

EPAN – European Public Administration Network. (2004). *Key principles of an interoperability architecture.* Ireland.

Ess, Charles and Sudweeks, Fay (1998). "Computer-mediated communication or culturally-mediated computing? Challenging assumptions of the electronic global village". *The Electronic Journal of Communication / La Revue Electronique de Communication*, N° 8. Retrieved from: http://www.cios.org/getfile%5CEss_V8N398

EU (2004). *eGov Research in Europe. European Commission.*. Retrieved December 15, 2005, from http://europa.eu.int/information_society/programmes/egov_rd/text_en.htm

Eugster, P., Th., Guerraoui, R., & Damm, C. H. (2001, October). On objects and events. In *Proceedings of the 16th ACM Conference on Object-Oriented Programming Systems, Languages and Applica-tions (OOPSLA 2001)* (pp. 131-146).

European Commission. (2002). *Vision and roadmaps for sustainable development in a networked knowledge society* (Report from the Information Society Directorate-General on new methods of work and electronic commerce). Retrieved April 24, 2008, from ftp://ftp.cordis.europa.eu/pub/ist/docs/ka2/visionsandroadmaps-final20020131.pdf

European Commission. (2003). *European Governance: A White Article.* Retrieved June 10, 2007, from http://europa.eu.int/eur-lex/en/com/cnc/2001/com2001_0428en01.pdf

European Commission. (2004). *4th European Conference on eGovernment, ECEG Dublin, Ireland, 17-18 June.* Retrieved June 10, 2007, from http://www.academic-conferences.org/eceg2004/eceg2004-home.htm

European Commission. (2005). *E-Government Communication.* Retrieved April 24, 2008, from http://europa.eu.int/information_society/eeurope/2005/

European Commission. (2005). *i2010 – A European information society for growth and Employment.* Brussels, Belgium: European Commission.

European Commission. (2007). *Fourth Ministerial eGovernment Conference: Reaping the benefits of e-government, 20-21 September 2007 in Lisbon.* Retrieved April 24, 2008, from http://ec.europa.eu/idabc/en/document/7196

Evans , G. (2003). *Implementing E-Government: An executive report for civil servants and their advisors.* Hampshire, England: Gower Publishing Limited.

Evans, P. (2006). How Local Authorities can motivate Councillors to update their websites – and how they can be promoted to the public. *The Councillor.info project.* Retrieve March 8, 2007, from http://www.popteltechnology.coop/Shared_ASP_Files/GFSR.asp?NodeID=89255&AttributeName=FileName

Fagan, M. (2006). *Exploring city, county and state E-Government initiatives: An east Texas perspective. Business Process Management Journal, 12*(1),101-112.

Faiola, Anthony and Matei, Sorin (2005). "Cultural cognitive style and web design: Beyond a behavioral inquiry into computer-mediated communication". *Journal of Computer-Mediated Communication,* N° 11. Retrieved from: http://jcmc.indiana.edu/vol11/issue1/faiola.html

Fairholm, M. R. (2004). Different perspectives on the practice of leadership. *Public Administration Review, 64*(5), 577–590. doi:10.1111/j.1540-6210.2004.00405.x

Falivene, G. (2004). Reformas de las políticas de formación directiva para el fortalecimiento institucional en contextos de crisis: aprendizajes realizados. *Reforma y Democracia, Revista del CLAD, 29,* 95-130.

Falivene, G., & Kaufman, E. (2005). Training and articulating public agencies in Argentina. In E. Coakes & S. H. Clarke (Eds.), *Encyclopedia of communities of practice and knowledge management*. Idea Group. Retrieved March 15, 2007, from http://www.idea-group.com/encyclopedia/details.asp?ID=458

Falivene, G., & Silva, G. (2003). Formación directiva para la creación de una cultura del conocimiento y de la calidad en las organizaciones públicas. *I° Congreso de Gestión de la Calidad de la Ciudad de Buenos Aires. Gobierno de la Ciudad Autónoma de Buenos Aires.* Buenos Aires, 2003. Retrieved March 15, 2007, from http://cffp.sgp.gov.ar/contenidos/inap/capacitacion/docs/falivene-silva.pdf

Falivene, G., & Silva, G. (2005). Formas de aprendizaje de directivos públicos en la Argentina. Estudio de casos, Informe de avance de investigación, Documento interno, Programa de Innovación de la Capacitación. Buenos Aires: INAP.

Falivene, G., Gurmendi, L., & Silva, G. (2003, October). El *e-learning* como mecanismo articulador de procesos de gestión del conocimiento y formación continua en las organizaciones públicas: el caso del Sistema de Información Universitaria (SIU). *1er. Premio del Concurso Internacional de Ensayos sobre Mecanismos de e-learning para Mejorar la Educación a Distancia de Funcionarios Públicos en Iberoamérica*, called by CLAD y co-sponsored by the government of Spain (MAP-AECI-FIIAPP).

Fandy, M. (1999). CyberResistance: Saudi opposition between globalization and localization. *Comparative Studies in Society and History, 41,* 124-147.

Feenburg, A. (1999). *Questioning Technology*. London: Routledge.

Fernández Parratt, Sonia (2002). "La glocalización de la comunicación". *Ámbitos, Revista Andaluza de Comunicación*, N° 7-8. Retrieved from: http://www.comunicacionymedios.com/Reflexion/teorias/glocalizacion.htm

Filzmaier, P., Stainer-H¨ammerle, K., & Snellen, I. (2004). Information management of MPs: Experiences from Austria, Denmark and the Netherlands. *Information Polity*, 9(1/2), 17–28

Finger, M. and Pecoud, G. (2003) 'From e-government to e-governance? towards a model of e-governance', 3rd European Conference on E-government, Trinity College Dublin, 3–4 July, Ireland.

Finin, T., Fritzson, R., McKay, D., & McEntire, R. (1994). KQML as an agent communication language. In *Proceedings of the 3rd International Conference on Information and Knowledge Management* (pp. 456-463).

Fink, Dieter and Laupase, Ricky (2000). "Perceptions of Web site design characteristics: a Malaysian/ Australian comparison". *Internet Research: Electronic Networking Applications and Policy*, N° 10. Retrieved from: http://www.emeraldinsight.com/Insight/ViewContentServlet?Filename=Published/EmeraldFullTextArticle/Articles/1720100104.html

Flick, U. (2006). An introduction to qualitative research, Third Edition. Thousand Oaks, London: Sage Publications.

Fountain, J. E. (1995). *Enacting Technology: An Institutional Perspective*. Cambridge, MA: John F. Kennedy School of Government, Harvard University.

Fountain, J. E. (2001). *Building the virtual state: Information technology and institutional change*. Washington, D.C: Brookings Institution Press.

Fountain, J. E. (2004). *Prospects for the Virtual State*. Working papers. Retrieved May, 2006, from http://www.j.u-tokyo.ac.jp/coeps/pdf/040710.pdf

Fountain, J. E. (2008). Bureaucratic Reform and E-Government in the United States: An Institutional Perspective. In A. Chadwick & P. N. Howard (Eds.), *The Handbook of Internet Politics*. New York: Routledge.

Fountain, J. E., McKinnon, R., & Park, E. (2003). *E-Government Cross-Agency and Intergovernmental Initiatives Research Project: Web Survey Results*. Boston, MA: Working Papers Series, National Center for Digital Government, John F. Kennedy School of Government, Harvard University.

Fountain, J.E. (2001). *Building the Virtual State: Information Technology and Institutional Change*. Brookings Institution Press: Washington, DC.

Fraga, E. (2002) "Trends in e-government: how to plan, design, and measure e-government", paper presented at the Government Management Information Sciences (GMIS) Conference, Santa Fe, NM, 17 June.

Front Line. (2006). Special feature on Chhattisgarh. *Front Line, November*. Retrieved September 23, 2007, from http://pay.hindu.com/ebook%20-%20ebfl20061103part6.pdf

Fundación Universidad Empresa de Valencia (sponsored by the European Commission within the framework of the Socrates-Minerva project). (n.d). MECA-ODL, Guía metodológica para el análisis de la calidad de la formación a distancia en Internet. Retrieved March 15, 2007, from www.adeit.uv.es/mecaodl

Fustes, M. (2003, July). The unconstrained business. *Insight, 3*, 15-17.

Ganapati, S., & Schoepp, C. F. (2008). The wireless city. *International Journal of Electronic Government Research, 4*, 54–68.

Gandhi, S., & Cross, C. (2001, October). E-Government initiative at city of Orlando: Current trends and future directions. *Proceedings of the URISA conference*, 1-12.

García Canclini, Néstor (2003). "Noticias recientes sobre la hibridación". *Revista Transcultural de Música*, N° 7, 2003. Retrieved from: http://www.sibetrans.com/trans/trans7/canclini.htm

Garnham, N. (2000) Amartya Sen's "Capabilities" Approach to the Evaluation of Welfare and its Application to Communications, in Beyond Competition: Broadening the scope of telecommunications policy, Cammaerts, B. and Burgelmans, J.C (Eds.), VUB University Press, 25-37.

Garson, G. D. (2003). Technological telelogy and the theory of technology enactment. *Social Science Computer Review, 21*(4), 425–431. doi:10.1177/0894439303256371

Garud, R., Jain, S., & Kumaraswamy, A. (2000). Institutional entrepreneurship in the sponsoring of common technological standards: the case of Sun Microsystems and Java. *Academy of Management Journal*.

Ghosh, A. and Banerjee, G. (2006) A Study of E-governance in Rural India, Fourth International Conference on Electronic Governance.

Giddens, A. (1979). *Central Problems in Social Theory. Action, Structure and Contradiction in Social Analysis*. Berkeley and Los Angeles, CA: University of California Press.

Giddens, A. (1984). *The Constitution of Society*. Berkeley and Los Angeles, CA: University of California Press.

Gil-Garcia, J. R. (2005, September 1-4). *Do Citizens' Expectations Matter for E-Government? Exploring the Determinants of the Functionality of State Web Sites*. Paper presented at the 2005 APSA Annual Meeting, Washington, DC.

Gil-Garcia, J. R. (2006, January 4-7, 2006). *Enacting State Websites: A Mixed Method Study Exploring E-Government Success in Multi-Organizational Settings*. Paper presented at the 39th Hawaii International Conference on System Sciences (HICSS).

Gil-Garcia, J. R., & Helbig, N. (2006). Exploring e-government benefits and success factors. In A.-V. Anttiroiko & M. Malkia (Eds.), *Encyclopedia of digital government*. Hershey, PA: Idea Group Inc.

Gil-García, J. R., & Luna-Reyes, L. F. (2006). Integrating Conceptual Approaches to E-Government. In M. Khosrow-Pour (Ed.), *Encyclopedia of E-Commerce, E-Government, and Mobile Commerce* (pp. 636-643). Hershey, PA: Idea Group Reference.

Global e-Policy eGovernment Institute. (2003). *Digital governance in municipalities worldwide: An assessment of municipal web sites throughout the world*. Retrieved April 10, 2008, from http://unpan1.un.org/intradoc/groups/public/documents/aspa/unpan012905.pdf

Goldkuhl, G. (2008). *The challenges of interoperability in e-government: towards a conceptual refinement*. Pre-ICIS 2008 SIG e-Government Workshop, Paris.

Goldsmith, A. (2005). *Wireless communications*. UK: Cambridge University Press.

Golebiowska, J., Dieng-Kuntz, R., Corby, O., & Mousseau, D. (2001). Building and exploiting ontologies for an automobile project memory. In *Proceedings of the 1st International Conference on Knowledge Capture K-CAP* (pp. 52-59).

González Chávez, José Ramón (2004). "Simbolismo de la bandera nacional de México". *Derecho y Cultura*, N° 13. Retrieved from: http://www.juridicas.unam.mx/publica/librev/rev/derycul/cont/13/ens/ens7.pdf

González, Adriana (2002). "Análisis semiótico de las campañas electorales". *Razón y Palabra*, N° 25. Retrieved from: http://www.cem.itesm.mx/dacs/publicaciones/logos/anteriores/n25/agonzal.html

Goodin, R. (Ed.) (1996). *The theory of institutional design*. Cambridge: Cambridge University Press.

Gore, A. (1993). Reengineering through Iiformation technology. Accompanying *Report of the National Performance Review*. Washington: Office of the Vice President.

Goss, S. & Corrigan, P. (1999). *Starting to Modernise: Developing New Roles for Council Members*. London: New Local Government Network.

Gottschalk, P., & Solli-Saether, H. (2009). *E-government interoperability and information resource integration: Frameworks for aligned development*. Hershey, PA: Information Science Reference.

Governance Knowledge Center. (2004). *E-setu in Assam*. New Delhi: Department of Administrative Reform and Public Grievances, Ministry of Personnel, Public Grievances and Pensions, Government of India. Retrieved May 22, 2007, from http://203.200.1.75/GKC/GKC_WebUI/Portal/TaxonomyShowcase/ShowCaseStudy.aspx?CSID=404&tid=389

Government Accounting Office. (2001) *Telecommunications: Research and regulatory efforts on mobile phone health issues*. Retrieved February 15, 2009, http://www.gao.gov/new.items/d01545.pdf.

Government Accounting Office. (2005). *Information security: Federal agencies need to improve controls over wireless networks*. Retrieved February 15, 2009, http://www.gao.gov/new.items/d05383.pdf.

Government of Hong Kong Special Administrative Region. (2008). *M-government*. Retrieved February 15, 2009, from http://www.info.gov.hk/digital21/e-gov/eng/init/mgov.htm

Graham, I., Spinardi, G., Williams, R., & Webster, J. (1995). The Dynamics of EDI standard development. *Technology Analysis and Strategic Management*, 7(1), 3–20. doi:10.1080/09537329508524192

Grant G. (2005) Realizing the Promise of Electronic Government, Editorial Preface, Journal of Global Information Management, 13(1), January-March.

Grant G. and Chau D. (2005) Developing a Generic Framework for E-Government, Journal of Global Information Management, 13(1), 1-30, Jan - March, Idea Group Publishing.

Grant, G., & Chau, D. (2005, January-March). Developing a generic framework for E-Government. *Journal of Global Information Management, 13*(1), 1-30.

Gronlund, A. (2001) "Democracy in an IT-framed society", Communications of the ACM, Vol. 44 No. 1, pp. 23-6.

Grönlund, Å. (2002). *Electronic government – Design, applications, and management*. Hershey, PA: Idea Group.

Grönlund, Å. (2004). The E-Service model - As implemented at Swedish National Labour Market Administration. In K Mark Weaver (ed), *Proceedings of Academy of Mangement*, New Orleans August 11-13, 2004. www.aomonline.org

Grönlund, Å. (2005). Introducing W-Gov: History, definitions, and issues. *Communications of AIS, 15*(electronic journal, www.cais.org).

GSA. (2002). *Government without boundaries: A management approach to inter-governmental programs*. Washington, D.C: Office of Intergovernmental Solutions.

Guffey, K. M. (2003). Collaborative networks: the initial design strongly influences the outcome. *Public Management, 32*(2), 42.

Guffey, K. M. (2006). Empowering collaborations in the hollow state. *International Journal of Public Administration, 29*(8), 561–575. doi:10.1080/01900690500455271

Gulledge, R. R., & Sommer, R. A. (2002). Business process management: Public sector implications. *Business Process Management Journal, 8*(4), 364–376. doi:10.1108/14637150210435017

Gupta M.P., Kumar. P. and Jaijit B. (2004) Government Online, Opportunities and Challenges, Tata McGraw-Hill, New Delhi.

Gupta, D.N. (2006). *Business process re-engineering and change management: Learning from e-governance projects*. In R. K. Mitra (Ed.), *E-government: Macro issues*. New Delhi: Gift Publishing.

Gupta, M. P., & Jana, D. (2003). E-Government evaluation: A framework and case study. *Government Information Quarterly, 20*, 365-387.

Gurmendi, L. (2005). SIU—data warehouse: herramientas para la toma de decisiones. *Info SIU, Sistema de Información Universtaria*, Monthly Bulletin, June 2005. Retrieved March 15, 2007, from http://www.siu.edu.ar/infosiu/nota.php?nw=5&nota=37

Haarslev, V., & Moller, R. (2003). Racer: An OWL reasoning agent for the Semantic Web. In *Proceedings of the International Workshop on Applications, Products and Services of Web-based Support Systems, in conjunction with the 2003 IEEE/WIC International Conference on Web Intelligence* (pp. 91-95).

Hacker, K.L. & Van Dijk, J. (Eds.) (2000). *Digital Democracy, Issues of Theory and Practice*. London: Sage Publications.

Hackney, R., & Jones, S. (2002, April). Towards E-Government in the Welsh (UK) Assembly: An Iiformation systems evaluation. *ISOneWorld Conference and Convention*, Las Vegas, USA.

Hague, B.N. & Loader, B.D. (Eds.) (1999). *Digital Democracy: Discourse and Decision Making in the Information Age*. London: Routledge.

Halavais, Alexander (2000). "National borders on the World Wide Web". *New Media & Society*, Nº 2.

Hammer, M., & Champy, J. (1993). *Reengineering the corporation: A manifesto for business revolution*. New York: Harper Business.

Hanseth, O., & Monteiro, E. (1998). Standards and standardization processes. In *Understanding information infrastructure* (manuscript).

Harding, A. (1998). Regime formation in Manchester and Edinburgh. In G. Stoker (Ed.), *The new politics of British local governance*. London: Macmillan.

Harris, R., & Rajora, R. (2006). *Empowering the poor: Information and communications technology for governance and poverty reduction, a study of rural development projects in India*. Bangkok: UNDP, Asia Pacific Development Information Programme (APDIP). Retrieved May 23, 2007, from http://www.apdip.net/publications/ict4d/EmpoweringThePoor.pdf

Haseloff, Otto W. (1970). "Sobre las condiciones del efecto de la comunicación política y publicitaria". In Otto W. Haseloff (ED), *La comunicación*. Editorial Nuevo Tiempo, Venezuela.

Hassan, S., & Gil-Garcia, J. R. (2008). Institutional Theory and E-Government Research. In G. D. Garson & M. Khosrow-Pour (Eds.), *Handbook of Research on Public Information Technology*. Hershey, PA: IGI Global.

Healey, P. (2007). The new institutionalism and the transformative goals of planning. In N. Verma (ed.), *Institutions and planning*. Amsterdam: The Elsevier.

Heeks R. (2003) Most e-Government–for-Development Projects Fail: How can Risks be Reduced? i-Government Working Paper Series Paper No. 14, Available at www.sed.manchester. ac.uk/ idpm/publications/wp/igov/igov-wp14.pdf.

Heeks, R. (2001) "Understanding e-governance for development", paper no. 11, i-Government Working Paper Series, Institute for Development Policy and Management, University of Manchester, Manchester.

Heeks, R. (2002) E-government for Development, Institute for Development Policy and Management (IIPM), University of Manchester, UK.

Heeks, R. (2003). *E-government for development: Success and failure rates of e-government in developing/transitional countries: Overview*. Manchester: University of Manchester.

Heeks, R. (2003a). *Understanding e-governance for development. IDPM i-government* (working paper 11). University of Manchester. Retrieved January 20, 2006, from http://www.sed.manchester.ac.uk/idpm/publications/wp/igov/igov_wp11.pdf

Heeks, R. (2003b). *Most e-government-for-development projects fail: How can risks be reduced?* (IDPM i-government working paper 14). University of Manchester. Retrieved January 20, 2006, from http://www.sed.manchester.ac.uk/idpm/publications/wp/igov/igov_wp14.pdf

Heeks, Richard (2004) "eGovernment for Development: Transparency Definitions Page". DoWire Democracies Online. Retrieved from: http://www.egov4dev.org/transpdefn.htm

Heras Gómez, Leticia (2002). "Cultura política: El estado del arte contemporáneo". *Convergencia*, N° 30. Retrieved from: http://editorial.unab.edu.co/revistas/reflexion/pdfs/dem_48_4_c.pdf

Hexmoor, H., & Sabaa, H. (2006). Towards semantically coherent collaboration. In *Proceedings of the International Symposium on Collaborative Technologies and Systems* (pp. 264-269). Washington, DC: IEEE Computer Society.

Hiller, J., & Belanger, F. (2001). *Privacy strategies for electronic government*: The PricewaterhouseCoopers Endowment for the Business of Government.

Ho, A. (2002). Reinventing local governments and the e-government initiative. *Public Administration Review*, *62*(4), 434–444. doi:10.1111/0033-3352.00197

Ho, A. T. (2002). Reinventing local governments and the e-government initiative. *Public Administration Review*, *62*(4), 434-441.

Hoff, J. (2004). The Democractic Potentials of Information Technology: Attitudes of European MPs towards new technology. *Information Polity*, 9(1/2), 55-66.

Hoff, J., Horrocks, I. & Tops, P. (Eds.) (2000). *Democratic Governance and New Technology, Technologically Mediated Innovations in Political Practices in Western Europe*. London: Routledge.

Hofstede, Geert (1999). *Culturas y Organizaciones: El Software Mental*. Alianza Editorial, Madrid.

Holden, S. H., Norris, D. F., & Fletcher, P. (2003). Electronic government at the local level: progress to date and future issues. *Public Performance & Management Review*, *26*(4), 325–344. doi:10.1177/1530957603026004002

Holden, S. H., Norris, D. F., & Fletcher, P. D. (2003). Electronic government at the local level: Progress to date and future issues. *Public Performance and Management Review*, *26*(4), 325-344.

Holden, S. H., Norris, D., & Fletcher, P. (2003). Electronic government at the local level. *Public Performance and Management Review*, *26*(4), 325-344.

Holmes, D. (2001). *E-government: E-business strategies for government*. London: Nicholas Brealey Publishing.

Holzer, M., & Callahan, K. (1998). *Governments at work: Best practice and model programs*. London: Sage.

Holzer, M., & Kim, S.T. (2005). Digital governance in municipalities worldwide (2005): UN/ASPA.

Hongladarom, Soraj (1998). "Global culture, local cultures, and the Internet: The Thai example". *En "Proceedings Cultural Attitudes Towards Communication and Technology '98", University of Sydney, Australia*. Retrieved from: http://www.it.murdoch.edu.au/~sudweeks/catac98/pdf/19_hongladarom.pdf

Hu, P., Cui, D., & Sherwood, A. (2006). Examining cross-agency collaborations in E-Government initiatives. *Proceedings of the 39th Hawaii International Conference on System Sciences*, pp.1-11

Hughes, M., Scott, M., & Golden, W. (2006). The role of business process redesign in Ireland. *Business Process Management Journal*, *12*(1), 76–87. doi:10.1108/14637150610643779

Hungarian algorithm. (2007). Retrieved July 23, 2007, from http://en.wikipedia.org/wiki/Hungarian_algorithm

Hurd, J. D., Civco, D. L., Gilmore, M. S., Prisloe, S., & Wilson, E. H. (2006, May 1-5). *Tidal wetland classification from landsat imagery using an integrated pixel-based and object-based classification approach*. Paper presented at the ASPRS 2006 Annual Conference, Reno, NV.

Huxham, C. (1996). Collaboration and collaborative advantage. In C. Huxham (Ed.), *Creating collaborative advantage* (pp. 1-18). Thousand Oaks, C.A: Sage Publications, Inc.

Huxham, C., & Vangen, S. (2000). Leadership in the shaping and implementation of collaboration agendas: How things happen in a (not quite) joined-up world. *Academy of Management Journal*, *43*(6), 1159-1166.

IBP (2003). "Índice latinoamericano de transparencia presupuestaria". *International Budget Project* (IBP). Retrieved from: http://www.internationalbudget.org/themes/BudTrans/Spanish.pdf

IDD (2005). Índice de Desarrollo Democrático de América Latina 2005. Konrad Adenauer Foundation. Retrieved from: http://www.idd-lat.org

IdeA, & Socitm. (2002). Local e-government now: A worldwide view. Retrieved August 15, 2006, from http://www.locregis.net/aaa/LEGNUK.PDF

IEEE Standards Information Network. (2000). *IEEE 100: The authoritative dictionary of IEEE standards terms*, Seventh Edition. New York: IEEE.

Ihrke, D., Proctor, R., & Gabris, J. (2003). Understanding innovation in municipal government: city council member perspectives. *Journal of Urban Affairs*, *25*(1), 79–90. doi:10.1111/1467-9906.t01-1-00006

Ilyas, M., & Ahson, S. A. (2006). *Smartphones: Research report*. Chicago: International Engineering Consortium.

Information Technologies Group. (2000). *Readiness for the networked world: A guide for developing countries* (Online Guide on Assessing Readiness). Bethesda, MD: Harvard University, Centre for International Development.

Ingraham, P. (2001). *Linking leadership to performance in public organizations*. Paris: Organization for Economic Co-Operation and Development.

Intanagonwiwat, C., Govindan, R., & Estrin, D. (2000, August). Directed diffusion: A scalable and robust communication paradigm for sensor networks. In *Proceedings of the Sixth Annual International Conference on Mobile Computing and Networking (MobiCOM '00)*, Boston, MA.

INTELCITIES. (2004-2006). *Intelligent Cities project* (N°: IST.2002-507860). EU VI Framework, Information Society Technologies, http://www.intelcitiesproject.com

Intelligence Community Forum. (2006). The top seven intelligent communities of 2006. Retrieved September 20, 2006, from http://www.intelligentcommunity.org/associations/5315/files/TopSevenIC-2006.pdf

International Telecommunications Union. (2008) *International Telecommunications Union/ ICT Indicators Database*. Retrieved February 15, 2009, from http://www.itu.int/ITU-D/ICTEYE/Indicators/Indicators.aspx#.

Irani, Z., Al-Sebie, M., & Elliman, T. (2006). Transaction stage of E-Government systems: Identification of its location & importance. *Proceedings of the 39th Hawaii International Conference on System Sciences, IEEE*, 1-9.

ITU, International Telecommunication Union. (2006). *World telecommunication lindicators database* (9th ed.). Geneva: ITU. Retrieved April 20, 2006, from http://www.itu.int/ITU-D/ict/publications/world/world.html

Ivatury, G., & Pickens, M. (2006). *Mobile phone banking and low-income customers: Evidence from South Africa*. Washington, DC: CGAP, United Nations Foundation, and Vodafone Group Foundation. Retrieved February 15, 2009, from http://go.worldbank.org/43SKY07120.

Jaeger, P. (2003). The endless wire: E-government as global phenomenon. *Government Information Quarterly*, *20*(4), 323–331. doi:10.1016/j.giq.2003.08.003

Jaeger, P. T., Shneiderman, B., Fleischmann, K. R., Preece, J., Qu, Y., & Wu, P. F. (2007). Community response grids: E-government, social networks, and effective emergency management. *Telecommunications Policy*, *31*, 592–604. doi:10.1016/j.telpol.2007.07.008

Jain, P. (2002). The catch-up state: E-Government in Japan. *Japanese Studies, 22*(3), 237-255.

Japas, D. (2005, July 10). Internet: wikimanía. *Revista La Nación*, Buenos Aires.

Jarvis, S., & Wilkerson, K. (2005). Congress on the Internet: Messages on the homepages of the U.S. House of Representatives, 1996 and 2001. *Journal of Computer-Mediated Communication, 10* (2), article 9. Retrieve March 8, 2007, from http://jcmc.indiana.edu/vol10/issue2/jarvis.html

Jefatura de Gabinete de Ministros, Subsecretaría de la Gestión Pública, *Plan Nacional de Gobierno Electrónico*, Decree 378/2005.

Jena–A Semantic Web Framework for Java. (n.d.). Retrieved December 4, 2006, from http://jena.sourceforge.net/index.html

Jervall, L., & Persson, T. (2006). *IT-stöd inom landstingen i Sverige*.

Jessop, B. (1997). Capitalism and its future: Remarks on regulation, government and governance. *Review of International Political Economy*, *4*(3), 561-581.

JiWire.com. (2009) *Wi-Fi Finder*. Retrieved February 15, 2009, from http://www.jiwire.com/search-hotspot-locations.htm.

Joseph, D. A. Manoj, B. S., and Murthy, C. S. R. (2004) Interoperability of WiFi hotspots and cellular networks. WMASH '04: In *Proceedings of the 2nd ACM international workshop on Wireless mobile applications and services on WLAN hotspots*. New York: ACM.

JPEG Metadata Discovery Tool (JMDT). (2007). Retrieved July 23, 2007, from http://metadata.solers.com

Ju-Pak, Kuen-Hee (1999). "Content dimensions of Web advertising: a cross-national comparison". *International Journal of Advertising*, N° 18.

Justice, J.,, & Melitski, J., & Smith, Daniel L. (2006). E-government as an instrument of fiscal accountability and responsiveness: Do the best practitioners employ the best practices? *American Review of Public Administration, 36*(3), 301–322. doi:10.1177/0275074005283797

Kalyanpur, A., Parsia, B., Sirin, E., Grau, B. C., & Hendler, J. A. (2006). Swoop: A Web ontology editing browser. *Journal of Web Semantics, 4*(2), 144-153.

Kannabiran, G., Xavier, M. J., & Anantharaaj, A. (2004) Enabling e-governance through Citizen Relationship Management - concept, model and applications, Journal of Services Research, Vol. 4-2, 2004 223-240.

Kanungo, V. & Umashankar, C. (2006) RASI Project- E-Democracy, The Society for promotion of eGovernance, New Delhi, 2005.

Kaplan, B., & Duchon, D. (1988). Combining qualitative and quantitative methods in information systems research: A case study. *MIS Quarterly, 12*(4), 571-586.

Karyda, M., Balopoulos, T., Gymnopoulos, L., Kokolakis, S., Lambrinoudakis, C., Gritzalis, S., et al. (2006). An ontology for secure e-government applications. In *Proceedings of the First International Conference on Availability, Reliability and Security (ARES'06), 00* (pp. 1033-1037).

KatrinVerclas. (2008). *SMS Critical in Election Monitoring in Ghana*. Retrieved February 15, 2009, from http://mobileactive.org/sms-critical-election-observation-ghana.

Katz, R., & Brewer, E. (1996). Wireless overlay networks and adaptiveApplications. In *Proceedings of MobiCom.*

Kaufman, E. (2005). Los modelos participativos de gobierno electrónico: Formación de funcionarios y constitución de redes interorganizacionales público-privadas. In S. Finkielevich (coord.), *TIC y desarrollo local. Municipios e Internet.* Buenos Aires: Ed. La Crujía.

Kawalek, P., & Wastell, D. (2001). The Informed Representative: The Information Needs of Local Elected Decision Makers. In Remenyi, D., & Bannister, F., *European Conference on e-Government*. Reading: MCIL:

Kaylor, C., Deshazo, R., & Van Eck, D. (2001). Gauging e-government: A report on implementing services among American cities. *Government Information Quarterly, 18*(4), 293–307. doi:10.1016/S0740-624X(01)00089-2

Ke, W., & Wei, K. K. (2004). Successful e-government in Singapore. *Commnications of ACM, 47,* 95-99.

Kearns, I., Bend, J. & Stern, B. (2002). *e-Participation in Local Government*. London: Institute for Public Policy Research.

Kernaghan K., Riehle, N. & Lo, J. (2003). Politicians's use of ICTs: a Survey of Federal Parliamentarians. *Crossing Boundaries*. Retrieved March 8, from www.publicsectorit.ca/publications/CBStudy.pdf

Kettl, D. F. (2004). *System under stress: Homeland security and American politics*. Washington: CQ.

Khadaroo, M. I. (2005). An institutional theory perspective on the UK's Private Finance Initiative (PFI) accounting standard setting process. *Public Management Review, 7*(1), 69–94. doi:10.1080/1471903042000339428

Kherfi, M. L., Ziou, D., & Bernardi, A. (2004). Image retrieval from the World Wide Web: Issues, techniques, and systems. *ACM Computing Surveys, 36*(1), 35-67.

Kieley, B., Lane, G., Paquet, G., & Roy, J. (2002). E-government in Canada: Services online or public service renewal? In Å. Grönlund (Ed.), *Electronic government: design, applications, and management* (pp. 340-355). Hershey, PA: Idea Group Publishing.

Kim, H., Pan, G., & Pan, S. (2007). Managing IT-enabled transformation in the public sector: Case study on E-Government in South Korea. *Government Information Quarterly, 24*, 338-352.

King, S. F. (2007). Citizens as customers: Exploring the future of CRM in UK local government. *Government Information Quarterly, 24*(1), 47–63. doi:10.1016/j.giq.2006.02.012

Klischewski, R. (2004). Information integration or process integration? How to achieve interoperability in administration. In R. Traunmüller (Ed.), *EGOV 2004* (LNCS 3183, pp. 57-65).

Klischewski, R., & Scholl, H. (2006). Information quality as a common ground for key players in e-government integration and interoperability. In *Proceedings of the 39th Hawaii International Conference on System Sciences.*

Knoblock, C.A. & Ambite, J.L. (1997). *Agents for Information Gathering, Software Agents.* J. Bradshaw, (Ed.), MIT Press, Menlo Park, CA.

Knott, G., & Waites, N. (1998). *Computer studies*, 4th Edition. Sunderland, England: Business Education Publishers Limited

Knowles, M. (1980). *The modern practice of adult education.* New York: Cambridge University Press.

Kolsaker, A. (2006). Reconceptualising e-government as a tool of governance: The UK case. *International Journal of Electronic Government, 3*(4), 347-355.

Kolsaker, A. (2007). Understanding e-government (G2C) in the knowledge society. *International Journal of Information Technology and Management, 6*(2-4), 138-147.

Komarek, P. (2004, May). *Logistic regression for data mining and high-dimensional classification* (Tech. Rep. No. CMU-RI-TR-04-34). Pittsburgh, PA: Carnegie Mellon University, Robotics Institute.

Korotkiy, M., & Top, J. (2006). Onto SOA: From ontology-enabled SOA to service-enabled ontologies. In *IEEE International Conference on Internet and Web Applications and Services.*

Kothari, A., Sabhash, S., & Zhou, Y. (2003). Bandwidth-constrained allocation in grid computing. In *Proceedings of WADS.*

Kraemer, K. L., & John, L. K. (2006). Information technology and administrative reform: Will E-Government be different? *International Journal of Electronic Government Research 2*(1), 1-20.

Kraemer, K. L., King, J. L., Dunkle, D. E., & Lane, J. P. (1989). *Managing Information Systems. Change and Control in Organizational Computing.* San Francisco, CA: Jossey-Bass.

Kraemer, K., & King, J. (2003). Information technology and administrative reform: Will the time after e-government be different? *Center for Research on Information Technology and Organizations. IT in Government.* Paper 337.

Kraemer, K.L. & King, J.L. (1994). Social analysis of information systems: the Irvine School, 1970–1994. *Informatization and the Public Sector*, 3(2), 163–182.

Ksantini, R., Ziou, D., Colin, B., & Dubeau, F. (2007). *Logistic regression models for a fast CBIR method based on feature selection.* Paper presented at the International Joint Conference on Artificial Intelligence.

Kumar P., Sushil and Gupta M.P. (2004) Towards E-Government, Management Challenges, Tata McGraw-Hill, New Delhi.

Kuscu, M. H., Kuschu, I., & Yu, B. (2007) Introducing mobile government. In I. Kushcu (Ed.), *Mobile government: An emerging direction in e-government.* Hershey, PA: IGI Publishing.

Ladner, R., Warner, E., Petry, F., Gupta, K., Moore, P., & Aha, D. (2006a). Design of an integrated Web services brokering system. *International Journal of Web Services Research.*

Ladner, R., Warner, E., Petry, F., Gupta, K., Moore, P., & Aha, D. (2006b). Soft computing techniques for Web services brokering. *Web Intelligence Journal.*

Lamont, J. (2006, May 26). *E-government: Enhancing national security.* Retrieved February 22, 2007, from http://www.kmworld.com/Articles/ReadArticle.aspx?ArticleID=15806

Landsbergen, D., & Wolken, G. (1998). *Eliminating legal and policy barriers to interoperable government systems.*

Landsbergen, D., & Wolken, G. (2001). Realizing the promise: government information systems and the fourth generation of information technology. *Public Administration Review*, *61*(2), 205–218.

Larsen, M., & Klischewski, R. (2004). Process ownership challenges in IT-enabled transformation of interorganizational business processes. *Proceedings of the 37th Hawaii International Conference on System Sciences, IEEE*, 1-11.

Latinobarómetro (2004). Latinobarómetro 2004: una década de mediciones. Retrieved from: http://www.latinobarometro.org

Lau, Edwin (2006). Electronic government and the drive for growth and equity. In Mayer-Schönbeger & Lazer (Eds.), *From Electronic Government to Information Government*, 39-58. Cambridge, Massachusetts: MIT Press

Lavallee, A. (2008, December 8). A second look at citywide Wi-Fi. *Wall Street Journal*. Retrieved February 15, 2009, from http://online.wsj.com/article/SB122840941903779747.html.

Lave, J., & Wenger, E. (1991). *Situated learning. Legitimate peripheral participation*. New York: Cambridge University Press.

Layne, K., & Lee, J. (2001). Developing fully functional e-government: A four stage model. *Government Information Quarterly*, *18*, 122–136. doi:10.1016/S0740-624X(01)00066-1

Le Botertf, G. (1991). *Cómo invertir en formación*. Barcelona: EADA Gestión.

Le Gales, P. (1998). Regulation and governance in European cities. *International Journal of Urban and Regional Research*, *22*(3), 482-506.

Leavitt, N. (2005, April). Mobile phones: The next frontier for Hackers? *Computer*, 38(4), 20–23.

Lee, S. M., Tan, X., & Trimi, S. (2005). Current practices of leading e-government countries. *Communications of ACM*, *48*, 99-104.

Lehr, W., & McKnight, L. W. (2003). Wireless Internet access: 3G vs. WiFi? *Telecommunications Policy*, *27*, 351–370. doi:10.1016/S0308-5961(03)00004-1

Li, B. (2005). *On the barriers to the development of E-Government in China. Communications of ACM*, 549-552

Li, J., & Wang, J. Z. (2006). *Real-time computerized annotation of pictures*. Paper presented at the ACM Multimedia Conference, Santa Barbara, CA.

Li, J., Wang, J. Z., & Wiederhold, G. (2000). *IRM: Integrated region matching for image retrieval*. Paper presented at the ACM Multimedia Conference, Los Angeles, CA.

Lim, J. H., & Tang, S.-Y. (2008). Urban e-government initiatives and environmental decision performance in Korea. *Journal of Public Administration: Research and Theory*, *18*(1), 109–138. doi:10.1093/jopart/mum005

Lim, T. S., Loh, W. Y. & Shih, Y. S. (2000). A comparison of prediction accuracy, complexity, and training time for thirty-three old and new classification algorithms. *Machine Learning*, *40*, 203-228.

Linden, R. M. (2002). *Working across boundaries: Making collaboration work in government and nonprofit organizations*. San Francisco: Jossey-Bass.

Littman, M., & Boyan, J. (1993). *A distributed reinforcement learning scheme for network routing* (Tech. Rep. No. CMU-CS-93-165).

Logan, R. K. (2000). *The extended mind: Understanding language and thought in terms of complexity and chaos theory*. University of Toronto. Retrieved March 15, 2007, from http://www.upscale.utoronto.ca/GeneralInterest/Logan/Extended/Extended.html

Logan, R. K. (2004). *The sixth language: Learning a living in the internet age*. Caldwell: Blackburn Press.

Lonti, Z., & Verma, A. (2003). The determinants of flexibility and innovation in the government workplace: Recent evidence from Canada. *Journal of Public Administration: Research and Theory*, *13*(3), 283–309. doi:10.1093/jopart/mug025

López de la Roche, Fabio (2000). "Aproximaciones al concepto de cultura política". *Convergencia*, Nº 22. Retrieved from: http://redalyc.uaemex.mx/redalyc/src/inicio/ArtPdfRed.jsp?iCve=10502205&iCveNum=17

Lozada, Mireya (2004). "El Ciberciudadano: Representaciones, redes y resistencias en Venezuela y América Latina". Colección Monografías, Nº 10. Retrieved from: http://globalcult.org.ve/doc/Monografias/Monografia-Lozada.doc

Lull, James (1995). *Medios, comunicación y cultura*. Amorrortu Editores, Buenos Aires.

Luna-Reyes, L. F., Gil-García, J. R., & Cruz, C. B. (2006, August 4-6). *Collaborative Digital Government in Mexico: Some Lessons from Federal Web-Based Inter-Organizational Information Integration Initiatives*. Paper presented at the 12th Americas Conference on Information Systems, Acapulco, Mexico.

Lynn, L. E. Jr. (2001). The myth of the bureaucratic paradigm: what traditional public administration really stood for. *Public Administration Review*, *61*(2), 144–160. doi:10.1111/0033-3352.00016

Ma, W. Y., & Manjunath, B. (1997). *NaTra: A toolbox for navigating large image databases*. Paper presented at the IEEE International Conference on Image Processing.

Macintosh, A. & Whyte, A. (2006). Evaluating how Participation Changes Local Democracy. *eGovernment Workshop '06 (eGOV06)*. September 11 2006, Brunel University, West London

Macintosh, A. (2006). E-participation in policy-making: the research and the challenges. In P. Cunningham & M. Cunningham, (Eds.), *Exploiting the knowledge economy: Issues, applications and case studies*. IOS press.

Macintosh, A., Coleman, S. & Lalljee, M. (2005). E-Methods for Public Engagement: Helping Local Authorities Communicate with Citizens. *Local e-Democracy National Project*. Retrieved March 8, from http://itc.napier.ac.uk/ITC/Documents/eMethods_guide2005.pdf

Macumber, H., & Cheung, B. (2007). A secure wireless data access service for the government of Canada. In I. Kushcu (Ed.), *Mobile government: An emerging direction in e-government*. Hershey, PA: IGI Publishing.

Madon S (2004) Evaluating the Developmental Impact of E-Governance Initiatives, Vol. 20, No. 5, pp. 1-13.

Madon, S. (2004). Evaluating the development impact of e-governance initiatives: An explanatory framework. *Electronic Journal of Information System in Developing Countries, 20*(5).

Madon, S. and Kiran, G. (2002) Information Technology for Citizen-Government Interface: A study of FRIENDS project in Kerala. World Bank Global Knowledge Sharing Program(GKSP). http://www1.worldbank.org/publicsector/bnpp/egovupdate.htm.

Magnuson, S. (2006, August). Homeland security mission creates more complications. *National Defense Magazine*. Retrieved April 20, 2007, from http://www.nationaldefensemagazine.org/issues/2006/August/HomelandSecurity.htm

Maguire, M. C., (1999) A review of user-interface design guidelines for public information Kiosk systems, Int. J. Human-Computer Studies, 50, 263–286.

Mahrer, H. & Krimmer, R. (2005). Towards the enhancement of e-democracy: identifying the notion of the 'Middleman Paradox'. *Information Systems Journal*, 15, 27–42.

Maistre, F. (2003). *JORAM*. Retrieved May 2005, from http://joram.ob-jectweb.org

Malmer, G. (2007). *IT-strategi för vård och omsorg*. http://www.skl.se/artikel.asp?C=5235&A=48864, visited Jan 15, 2008.

Mann, S., Nolan, J., & Wellman, B. (2003). Sousveillance: Inventing and using wearable computing devices for data collection in surveillance environments. *Surveillance & Society*, *1*, 331–355.

Mansar, S. (2006). E-Government implementation: Impact on business processes, *IEEE*, 1-5.

Mansell, R. (2001) New Media and the Power of Networks. First Dixons Public Lecture. The London School of Economics and Political Science, 23rd October.

ManTech awarded disaster-mapping contract from DHS. (2006, November 12). *SOAWorld Magazine*. Retrieved February 22, 2007, from http://webservices.sys-con.com/read/299259.htm

Marche, S. and McNiven, J.D. (2003) "E-government and e-governance: the future isn't what it used to be", Canadian Journal of Administrative Science, Vol. 20 No. 1, pp. 74-86.

Maria, E. D. & Micelli, S. (eds.) (2005). *On Line Citizenship. Emerging Technologies for European Cities.* New York: Springer.

Marks, E., & Bell, M. (2006). *Executives' guide to service-oriented architecture (SOA): A planning and implementation guide for business and technology.* Wiley.

Markus, Aaron y Gould, Emilie (2000). "Crosscurrents: Cultural dimensions and global web user- interface design". *Interactions*, Vol. 7, Issue 4. Retrieved from: http://portal.acm.org/citation.cfm?id=345238

Markus, Aaron, Armitage, Joh, Volker, Frank and Guttman, Edward (1999). "Globalization of User Interface Design for the Web". Retrieved from: http://zing.ncsl.nist.gov/hfweb/proceedings/marcus

Martín- Barbero, Jesús (2003). *De los medios a las mediaciones.* Editorial Nomos-Convenio Andrés Bello, Santa Fe de Bogotá.

Martínez, Gildardo (2004) "Internet y ciudadanía global: procesos de producción de representaciones sociales de ciudadanía en tiempos de globalización". In Daniel Mato (ED), *Políticas de ciudadanía y sociedad civil en tiempos de globalización.* Caracas: FACES, Universidad Central de Venezuela. Retrieved from:: http://globalcult.org.ve/pub/Rocky/Libro2/Martinez.pdf

Mattessich, P. W., Murray-Close, M., & Monsey, B. R. (2001). *Collaboration: What makes it work* (2 ed.). St. Paul, Minnesota: Amherst H. Wilder Foundation.

Maturana, León (1991). *Comunicación, Sistema y Cultura*; Editorial Almogesto, Buenos Aires.

McClure, D. (2000). *Statement of David L. McClure, U.S. General Accounting Office, before the Subcommittee on Government Management, Information and Technology.* Committee on Government Reform, House of Representatives. Retrieved December 15, 2007 from http://www.gao.gov

McDaniel, E. A. (2003). *Facilitating cross-boundary leadership in emerging e-government leaders.* Paper presented at the Informing Science + IT Education Conference, Fori, Finland.

McGrath, K. (2002). The golden circle: A way of arguing and acting about technology in the London ambulance aervice. *European Journal of Information Systems, 11*(4). 251-266.

McGuinness, D. L., & Harmelen, F. V. (Eds.). (2004). *OWL Web ontology language overview.* Retrieved December 4, 2006, from http://www.w3.org/TR/owl-features/

Mclvor, R., McHugh, M., & Cadden, C. (2002). Internet technologies: Supporting transparency in the public sector. *The International Journal of Public Sector Management, 15* (3), 170-187.

McNeil, R. S., Tolbert, C. J., Mossberger, K., & Dotterweich, L. J. (2003). Innovating in digital government in the American states. *Social Science Quarterly, 84*(1), 52-70.

McNurlin, B. C., & Sprague, R. H. (2006) *Information systems management in practice* (6th ed.). Upper Saddle River, NJ: Prentice Hall.

McSweeney, Brendan (2002). "Hofstede's model of national cultural differences and their consequences: A triumph or faith – A failure of analysis". *Human Relations*, Vol. 55, N° 1, [January] 2002, pp. 89-118. Retrieved from: http://geert-hofstede.international-business-center.com/mcsweeney.shtml

Medjahed, B., & Bouguettaya, A. (2005). Customized delivery of e-government Web services. *IEEE Intelligent Systems, 20*(6), 77-84.

Merino, Mauricio (2003). "La formación del Estado nacional mexicano. El pasado colonial, las ideas liberales y los gobiernos locales como elementos delineadores del Estado". Retrieved from: http://bv.gva.es/documentos/Merino.doc

Meso, P., Checchi, R., Sevcik, G., Loch, K., & Straub, D. (2006). Knowledge spheres and the diffusion of national IT policies. *The Electronic Journal of Information Systems in Developing Countries, 23.*

Miikkulainen, R., & Kumar, S. (1999). Confidence based dual reinforcement q-routing: An adaptative on-line routing algorithm. In *Proceedings of the Sixteenth International Joint Conference on Artificial Intelligence* (pp. 758-763).

Miles, M. B. and Huberman, A. M. (1994). *An Expanded Sourcebook: Qualitative Data Analysis,* 2nd edition. London: Sage Publications.

Millard, J., & Iversen, J. (2004). *Reorganization of government back offices for better electronic public services – European good practices*. Final report to the European Commission, January.

Miller, A. G. (1995). WordNet: A lexical database for English. *Communications of ACM, 38,* 39-41.

Miller, J. A., Baramidze, G. T., Sheth, A. P., & Fishwick, P. A. (2004). Investigating ontologies for simulation modeling. In *Proceedings of the 37th Annual Symposium on Simulation ANSS* (p. 55).

Milward, H. B., & Snyder, L. O. (1996). Electronic government: linking citizens to public organizations through technology. *Journal of Public Administration: Research and Theory, 6*(2), 261–276.

Mingers, J. (2001). *Combining IS research methods: Towards a pluralist methodology. Information Systems Research, 12*(3), 240-259.

Ministry of Information Communication Technologies. (2005). *E-preparedness of states of India*. Retrieved August 25, 2007, from http://www.mit.gov.in/download/eready/EX_sum.PDF

Mistri, M. (1999). Industrial districts and local governance in the Italian experience. *Human Systems Management, 18*(2), 131-139.

Mitchell, T. (2005). *Generative and discriminative classifiers: Naïve Bayes and logistic regression.* Retrieved from http://www.cs.cmu.edu/~tom/mlbook/NBayesLogReg.pdf

Montjoy, R. S., & Watson, D. J. (1995). A case for reinterpreted dichotomy of politics and administration as a professional standard in council-manager government. *Public Administration Review, 55*(3), 231–239. doi:10.2307/3110241

Moon, J. (2002). The evolution of e-government among municipalities: Rhetoric or reality? *Public Administration Review, 62*(4), 424–433. doi:10.1111/0033-3352.00196

Moon, J., & Welch, E. (2005). Same bed, different dreams? A comparative analysis of citizen and bureaucrat perspectives on e-government. *Review of Public Personnel Administration, 25*(3), 243–264. doi:10.1177/0734371X05275508

Moon, M. J. (2002). The evolution of e-government among municipalities: Rhetoric or reality? *Public Administration Review, 62*(4), 424-433.

Moon, M. J. (2004) *From e-government to m-government? Emerging practices in the use of mobile technology by state governments.* Washington, DC: IBM Center for the Business of Government.

Moore, M. (1995). *Creating public value: Strategic management in government.* Harvard University Press: Cambridge, MA, 1995.

Moragás, Miguel de (1985). "Transformación tecnológica y tipología de los medios. Importancia política de la noción de ámbito comunicativo" In Moragás, Miguel de (1985), *Sociología de la comunicación de masas, IV: Nuevos problemas y transformación tecnológica* Editorial Gustavo Gili, Barcelona.

Moragás, Miguel de (n.d.). "Internet: facilidades tecnológicas, dificultades de comunicación". Retrieved from: http://www.comminit.com/la/teoriasdecambio/teorias2004/teorias-24.html

Morgan, D. R., & Watson, S. S. (1992). Policy Leadership in council-manager cities: comparing mayors and managers. *Public Administration Review, 52*(5), 438–446. doi:10.2307/976803

Morgan, G. (1997). *Images of organization.* California: Sage Publications.

Morin, E. (1996). *Introducción al pensamiento complejo.* Barcelona: Gedisa.

Morris et al, Kiosks: A technological overview. Available: http:// www.visi.com/~keefner/pdfs/Kiosk_paper.html#PTFToC2, 1995, accessed April 14, 2004.

Mossberger, K., Tolbert, C. J., & Stansbury, M. (2003). *Virtual inequality: Beyond the digital divide.* Washington, DC: Georgetown University Press.

Moulaert, F., & Delladetsima, P. (2002). *Globalisation and integrated area development in European cities.* Oxford: Oxford University Press.

MovIT – Steering Committee. (2007). *Medborgarorienterad verksamhetsutveckling med stöd av IT*

Moynihan, Donald P., & Ingraham, P. (2004). Integrative leadership in the public sector: A model of performance-information use. *Administration & Society, 36*(4), 427–453. doi:10.1177/0095399704266748

Mumford, E. (1994). New treatments or old remedies: Is business process reengineering really Socio-technical design? *Journal of Strategic Information Systems, 3*(4), 313-326.

Murphy, J. (MP Parliamentary Secretary Cabinet Office Report) (2005). Beyond E-Government the world's most successful technology-enabled transformations. *Executive summary, INSEAD the business school for the world,* 1-124, available at: www.localtgov.org.uk

Myers, M. D. (1997). Qualitative research in information systems. *MIS Quarterly, 21*, 241-242.

Nalbandian, J. (1989). The contemporary role of city managers. *American Review of Public Administration, 19*(4), 261–279. doi:10.1177/027507408901900401

Nalbandian, J. (1991). Professionalism in local government. San Francisco: Jossey-Bass.

Nalbandian, J. (1999). Facilitating community, enabling democracy: new roles for local government managers. *Public Administration Review, 59*(3), 187–197. doi:10.2307/3109948

Nalbandian, J. (2005). Professionals and the conflicting forces of administrative modernization and civic engagement. *American Review of Public Administration, 35*(4), 311–326. doi:10.1177/0275074005279897

NASCIO. (2005). Connecting the silos: Using governance models to achieve data integration. Retrieved July 10, 2006, from www.nscio.org

Nath, V. (2006) Building and Sustaining Democratic and Accountable Governance Institutions using ICT- Models of Digital Governance, http://www.cddc.vt.edu/digitalgov/gov-models.html, accessed in March 2007

National Security Agency. (n.d.). *Global information grid, Scope and objectives.* Retrieved February 22, 2007, from http://www.nsa.gov/ia/industry/gigscope.cfm?MenuID=10.3.2.2

Natsev, A. (2001). *Multimedia retrieval by regions, concepts, and constraints.* Unpublished PhD thesis, Duke University, Durham, NC.

Natsev, A., Chadha, A., Soetarman, B., & Vitter, J. S. (2001). *CAMEL: Concept annotated iMagE libraries.* Paper presented at the Storage and Retrieval for Image and Video Databases, SPIE, San Jose, CA.

Natsev, A., Rastogi, R., & Shim, K. (2004). WALRUS: A similarity retrieval algorithm for image databases. *IEEE Transactions on Knowledge and Data Engineering, 16*(3), 301-316.

Navy PEO C4I & Space RAPIDS Team, Air Force ESC C2ERA Team. (2004, December). *Net-centric enterprise solutions for interoperability.* Retrieved April 17, 2007, from http://nesipublic.spawar.navy.mil/files/NESI-Overview-v1e.ppt

Netcentric Enterprise Solutions for Interoperabilty. (2006, June). *Netcentric enterprise solutions for interoperability part 5: Developer guidance* version 1.3. Retrieved April 20, 2007, from http://nesipublic.spawar.navy.mil/part5/releases/1.3.0/WebHelp/nesi_part5_v1_3.htm

New Millennium Research Council. (2005). *Not in the public interest – The myth of municipal Wi-Fi networks.* Washington, D.C. Retrieved February 15, 2009, from http://www.newmillenniumresearch.org/archive/wifireport2305.pdf.

Newland, C. A. (1989). The future of council-manager government, In H. George Frederickson (Ed.), *Ideal and Practice in Council-Manager Government.* Washington, DC: International City Management Association.

Ni, Y. N. & Ho, A. T. (2005) Challenges in e-government development: Lessons from two information Kiosk projects, Government Information Quarterly, 22, 58–74.

Nicholas, D., Huntington, P. & Williams, P. (2003) Three years of digital consumer health information: a longitudinal study of the touch screen health Kiosk, Information Processing and Management, 39, 479–502.

NISG & i4D. (2006). ICTD project review workshop (Electronic version). *ICTD project newsletter, June.* Retrieved April 12, 2007, from http://www.i4donline.net/articles/current-article.asp?articleid=705&typ=Features

Nonaka, I., & Takeuchi, H. (1999a). *The knowledge-creating company.* New York: Oxford University Press.

Nonaka, I., & Takeuchi, H. (1999b). *La organización creadora de conocimiento: Cómo las compañías japone-*

sas crean la dinámica de la innovación. México City: Oxford Press.

Norris, D. F., & Moon, M. J. (2005). Advancing E-Government at the grass roots: Tortoise or hare? *Public Administration Review, 65*(1), 64-75.

Norris, D., & Jae Moon, J. (2005). Advancing e-government at the grassroots: tortoise or hare? *Public Administration Review, 65*(1), 64–75. doi:10.1111/j.1540-6210.2005.00431.x

Norris, D., & Jae Moon, J. (2005). Does managerial orientation matter? The adoption of reinventing government and e-government at the municipal level. *Information Systems Journal, 15*(1), 43–60. doi:10.1111/j.1365-2575.2005.00185.x

Norris, D., Holden, S. H., & Fletcher, P. D. (2001). *E-government: Web sites and web access*. Washington, D.C: International City/County Management Association.

Norris, P. (2005). The Impact of the Internet on Political Activism: Evidence from Europe. *International Journal of Electronic Government Research*, 1(1), 20-39.

North, D. C. (1999). *Institutions, Institutional Change, and Economic Performance*. New York: Cambridge University Press.

Ntaliani, M., & Costopoulou, C., C., Karetsos, S. (2008). Mobile government: A challenge for agriculture. *Government Information Quarterly, 25*(4), 699–716. doi:10.1016/j.giq.2007.04.010

O'Rourke, R. (2005, June 2). *Homeland security: Navy operations—Background and issues for Congress*. Retrieved February 22, 2007, from http://www.history.navy.mil/library/online/homeland_security.htm

Oberle, D., Eberhart, A., Staab, S., & Volz, R. (2004). Application servers, enterprise computing and software engineering: Developing and managing software components in an ontology-based application server. In *Proceedings of the 5th ACM/IFIP/USENIX International Conference on Middleware* (pp. 459-477).

Obrst, L., Wray, R. E., & Liu, H. (2001). Ontological engineering for B2B e-commerce. In *Proceedings of the International Conference on Formal Ontology in Information Systems, 2001* (pp. 117-126).

OECD (2003). *The E-Government imperative*. Paris: OECD E-Government Studies. ISBN 92-64-10117-9

OECD. (2003). *OECD e-Government Studies: The E-Government Imperative*. Paris, France: OECD Publishing.

OECD. (2003a). *Checklist for e-government leaders* (OCDE Policy Brief on September 2003). Paris: OECD Observer. Retrieved June 10, 2007, from http://www.oecd.org/dataoecd/62/58/11923037.pdf

OECD. (2003b). *Engaging citizens online for better policy-making* (OCDE Policy Brief on March, 2003). Paris: OECD Observer. Retrieved June 10, 2007, from http://www.oecd.org/dataoecd/62/23/2501856.pdf

OECD. (2003c). *The E-Government imperative: Main findings* (OCDE Policy Brief on March, 2003). Paris: OECD Observer. Retrieved June 11, 2007, from http://www.oecd.org/dataoecd/60/60/2502539.pdf

OECD. (2005). *OECD e-Government Studies: Mexico*. Paris, France: OECD Publishing.

Office of the e-Envoy. (2002). UK online Annual Report 2002. Retrieved April 24, 2008, from http://archive.cabinetoffice.gov.uk/e-envoy/reports-annrep-2002/$file/04-01.htm

Okot-Uma, R.W. (2000) Electronic Governance: Re-Inventing Good Governance, Commonwealth Secretariat, London.

Okot-Uma, R.W. (2001) "Electronic governance: (leading to good government)", Electronic Governance and Electronic Democracy: Living and Working in the Connected World, The Commonwealth Centre for Electronic Governance, Ottawa, available at: www.electronegov.net (accessed 7 August 2003).

OpenID. (2007). *OpenID—Free secure identity*. Retrieved July 23, 2007, from http://www.openid.org

Opsahl, A. (2008). Cities use WiMAX to create municipal wireless networks. *Government Technology*. Retrieved February 15, 2009, from http://www.govtech.com/gt/241661?id=&story_pg=1

Örebro City Administration Office. (2007). *Servicepolicy och Tillgänglighetsgaranti för Örebro Kommun*.

Örebro City executive board. (2006). *Budget 2007 med prioriterade mål (Budget with priorities)*. Örebro kommun.

Örebro City. (2007a). *Dialogen kring Klagomål*

Örebro City. (2007b). *Klagomålshantering i Örebro Kommun*

Organization for Economic Co-operation and Development. (2003). *The e-government imperative*. Paris: OCDE.

Organization of Economic Co-Operation and Development (2003). Checklist for e-government leaders. Retrieved October 10, 2005, from http://www.oecd.org/publications/Pol_brief

Orlikowski, W.J. (1992). The duality of technology: rethinking the concept of technology in organizations. *Organisational Science*, 3(3), 398–427.

Orlikowski, W.J. (2000). Using technology and constituting structures: a practice lens for studying technology in organizations. *Organizational Science*, 11(4), 404–428.

Osborne, D., & Gaebler, T. (1993). *Reinventing government: how the entrepreneurial spirit is transforming the public sector*. New York: Plume.

Palanisamy, R. (2004). Issues and challenges in e-governance planning. *Electronic government, 1*(3), 253-273.

Panamá. Retrieved March 15, 2007, from http://www.clad.org.ve/fulltext/0048201.pdf

Panebianco, Angelo (1982). "Comunicación política". En Bobbio y Mateuci (ED), *Diccionario de Ciencia Política*, Editorial Siglo XXI, Madrid.

Pannekoek, F., Bernard, P., Mitchell, D., Martin, C. and Dickin, J. (2002) 'The internet as a site of citizenship: the final report (Information Deficit Canadian Solutions 2001)', Canadian Journal of Communication, Toronto, Vol. 27, No. 4, pp.509–527.

Paolucci, M., Soudry, J., Srinivasan, N., & Sycara, K. (2004). A broker for OWL-S Web services. In *Proceedings of the AAAI Spring Symposium on Semantic Web Services* (pp. 562-567).

Parkhomenko, O., Lee, Y., & Park, E. K. (2003). Ontology-driven peer profiling in peer-to-peer enabled semantic Web. In *Proceedings of the Twelfth International Conference on Information and Knowledge Management* (pp. 564-567).

Parvez, Z. & Ahmed, P. (2006). Towards Building An Integrated Perspective of e-Democracy in Practice. *Information, Communication & Society*, 9(5), 612–632.

Parvez, Z. (2006a). Examining e-Democracy Through A Double Structuration Loop. *Electronic Government*, 3(3), 329–346.

Parvez, Z. (2006b). Informatization of Local Democracy: A Structuration Perspective. *Information Polity*, 11(1), 67-83.

Paskaleva-Shapira, (2007). E-City Europe: Status, propositions and opportunities. *Proceedings of the 3rd IET International Conference on Intelligent Environments, IE 07*, IEEE, 510-516.

Paskaleva-Shapira, K. (2005). City E-Governance as an innovative urban public policy framework. In M. Böhlen, J. Gamper, W. Polasek and M. Wimmer (Eds.), *Proceedings of the TED Conference on e-Government: Electronic Democracy: The Challenges Ahead*. IFIP, 3-11.

Paskaleva-Shapira, K. (2008). Urban sustainability and governance: Challenges of the knowledge society. In Vreeker, R., Deakin, M. & Curwell, S. (Eds.). *Sustainable Urban Development*, Routledge, London (Forthcoming).

Paul, R. A. (2005). *DoD towards software services*. In *Proceedings of the 10th IEEE International Workshop on Object-Oriented Real-Time Dependable Systems (WORDS'05)* (pp. 3-6).

Pavlou, Paul y Chai, Lin (2002). «What drives electronic commerce across cultures? A crosscultural empirical investigation of the theory of planned behavior», *Journal of Electronic Commerce Research*, Vol. 3 N° 4. Retrieved from: http://www.csulb.edu/web/journals/jecr/issues/20024/paper4.pdf

Pechoucek, M., Marık, V., & Stepankova, O. (2001). Towards reducing communication traffic in multi-agent systems. *Journal of Applied Systems, 2*(1), 152-174.

Peng, F., & Deyun, Z. (2006). *Hybrid optimize strategy based QoS route algorithm for mobile ad hoc networks.* Department of Computer Science and Technology, Xi'an Jiaotong University, Xi'an, China.

Perina, Rubén (2002). "Gobernabilidad, cultura política y liderazgo: Esbozo para una teoría". Retrieved from: http://www.upd.oas.org/cursos/documentos/aspSmartUpload/files/Gobernabilidad%20Cult%20Pol%20y%20%20Liderazgo%20%20Sept%2005%20nuevo.doc

Peristeras, V., Tarabanis, K., & Goudos, S. K. (forthcoming). Model-driven eGovernment interoperability: A review of the state of the art. *Computer Standards & Interfaces*, 31(4), 613.

Perlich, C., Provost, F., & Simonoff, J. (2003). Tree induction vs. logistic regression: A learning-curve analysis. *Journal of Machine Learning Research, 4,* 211-255.

Peschard, Jaqueline (1996). *La cultura política democrática. Cuadernos de Divulgación de la Cultura Democrática*, N° 2; Instituto Federal Electoral, México. Retrieved from: http://www.ife.org.mx/InternetCDA/estaticos/DECEYEC/la_cultura_politica_democratica.htm

Peters, B. G. (2001). *Institutional theory in political science. The 'new' institutionalism.* London: Continuum.

Pierre, J. (1999). Models of urban governance: The institutional dimensions of urban politics. *Urban Affairs Review*, *34*(3), 372-96.

Pigato, M. (2001). *Information and communication technology, poverty, and development in sub-Saharan Africa and South Asia* (Africa region working paper series #20). Washington, DC: World Bank.

Plasser, Fritz (2004). "La comunicación política en los hemisferios Norte y Sur. ¿Qué intercambio reciproco puede esperarse?". *Diálogo Político*, N° 2, Marzo 2004, Argentina. Pp. 165-180.

Poder Ejecutivo. (2002). *Ley Federal de Transparencia y Acceso a la Información Pública Gubernamental.* Retrieved September, 2006, from http://www.elaw.org/resources/text.asp?id=1544

Poister, T. H., & Streib, G. (1999). Strategic management in the public sector: concepts, models, and processes. *Public Productivity and Management Review*, *22*(3), 308–325. doi:10.2307/3380706

Poister, T., & Streib, G. (1994). Municipal management tools from 1976 to 1993: An overview and update. *Public Productivity & Management Review*, *18*(2), 115–125. doi:10.2307/3380641

Poister, T., & Streib, G. (1999). Performance measurement in municipal government: Assessing the state of the practice. *Public Administration Review*, *59*(4), 325–335. doi:10.2307/3110115

Poister, T., & Streib, G. (2005). Elements of strategic planning and management in municipal government: status after two decades. *Public Administration Review*, *65*(1), 45–56. doi:10.1111/j.1540-6210.2005.00429.x

Polanyi, M. (1958). *Personal knowledge.* Chicago: The University of Chicago Press.

Powell, W. W., & DiMaggio, P. J. (1991). *The New Institutionalism in organizational analysis.* Chicago, IL: University of Chicago Press.

Prasad, K. (2006). *Indian administration: Politics, policies and prospects.* New Delhi: Dorling Kindersley.

Pratchett, L (2007). *Local e-Democracy in Europe: Democratic X-ray as the Basis for Comparative Analysis.* International Conference Direct Democracy in Latin America. 14-15 March, Buenos Aires, Argentina. Retrieved March 8, from http://www.dd-la.ch/download/Pratchett_Lawrence.pdf

Pratchett, L., Wingfield M. & Polat, R. K.(2005). Barriers to e-Democracy: Local Government Experiences and Responses. *Local e-Democracy National Project*, Retrieved March 8, from http://www.icele.org/downloads/Researchreport.pdf

Pratchett, L.; Wingfield, M. & Polat, R. K. (2006). Local Democracy Online: An Analysis of Local Government Web Sites in England and Wales. *International Journal of Electronic Government Research*, 2(3), 75-92.

PriceWaterhouseCoopers. (2001). *Position paper, Chhattisgarh, Chapter V.* Retrieved August 20, 2007, from http://chhattisgarh.nic.in/opportunities/Information%20Technology.pdf

Prud'hommeaux, E., & Seaborne, A. (Eds.). (2007). *SPARQL query language for RDF.* Retrieved June 16, 2007, from http://www.w3.org/TR/rdf-sparql-query/

Puron Cid, G., & Gil-Garcia, J. R. (2004). Enacting E-Budgeting in Mexico. *Public Finance and Management*, *4*(2), 182–217.

Pyati, A. (2005). WSIS: Whose vision of an information society? *First Monday, 10*(5). Retrieved May 1, 2007, from http://firstmonday.org/issues/issue10_5/pyati/index.html

Quinlan, J. R. (1993). *C4.5: Programs for machine learning*. San Francisco: Morgan Kaufmann.

Radhakumari (2006) Akshaya – A Grass Root Level IT Project in Kerala – An Unique Experiment with Broadband, Fourth International Conference on Electronic Governance.

Rahimi, S., Carver, N., & Petry, F. E. (2005). A multi-agent architecture for distributed domain-specific information integration. In R. Ladner & F. E. Petry (Eds.), *Net-centric approaches to intelligence and national security* (pp. 129-148). New York: Springer.

Rao, S. S. (2004) Role of ICTs in India's rural community information systems, Vol. 6, No. 4, pp. 261-269.

Reddick, C. (2004). A two-stage model of e-government growth: Theories and empirical evidence for U.S. cities. *Government Information Quarterly, 21*(1), 51–64. doi:10.1016/j.giq.2003.11.004

Reddick, C. (2005). Citizen-initiated contacts with government comparing phones and websites. *Journal of E-Government*, *2*(1), 27–53. doi:10.1300/J399v02n01_03

Reddick, C. G. (2004). A two-stage model of e-government growth: Theories and empirical evidence for U.S. Cities. *Government Information Quarterly, 21*(1), 51-64.

Reddick, C. G., & Frank, H. A. (2006). The perceived impacts of e-government on U.S. Cities: A survey of Florida and Texas city managers. *Government Information Quarterly, Corrected Proof, 23*(2), 249-266.

Reddick, C., & Frank, H. (2007). E-government and its influence on managerial effectiveness: A survey of Florida and Texas city managers. *Financial Accountability & Management*, *23*(1), 1–26. doi:10.1111/j.1468-0408.2007.00417.x

Rendleman, J. (2007). Navy CIO approves open-source software use. *Government Computer News*. Retrieved July 23, 2007, from http://www.gcn.com/print/26_14/44462-1.html

Rheingold, H. (2002). *Smart mobs: The next social revolution*. Cambridge, MA: Perseus Publishing.

Rhodes, R. (1996). The new governance: Governing without government. *Political Studies*, *44*(4), 652-667.

Riley (2005) E-Governanace Comes of Age in the Commonwealth, pp. 207-211.

Riley, T. B. (2007). Strategies for the effective implementation of E-Government projects. *Journal of Business and Public Policy*, *1*(1), 1-11.

Riley, T.B. (2001) "Electronic governance in context", Electronic Governance and Electronic Democracy: Living and Working in the Connected World, The Commonwealth Centre for Electronic Governance, Ottawa, available at: www.electronegov.net (accessed 7 August 2003).

Robbins, H. (1952). Some aspects of the sequential design of experiments. *Bulletin American Mathematical Society, 55*, 527-535.

Robinson, E. (2005). *Councillors' Websites: an analysis. Local e-Democracy National Project*. Retrieved, March 8, from, http://www.icele.org/downloads/Councillorswebsitesedit.pdf

Rocheleau, B. (1997). Governmental information systems problems and failures: a preliminary review. Public Administration and Management: An Interactive Journal, 2(3).

Rocheleau, B. (2003). Politics, Accountability, and Governmental Information Systems. In G. D. Garson (Ed.), *Public Information Technology: Policy and Management Issues* (pp. 20-52). Hershey, PA: Idea Group Publishing.

Rodriguez, H., Trainor, J., & Quarantelli, E. L. (2006). Rising to the challenges of a catastrophe: the emergent and prosocial behavior following Hurricane Katrina. *The Annals of the American Academy of Political and Social Science*, *604*(1), 82–101. doi:10.1177/0002716205284677

Rojas Mix, Miguel (2003). "El imaginario nacional en las repúblicas latinoamericanas del siglo XIX". Retrieved from: http://bv.gva.es/documentos/Rojas.doc

Rojas, E. (1999, May-August). Las instituciones de formación profesional frente a desafíos teóricos inéditos. *Boletín CINTERFOR, 146*,

Rose, J. & Lewis, P. (2001). Structuration theory, action research, and information systems development. In L. Russo, B. Fitzgerald & J.I. DeGross (Eds.). *Realigning Research and Practice in Information Systems Development: The Social and Organizational Perspective*. Boston: Kluwer Academic Publishers.

Ross, J. W., Beath, C. M., & Goodhue, D. L. (1998). Develop long-term competitiveness through it assets. *Sloan Management Review, 38*(1), 31-43.

Rossel, P., Finger, M., & Misuraca, G. (2006). "Mobile" e-Government Options: Between Technology-driven and Usercentric. *The Electronic. Journal of E-Government, 4*, 79–86.

Roy, J. (2007). E-Government in Canada: Transition or Transformation? In D. F. Norris (Ed.), *Current Issues and Trends in E-Government Research* (pp. 44-67). Hershey, PA: CyberTech Publishing.

Ruby, Ruby on rails and Drupal, what is the difference? (2007). Retrieved July 23, 2007, from http://groups.drupal.org/node/2176

Rui, Y., Huang, T., & Chang, S. (1999). Image retrieval: Current techniques, promising directions and open issues. *Journal of Visual Communication and Image Representation, 10*(4), 39-62.

Rutgers-SKKU. (2005). *E-Governance Performance Report*. Retrieved April 23, 2008, from http://andromeda.rutgers.edu/~egovinst/Website/press2005.htm

Rutherford, M. (1999). *Institutions in economics. The old and the new institutionalism*. New York: Cambridge University Press.

Ruyter, K. D., & Scholl, N. (1998). Positioning qualitative market research: Reflections from theory and practice. *Qualitative Market Research: An International Journal, 1*(1), 7-14.

Rwanda Information Technology Authority, RITA. (2000). *Strategies towards the achievement of the missions for the realization of the vision for Rwanda by RITA*. Retrieved January 26, 2006, from http://www.rita.gov.rw/about/about_strategie.html

Rydin, Y., & Pennington, M. (2000). Public participation and local environmental planning: The collective action problem and the potential of social capital. *Local Environment, 5*(2), 153-169.

Sackmary, Benjamin y Scalia, Lynne (1999). "Cultural patterns of WWW business sites: A comparison of Mexican and USA companies". Retrieved from: http://marketing.byu.edu/htmlpages/ccrs/proceedings99/sackmary.htm

Sagawa, S., & Segal, E. (2000). *Common interest common good: Creating value through business and social sector partnerships*. Boston, M.A: Harvard Business School Press.

Sahay, S., & Walsham, G. (1997). Social structures & management agency in India. *Organisation Studies, 18*, 415-444.

Saint-Onge, H., Wallace, D. (2003). *Leveraging communities of practice for strategic advantage*. Boston: Butterworth-Heinemann.

Salton, G., & McGill, M. (1983). *Introduction to modern information retrieval*. McGraw-Hill.

Sánchez Ovcharóv, S. (2004). *Qué es el data mining*. Data Mining Institute. Retrieved March 15, 2007, from http://www.estadistico.com/arts.html?20010219

Sánchez Ruiz., Enrique (2000). "Televisión, cultura política, autoritarismo y violencia: La formación ciudadana de todos los días". *Razón y Palabra*, 17, Febrero-Abril. Retrieved from: http://www.cem.itesm.mx/dacs/publicaciones/logos/anteriores/n17/17ssanchez.html

Sandy, H. (2002). E-*government in the Arab world: Between reality and ambition*. Retrieved May 3, 2007, from http://unpan1.un.org/intradoc/groups/public/documents/ARADO/UNPAN005603.pps

Sannarnes, M. K., Henriksen, H. Z., & Andersen, K.V. (2006). The E-Government melting pot: Lacking new public management and innovation flavor? In M.A. Wimer, H.J. Scholl, A. Gröndlund, and K.V. Andersend (Eds.), *Proceedings of Electronic Government: 5th International Conference, EGOV 2006, Krakow, Poland, September 4-8, 2006* (pp.25-36). Heidelberg: Springer Berlin.

Santamaría Glez, F. (2006). La Web 2.0: caracterísiticas, implicancias en el entorno educativo y algunas de sus herramientas, Seminario Internacional Virtual Educa Cono Sur, Buenos Aires. Retrieved March 15, 2007, from http://www.iesevevirtual.edu.ar/virtualeduca/ponencias2006/La%20Web20_Santamaria.pdf

Santos, E., Jr., Santos, E., Nguyen, H., Pan, L., & Korah, J. (2005). Large-scale distributed foraging, gathering, and matching for information retrieval: Assisting the geospatial intelligent analyst. In *Proceedings of the SPIE* (Vol. 5803, pp. 66-77).

Santos, E., Jr., Santos, E., Nguyen, H., Pan, L., Korah, J., Zhao, Q., et al. I-FGM information retrieval in highly dynamic search spaces. In *Proceedings of SPIE* (Vol. 6229, pp. 1-12).

Santos, E., Jr., Santos, E., Nguyen, H., Pan, L., Korah, J., Zhao, Q., et al. (2007). Applying I-FGM to image retrieval and an I-FGM system performance analyses. In *Proceedings of the SPIE: Defense \& Security Symposium* (Vol. 6560), Orlando, FL.

Saorín Pérez, T. (2002). Modelo conceptual para la automatización de bibliotecas en el contexto digital (Doctoral dissertation, School of Information and Data Sciences, University of Murcia, 2002).

Sargent, G. & McLvor, J. (1996) Public access information: A prototype web Kiosk, Managing Information, 3(4), 32-35.

Sarikas, O. D., & Weerakkody, V. (2007). Realising integrated E-Government services: A UK local government perspective. *Transforming Government: People, Process and Policy, 1*(2). Emerald

Saunders, M., Lewis, P., & Thornhill, A. (2002). Research methods for business students, 3rd Edition, London: Prentice Hall.

Sauter, R., & Watson, J. (2008) Technology leapfrogging: A review of the evidence. A report for DFID. Brighton, UK: Sussex Energy Group. Retrieved February 15, 2009, from http://www.dfid.gov.uk/pubs/files/DFIDLeapfroggingReportWeb.pdf.

Saxena, A., & Wadhwa, S. (2004). E-business perspective of e-governance. In M. P. Gupta (Ed.), *Promise of e-governance*. New Delhi: Tata McGraw Hill.

Saxena, K. B. C. (2005) Towards excellence in e-governance, International Journal of Public Sector Management, Vol. 18 No. 6, pp. 498-513.

Scharmer, C. O. (1996, February 23). Knowledge has to do with truth, goodness, and beauty. Conversation with professor Ikujiro Nonaka. *Dialog on Leadership*, Tokyo, Japan. Retrieved March 15, 2007, from http://www.dialogonleadership.org/Nonaka-1996.pdf

Scheela, W., & Van Dinh, N. (2004). Venture capital in a transition economy: the case of Vietnam. *Venture Capital - An international journal of entrepreneurial finance, 6*(4), 333-350.

Schelin, S. H. (2003). E-Government: An Overview. In G. D. Garson (Ed.), *Public Information Technology: Policy and Management Issues* (pp. 120-137). Hershey, PA: Idea Group Publishing.

Schellong, A. (2007). *Extending the Technology Enactment Framework*. Boston, MA: Harvard University, Kennedy School of Government, Program on Networked Governance, Working Paper No. PNG07-003.

Schneider, M., & Teske, P. (1994). The bureaucratic entrepreneur: The case of city managers. *Public Administration Review, 54*(4), 331–340. doi:10.2307/977380

Scholl, H. (2002). *Current practices in E-Government-induced business process change (BPC): An empirical study of Current Practices*, 1(2), 27-49.

Scholl, H. (2005) Interoperability in e-government: More than just smart middleware. In *Proceedings of the 38th Annual Hawaii International Conference on System Sciences (HICSS'05) - Track 5 - Volume 05*. Washington, DC: IEEE Computer Society. Retrieved February 15, 2009, from http://portal.acm.org

Scholl, H. (2005). Organizational transformation through E-Government: Myth or reality? *Lecture Notes in Computer Science, LNCS 3591/2005*, 1-11, Springer.

Scholl, H. J. (2002). *Executive Briefing on Electronic Government and Business Process Change*. Albany, NY: Center for Technology in Government.

Scholl, H. J., Fidel, R., Liua, S., Paulsmeyer, M., & Unsworth, K. (2007). E-government field force automation: Promises, challenges, and stakeholders. In M. A.Wimmer, J. Scholl, & A. Grönlund (Eds.), *Electronic Government. 6th International Conference, EGOV 2007 Regensburg, Germany, September 3-7, 2007 Proceedings*. Berlin: Springer-Verlag.

Scholl, H., & Klischewski, R. (2007). E-government integration and interoperability: framing the research agenda. *International Journal of Public Administration, 30*(8), 889–920. doi:10.1080/01900690701402668

Scott, J. (2006). "E" the people: Do U.S. municipal government web sites support public involvement? *Public Administration Review, 66*(3), 341–353. doi:10.1111/j.1540-6210.2006.00593.x

Scott, W. R. (2001). *Institutions and organizations* (2nd ed.). Thousand Oaks, CA: Sage.

Seaborne, A. (2004). *RDQL—A query language for RDF.* Retrieved December 4, 2006, from http://www.w3.org/Submission/RDQL/

Sealy, W.U. (2003) 'Empowering development through e-governance: creating smart communities in small island states', International Information & Library Review, Vol. 35, No. 2, pp.335–358.

Searle, J. (1969). *Speech acts: An essay in the philosophy of language.* London: Cambridge University Press.

Sears, Andrew; Jacko, Julie; y Dubach, Erica (2000). "International aspects of World Wide Web usability and the role of high-end graphical enhancements". *International Journal of Human-Computer Interaction,* Vol. 12, Issue 2. Retrieved from: http://www.leaonline.com/doi/abs/10.1207%2FS15327590IJHC1202_5

Seifert, J., & Petersen, E. (2002). The promise of all things E: Expectations and challenges of emergent electronic government. *Perspectives on Global Development and Technology, 1*(2). 193-213.

Selden, C. S., Brewer, G., & Brudney, J. (1999). The role of city managers: Are they principals, agents, or both? *American Review of Public Administration, 29*(2), 124–148. doi:10.1177/02750749922064319

Serrao, S. A., & Sujatha, B. R. (2004). *Birth registration: A background note.* Bangalore, India: Community Development Foundation. Retrieved January 28, 2007, from http://www.ilpnet.org/news/BRWorkshop/BirthRegistration_Background.pdf

Servicio Público de Empleo Estatal. *Servicio de Observatorio Ocupacional. (2004). Incidencia de la Sociedad de la Información en el mercado de trabajo. Ocupaciones afectadas por las nuevas formas de trabajo.* Madrid:

Sethi, N. and Sethi, V. (2006) Public-Private-People Partnerships in E-government: A case study of Singapore Tracks, Fourth International Conference on Electronic Governance.

Shackleton, P., Fisher, J., & Dawson, L. (2006). E-government services in the local government context: An Australian case study. *Business Process Management Journal, 12*(1), 88–100. doi:10.1108/14637150610643788

Sharma, K. S., & Palvia, S. (2004). Organizational and cultural barriers to e-governance implementation in India. In M. P. Gupta (Ed.). *Towards e-governance.* New Delhi: Tata McGraw Hill.

Sheppard, Charles y Scholtz, Jean (1999). "The Effects of Cultural Markers on Web Site" Paper presented at Proceedings of the Fifth Conference on Human Factors & the Web, Gaithesburg, Maryland. Retrieved from: http://zing.ncsl.nist.gov/hfweb/proceedings/sheppard/index

Sienkiewicz, Z. J., & Kowalczuk, C. I. (2005). *A summary of recent reports on mobile phones and health (2000-2004).* NRPB-W65. National Radiological Protection Board, U.K.

Silverman, D. (2000). *Doing qualitative research: A practical handbook.* London: Sage Publications.

Simon, Steven J. (1999). "A Cross Cultural Analysis of Web Site Design: An Empirical Study of Global Web Users" Paper Presented at the Seventh Cross-Cultural Consumer Business Studies Research Conference, Cancun, Mexico. Retrieved from: http://marketing.byu.edu/htmlpages/ccrs/proceedings99/simon.htm

Singh, A. (2005). Sidestepping pitfalls. Data-Quest, May 21, 2005. Retrieved August 29, 2008 from http://www.dqindia.com/content/egovernance/2005/105052101.asp

Singh, Nitish (2000). "Analyzing Cultural Sensitivity of Websites: A Normative Framework". Journal of Practical Global Business. Retrieved from: http://iiei.edu/journal/Jour_2/journalv1_p32.pdf

Singh, Nitish; Kumar, Vikas; y Baack, Daniel (2005). "Adaptation of cultural content: evidence from B2C ecommerce firms" *European Journal of Marketing,* Vol. 39, Issue 1/2. Emerald Group Publishing Limited. Retrieved from: http://www.emeraldinsight.com/Insight/viewPDF.jsp?Filename=html/Output/Published/EmeraldFullTextArticle/Pdf/0070390105.pdf

Singh, V. S. (2002). *SETU: A citizen facilitation center in India. E-government for development information exchange*. University of Manchester: IDPM. Retrieved February 2, 2007, from http://www.egov4dev.org/setu.htm

Singla, M. L. (2002) E-Governance- Transforming the National Bone Marrow, Journal of Management Research, Vol. 2, No. 3, 165-175

Sirin, E., Parsai, B., Grau, B. C., Kalyanpur, A., & Katz, Y. (n.d.). *Pellet: A practical OWL-DL reasoner*. Retrieved December 4, 2006, from http://mindswap.org/papers/PelletJWS.pdf

Smeulders, A. W. M., Worring, M., Santini, S., Gupta, A., & Jain, R. (2000). Content-based image retrieval at the end of the early years. *IEEE Transactions on Pattern Analysis and Machine Intelligence, 22*(12), 1349-1380.

Snellen, I. TH. M., & Van Der Donk, W. B. H. J. (Eds.). (1998). *Public administration in an information age, a handbook*. Amsterdam: IOS Press.

Snyder, W. M., & Wenger, E. (2003). *Communities of practice in government the case for sponsorship*. (Report to the CIO Council of the U.S. Federal Government). Retrieved March 15, 2007, from http://www.ewenger.com/pub/pubusfedciodownload.htm

Søndergaard, Mikael (n.d.). "In my opinion". Opinion Article, European Business Forum. Retrieved from: http://geert-hofstede.international-business-center.com/Sondergaard.shtml

Souza, C. (2001). Participatory budgeting in Brazilian cities: Limits and possibilities in building democratic institutions. *Environment & Urbanization, 13*(1).

Special Committee for E-government. (2003). Korea's e-government: Completion of e-government framework: Special Committee for E-government, Republic of Korea.

Srinivasan, J (2004) Sustainable Access in Rural India (SARI) project-Madurai, Tamilnadu, www.iiitb.ac.in/ICTforD/SARI%20final.pdf accessed during October 2005.

Stake, R. E. (2000). *The art of case study research*. Thousand Oaks, CA: Sage Publications.

State Services Commission. (2007). *New Zealand e-government interoperability framework*. Retrieved from http://www.e.govt.nz.

Stengers, Hélene ; De Troyer, Olga ; Mushtaha, Abdalghani; Baetens, Martine ; y Boers, Frank. (2004). "Localization of Web Sites: Is there still a need for it?". Retrieved from: http://www.ht04.org/workshops/WebEngineering/HT04WE_Stengers.pdf

Stensgaard, A. (2005). *International case studies*. In *Proceedings of the 11th GCC e-Government Forumin Dubai*.

Stevens, L. (2007, February). *The in and out of SOA*. Retrieved April 20, 2007, from http://www.fedtechmagazine.com/article.asp?item_id=257

Steyaert, J. C. (2004). Measuring the performance of electronic government services. *Information & Management, 41*(3), 369–375. doi:10.1016/S0378-7206(03)00025-9

Stoker, G. (1998). Governance as a theory: Five propositions. *International Social Science Journal, 50*(155), 17-28.

Stoker, G. (2000). Urban political science and the challenge of urban governance. In J. Pierre (Ed.), *Debating governance: Authority, steering and democracy*. Oxford: Oxford University Press.

Stone, P. (2000). Tpot-rl applied to network routing. In *Proceedings of the 17th International Conference on Machine Learning*.

Stowers, G. (2004). *Measuring the Performance in E-Government*. Washington, DC: IBM Center for the Business of Government.

Streib, G. (2005). Quantifying the knowledge of public management professionals: Developing an assessment tool for local government managers. *Public Performance & Management Review, 28*(3), 418–436.

Streib, G., & Navarro, I. A. (2006). Citizen demand for interactive e-government: The case of Georgia consumer services. *American Review of Public Administration, 36*(3), 288–300. doi:10.1177/0275074005283371

Student Loan Company (2006). Student support for higher education in England. *Academic Year 2006/07 (Provisional), Student Load Company,* ww.slc.co.uk/pdf/slcsfr032006.pdf

Sun, Huatong (2001). "Building a Culturally Competent Corporate Web Site: An Exploratory Study of Cultural Markers in Multilingual Web Design". Paper presented at Proceedings of SIGDOC 2001. Retrieved from: http://faculty.gvsu.edu/sunh/resch/acm01.pdf

Suri P.K. (2005) NICNET based Agricultural Marketing Information Network - A Farmers Centric Portal on Agricultural Marketing in India and a Step towards Globalizing Indian Agriculture, Agricultural Marketing Journal, XLV(4) January-March.

Sutton, R. S., & Barto, A.G. (1998). *Reinforcement learning: An Introduction*. Cambridge, MA: MIT Press/Bradford Books.

Svara, J. (1998). The politics-administration dichotomy model as aberration. *Public Administration Review, 58*(1), 51–58. doi:10.2307/976889

Svara, J. (2003). Effective mayoral leadership in council-manager cities: Reassessing the facilitative model. *National Civic Review, 92*(2), 157–172. doi:10.1002/ncr.14

Svara, J., et al. (1994). *Facilitative leadership in local government: Lessons from successful mayors and chairpersons*. San Francisco: Jossey-Bass Publishers.

Symonds, M. (2000) "A survey of government and the internet", The Economist, Vol. 355 No. 8176, pp. S3-S5.

Tan C.W., Shan L., Pan S.L. and Lim E.T.K. (2005) Managing Stakeholder Interests in e-Government Implementation: Lessons Learned from a Singapore e-Government Project, Journal of Global Information Management 13(1), 1-30, Jan-March.

Tan, C. W., & Pan, S.L. (2003). Managing e-transformation in the public sector: An e-government study of the inland revenue authority of Singapore (IRAS). *European Journal of Information Systems archive, 12*(4), 269-281.

Tao, N., Baxter, J., & Weaver, L. (2001). A multi-agent, policy-gradient approach to network routing. In *Proceedings of the 18th International Conference on Machine Learning.*

Tapscott, Mark (2004). "Internet Revolution is Forcing Transparency". Center for Media and Public Policy, Heritage Foundation. Retrieved from: http://www.developmentgateway.org/egovernment/rc/ItemDetail.do~1024669

Tassey, G. (2000). Standardization in technology-based markets. *Research Policy, 29*(4-5), 587–602. doi:10.1016/S0048-7333(99)00091-8

Tat-Kei Ho, A. (2002). Reinventing local governments and the E-Government initiative. *Public Administration Review, 62*(4), 410-420.

Technology CEO Council. (2002). The CSPP readiness guide: For living in the networked world. Retrieved April 24, 2008, from http://www.techceocouncil.org/documents/NW_Readiness_Guide.pdf

Teitelbaum, J. (2002). Dueling for Da'wa: State vs. society on the Saudi Internet. *Middle East Journal.*

Tesoro, J. L. (2003, February). La probidad, el civismo y la equidad como determinantes básicos del desempeño del gobierno electrónico. *Revista Probidad, 21*. Retrieved March 15, 2007, from http://www.revistaprobidad.info/021/002.html

Tesoro, J. L. (2004). *El gobierno electrónico en la argentina: indagación comparativa y apreciación estratégica*. Retrieved March 15, 2007, from http://www.infoleg.gov.ar/basehome/noticias/Tesoro_16-01-04.htm

The World Bank. (2007). *Definition of e-government*. Retrieved May 24, 2007, from http://go.worldbank.org/M1JHE0Z280

Thomas, J., & Streib, G. (2003). The new face of government: Citizen-initiated contacts in the era of e-government. *Journal of Public Administration: Research and Theory, 13*(1), 83–102. doi:10.1093/jpart/mug010

Thomas, J., & Streib, G. (2005). E-democracy, e-commerce, and e-research: Examining the electronic ties between citizens and governments. *Administration & Society, 37*(3), 259–280. doi:10.1177/0095399704273212

Thorleifsdottir, A., Paskaleva-Shapira, K., Forseback, L., Tzovaras, D., Christodoulou, E., & Schnepf, D. (2004). *Best practices in e-governance*. ('IntelCities' Project Report D15.2.2). Retrieved from 'IntelCities' Project official web site: http://www.intelcitiesproject.com

TI (2004). "Índice de percepción de la corrupción". Transparencia Internacional América Latina y el Caribe (TILAC), Transparencia Internacional (TI). Retrieved from: http://www.transparency.org/policy_research/surveys_indices/cpi/2004

Tierney, K. J., & Trainor, J. (2004). *Networks and resilience in the World Trade Center disaster*. Buffalo, New York: Multidisciplinary Center for Earthquake Engineering Research.

Tiku, K. M. (2004). *E-setu brings digital opportunities to Majuli helps island emerge out of time warp*. New Delhi: UNDP India News. Retrieved March 3, 2007, from http://209.85.165.104/search?q=cache:sDjuGxtf8rAJ:www.undp.org.in/UNDPNEWS/Jan-04/j-pg02.htm+undp+india+news+e-setu&hl=en&gl=us&ct=clnk&cd=1&client=firefox-a

Timmers, P. (2004). *European Commission perspectives on E-Government* [PowerPoint slides]. Presentation at IntelCities project kickoff meeting, 12 March, Brussels. Retrieved from 'IntelCities' Project official web site: http://www.intelcitiesproject.com

Tolbert, C., & Mossberger, K. (2003). The effects of e-government on trust and confidence in government. *Public Administration Review, 66*(3), 354–369. doi:10.1111/j.1540-6210.2006.00594.x

Toyama, K., K. Kiri, M. Lakshmi Ratan, A. Nileshwar, R. Vedashree, R. F. MacGregor. (2005) Rural Kiosks in India, Microsoft Research Technical Report, MSR-TR-2004-146.

Trahant, B. (2007). Debunking five myths concerning employee engagement. *Public Management, 36*(1), 53–59.

Traunmüller, R. (Ed.). (2004). *Electronic government: Third International Conference, EGOV 2004, Zaragoza, Spain, August 30-September 3, 2004, Proceedings*. Linz: Sprinter.

Trouvé, A. T., & García Acosta, A. (2004, November 2-6). Proyecto Padrinazgo de Publicaciones Periódicas Argentinas (4P-AR): reconocimiento de las competencias desplegadas en el trabajo en redes. *IXº Congreso Internacional del CLAD sobre la Reforma del Estado y de la Administración Pública*, Madrid, Spain.

Tsagarousianou, R., Tambini, D. & Bryan, C. (1998). *Cyberdemocracy: Technology, Cities and Civic Networks*. London: Routledge.

Tsikriktsis, Nikos (2002). "Does culture influence web site quality expectations? An empirical study", *Journal of Service Research*, Vol. 5 No.2. Retrieved from: http://jsr.sagepub.com/cgi/content/abstract/5/2/101

Tsymbalenko, Y., & Munson, E. V. (2001). *Using HTML metadata to find relevant images on the Web*. Paper presented at the Internet Computing, Las Vegas, NV.

Tulip, S. (2000) 'Local launch pad', Supply Management, Vol. 5, No. 16, pp.34, 35.

Tung, L. L. & Tan, J. H., (1998) Model for the classification of Information Kiosks in Singapore, International Journal of Information Systems, Vol. 18, No. 4, 255-264.

U.S. Department of Defense (DoD). (2007). *DoD directive 3000.05, Military support for stability, security, transition, and reconstruction (SSTR) operations*. Retrieved July 23, 2007, from http://www.dtic.mil/whs/directives/corres/html/300005.htm

U.S. Department of Education. (2005). *EDGAR version*. Retrieved June 23, 2005, from http://www.ed.gov/index.jhtml?src=a

U.S. Department of Homeland Security. (2007). *National response plan*. Retrieved July 23, 2007, from http://www.dhs.gov/xprepresp/publications

UN (2004). *Towards access for opportunity. Global E-Government Readiness Report 2004*. New York: United Nations, Department for Economic and Social Affairs, Division for Public Administration and Development Management. Retrieved December 29, 2005, from www.unpan.org/eGov4.asp

UN (2005). *World public sector report: Global E-government Readiness: From E-Government to E-Inclusion*. United Nations, New York.

UN. (2005). Global e-government readiness report 2005. Towards access for opportunity. New York: United Nations, Department for Economic and Social Affairs, Division for Public Administration and Development Management. Retrieved December 29, 2007, from http://www.unpan.org/egovernment4.asp

UNDESA (2003) *e-Government at the Crossroads. World Public Sector Report 2003*. United Nations Department of Economic and Social Affairs. United Nations, New York. Retrieved December 29, 2005, from www.un.org/esa/desa/desaNews/desa94.html

UNDESA. (2003). *World public sector report 2003: E-government at the crossroads*. New York: United Nations.

UNDESA. (2005). *Global e-governance readiness report*. New York: United Nations. Retrieved March 3, 2007, from http://www.lidec.futuro.usp.br/downloads/egovUN.pdf

UNDP (2004). *Final evaluation report on sustainable development networking programme*. Retrieved January 28, 2006, from http://sdnhq.undp.org/docs/evals/SDNP-assessment-report-Final.pdf

UNDP (2005). *Global E-Government E-Readiness Report 2005: From E-Government to E-Inclusion*. Department of Economic and Social Affairs, United Nations. Retrieved from:: http://www.unpan.org/egovernment5.asp

UNDP. (2003). *Project e-setu: reaching the unreached*. New Delhi: UNDP India. Retrieved January 25, 2006, from http://www.undp.org.in/events/ict-goa/e-setu15-16dec03goa.PPT

UNDP. (2004). *Assam human development report 2003*. New Delhi: UNDP India. Retrieved January 25, 2006, from http://hdr.undp.org/docs/reports/national/IND_India/INDIA_2003_en.pdf

UNHCHR. (1989). *Convention on the rights of the child*. Geneva: United Nations. Retrieved January 28, 2006, from http://www.unhchr.ch/html/menu3/b/k2crc.htm

United Nations and American Society for Public Administration (2002), Benchmarking E-Government: A Global Perspective, UN/ASPA, New York, NY.

United Nations Department of Economic and Social Affairs Report, World public sector report 2003: E-Government at the crossroads. New York, United Nations Publication, 2003.

United Nations. (2000). *Millennium development declaration*. Retrieved January 22, 2007, from http://www.un.org/millennium/declaration/ares552e.pdf

United Nations. (2005). *National profile for the information society in Saudi Arabia*. New York: United Nations Economic and Social Commission for Western Asia (ESCWA). Retrieved August 2, 2007, from http://www.escwa.org.lb/wsis/reports/docs/SaudiArabia_2005-E.pdf

United Nations/American Society for Public Administration (UN/ASPA). (2002). *Benchmarking e-government: a global perspective*. New York: United Nations/American Society for Public Administration.

United States Office of Management and Business (OMB). (2002, February 27). *Implementing the President's management agenda for e-government*. Retrieved January 19, 2007, from http://www.usa.gov/Topics/Includes/Reference/egov_strategy.pdf

Urbina, I. (2008, March 22). Hopes for wireless cities fade as Internet providers pull out. *The New York Times*, pp. A1, A10.

van Dam, Nik; Evers, Nik; y Arts, Florann A. (2005). "Cultural User Experience Issues in E-Government: Designing for a Multi-Cultural Society". *Lecture Notes in Computer Science*, Vol. 3081. Retrieved from: http://hcs.science.uva.nl/usr/evers/DamEversArts.pdf

Van de Donk, W.B.H.J., Snellen, I.M. & Tops, P.W. (1995). *Orwell in Athens: A Perspective on Informatization and Democracy*. Netherlands: IOS Press.

Van Den Berg, L., & Van Winden, W. (2002). *Information and communication technology as potential catalysis for sustainable urban development: Experiences in Eindhoven, Helsinki, Manchester, Marseilles and The Hage*. Aldershot: Ashgate Publishing Ltd.

Van Den Berg, L., Van Der Meer, I., & Pol, P. (2004). *Social challenges and organizing capacities in cities: Experiences in eight European cities*. Aldershot: Ashgate Publishing Ltd.

Van Der Meer, L., & Van Winden, W. (2003). E-governance in cities: A comparison of urban ICT policies. *Regional Studies, 37*(4), 407-419.

van Deursen, A., van Dijk, J., & Ebbers, W. (2006). *Why e-government usage lags behind: Explaining the gap between potential and actual usage of electronic public services in the Netherlands* (LNCS, pp. 269-280). Berlin: Springer, Heidelberg.

Vapnik, V. (1999). *The nature of statistical learning theory* (2nd ed.). Springer Verlag.

Vega, Hannia (2002). "La comunicación de gobierno en Internet". In *Estrategias de Comunicación para Gobiernos*, de Izurieta, Z., Perina, R., y Arteton, C. (Editores); La Crujía Ediciones, Buenos Aires

Veltkamp, R. C., & Tanase, M. (2000). *Content-based image retrieval systems: A survey* (Tech. Rep. No. UU-CS-2000-34). The Netherlands: Utrecht University, Department of Computer Science.

Verón, Eliseo (1971). "Ideología y comunicación de masas: La semantización de la violencia política". Nueva Visión, Buenos Aires. Retrieved from: http://www.nombrefalso.com.ar/apuntes/pdf/veron.pdf

Verón, Eliseo (1985). "La palabra adversativa: Observaciones sobre la enunciación política". In *El discurso político: lenguajes y acontecimientos*. Editorial Hachette, Buenos Aires.

Verón, Eliseo (2004). *Fragmentos de un tejido*; Colección "El mamífero parlante". Editorial Gedisa, Barcelona.

Verva (2007) *Utgå från målgruppernas behov.* Retrieved February 1, 2008, from http://www.verva.se/verksamhetsstod/webb/vl24/2006/2/1/3/

Victor, Stephen P. (n.d.). "Information Architecture and the Construction of Ideology: A Proposal for a Qualitative Study of a School District's Web Pages". College of Education, University of Houston Houston. Retrieved from: http://itech1.coe.uga.edu/itforum/paper59/paper59.htm

Vittal, N. (n.d.). *Change management and process re-engineering.* Paper presented in the CII e-governance summit, September 21, 2001, New Delhi. Retrieved May 30, 2006 from http:/

Vizer, Eduardo A. (2003). *La trama (in)visible de la vida social. Comunicación, sentido y realidad.* Ediciones La Crujía, Buenos Aires.

Walker, D. M. (2001). *E-government in the information age: The long view.* Retrieved May 3, 2007, from http://www.gao.gov/cghome/ia/sld008.htm

Walsham, G. (1997). Actor-network theory and IS research: current status and future prospects. In Lee, A., S., Liebenau, J., and DeGross, J., I. (eds.). *Information Systems and Qualitative Research.* London: Chapman & Hall.

Wang, J. Z., Li, J., & Wiederhold, G. (2001). SIMPLIcity: Semantics-sensitive integrated matching for picture libraries. *IEEE Transactions on Pattern Analysis and Machine Intelligence, 23*(9), 947-963.

Ward, J., & Peppard, J. (2002). *Strategic planning for information systems.* New York: John Wiley & Sons, LTD.

Wassenaar, A. (2000). E-Governmental value chain models. DEXA, IEEE Press, 289-293.

Weerakkody, V. J. P., & Hinton, C. M. (1999). Exploiting information systems & technology through business process improvement. *Knowledge and Process Management: The Journal Of Corporate Transformation, 6*(1). UK: John Wiley & Sons, Ltd..

Weerakkody, V., & Currie, W. (2003). Integrating business process reengineering with information systems development: Issues & implications. *Lecture Notes in Computer Science, LNCS 2678*, 302-320. Springer.

Weerakkody, V., Baire, S., & Choudrie, J. (2006, January). E-Government: A case for process improvement in the public sector. *Hawaii International Conference on Systems Sciences (Hicss-39).*

Weerakkody, V., Janssen, M., & Hjort-Madsen, K. (2007). Realising integrated E-Government services: A european perspective. *Journal of Cases in Electronic Commerce,* 3(2), 14-38. Idea Group, ISSN 1548-0623.

Welch, E. W., & Pandey, S. K. (2007). E-government and bureaucracy: Toward a better understanding of intranet implementation and its effects on red tape. *Journal of Public Administration: Research and Theory, 17*(3), 379–404. doi:10.1093/jopart/mul013

Wenger, E. (1998). *Communities of practice. learning, meaning and identity.* New York: Cambridge University Press.

Wenger, E. (2000). Communities of practice and social learning systems. *Organization Articles, 7.*

Wenger, E. (2001). Comunidades de práctica: aprendizaje, significado e identidad. *Cognición y Desarrollo Humano*, 38.

Wenger, E., McDermott, R., & Snyder, W. (2002). *Cultivating communities of practice.* Boston: Harvard Business School Publishing.

West, D. (2004). E-government and the transformation of service delivery and citizen attitudes. *Public Administration Review, 64*(1), 15–27. doi:10.1111/j.1540-6210.2004.00343.x

West, D. (2005). *Global e-government 2005.* Providence, RI: Brown University.

West, D. M. (2003). *Global E-Government*, http://www.insidepolitics.org/egovt03int.pdf; (visited August December 29, 2005)

West, D. M. (2004). E-government and the transformation of service delivery and citizen attitudes. *Public Administration Review, 64*(1), 15-27.

Westley F., & Mintzberg, H. (1989). Visionary leadership and strategic management, Strategic Management Journal, 10(summer), 17-32

What is e-government? (n.d.). Retrieved January 19, 2007, from http://www.wisegeek.com/what-is-e-government.htm

What is Jabber? (2007). Retrieved July 23, 2007, from http://www.jabber.org/about/overview.shtml

Whitaker, G., Henderson, M., & Altman-Sauer, L. (2004). Collaboration: Calls for mutual accountability. *Public Management, 86*(11), 16–20.

Whitman, M., & Woszczynski, A. (2004). The handbook of information systems research. Hershey: Idea group publishing.

Wiesner Salamanca, Santiago (n.d.). "Internet: ¿Cómo se dice / cómo se usa?". Research Paper, Project "Usos de las nuevas tecnologías de comunicación e información para la construcción de la paz en Colombia", Facultad de Comunicación Social para la Paz de la Universidad Santo Tomás- Facultad de Humanidades de la Pontificia Universidad Javeriana. Retrieved from: http://www.colnodo.apc.org/aa/img_upload/13e08f09d1591809155e45a9932c599f/WIESNER.pdf

Wilhelm, A. (2005). *Digital nation: Towards an inclusive information society.* MIT Press, 133-134.

Willcocks, L. (1995). False promise or delivering the goods? Recent findings on the economics and impact of business process reengineering. *Proceedings of The 2nd European Conference On IT Investment Evaluation.* UK

Williams, M. (2009). Governments use Twitter for emergency alerts, traffic notices and more. *Government Technology.* Retrieved February 15, 2009, from http://www.govtech.com/gt/579338?topic=117680.

Williams, R. (1997). Universal solutions or local contingencies: tensions and contradictions in the mutual shaping of technology and work organization. In I. Mcloughlin & D. Mason (Eds.), *Innovation organizational change and technology* (pp. 170-185). London: International Thompson Business Press.

Williams, R., Bunduchi, R., Gerst, M., Graham, I., Pollock, N., Procter, R., & Voß, A. (2004). Understanding the evolution of standards: alignment and reconfiguration in standards development and implementation arenas. In *Proceedings of the 4S & EASST Conference. Paris.*

Wilson, W. (1887). The study of an administration. *Political Science Quarterly, 2*(2), 197–222. doi:10.2307/2139277

Wimmer, M. (2004). A European perspective towards online one-stop government: The eGov project. *Electronic Commerce Research and Applications*, 92-103.

Wimmer, M., & Traunmuller, R. (2000). Trends in electronic government: Managing distributed knowledge. *Proceedings from 11th International Workshop on Database and Expert Systems Applications*, 340-345. New York: Springer.

Winner, Langdom (1987). *La ballena y el reactor* Editorial Gedisa, Barcelona.

Witten, I. H., & Frank, E. (2005, June). *Data mining: Practical machine learning tools and techniques* (2nd ed.). Morgan Kaufmann.

Wolton, Dominique (2000). *Internet, ¿y después? Una teoría crítica de los nuevos medios de comunicación.* Editorial Gedisa, Barcelona.

Wood, D., & Gray., B. (1991). Toward a comprehensive theory of collaboration. *Journal of Applied Behavioral Science, 27*(1), 139-162.

Woodrow, E., & Heinzelman, W. (2001). *SPIN-IT: A data centric routing protocol for image retrieval in wireless networks.* Retrieved November 20, 2003, from http://www.ece.rochester.edu/~wheinzel/GroupWeb/papers/spin-it_icip02.pdf

World Bank (2001) Working Group on e-Governance, Discussion Forum, The World Bank, Washington, DC.

World Bank (2004) *World Bank E-Government.* Retrieved December 29, 2005, from http://www1.worldbank.org/publicsector/egov/

World Bank. (2003). *World development report 2004: Making services work for poor people*. Washington, DC: World Bank. Retrieved Fabruary 3, 2007, from http://econ.worldbank.org/external/default/main?menuPK=477704&pagePK=64167702&piPK=64167676&theSitePK=477688

World Economic Forum. (2007). *Global competitiveness report 2007-2008.* Houndmills, Baingstoke, Hampshire: Macmillan Publishers Limited.

Xavier, M. J. & Pillai, R. P. (2003) Indian Experience in G2C Service Delivery Models: Select Case Studies and Lessons for Future Developments, International Conference on Electronic governance, New Delhi, 32-41.

Yang, K. (2003). Neoinstitutionalism and e-government: Beyond Jane Fountain. *Social Science Computer Review*, *21*(4),432–442. doi:10.1177/0894439303256508

Yildiz, M. (2007). E-government research: reviewing the literature, limitations, and ways forward. *Government Information Quarterly*, *24*(3), 646–665. doi:10.1016/j.giq.2007.01.002

Yin, R. K. (2003). *Case study research: Design and methods*, 3rd Edition. London: Sage Publications.

Young J.S.L (2003) E-Government in Asia: Enabling Public Service Innovation in the 21st Century, Times Media, Singapore.

Zahedi, Fatemeh; van Pelt, William; y Song, Jaeki (2001). "A conceptual framework for international web design". *IEEE Transactions on Professional Communication*, Vol. 44, Issue 2. Retrieved from: http://tc.primaryspaces.com/zahedi.pdf

Zahir, Sajjad; Dobing, Brian; y Hunter, Gordon (2002), "Cross-cultural dimensions of internet portals", *Internet Research: Electronic Networking Applications and Policy*, Vol. 12 N° 3. Retrieved from: http://www.emeraldinsight.com/Insight/ViewContentServlet?Filename=Published/EmeraldFullTextArticle/Articles/1720120301.html

Zhang, J., Jin, R., Yang, Y., & Hauptmann, A. G. (2003). Modified logistic regression: An approximation to SVM and its application in large-scale text categorization. In *Proceedings of the Twentieth International Conference on Machine Learning 2003,* Washington DC.

Zhang, M., & Wolff, R. S. (2004, February). Crossing the digital divide: Cost-effective broadband wireless access for rural and remote areas. *IEEE Communications Magazine*, 99–105. doi:10.1109/MCOM.2003.1267107

Zhang, T., Ramakrishnan, R., & Livny, M. (1996). *BIRCH: An efficient data clustering method for very large databases.* Paper presented at the ACM SIGMOD International Conference on Managment of Data, Montreal, Canada.

Zhao, Wenyong; Massey, Brian L.; Murphy, Jamie; y Fang, Liu (2003). "Cultural Dimensions of Website Design and Content". *Prometheus*, Vol. 21, N° 21. Carfax Publishing, Taylor and Francis Ltd. Retrieved from: http://web.biz.uwa.edu.au/staff/jmurphy/Cultural_Dimensions.pdf

Zhiyuan, F. (2002). E-Government in digital era: Concepts, practice and development. *International Journal of The Computer, The Internet and Management, 10*(2), 1-22.

Zhu, X., Sun, S., Cheng, S. E., & Bern, M. (2004). *Classification of protein crystallization imagery.* Paper presented at the 26th Annual International Conference of IEEE Engineering in Medicine and Biology Society, San Francisco.

Zimmermann, W. (2005). 'eStrategy' for E-Government in cities: An introduction. *UMP-Asia Occasional* (Article No. 62). Retrieved April 24, 2008, from http://www.serd.ait.ac.th/ump/OP%20Dr.%20Willie%20ed%20vers%202005%20from%20GS.pdf

Zipf, M. (2001) 'E-government', Deutschland, Vol. 3, pp.62–65.

Zouridis, S., & Thaens, M. (2003). E-government: Towards a public administration approach. *The Asian Journal of Public Administration*, *25*(2), 159–183.

Zuboff, S. (1988). *In the Age of the Smart Machine*. New York: Basic Books.

Zwahr T., Finger M. and Mueller P. (2005) More than Digitization-The Transformative Potential of E-Governance: An Exploratory Case Study, Proceedings of the 38th Hawaii International Conference on System Sciences, Available at www.computer.org.

About the Contributors

Vishanth Weerakkody is a full time faculty member in the Business School at Brunel University, UK. He holds an MSc in 'Business Systems Analysis and Design' from City University in London and a PhD in 'Business Process and Information Systems Reengineering' from the University of Hertfordshire. VW currently teaches organisational behaviour and analysis and innovation and knowledge management at Brunel Business School. He was previously a faculty member in the department of IS and Computing at Brunel University where he participated and project managed a number of research assignments on e-business and application outsourcing. His current research interests include public sector process transformation and change, technology adoption and diffusion in the public sector and electronic government. He has published over thirty journal articles, guest-edited seven special issues of leading journals and co-chairs sessions at major international conferences on these themes. VW has also held various IT positions in multinational organisations during the period 1989 to 1995 mainly in the area of software development and systems design and his final appointment in industry was as a 'methods and process analyst' at IBM UK. VW is a Chartered IT professional, Member of the British Computer Society, the Institute for the Management of Information Systems, the UK Association of Computer Professionals and a Fellow of the UK Higher Education Academy. He is the current Editor-in-Chief of the International Journal of Electronic Government Research.

***

Susheel Chhabra is Associate Professor, Information Technology at Lal Bahadur Shastri Institute of Management, Delhi, India and has been a Programme Coordinator, PGDM (MBA) in the same Institute. His areas of research & consultancy include e-government, e-business, Computer Networks & Software Engineering. He has published several research papers in International & National level Journals. He has co-authored a text book on *Human Resource Information Systems*, edited a special issue on *Strategic e-Business Model for Government, International Journal of E-Government Research* and also co-authored an edited book on *Integrating E-Business Models for Government Solutions: Citizen-Centric Service Oriented Methodologies and Processes* (also published by IGI Global). He is acting as Editor-in-Chief of the *International Journal of Information Communication Technologies and Human Development*. He is currently engaged in several consultancy & training assignments on e-governance and management information systems.

Ernani Marques dos Santos is a researcher at the School of Economics, Administration and Accounting of the University of São Paulo, Brazil. He was a Visiting Researcher in the Information System and Innovation Group at London School of Economics and Political Science, London, UK. His research interests and publications are related to Information Technology adoption, Information Technology value and use of Information Technology in Public Sector (Electronic Government). He holds PhD degree and MSc degree in Management, and Bachelor's degrees in Informatics and Management. Besides being a researcher, he works as an electronic government project manager in a Brazilian state government agency.

Sukumar Ganapati is an Assistant Professor in the Public Administration department at Florida International University (FIU). He has a Ph.D. in Planning from the University of Southern California, where he was also the Assistant Director of the Center for International Policy, Planning, and Development. Dr. Ganapati teaches a course on Information Technology and E-government in FIU. His research interests include Geographic Information Systems (GIS), and the role of institutions in housing and community development.

J. Ramon Gil-Garcia is an Assistant Professor in the Department of Public Administration and the Director of the Data Center for Applied Research in Social Sciences at Centro de Investigación y Docencia Económicas (CIDE) in Mexico City. He is also a Research Fellow at the Center for Technology in Government, University at Albany, State University of New York. Dr. Gil-Garcia is the author or co-author of articles in various journals including the *European Journal of Information Systems*, *Journal of the American Society for Information Science and Technology* (JASIST), *The International Public Management Journal*, and *Government Information Quarterly*. His research interests include electronic government, inter-organizational information systems, institutional approaches to IT in organizations, and multi-method research approaches.

M P Jaiswal is currently Professor of Information Systems at Management Development Institute, Gurgaon, India and has been a Visiting Professor cum Sr. Fulbright Fellow at Carnegie Mellon University, USA during 2004-05. His area of research includes Business Value of Enterprise Systems, ERP Enabled Process Reengineering, e-Government Implementation Models. He has published over 50 research papers and case studies in various International Journals. He is currently working on several ERP and Business Process Reengineering consulting projects. He is co-author of six books: *Management Information Systems* (Oxford), *Enterprise Resource Planning* (Macmillan), *Customer Relationship Management* (Asian), *e-Business Models: Success Strategies* (Excel), *Bridging Digital Divide* (Macmillan), *Enterprise Systems and Business Process Management* (Macmillan)

Luis Felipe Luna-Reyes is a Professor of Business at the Universidad de las Américas-Puebla in México. He holds a Ph.D. in Information Science from the University at Albany. Luna-Reyes is also a member of the Mexican National Research System. His research focuses on electronic government and on modeling collaboration processes in the development of information technologies across functional and organizational boundaries.

Ignacio Navarro is a recent graduate of the Georgia State University/Georgia Institute of Technology joint Public Policy Program. His research interests include urban policy, local governments, and economic development policy.

Gregory Streib is a professor of public administration at Georgia State University, specializing in public management and applied research methods. His research has addressed a variety of public management topics, including strategic planning, pay-for-performance, health care cost reduction, performance measurement, reinventing government, and the implementation of E-governance initiatives.

Index

E

F

G

H

I

K

L

M

N

O

P

Q

R

S